Consumers, Corporations, and Public Health

Consumers, Corporations, and Public Health

A Case-Based Approach to Sustainable Business

John A. Quelch

OXFORD
UNIVERSITY PRESS

Oxford University Press is a department of the University of Oxford. It furthers the University's objective of excellence in research, scholarship, and education by publishing worldwide. Oxford is a registered trade mark of Oxford University Press in the UK and certain other countries.

Published in the United States of America by Oxford University Press
198 Madison Avenue, New York, NY 10016, United States of America.

First Edition published in 2016

Library of Congress Cataloging-in-Publication Data
Consumers, corporations and public health: a case-based approach to
sustainable business / edited by John A. Quelch.
p. ; cm.
ISBN 978–0–19–023512–3 (alk. paper)
I. Quelch, John A.
[DNLM: 1. Commerce. 2. Public Health—economics. 3. Health Promotion—methods.
4. Health Services. 5. Professional Corporations. WA 100]
RA427.8
362.1—dc23
2015029317

1 3 5 7 9 8 6 4 2

Printed by Webcom, Canada

CONTENTS

PREFACE

The case studies in this book, cobranded by Harvard Business School and Harvard T. H. Chan School of Public Health, were all developed during the last three years for use in my new Consumers, Corporations, and Public Health course. This course was offered for the first time in 2015 to students enrolled in both Harvard Business School's MBA program and Harvard T. H. Chan School of Public Health's MPH and MS programs.

The principal aim of the course and of this book is to encourage dialogue and mutual understanding between these two groups, which typically bring very different assumptions and worldviews to the discussion of public health problems. Both groups can agree on one thing: the consumer interest is an appropriate starting point for determining both good business practice and good public policy.

I especially thank Harvard Business School Research Associate Margaret L. Rodriguez for helping to develop many of the cases in this collection. She has been not only highly productive but also creative and meticulous in her work. Thanks are also due to other Harvard Business School Research Associates who have contributed to individual case studies: Carin-Isabel Knoop, Michael Norris, and Christine Snively. Harvard Business School faculty members Robert Huckman and Leslie John also contributed materials.

My office assistant, Elaine Shaffer, worked diligently to organize the site visits and executive interviews that many of the case studies required. She also collaborated closely with Amy Iakovou at Harvard Business School Publishing to organize the manuscript for delivery to my editor at Oxford University Press, Chad Zimmerman. Chad's support throughout the development and editing process is much appreciated.

This project has also received considerable support from Dean Nitin Nohria and the Division of Research at Harvard Business School and Dean Julio Frenk of the Harvard T. H. Chan School of Public Health.

John A. Quelch
Boston, June 2015

CONTRIBUTORS

Robert Huckman
Harvard Business School
Boston, MA

Leslie K. John
Harvard Business School
Boston, MA

Carin-Isabel Knoop
Harvard Business School
Boston, MA

Michael Norris
Harvard Business School
Boston, MA

Margaret L. Rodriguez
Harvard Business School
Boston, MA

Christine Snively
Harvard Business School
Boston, MA

INTRODUCTION

In 2014, a wave of Ebola killed over 3,000 people in West Africa. Nine months after the first patient appeared in Guinea, the World Health Organization (WHO) belatedly declared a "public health emergency of international concern." Meanwhile, fear of the deadly virus disrupted trade, commerce, and international air service. The World Bank estimated a $33 billion hit to regional economies over 18 months. The Liberian economy, as one example, was forecast to contract by 12% in 2015.

The disease spread quickly. As family members and, indeed, health workers cared for the sick, they came into contact with body fluids and subsequently became infected. Hospitals were overwhelmed, and isolation wards were in short supply. Once deceased, bodies were, according to local custom, again touched by loved ones and friends prior to burial, resulting in further contamination. The speed with which preventive information could be effectively communicated to people was often inadequate, especially to those living in poor, rural villages.

The Ebola outbreak put both local businesses and multinational companies at risk. Many small businesses shut and, by November 2014, half of Liberia's workers were no longer on the job. One fast food chain, Monroe Chicken, saw its cost of raw materials increase as borders closed. But, determined to continue operations despite fewer customers, Monroe instituted daily employee temperature checks, installed handwashing buckets, and required employees to eat free meals at the restaurants and avoid all street food. Monroe laid off no workers during the crisis, maintaining employee morale and reassuring customers with familiar faces.

In Liberia, ArcelorMittal had invested $700 million in a vast iron ore mine that would produce 5 million tons per year. In the face of the Ebola crisis, the company built a new medical clinic, implemented daily temperature checks and handwashing, limited access to one point of entry per facility, and organized daily morning meetings so employees could share information and concerns. Since its operations were spread across a community of 25,000 people, ArcelorMittal mapped exactly where each employee lived and established a 30-kilometer buffer zone around its mining concession. The company invested heavily in educating schoolteachers in the area about how to avoid the disease.

Supporting public health means supporting social cohesion and political stability, both essential to the free flow of commerce. These two examples illustrate how corporations, large and small, can be impacted by public health events, and how they can respond in ways that not only defend their own interests but contribute by deed and by example to solve public health problems. Meanwhile, GSK and NewLink Genetics began to accelerate the development and production of vaccines to counter the Ebola virus, once the WHO requested that they do so and nongovernmental agencies guaranteed that they would make bulk purchases of the vaccine.

New medicines, new medical devices, and new approaches to insurance and care management stem from the efforts of the private sector, but are often stimulated by basic research funding from public agencies such as the National Science Foundation and National Institutes of Health. Public health has improved dramatically as a result. Over the last six decades, global life expectancy has increased by 23 years and infant mortality has decreased by 70%. Nevertheless, 6.3 million children died before their fifth birthday in 2013. Even more troubling, success is spawning new problems: aging populations in developing countries are increasingly suffering from the same sedentary lifestyles, consumption of processed foods, and consequent chronic health problems, such as diabetes, that have been boosting healthcare costs in developed countries. While infectious diseases remain a problem, health systems in emerging economies are having to adapt to a new demand profile. State budgets are often inadequate to respond, and doctors are underpaid and in short supply, opening opportunities for creative solutions from the private sector and/or public-private partnerships to fill the gaps.

In the United States, 18% of gross domestic product (GDP) is spent on health care. Critics argue that this is due to the significant participation of the for-profit sector. Drug companies try to persuade doctors to prescribe more drugs than patients need. Hospitals with spare beds are motivated to extend patient stays and charge their insurers. Second opinions and batteries of tests are needed to ward off malpractice suits in the event a treatment goes wrong. Poor information technology connectivity among competing private health providers makes joined-up patient care inefficient.

Others contend that US consumers (at least those who can pay) have access to the best cutting-edge and consumer-responsive health care in the world. While European and Japanese consumers benefit from the promise of universal coverage and the buying power of their single-payer national health insurance systems, these cumbersome bureaucracies may be subject to diseconomies of scale, as well as employee demotivation and rationing of services to patients due to inadequate or uncertain funding. It is common in the United Kingdom, for example, for patients to have to wait to see a specialist or to wait months for a non-emergency operation. In addition, the elderly are more likely to receive palliative care than expensive treatments that prolong their lives. It may be true in the United States that 80%–90% of healthcare costs are spent in the last six months of life. But how do we know if this is good or bad? There are, to be sure, inefficiencies and fraud in the fragmented US healthcare system. But there are also inefficiencies in any bureaucratic and nationally standardized healthcare system that consumes perhaps only 10% of GDP. In a prosperous and civilized nation, what (other than education) could be more important to spend money on than health care?

The motivation for this book is threefold. The first objective is to highlight the importance to public policymakers and private sector executives in health care of understanding consumer attitudes and behaviors when shaping their interventions. Not all consumers are likely to respond in the same manner, and some may respond in ways that are seemingly contrary to their best interests. Researching consumer behavior in advance can result in more effective interventions. The second objective is to highlight the different mindsets of public health and private sector executives and to stress the need for mutual understanding. Private sector executives have the luxury of being able to target profitable sub-segments of the population who can afford to pay for their products and services, while public health officials are responsible for the health of the entire population, especially the most vulnerable. Many public health problems can benefit from public and private organizations working in partnership on solutions; for such engagements to be effective, mutual understanding and respect are essential. The third objective of this collection of case studies is to demonstrate the value of engaging and empowering consumers to take charge of their health care. The results can be both lower costs and improved quality of patient outcomes, invariably resulting in higher consumer satisfaction.

The book is organized into six modules of case studies. The following sections summarize the themes and key issues of each module.

CORPORATE STRATEGY AND PUBLIC HEALTH

Every corporation is a player in public health. The products and services delivered to customers must be safe. Any claims made to customers regarding health and safety must be valid. Advice must be given regarding proper use to ensure against excessive or inappropriate consumption. Dosage advice on the packages of over-the-counter pharmaceuticals and regulations regarding the design and packaging of children's toys are two areas where government regulators, working in cooperation with industry, develop processes, guidelines, and rules that prevent accidents.

A corporation's public health footprint has three pillars: safety, *sanitas*, and sustainability. Safety refers to the in-use safety of the products or services that the consumer is purchasing. It depends largely on the existence of quality control protocols in sourcing, production, and distribution. *Sanitas* refers to the health and wellness of employees and family members, not merely direct employees but all workers involved in the supply chain, from ingredient producers to after-sales service people. Under cost pressure from foreign competitors, many companies are downsizing, placing more work (and often stress) on those employees whom they retain. Investing in physical and mental health and wellness can attract and retain good employees, boost their motivation and productivity, and lower health insurance costs. Sustainability refers to the impact of the company's operations on environmental health, from carbon dioxide emissions to water usage. DuPont appointed the first chief sustainability officer in 2004, and leading corporations are now expected by investors to publish an annual sustainability report alongside their financial statements.

Companies that pursue a positive public health footprint may not always see an immediate payback in performance or investor support. There is skepticism among investors that the inclusion of a public health perspective may be a distraction to management and a drag on earnings. However, the chief executives of Pepsi and Unilever would argue that the attention they pay to public health issues in shaping their product portfolios and company operations will be a point of differentiation that will benefit their shareholders in the long run.

For most corporate leaders, it may not seem advisable to market superior comparative performance on something like safety. First, to advertise that your airline is the safest highlights a negative that might deter some consumers from flying. Second, if a safety issue arises, the company that touts safety is going to be severely embarrassed. Third, most companies interested in advancing safety standards prefer to work within industry and trade associations rather than breaking ranks and promoting their own capabilities.

BP's green energy advertising campaign was upended by a series of safety problems that culminated in the loss of life and severe pollution in the Gulf of Mexico resulting from the Deep Water Horizon disaster. Volvo, on the other hand, successfully equated its brand name with pro-safety auto design and touted this superiority to middle-class families with young children.

Companies both within and outside the healthcare sector are focused on the health and safety of both their consumers and their employees. Health insurance is often second only to payroll among corporate expenses. Starbucks spends more on health insurance each year than on coffee. If health insurance costs can be reduced by improving the physical and mental wellness of employees, that should boost a company's competitiveness and productivity as well as improving employee and, thereby, customer satisfaction. However, three problems can arise if a culture of wellness is taken too far. First, it may encourage selection bias toward the recruitment of a younger, healthier workforce. Second, it may keep the well healthy (certainly a valuable outcome) but may unnerve employees who are sick and in need of help. Third, it often overemphasizes physical activity and underappreciates the value of stress-free work.

In 2014, Colgate-Palmolive launched a superior anti-cavity toothpaste, the first demonstrable improvement in cavity prevention since fluoride was added to toothpaste 50 years ago. Rather than launching the product at premium prices in developed countries, Colgate decided to launch at accessible prices in emerging markets. In Brazil, thanks to decades of relationship building by Colgate with the Brazilian Ministry of Health, free samples of the new toothpaste were distributed to hundreds of thousands of schoolchildren who are required to brush every day after school lunch. These samples connect the Colgate brand to future purchasers, and the children take the samples home to their parents. This is a clear case where doing the right thing is both good for public health and good for business.

The case of Royal Caribbean cruise lines brings together all three strands of the corporation's public health footprint. The company has taken the lead in environmental health, developing and installing progressively advanced emission purification systems known as scrubbers on each new class of vessel it brings into service. In addition, Royal Caribbean has led the industry in implementing advanced on-board water purification systems that treat waste water before it is released into the ocean. Royal Caribbean has not waited to respond to new regulations. It has shaped industry regulations and has implemented improvements several years ahead of regulatory deadlines, all part of its "above and beyond compliance" (ABC) philosophy.

Royal Caribbean has shown similar leadership in workplace and passenger safety. Crews come from many countries and cultures, and have to be trained not only in the niceties of customer service but in being vigilant and speaking up on any matters that pertain to passenger and employee safety and security. In addition, Royal Caribbean, under the direction of its chief medical officer, takes special precautions to prevent outbreaks of disease or medical emergencies on board its vessels. An outbreak of norovirus in the middle of a cruise can result in damage control and customer compensation costs, even after insurance payouts, approaching 5% of the annual profits of the company. Preventive measures, from screening of passengers when they board to rigorous cleanliness procedures, to activating prescribed protocols in the event of an outbreak, can all enhance public health and reduce the risk of lost profits.

The Royal Caribbean case illustrates how companies not in the health sector nevertheless have multiple public health impacts and responsibilities: on passenger and workforce health and safety, on disease prevention and control, and on environmental sustainability. Collectively, we call these impacts, both actual and potential, the public health footprint of the corporation. Every company has a public health footprint. But, often, the elements of the footprint are not seen as connected. Increasingly, however, we see the appointment of a senior corporate executive to oversee health, safety, and the environment. This executive is charged with ensuring that the net public health footprint of the company is positive.

CONSUMER ANALYTICS AND HEALTHCARE OUTCOMES

In many industries, rising costs have prompted creative thinking that results in consumers taking on more responsibility, and being rewarded for doing so by lower prices. In supermarkets, for example, consumers gather their own merchandise rather than asking for assistance from store clerks (except in the baked goods, meat, and seafood departments). In some stores, they may even be encouraged to check themselves out and to bag their own groceries. The consequent savings in store labor facilitate lower retail prices. In the world of financial services, some consumers are confident enough in their financial acumen or skeptical enough of traditional brokers that they invest with lower cost providers like Vanguard and manage their own money.

A similar transition is occurring in health care. Thanks to the aging of the population and more prevalent chronic diseases, plus advances in technology, healthcare costs are rising faster than general inflation. Confronted by rising health insurance premiums, and uncertain quality of health outcomes, more and more consumers are investigating through online research, or by asking around, which insurance plan, which hospital, or which doctor makes sense for them. Governments, not-for-profits, and commercial websites are facilitating this trend by aggregating performance and rating information to make such comparisons easier. A final issue is that engaged consumers disproportionately include the worried well, while truly sick people lack the energy, ability, or inclination to help themselves.

Of course, not all consumers have the time or inclination to be this involved. And some may simply be too ill, mentally or physically, to help themselves. Others continue to defer to the doctor as an authority figure without doing their own research. There is also concern that engaged consumers may eat up their doctors' time (and thereby increase healthcare costs) by questioning their diagnoses and treatments. Others who are empowered may end up making healthcare decisions that are not in their best health interests. Many patients with chronic mental conditions, for example, believe that they can calibrate the dose of their medications better than their physicians.

To benefit the healthcare system, empowerment must be accompanied by education. Simply delegating decision-making responsibility to consumers without giving them relevant, accessible information and educating them in how to use it simply causes more anxiety and distrust. The best insurance exchanges established by the Affordable Care Act presented consumers with a simple set of healthcare insurance plan options, typically bronze, silver, and platinum, plus website information and trained "navigators" and insurance brokers to help them make their choices.

As the prevalence of chronic diseases such as diabetes increases, effective education becomes all the more important in controlling healthcare costs. In the United States, treating chronic diseases accounts for 75% of all healthcare costs, and 5% of Medicare patients account for 42% of program costs. If patients with chronic conditions—and their family members and caregivers—can be educated on the benefits of behavior changes such as improved diet and more exercise, hospital readmissions and health system costs can be reduced. In the case of high-cost patients with multiple conditions, investing in a customized behavior-change plan may pay off. For most chronic patients, enrollment in a standard, regular exercise program or similar intervention is sufficient.

Consumer segmentation analysis is as essential in health care as it is in explaining consumer behavior in other spheres. Consider shopping. One segment of consumers prefers to shop online for the lowest prices, while another segment would rather pay a little more to touch and feel the merchandise and interact with a salesperson before buying in a department store. Or take financial services. One segment is prepared to pay more for personalized handholding by a stockbroker or financial planner. Consumers in a second segment are confident enough to avoid these costs and manage their own investments. Something similar is true in health care, with two important contextual differences. First, health care and health insurance are grudge purchases that consumers make only reluctantly. Second, consumers can only help themselves up to a certain point, at which a doctor's intervention becomes essential.

Imagine that we could profile all consumers in the population, overlaying all their clinical records and all their health insurance claims data on top of demographic information, family medical history, lifestyle data relating to exercise and food consumption, plus attitudes and opinions that determine their overall optimism. Ideally, we would then tailor our wellness messaging and interventions according to who is in most need, who is most likely to respond, and where the payback to intervening in terms of reduced healthcare costs and improved health outcomes is likely to be greatest.

Privacy laws, the integration of multiple databases, and an actuarial mindset that views patients as numbers rather than people are all challenges in this effort. However, at least one life insurance company, Humana, is pursuing this consumer-centric strategy. Many of their members qualify for Medicare Advantage government health insurance, which reimburses at standard rates based on each member's health conditions. Humana believes that, through consumer segmentation research, it can discover how to motivate members to change their behaviors, lifestyles, and medical conditions and so save money through fewer doctor visits, hospital readmissions, drugs, and procedures.

Not only payers but also providers are increasingly focusing on the consumer. Carolinas Healthcare, a major hospital network, is also using big data analytics to integrate multi-source health information and then customize interventions for specific consumers, such as those at high risk of hospital readmission. Motivating doctors and nurses to let data analytics guide their patient workflows is critical to achieving the dual objectives of reducing costs and improving patient health outcomes.

Medical device companies such as Philips have millions of products worldwide remote monitoring consumers' vital signs and health metrics every day. Philips believes it, too, can be a force for patient data integration, especially as a trusted brand known to many consumers. Emergency medical records companies such as Epic and even IBM, through its Watson health project, are taking the same view. It remains to be seen who will be the most powerful data integrator in health care.

PREVENTION AND ADHERENCE

Consumer attitudes and behaviors are important drivers of health and wellness. Regular exercise, avoiding tobacco and alcohol addiction, and good diet can go a long way to sustaining an individual's health. The French author Anthelme Brillat-Savarin famously stated, "Tell me what you eat and I will tell you who you are." Minimal stress, a spirit of optimism, and mindfulness are equally important. The will to live, often correlated with the support of family and friends, can make the difference in seeing someone through a serious illness.

Although an ounce of prevention is worth a pound of cure, few among us are doing our part. Only 5% of Americans eat in accordance with the national dietary guidelines. Warren Buffett, for example, claims that the secret to his success is that he eats like a six-year-old. Rising per capita incomes go hand in hand with a more sedentary lifestyle, thanks to the automobile and the substitution of knowledge economy desk jobs for those involving physical labor. Corporations selling us convenient, tasty, and potentially addictive processed foods heavy on sugar, salt, and bad cholesterol, and heavily advertised, also contribute.

Persuading consumers to take preventive action on behalf of their health is difficult. First, short-term gratification has to be sacrificed for the uncertain prospect of longer-term gain. Second, with the exception of quitting smoking, it is hard to identify the simple rule (avoiding one thing) that will make a significant difference to health outcomes. Perhaps avoiding trans fats is approaching avoiding tobacco as a second straightforward discipline. Third, average life spans continue to advance thanks to simply administered diagnostics that allow for early disease detection. Fourth, therapeutic technologies suggest that we can live carefree until we run into trouble and still have a good chance of being cured.

Changing the attitudes and behaviors of people who are set in their ways is difficult. But there are at least three ways to motivate change. The first is information, including public service advertising, media stories, and well-designed nutrition labels. Such messages often rely on fear appeals delivered through traditional media, which turn consumers off, rather than on humorous messages delivered through social media, which can engage consumers on their own terms. In addition, the media weight supporting preventive messages is invariably insufficient to counter the volume of commercial advertising pushing potentially harmful products.

A second approach is to use financial incentives. An insurance premium reduction may be offered to a consumer for completing an annual health profile and health checkup. Likewise, out-of-pocket copayments by insured consumers for accessing health services will motivate some to stay healthy (though copayments should not be so high that they dissuade consumers from seeking timely care when they need it). However, it is politically unacceptable to charge sick people more for health insurance: consumers with preexisting conditions, some perhaps genetically induced through no fault of the individual, cannot be excluded from insurance pools in the United States following passage of the Affordable Care Act.

In addition to individualized consumer incentives, public policymakers may elect to increase the cost of using a harmful product. For example, they can impose taxes or distribution restrictions on commercial products, such as cigarettes, alcoholic beverages, and, increasingly, sugary soft drinks, that are considered deleterious to health.

A third approach to prevention is regulation. The Food and Drug Administration and the Consumer Product Safety Commission, for example, set standards for product quality and manage a process of review and approval of what can be marketed to consumers. In these cases, the government regulates the market in the interests of public health, preventing harmful and untested (and therefore potentially harmful) products from reaching consumers.

In sum, there is no doubt that consumer marketing has promoted the use of products and services that collectively contribute—consumer freedom of choice notwithstanding—to an unhealthy lifestyle. But for-profit corporations can also be part of the solution. First, new food products can be developed that are healthy, tasty, and affordable. New medical devices for in-home use can be better designed for ease of use. Second, Fitbit and a host of other products linked to computer and phone apps can help consumers monitor key health data and take preventive action. Third, for-profit advertising agencies and market research firms regularly offer pro bono creative and research services to develop public service advertising campaigns in collaboration with nonprofit organizations such as the Advertising Council.

More important to positive health outcomes than initiating preventive action is adherence, the sustained commitment to a preventive behavior. The consumer cannot quit smoking for a week; she must quit forever. Likewise, regular exercise must become a way of life. Fitbit and other similar products linked to computer and phone apps enable engaged consumers to monitor health data and sustain preventive action. These products, however, are largely used by people who are already healthy. What about those who are sick and on prescription drugs?

Around a third of first-time prescriptions written in the United States are never filled. And half the prescriptions for chronic conditions that are filled are not completed and refilled. Apart from the enormous wasted effort and the cost of unused drugs, health outcomes are not being improved and health costs are not being reduced because so many consumers do not adhere to the drug prescriptions given to them by doctors. In some cases, the cost may be too high. In other cases, there is a lack of confidence in the doctor, a skepticism regarding the drug's efficacy, a tendency to self-medicate, or simple forgetfulness—hence the commercial development of electronic pill dispensers that glow or that notify a family member if unopened. In addition, CVS Health has retrained pharmacists in its 7,800 stores to engage with consumers when dispensing prescriptions and to follow up by phone, email, or text message if they are not refilled on time. CVS aims to make sure that the right patient is on the right therapy at the right time at the right dosage.

CONSUMER ACCESS AND AFFORDABILITY

Despite the benefits of globalization in lifting billions out of abject poverty and spawning an emerging middle class in developing economies, many remain firmly at the bottom of the pyramid without access to potable water, let alone vaccines and basic health care. Though access to health care is not included in the United Nations Declaration of Human Rights, a majority of Western policymakers and corporate executives believe, on both moral and economic grounds, that the needs of the global poor should not go unaddressed. Solutions include the manufacture of low-cost generic drugs and medical devices, and innovations that overcome the infrastructure and environmental barriers that prevent solutions from traversing "the last mile" to reach the world's poorest.

For example, several water purification devices have been developed that use solar power to produce potable water from contaminated water for a home or for a village. The challenge is funding their manufacture, distributing them, and training people in their use and maintenance, often in remote locations. The need to refrigerate most vaccines and many drugs from the factory to the point of use adds significant cost. In addition, the unreliability of the cold chain in developing countries means that many vaccine doses go to waste and others that are administered are ineffective. Vaxess is one company that seeks to economically heat-stabilize vaccines in the production process, removing the need for refrigeration and increasing the odds of access and affordability for last-mile consumers.

As with any innovation, the adoption of such new technologies depends on their relative advantage, their complexity, their compatibility with existing practices, the ease with which their benefits can be understood, and the ease with which consumers can try them out at minimal risk. These five criteria were identified by Everett Rogers in his 1962 book *The Diffusion of Innovation*. The five diffusion criteria can be applied across all stakeholder groups to assess the likelihood of new product adoption. The benefits of non-refrigerated vaccines, for example, must be seen clearly not only by consumers but by the vaccine manufacturers, by the regulators who must approve them, by the international organizations like UNICEF that buy them in large volumes, by the insurance companies and payers in the developed world, and by the hospitals, doctors, and nurses who administer them.

Access and affordability present important ethical and practical challenges in developed countries as well. Disparities exist even in countries with single-payer, taxpayer-funded national health systems that provide care to all citizens. Rural areas may not be well served by doctors, and specialized help may be limited. The poor may find even modest copayments unaffordable and a deterrent to using health services, perhaps resulting in more expensive emergency room treatment later. A major criticism of single-payer systems is that governments focus on controlling healthcare expenditures with unfortunate results. They may ration care, causing patients lengthy waiting times to see a specialist or to receive a non-emergency surgery, or they may limit their citizens' access to new drugs and expensive or discretionary treatments.

In the United States, around 40 million people had no health insurance prior to the passage of the Affordable Care Act in 2010. Many were unemployed or underemployed and therefore had no access to an employer health plan. Others were unable to obtain health insurance due to preexisting medical conditions. Many healthy young adults viewed themselves as invincible and saw health insurance as a grudge purchase. They chose not to buy it even if they could afford it; their non-participation in the risk pool raised costs for everyone else.

The Affordable Care Act established minimum standards for health insurance plans and set up an electronic marketplace in each state where private insurance companies could offer qualifying plans that varied in pricing and benefits. Consumers were able to comparison shop, and many received government subsidies toward their annual premiums based on their incomes.

Yet, despite two years of marketing efforts, the number of uninsured was reduced by only around 10 million. Many people simply found health insurance too difficult a subject to deal with and continued to use public hospital emergency rooms—at great cost to the system—when they were unwell. Others were philosophically opposed to participating in any "big government" program. Undocumented immigrants were afraid to sign up. Many young people chose to remain uninsured. Understanding the consumer mindset of these various population segments is essential to crafting messages, incentives, and regulations to bring them into the ranks of the insured.

Access to expensive new drugs that target serious diseases with limited prevalence presents pharmaceutical manufacturers with financial, marketing, and ethical challenges. In 2013, 19 of 28 new drugs approved by the US Food and Drug Administration were specialty drugs with an average development cost of $2.6 billion. The higher prices of these drugs, especially those targeting diseases with lower incidence, were highlighted when Gilead Sciences charged $80,000 for a single treatment course of Solvadi for hepatitis C patients. While justifiable on a value pricing basis (Solvadi cured rather than controlled the disease), many insurers and employers balked at covering the cost of the drug for their members. Gilead offered lower prices for needy patients in the United States, charged less in other developed countries with single-payer government agencies that leveraged their procurement clout, and licensed generic production at a fraction of the US price in developing economies. A generic version priced at $10 emerged in Bangladesh in 2015.

By responding in this way, Gilead followed a common pattern of price discrimination for drugs and vaccines, whereby prices in developing countries are set well below those in developed countries. This is one reason that 18% of US GDP is spent on health care, compared to 10% worldwide; the US consumer cross-subsidizes the drug and vaccine purchases of consumers in other countries.

The major pharmaceutical companies continue to allocate most of their funds on research and development of new blockbuster drugs. Few funds are devoted to improving access and affordability. Yet the manner in which a drug has to be taken (e.g., by vaccine, pill, or patch), the frequency of dosage, the duration of the treatment, and the availability of the drug in remote areas all bear upon the new drug's ability to influence healthcare outcomes. Even when they add value, important innovations that improve patient access and adherence take a back seat to the new products. The reality is that there is no Nobel Prize in Medicine for improving access or distribution.

CONSUMERISM AND PATERNALISM

From online shopping to managing financial assets, increasingly large segments of consumers are willing, indeed eager, to gather information and make decisions, largely unassisted by others. They have sufficient experience to be confident in their judgments, and these judgments can be reversed; products bought online can be returned, mutual funds can be sold.

Healthcare decisions are not so easy. In emergencies, there is no time for shopping around and price comparisons are not high on the agenda, especially if an insurance company is paying. Some comparative performance information on doctors and hospitals is available, but it is likely incomplete and possibly out of date. Sampling alternatives is often impractical, and some decisions (e.g., elective surgery) cannot be reversed once implemented, while others (e.g., non-adherence to a prescription) can. Most important, the consumer cannot do it all herself: doctors, hospitals, and insurance companies all must be selected and worked with.

Nevertheless, there is a myriad of new web-based sources of health information to interest the engaged consumer. The British National Health Service publishes performance ratings of all its hospitals on multiple dimensions. There are websites such as WebMD that provide information about disease symptoms and treatments or drug side effects. Other websites, including Patients Like Me, organize communities of patients who share information about the efficacy of drugs and other treatments for various diseases, often providing comfort and hope as well as empowering patients and their caregivers.

Some consumers, often those more interested in prevention, soak up this information and feel empowered by it to the point of raising questions with their doctors. Others try to avoid the information overload and are comfortable viewing their doctors as superiors rather than equals. For their part, doctors are also divided. Some welcome patients who take an interest in their health, conduct research online, and ask intelligent questions in office visits. Others find that over-curious patients detract from their efficiency and worry that patients may become confused by the information or may try to treat themselves in ways that could be harmful.

John Stuart Mill objected to paternalism, the curtailment of freedom of choice, unless free choice harms others. In the case of health care, consumers unprotected might make choices that cause themselves harm. But, in causing such harm, they may consume services that might be better allocated to others and diminish their ability to be productive members of society. As such, the consumer who doesn't exercise, eats unwisely, and doesn't adhere to prescribed medications is causing financial harm to others.

In late 2013, the Food and Drug Administration prohibited 23andMe, a direct-to-consumer genetics testing company, from continuing to provide disease-risk information to its paying customers. The FDA contended that 23andMe was marketing a medical device and that the analytical and clinical validity of the algorithms underlying the disease-risk assessments were unproven and risked misleading consumers into taking harmful medical action. Many of 23andMe's 450,000 consumers defended the right to know their DNA and to purchase information that interpreted it.

This case highlights the mindset contrasts between healthcare regulators and entrepreneurs. Regulators are naturally conservative and write rules to protect all citizens, including the most vulnerable and those unable to look out for themselves. Their worst nightmare is to approve the sale and marketing of a drug or medical advice, only to find that it causes injury or death, to however small a minority of users. The entrepreneur, by contrast, often embraces a Benthamite philosophy of greatest good for the greatest number; if a drug cures a severe illness but one in a thousand users dies, the entrepreneur might push ahead. Finally, the entrepreneur is used to targeting her product at the market segment that most needs it. The regulator, however, has to regulate for all citizens and must consider the possibility that the product may be acquired by some for whom it is not appropriate.

Public health policymakers often think they know what is best for people and rarely make a move without believing that they have science on their side. The problem is that they often investigate insufficiently the various consumer behavior responses and underestimate the messaging necessary to motivate behavior change. When Mayor Bloomberg tried to cap at 16 ounces the serving size of sugary drinks sold in New York City restaurants, he may have presumed that all consumers who previously ordered 24- or 32-ounce servings would knuckle under. But surely there would be some who would order two 16-ounce servings, especially if the soft drink manufacturers priced this option attractively? Giving consumers a nudge is not quite the same as limiting their freedom of choice. When consumer protection morphs into paternalism, some citizens respond with defiance, often counter to their own well-being.

EMERGING MARKETS, CONSUMER BEHAVIOR, AND PUBLIC HEALTH

Despite an ever-increasing mountain of scientific evidence regarding the deleterious effects of tobacco smoking, cigarettes continue to be sold. For 50 years, the tobacco industry has steadfastly resisted all efforts to curtail its marketing activity. The industry has compensated for the decline in smoking in developed economies by promoting cigarette consumption in emerging markets such as China and India, where the taxes generated on tobacco sales often reflect the interests of the finance ministry overriding those of the health ministry.

In Western countries, public health officials have used the complete arsenal of available measures to gradually curtail the incidence of tobacco consumption. These include messaging from public service announcements to warnings on packaging and in advertising; restrictions on where and how tobacco products can be sold to manage the "choice architecture" presented to consumers; pricing nudges in the form of higher taxes to dampen consumption; and, in some jurisdictions, outright bans on where smoking can occur or on the sale of some or all tobacco products. Objections to paternalism and in defense of individual freedom fall short since the health costs to address the harmful consequences of tobacco smoking largely fall on taxpayers as a whole, not on the individual smoker.

The tobacco companies have worked hard to improve the efficacy of filtered cigarettes in catching carcinogens before they are inhaled. They have also focused their promotion on menthol and "lite" cigarettes. In other words, they have shaped their product portfolios and their allocation of marketing effort across products in response to declining consumer interest and pressure from public health officials.

The accelerating emergence of the markets for e-cigarettes and recreational marijuana use both offer substantial opportunities for the survival of the big tobacco companies. E-cigarettes offer consumers the opportunity to smoke without inhaling the carcinogens that accompany the burning of tobacco. Not surprisingly, big tobacco companies interested in diversifying their risk have been purchasing fledgling, independent e-cigarette brands, catapulting them rapidly to national distribution and increased sales.

For public health policymakers, e-cigarettes present a difficult dilemma. On the one hand, they represent a potential path away from cigarettes for smokers trying to quit. Though exposure to nicotine remains an important medical concern (and there is insufficient research on the consequences of nicotine addiction), it is preferable that the traditional cigarette smoker who switches will no longer be ingesting carcinogens into her lungs. On the other hand, many are concerned that e-cigarettes will become a halfway house in the opposite direction on the road from not smoking to smoking cigarettes, with the cool technology of vaping attracting young people who would have otherwise eschewed the by-now dirty habit of cigarette smoking. These two approaches can be seen in the marketing of different e-cigarette brands, with some aiming to help the intelligent cigarette smoker to quit and others focusing on vaping pleasure.

Worldwide, public health officials have been scrambling fast to regulate the marketing of e-cigarettes and to place some limits on the permissible nicotine content. Legalization of marijuana for recreational as well as medicinal uses has also proven controversial, not least because of medical evidence of pain relief benefits being offset by evidence of reduced IQ among young people who smoke regularly. Add to this the fact that marijuana remains an illegal drug in the United States under federal law; the market is developing slowly, one referendum in one state at a time. In Colorado, recreational marijuana sales became legal on January 1, 2014. Through the licensing of retail dispensaries and the electronic tagging of individual plants, the market remains tightly controlled. There are, in fact, four submarkets, each characterized by different consumer behaviors; the preexisting medicinal market involving frequent users who are loyal to a particular strain or supplier that relieves their pain; the recreational market involving occasional users (including tourists) who are less price sensitive and value a "Starbucks-like" retail experience; the individual grower market, consumers growing for themselves but perhaps illegally selling their surplus privately to others; and the illegal market, which continues to exist because of high recreational marijuana prices stemming from greedy state and local governments imposing high sales and excise taxes. Meanwhile, public health officials are scrambling to regulate the new product categories of marijuana edibles and drinkables that can be tempting to non-users and children, as well as attractive to current users who, in some circumstances, do not want to be seen smoking.

It will be perhaps 5 to 10 years before a sufficient number of states legalize recreational marijuana to attract the direct investment interest of the big tobacco companies. At present, the market size is too inconsequential and federal law prevents the legal movement of marijuana across state lines. But for sure, the major tobacco companies are plotting their strategies to maintain shareholder value in their companies by investing in both marijuana and e-cigarette brands. Public health officials must be cognizant of such emerging markets and plan their future responses rather than scrambling to react once the genie is out of the bottle.

CONSUMER POWER IN SHAPING PUBLIC HEALTH

Healthcare and education are two issues in which citizens around the world, rich and poor, are passionately interested. It has long been appreciated that the way that a society treats its youngest and oldest members says much about its moral maturity. Economic development specialists also attest to the importance of health care in determining productivity. The connection between child health and nutrition and readiness to learn in school is also well established. Forthcoming revisions to the Millennium Development Goals are expected to again highlight the importance of disease prevention and health care to the global community.

Nevertheless, the pressures of commercial competition all too often still result in decisions that take scant account of public health and whether the health of individual citizens is being advanced. When worker safety is jeopardized by unenforced building codes or exposure to harmful industrial chemicals, that becomes a public health issue. Bangladesh garment factory owners engaged in cutthroat price competition to secure orders from Western manufacturer and retailer brands. These brands conveniently sourced their requirements at arm's length through third-party intermediaries to avoid any responsibility for workplace conditions. Then, the Rana Plaza disaster that killed over 1,000 factory workers in Bangladesh in 2013 highlighted to Western consumers the challenging conditions faced by the workers who made their clothes. Consumer pressure on Western retailers worked its way back up the supply chain to force improvements in workplace conditions. In this case, Western consumers were taking responsibility not for their own health but for the health and safety of workers in a foreign land thousands of miles away.

Consumer power has not been that evident a criterion in shaping the financial decisions of major multinationals. Merger and acquisition activity in the healthcare sector invariably occurs with scant regard for the impact on public health or the end consumer. Pfizer's attempted takeover of the British company, AstraZeneca, in 2014 was criticized widely for being motivated by financial engineering; the combined company would be headquartered in England in order to achieve a lower corporate tax rate. The British government favored the merger as it would boost the high-priority life sciences sector, but little attention was paid to whether the integration of the two company research groups would delay the development and commercialization of important new drugs to the detriment of consumers. Interestingly, though, at public hearings, the AstraZeneca chief executive championed the interests of patients in opposing the proposed merger.

Consumers worldwide are increasingly taking charge of their health. As populations age, there are more consumers than ever before suffering from chronic conditions. Most no longer see disease and the timing of their death as inevitable. Supported by the Internet, many actively seek out information to increase their odds of staying alive. Aided by family and friends, they research their conditions and possible treatments, often sharing their experiences with others in online communities. They are more inclined to question authority, and to raise issues with their doctors, care providers, and pharmacists. Some providers view such patients as wasting their time, but most recognize that patients know themselves better than anyone and therefore value their insights. Of course, not everyone is interested in or capable of engaging in the management of his or her own health. Some are fatalistic; others avoid doctors and hospitals at all costs; still others are simply too sick to help themselves. Any public health system must respect the reality of these consumer differences and not withhold care from people simply because they do not engage and do not speak up. As Atul Gwande has stated elegantly, "Patients are pleased to have their autonomy respected but exercise of autonomy includes the right to relinquish it."

Consumer empowerment is perhaps more evident in the United States than other developed economies served by single-payer national health systems. In the United States, most citizens see each month on their paystubs a significant dollar sum deducted for health insurance. Every year, they have to review alternative health insurance plans, make risk-return tradeoffs, and choose the ones they prefer for themselves and their families. In Japan and Western Europe, most citizens receive their health care "for free" through a national health system, funded by taxpayers. The result can sometimes be a less empowered, more quiescent patient population. Interestingly, many developing countries operate more like the United States. Lacking the resources to fund meaningful national health programs, individual consumers are left to fend for themselves, seeking private treatment that they and their families can afford. In poor countries, consumers are best advised to keep their own medical records since nothing approaching an electronic record-keeping system is available.

As a result, enormous innovation in the delivery of good quality but low cost healthcare services is taking place from Asia to Africa. In India, the Avarind Eye Hospital provides routine eye surgeries to the highest quality standards at perhaps a tenth of the developed country price. A mass production approach to other routine surgeries, such as hernia operations, provides similar savings. In the area of prevention, the spread of ever-cheaper mobile smart phones enables citizens in remote rural areas to receive online medical consultations, treatment suggestions, and prescriptions. Readings on diagnostic machines in clinics can be taken by nurses or community workers, transmitted electronically and interpreted by specialist doctors working in city hospitals. When the time from data collection to treatment can be cut thanks to mobile health care, lives can be saved.

Mobile health is gaining traction in developed economies as well. The Fitbit and other wristband products that enable consumers to self-monitor exercise levels, sleep patterns, and blood pressure have sold briskly. Despite Google Health's failed effort to facilitate patients' collecting their medical records electronically in one place, there were around 40,000 health apps available by 2015 for 1.6 billion mobile smart phones, and the advent of Apple's Healthkit, also deployed in the new Apple Watch, promised to stimulate broader use and more innovation. Many of these products, sometimes faddish in nature, appealed to a younger generation of healthcare enthusiasts or to the worried well—those who are basically fit but who make an effort to look after themselves. The importance of consumers working to preserve their health through sensible, preventive measures cannot be underestimated; these consumers are reducing or at least postponing their eventual burden on the healthcare system.

For those already sick, mobile health adds equally important benefits. From remote monitoring to in-body sensors, mobile health innovations enable patients to spend fewer expensive and less than pleasant days in hospitals and more days getting better or managing their illness in the comfort of their own homes. The temptation to undertake continuous rather than snapshot monitoring can, in some cases, be unproductive and costly, and risks turning patients into hypochondriacs. Mobile health innovations should be adopted widely only after controlled consumer experiments have demonstrated their value added in terms of improved patient outcomes.

CONCLUSION

Demographic changes are powerful forces. Equally powerful are the dramatic improvements in public health over the last century that have lengthened life expectancies and so contributed to the aging of populations and deteriorating dependency ratios. The invisible hand of the market responds to such shifts by reallocating resources and creative efforts to take advantage of new business opportunities. At the same time, there are many poor and vulnerable citizens whose income levels are not that attractive to the private sector. Humanity requires that their health needs be addressed but, in an era of resource constraints, both rich and poor can be part of the solution by taking care of themselves, living a lifestyle that promotes rather than challenges good health, and availing themselves of medical care when needed but receiving that care from the correct providers.

For those consumers who are not self-motivated, who is in the best position to nudge them to make the right choices? Is it the family doctor or the front-line team of doctors and nurses who are employed by the hospital where they are being treated? Or the insurance companies that are motivated to lower the costs of their care by persuading patients to take preventive measures? Or perhaps the pharmacists who can influence consumers to stick to prescribed drug regimens? Who does the consumer trust more? The public health policymaker who is simultaneously trying to improve patient outcomes and lower costs has many private-sector allies to influence patient behavior if she knows how to engage them. While philosophical and stylistic differences between public and private sector executives in the healthcare sector may remain, mutual understanding and partnership-driven solutions can always be advanced when both groups focus on the common theme of consumer needs, consumer decision-making, and better consumer health outcomes.

PART I

Corporate Strategy and Public Health

1

JOHNSON & JOHNSON
THE PROMOTION OF WELLNESS

John A. Quelch and Carin-Isabel Knoop

To be the world's healthiest company is an ambitious goal. Our mission is to deliver high-quality value-added health care in a sustainable manner, so we must serve as the role model with our own employee population. How are we as a society going to pay for health care in the next 20 to 30 years? We want to be an integral part of the solution and already have a significant track record in this space.
Alex Gorsky, *Chief Executive Officer*.

We want to make health the default because the health of the employee is inseparable from the health of the business.
Fikry Isaac, *Vice President Global Health Services, and Chief Medical Officer*.

In January 2014, Dr. Fikry Isaac, Vice President Global Health Services, Johnson & Johnson (J&J), and Chief Medical Officer, Wellness & Prevention, Inc., was about to meet with J&J Chief Executive Officer Alex Gorsky. In 2014, J&J's "Culture of Health" 12-program framework was launched globally throughout J&J, and customized according to location, culture, and specific health needs. All business locations were to participate regardless of size. The health programs included a tobacco-free workplace, free health profiles, an employee assistance program, medical surveillance, physical activity, health promotion, stress and energy management, cancer awareness, HIV/AIDs awareness, healthy eating, modified duty/return to work, and travel health. Tools were prevention-focused education, rewards for healthy behaviors, and environments that made it natural for employees to engage in healthy behaviors. "Successful health and wellness programs take a holistic view of 'health' that includes physical, occupational, intellectual, social/spiritual, and emotional components," Isaac noted, "because there's a clear connection between wellness, productivity and competitiveness."[1]

[1] Fikry W. Isaac MD, MPH, Vice President Global Health Services, Johnson & Johnson and Chief Medical Officer, Wellness & Prevention, Inc., and Scott C. Ratzan MD, MPA, MA, Vice President of Global Health, Government Affairs & Policy for Johnson & Johnson, "Corporate Wellness Programs: Why Investing In Employee Health and Well-Being Is an Investment in the Health of the Company," internal J&J paper.

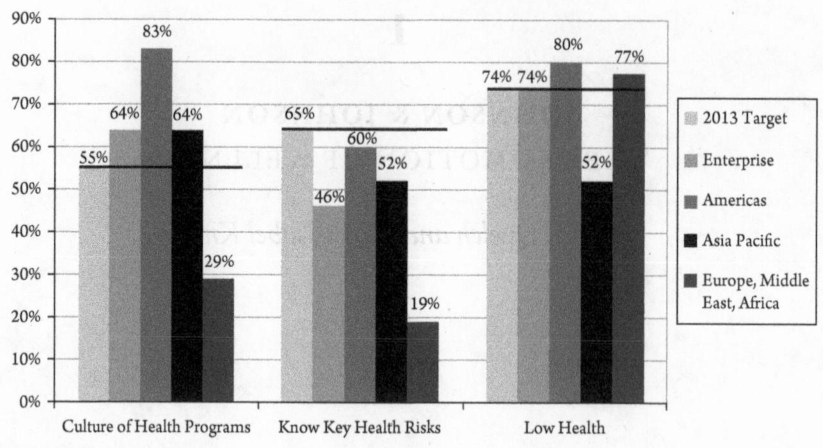

I: Culture of Health (COH)
Reached 30% more employees enterprise-wide since 2010 (with a 43% increase outside of the U.S.)
–84,000 employees (64%) have access to all 12 COH programs
–100,000 employees (86%) have access to 10/12 COH programs
II: Health Profile Participation (Know Key Health Risks)
Outside of the U.S. has increased by 24% since 2010–expect further increase with greater profile availability
III: Low Health Risk
Has remained relatively stable with slight decreased trend due to increased participation

Notes:

The "Enterprise"category referred to the entire J&J organization.

The three black bars indicate the 2013 company-wide targets.

Figure 1.1 Exhibit 1a Johnson & Johnson Healthy Future 2015 Goals, 2013 Results.

By the end of 2015, Isaac and his Global Health Services organization were responsible for delivering three Healthy Future 2015 performance goals: (1) 90% of employees with access to fully implemented Culture of Health programs; (2) 80% of employees with a completed health risk profile and knowledge of their key health indicators (e.g., blood pressure, weight, blood sugar, cholesterol, etc.); and (3) 80% of employees with a health risk profile in the "low risk" (0–2 of the 11 health risks) category. With Gorsky, Isaac would have to review progress toward achieving these goals (see Figure 1.1 and Table 1.1) and set priorities to further improve the health and well-being of J&J's 128,000 employees (about two-thirds of whom were outside the United States).

COMPANY BACKGROUND

Since its 1885 founding as an antiseptic surgical dressing manufacturer, J&J had introduced many household medical products, such as the Band-Aid® bandage, birth control, acetaminophen (Tylenol®), and contact lenses.[2] In the 1990s, acquisitions and investments strengthened the company's foothold in the skin-care and medical device industries, making J&J one of the most well-known household names within health care. Based in New Brunswick, New Jersey, J&J controlled 275 companies based in 60 countries. With $67 billion in revenues in 2012, the "family of companies" reported into three

[2] Anne Law, "Johnson & Johnson: History," Hoovers, Inc., www.hoovers.com, accessed January 2014.

Table 1.1 Exhibit 1b Percentage of Sites Worldwide (n = 400) Implementing All 12 Culture of Health Programs, 2010 and 2013

Culture of Health Program	*2010*	*2013*
Tobacco Free	70%	77%
HIV/AIDS	50%	79%
Health Profile	52%	78%
EAP	76%	90%
Medical Surveillance	79%	82%
Physical Activity	71%	88%
Health Promotion	66%	85%
Stress & Energy Management	70%	74%
Cancer Awareness	60%	88%
Healthy Eating	54%	84%
Modified Duty	68%	83%
Travel Health	65%	71%

Source: Company documents.

divisions: Pharmaceuticals (40% of sales), Medical Devices & Diagnostics (40%), and Consumer (20%).[3] (See financials in Table 1.2 and share price trends in Figure 1.2)

"Wait a Minute, This Is a Credo Issue!"

Discussions of wellness at J&J often evoked the memory of Robert Wood "General" Johnson, the founder's son—the gym he maintained on-site, the clinic he had in his office, and the physicians who worked for J&J whom he authorized to make house calls to help sick employees. Johnson also offered his employees one of the first pension plans in the U.S. and brought in a chef to cook for employees working late. When women took over factory jobs as men left to fight in World War II, he organized a women's volleyball team. Worried that J&J might lose its moral compass by going public in 1944, then-CEO General Johnson wrote the firm's Credo (see Box 1.1). Current CEO Gorsky explained:

> General Johnson took a stand for employees in the 1940s when the employee-management relationship in general in the U.S. was not great. He took a stand on fair pay and good treatment, and this was a very progressive idea. But the Credo is as relevant today as it has always been. We just completed a Credo Challenge—started by former CEO Jim Burke. He said if the Credo does not mean anything we will take it off the wall. We went through the Credo with our board and our management committee line by line and asked ourselves: "How do we think about that?" We used real world case studies where we did not live up to these commitments. People took the Credo, signed it, and posted it in their offices, factory cafeterias, or warehouses. Lots of [other] companies have some kind of statement of company values, but we really live it.

[3] Anne Law, "Johnson & Johnson: Description," Hoovers, Inc., www.hoovers.com, accessed January 2014.

Table 1.2 Exhibit 2 Johnson & Johnson and Subsidiaries: Consolidated Statement of Earnings (in millions except per share figures), 2008–2012

	2012[a]	*2011*[a]	*2010*[a]	*2009*[a]	*2008*[a]
Sales to customers	$67,224	$65,030	$61,587	$61,897	$63,747
Cost of products sold	21,658	20,360	18,792	18,447	18,511
Gross profit	45,566	44,670	42,795	43,450	45,236
Net earnings	10,514	9,672	13,334	12,266	12,949
Add: Net loss attributable to non-controlling interests	339				
Net earnings attributable to Johnson & Johnson	10,853	9,672	13,344	12,266	12,949
Basic net earnings per share attributable to J&J	$3.94	$3.54	$4.85	$4.45	$4.62
Diluted net earnings per share attributable to J&J	$3.86	$3.49	$4.78	$4.40	$4.57

Source: Company documents.

[a] Adjusted earnings (before and after tax) and adjusted EPS.

The Credo also reflected the centrality of employee well-being. "The Credo tells us we should be taking care of our employees—this is more than having access to a fitness center," noted Pamela Corson, director of J&J's global Employee Assistance Program (EAP) and mental well-being. "Our focus has been on improving lifestyles, not just for the dollars saved, but also because it is the right thing to do," she explained. J&J managers believed that the Credo motivated not only J&J's early involvement in caring about

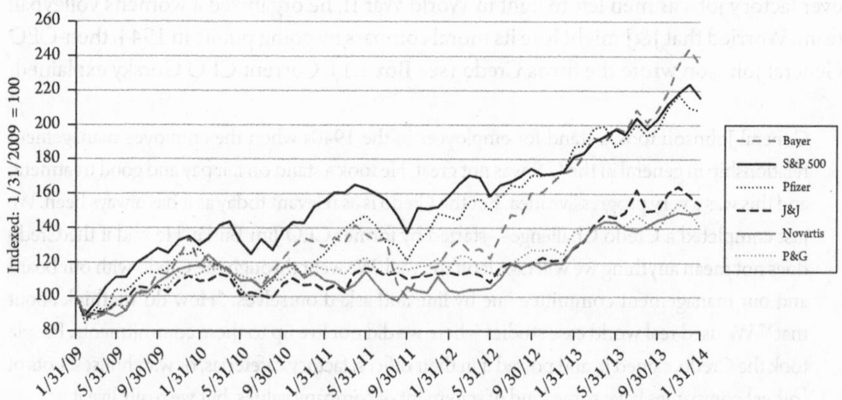

Figure 1.2 Exhibit 3 Johnson & Johnson Share Price vs. Competitors and S&P 500 Composite Index, 2009–2014.

Source: Thomson Reuters Datastream, accessed March 10, 2014.

Box 1.1 Exhibit 4 Johnson & Johnson Credo

We believe our first responsibility is to the doctors, nurses and patients, to mothers and fathers and all others who use our products and services. In meeting their needs everything we do must be of high quality. We must constantly strive to reduce our costs in order to maintain reasonable prices. Customers' orders must be serviced promptly and accurately. Our suppliers and distributors must have an opportunity to make a fair profit.

We are responsible to our employees, the men and women who work with us throughout the world. Everyone must be considered as an individual. We must respect their dignity and recognize their merit. They must have a sense of security in their jobs. Compensation must be fair and adequate, and working conditions clear, orderly and safe. We must be mindful of ways to help our employees fulfill their family responsibilities. Employees must feel free to make suggestions and complaints. There must be equal opportunity for employment, development and advancement for those qualified. We must provide competent management, and their actions must be just and ethical.

We are responsible to the communities in which we live and work and to the world community as well. We must be good citizens—support good works and charities and bear our fair share of taxes. We must encourage civic improvements and better health and education. We must maintain in good order the property we are privileged to use, protecting the environmental and natural resources.

Our final responsibility is to our stockholders. Business must make a sound profit. We must experiment with new ideas. Research must be carried on, innovative programs developed and mistakes paid for. New equipment must be purchased, new facilities provided and new products launched. Reserves must be created to provide for adverse times. When we operate according to these principles, the stockholders should realize a fair return.

Source: Johnson & Johnson Company, "Our Credo," http://www.jnj.com/sites/default/files/pdf/jnj_ourcredo_english_us_8.5x11_cmyk.pdf, accessed January 2014.

employee well-being but also its sustained commitment. The Credo was set in stone at the entrance of global headquarters and displayed at every location globally. General Johnson's philosophy on management (see Box 1.2) also hung in many headquarter offices.

CARING FOR EMPLOYEES: A LEGACY OF HEALTH AND WELLNESS PROGRAMS

In 1979, J&J began offering employees its "Live for Life" wellness program. The aim was to cut health-care costs by focusing on reducing risks that contributed most to these costs: obesity, hypertension, blood glucose, inactivity, cholesterol, tobacco use, and stress. Employees were asked to voluntarily complete a health assessment questionnaire. The company set up on-site clinics to deliver occupational health services, perform medical evaluations, advise on nutrition and weight management, provide flu shots and vaccinations, and manage smoking cessation programs. J&J

Box 1.2 Exhibit 5 Johnson & Johnson Management Philosophy

Our Management Philosophy

Our concept of modern management
may be summarized in the expression "to serve."
It is the duty of the leader
to be a servant to those responsible to him.
He accepts the problems of others
and the right of others to help and advise.
High position does not imply the wielding of authority
but rather to inspire others by effort
within the framework of the corporation policy.

We expect little of the organization chart
but much of policies and objectives.

Once these are understood and accepted
we expect management to reach its peak efficiencyby its own energy.

To lead in any human situation
means to give direction to human energy.
It means to be ahead of others in perception of the goal,
which means reaching such goals in the face of new problems.
It is the duty of management
to stimulate and develop the aptitudes of others.

To be responsible to others for their progress
is a far cry from the concept of authority with
autocratic control.

It is a question of giving subordinates
not only an understanding of policy
but of thinking independently.

It is a process of participating in other men's
initiatives, stimuli, ideas and incentives.

This concept of command helps to overcome intellectual stagnation,
the great problem of large organizations,
thus increasing their fertility in the field of ideas.
The greatest responsibility of modern management
is to develop the human intellect
in order that it may express its talent.

—Robert Wood Johnson, 1957

Source: Company documents.

Table 1.3 The table below shows company-wide targets from 2011 to 2015

Bridging Targets	*2011*	*2012*	*2013*	*2014*	*2015*
Culture of Health Programs	25%	40%	55%	70%	90%
Health Profile Participation	45%	55%	65%	75%	80%
Low Health Risks	70%	72%	74%	77%	80%

Source: Company documents.

opened gyms on-site and set up one of the first-ever programs to provide employee counseling.[4]

This laid the groundwork for a more comprehensive health and wellness (H&W) program in 1995. A task force looking into the delivery of services in the U.S. saw expensive duplications in the provision of Live for Life services across business units. Those services were subsequently brought under the H&W umbrella, and health assessments were linked to benefits plan design. H&W integrated employee health, disability management, employee assistance, and occupational medicine programs, focusing on prevention, self-care, and risk-factor reduction.[5] The J&J clinics also expanded their offerings; in 2013, the clinics reported 48,751 new cases and a total of 63,400 visits.

In 2004, then-Chairman and CEO William Weldon called for extending J&J's global wellness programs from the U.S. to the rest of the world. In 2007, J&J implemented a worldwide tobacco-free campus policy, banning smoking and tobacco products on all premises worldwide. By 2014, more than 98% of J&J worldwide workplaces were tobacco free. Smoking was also prohibited in company vehicles and at company-sponsored meetings. In 2013, the smoking rate among all U.S. employees participating in a health risk assessment dropped to 3.2%. (See Table 1.4.)

THE GLOBAL HEALTH SERVICES GROUP

In 2008, J&J set up a new business unit, Wellness & Prevention, as part of the Consumer business to provide these services to other employers, combining internal staff with acquired companies such as HealthMedia, Inc., and the Human Performance Institute (HPI). Meanwhile, Global Health Services (GHS) continued to innovate and provide enhanced health services internally. In 2013, the GHS team (which reported through the Total Rewards & Performance framework as a part of Global Human Resources) provided central leadership to H&W services for J&J employees. The team had 358 people in 262 full-time equivalent positions and included experts in occupational

[4] Isaac and Ratzan, "Corporate Wellness Programs."

[5] Ronald J. Ozminkowski, et al., "Long-Term Impact of Johnson & Johnson's Health & Wellness Program on Health Care Utilization and Expenditures," *Journal of Occupational and Environmental Medicine* 44, no. 1 (2002), http://www.thehealthproject.com/documents/2003/johnson_johnson_utilization_expenditure.pdf, accessed January 2014.

Table 1.4 Exhibit 6 Excess Johnson & Johnson Health-Care Costs Based on Employee Risk Portfolio, 2013

Category	*Excess Health Care Cost per Risk*[a]	*# of High-Risk Employees*[b]	*Excess Health Care Costs*	*# of High-Risk Employees*[c]	*Excess Health Care Costs*
Obesity (BMI 30.0+)	$2,764	6,178	$17,075,992	7,603	$21,014,692
Hypertension (Blood pressure 140+/90+ mmhg)	$1,505	1,976	$2,973,880	2,429	$3,655,645
Glucose (Fasting 126+ mg/dl)	$3,357	823	$2,762,811	1,021	$3,427,497
Inactivity (Moderate Activity = 0 days per week)	$1,642	1,565	$2,569,730	1,936	$3,178,912
Cholesterol (Total Cholesterol 240+ mg/dl)	$1,051	1,656	$1,740,456	2,041	$2,145,091
Tobacco Use (Any use)	$1,652	922	$1,523,144	1,126	$1,860,152
Stress (Heavily or Excessively Stressed)	$2,621	377	$988,117	458	$1,200,418
Total			**$29,634,130**		**$36,482,407**

Source: Company documents.

[a] Health Care Costs used in the Results Calculator software.

[b] 2013 Health Profile participation = 28,654 Choices Eligible employees.

[c] Data extrapolated to J&J total Choices Eligible population of 35,197.

medicine, health promotion, energy management, and employee assistance. (See Figure 1.3.)

GHS staff reported to regional groups (Americas; Europe, the Middle East, and Africa (EMEA); and Asia-Pacific). The GHS configuration depended on the density of J&J operations, resulting in six campuses—clusters of sites—in the U.S., three in EMEA, and three in Asia-Pacific. Services were provided via a hybrid model of J&J health professionals and local contractors. Resources outside the U.S. historically focused mostly on occupational health to meet business and regulatory needs.

Within GHS, J&J maintained a separate central budget dedicated to providing resources, communications, program development, and regional oversight. Outside the U.S., each operating company had to invest financial and human resources to ensure programs were customized to meet the health needs of their populations and enhance the health culture within their organizations.[6] At newly acquired companies, the GHS team

[6] GHS case study.

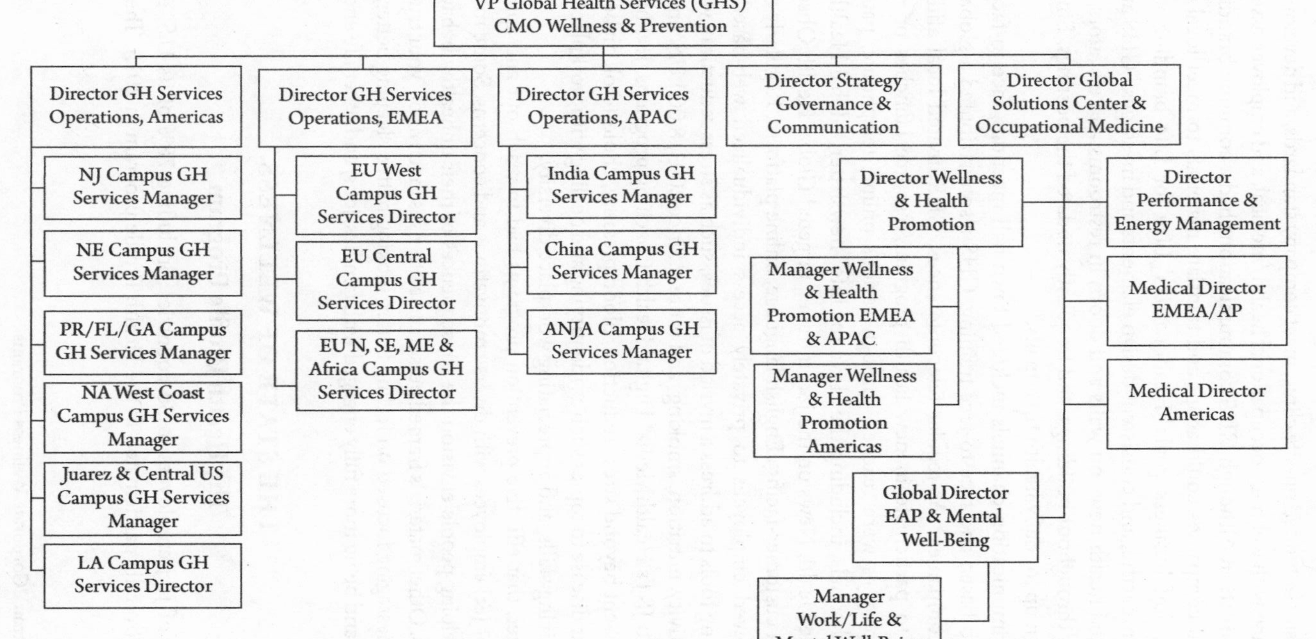

Figure 1.3 Exhibit 7 Johnson & Johnson Global Health Services Organization.
Source: Company documents.

would help management understand J&J's Culture of Health philosophy and develop a one- to three-year plan to align them with the rest of J&J. The campus lead (usually a nurse or health-care professional) would help each acquired location to recruit, train, and establish a business-funded on-site clinic, meet company standards, and develop an integrated approach with wellness, occupational health/medical, and employee assistance.

Communication Although GHS communications had a common branding look and feel, local companies could adapt and translate materials to meet local cultural requirements and business goals. Headquarters' Live for Life branding included memorable, impactful, and consistent design elements and messages.[7] GHS and local partners posted health news on walls and doors, in restrooms and elevators, and on TV monitors throughout buildings, and frequently updated the postings. Employees could also sign up for daily health tip e-mails.[8]

GHS communication channels included town hall meetings, face-to-face meetings, plus web-based and face-to-face training. GHS also distributed a global newsletter to all companies.[9] At regular teleconferences, GHS invited local affiliates or stakeholders to participate in new health program/resource launches or regional updates. Employees were reached through various online, telephonic, paper, and face-to-face channels, including the "Live for Life" newsletter, Global Health calendar, Employee Health News on the J&J intranet, targeted Global Health Observance e-mails, and a customer-facing, English language, online platform. Regularly updated websites allowed employees to privately access individualized web-based digital health coaching tools to address a myriad of issues, such as stress reduction, work/life balance, inactivity, nutrition, smoking, and more.[10] Since 2003, 8,000 U.S. employees participated in J&J's HealthMedia® Digital Health Coaching programs. J&J health literacy efforts went beyond stress reduction, blood pressure, cholesterol, diabetes, and cardiovascular disease to topics such as identifying and dealing with workplace bullies, improving driving skills, and appreciating workplace diversity.[11]

Isaac argued that effective prevention programs had to reach out and appeal to a broad range of J&J employees with diverse motivations and concerns. Some messaging focused on helping people envision the consequences of their unhealthy behaviors on their life goals. Other materials framed personal health risks in terms of "your true health age." Other messaging focused on feeling better, looking better, sleeping better, having more energy, and being more fully engaged with families, jobs, and other life endeavors.

THE STATE OF WELLNESS

The Health Profile Program

Around 59% of J&J employees in 36 countries (including 78% of its U.S. employees and 47% overall) participated in the Health Profile program in 2013. The survey

[7] Isaac and Ratzan, "Corporate Wellness Programs."
[8] Isaac and Ratzan, "Corporate Wellness Programs."
[9] CHS case study, J&J internal document.
[10] Isaac and Ratzan, "Corporate Wellness Programs."
[11] Isaac and Ratzan, "Corporate Wellness Programs."

was annual in the U.S. and biannual internationally. Some locations had 100% participation; others had not yet launched. Annual reports revealed trends and levels of participation and risk. In the U.S., the top-three risks based on self-reporting were: (1) **unhealthy eating**, defined as not eating five servings of fruits and vegetables a day (55% of U.S. respondents); (2) **physical activity**, defined as less than 150 total minutes of moderate physical activity a week (21% did not exercise sufficiently); and (3) **obesity**, defined as a body mass index (BMI)[12] over 30 (20.5%). In some developing countries, the third most-salient risk was tobacco use. Over 40% of U.S. participants believed the Health Profile helped them discover an unknown health issue, while 73% said it helped them improve or maintain a healthy lifestyle.[13]

Upon completing the Health Profile, all domestic J&J employees with one or more of the following seven Global Population Health Risks were eligible for telephonic health advising: tobacco, inactivity, blood pressure, cholesterol, glucose, BMI, and stress. Available through Health Fitness, Health Advising consisted of one confidential phone conversation with a professional health educator who reviewed a participant's Health Profile results, answered questions, and provided referrals to resources and support. In 2012, 86% of eligible Health Advising participants completed a Health Advising session through Professional Health Advisors.[14]

The Health Profile was developed and managed by an outside vendor. "This tool provides us good insights into the health risks of J&J employees around the world," said Lina Uribe, global director for wellness and health promotion. J&J outperformed the vendor's composite company benchmark for several health risks. Overall, J&J employee health risk trends were significantly better than national norms for the U.S. (see Table 1.5 and Table 1.6). The factors driving global results could be challenging—while vegetarians in India might easily eat five servings of vegetables a day, these might be prepared in saturated fats, impacting obesity. (See Table 1.7 for regional variations.)

Health risk assessments for program participants enabled J&J to monitor trends in employee health. J&J in turn supported local managers in organizing interventions to address the top health risks for their locations. Employees participating in the U.S. Health Profile program received a $500 discount toward their health insurance premiums.[15] If a health risk was identified, the employee had to participate in a Health Advising session to retain the $500 credit. "Outside the U.S., we adjust the incentives according to local benefit programs and customs, but in general we offer much smaller financial incentives," noted Vice President of Global Total Rewards and Performance Susan Podlogar.

12 Body mass index (BMI) was a measure of body fat based on a person's weight and height measured as kilograms of weight divided by meters of height squared, kg/m^2.

13 Johnson & Johnson 2012 Citizenship and Sustainability Report, http://www.jnj.com/sites/default/files/pdf/2012-JNJ-Citizenship-Sustainability-ANNUAL-REPORT-June2013-FINAL062413.pdf, accessed January 2014.

14 Johnson & Johnson 2012 Citizenship and Sustainability Report.

15 Sophie Quinton, "The Johnson & Johnson Workout Program: Improving Productivity with Diet and Exercise," *The National Journal*, June 27, 2013, http://www.nationaljournal.com/next-economy/solutions-bank/the-johnson-johnson-workout-program-improving-productivity-with-diet-and-exercise-20130627, accessed January 2014.

Table 1.5 Exhibit 8a Johnson & Johnson Employee Health Risk Factors Compared to U.S., 2009

Health Risk Factor	*J&J 2009*	*CDC US Data*[a]	*Vendor Book of Business (vendor data on other U.S.-based MNCs)*
Unhealthy Eating (<5 Servings / Day)	60.0%	75.6% (2007)	70.2%
Obesity (BMI 30.0+)	20.4%	34.1% (2003–06)	33.5%
Inactivity (<150 Moderate Minute Equivalents)	20.4%	30.5% (2005–06)	NA
Hypertension (Blood Pressure 140+/90+ mmhg)	6.3%	17.9% (2003–06)	8.1%
Cholesterol (Total Cholesterol 240+ mg/dl)	5.3%	16.3% (2003–06)	6.4%
Tobacco Use (Current User of Any Tobacco)	3.9%	29.6% (2006)	14.9%
Glucose (126+ when fasting—close to diabetes)	2.5%	NA	NA
Stress (Heavily or Excessively Stressed)	1.6%	NA	2.8%

[a] Based on "Health, United States, 2009," a publication by the Centers for Disease Control and Prevention and National Center for Health Statistics (except for "Unhealthy Eating," which is based on the Behavioral Risk Factor Surveillance System (BRFSS) data from 2007).

J&J also offered, since 2009, financial incentives to at-risk U.S. employees for participation in CareConnect care management programs; these included a maternity program, a healthy weight program, and preventive colonoscopies.[16] Poor results and low participation led J&J to suspend its healthy weight program that gave employees with BMIs of over 30 a credit toward their health plan contribution for losing 10% of their weight in a year. The CareConnect program also helped employees manage chronic or acute conditions, offering a customized and integrated approach that addressed each individual's health issues.

To test for the connection between corporate focus on better health and employee actions, J&J, starting in 2012, included a new question in its biannual Credo survey. In 2013, 82% of respondents agreed: "My company helps me in my efforts to achieve good health and well-being." Responses covered 98% of employees. "This enables us to see how the caring theme is playing out," a manager explained. GHS also gathered data through J&J's management assessment and action review program at manufacturing locations, which surveyed employees about health programs and hazards in the workplace.

[16] Isaac and Ratzan, "Corporate Wellness Programs."

Table 1.6 Exhibit 8b Johnson & Johnson Employee Health Risk Factors Compared to U.S., 2013

Health Risk Factor (in descending order by High Risk Prevalence)	*J&J 2013*	*CDC US Data*	*Vendor Book of Business (2013)*
Unhealthy Eating (<5 Servings / Day)	55.5%	76.6% (2009)	56.1%
Obesity (BMI 30.0+)	21.6%	34.9% (2011–2012)	34.0%
Inactivity (<150 Moderate Minute Equivalents)	21.1%	47.6% (2011)	42.2%
Hypertension (Blood Pressure 140+/90+ mmhg)	6.9%	30.6% (2007–2010)	7.7%
Cholesterol (Total Cholesterol 240+ mg/dl)	5.8%	13.7% (2007–2010)	7.2%
Tobacco Use (Current User of Any Tobacco)	3.2%	27.4% (2010)	8.9%
Glucose (126+ Fasting)	2.9%	NA	5.7%
Stress (Heavily or Excessively Stressed)	1.3%	NA	1.2%

Source: Company documents.

Table 1.7 Exhibit 9 Population Health Risks by Region 2013—Health Profile Participants (self-reported and professionally collected data)

High Risk Factor	*Global*	*Americas*	*EMEA*	*Asia Pacific*
Unhealthy Eating	61.7%	57.1%	61.0%	77.9%
Inactivity	36.3%	28.4%	36.7%	63.3%
Obesity	17.9%	22.5%	12.3%	5.5%
Hypertension	9.0%	7.3%	16.7%	10.1%
Cholesterol	7.3%	6.2%	8.8%	10.3%
Depression	7.0%	7.2%	3.2%	8.7%
Tobacco Use	9.3%	5.3%	14.9%	19.9%
Stress	12.9%	10.4%	13.0%	21.4%
Seat Belt	6.2%	3.1%	1.4%	21.8%
Glucose	2.7%	2.8%	0.8%	3.5%
Alcohol	2.8%	2.4%	2.3%	4.1%

Source: Company documents.

Energy for Performance in Life Program

Another core program was Energy for Performance in Life (E4PIL), launched in 2008, which taught energy management strategies. Around 33,000 employees were reached by 2013,[17] with the aim of reaching 50% of all employees by the end of 2015. The goal was to teach participants how to maximize their personal energy; to feel physically energized, emotionally connected, and mentally focused; and to obtain "full engagement in work and life."[18] The program identified four dimensions of full employee engagement. At its base were the physical aspects ("Are your nutrition, fitness, sleep and recovery patterns adequate to support you?"), followed by the emotional ("Are you effective in your interpersonal relationships?"), mental ("Are you present in the moment, focused, and fully aware?"), and spiritual ("Are you purpose-driven, committed, passionate, and principled?").[19] As part of E4PIL training, a "360 Review" incorporated participants' key health indicators. Family members and coworkers completed questionnaires about individuals' self-care and energy levels. "This is in part how program participants gauge the effectiveness of their relationships and evaluate whether their self-image is keeping them from being the person they wish to be," Isaac explained.[20]

Participants had to "honestly assess" their daily choices. Workbooks helped employees plan meals and energy-enhancing snacks. They also included sample plans, adequate recovery-time breaks, relaxation exercises, and sleep. A meeting guide helped participants coordinate meetings to include stretch breaks and snacks.[21] Participants used journaling and storytelling to identify who and what had consumed their energy each day. They developed plans for change, measured progress after 90 days, and repeated the process. Ideally, the new cycle would become habit. After participating in E4PIL, every participant received follow-up support including an e-mail from a GHS employee every 30, 60, and 90 days. A refresher course six months after the initial session was being tested in Europe.

E4PIL was offered in several formats, varying in length from two days to 60 minutes. As of 2014, most E4PIL graduates were from North America and Europe, but the team pushed for more international exposure. Participation often cascaded through the ranks of organizations once their leaders participated. One business unit leader in Florida, for example, credited the program for his losing 100 pounds and changing his life. He then encouraged all of his employees to attend. "This has changed the culture of that location," Kathleen Koch, director, performance and energy management, explained. "You can feel the energy." A finance director at a logistics center sent all his 600 staff. Gorsky and seven of his family members also attended. According to Koch, "the program teaches people how to make personal changes for their well-being and how to sustain habits and live the rituals they promise to follow."

17 Johnson & Johnson 2012 Citizenship and Sustainability Report.

18 Isaac and Ratzan, "Corporate Wellness Programs."

19 Isaac and Ratzan, "Corporate Wellness Programs."

20 Isaac and Ratzan, "Corporate Wellness Programs."

21 Isaac and Ratzan, "Corporate Wellness Programs."

Sensitivity to cultural differences was critical to success. "We are translating emotional concepts and personal feelings for E4PIL. They mean different things in different languages; for example 'spiritual energy' is difficult to translate," Koch explained. J&J was also developing local contractors to run training programs locally at less expense than having HPI staff traveling to the regions.

Fitness and Healthy Eating

J&J ensured employees could act on the education they received from their health profiles and E4PIL courses. In 2012, 84% of employees worldwide had access to a physical activity program and/or on-site fitness centers, or reimbursement toward the cost of external exercise programs. Whenever feasible, employees were encouraged to use these resources during the day, not just before or after work. When building on-site facilities was not possible, J&J supported alternative approaches such as the creation of "energy and recovery spaces"—rooms that could contain stretching and movement-encouraging tools, electronic health and sports gaming devices,[22] massage chairs, headphones, or Ping-Pong tables.

Further, J&J's U.S. healthy eating initiative, *eatcomplete*, ensured that food in company cafeterias met certain health standards.[23] This included healthy portion sizes and easy access to healthy foods, and food preparation practices that reduced the use of salt, sugars, and fats. The initiative included multiple nutritionist-led awareness events in coordination with cafeteria samplings, point-of-sale signage in cafeterias and designated vending areas, and seasonal catering menus with *eatcomplete* options featured. U.S. cafeterias were audited up to six times a year for compliance with *eatcomplete* criteria and with key performance indicators J&J established in its food service vendor contracts. By 2012, 89% of J&J cafeterias worldwide incorporated healthy eating principles in their food preparation and menus.

The behaviors J&J wanted to encourage were specifically defined, but success depended on offering a broad range of materials, programs, and events to keep employees engaged. "Our approach is to engage people wherever they are now, rather than where we want them to be," Isaac explained. "We continuously develop, test, and measure new ways to engage employees (and their families). The single biggest challenge to changing unhealthy behaviors is lack of employee engagement."[24,25] Asia-Pacific Regional Vice President Kim Taylor saw the need to establish alternatives to unhealthy behaviors: "If you ban smoking during working hours, you face the issue of the lunch break. It is crucial to provide alternatives such as lunch-time walks."

22 Isaac and Ratzan, "Corporate Wellness Programs."

23 Johnson & Johnson 2012 Citizenship and Sustainability Report.

24 "Purchasing Value in Health Care, Selected Findings From the 15th Annual National Business Group on Health," Towers Watson Survey Report, 2010.

25 Isaac and Ratzan, "Corporate Wellness Programs."

Mental Well-Being

J&J's Employee Assistance Program (EAP) provided employees and their families with confidential and culturally sensitive assistance to cope with work-related and personal problems. Since 2005, 98% of employees worldwide had access to local EAP services, delivered in over 350 locations, in many cases by local contractors. EAP professional services were available 24 hours a day. Additionally, coaching was offered to managers to help them promote a positive workplace. Psychological assistance was offered to support employees following traumatic events; in 2013, EAP services responded to over 200 such traumas affecting J&J employees. Training and information were available on multiple topics, with emphasis on building personal skills to increase resilience.

In 2013, the percentage of employees using EAP was over 7% (7% for North America and EMEA, 6% in Asia-Pacific, and 13% in Latin America), higher than the industry norms of 3% to 4%. "Our goal is 100% access, but we are also focused on reducing stigma about mental health–related issues as well as on communicating the value that EAP can bring to our organization," Corson noted. In the U.S. (based on survey responses related to impact on absenteeism and presenteeism as a result of EAP interventions), there was a savings of $2.57 for every EAP dollar spent.

The top-four clinical issues addressed through EAP in 2013 were mental health concerns (29%), work-related issues (19%), relationship concerns (15%), and family concerns (14%). Requests for support in legal matters, child-care needs, and housing concerns were also significant. "We have an on-site counseling presence at many locations, which makes it even easier for employees to access services," Corson noted. "An employee might ask for a child-care referral. The conversation could reveal an impending divorce, in which case we will help with both issues." The most common work-related issues involved supervisor conflict, work overload, and colleague conflict.

As part of a larger mental well-being strategy beyond EAP, other programs included online mental health screenings, work/life balance websites, digital coaching programs, 24/7 telephone and online counseling, mindfulness training, yoga, and online meditation. Online EAP manager training provided an overview of services to help them better support their teams.

Modeling Wellness

Many J&J managers reiterated that the commitment to wellness came from the top—from the image of a trim, disciplined, Fitbit[26]-toting CEO. "From the time Gorsky gets off the plane and meets with people and new leaders, he models these behaviors," Podlogar said. "It is hard to get traction if leadership is not walking the talk," she added. However, Gorsky noted, "You cannot [just] put a gym in the corner and tell people to use it, or [just] put a salad bar in the cafeteria. You need to give people multiple tools. It takes all of that, and leadership role models. I talk about this at many meetings, I talk to our leaders about taking care of themselves and I tell people

[26] A Fitbit was a digital fitness tracker wristband that measured the wearer's physical activity and quality of sleep.

[they] can leave the office at 2:00 p.m. to go home or to the gym, but they only do it if I do."

GHS also recruited volunteer "health champions," often regional executive vice presidents, to spread the H&W message. To Isaac, exemplary leadership gave the "impression that everyone is living more healthfully—healthful behaviors become the default, not the exception. This is important because many people naturally engage in the behaviors exemplified by their peers and managers."[27]

CHALLENGES

Proving Value

J&J spent an estimated $60 million yearly to deliver Global Health Services to its employees, plus additional investment in occupational health, wellness, and mental well-being, including EAPs. It was difficult to calculate global H&W spending because of different reporting and IT systems. As a result, funding and prioritizing the H&W programs was challenging. Podlogar explained: "How can we make sure the businesses see the value and fund our programs? When a computer system breaks down, you need to get it back up. But when a stressed person shows up at work, it's tough to clearly show that this will negatively impact business results."

J&J began to collect data on health-related savings in the 1990s. In 1995, medical claims for roughly 19,000 U.S.-based employees participating in the H&W program showed an average total savings of $224.66 per employee across all expenditure categories.[28] (See Table 1.8.) A slight increase in emergency room expenditures per employee per year ($10.87) was offset by an overall decrease in expenditures per employee for outpatient and doctors' office visits ($45.17), mental health visits ($70.69), and inpatient hospital days ($119.67).[29] These savings became progressively more significant in years three and four.[30]

More than 10,000 U.S. J&J employees participated in a longitudinal study between 2002 and 2008 to determine the relationship between weight gain or loss and health-care costs. The study participants were classified into two risk groups in 2002 (high risk or low risk) across nine health factors (obesity, high blood pressure, high total cholesterol, tobacco use, excessive alcohol consumption, poor nutrition, physical inactivity, high stress, and poor emotional health). In 2008, the employees were then reassigned to four groups across the nine factors: stayed at high risk, moved from high risk to low risk, stayed at low risk, or moved from low risk to high risk.

The study found that employees who added weight risk (BMI ≥ 30) had an increase in their annual medical costs of $1,267, which was about $982 more than those who

[27] Isaac and Ratzan, "Corporate Wellness Programs."

[28] Ozminkowski, et al., "Long-Term Impact of Johnson & Johnson's Health & Wellness Program on Health Care Utilization and Expenditures."

[29] Ozminkowski, et al., "Long-Term Impact of Johnson & Johnson's Health & Wellness Program on Health Care Utilization and Expenditures."

[30] Ozminkowski, et al., "Long-Term Impact of Johnson & Johnson's Health & Wellness Program on Health Care Utilization and Expenditures."

Table 1.8 Exhibit 10 Annual Savings per Employee after Start in Health & Wellness Program, 1995

Type of Care	*1 Year After Start ($)*	*2 Years After Start($)*	*3 Years After Start($)*	*4 Years After Start($)*	*Weighted Average per Employee per Year ($)*
Overall savings	91.99	131.02	355.54	413.10	224.66
Emergency dept visits	−12.15	−14.43	−7.27	−8.06	−10.87
Outpatient/doctors' office visits	−35.04	−3.85	146.60	121.93	45.17
Mental health visits	78.42	55.05	51.49	103.43	70.69
Inpatient days	60.76	94.25	164.72	195.80	119.67

Source: Ronald J. Ozminkowski, et al., "Long-Term Impact of Johnson & Johnson's Health & Wellness Program on Health Care Utilization and Expenditures," *Journal of Occupational and Environmental Medicine* 44, no. 1 (January 2002): 26.
Note: Savings are cumulative in each column.

remained at low risk.[31] Employees who added weight risk started out with higher health-care costs, suggesting that they initially had more medical problems than those in the low-risk group.[32] Employees who lost weight risk had an annual health-care cost growth rate that was $101 lower than those who remained at higher risk, though the difference was not statistically significant.[33] Two other health risks—tobacco use and alcohol consumption—exhibited a significant relationship between risk and cost, though in the opposite direction: employees who quit smoking or reduced their alcohol consumption had significantly higher health costs over time.[34] "If you lose weight, it is mostly very positive," GHS Director Mark Cunningham-Hill explained, "but if you lower your blood pressure risk, it could be a secondary effect of losing weight, lowering stress levels and so on, or it can be because you sought medical treatment which increased short-term health costs." More dramatically, stopping smoking or reducing alcohol might occur after a major health event such as a stroke or heart attack; the costs associated with the health event could explain the increased costs after these risk behaviors ceased. Similarly, a woman might stop smoking when pregnant, improving her health but recording higher health-care expenses at least temporarily. (Tables 1.9, 1.10, **and** 1.11 show data on the frequency of risk and risk changes, health-care costs per risk, and the impact of increasing/lowering risk on costs.)

[31] Ginger Smith Carls, Ron Z. Goetzel, Rachel Mosher Henke, Jennifer Bruno, Fikry Isaac, and Janice McHugh, "The Impact of Weight Gain or Loss on Health Care Costs for Employees at the Johnson & Johnson Family Companies," *Journal of Occupational and Environmental Medicine* 53 (January 2011): 8–16.

[32] Smith Carls, et al., "The Impact of Weight Gain or Loss on Health Care Costs for Employees . . ."

[33] Smith Carls, et al. "The Impact of Weight Gain or Loss on Health Care Costs for Employees . . ."

[34] Smith Carls, et al. "The Impact of Weight Gain or Loss on Health Care Costs for Employees . . ."

Table 1.9 Exhibit 11 Frequency of Risk and Risk Changes, 2002–2008

Risk	*Add Risk(%)*	*Lose Risk(%)*	*Stay at Risk (%)*	*Stay Not at Risk (%)*	*Unknown*[a] *(%)*
Weight	4	4	16	76	1
Blood pressure	4	7	2	78	8
Cholesterol	4	6	3	86	1
Alcohol	2	1	1	94	2
Tobacco	1	4	3	92	0
Exercise	13	19	18	46	4
Nutrition	11	18	50	17	5
Emotional health	6	4	1	86	3
Stress	7	5	3	65	21

Source: Ginger Smith Carls, Ron Z. Goetzel, Rachel Mosher Henke, Jennifer Bruno, Fikry Isaac, and Janice McHugh, "The Impact of Weight Gain or Loss on Health Care Costs for Employees at the Johnson & Johnson Family Companies," *Journal of Occupational and Environmental Medicine* 53 (January 2011): 11.

Note: n = 10,601 employees. Surveyed employees completed from two to four health risk assessments for the period of 2002 to 2008.

Note: The percentage of employees who changed their risk status during the study was relatively low. Generally less than 10% changed risk, with the exception of exercise and nutrition habits. The study also showed correlations among each of the health risks. All of the risk factors were positively correlated with weight risk, except for alcohol risk. The risks most strongly related to weight risk were blood pressure, lack of exercise and poor diet.

[a] Unknown includes employees who have added and lost the risk during the study, and employees who did not have complete information about their risk status for at least two health risk assessments.

Participating employees at the outset of the study averaged 40.2 years old; 44% were female and 56% were male; 92% were salaried workers, as opposed to hourly. A majority of employees (67%) used a preferred provider organization (PPO) health plan, with others using point-of-service plans (14%), comprehensive plans (18%), or other plans (1%).[35]

The H&W program saved an annual $565 (in 2009 dollars) in health-care costs per U.S.-based employee over the seven-year period.[36] Health program investments during this period averaged $300 per year. The study compared J&J data with data from 16 other company wellness programs. J&J employees had a lower average predicted probability of being at high risk for high blood pressure, high cholesterol, poor nutrition, obesity, physical inactivity, and tobacco use.[37] However, the study noted that J&J employees were at higher risk for depression and stress than those in the comparison group. J&J's medical

[35] Smith Carls, et al. "The Impact of Weight Gain or Loss on Health Care Costs for Employees . . ."

[36] Quinton, "The Johnson & Johnson Workout Program."

[37] Rachel M. Henke, Ron Z. Goetzel, Janice McHugh, and Fik Isaac, "Recent Experience in Health Promotion at Johnson & Johnson: Lower Health Spending, Strong Return On Investment," *Health Affairs* 30, no. 3 (March 2011), via ProQuest Business Collection, accessed January 2014.

Table 1.10 Exhibit 12 Changes in Health-Care Costs for Employees in Four Risk Groups, 2002–2008

	Add Risk	*Stay Not at Risk*	*Lose Risk*	*Stay at Risk*
		Weight risk		
Number of employees	405	8,015	384	1,699
Average annual medical/ Rx costs—first year	$3,742	$3,154	$4,256	$4,358
Average annual change in medical/RX costs	$1,267	$285	$429	$530
Impact	$982		-$101	
95% Confidence interval	($255–$1,710)		(–$468 to $256)	
		Blood pressure risk		
Number of employees	436	8,304	773	192
Average annual medical/ Rx costs—first year	$2,896	$3,349	$4,040	$4,725
Average annual change in medical/RX costs	$682	$601	$300	–$215
Impact	$297		$515	
95% Confidence interval	($9–$585)		(–$298 to $1,329)	
		Cholesterol risk		
Number of employees	464	9,072	650	286
Average annual medical/ Rx costs—first year	$3,737	$3,401	$3,485	$3,084
Average annual change in medical/RX costs	$436	$354	$429	$533
Impact	$82		–$104	
95% Confidence interval	(–$226 to $390)		(–$1,066 to $858)	
		Tobacco risk		
Number of employees	79	9,722	432	328
Average annual medical/ Rx costs—first year	$3,133	$3,421	$2,577	$4,401
Average annual change in medical/RX costs	$321	$343	$856	$466

Table 1.10 Continued

	Add Risk	*Stay Not at Risk*	*Lose Risk*	*Stay at Risk*
Impact	−$31		390	
95% Confidence interval	(−$416 to $354)		(−$126 to $907)	
		Alcohol risk		
Number of employees	200	9,971	113	91
Average annual medical/Rx costs—first year	$3,225	$3,430	$4,497	$3,216
Average annual change in medical/RX costs	$551	$366	-$35	$571
Impact	$185		−$233	
95% Confidence interval	(−$190 to $559)		($−1,417 to $951)	
		Stress risk		
Number of employees	730	6,875	487	279
Average annual medical/Rx costs—first year	$3,883	$3,412	$4,089	$4,284
Average annual change in medical/RX costs	$362	$315	$371	$672
Impact	$47		−$300	
95% Confidence interval	(−$180 to $274)		(−$576 to $155)	
		Exercise risk		
Number of employees	1,336	4,989	2,049	1,895
Average annual medical/Rx costs—first year	$3,666	$3,338	$3,567	$3,266
Average annual change in medical/RX costs	$383	$289	$405	$483
Impact	$94		−$78	
95% Confidence interval	(−$157 to $344)		(−$300 to $144)	
		Emotional health risk		
Number of employees	624	9,066	475	140
Average annual medical/Rx costs—first year	$3,529	$3,398	$4,059	$3,504

(continued)

Table 1.10 Continued

	Add Risk	*Stay Not at Risk*	*Lose Risk*	*Stay at Risk*
Average annual change in medical/RX costs	$543	$339	$538	$469
Impact	$204		$69	
95% Confidence interval	(–$38 to $445)		(–$332 to $470)	
		Nutrition risk		
Number of employees	1,147	1,751	1,881	5,314
Average annual medical/Rx costs—first year	$3,560	$3,635	$3,700	$3,253
Average annual change in medical/RX costs	$288	$274	$522	$337
Impact	$13		$185	
95% Confidence interval	(–$267 to $294)		(–$13 to $383)	

Source: Ginger Smith Carls, Ron Z. Goetzel, Rachel Mosher Henke, Jennifer Bruno, Fikry Isaac, and Janice McHugh, "The Impact of Weight Gain or Loss on Health Care Costs for Employees at the Johnson & Johnson Family Companies," *Journal of Occupational and Environmental Medicine* 53 (January 2011): 12.
Exhibit 12 on page 20 shows unadjusted changes in the health-care costs for employees in each risk group without controlling for confounders. As an illustration, employees who *added* weight risk increased their average annual medical costs by $982 more than employees who remained at lower risk, whose average annual medical costs increased by $285. Employees who lost weight risk experienced annual cost growth that was $101 lower than their peers who remained at a higher weight risk level (but the authors of the study pointed about that this was not statistically significant).

spending grew at a 3.7% lower annual rate than at comparable U.S. companies during the seven-year period.[38]

Some impacts could not be measured. Paul McKenzie, the vice president of manufacturing at Janssen Supply Chain (a J&J company), observed that employees had started to organize walk breaks or schedule lunch so that they could go for a walk, rather than just stay in the break room to play cards. "The camaraderie among associates who adopt the Energy for Performance in Life approach has a unique impact," he explained. "We have trained 70% of staff already but are aiming for 80%. We have reduced lost work days and short-term disability time. In fact, we are 80% below an industry benchmark for lost work days. Our cafeterias have created easy ways for us to eat smaller portions. We give people more time to develop as individuals. We work on the ergonomics of work spaces. This is a strategic approach. This is not just a box checking exercise; it is part of our strategy for delivering on the Credo."

[38] Henke, et al., "Recent Experience in Health Promotion at Johnson & Johnson."

Table 1.11 Exhibit 13 Impact of Adding or Losing Risk on Costs, Regression-Adjusted Estimates

Outcome	*Category*	*Estimated Costs, 2002*	*Percent Growth*	*% Points Change (95% Confidence Interval)*
Weight	Lose risk (*n* = 384)	$4,204	7.1	−2.3% (−7.4% to 2.7%)
	Stay at risk (*n* = 1,699)	$3,670	9.4	
	Add risk (*n* = 405)	$2,978	17.8	9.9% (3.0% to 16.8%)
	Stay not at risk (*n* = 8,015)	$2,920	7.9	
Blood pressure	Lose risk (*n* = 773)	$3,452	10.9	1.8% (−11.8% to 15.4%)
	Stay at risk (*n* = 192)	$3,077	9.1	
	Add risk (*n* = 436)	$2,734	9.9	1.5% (−3.7% to 6.7%)
	Stay not at risk (*n* = 8,304)	$3,086	8.5	
Cholesterol	Lose risk (*n* = 650)	$2,871	13.6	0.1% (−9.3% to 9.7%)
	Stay at risk (*n* = 286)	$2,266	13.5	
	Add risk (*n* = 464)	$2,912	8.8	1.1% (−3.8% to 6.0%)
	Stay not at risk (*n* = 9,072)	$3,199	7.7	
Tobacco	Lose risk (*n* = 432)	$2,357	22.0	17.8% (9.1% to 26.6%)
	Stay at risk (*n* = 328)	$3,794	4.1	
	Add risk (*n* = 79)	$2,913	13.4	5.4% (−3.6% to 14.3%)
	Stay not at risk (*n* = 9,722)	$3,130	8.0	
Alcohol	Lose risk (*n* = 113)	$2,605	17.0	15.3% (0.3% to 30.2%)

(*continued*)

Table 1.11 Continued

Outcome	*Category*	*Estimated Costs, 2002*	*Percent Growth*	*% Points Change (95% Confidence Interval)*
	Stay at risk ($n = 91$)	$2,772	1.7	
	Add risk ($n = 200$	$2,499	13.2	4.9% (−3.7% to 13.4%)
	Stay not at risk ($n = 9,971$)	$3,152	8.3	
Stress	Lose risk ($n = 487$)	$3,734	7.5	−3.3% (−10.6% to 4.1%)
	Stay at risk ($n = 279$)	$3,918	10.8	
	Add risk ($n = 730$)	$3,584	6.6	1.5% (−4.9% to 1.8%)
	Stay not at risk ($n = 6,875$)	$3,024	8.2	
Exercise	Lose risk ($n = 2,322$)	$3,187	9.1	−0.1% (−4.0% to 3.7%)
	Stay at risk ($n = 1,662$)	$3,160	9.2	
	Add risk ($n = 1,044$)	$3,204	7.8	0.4% (−3.3% to 4.1%)
	Stay not at risk ($n = 5,268$)	$3,066	7.4	
Emotional health	Lose risk ($n = 475$)	$3,650	9.8	1.9% (−7.1%% to 10.8%)
	Stay at risk ($n = 140$)	$3,494	7.9	
	Add risk ($n = 624$)	$3,312	12.5	4.5% (−0.3% 9.3%)
	Stay not at risk ($n = 9,066$)	$3,079	8.0	
Nutrition	Lose risk ($n = 1,881$)	$3,142	10.5	3.1% (−0.4% to 6.5%)
	Stay at risk ($n = 5,314$)	$3,187	7.4	

Table 1.11 Continued

Outcome	*Category*	*Estimated Costs, 2002*	*Percent Growth*	*% Points Change (95% Confidence Interval)*
	Add risk (*n* = 1,147)	$3,035	8.1	0.7% (3.3% to 4.7%)
	Stay not at risk (*n* = 1,751)	$3,090	7.4	

Source: Ginger Smith Carls, Ron Z. Goetzel, Rachel Mosher Henke, Jennifer Bruno, Fikry Isaac, and Janice McHugh, "The Impact of Weight Gain or Loss on Health Care Costs for Employees at the Johnson & Johnson Family Companies," *Journal of Occupational and Environmental Medicine* 53 (January 2011): 13.

Exhibit 13 on page 21 shows the regression-adjusted impact of adding and losing each risk. The results were adjusted for age, gender, and geographic region, factors that were all very predictive of costs. The chart shows that adding weight risk, losing tobacco risk, and losing alcohol risks were associated with significant cost increases, relative to employees whose health risks did not budge. Employees adding weight risk experienced 9.9% point higher cost growth compared to those who stayed at the same risk level.

Integrating Acquisitions

Bringing in newly acquired businesses brought unique challenges. One example was the $19.7 billion acquisition of the biotech firm Synthes, based in Switzerland. "They did not have any health [programs], no clinic operations," said Cunningham-Hill. "Some of their plants in Europe are not smoke free; we will need to work on this with management and the work councils. Once they agree to fund the program, [GHS] can execute it for them." The goal was to introduce all the J&J health programs to newly acquired companies within three years.

Alignment with J&J values mattered in acquisitions and made it easier to roll out the wellness programs, as Gorsky explained: "We examine their strategy and general direction first, then we look at whether they have a value system consistent with J&J and what the leaders are like. If both look good, the chances are we will have a successful acquisition. In the case of Synthes, their value statement indicates the same fundamental philosophy as our Credo."

Sustaining Interest

Finding ways to attract and retain employee attention was the greatest challenge. "You can send newsletters, and you will only reach those who read the newsletters," Taylor explained. Alternative approaches, such as team-based competitions, were found to work well and create "an almost viral impact," especially in engaging employees in the Asia-Pacific region.

Since 2005, J&J employees participated in the annual Million Step Challenge, or similar pedometer challenges, aimed at increasing movement during the work day. Over 30,000 pedometers were given to employees, with the goal of at least 10,000 steps per person each day. By 2013, more than 55,000 employees had participated. In 2012 alone, 7,300 U.S. employees participated in the challenge. Of U.S. participants, 60% reported more energy; 40%, lower weight; and 27%, lower stress.[39]

At one such challenge in Asia in 2013, 50 teams were expected, but 500 signed up. Taylor noted: "We had a major meeting of pharma group companies with leaders going up on stage and saying, 'This is my pedometer, where is yours?'" Many teams continued with daily step counts. "If you can have a few initiatives become mainstream across our network, you can achieve impact," she added. "Competition and recognition of winners were key to getting it going."

Connecting fitness to charity also worked. "When we have a charitable donation with a health focus attached to the activity, this can motivate some employees. Also, if there is a link to a community benefit, we see more discretionary funds approved by the business units," Taylor noted. Some countries organized mental health events to give access to resources for communities and to enable employees to volunteer information discreetly.

Some said J&J's wellness focus improved recruiting and could be integrated into onboarding. While GHS was part of HR, Isaac noted: "We don't ask if our focus on wellness helped persuade you to come to J&J." However, there was a slight concern that the wellness focus might discourage applications from potential high-quality hires who did not have the same focus on health. "It would be a real stretch to say that we are such a fit and healthy workforce that an obese person could not walk through the door, be accepted, and succeed. J&J is very different from an athletic company or fashion house where the expectation of a certain body shape might be the norm," Taylor noted. "Our policies should never be used to foster intolerance."

Reaching the Unwell

Another focus was disease prevention: "Keeping the well well is very critical," said Isaac. "We see many cases of employees who are well but then gain weight, experience health problems, and then need to lose weight as part of managing their condition. A significant cost saving to our health plan is keeping employees from becoming overweight." Because obesity and poor eating habits could be associated with underlying stress, J&J aimed to do even more to help employees ensure their overall health—including physical, mental, and spiritual. "As you address lifestyle management, working toward keeping the well well and reducing the consequences of unhealthy behaviors, you can achieve good gains by year three," Isaac noted. "As a culture of health becomes the norm, this helps bring in those who at first don't trust the process, are not motivated, or want to defer."

Health did not stop at the workplace. "What about the health of family members and communities?" Isaac added. "How can we take the program beyond the walls of J&J?" In the U.S., retirees had access to health benefits, digital health coaching, and fitness centers in some J&J locations. "We have not expanded the health risk assessment to retirees at this time," said Isaac.

[39] Johnson & Johnson 2012 Citizenship and Sustainability Report.

Table 1.12 Table A Global Implementation of J&J Health Programs, 2013

	Number of Employees	*Culture of Health Implementation*[a]	*Health Risk Assessment Participation*	*Low Health Risk Population*
U.S.	36,755	84%	78%	88%
Brazil	6,283	58%	47%	75%
China	8,942	88%	34%	57%
India	2,772	26%	82%	19%
Mexico	1,122	91%	72%	55%
U.K.	5,429	37%	16%	76%

Source: Company documents.

[a] Measured by access to the 12 Culture of Health Programs.

Finally, managers felt J&J could do more to ensure the mental health of employees and counter the stigma associated with mental health problems. Often, people who had gone through crises could become the greatest champions for good mental health at work. At J&J, depression was the third most common reason for short-term disability in the U.S. after pregnancy and musculoskeletal ailments. Overall, stress and depression were the greatest productivity drains, although this varied by region. Employee health profiles provided some risk information. For example, there was a correlation between heavy alcohol use and stress and depression. "We think it is all connected. The healthier you are physically, the better your mental health and vice versa," Gorsky said. "We are in mental health as a business so we understand that."

Globalizing Wellness

From 2006 to 2013, the percentage of "low risk" U.S. employees increased from 78% to 88%, with a corresponding drop in the "high risk" category. U.S. J&J employees had 41% less incidence of heart disease and 75% less incidence of high blood pressure than the national average, and they exercised more and smoked less. Table 1.12 shows global results.

Some programs and support materials were localized to address cultural differences, especially those on sensitive topics such as depression. For example, in China, exercise as a centerpiece of a fitness regime did not work as well as in the U.S. As McKenzie explained, "Young people focus on academics and not sports. At our plant in Xian we don't have a fitness center but we do make time available for workers to stretch or practice Tai-Chi."

In Europe, the Culture of Health message was clearly understood, but employees reliant on free public health for care were less motivated to participate. In countries with self-pay health-care systems, such as the Philippines, engagement was stronger.

All over the world, earning employees' trust regarding the confidentiality of personal health information was critical. J&J also had to comply with local regulations and with its own standards, which were almost always stricter. "We have a global privacy policy. Employee data is confidential. We only analyze aggregate data," a J&J manager said. "You also have to consider the government's information access rights when you are collecting health data." Taylor suggested that in countries with stronger central governments, such as China, Vietnam, or Myanmar, "people hesitate because they are more attuned to centralized control. The notion that one government agency would not share information with another would be like dreaming." Korea, for example, had strict privacy rules, so GHS had to work directly with J&J's Asia-Pacific privacy officer. In Europe, "it is harder to achieve high health profile participation because some unions see it as an intrusion on privacy," said Cunningham-Hill. "How can J&J reduce variations in adoption of our best practices because of differences in culture, program longevity, and resources across countries?"

2

COLGATE-PALMOLIVE COMPANY

MARKETING ANTI-CAVITY TOOTHPASTE

John A. Quelch and Margaret L. Rodriguez

In October 2013, Colgate-Palmolive Company (Colgate), the world's leading oral care company, was about to launch its new Colgate® Maximum Cavity Protection™ plus Sugar Acid Neutralizer™ toothpaste in Brazil (CMCP+SAN). The oral care category accounted for 46% of Colgate's $17.4 billion sales worldwide in 2013. The new CMCP+SAN toothpaste contained 1.5% arginine, an insoluble calcium compound, and fluoride, and was clinically proven to reduce and prevent cavities more effectively than toothpaste with the same level of fluoride alone. The key innovation in the toothpaste category introduced nearly sixty years earlier to prevent cavities was fluoride. All major industry players, including Procter & Gamble, GlaxoSmithKline and Colgate itself, had long ago launched products with the maximum amount of fluoride allowed by health authorities. Yet caries remained a significant threat to public health in many countries, both developing and developed.

As Suzan Harrison, Colgate's president of Oral Care, prepared to launch CMCP+SAN in Brazil, the world's third largest oral care market, her executive team considered the product's positioning and pricing. In particular, would the patent-protected CMCP+SAN technology motivate consumers who sought superior cavity protection to pay more and switch from the existing base Colgate® Maximum Cavity Protection™ product which already offered the maximum allowable level of fluoride. As Harrison prepared for her meeting with Ian Cook, Colgate's chief executive, to discuss the CMCP+SAN launch strategy in Brazil, she weighed Colgate's public health and sustainability goals alongside maximizing the economic value to Colgate's shareholders.

COLGATE-PALMOLIVE ORAL CARE

In 2013, Colgate was a $17.4 billion consumer products company with operating profit over $3.5 billion. (See Table 2.1 for Colgate's summary financials). Colgate's products were marketed in over 200 countries and it employed more than 37,000 people. Eighty percent of Colgate's revenue was generated outside the U.S., with more than 50% coming from emerging markets (in OC, PC and HC categories). The company had four core businesses: oral care (OC), personal care (PC), home care (HC) and

Table 2.1 Exhibit 1 Colgate-Palmolive Summary Financials (millions), 2011–2013[a]

	2013	*2012*	*2011*
Net Sales	17,420	17,085	16,734
Cost of Sales	7,219	7,153	7,144
Gross Profit	10,201	9,932	9,590
Selling, general and administrative expenses (SG&A)	6,223	5,930	5,758
Operating profit	3,556	3,889	3,841
Net Income	2,241	2,472	2,431

Source: Company documents.

[a] Colgate's 2013 fiscal year concluded in December 2013.

pet nutrition. (See Table 2.2 for the proportion of net sales each business generated).[1] Colgate's oral care category included toothpaste, toothbrushes, mouthwash and interdental devices (as well as floss and pharmaceutical products sold directly to dentists). Colgate tailored its product mix for emerging markets by emphasizing smaller sizes and value options. Colgate's frequent product innovations and effective marketing helped achieve strong brand penetration and distribution worldwide.

Colgate's Organizational Structure[2]

Colgate regional managers across the five operating regions[3] reported to the chief executive officer or chief operating officer (See Table 2.3 for financial results by region). Country managers in each market reported to the regional managers (who held the P&L) and were responsible for developing and funding the marketing efforts for their country's product portfolio. Global category teams focused on transferring best practices across markets and developing worldwide strategies for each category. Global category teams were evaluated based upon Colgate's global market share. The global team for oral care included a professional relations team and a consumer marketing team. In addition to the global and local teams, nine Consumer Innovation Centers (CICs), staffed by product developers and marketers, supplied the regions with new products. The new products incorporated both global innovations and local market knowledge. In 2013, Colgate spent $267 million on research and development activities across all

[1] Personal care and home care accounted for 21 percent and 20 percent of Colgate's total net sales in 2013, respectively. Each division's contribution to sales varied by market; for example, in Asia, oral care accounted for 86 percent of 2013 net sales.

[2] Quelch, John A., and Jacquie Labatt-Randle. "Colgate Max Fresh: Global Brand Roll-Out." HBS No. 508-009. Boston: Harvard Business School Publishing, 2007.

[3] The five regions were: North America, Latin America, Europe/South Pacific, Asia and Africa/Eurasia excluding Hill's® Pet Nutrition.

Table 2.2 Exhibit 2 Distribution of Company Net Sales, by Business Segment

	2013	*2012*	*2011*
Oral Care	46%	44%	43%
Personal Care	21%	22%	22%
Home Care	20%	21%	22%
Pet Nutrition	13%	13%	13%

Source: Company documents.

four of its businesses. Colgate's primary research center for oral care products (as well as home and personal care products) was located in Piscataway, New Jersey.

Colgate's management monitored a variety of key indicators to assess business performance, including: market share, net sales (including volume, pricing and foreign exchange components), gross profit margin, operating profit, net income, organic sales growth (net sales growth excluding the impact of foreign exchange, acquisitions and divestments), and earnings per share, as well as metrics on working capital, capital expenditures, cash flow and return on capital. The focus on these indicators, as well as the company's four strategic initiatives: "engaging to build our brands; innovation for growth; effectiveness and efficiency; and leading to win," drove the company's growth agenda.

History of Colgate Toothpaste

In 1873, Colgate launched the first toothpaste, Colgate® Dental Cream. For nearly 100 years, toothpaste served a cosmetic purpose as an oral cleanser. Therapeutic benefits, like caries-prevention, were not discussed in the toothpaste category until Procter & Gamble (P&G) launched Crest®, its patented fluoride toothpaste, in 1955.[4] Research conducted found that use of fluoride toothpaste resulted in 20% fewer cavities.[5] Crest® toothpaste led the shift to marketing toothpaste based upon therapeutic benefits by obtaining the endorsement of the American Dental Association in 1960. As a consequence of P&G's patents on Crest® toothpaste, competitors, including Colgate, were unable to launch their own fluoride toothpaste products until 1967. One year later, Colgate added fluoride to its toothpaste, but by that time many consumers considered Crest® the leading therapeutic toothpaste.[6]

By the 1990s, almost all U.S. toothpaste products contained fluoride. Marketing toothpaste on the basis of caries prevention was no longer a basis for differentiation; consumers instead sought solutions for halitosis, tooth discoloration, and sensitive teeth.[7] In 1997, Colgate launched its premium Colgate Total® product with a

[4] Quelch, Labatt-Randle. "Colgate Max Fresh: Global Brand Roll-Out." HBS No. 508-009. 2007.

[5] Quelch, Labatt-Randle. "Colgate Max Fresh: Global Brand Roll-Out." HBS No. 508-009. 2007.

[6] Quelch, Labatt-Randle. "Colgate Max Fresh: Global Brand Roll-Out." HBS No. 508-009. 2007.

[7] Quelch, Labatt-Randle. "Colgate Max Fresh: Global Brand Roll-Out." HBS No. 508-009. 2007.

Table 2.3 Exhibit 3 Financial Performance of Oral, Personal and Home Care, by Region

	Net Sales, $B	*Operating Profit, $B*	*Organic Sales Growth*
North America	3.07	0.93	3.5%
Latin America	5.01	1.39	9.5%
Europe and South Pacific	3.40	0.81	(0.5%)
Asia	2.47	0.70	10.5%
Africa and Eurasia	1.26	0.27	7.0%
Total Oral, Personal and Home Care	15.21	4.08	6.0

Source: Company documents.

$100 million marketing campaign.[8] Colgate Total® offered therapeutic benefits[9] for an array of oral health issues, including plaque and gingivitis,[10] and quickly became the leading toothpaste in the U.S., and propelled Colgate to share leadership.[11] In 2013, Colgate held 45% value share of the worldwide toothpaste category (see Figure 2.1 for competitive oral care market shares/competitor sizes/marketing budgets). In 2013, Colgate's toothpaste market shares had increased in Europe/South Pacific, Asia and Africa/Eurasia and decreased in North America and Latin America versus 2012.

In 2013, Colgate's toothpaste sub-brands included Colgate® Sensitive Pro-Relief™, Colgate® Maximum Cavity Protection™ (also known internally as "Big Red"), Colgate® Max Fresh™, Colgate® Optic White™, Colgate® Luminous White™ and Colgate Total®.[12] Colgate Total® was Colgate's leading toothpaste brand. The 20 year-old, exclusive formula contained 0.3% triclosan and 2% PVM/MA copolymer, and offered best-in-class protection against plaque and gingivitis. Colgate estimated that between 50 and 75% of people worldwide suffered from gingivitis. For the 15%of consumers who suffered from sensitivity,[13] Colgate sold a line of Colgate® Sensitive Pro-Relief™ products, which included the active ingredient arginine, at 8% in a calcium carbonate-based fluoride formula. Colgate also offered a whitening product under the Colgate® Optic White™ brand, (although the hydrogen peroxide-based formula was available only in select countries—of which the U.S. was one). Roughly 25% of the worldwide toothpaste market by value[14] was in "mainstream anti-caries products", such as Colgate® "Big Red" and Colgate® Triple Action toothpastes. The largest share of Colgate's volume sales came from this

[8] Quelch, Labatt-Randle. "Colgate Max Fresh: Global Brand Roll-Out." HBS No. 508-009. 2007.

[9] Colgate Total® toothpaste's therapeutic benefits included strengthening enamel, fighting cavities, reducing plaque, protecting against tartar build-up, reducing gingivitis, whitening, removing stains and reducing bad breath.

[10] Quelch, Labatt-Randle. "Colgate Max Fresh: Global Brand Roll-Out." HBS No. 508-009. 2007.

[11] Quelch, Labatt-Randle. "Colgate Max Fresh: Global Brand Roll-Out." HBS No. 508-009. 2007.

[12] Colgate retailed other toothpaste brands in select markets, including: Sorriso®™, Kolynos®™, elmex®, ™ and Tom's of Maine™.

[13] Those suffering from sensitivity could include those who were sensitive to cold, hot, sweet or sour foods or beverages.

[14] Casewriter estimates.

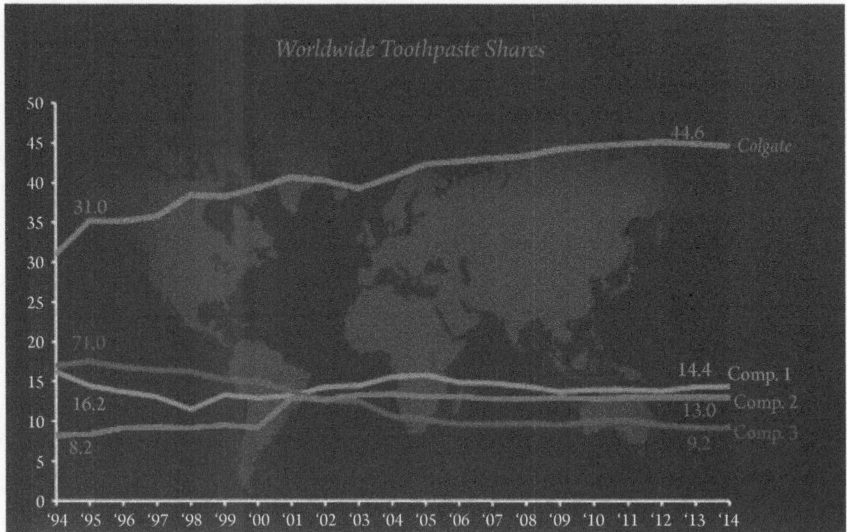

Figure 2.1 Exhibit 4 Colgate Global Toothpaste Value Market Share, 2013.
Source: Company documents.

segment, but it was growing at a slow rate. Most toothpaste category growth was driven by innovation in the premium tier, which aimed to trade consumers up to higher value products. Price guidance for Colgate's sub-brands was issued by corporate, but general managers in the country markets had the flexibility to adjust prices. Colgate also tracked the purchasing power of low income consumers in all emerging markets to ensure its products were priced affordably.

ORAL CARE AND PUBLIC HEALTH

Sufferers of oral disease often experienced pain in the mouth and face, periodontal (gum) diseases, tooth decay, tooth loss, or other diseases that limited their ability to chew, smile or speak. Oral diseases were most prevalent among individuals who had diets heavy in sweet and sticky foods and beverages, used tobacco, used alcohol to excess and/or practiced poor oral hygiene. Although oral health issues were more common in poorer countries, oral health was also a significant concern in high-income countries—often accounting for five to ten percent of total public health spending.[15] In the U.S. alone, children missed more than 51 million school hours each year due to dental-related reasons, with poor children suffering nearly 12 times more restricted-activity days than children from higher-income families.[16]

[15] World Health Organization, "Oral Health Factsheet Number 318," April 2012, http://www.who.int/mediacentre/factsheets/fs318/en/, accessed April 2015.

[16] U.S. Department of Health and Human Services, "A National Call to Action to Promote Oral Health," Rockville, MD: U.S. Department of Health and Human Services, Public Health Service, Centers for Disease Control and Prevention, and the National Institutes of Health, National Institute of Dental and Craniofacial Research. NIH Publication No. 03-5303, May 2003. http://www.nidcr.nih.gov/DataStatistics/SurgeonGeneral/NationalCalltoAction/Documents/NationalCallToAction.pdf

Dental caries, or cavities, were the most common chronic disease worldwide.[17] Caries were caused by bacteria which metabolized carbohydrates in the food and beverages people consumed. As they metabolized the carbohydrates, the bacteria produced acids which could dissolve the tooth enamel. People living in areas with poor access to oral health facilities, with aging populations or with high consumption of sugary foods and beverages were most likely to suffer from caries. Untreated caries could result in the breakdown of the enamel and tooth decay which could only be treated by filling or removing afflicted teeth.[18] According to estimates from the World Health Organization, 60 to 90% of school-aged children, and nearly all adults, suffered from caries and Colgate estimated that 5.4 billion people would suffer from active caries at some point in their lives. Many U.S. consumers believed caries was no longer a threat. However, caries affected over 78% of U.S. children and adolescents aged 6 to 19 years (compared to, for example, 94% in the Philippines), making it the most common chronic disease in this age group in the U.S.[19]

Dental caries could be prevented by regular and thorough tooth brushing,[20] reducing sugar consumption and effective exposure to fluoride (through toothpaste, fluoridated drinking water or fluoride treatments performed by dental professionals). Fluoride prevented dissolution of tooth enamel by replenishing natural calcium ions from saliva, resulting in re-mineralization of weakened enamel.[21] The fluoridation of community drinking water helped reduce caries and was named by the U.S. Centers for Disease Control and Prevention as one of the ten greatest public health achievements of the 20th century.[22] Studies showed water fluoridation reduced the amount of decay in children's teeth by 18 to 40%.[23] In developing markets, the availability of affordable fluoride toothpaste was a key source of exposure to fluoride and a driver of caries-prevention.[24]

COLGATE'S SUSTAINABILITY PROGRAMS

Colgate's leadership in sustainability was supported by the vision of its chief executive, Ian Cook,[25] and captured in the company's 2011 to 2015 Sustainability Strategy

[17] "The Oral Health Atlas," FDI World Dental Federation, 2009, referenced in company interviews.

[18] Worldwide, roughly 30 percent of adults between 65 and 74 years of age had no natural teeth.

[19] Centers for Disease Control and Prevention and the American Dental Association. Fluoridation: nature's way to prevent tooth decay. Available at http://www.cdc.gov/Fluoridation/pdf/natures_way.pdf

[20] Worldwide penetration of toothpaste was high, with nearly 90 percent of people brushing at least once per day (with a few notable exceptions, like India, where penetration was 70 percent).

[21] Featherstone JD. Prevention and reversal of dental caries: role of low level fluoride. Community Dent Oral Epidemiol 1999;27:31–40.

[22] U.S. Centers for Disease Control and Prevention, "Ten Great Public Health Achievements in the 20th Century," April 2013, http://www.cdc.gov/about/history/tengpha.htm, accessed April 2015.

[23] U.S. Department of Health and Human Services, (2000). Oral Health in America: A Report of the Surgeon General. National Institute of Dental Craniofacial Research, National Institutes of Health. Rockville, MD

[24] World Health Organization, "Strategies and approaches to oral disease prevention and health promotion," http://www.who.int/oral_health/strategies/cont/en/, accessed April 2015.

[25] Cook had joined the company's U.K. division in 1976 and assumed the role of chief executive in 2007.

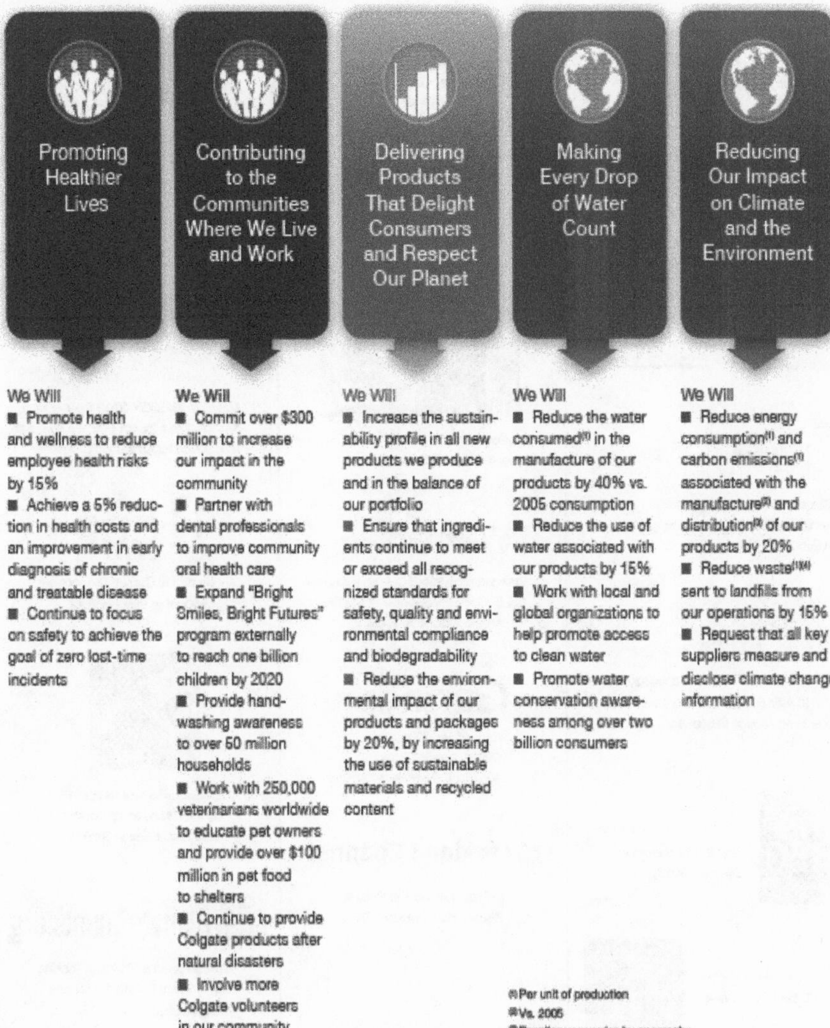

Promoting Healthier Lives
We Will
■ Promote health and wellness to reduce employee health risks by 15%
■ Achieve a 5% reduction in health costs and an improvement in early diagnosis of chronic and treatable disease
■ Continue to focus on safety to achieve the goal of zero lost-time incidents
Contributing to the Communities Where We Live and Work
We Will
■ Commit over $300 million to increase our impact in the community
■ Partner with dental professionals to improve community oral health care
■ Expand "Bright Smiles, Bright Futures" program externally to reach one billion children by 2020
■ Provide hand-washing awareness to over 50 million households
■ Work with 250,000 veterinarians worldwide to educate pet owners and provide over $100 million in pet food to shelters
■ Continue to provide Colgate products after natural disasters
■ Involve more Colgate volunteers in our community programs
Delivering Products That Delight Consumers and Respect Our Planet
We Will
■ Increase the sustainability profile in all new products we produce and in the balance of our portfolio
■ Ensure that ingredients continue to meet or exceed all recognized standards for safety, quality and environmental compliance and biodegradability
■ Reduce the environmental impact of our products and packages by 20%, by increasing the use of sustainable materials and recycled content
Making Every Drop of Water Count
We Will
■ Reduce the water consumed(1) in the manufacture of our products by 40% vs. 2005 consumption
■ Reduce the use of water associated with our products by 15%
■ Work with local and global organizations to help promote access to clean water
■ Promote water conservation awareness among over two billion consumers
Reducing Our Impact on Climate and the Environment
We Will
■ Reduce energy consumption(1) and carbon emissions(1) associated with the manufacture(2) and distribution(3) of our products by 20%
■ Reduce waste(1)(4) sent to landfills from our operations by 15%
■ Request that all key suppliers measure and disclose climate change information
(1) Per unit of production
(2) Vs. 2005
(3) Baseline year varies by geography
(4) Vs. 2010

Figure 2.2 Exhibit 5 Colgate's 2011 to 2015 Sustainability Strategy.
Source: Company documents.

(Figure 2.2) which established Colgate's approach to improving outcomes in the "People," "Performance," and "Planet" pillars. Colgate's sustainability strategy set targets to improve the health of its employees around the world, improve the sustainability profile of its products and reduce its manufacturing environmental footprint (including specific goals related to reduction of water usage, greenhouse gases, and waste production), as well as contribute to the communities in which it operated, including expanding the Company's flagship "Bright Smiles, Bright Futures" oral health education program. Colgate's total charitable donations for 2013 exceeded $35 million (over $25 million in cash, and over $10 million in kind). In 2012, Colgate established a "Sustainability Excellence Award" for the division with the greatest contribution to sustainability. In 2013, Colgate instituted an annual Colgate Cares Day,

Figure 2.3 Exhibit 6 Sustainability Accolades Received by Colgate from Independent Organizations, 2013.
Source: Company documents.

in which over 800 Colgate employees in the U.S. devoted their time to community service. By 2013, the company had received numerous accolades from independent organizations for its various initiatives (see Figure 2.3).

This progress laid the groundwork for Colgate's 2015 to 2020 Sustainability Strategy, developed in 2013 and published in 2014, which outlined "commitments for the coming years in line with the needs of our times." Colgate made new People, Performance and Planet commitments, expanding the goal for the number of children to be reached through its "Bright Smiles, Bright Futures" program, to 1.3 billion by 2020; improving the sustainability profile in new products and product updates; and committing to reduce greenhouse gas emissions on an absolute basis by 25% compared to 2002, with a longer term goal of a 50% absolute reduction by 2050. Colgate also committed to reduce manufacturing water intensity by half and to promote water conservation awareness to all of its global consumers.

Product and Supply Chain Sustainability

Colgate established a Product Sustainability Scorecard in 2012 to measure progress against its 2015 sustainability goals. The scorecard evaluated products against 25 criteria in seven categories: responsible sourcing and raw materials, ingredient profile, water, social impact, packaging, energy and greenhouse gases and waste. Performance on the 25 criteria was measured across a portfolio of comparable Colgate products. In 2013, Colgate improved the sustainability profile of 48% of new products through activities such as sourcing packaging materials for its Colgate Total Advanced Pro-shield™ mouthwash in the U.S. (which resulted in lower greenhouse gas emissions). In 2014, Colgate published a Policy on No Deforestation, joining the Consumer Goods Forum commitment to help achieve zero net deforestation by 2020. In the policy, Colgate laid out concrete commitments to improve the sourcing of pulp and paper, palm oil and derivatives, soy and soy oil and beef tallow.

Community Outreach Programs

Many of the community programs Colgate operated were closely aligned to its lines of business. For example, Hill's® Pet Nutrition donated over $275 million worth of pet food to nearly 1,000 animal shelters, which aided in the adoption of seven millions dogs and cats, between 2002 and 2013. Colgate also funded hand-washing education under its "Clean Hands, Good Health," campaign (which was co-branded with the Softsoap™ brand in the U.S.) In 2013, Colgate's program taught 62.5 million people worldwide about the importance of washing hands with soap via advertising, in-store hand-washing demonstrations and school-based programs.

In many of the communities it served, Colgate's longest running outreach program was its oral health education and outreach program. In 1911, Colgate launched its first oral health education initiative, "Good Teeth, Good Health," which trained U.S. teachers on proper oral care practices. In the 1940s, Colgate launched the "Mama Colgate" program in South Africa, wherein a trained representative visited schools to teach children about oral health via flipcharts. For many years prior to 1995, in Latin America, a brown rabbit called "Dr. Muelitas,"taught children about oral health. Dr. Muelitas, or "Dr. Rabbit," visited schools and appeared in Colgate educational materials (see Figure 2.4 for an example). Colgate also partnered with other organizations for oral health outreach: Colgate was a founding sponsor of the Global Child Dental Fund, an organization which partnered with the World Health Organization (WHO) to help eliminate caries among all children by 2026. In the U.S., Colgate partnered with the American Dental Association on its "Give the Kids a Smile" program to donate 300,000 toothbrushes and toothpaste samples each year.

Bright Smiles, Bright Futures™ In 1990, Colgate had observed significant disparate oral health outcomes by ethnic group in the U.S. Colgate's existing school-based programs did not have sufficient resources to address the disparities, so Colgate hired

Figure 2.4 Exhibit 7 Colgate's Dr. Rabbit, 2013.
Source: Company documents.

Dr. Marsha Butler to lead a new initiative which aimed to raise oral health literacy among at-risk youth in the U.S. Butler created the "Bright Smiles, Bright Futures™" program (BSBF), which brought Dr. Rabbit health education program to kids in Head Start[26], pre-school, and 1st through 3rd grade students to help them learn good oral health habits: brushing twice per day with fluoride toothpaste, visiting the dentist regularly, and limiting sugary foods. Butler and her team worked with the U.S. Surgeon General to create the "Seven Steps to a Bright Smile" guide.

By 1994, Marsha and her team had scaled the standardized BSBF programs to many countries worldwide. BSBF distributed free Colgate-branded product[27] and educational materials to children through a BSBF kit (co-branded with Colgate®); including a brushing calendar for children to use at home, which increased the entire family's engagement with the Colgate brand. BSBF enlisted volunteer professionals to provide free check-ups via mobile vans (essentially dental offices on wheels), to members of the community in over 30 countries. The BSBF program in each country used centrally developed materials and a standardized strategy; yet each market partnered with local dentists, educators and ministries of health to customize the materials and reach children in the most effective way. In Vietnam, Colgate partnered with the Ministry of Education and Training to provide Vietnamese primary school students with oral health education and samples of Colgate® products in the week following the national flag-raising ceremony.

In 1998, the first clinical study of BSBF's effectiveness found that children exposed to the curriculum showed statistically significant improvement in their plaque scores versus the control as a result of enhanced oral health practices learned through the

[26] The Head Start Program, administered by the U.S. Department of Health and Human Services, provided resources for early childhood education, nutrition and health to low-income families with children between birth and five years of age.

[27] In the U.S., coupons were distributed to school kids instead of toothpaste samples. Redemption rates for the coupons were three to four percent.

Box 2.1 Exhibit 8 Colgate Bright Smiles, Bright Futures (BSBF) Study in China, 2000

An eight week study was conducted in China with the support of the Ministry of Education. 844 participants between eight and nine years-old were selected from two primary schools. At the start of the study, the plaque score of each participant was measured by a trained dentist or nurse; and the oral health knowledge of the child was evaluated via a questionnaire. The 407 children in the experimental group received the BSBF program and the 437 in the control group received no oral health education. At the end of the eight weeks, the plaque score and oral health knowledge were tested for both the experimental and control group.

Results:

Table I Mean Plaque Index Scores for the Experimental and Control Groups

	Number of Subjects	*Mean Plaque Index Score*			*Sig.*
		Baseline	*Final*	*Change*	
Experimental Group	407	4.65	2.35	2.30	$p < 0.001$
Control Group	437	4.71	4.10	0.61	$p > 0.05$

Source: Company documents.

BSBF program.[28] Subsequent studies conducted among eight to nine year-olds in China, and three to five year-olds in India, demonstrated significant impact of BSBF on the reduction of plaque as a result of increased knowledge of dentistry and oral health best practices (see Box 2.1 for the results of the study conducted in China).

Colgate's professional relations teams, which were primarily responsible for providing outreach to dentists and the oral care community, were responsible for implementing BSBF in each country. Leadership in each market could translate or customize the BSBF program to fit the needs of their communities. In India, the Indian Dental Association partnered with Colgate to distribute its BSBF kits (which included oral health literature, as well as product samples). By 2013, BSBF had reached over 750 million children in over 80 countries, and BSBF educational materials had been translated into 30 languages. In 2013 alone, BSBF reached over 50 million children worldwide.

COLGATE® MAXIMUM CAVITY PROTECTION™ PLUS SUGAR ACID NEUTRALIZER™ TOOTHPASTE (CMCP+SAN)

Colgate's CMCP+SAN toothpaste relied on the anti-caries properties of arginine in combination with an insoluble calcium compound and fluoride. The foundational research on this technology was conducted by Dr. Israel Kleinberg. He worked for decades to

[28] SM Siegal, "Advances and Progress in Oral Health Through Oral Care Education—Scientific Proof of the Effectiveness of a Global Oral Health Education Initative" Colgate-Palmolive Company, 1998.

understand arginine's caries-prevention properties before achieving clinical results which showed that a product that incorporated arginine with an insoluble calcium compound was as effective as 1000 ppm fluoride. This research was first presented at the IADR conference in 2003 and was published in the scientific literature in 2005. Colgate acquired the rights to the technology, which Colgate referred to as Pro-Argin™ technology, around that same time. Colgate's Pro-Argin™ technology helped prevent the drop in pH levels caused by the acids derived from the carbohydrates found in many foods and beverages (particularly those high in sugar), which Colgate referred to as "sugar acids". Caries could form when sugar acids caused the pH level to drop on the surface of the teeth, resulting in repeated episodes of demineralization. As demineralization progressed, the tooth enamel eventually became irreversibly damaged, which often led to cavities.

Colgate began its research by taking Dr. Kleinberg's basic invention and combined it with fluoride to provide superior cavity prevention efficacy compared to the same level of fluoride alone. The initial research comprised short term in vivo studies evaluating the effects of CMCP+SAN as compared to toothpaste with the same level of fluoride alone on sugar acid induced demineralization and re-mineralization of demineralized enamel. The research progressed through 6 month studies evaluating the arrest and reversal of early coronal and root caries, and finally two-year studies were conducted to assess the ability to prevent the formation of new cavities. These clinical trials proved that the combination of 1.5% arginine, an insoluble calcium compound and 1450 ppm fluoride in CMCP+SAN prevented 20% more new cavities over a two year period compared to toothpaste with 1450 ppm fluoride alone.[29] Additionally, CMCP+SAN was proven to combat the effect of sugar acids on plaque pH levels, and to strengthen the tooth enamel to prevent damage from demineralization and to re-mineralize four times more effectively versus toothpaste with the same level of fluoride alone. Arginine was a well-known substance (and was already a key ingredient in Colgate® Sensitive Pro-Relief™ toothpaste). The specific combination of 1.5% arginine, an insoluble calcium compound, and fluoride used in CMCP+SAN was uniquely optimized for superior cavity prevention efficacy and was patent-protected. Raj Kohli, vice president of Oral Care Product Development, noted: "In R&D, we have several 'evergreen goals': goals which you may work your entire career to achieve. CMCP+SAN is the first evergreen we have seen on my watch: beating fluoride at caries-prevention." By 2013, Colgate had performed two clinical trials, in China and in Thailand.

CMCP+SAN Positioning Strategy

In early 2013, Colgate tested the new CMCP+SAN product in four markets: India, Colombia, Mexico and the UK. Although CMCP+SAN was initially created for sale primarily in emerging markets, the product tested well in developed markets so Colgate decided to roll-out CMCP+SAN worldwide. In launching CMCP+SAN, Colgate faced the challenge of turning the oral health conversation back to caries. Although caries was still a key public health issue, caries-protection was not a

[29] P Kraivaphan,, C Amornchat,, T Triratana,, LR Mateo, R Ellwood, D Cummins,, W DeVizio,, YP Zhang, "Two-Year Caries Clinical Study of the Efficacy of Novel Dentifrices Containing 1.5% Arginine, an Insoluble Calcium Compound and 1450 ppm Fluoride," *Caries Research*, via: http://www.colgateprofessional.co.uk/LeadershipUK/Research/2-year-Caries-Clinical_Thailand.pdf.

Table 2.4 Exhibit 9 Estimated Cost Structure for Colgate Toothpaste Price Tiers in Brazil, 2013

	Premium Tier	*Mid-Tier*	*Base Tier*
Manufacturer Sales per kilogram	$1.49	$0.77	$0.50
Ingredient Cost per kilogram	$0.27	$0.14	$0.12
Packaging Cost per kilogram	$0.36	$0.15	$0.10
Distribution Cost per kilogram	$0.15	$0.08	$0.05
Contribution per kilogram	$0.67	$0.39	$0.23
Promotion per kilogram	$0.04	$0.01	$0.002
Advertising per kilogram	$0.30	$0.11	$0.00[a]
Overhead per kilogram	$0.11	$0.11	$0.11
Profit per kilogram	$0.27	$0.17	$0.12

Source: Casewriter estimates.

[a] Base had not received advertising support in Brazil since 2005.

competitive differentiator within the toothpaste category, since fluoride was considered the best-in-class protection against cavities and most toothpaste sold had for decades contained the maximum-allowed level of fluoride. Colgate considered three positioning options for the global launch of CMCP+SAN:

Replace the Base Product Colgate could replace its existing anti-caries base brand ("Big Red") with the new CMCP+SAN formulation. In addition, Colgate explored the option of incorporating the CMCP+SAN formula into its entire product line-up, but found that there were technical hurdles with some of these formulations. The ingredients of CMCP+SAN were more expensive than those of Big Red (see Table 2.4 for cost of goods sold for CMCP+SAN and Big Red), so a higher price would be needed to maintain the same absolute and/or percentage margin. When Colgate performed a simulated test market to measure the potential demand for an upgraded Big Red product, it estimated that 4% of current Big Red consumers did not care for the "new" taste of CMCP+SAN.[30]

Make CMCP+SAN a Premium New Product Colgate could position CMCP+SAN as a premium innovation, priced just below Colgate's premium brand, Colgate Total®. Those in favor of the approach argued that a patent-protected, anti-caries toothpaste that was superior to fluoride provided a compelling value proposition to consumers and should command a higher price than Big Red. However, others were concerned that CMCP+SAN's superior caries-prevention would motivate some consumers to trade down from Colgate Total®. Colgate could not simply add SAN to the existing Colgate Total® formulation, due to technical hurdles.

Launch a Line Extension Colgate could add a line extension to its existing suite of anti-caries/"Big Red" products that would only feature the CMCP+SAN technology. A line extension would allow CMCP+SAN to be priced above the base product, but would be less likely to motivate trade downs from premium-priced Colgate Total®. Launching

30 Casewriter estimate.

CMCP+SAN as a line extension of the existing anti-caries products could ensure that superior cavity protection was accessible to consumers that needed it the most, which would produce greater public health benefits, and, over time, could trade-up consumers.

CMCP+SAN Launch Marketing

CMCP+SAN was slated to launch first in late 2013 in Turkey and then Brazil, under the brand name "Colgate® Maximum Cavity Protection™ plus Sugar Acid Neutralizer™."

Each Colgate subsidiary was responsible for paying for the costs of launching and marketing CMCP+SAN. Some Colgate country managers identified challenges with respect to CMP+SAN given the existing need to drive sales of the whitening, sensitivity, and basic product lines. Only two years before, Colgate rolled-out Colgate® Optic White™ beyond the U.S. to further strengthen leadership position in this fast growing toothpaste segment. In many markets, Big Red no longer received advertising support, so the country managers would need to divert funds that were previously allocated to higher priced products like Colgate Total®™ to promote CMCP+SAN. Country managers would also have to offer trade deal on CMCP + SAN to Colgate's retail customers or risk them delisting existing SKUs to make space for CMCP+SAN. Colgate used a simulated test market to estimate value sales, trial rate, repeat purchase rate and source of volume.

Product Since CMCP+SAN was originally conceived as an upgrade for the Big Red product line, the CMCP+SAN formulation was designed to have the same taste and texture as the original chalk-based variant of Big Red. By the time Colgate decided to explore whether to launch CMCP+SAN as a separate product line, Colgate's ability to change the formula was limited. A new formula would probably require additional clinical studies. The formula's similarity to Big Red would make it easier to migrate consumers to CMCP+SAN, but they might have difficulty understanding the value proposition of the higher-priced CMCP+SAN.

Pricing At Colgate, discussions continued on how to price the product. Arginine, the key active ingredient, was more expensive than the ingredients in Big Red, so CMCP+SAN would need to carry a higher price than Big Red in order to return the same margin. Should the breakthrough innovation offered by CMCP+SAN be priced at a premium to enhance margin, or, given the significant public health benefits of CMCP+SAN should the arginine-based technology replace traditional Big Red, with only a slight price increase sufficient to cover incremental costs? It was also noted that caries was no longer considered a "premium benefit" in the category (e.g. all other toothpastes sold on the basis of caries-protection were value-priced), so consumers might be unwilling to pay a higher price for additional caries-protection. Colgate's internal pricing studies suggested that consumer demand for CMCP+SAN would be highly sensitive to price.

Most general managers of Colgate's local markets, who were all profit and loss accountable, did not want to accept a scenario in which the incremental costs of producing CMCP+SAN were not covered in the price, so Colgate headquarters recommended a manufacturer price premium to base. The exact price premium would vary based on category and competitive price considerations and the Big Red market share. As CMCP + SAN rolled-out, Colgate struck a balance between an affordable launch price for higher public health benefit and a more premium pricing that helps drive credibility and profitability.

Figure 2.5 Exhibit 10 Colgate Maximum Cavity Protection with Sugar Acid Neutralizer™ Package, 2013.
Source: Company documents.

Advertising and Promotion In 2011, Colgate engaged Fletcher-Knight, a brand strategy consulting firm, to develop product positioning options for the CMCP+SAN technology. Fletcher-Knight offered different on-pack claims, all targeting mothers with young children, including "Makes teeth stronger" and "with Sugar Acid Neutralizer™." Colgate selected "with Sugar Acid Neutralizer™" as both the on-pack claim and the name of the technology; and "Colgate® Maximum Cavity Protection™ plus Sugar Acid Neutralizer™" as the full product name, to convey superiority versus the existing, basic anti-caries line. A purple color was selected for the package (see Figure 2.5 for CMCP+SAN pack shot), to help CMCP+SAN stand out at shelf where most packages were either red (Colgate®) or blue (Crest®). Colgate planned to launch three variants of CMCP+SAN over the long run: traditional/base, whitening, and junior (featuring child-friendly flavors).

Public health Colgate's team of public health professionals was especially engaged in the CMCP+SAN launch planning. According to Harrison, "Public health is more than just a good thing to do; it ultimately increases consumption." Marsha Butler, vice president of oral health and professional relations, who reported to Harrison, wanted to be sure that the breakthrough clinical results underlying CMCP+SAN came through strongly enough in commercial advertising. She recommended creating partnerships with public health-focused organizations and government health agencies to promote the healthcare benefits of CMCP+SAN to dentists, hygienists and dental schools.

In particular, Colgate's public health group partnered with a charitable organization, the Alliance for a Cavity-Free Future, dedicated to the goal that children born in 2026 and onward would never suffer from caries. Colgate was the ACFF's primary funder. The ACFF also received technical support from representatives of public health organizations such as the WHO, PAHO and the FDI World Dental Conference. The local ACFF chapters worked with Colgate to garner media to raise awareness of the caries threat, among both the general public and oral care professionals, and build a website to inform consumers about caries prevention.

COLGATE IN BRAZIL

In 2013, Brazil was the seventh largest economy ranked by total GDP, but was 95th in GDP per capita. Brazil's investment in infrastructure fell from over five percent of GDP in the 1970s to less than half of a percent in the 2000s,[31] and its poor infrastructure was considered a deterrent to international trade. Roughly 21% of Brazil's population of over 200 million lived in poverty in 2012.[32] Brazil's productivity was expected to drive annual growth of 1.2% in GDP per capita—which was below the estimated growth of 4.2% needed to reduce the population living in poverty or at-risk of poverty by half.[33]

In 2013, Brazil was the third largest oral care market worldwide.[34] Consumption of toothpaste in Brazil was high: 99% usage, 90% of people brushed twice or more times per day, and average use was over 600g[35] of toothpaste per person per year. Brazil's high per capita consumption of toothpaste partly resulted from school-based oral health care programs which required children to brush their teeth following lunch.

Colgate entered Brazil in 1927. By 2013, Colgate's value share of the toothpaste market was above 70%. Colgate's toothpaste sales in Brazil approached $1 billion in 2013.[36] For Colgate-Palmolive Brazil, roughly 45% of toothpaste volume, but only about 30% of Colgate's value, was in the basic tier. Table 2.5 and Figure 2.6 show market data and price tiers for Colgate's portfolio in Brazil). Colgate's market share in Brazil had increased over time thanks to the launch of premium innovations. Since 2004, Colgate has successfully implemented a premiumization strategy, using Colgate Total to develop a premium-priced multi-benefit segment and raise awareness of numerous oral care problems.

Colgate Sustainability Programs in Brazil

Colgate's community and oral health education programs were implemented by the professional relations team in Brazil (which reported to the Brazil vice president and general manager, Ricky Ramos). Members of the professional relations team, many of whom were trained as dentists, visited dental offices and spent time on product presentations ("detailing"),[37] which included giving samples for dentists and hygienists to distribute to patients. The professional relations budget was entirely funded by Colgate Brazil.

BSBF had been operating programs in Brazil since 1994, although the Dr. Rabbit health program had been taught in Brazilian schools since the mid-1950s. The program reached, on average, 20-30% of first through fourth grade school children each year (compared to roughly 80% of U.S. kindergarteners reached each year). Children

[31] "How Brazil Can Grow," McKinsey Global Institute, December 2006.

[32] U.S. Central Intelligence Agency, "The World Factbook," https://www.cia.gov/library/publications/resources/the-world-factbook/fields/2046.html#br, accessed April 2015.

[33] "Connecting Brazil to the World: A Path to Inclusive Growth," McKinsey Global Institute, May 2014.

[34] Market size based upon retail price.

[35] Casewriter estimate.

[36] Canadean, "The Future of the Oral Hygiene Market in Brazil to 2017," November 2013, Thomson ONE Banker, accessed January 2015.

[37] Detailing was composed of sharing the science behind the Colgate toothpaste formulations, describing the products with consumer friendly language, emphasizing the importance of public health and providing samples.

Table 2.5 Exhibit 11 Estimated Value and Volume Share for Colgate Toothpaste in Brazil by Price Tier, 2013

	Colgate Premium Tier[a]	*Colgate Mid-Tier*[b]	*Colgate Base Tier*[c]	*Total Category*
Retail Sales, $ Million	$268	$214	$201	$956
Value Share of Retail Sales	28%	22%	21%	71%
Manufacturer Sales, $ Million	$134	$107	$100	$478
Value Share of Manufacturer Sales	28%	22%	21%	71%
Volume Sales, kg Million	90	140	200	701
Volume Share	13%	20%	29%	62%

Source: Casewriter estimates.

[a] Premium Colgate Share of Toothpaste Category contains: Colgate Total®, Colgate Sensitive Pro-Relief™ and Colgate® Luminous White™.

[b] Mid-Tier Colgate Share of Toothpaste Category contains: Kolynos™/Sorriso™, all other.

[c] Value Colgate Share of Toothpaste Category contains: Big Red and Colgate Triple Action™.

received the BSBF oral health education from: Colgate dentists, dental associations and dental schools, community health workers, government dentists, non-profit organizations, churches and the "Health at School" program (which was a joint venture between the federal ministries of health and education). In 2009, hand-washing education was added to the "Health at School" program. Colgate provided sinks in schools for children to learn from dental and other health professionals proper hand-washing and teeth-brushing. BSBF volunteers also used mobile units to provide rural communities with dental education, partnered with retailers and distributed BSBF kits. The BSBF kits included a Colgate toothbrush, a 30g sample of toothpaste, a bar soap and an educational manual. The annual cost of BSBF and Colgate's other public health initiatives in Brazil was over $1 million (about 75% of which went towards the BSBF kits[38]).

Colgate's Partnership with the Brazilian Ministry of Health By 2014, Colgate had brought oral health education to 55 million children in Brazil. Colgate donated several hundred thousand BSBF kits. In 2011, Colgate developed a new BSBF oral health education manual to train thousands of Community Health Workers with input from the Ministry of Health, oral health experts and academics approved by the government. In 2012, a pilot test of the new manual was conducted with 1,200 trained CHWs; it carried the brands of BSBF, ACFF and the Ministry of Health.

In 2014, Colgate signed a five-year agreement with the Ministry of Health to train CHWs throughout Brazil and to run an oral health study on 500,000 citizens in Paraiba. First, Colgate trained thousands of CHWs in the capital city, Sao Paolo. Colgate determined which markets to target first by balancing input from the Ministry

[38] Casewriter estimate.

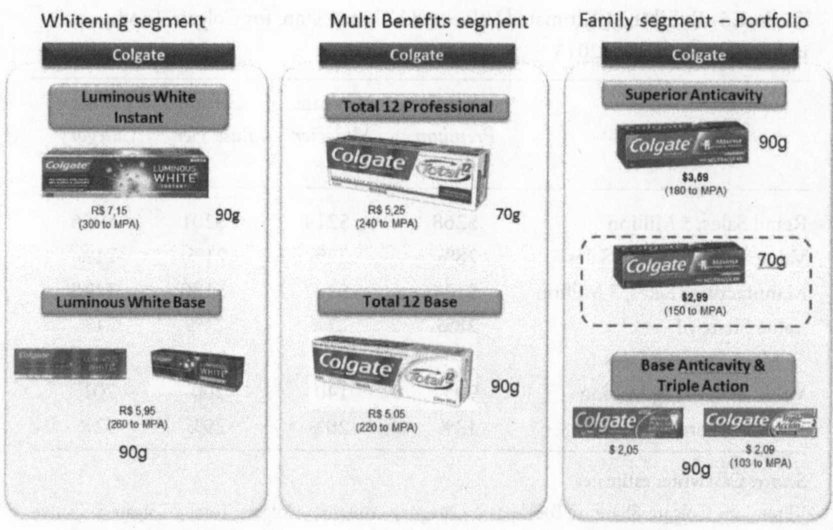

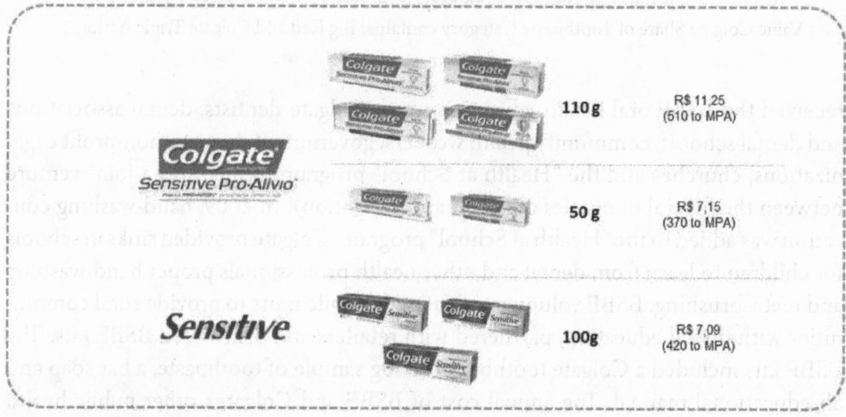

Figure 2.6 Exhibit 12 Colgate Product Tiers and Recommended Price Points in Brazil.[a]

Source: Company documents.

[a] All prices listed in Brazilian reals. One Brazilian real was equivalent to .39. All prices provided are indexed to Colgate Multi-Cavity Protection, referred to as MPA above, also known as "Big Red" or "base."

of Health on the areas with the highest need against the areas that offered upside for Colgate's business. By December 2014, Colgate planned to double the number of CHWs already trained who then served over 15 million Brazilian citizens.

CMCP+SAN LAUNCH IN BRAZIL

Prior to CMCP+SAN's launch in Brazil, Big Red and Triple Action held an estimated 29% volume share and 21% value share[39]; while Colgate Total® held a 12% volume

[39] Casewriter estimate.

Table 2.6 Exhibit 13 Estimated Trial, Repeat and Source of Volume for CMCP+SAN in Brazil, 2013

	CMCP+SAN	*Category Average*
Trial rate	10.6%	7.5%
Repeat rate	26%	22%
Volume sourced from competition	125 Index	100 Index

Source: Casewriter estimates.

share and 20% value share[40]. Big Red and Colgate® Triple Action™ were considered "base" products and had not been supported with media for several years. It was hoped that CMCP+SAN would source its volume disproportionately from base tier and competitive brands of toothpaste (see Table 2.6). Positioning CMCP+SAN in the premium tier would reduce the risk of loss-making cannibalization and trade-downs. Based on market simulation research, CMCP+SAN product was expected to obtain a share of over 1.5%[41] in year one. With the launch of CMCP+SAN, Colgate Brazil might have to allocate more funds to Colgate Total®, to re-emphasize its premium positioning. The plan was for CMCP+SAN to only be available in the 90g size at launch, but later a 70g size (retailing at less than 3 reals,[42] an entry level price point ideal for small, "mom and pop" retail outlets), would be launched. The on-pack technology name at launch was "Neutrazucar™,"changed from "Sugar Acid Neutralizer™" (which became cumbersome when translated into Portuguese).

Colgate faced an additional challenge with CMCP+SAN's launch: "Caries prevention is important, but currently consumers and dentists aren't that focused on caries," said Patricia Bella Costa, associate director of professional relations for Colgate Brazil, "so we had a great solution to a large global problem which, unfortunately, was not top-of-mind for dental professionals." Dentists and consumers were more concerned about other oral health problems like gingivitis and dental implants than caries. The launch of Colgate Total® in Brazil had propelled the category towards new therapeutic benefits; prior to Colgate Total®, the category had been driven by fresh breath and caries prevention.

The process of launching CMCP+SAN in Brazil began six to eighteen months before October 2013; and required the advance cooperation of the public relations, professional relations, and consumer marketing teams. Compared to earlier Colgate-brand toothpaste launches in Brazil, CMCP+SAN's launch involved a disproportionate investment in public and professional relations versus traditional consumer marketing. Nevertheless, the SAC launch advertising and promotion spend was expected to be between $3 million (for a value-priced product) and $6 million (for a premium-priced product) over the first three months[43].

[40] Casewriter estimate.

[41] Casewriter estimate.

[42] Three Brazilian reals were equivalent to roughly $1.17.

[43] The advertising and promotion budget for the first three months of the CMCP+SAN launch represented roughly 40 percent of the year one spend. The estimated overhead cost associated with CMCP+SAN in year one was roughly $5 million. All figures are casewriter estimates.

Professional relations

The professional relations budget in Brazil was roughly 2%[44] of oral care sales. It was used to fund the BSBF program, Colgate detailers, and training for community health workers. Many dentists believed that fluoride was still the best technology to fight caries. For the launch of CMCP+SAN, Butler and her team helped identify over 100 thought leaders and partners who could turn the oral health conversation back to caries, ahead of CMCP+SAN's launch. She created a caries expert board to look at what could be done to prevent caries, and how the issues would be communicated to professionals Colgate used more than 50 full-time detailers to visit dentists quarterly; they could demonstrate how the new technology worked, and distribute CMCP+SAN samples.

Colgate trained its commercial and professional teams to make joint calls on the major retailers (including Walmart, Carrefour and Casino) to introduce CMCP+SAN and explain the technology. Moira Loten, vice president of professional relations, noted that it was easier to motivate the salesforce, engage the professional community and sell to customers when the company was launching a truly breakthrough innovation. A sub-group within the professional relations team including dentists and the Scientific Affairs team (led by Bella Costa), were included in visits to large customers prior to the launch of CMCP+SAN. The CMCP+SAN message reached every dentist in the country, through a combination of dental visits, emails and dental conventions. Professional relations also helped to place stories targeted at dental professionals in industry publications. Professional relations created webinars with experts to demonstrate how CMCP+SAN worked to prevent cavities; which were then distributed to dentists and dental schools.

BSBF supported the launch of CMCP+SAN in Brazil by converting every toothpaste sample distributed via BSBF kits to CMCP+SAN (where previously, samples of Colgate® Maximum Cavity Protection™ or "Big Red," were used). Since children took the samples home, Colgate believed the adults in the family would also sample CMCP+SAN—which in turn influenced purchase decisions. A health promotion study in Thailand, conducted in collaboration with a leading global health agency, that included daily tooth-brushing with CMCP+SAN toothpaste and education from BSBF demonstrated that, over a two year period, the prevalence of caries dropped up to 41% among those children in the treatment group.

Public Relations

Brand-specific public relations and the activities of the Brazilian chapter of the ACFF aimed to teach consumers that the number one cause of caries was sugar acids in foods, and that CMCP+SAN was the most effective treatment. Digital public relations were designed to deliver one billion impressions by the time CMCP+SAN was launched. Nearly 230 articles were expected to appear on CMCP+SAN, (which contributed to the one billion impressions). Colgate budgeted $2 million[45] to spend on

[44] Casewriter estimate.

[45] Casewriter estimate.

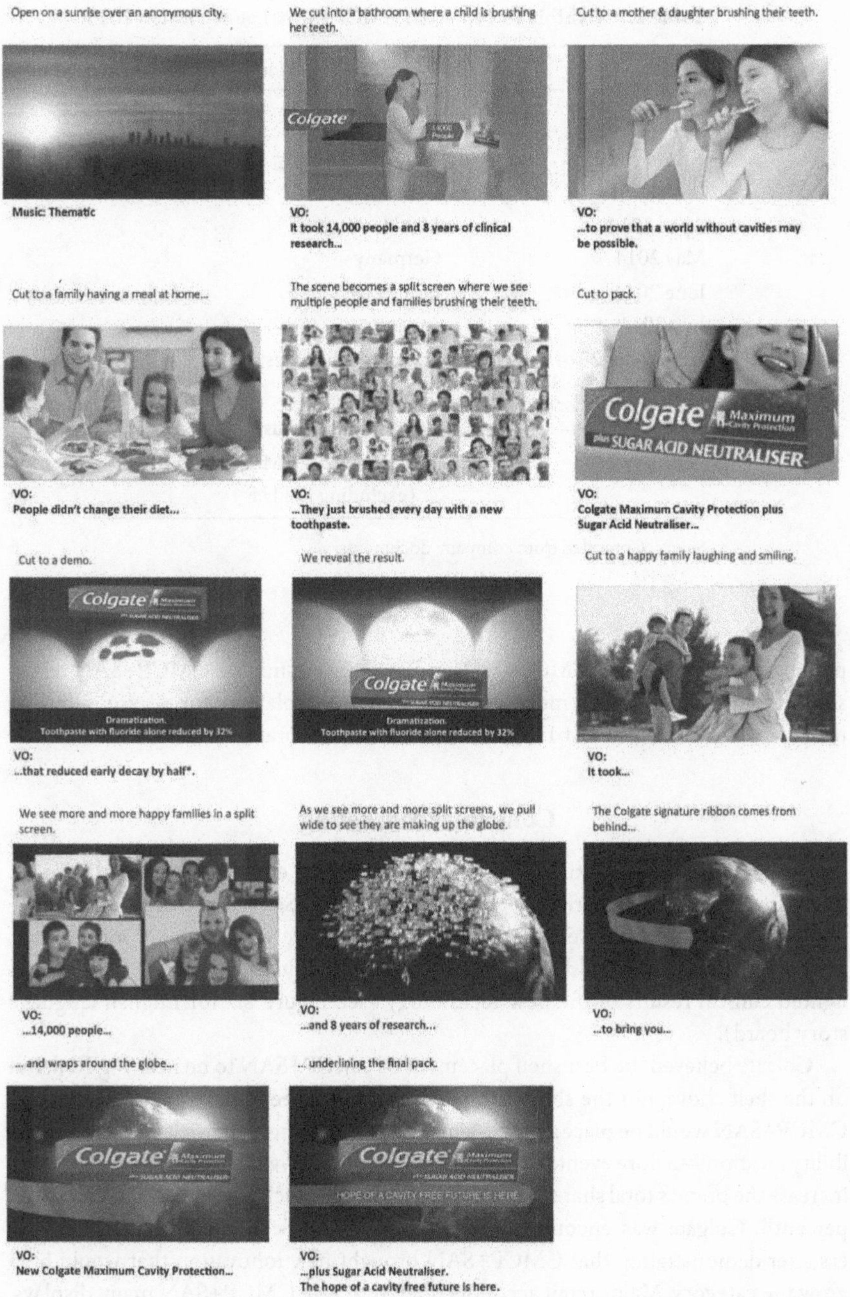
Open on a sunrise over an anonymous city.
Music: Thematic
We cut into a bathroom where a child is brushing her teeth.
Colgate
VO:
It took 14,000 people and 8 years of clinical research...
Cut to a mother & daughter brushing their teeth.
VO:
...to prove that a world without cavities may be possible.
Cut to a family having a meal at home...
VO:
People didn't change their diet...
The scene becomes a split screen where we see multiple people and families brushing their teeth.
VO:
...They just brushed every day with a new toothpaste.
Cut to pack.
Colgate Maximum Cavity Protection
plus SUGAR ACID NEUTRALISER
VO:
Colgate Maximum Cavity Protection plus Sugar Acid Neutraliser...
Cut to a demo.
Colgate
Dramatization.
Toothpaste with fluoride alone reduced by 32%
VO:
...that reduced early decay by half*.
We reveal the result.
Colgate
Dramatization.
Toothpaste with fluoride alone reduced by 32%
Cut to a happy family laughing and smiling.
VO:
It took...
We see more and more happy families in a split screen.
VO:
...14,000 people...
As we see more and more split screens, we pull wide to see they are making up the globe.
VO:
...and 8 years of research...
The Colgate signature ribbon comes from behind...
VO:
...to bring you...
... and wraps around the globe...
Colgate Maximum
VO:
New Colgate Maximum Cavity Protection...
... underlining the final pack.
Colgate Maximum
HOPE OF A CAVITY FREE FUTURE IS HERE
VO:
...plus Sugar Acid Neutraliser.
The hope of a cavity free future is here.

Figure 2.7 Exhibit 14 Colgate CMCP+SAN "Living Proof" TVC Story Board, 2013.
Source: Company documents.

Table 2.7 Exhibit 15 Projected CMCP+SAN Launch Dates, 2013

Date	*Market*
October 2013	Brazil, Turkey
February 2014	Malaysia, Norway, Sweden, Australia
March 2014	Greece, Spain
April 2014	Mexico
May 2014	Germany
June 2014	India, UK, Chile
July 2014	Argentina
September 2014	France, Philippines
October 2014	Italy
November 2014	Central Europe East
February 2015	Most Remaining Markets (excluding the U.S.)

Source: Compiled from company documents.

public relations to launch CMCP+SAN in Brazil. A one-minute CMCP+SAN television "infomercial" targeting mothers with children was planned for release following the product launch—the last 15 seconds of the ad was "branded" Colgate.

Consumer Marketing

Colgate's consumer marketing activities built upon the efforts of public relations to emphasize the threat of caries by positioning CMCP+SAN as the best-in-class caries solution. After public relations aired its one-minute CMCP+SAN infomercial, consumer marketing would initiate traditional television advertising which highlighted clinical results of the new technology (see Figure 2.7 for English language story board).

Colgate believed the best shelf placement of CMCP+SAN to be near Big Red, but on the shelf above, not the shelf below. For the first three months following launch, CMCP+SAN would be placed in the "window of innovation" at eye level—a high visibility location—before eventually moving next to or above Big Red. Colgate hoped to increase the brand's total share of shelf space with the launch of CMCP+SAN by seven percent[46]. Colgate was encouraged by positive feedback from large retail customers after demonstrating that CMCP+SAN brought new innovation that would help grow the category. Major retail accounts offered to give CMCP+SAN many displays, end-caps, promotional "islands" in-store. Colgate hired in-store demonstrators using iPads in-store to share the results of public health tests that showed CMCP+SAN's efficacy.

[46] Casewriter estimate.

CONCLUSION

The CMCP+SAN launch was planned to occur in October 2013, at a dental convention in Brazil. A three minute "mode of action" video, which demonstrated the technology, would be shown to the audience, and key articles on caries management would be distributed. Colgate would ensure that key thought leaders: customers, journalists and government officials were invited to the launch.

The question remained as to whether CMCP+SAN should be positioned and launched as a premium innovation or as a base product that could significantly improve oral health for a much broader segment of the Brazilian population. If CMCP+SAN achieved success, Harrison and Butler believed that public health initiatives could become an even more important part of Colgate's marketing effort for future toothpaste launches. Harrison and her colleagues in New York planned to monitor closely the early CMCP+SAN results in Brazil as they would inform the launch strategies in subsequent roll-out markets (see Table 2.7).

3

ROYAL CARIBBEAN CRUISES LTD.
SAFETY, ENVIRONMENT, AND HEALTH

John A. Quelch and Margaret L. Rodriguez

While there is no such thing as perfect safety, there can be a perfect dedication to safety and we work every day to achieve that.
Richard Fain, *chairman and chief executive officer of Royal Caribbean Cruises Ltd.*

In January 2014, Gary Bald, senior vice president of Safety, Environment, and Health at Royal Caribbean Cruises Ltd. (RCL), prepared for a review meeting with Richard Fain, the company's chairman and chief executive officer since 1988, and Adam Goldstein, president and chief executive officer of Royal Caribbean International (RCI), RCL's principal cruise line. Before joining RCL in 2006, Bald had spent 29 years with the Federal Bureau of Investigation. After seven years of upgrading security for the cruise line, Bald stated, "We've come a long way, but what keeps me up at night is what I don't know." As he prepared for his meeting with Fain and Goldstein, Bald considered whether his department's current initiatives would be sufficient to maintain RCL's position at the cutting edge of cruise industry best practice, and whether RCL could and should market to differentiate itself from its competitors in the areas of safety, environment, and health.

COMPANY BACKGROUND

Royal Caribbean International (RCI) was founded in 1968 by three Norwegian shipping companies to cater to the elite customers who sought transoceanic or around-the-world cruises.[1] In 1970, RCI offered its first cruise. In 1985, the parent company was incorporated in the Republic of Liberia. In 1990, the firm's operations were consolidated into a new Miami headquarters. In 1996, RCL acquired Celebrity Cruise Line Inc. for around $515 million.[2] By 2013, the company had grown to a fleet

[1] Ellen D. Wernick, "Royal Caribbean Cruises Ltd.," *International Directory of Company Histories*, vol. 74, ed. Tina Grant (Detroit: St. James Press, 2006), pp. 277–281, Gale Virtual Reference Library, Web, November 13, 2013.

[2] Wernick, "Royal Caribbean Cruises Ltd."

Table 3.1 Exhibit 1 Royal Caribbean Summary Financials ($ billion), 2008–2013

	2008	*2009*	*2010*	*2011*	*2012*	*2013*
Revenue	6.53	5.89	6.75	7.54	7.69	7.74
Cost of Goods Sold	4.40	3.99	4.42	4.94	5.16	5.13
SG&A	0.762	0.762	0.848	0.961	1.01	1.00
Depreciation and Amortization	0.520	0.568	0.644	0.702	0.73	0.75
Gross Income	1.61	1.33	1.69	1.73	1.58	1.48
EBITDA	1.35	1.06	1.45	1.63	1.52	1.62

Source: Adapted from company documents.

of 41 ships that held 98,500 passenger berths across six brands: Royal Caribbean International, Celebrity Cruises, Pullmantur Cruises, Azamara Club Cruises, Croisières de France, and TUI Cruises (of which Royal Caribbean owned a 50% share). In 2013, RCL welcomed over 5 million guests on cruises that visited over 460 ports of call. U.S. consumers accounted for 51% of RCL's passenger ticket revenue in 2013,[3] partly because of the popularity of the Caribbean as a destination. RCL employed about 62,000 people worldwide with revenues approaching $8 billion (see Table 3.1 for a summary of RCL's financial performance by year).

RCL's vision was "to empower and enable our employees to deliver the best vacation experience to our guests, thereby generating superior returns to our stakeholders and enhancing the wellbeing of our communities." RCL's mission, built upon its logo of the white-and-blue crown and anchor (see Figure 3.1), was captured in "Anchored in Excellence":

> We always provide service with a friendly greeting and a smile. We anticipate the needs of our customers. We make all efforts to exceed our customers' expectations. We take ownership of any problem that is brought to our attention. We engage in conduct that enhances our corporate reputation and employee morale. We are committed to act in the highest ethical manner and respect the rights and dignity of others. We are loyal to Royal Caribbean and Celebrity Cruises, and strive for continuous improvement in everything we do.

RCL's six brands were differentiated from each other based on their geographic regions of operation and the sizes or price points of their cruise ships. The flagship Royal Caribbean International (RCI) brand, with 21 ships, accounted for over 60% of RCL revenues. It offered cruises to destinations across the globe at accessible prices. Celebrity Cruises, with five new ships added to its fleet since 2008, offered premium cruises to customers from North America, Australia, and the U.K. Pullmantur Cruises catered to customers located in Latin America and Spain with accessible cruise prices. Azamara Club Cruises offered luxury cruises on small ships to exotic, less-traveled cruise destinations worldwide. Croisières de France was developed by RCL to appeal to French passengers; French was spoken onboard as the first language, and the food

[3] Geoffrey Kaicher, "Industry Report 48311, September 2013," IBISWorld, accessed November 2013.

Figure 3.1 Exhibit 2 Royal Caribbean Cruises Ltd. and Royal Caribbean International Logos, 2013
Source: Company documents.

and décor took cues from French culture. TUI Cruises was a joint venture between TUI (a German tourism company) and RCL designed to appeal to German-speaking travelers. (See Table 3.2 for a full list of RCL ships by brand.)

In 2013, RCI offered 85 cruise itineraries. Most were offered between 5 and 10 times. RCI's published prices in its catalog for a typical 7-night Caribbean cruise ranged from $649 per person for double occupancy for an interior (windowless) room, to $1,049 for an ocean view room with balcony, to $2,099 for a suite. Comparable prices for a 14-night Mediterranean cruise were $1,749, $2,659, and $3,699. On average, passengers spent an extra 30% over the ticket price on shore excursions, onboard shopping, and drinks.

COMPETITION AND INDUSTRY DEMAND

RCL was one of four cruise firms that accounted for over 93% of passenger nights.[4] (See Table 3.3 for cruise brands.) The largest operator was Carnival Corporation, with a portfolio of 12 leading cruise brands in North America, Europe, and Australia.[5] In 2013, Carnival's revenue was $15.5 billion. In 2013, Carnival operated 100 ships with capacity for over 200,000 passengers, and was expected to add a further 9 ships to its fleet by 2016. Carnival operated six brands in North America—Carnival Cruise Lines, Princess Cruises, Holland America Line, Seabourn, Cunard, and Costa Cruises—that together accounted for over 70% of the company's revenue.

Like RCL, Carnival's portfolio of brands was differentiated based on geographic regions of operation and price tiers. Carnival was Carnival Corporation's most

[4] U.S. Department of Transportation Maritime Administration, "North American Cruise Statistical Snapshot," 2011, accessed November 2013.

[5] Kaicher, "Industry Report 48311, September 2013."

Table 3.2 Exhibit 3 RCL Fleet by Year of Service, Guest Berths, and Areas of Operation, 2012

Ship	*First Year of Service*	*Guest Berths*[a]	*Areas of Operation*
Royal Caribbean			
Allure of the Seas	2010	5,400	Caribbean
Oasis of the Seas	2009	5,400	Caribbean
Independence of the Seas	2008	3,600	Caribbean/Europe
Liberty of the Seas	2007	3,600	Caribbean/Europe
Freedom of the Seas	2006	3,600	Caribbean
Jewel of the Seas	2004	2,100	Caribbean
Mariner of the Seas	2003	3,100	Asia/Caribbean
Serenade of the Seas	2003	2,100	Caribbean/Europe/Middle East
Navigator of the Seas	2002	3,100	Caribbean/Europe
Brilliance of the Seas	2002	2,100	Canada/Caribbean/Europe
Adventure of the Seas	2001	3,100	Caribbean/Europe
Radiance of the Seas	2001	2,100	Alaska/Oceania
Explorer of the Seas	2000	3,100	Bermuda/Canada/Caribbean
Voyager of the Seas	1999	3,100	Asia/Oceania
Vision of the Seas	1998	2,000	Caribbean/Europe/Panama
Enchantment of the Seas	1997	2,250	Caribbean/ Bahamas
Rhapsody of the Seas	1997	2,000	Alaska/Oceania
Grandeur of the Seas	1996	1,950	Bermuda/Canada/Caribbean
Splendor of the Seas	1996	1,800	Brazil/Europe
Legend of the Seas	1995	1,800	Asia/Caribbean/Europe/ Panama
Majesty of the Seas	1992	2,350	Bahamas
Celebrity Cruises	2012	3,000	Caribbean/Europe
Celebrity Silhouette	2011	2,850	Caribbean/Europe
Celebrity Eclipse	2010	2,850	Caribbean/Europe
Celebrity Equinox	2009	2,850	Caribbean/Europe
Celebrity Solstice	2008	2,850	Alaska/Oceania
Celebrity Constellation	2002	2,050	Caribbean/Europe
Celebrity Summit	2001	2,150	Bermuda/Canada/Caribbean/ New England
Celebrity Infinity	2001	2,150	Europe/Panama/South America
Celebrity Millennium	2000	2,150	Alaska/Asia/Panama
Celebrity Century	1995	1,800	Alaska/Hawaii/Panama/ Pacific Coast
Celebrity Xpedition	2004	96	Galapagos Islands

Table 3.2 Continued

Ship	*First Year of Service*	*Guest Berths*[a]	*Areas of Operation*
Azamara Club Cruises	2004	700	Asia/Europe
Azamara Journey	2006	700	Europe/South and Central America/Panama
Azamara Quest	1992	1,400	Brazil/Europe
Pullmantur	1990	1,600	Brazil/Europe
Zenith	1988	2,300	Brazil/Europe
Empress	1991	2,350	Caribbean/South America
Sovereign	1990	1,350	Caribbean/Europe
Monarch of the Seas	2009	1,900	Caribbean/Europe
CDF Croisieres de France	2011	1,900	Caribbean/Europe/Middle East
Horizon			
TUI Cruises			
Mein Schiff			
Mein Schiff 2			

Source: Adapted from company documents.

[a] Most rooms were double occupancy and included two berths. Prices were quoted per person based on double occupancy.

popular brand and competed alongside RCI in the "contemporary" tier. It served the North American market and offered cruises to the Caribbean, Europe, Mexico, and Alaska at accessible prices (typically below those of RCI). Princess Cruises competed with Celebrity and offered premium cruises to destinations around the globe. Holland America Cruises catered to premium customers with five-star dining and gracious service. Seabourn Cruises offered luxury vacations aboard small ships with large suites, spas, and a one-to-one staff-to-passenger ratio. Cunard offered luxury cruises featuring top-quality British service aboard its famous fleet, which included the *Queen Victoria*, the *Queen Elizabeth*, and the *Queen Mary 2*. Costa Cruises was Europe's largest contemporary cruise line and offered cruises to destinations worldwide at accessible price points. Carnival also owned Ibero Cruceros (for Spanish- and Portuguese-speaking guests), AIDA Cruises (for German-speaking guests), and P&O Cruises (which originally catered to travel between the U.K. and Australasia, and later offered separate cruises to the European and Australasian markets).

Norwegian Cruise Line was the third-largest cruise line and competed in the contemporary tier. Founded in 1966, Norwegian's revenue reached $2.3 billion in 2012. Norwegian had roughly 14,000 employees and operated 12 ships. Since RCL and Carnival led in the U.S. market, Norwegian's strategic focus was on the fast-growing European market.[6,7] Norwegian was named "Europe's Leading Cruise Line" for five years in a row,

[6] Although Norwegian Cruise Line planned to grow in the European market, 82% of its 2012 revenue came from North American cruises.

[7] Norwegian Cruise Line, 2012 Annual Report, http://www.investor.ncl.com/annuals.cfm, accessed February 2014.

Table 3.3 Exhibit 4 Illustrative Cruise Brands by Tier, 2013

Parent Corporation	*Contemporary*	*Premium*	*Luxury*	*Specialty*
Carnival	Carnival	Princess	Cunard	
	Costa	Holland America	Seabourn	
Royal Caribbean	Royal Caribbean	Celebrity	Azamara	
Norwegian	Norwegian	—	—	
Other		MSC	Crystal	Disney
			Regent Seven Seas	Windstar
			Oceania	Viking River
				AmaWaterways

Source: Compiled from "Cruises, US," Mintel, October 2013, accessed November 2013; and U.S. Dept. of Transportation Maritime Administration, "North American Cruise Statistical Snapshot," 2011, accessed November 2013.

between 2008 and 2013, by World Travel Awards.[8] Norwegian focused on cost-saving initiatives between 2008 and 2013, which resulted in net cruise cost per passenger day falling 21.6% during this period.[9] Norwegian had recently invested in several new vessels and, overall, had a younger fleet of ships (average age of 5 years) than RCL (average age of 7 years), which, in turn, was younger than the Carnival fleet (average age of 12 years). Revenues were expected to increase 2.6% in 2013.[10]

The basis for competition among cruise brands varied by price tier. Contemporary cruise lines typically offered attractions appealing to young and old on very large vessels. Ticket prices were relatively low, but extra charges were commonplace. At the other end of the spectrum, luxury cruise lines appealed primarily to adults (rather than young families), emphasized fine dining and low passenger-to-staff ratios on smaller ships, and were often priced on an all-inclusive basis.

Cruise ship operations had high fixed costs and minimal variable costs. Cruise ship companies therefore aimed to keep their vessels earning revenues 360 days per year. The ships would be in dry dock only one week every five years with a once-in-a-lifetime major retrofit taking five weeks. Fuel, labor, food, and onboard entertainment were RCL's principal operating costs. (See Table 3.4 for RCL's operating costs.) These varied little, depending on the number of passengers on board. Cruise ships

[8] World Travel Awards, "Norwegian Cruise Line," 2013, http://www.worldtravelawards.com/profile-1839-norwegian-cruise-line, accessed November 2013.

[9] World Travel Awards, "Norwegian Cruise Line."

[10] World Travel Awards, "Norwegian Cruise Line."

Table 3.4 Exhibit 5 Illustrative Royal Caribbean Revenues, Operating Costs, and Income per Passenger, 2013

Revenues, Costs, and Profit	
Retail Ticket Price[a]	$1,150
Travel Agent Commission	($150)
Operating Costs[b]	($680)
Selling, General, and Administrative Costs	($120)
Interest and Depreciation	($100)
Operating Profit	$100

Source: Company documents.

[a] On average, a passenger on RCL spent 30% over the ticket price on extras, yielding a similar percentage of operating profit.

[b] Costs include fuel, labor, entertainment, and food.

therefore aimed to always sail full. Unbooked rooms were sold through brokers at a discount as the sail date approached.

Cruises were high-ticket items, so demand was closely tied to economic conditions and consumer confidence. Following the 2008 recession, demand (and the financial performance of the cruise lines) declined sharply in 2009.[11] Cruise lines had to offer large discounts, cabin upgrades, vouchers for onboard spending, and free onshore excursions to maintain occupancy rates. As a result, cruise profit per passenger per day declined, even though occupancy rates were sustained.[12]

Despite poor economic conditions, the cruise line industry continued to expand. According to RCL estimates, the global cruise industry welcomed 20.8 million guests in 2012, compared to 20.2 million guests in 2011, and 18.8 million guests in 2010. By 2013, the global cruise fleet was estimated to have about 351,000 passenger berths. Passenger berths industrywide were expected to increase by 8.7% by 2015, as 13 new ships were due to come online.[13] (See Figure 3.2 for cruise industry capacity between 2001 and 2015.) Analysts estimated cruise line revenues at $33.2 billion in 2013, growing to $49.5 billion by 2018.[14]

CONSUMER BEHAVIOR

For most cruise ship passengers, taking a cruise was a special vacation often timed around a honeymoon, an anniversary, or a birthday celebration, and frequently involved several generations of family members. Advance planning was commonplace,

[11] Kaicher, "Industry Report 48311, September 2013."

[12] Kaicher, "Industry Report 48311, September 2013."

[13] "Cruises, Issues and Insights, US," Mintel, October 2013, accessed November 2013.

[14] "Cruises, Issues and Insights, US," Mintel.

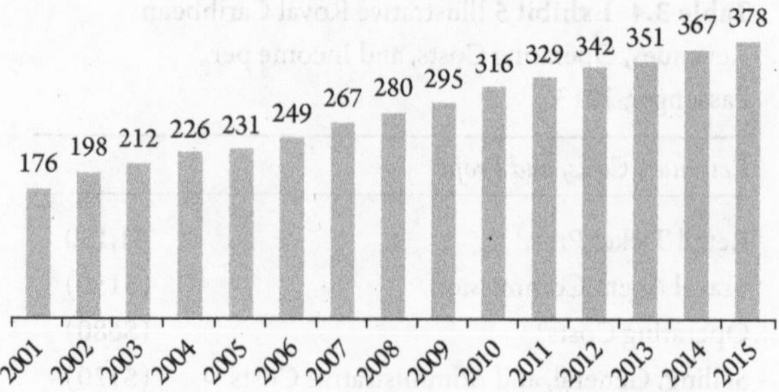

Figure 3.2 Exhibit 6 Cruise Industry Capacity (thousands of berths), 2001–2015.[a]
Source: Adapted from "Cruises, US," Mintel, October 2013, accessed November 2013; and CLIA Five-Year Capacity Report and Passenger Carrying Report, accessed November 2013.
[a] Estimates for 2014 and 2015 were based upon the number of berths for contracted and planned ships.

with many bookings made six months or more in advance. Cruisers typically first selected a destination or itinerary and time of year when they could travel. They would then consider the length of cruise and brand options according to budget constraints. The range of entertainment and recreational options and brand, or even specific vessel reputation (researchable online or via recommendations from friends), were also important.

A 2013 survey reported that 1 in 10 adults in the U.S. had cruised within the previous three years and had taken an average of 1.5 cruises.[15] Among those who cruised on RCL, 30% booked a second RCL cruise by the end of following year. Repeat cruisers were well aware of the benefits of cruising and were typically interested in cruising again in the future. Passengers who did not book a subsequent cruise within five years were considered as hard to reacquire as new cruisers. As revealed in Table 3.5, consumers who had never cruised harbored many concerns about investing in a cruise vacation. Many non-cruisers harbored the prejudice that cruising was not a good vacation choice for active people and that most cruise passengers fell into one of three categories: the newlywed, the almost dead, and the overfed.

Around 30% of cruisers booked their vacations directly on a cruise line website or by calling the cruise line. An equal percentage booked through travel agents. A further 10% booked through third-party brokers and consolidators such as Cruise Direct and Expedia.[16] Before purchasing a cruise, the typical customer visited 19 websites.

The increased popularity of booking cruises directly with the cruise lines amplified the marketing importance of the cruise line's social media and online presence, particularly among those who had not cruised within the last three years. RCL's blog, written by CEO Adam Goldstein, highlighted the features of new ships and new destinations, and answered fans' questions.

[15] "Cruises, US," Mintel, October 2013, accessed November 2013.
[16] Adapted from "Cruises, US," Mintel, October 2013, accessed November 2013.

Table 3.5 Exhibit 7 Consumer Opinion Survey on Cruising, 2013
Question: Which, if any, of the following statements about cruises do you agree with?

	Recent Cruiser[a]	*Cruised Before*[b]	*Never Cruised*	*All*
They are a good way of visiting and exploring destinations.	60	60	36	46
They offer a good variety of activities (i.e., something for everyone).	56	60	36	45
They are good value for money.	55	49	17	32
They are good for commemorating special-occasions.	36	38	23	29
They are a good place to meet new people.	38	34	24	29
Recent safety issues, such as *Costa Concordia*, have put me off taking a cruise.	15	28	30	27
You don't get to see enough of the local culture/places you visit.	18	24	17	19
They are too crowded.	15	17	20	18
I would be more likely to use a cruise line that voluntarily adopted a passenger bill of rights.	22	19	15	17
They are reliable.	35	23	7	16
The itineraries don't give me the flexibility I would like for my vacation.	15	14	12	13
None of these.	2	4	26	16

Source: Adapted from "Cruises, US," Mintel, October 2013, accessed November 2013.
[a] Those who cruised within the past three years, 364 participants.
[b] Those who cruised more than three years ago, 485 participants.

Two factors were often underestimated in driving brand choice: innovations and service quality. "Wow" innovations were especially important in differentiating RCL ships. "Our ships are destinations in their own right. Innovation is in our DNA," said executive vice president of maritime, Harri Kulovaara, who had spearheaded the design of bigger and better classes of RCL ships over 30 years, working with shipyards in Finland, France, and Germany (see Figure 3.3 for fleet evolution).

RCL was the first cruise line to introduce ships designed for warm-weather cruising. Its Voyager class ships included then-unique attractions like ice skating rinks and rock climbing walls.

RCL's Oasis class ships, launched in 2009, featured open atriums and were 50% larger than the next largest cruise ship then in service, costing $1.5 billion each and accommodating 5,400 passengers. Each Oasis class ship featured a surfing simulator and flow rider, a zip-line, a climbing wall, an ice skating rink, outdoor gardens, designer shops, a Starbucks, and Broadway shows. Designed for maximum cruising stability and with GPS navigation systems that enabled them to be turned in tight ports with inches to spare, three Oasis class ships would be in service by 2017.

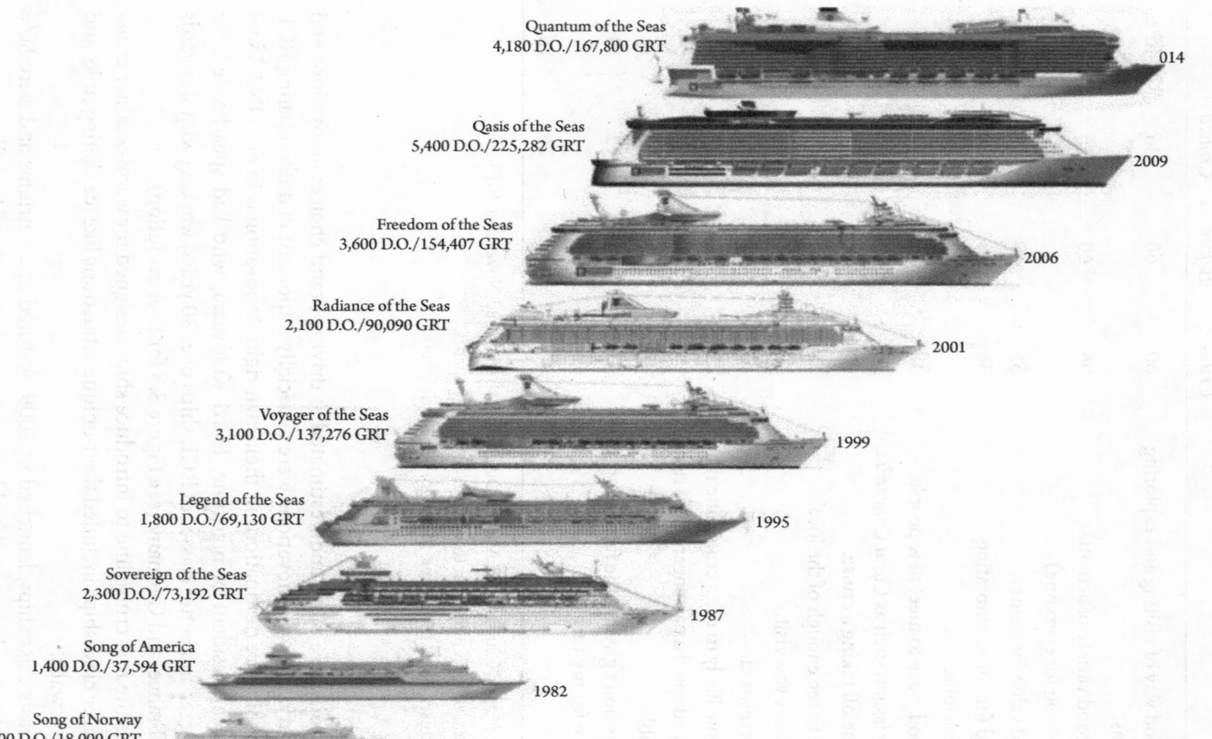

Figure 3.3 Exhibit 8 Royal Caribbean Fleet Evolution, 1970–2013.[a]

Source: Company documents.

[a] GRT is gross tonnage, a measure of volume, where one "ton" is equal to 100 cubic feet. D.O. referred to passenger berths.

RCL's Quantum class ships, the first of which would be launched in late 2014, would include the 100-foot high North Star observation arm inspired by the London Eye that lifted up to 14 passengers at a time (see Figure 3.4); the Seaplex with virtual skydiving, bumper cars, and circus act training; an interior 270-degree floor-to-ceiling panoramic viewing space during the day that became an entertainment center at night; and virtual balconies for 373 interior cabins that offered real-time ocean views.

RCL was also continuously upgrading the speed of Internet connections for passengers. In partnership with O3b Networks, RCL expected to match land speed connectivity in 2014.

Service excellence was also critical, especially to attract repeat business. RCL's quality code (see Figure 3.5) captured the "7 Cs of Quality" at RCL, including the "commitment" to exceeding "our guests' expectations" and a culture that emphasized: "We treat our co-workers with respect and are proud to be Anchored in Excellence."

"Human capital is critical to RCL's success. Guests will not come back to us on the basis of superior hardware. Repeat business all depends on the customer experience," said Maria del Busto, RCL's global chief human resources (HR) officer. Customer service heavily influenced RCL customers' satisfaction. RCL measured the percentage of recent guests whom it considered secure: guests who were "very satisfied," "definitely would recommend RCL," and "definitely would cruise again on RCL." In 2013, the secure guests index (SGI) reached an all-time high of 54%.

RCL's HR department focused on managing each employee's experience at the company. Prospective employees, whether front-line or behind-the-scenes staff, were screened to ensure they possessed the appropriate service orientation and language skills to deliver the quality that guests expected from RCL. Subcontractors around the world helped RCL recruit its multinational crew (e.g., 20% of employees were Filipino). The centers performed the initial screenings, but each remaining candidate was interviewed by RCL personnel before being made an offer. After hiring, employees received extensive onboarding to help them understand the role they played in "wowing" the customer and delivering a top-quality vacation experience.

RCL's crew turnover was a remarkably low 25%, partly resulting from the six-months-on, two-months-off assignment rotation for crew (it was two months on, two months off, for senior officers and captains). An HR officer on each ship was part of the captain's executive committee and was evaluated in part on both employee satisfaction and engagement. In 2012, RCL's companywide survey found 83% of employees felt very engaged.

THE SAFETY CHALLENGE

Two accidents in 2012 damaged the cruise industry's reputation. In January, the *Costa Concordia* (a Carnival ship) sank after colliding with a reef off the Italian coast, killing 32 passengers and injuring 64 more.[17] The ship carried 4,200 passengers and crew members at the time.[18] Later that year, the *Costa Allegra,* from the same fleet, suffered a fire that left more than 1,000 people onboard without power in the Indian Ocean

[17] Kaicher, "Industry Report 48311, September 2013."

[18] Kaicher, "Industry Report 48311, September 2013."

Figure 3.4 Exhibit 9 Quantum Class North Star 360° Observation Capsule, 2013.
Source: Royal Caribbean, "Quantum of the Seas," http://www.royalcaribbean.com/findacruise/ships/class/ship/home.do?shipClassCode=com.rccl.value.catalog.ShipClassValue%40a437a1e&shipCode=QN&br=, accessed December 2013.

(the accident did not result in fatalities). According to a Cruise Critic poll conducted after the accidents, 66% of readers booked on future cruises said the incidents did not have an impact on their cruise trip plans, while 30% said the accident made them more aware of their own safety, with no change of plans.[19]

Following the two Costa incidents, Carnival committed to increase the safety requirements for its fleet. However, in February 2013, Carnival's *Triumph* had a generator fire that left the ship and its passengers stranded for four days in the Gulf of Mexico. After the incident, Carnival canceled all trips on the *Triumph* until repairs were completed and began overhauling 24 of its ships to add emergency generators, upgrade fire safety, and improve engine rooms. Carnival announced it would invest $700 million to improve the safety of its fleet.[20] Carnival also introduced the "Great Vacation Guarantee," which offered guests a 110% refund, transportation home, and shipboard credit for future cruises in the event they were dissatisfied and wished to end their cruise early.[21]

RCL was not incident-free. In May 2013, RCL's *Grandeur of the Seas* caught fire en route to the Bahamas. At the time, the ship carried over 3,000 passengers and crew, none of whom was injured.[22] The ship never lost power, thanks to backup systems, and reached the Bahamas within seven hours of the start of the fire. RCI's chief executive flew out to the ship. After the damage was assessed, RCL decided to end the cruise and, within 18 hours, announced the issuance of refunds and vouchers for future cruises to all passengers. Their flights home all had to be rebooked, with RCL absorbing costs. Passengers booked on subsequent cruises were also compensated, as the *Grandeur* underwent six weeks of repairs before returning to rotation. The total cost to RCL after insurance payments was $24 million.

Senior RCL executives played important roles in the Cruise Lines International Association (CLIA), which represented the interests of the industry before

[19] Kaicher, "Industry Report 48311, September 2013."

[20] Tess Stynes, "Carnival Profit Down 30% Amid Weaker Revenue, Asset Write-Downs," *Wall Street Journal* (Online), September 24, 2013, http://online.wsj.com/article/BT-CO-20130924-706461.html, accessed November 2013.

[21] "Cruises, US," Mintel.

[22] Gene Sloan, "Cause of cruise ship fire remains a mystery," *USA Today*, July 12, 2013, http://www.usa today.com/story/travel/news/2013/07/12/cruise-ship-fire-mystery/2513097/, accessed December 2013.

Our Company takes pride in being one of the world's leading cruise vacation providers, and in our commitment to the 7 Cs of our quality management system.

7 Cs of Quality

Commitment	We are committed to exceeding our guests' expectations.
Customers	We are attentive to our guests' needs.
Compliance	We meet or exceed applicable regulations and voluntary standards and strive to be *Above and Beyond Compliance* in our shipboard and shoreside operations.
Conscientious	Our livelihood depends upon the environment and the safe, secure operation of our business.
Culture	We treat our co-workers with respect and are proud to be *Anchored in Excellence*.
Communication	We encourage all employees, vendors and suppliers to meet our quality objectives.
Continuous Improvement	We seek to continuously improve our quality performance.

Figure 3.5 Exhibit 10 Royal Caribbean Quality Code, 2013.
Source: Company documents.

international and national regulators. It also marketed cruising to the travel industry and trained travel agents. The CLIA led an industrywide review of safety policies following the *Costa Concordia* event. New safety procedures were agreed to for all ships controlled by the 26 CLIA members, which included RCL and Carnival. (See Box 3.1 for CLIA's passenger bill of rights, instituted in 2013.) The bill of rights largely consolidated policies already in place, but no longer allowed cruise lines to treat the breakdown of a ship as an act of God. The bill of rights was thought likely to help first-time cruise passengers feel more confident about choosing to cruise. However, a report by the U.S. Coast Guard stated that the growing size of cruise ships made fighting fires and other disasters more complicated; and some observers questioned whether the larger life boats needed for passengers on mega-ships could be boarded within 30 minutes of the alarm, as required by International Maritime Organization (IMO) regulations.

CRUISE LINE REGULATIONS

Cruise lines were subject to numerous regulations administered by governments, international organizations, and maritime law. Cruise line safety regulations were enforced by the IMO. A key requirement for passenger ships was "safe return to port," which stipulated ships must be designed with sufficient backup power systems to enable them to return to port.[23] The IMO worked closely with industry organizations

[23] International Maritime Organization, "Passenger ships," 2013, http://www.imo.org/OurWork/Safety/Regulations/Pages/PassengerShips.aspx, accessed November 2013.

Box 3.1 Exhibit 11 CLIA's International Cruise Line Passenger Bill of Rights, 2013

"The Members of the Cruise Lines International Association are dedicated to the comfort and care of all passengers on oceangoing cruises throughout the world. To fulfill this commitment, our Members have agreed to adopt the following set of passenger rights:

- The right to disembark a docked ship if essential provisions such as food, water, restroom facilities and access to medical care cannot adequately be provided onboard, subject only to the Master's concern for passenger safety and security and customs and immigration requirements of the port.
- The right to a full refund for a trip that is canceled due to mechanical failures, or a partial refund for voyages that are terminated early due to those failures.
- The right to have available on board ships operating beyond rivers or coastal waters full-time, professional emergency medical attention, as needed until shore side medical care becomes available.
- The right to timely information updates as to any adjustments in the itinerary of the ship in the event of a mechanical failure or emergency, as well as timely updates of the status of efforts to address mechanical failures.
- The right to a ship crew that is properly trained in emergency and evacuation procedures.
- The right to an emergency power source in the case of a main generator failure.
- The right to transportation to the ship's scheduled port of disembarkation or the passenger's home city in the event a cruise is terminated early due to mechanical failures.
- The right to lodging if disembarkation and an overnight stay in an unscheduled port are required when a cruise is terminated early due to mechanical failures.
- The right to have included on each cruise line's website a toll-free phone line that can be used for questions or information concerning any aspect of shipboard operations.
- The right to have this *Cruise Line Passenger Bill of Rights* published on each line's website."

Source: Cruise Lines International Association (CLIA), "Cruise Industry Adopts Passenger Bill of Rights," May 22, 2013, http://www.cruising.org/news/press_releases/2013/05/cruise-industry-adopts-passenger-bill-rights, accessed November 2013.

like CLIA to continuously improve the safety standards for passenger vessels.[24] In addition, ships were subject to the safety standards stipulated by each port of call. For example, all ships docking in U.S. ports were subject to safety inspections conducted by the U.S. Coast Guard before launch and routinely over the life of the ship.[25]

[24] "International Maritime Organization (IMO) Adopts Additional Measures from Global Cruise Industry to Enhance Passenger Ship Safety," PR News Wire, July 1, 2013, http://www.prnewswire.com/news-releases/international-maritime-organization-imo-adopts-additional-measures-from-global-cruise-industry-to-enhance-passenger-ship-safety-213841031.html, accessed November 2013.

[25] U.S. Senate, Testimony Before the Committee on Commerce, Science and Transportation, Passenger Safety and Regulation of Cruise Ships, July 24, 2013, http://www.c-spanvideo.org/program/Cruisei, accessed November 2013.

In 2010, U.S. President Obama signed into law the Cruise Vessel Security and Safety Act.[26] The act was drafted to improve the safety of cruise ships for their passengers. The act required cruise ships to install the appropriate technology to keep passengers safe (e.g., video surveillance, time-restricted cabin keys, passenger overboard detectors,) provide medical personnel and equipment to assist victims of sexual assault, and keep records of all suspicious deaths and disappearances (to be shared publicly online by the U.S. Coast Guard once investigations were complete).[27] Civil and criminal penalties for noncompliance were included in the act. The act also required cruise lines to have at least one crew member on each vessel who had received FBI training in crime detection, evidence preservation, and reporting.[28] Most cruise ships in service in 2010 were already in compliance.[29] The incremental investment required to bring all ships that visited U.S. ports up to standard was estimated at around $140 million in 2009.[30]

In July 2013, Senator Jay Rockefeller held hearings regarding cruise line passenger safety.[31] The CEOs of RCI and Carnival Cruises were invited to give testimony. They voluntarily agreed to expand reporting on their websites of alleged crimes committed onboard their vessels. Following the hearing, Senator Rockefeller proposed the "Cruise Passenger Protection Act," which would require cruise lines calling at U.S. ports to establish victim support services (including a 24-hour helpline) for passengers who became victims of onboard crime.[32] Rockefeller also proposed new legislation to repeal tax anomalies for foreign cruise lines that embarked or disembarked passengers from U.S. ports to help remunerate the Coast Guard and other U.S. agencies that provided assistance with the rescue of stranded cruise ships.[33]

The cruise industry was responsible for meeting the public health standards of a number of agencies, including the U.S. Centers for Disease Control and Prevention and ANVISA,[34] to ensure the safety of passengers. The American College of Emergency Physicians' Cruise Ship and Maritime Medicine Section set guidelines for health codes aboard passenger ships. Maritime law prescribed employer responsibilities for the care of employees.

Cruise lines were also subject to stringent environmental regulations. U.S. and international laws prohibited the discharge of certain materials, such as petrochemicals and plastics, into waterways. The IMO regulations under the International Convention for the Prevention of Pollution from Ships (the "MARPOL Regulations")

[26] "H.R. 3360—111th Congress: Cruise Vessel Security and Safety Act of 2010," 2009, http://www.govtrack.us/congress/bills/111/hr3360, accessed December 2013.

[27] "H.R. 3360—111th Congress: Cruise Vessel Security and Safety Act of 2010."

[28] "H.R. 3360—111th Congress: Cruise Vessel Security and Safety Act of 2010."

[29] "H.R. 3360—111th Congress: Cruise Vessel Security and Safety Act of 2010."

[30] "H.R. 3360—111th Congress: Cruise Vessel Security and Safety Act of 2010."

[31] U.S. Senate, Testimony Before the Committee on Commerce, Science and Transportation, Passenger Safety and Regulation of Cruise Ships.

[32] S. 1340—113th Congress: Cruise Passenger Protection Act, 2013, http://www.govtrack.us/congress/bills/113/s1340, accessed December 4, 2013.

[33] Hannah Sampson, "Sen. Rockefeller aims tax bill at cruise lines," *Miami Herald*, August 1, 2013, http:// www.miamiherald.com/2013/08/01/3537382/sen-rockefeller-aims-tax-bill.html, accessed November 2013.

[34] Brazil's public health agency.

aimed to minimize pollution by oil, sewage, garbage, and air emissions. In 2012, new MARPOL regulations reduced the amount of permitted sulfur from 4.5% to 3.5%, and targeted 0.5% by 2020 (subject to a feasibility review to be completed by the IMO).

In addition, MARPOL regulations established special Emission Control Areas (ECAs), which placed stringent limits on sulfur and nitrogen oxide emissions. As of July 1, 2010, ships that operated in ECAs were required to operate on fuel with a sulfur content of 1% or less, and to reduce the sulfur content to 0.1% by 2015. As of February 2013, there were three ECAs: the Baltic Sea, the North Sea/English Channel, and certain waters surrounding the North American coast (extending to the waters surrounding Puerto Rico and the U.S. Virgin Islands in 2014). In 2011, MARPOL stipulated measures to reduce greenhouse gas emissions. These included use of an energy-efficiency design index (EEDI)[35] for new ships as well as the establishment of an energy management plan for all ships, effective 2013.

ROYAL CARIBBEAN'S SAFETY, ENVIRONMENT, AND HEALTH INITIATIVES

Richard Fain, who had been both RCL's chief executive and chairman since 1988, spearheaded the company's commitment to safety, environment, and health:

> Every time I visit an RCL ship, I talk safety to the crew. That goes for all of our senior executives. We have a safety, environment, and health committee of our board of directors, chaired by former Environmental Protection Agency administrator Bill Reilly, which follows quarterly ship and fleet trends and investigates any spikes. Then we have our performance bonuses for the top 200 company executives that are based not just on financial performance and customer satisfaction, but also on company-wide safety results.
>
> In 2005, we set up an incident room at company headquarters. Any serious onboard emergency triggers the incident room to become operational. We communicate with the affected vessel and decide collectively how to trouble-shoot or respond to the problem. If a cruise has to be cancelled, the experienced staff in the incident room handles all communications with passengers and their relatives on shore, with the media, and with passengers booked on future cruises on the ship. We use the incident room at least twice per year to run desktop simulations of crises that may arise.

Gary Bald was responsible for RCL's safety, environment, and health initiatives. Bald also served as the head of the security team. Two vice presidents reported to Bald: Dr. Art Diskin and Richard Pruitt led the medical-public health and safety and environment groups, respectively. (See Figure 3.6 for organization chart.) Bald reported to the CEO and chairman, and was responsible for the design and implementation of all safety, security, public health, and environment policies across all RCL cruise line brands. Bald commented: "We have accidents, but I will not be satisfied until we have zero. We have policies to prevent accidents and to prevent problems escalating if they arise. But, more importantly, we aim to create a perpetual culture of

[35] EEDI is a performance-based mechanism that requires a specific minimum energy efficiency in new ships.

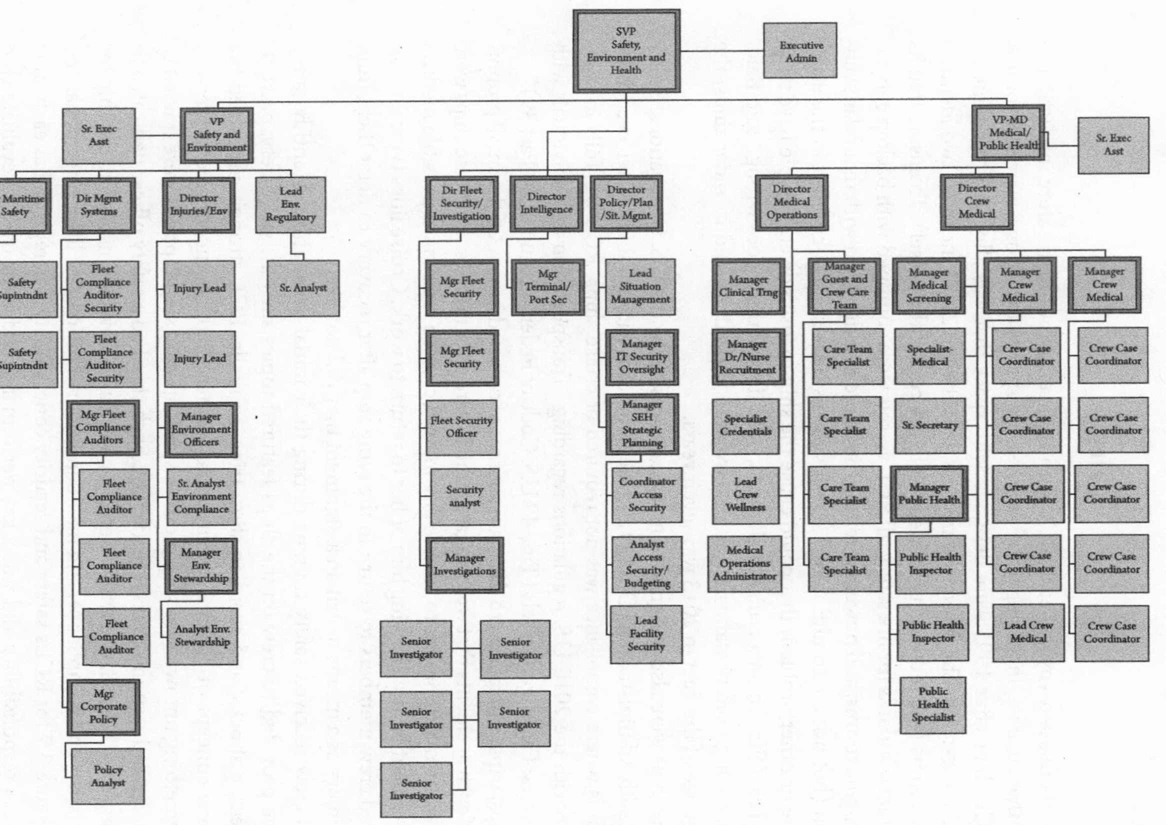

Figure 3.6 Exhibit 12 Royal Caribbean Safety, Environment, and Health Organization Chart, 2013.

Source: Company documents.

safety. Our crew have to be concentrating on safety all the time." Part of the culture was RCL's philosophy of "Above and Beyond Compliance" (ABC). Bald stated: "Most new safety regulations in the cruise industry take six years from idea to mandatory implementation. We at RCL always aim to be ahead of the curve—we regularly implement new regulations well before they become mandatory."

Safety

Before its maiden voyage, each RCL ship received a thorough safety inspection to verify that all areas, including water features and special attractions, were safe for use. All RCL ships after 1995 were designed with space that was allocated to redundant or backup systems. The *Voyager of the Seas*, launched in 2000, included two identical engine rooms (the redundancy added 1% to the cost of the vessel). To ensure that its ships met standards for fire safety, all RCL vessels were equipped with backup generators, engine rooms, and power switches. They were also designed with redundant ventilation (but not air-conditioning) systems to ensure passenger comfort in the event of a fire or other problem that could cause the ship to lose power. "People have to be treated as if they're on a cruise at all times, even if something goes wrong," said Bald. To ensure high safety standards, RCL retrofitted, retired, or sold its older ships; the average age of the fleet in 2013 was seven years.

The ships were also designed to meet standards set by the U.S. Occupational Safety and Health Administration (OSHA) and the Americans with Disabilities Act, even those standards where compliance was not required of cruise ships. RCL was fully in compliance with the 2010 U.S. regulations regarding "Transportation for Individuals with Disabilities: Passenger Vessels (Title 49 U.S. Code of Federal Regulations, Part 39)."

Slips, trips, and falls were the main sources of onboard injury. Of the small proportion of such accidents that were litigated, most were crew injuries. All cruise ships were required by maritime law to restore any injured crew to maximum possible medical improvement before allowing him or her to return to work. Cruise lines typically also required crew members to return to the same ship after recovery to deter them from using injury as a means to exit an assignment they did not like.

All crew received safety training during their initial orientation. Monthly safety training provided to crew on the ships featured topics such as back safety, preventing electric shocks, and avoiding slips, trips, and falls. RCL strongly promoted the maritime concept of "bridge resource management," which encouraged those who saw something untoward or suspicious to speak up (and ship captains were trained to encourage and respond to crew feedback). Each ship had a safety officer dedicated to ensuring crew compliance with emergency standards training, inspecting the ship for safety issues and compliance, and maintaining certifications for lifesaving appliances. (See Figure 3.7 for RCL's safety and security code.) Safety was regarded as each crew member's responsibility and was a key performance indicator used to evaluate ship officers. (See Box 3.2 for RCL's key performance indicators across 27 safety metrics.)

RCL followed the principles of the United Nations Declaration of Human Rights and the Labor Rights conventions of the International Labor Organization when interacting with workers. (See Box 3.3 for RCL's human rights statement and core labor principles.) All RCL employees worldwide were accorded the rights specified by the principles. RCL required its contractors and suppliers to also observe the principles.

Our Company is committed to providing a safe and secure environment for its guests and employees. As a primary business objective, it is the responsibility of every employee, shipboard and shoreside, to ensure that effective safety and security standards are practiced at all times.

Principles of Safety and Security

Culture	We maintain a corporate policy that emphasizes the *Safety of Life* and *Safety of the Ship* and sustain a company-wide culture where the prevention of safety and security incidents is a way of life.
Commitment	We select personnel for safety and security activities who are knowledgeable and committed and then provide them with training and resources to fulfill their duties.
Compliance	We meet or exceed applicable regulations and voluntary standards and strive to be *Above and Beyond Compliance* in our shipboard and shoreside safety and security operations.
Care	We maintain an effective preparedness and response capability that includes care of those affected by incidents.
Continuous Improvement	We implement safety and security practices and programs that promote the Company's commitment to continuously improve.

Figure 3.7 Exhibit 13 Royal Caribbean Safety and Security Code, 2013.
Source: Company documents.

Security

RCL divided security issues into two categories: access (off ship, relationship with ports) and guest security (on ship, including crimes, suspicious deaths, and overboards).

At RCL's headquarters in Miami, two teams supported on-ship safety: the fleet security officer (who served as the resident expert on crimes) and the intelligence expert (who monitored global risk factors that had an impact on the safety of RCL cruise ships at ports of call). RCL also provided or required physical security at each port, including fencing around the boarding areas and qualified security personnel. All guests and crew were provided with electronic identity cards to prevent unauthorized personnel from boarding the ships.

Each RCL ship had an onboard chief security officer (CSO), tasked with investigating security issues, who reported to the staff captain (the second in command). Most CSOs were former members of either the British Royal Navy or Israeli Security Forces.

Since joining RCL, Bald had implemented an electronic record-keeping system to track onboard security incidents and identify the contributing factors. Bald had new CCTV cameras installed aboard RCL's fleet at a cost of $27 million. These helped the security team to better record incidents, and deterred or uncovered those inclined to

Box 3.2 Exhibit 14 Royal Caribbean's Safety, Environment, and Health Key Performance Indicators

Metric 1: Incidents

Metric 1 measures the change in incident occurrence rate versus year ago. Incidents range in severity from high to moderate and cover the following categories: safety, environment, guest and crew injuries, security and medical/public health. For example, a high severity medical incident would be back-to-back norovirus outbreaks, whereas a moderate severity medical incident would be a pest infestation identified by a guest and confirmed by the ship.

Metric 2: Safety and Security Audits

Results of the safety, security and environmental audits for each ship are examined to determine: 1) the rate at which identified problems are fixed before their deadline, 2) problems identified in prior audits that still appear in subsequent audits, 3) problems found on one ship that appear on another in the fleet.

Metric 3: Objectives and Targets

Objectives and targets are assigned to different leaders each year, such as developing global quality assurance standards for the maintenance and operation of life boats, developing an improved communication program to better educate guests on potential shipboard hazards, and completing installation of AWP systems across the fleet.

Metric 4: Outcome Trends

Trends in the ratio of claims to incidents, and the cost of claims are measured over one year. Positive trends are rewarded.

Source: Adapted from company documents.

make false injury claims against the cruise line. There was frequent pilot testing of new technologies that might increase security on RCL vessels.

Bald's team was also responsible for investigating allegations of crew-on-guest crimes. These allegations represented a significant risk to the company, as cruise lines were subject to strict liability regarding staff transgressions.[36] Staff received extensive training on how to interact with guests, in particular how to discourage passenger advances. The incidence of guest-crew entanglements had declined in recent years, thanks to efforts to "drive out Love Boat expectations."[37] RCL also had programs in place to detect crew behaviors that could portend workplace violence, and all staff received biannual ethics training.

[36] All cruise lines were subject to strict liability legal standards that held cruise lines responsible for crimes committed by crew members, regardless of whether there was proof of negligence or fault on the part of the cruise line. These standards were higher than those that hotels would be subject to onshore.
[37] *The Love Boat* was a fictional American TV series that ran in the 1970s and 1980s and focused on romantic relationships aboard a cruise ship.

Box 3.3 Exhibit 15 Royal Caribbean Human Rights Statement and Core Labor Principles

Human Rights Statement

As a global enterprise and a leader in the cruise industry, RCL has been dedicated throughout its history to employing a multicultural shoreside and shipboard workforce of employees from every corner of the world and to enriching the places it visits and the lives of the people who live there.

Principles

- **Forced Labor:** There shall not be any use of forced labor, whether in the form of prison labor, indentured labor, bonded labor or otherwise.
- **Child Labor:** There shall not be use of any child labor.
- **Harassment or Abuse:** Every employee should be treated with respect and dignity. No employees shall be subject to any physical, psychological, or verbal harassment or abuse.
- **Nondiscrimination:** We are committed to attracting and developing a diverse, motivated and dedicated workforce, without regard to race, color, age, religion, gender, sexual orientation and disability. No person shall be subject to any discrimination in respect of employment and occupation.
- **Health and Safety:** We provide a safe and healthy working environment with opportunities for our employees to express their opinions without fear of retaliation.
- **Freedom of Association and Collective Bargaining:** We recognize and respect the right of employees to freedom of association and collective bargaining.
- **Wages and Benefits:** We recognize that wages are essential to meeting employees' basic needs. We guarantee employees will receive fair compensation and benefits in accordance with applicable law and/or union-negotiated agreements.
- **Hours of Work:** Employees shall not be required to work more than legally permitted limits.

Source: Company documents.

RCL reported a number of security incidents to law enforcement in 2012. (See Table 3.6 for a comparison of RCL's incident rate versus comparable rates for the U.S.) Although the rate of incidents was lower aboard RCL's ships than for the U.S. in total, RCL was dedicated to prevent all crimes (perceived or real). Bald cautioned against reading too much into the statistics: "We like to see trend lines going down, but we have to be careful about complacency. We are dealing with small numbers and there's a certain randomness to safety incidents."

Guests also played a role in ensuring security onboard RCL's ships. Before embarking, each passenger had to sign RCL's "Guest Policy," which outlined unsafe behaviors that were prohibited aboard RCL's vessels. Guests who violated the policy could be asked to leave the ship and/or be barred from future cruises. Unsafe behaviors prohibited by the Guest Policy included abusive or disruptive behavior, inappropriate interactions with crew, and failure to uphold parental or guardian responsibilities. Passengers could not board if they were over 24 weeks pregnant.

Table 3.6 Exhibit 16 Royal Caribbean Onboard Crime Allegations versus U.S. population per 100,000, 2011

	Rape	*Other Sexual Assault*[a]	*Assault*
Royal Caribbean	6.4	9.0	2.4
U.S.	26.8	N/A	241

Source: Adapted from the Royal Caribbean International, "2012 Stewardship Report," http://media.royalcaribbean.com/ content/en_US/pdf/13034530_ROYAL CARIBBEAN_2012StwrdshpTwoPgrs_v4.pdf; and "Crime in the U.S." Federal Bureau of Investigation, 2011, accessed November 2013.

[a] Excludes rape.

Public Health

RCL's medical and public health division (headed by Diskin) was responsible for maintaining health onboard. RCL ships were subject to health inspections by numerous agencies; in 2012, RCL's companywide score on the inspections performed by RCL's Medical and Public Health department and the U.S. Public Health Department was 97.1 (which exceeded the company's goal of 96).

Norovirus[38] was the leading cause of disease outbreaks on cruise ships; RCL developed an "outbreak prevention plan" to contain and treat norovirus (and other diseases). The plan's eight stages included screening, surveillance, sanitation, communication, isolation, treatment, reporting, and selected disembarkation (see Box 3.4 for the plan). During the boarding process at the beginning of the cruise, staff would monitor passengers and restrooms for signs of illness, and could deny boarding to any passenger believed to pose a medical risk.

As infectious diseases took some days to incubate, an outbreak could occur when a cruise was well underway. The U.S. Centers for Disease Control and Prevention (CDC) defined an outbreak as a disease that infected at least 3% of guests and/or crew on board. If a cruise had to be curtailed, costs to RCL would be substantial and customer dissatisfaction would be high. The costs of canceling a cruise would typically include refunds or vouchers to passengers (which could include airfare refunds and/or flight rebooking fees), food losses, extra labor for cleanup and inspections (including cleanup for everything, to a move to waiter service instead of buffets to cleaning buttons in the elevators), delays to subsequent cruises, lost excursion and add-on revenue (up to 30% of total revenue per person), and loss of future bookings due to reputation damage. Diseases discovered during a cruise had to be declared in writing at most ports of call.

Each RCL ship possessed a medical facility serving guests and crew that met or exceeded standards set by the American College of Emergency Physicians' Cruise Ship and Maritime Medicine Section. All vessels, regardless of size, had similar medical facilities, including up to three doctors and five nurses. The doctors exceeded

[38] A type of gastrointestinal illness. Norovirus was known as the "cruise ship sickness," but fewer than 1% of Americans affected by norovirus each year were cruise ship passengers.

Box 3.4 Exhibit 17 Royal Caribbean Outbreak Prevention Plan, 2013

Our Outbreak Prevention Plan (OPP) is a two-tiered approach to effectively prevent and guide response should an outbreak of communicable illness occur onboard any of our ships. Level 1 is designed to prevent outbreaks; while Level 2 (activated when three percent of people on board become ill) is focused on halting the spread of any such illness.

Our OPP consists of an eight-step strategy we call the RCL Paradigm:

- Routine *screening* all guests, crew and visitors before they board any of our ships
- Active *surveillance* of guest and crew health to quickly recognize the first indicators of an outbreak, especially any instance of public vomiting
- Enhanced *sanitation* and cleaning of the ship beginning with the first indication of an outbreak
- Effective *communication* with guests and crew to promote proper hygiene and hand washing; to encourage immediate reporting of illness; and to inform guests during an outbreak
- *Isolation* of affected guests and crew, as medically appropriate
- Complimentary medical assessment and *treatment*;
- Transparent *reporting* of outbreaks to our Chief Medical Officer as well as regulatory agencies to aid in the identification of the source of the outbreak (including possible shoreside sources)
- *Disembarkation* of any guest or crew member who requires medical care beyond the capabilities of the onboard medical facility

Some of the specific Level 2 measures we implement when an outbreak occurs include:

- Examining epidemiological patterns of guest staterooms, dining locations, foods eaten, shore activities, etc.
- Increasing the cleaning rate of handrails, elevator buttons, public restrooms and ice machines. This includes the strategic use of electrostatic sprayers and steam cleaners.
- Stationing cleaners in public restrooms to help identify ill guests and keep touch surfaces clean.
- Making medical house calls to staterooms to avoid ill guests interacting with healthy guests.
- Rotating serving utensils and eliminating self-service in the buffet

Our OPP goal is to prevent illness outbreaks; quickly respond to limit the extent of an outbreak; and to assure there are no infected surfaces that can allow an outbreak to carry over to the next cruise guests.

Source: Company documents.

general practitioner requirements, were certified in advanced life support, and had access to specialist technology. In 2010, RCL installed the technology needed to perform blood transfusions aboard its ships by sourcing blood matches from passengers and crew. RCL performed 35 successful transfusions at sea between 2010 and 2012. Medical staff onboard RCL's fleet also used high-speed Internet connections to transmit digital x-rays (which could be read by shoreside specialists to confirm diagnoses) and tele-dermatology to address onboard medical needs. RCL partnered with Dialysis at Sea, a dialysis care provider, to enable passengers with end-stage renal disease to receive dialysis treatment under the supervision of trained medical staff while at sea. Finally, women could not board if they were over 24 weeks pregnant.

Before being hired, all crew candidates received a medical evaluation to ensure that each was healthy and physically capable of performing required duties. RCL partnered with medical evaluation providers in over 30 countries to screen prospective crew members. Each crew member received a medical checkup every 24 months, and each year, every ship and RCL headquarters in Miami conducted health fairs to offer complementary health tests and health education resources to employees. Roughly 90% of shipboard employees participated. In 2012, RCL instituted electronic health records for its crew members.

Maritime law stipulated that any employee who became ill or injured while working must be treated until "maximum medical improvement" was achieved. Treatment of crew could include on-ship care at the medical facility and continuing care at a shoreside, quality medical institution. Off-ship treatments took place at centers of medical excellence identified by RCL that provided high-quality medical care in Panama, Croatia, the Dominican Republic, Brazil, Australia, the U.K., and the U.S.

RCL also offered mental wellness services to guests and crew. The CareTeam provided support in the event of onboard emergencies, family illnesses at home, or serious incidents. Over 400 trained CareTeam specialists across RCL's fleet could provide 24-hour assistance. In 2012, the CareTeam managed over 1,800 cases. After typhoon Haiyan struck the Philippines in November 2013, the CareTeam offered counseling and assistance to Filipino crew members whose families were affected by the storm.

Environment

In 1998, RCL pled guilty to obstruction of justice when rogue ship engineers attempted to cover up illegal dumping practices; it was sentenced to five years' probation and a $9 million fine.[39] In 1999, RCL was indicted on charges of dumping toxic solvents, oils, and chemicals in New York Harbor, Miami, the U.S. Virgin Islands, Los Angeles, and the Inside Passage of Alaska.[40] RCL pled guilty to 21 counts of polluting and was fined $18 million.[41] In 2000, the firm paid a further $3.3 million to the state of Alaska.[42]

Following the embarrassment of these lawsuits, RCL chose to invest in increased environmental protections. (See Figure 3.8 for Royal Caribbean's environmental code.) In 1996, RCL appointed an environmental officer (EO) on each vessel. EOs were required to attend training programs on RCL's environmental policies and initiatives, train and oversee other crew members in RC's environmental policies, and provide educational programs for the cruise line's guests. By 2013, following a series of environmental initiatives (see Table 3.7), RCL was considered an industry leader.

[39] Wernick, "Royal Caribbean Cruises Ltd."

[40] Wernick, "Royal Caribbean Cruises Ltd."

[41] Wernick, "Royal Caribbean Cruises Ltd."

[42] Wernick, "Royal Caribbean Cruises Ltd."

Our Company values the environment and is committed to protecting and conserving environmental resources, preventing pollution and continuously improving our environmental management. As a primary business objective, it is the responsibility of every employee, shipboard and shoreside, to ensure environmental stewardship is practiced at all times.

Principles of Environmental Stewardship

Culture	We strive to use natural resources efficiently and responsibly, with particular emphasis on reducing our air emissions including: NO_X, SO_X, CO_2 and other greenhouse gases. We consider environmental issues in design and development projects.
Commitment	We reduce, reuse and recycle, as much as possible and practical. We seek to purchase goods which have a content of recycled material without sacrificing efficiency and quality. We encourage vendors and suppliers to make a commitment to the environment and to provide us with greener products and services.
Compliance	We meet or exceed applicable regulations and voluntary standards and strive to be *Above and Beyond Compliance* in our shipboard and shoreside operations.
Continuous Improvement	We establish environmental objectives that challenge the Company to continuously improve environmental stewardship.
Collaboration	We promote stewardship of the marine environment through internal and external initiatives such as **Save the Waves®** and **The Ocean Fund℠**. We communicate our environmental commitment to the public and ask our guests to join us in respecting the environment.

Figure 3.8 Exhibit 18 Royal Caribbean Environmental Code, 2013.
Source: Company documents.

RCL's environmental sustainability efforts were a natural extension of its company vision. In addition, 36% of shore excursions in 2012 were conducted by third-party operators that were aligned with RCL's sustainability standards.

RCL's "Save the Waves" program was initially tasked with increasing compliance with "reduce, reuse and recycle" policies. Later, Save the Waves expanded to include pollution prevention, continuous improvement, and promoting "Above and Beyond Compliance" (ABC). The ABC philosophy required RCL to implement environmental improvements over and above those required by law and often several years in advance of upgraded requirements becoming mandatory. By 2012, 80% of RCL's guests and 100% of the crew reported awareness of the Save the Waves program. One of the program's initiatives was the Ocean Fund, which contributed over $12 million to ocean conservation societies between 1996 and 2012.

Solid waste management RCL's policy was to ensure that solid waste was never discharged into the ocean. The cruise line worked with its suppliers to reduce the volume of packaging materials needed for supplies delivered to the ships (and convert them to recyclable materials, where possible). RCL also worked to identify partners at its ports that could receive donations of items, such as mattresses, towels, and furniture, for reuse. Between 2007 and 2012, RCL reduced the amount of solid waste deposited in landfills from its ships by over 70%. Refrigerated units stored used bottles and cans onboard to prevent growth of bacteria and enable them to be recycled when the ship reached land. By 2012, further landfill waste reductions were proving harder

Table 3.7 Exhibit 19 Royal Caribbean Environmental Initiatives, 1992–2012

Year	*Initiatives*
1992	Established "Save the Waves" program to reduce, reuse and recycle.
1996	Environmental Officer position created; Launched the "Ocean Fund" to give grants for marine preservation.
1997	Obtained ISO 14001 Environmental and ISO 9001 Quality Certifications.
1998	Environmental Committee of the Board of the Directors founded.
1999	First generation advanced wastewater purification systems installed; Competition for "Environmental Ship of the Year" and "Innovative Ship of the Year" begun fleet-wide.
2000	Partnered with U. of Miami to equip Explorer of the Seas with laboratories for visiting scientists.
2000–2004	Smoke-less gas turbine engines installed on four Millennium-class and four Radiance-class ships.
2006	Galapagos Fund created to fund conservation efforts in the Galapagos Islands
2007	Partner with Conservation International to develop environmental stewardship strategy.
2008	Chief environmental officer position established; partnered with Sustainable Travel to develop stewardship strategy; Solstice ship equipped with solar panels, "green" roof and environmental educational space.
2009	Piloted "Sustainable Marine Tour Operators Standards"; hosted "Destination Stewardship Think Tank" to unite tour operators, conservationists and hospitality providers.
2010	Won the Conde Nast traveler "World Savers Award" in the cruise category; hosted the founding meeting of the Sustainable Travel Leadership Network.
2011	Celebrity Cruises won the Conde Nast traveler "World Savers Award" in the cruise category; new "Save the Waves" crew training launched; Emission "scrubbers" piloted on two ships.
2012	Next generation scrubber certified to International Maritime Organization standards; all ships equipped with interactive environmental data management systems; tours and operations at CocoCay© received gold level certification from Sustainable Travel International's tourism education program.

Source: Adapted from company documents.

to achieve (see Figure 3.9 for waster per passenger day), so RCL set up a waste management team tasked with increasing recycling, obtaining proof of recycling across worldwide operations, and helping to achieve "zero landfill" deposits on Oasis-class ships.

Many RCL vendors supplied food products or cleaning agents in reusable and returnable containers. In 2012, the crew aboard one RCL ship partnered with its food suppliers to eliminate Styrofoam packaging in favor of more easily recycled cardboard containers. RCL dedicated staff and resources to its recycling program. All trash aboard the ships was hand-sorted by crew to identify recyclable materials. Recyclables were

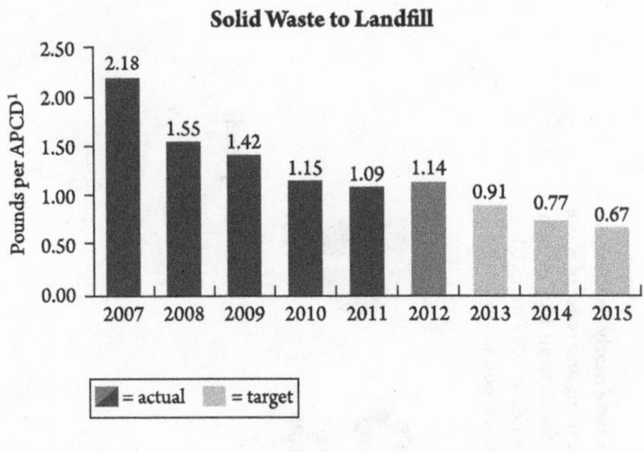

In 2012, we increasesd the amount of waste going to landfill by 0.05 pounds per APCD) for the first time since 2007.

The average person in the U.S. generates about 4.3 pounds of solid waste per day. On our ships, we produced and landed ashore approximately 1.14 pounds of waste per person per day in 2012.

U.S. average[2] 4.30 pounds

RCL 1.14 pounds

Figure 3.9 Exhibit 20 Royal Caribbean Landfill Waste per Passenger Day, 2007–2012.
Source: Company documents.

compacted and stored in climate-controlled areas until a port with recycling facilities was reached. In 2011, RCL held its first recycling competition to reward crews on the ships, which produced the largest amount of recyclables by weight over the year. During the five-year period between 2007 and 2012, RCL increased the total amount of recycled or reused waste by 75% (see Figure 3.10 for recycled waste per passenger day).

Wastewater management RCL's fleet of ships generated three different types of wastewater: bilge water, gray water, and black water (see Figure 3.11 for ship wastewater systems diagram). Bilge water was the drainage collected internally, including runoff from machinery. The water was collected in the lowest area of the ship, the "bilge," before being processed in special holding tanks where contaminants were removed. In the early 1990s, rogue engineers on one RCL ship illegally jerry-rigged several bilge water pipes to bypass the oily water separators, causing the unprocessed bilge water to be dumped into the ocean. Subsequently, RCL took steps to monitor and enforce compliance with the filtration process for bilge water. By 2013, the bilge water produced onboard RCL's ships was three times cleaner than the level required by international regulations. (See Figure 3.12 for bilge water treatment standards.)

Gray water was the runoff produced by the showers, sinks, baths, laundry, dishwashers, pools, spas, and kitchens on the ship, as well as condensate from the air-conditioning systems. International laws stated that untreated gray water could be disposed of within 12 nautical miles of land, in most locations. Since 1998, RCL always disposed of gray water no less than 12 nautical miles from shore. Black water was the drainage from urinals, toilets, and medical facilities. International standards required the disposal of untreated black water beyond 12 nautical miles from land, at a speed of at least four knots (the speed requirement ensured that the black water was dispersed throughout the water column). RCL stipulated that its black water be disposed of at speeds no less than six knots.

In 1999, RCL began sourcing and installing advanced water purification (AWP) systems. The AWP systems were designed to treat black water and gray water before they were disposed of, to produce output cleaner than required by international law (and cleaner than the output of most municipalities). As part of the ABC policy, RCL

Increased the volume of waste recycled from our ships by 125% over 2007 baseline
ORIGINA L GOAL:
Increase the volume of waste recycled by 50% over a 2007 baseline

We have nearly boubled our recycling and reuse of waste materials from 12.9 million pounds in 2007 to 25.10 million pounds in 2012.

Pounds (in millions)

millaian pounds

[1]APCD Refers to Available Passenger Cruse Days, which is the number of lower berths on a ship times the number of days that those berths are available to passenger per year.

[2]Environmental protection Agency Report-Municipal Soild waste (MSW) in the United Static Facts and Figures

Figure 3.10 Exhibit 21 Royal Caribbean Total Recycled Waste per Passenger Day, 2007–2012.

Source: Company documents.

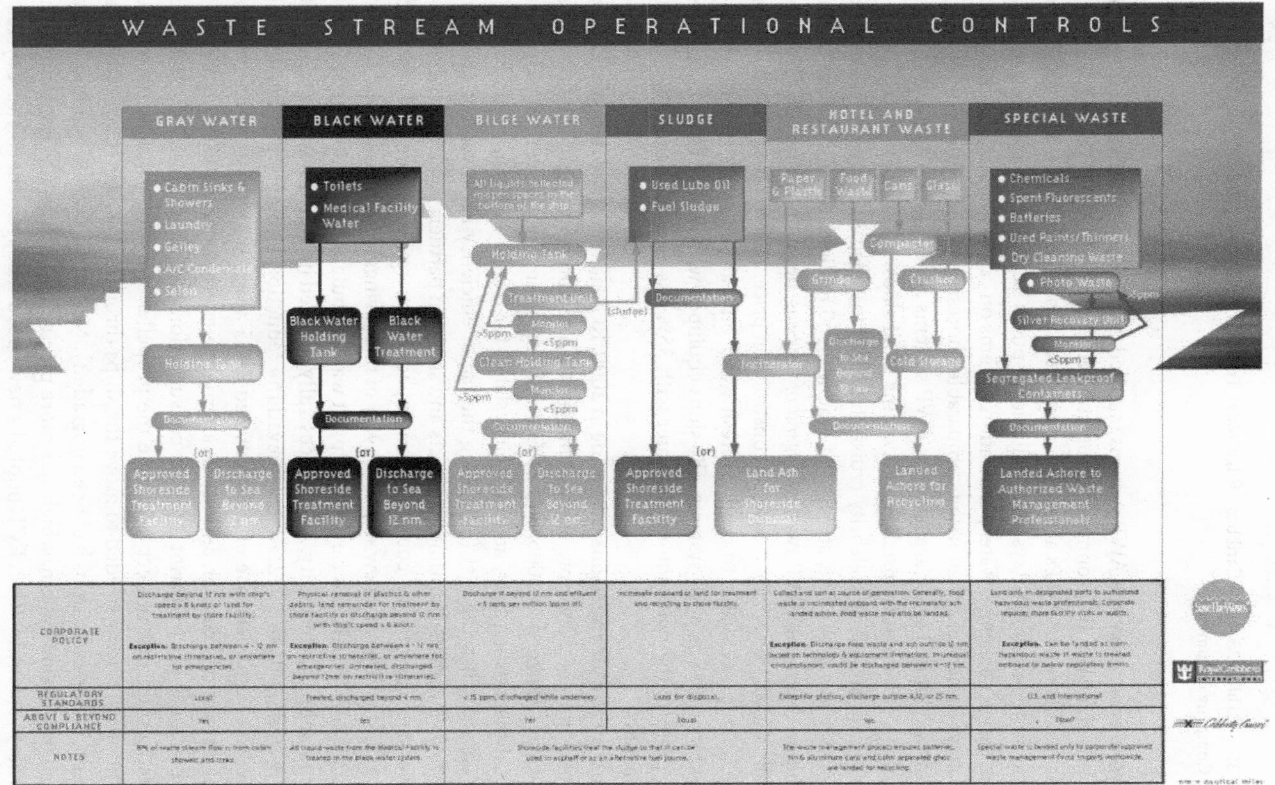

Figure 3.11 Royal Caribbean Ship Wastewater Systems.

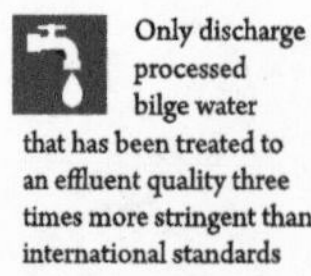

Only discharge
processed
bilge water
that has been treated to
an effluent quality three
times more stringent than
international standards

The IMO standard for discharging treated bilge water is 15 parts per million. In 2012, RCL ships discharged processed bilge water treated to an average of less than 1.5 parts per million.

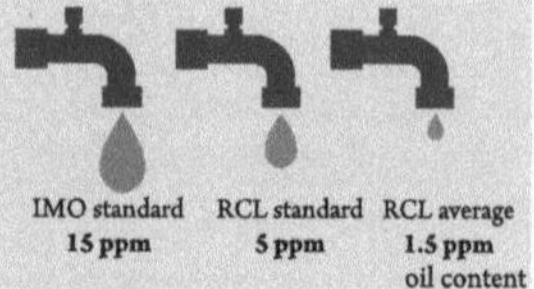

Figure 3.12 Exhibit 23 Royal Caribbean Bilge Water Treatment Standards, 2012.
Source: Company documents.

worked to ensure that the AWP systems installed on the fleet exceeded the discharge standards of the U.S. Environmental Protection Agency and MARPOL. However, scaling the installation of AWPs across the entire fleet proved difficult. At the time, there were no off-the-shelf AWP systems available for purchase and cruise ships presented a unique design challenge. Water purification systems on cruise ships had sharper peaks and valleys in demand than many comparable shoreside systems; the movement of the ship and limited space available for AWP systems added further challenges. RCL pledged $150 million to install AWP systems in all ships. By 2012, 19 of 21 ships in the RCI fleet and all 11 Celebrity cruise ships had installed AWPs, many more than any competitive cruise line, at a cost of around $160 million. The installation on the last ship to receive an AWP system, *Legend of the Seas,* began in January 2013. AWPs typically added 1% to 1.5% to a ship's construction price.

RCL's ships were able to produce fresh water onboard either by steam desalination or by reverse osmosis systems. The ships equipped with reverse osmosis systems could produce the same amount of water with 35% less electricity than those using desalination.

Energy and air emissions Beginning in 2000, RCL had set out to design each new class of ship to be 20% more energy efficient than the previous class. The first Oasis class vessel, designed in 2006, was 20% to 30% more energy efficient per passenger day than the existing fleet, and the third, slated for launch in 2016, would be 21% more efficient than the first (exceeding the target efficiency improvement of 15%). RCL worked with its maritime architects and shipyard partners to identify new technologies and designs that could have an impact on energy efficiency, and rewarded them with the value of a new ship's first year of fuel savings from innovations.

In 2012, 97% of RCL's carbon footprint was attributable to fuel used for propulsion and onboard electricity. RCL successfully reduced its greenhouse gas footprint by 19% from 2005 to 2012. RCL achieved the reduction through a combination of reduced fuel use (decrease of 19% between 2005 and 2012), purification systems to make emissions cleaner, and use of alternative energy sources. (See Figure 3.13 for greenhouse gas footprint and fuel consumption over time.) In 2005, RCL had initiated a multiyear project to update the propeller and rudder system to reduce the amount of energy needed to move the ships through the water (as of 2012, five of the six Vision-class ships had been upgraded). New vessels would be fitted with a podded propulsion system, which was more precise and energy efficient than older propeller systems. In 2012, RCL piloted a new speed-management software system to optimize the engine use of its ships; the system was slated to be rolled out to the fleet in 2013. All energy efficiency investments were designed to pay back in three years.

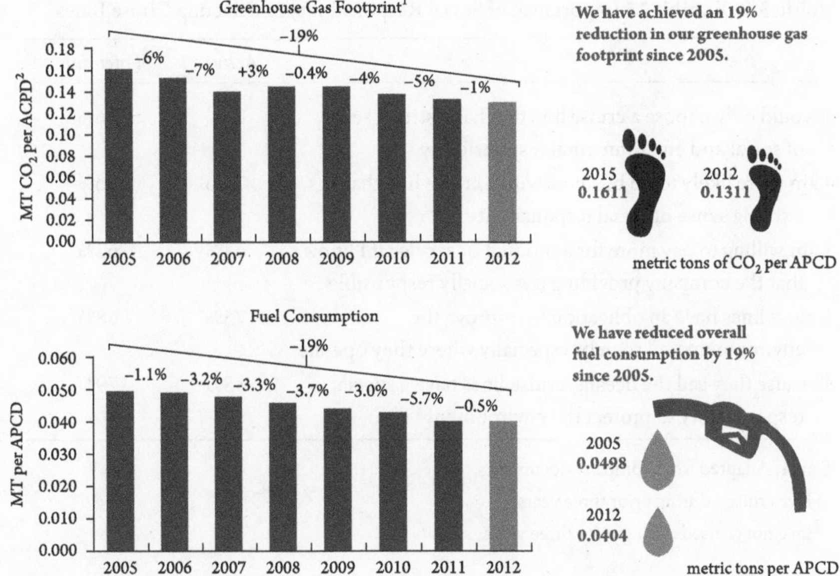

Figure 3.13 Exhibit 24 Royal Caribbean Greenhouse Gas Footprint and Fuel Consumption, 2007–2012.
Source: Company documents.

In 2011, RCL began piloting advanced emission purification (AEP) systems, known as "scrubbers" aboard the *Independence of the Seas*. Although the result of the pilot showed a decrease in sulfur dioxide emissions of around 90% (depending upon the load on the engine), the test revealed critical technical issues that prevented RCL from scaling the technology to the entire fleet. RCL piloted a different type of scrubber in 2012, which reduced sulfur dioxide emissions by 99.9%, but the test revealed the susceptibility of key components to corrosion. RCL continued testing by placing third and fourth variants of scrubbers on two new ships.

THE MEETING

Cruise line executives acknowledged that investments in projects to improve public health, safety, and the environment often went unnoticed by passengers. A July 2013 survey asked active and potential cruisers about the perceived safety of cruises versus other vacations. Six percent of actives and 27% of potentials stated cruises were somewhat or much less safe. Twenty-six percent of actives and 72% of potentials were much or somewhat more negative about cruising following recent events. During an observation period between September 2012 and September 2013, consumer online conversations regarding their cruise experiences were tagged by subject: experience was mentioned the most, over 463,000 times, whereas safety received just over 103,000 mentions (out of nearly 2 million total mentions).[43]

43 "Cruises, US," Mintel.

Table 3.8 Exhibit 25 Importance of Social Responsibility in Selecting Cruise Lines

	Actives[a]	*Potentials*[b]
I would only choose a cruise line that has a strong sense of social and environmental responsibility	21%	16%
I am more likely to do business with a cruise line that has a strong sense of social responsibility	74%	76%
I am willing to pay more for a product or service if I know that the company providing it is socially responsible	64%	62%
Cruise lines have an obligation to improve the environment and society, especially where they operate	75%	68%
Because they sail the oceans, cruise lines have a special responsibility to protect the environment	85%	79%

Source: Adapted from company documents.
[a] Have cruised during prior three years.
[b] Have not cruised during prior three years.

A July 2013 RCL survey examined the importance of social and environmental responsibility to active and potential cruisers (see Table 3.8 for survey results). In addition, the survey asked consumers to rate different cruise brands on social responsibility and safety (see Table 3.9 for results).

On the agenda for Bald's upcoming meeting with Fain and Goldstein was the issue of "differentiation." To what extent could or should RCL try to differentiate itself from

Table 3.9 Exhibit 26 Comparative Social Responsibility and Safety Perceptions of Cruise Lines

	"Most Socially Responsible Cruise Line"		*"More/Somewhat More Safe Than Others"*[c]		*"Brand I Trust"*	
	Actives[a]	*Potentials*[b]	*Actives*	*Potentials*	*Actives*	*Potentials*
Royal Caribbean	21%	17%	35%	25%	68%	72%
Celebrity	7%	2%	26%	18%	45%	49%
Carnival	11%	9%	9%	4%	41%	51%
Princess	5%	5%	41%	31%	54%	53%
Disney	31%	39%	24%	23%	35%	43%
Holland America	4%	4%	26%	20%	34%	38%
Norwegian	14%	17%	29%	29%	51%	55%

Source: Adapted from company documents.
[a] Have cruised during prior three years.
[b] Have not cruised during prior three years.
[c] Based on respondents aware of each cruise line.

other cruise lines on the basis of its "above and beyond compliance" initiatives and superior track records in safety, environment, and health.

Some executives believed RCL's consistent track record in these areas justified more aggressive promotion of RCL's commitments and achievements as part of its marketing strategy.

Others argued that RCL should not break ranks with industry tradition and should not exploit its progress at the expense of its competitors. Instead, RCL should cement its leadership of CLIA and other industry associations by quietly setting an example that would raise performance standards for all cruise lines.

A third group advocated selectively promoting RCL initiatives (e.g., environmental improvements) if market research suggested that doing so would significantly increase RCL's appeal to a large enough segment of target consumers.

As Gary Bald prepared for the meeting, he found himself conflicted. He was proud of RCL's track record and leadership and wanted the story told. On the other hand, he knew that RCL would never be 100% incident-free. He worried that promoting RCL's accomplishments in safety, for example, could backfire if and when a problem drew public scrutiny.

PART II

Consumer Analytics and Healthcare Outcomes

4

CAROLINAS HEALTHCARE SYSTEM CONSUMER ANALYTICS

John A. Quelch and Margaret L. Rodriguez

In 2014, Dr. Michael Dulin, chief clinical officer for analytics and outcomes research and head of the Dickson Advanced Analytics (DA^2) group at Carolinas HealthCare System (CHS), was preparing for a planning meeting with Carol Lovin, executive vice president and chief strategy officer at CHS. In the three years since DA^2 was formed, the team had successfully unified all analytics talent and resources into one group that served CHS. Rapid increases in computing power and decreases in data storage costs had enabled DA2's data architects to build predictive models incorporating complex clinical, financial, demographic, and claims data that would have been impossible to create only a few years before. Although DA^2 had blazed the trail for applied analytics in healthcare, other players in the value chain were making increased investments in their own modelling capabilities.

Healthcare payers, such as Humana and UnitedHealth, were increasingly making analytics the focus of a strategic shift towards consumer-centric healthcare; going so far as to create targeted communications strategies for different patient segments and engaging behavioral health companies to provide exercise, nutrition and other programs that would reduce the healthcare costs of their highest-risk patients. While many agreed that analytics could help the healthcare industry reduce costs and increase access to care, CHS recognized that privacy protections on patient data, as well as competitive rivalries, restricted the sharing of data among the various healthcare stakeholders.

Dulin also noted the entry of consumer tech companies into the healthcare space; in 2014, both Apple and Google announced features in their new mobile operating systems that aggregated and tracked the output from various health-wearables (like heart-rate monitors or step-counters), as well as electronic medical record (EMR) data. Apple's Healthkit could even incorporate the results of lab-tests into the dashboard (with the user's permission). Although the tech giants did not yet have access to claims or clinical data, they could potentially enter the field by acquiring an EMR company. Their expertise in analytics, access to demographic and location data, as well as the broad consumer-adoption of their devices, led Dulin to consider which industry players consumers would trust to integrate their healthcare data in the future and what role DA^2 could play.

CAROLINAS HEALTHCARE SYSTEM BACKGROUND

In 2014, the Carolinas HealthCare System, headquartered in Charlotte, owned and managed hospitals and acute care facilities that served over 2.2 million patients[1] per year across three states (North Carolina, South Carolina and Georgia). CHS was one of the oldest healthcare systems in the U.S.: its origins could be traced to the state's first civilian hospital, Charlotte Home and Hospital, established in 1876. The Charlotte Home and Hospital operated until 1940 (although the name was later changed to St. Peter's Hospital), when it was replaced by a new facility, the Charlotte Memorial Hospital, in a different location. During WWII, the hospital's financial difficulties led Rush S. Dickson, a local businessman, to lobby the city and county governments for larger reimbursements for emergency and indigent patients, and solicited financial support from local non-profits and corporations. In 1943, the Charlotte-Mecklenburg Hospital Authority was organized under the North Carolina Hospital Authorities Act, which provided for oversight mechanisms for Charlotte Memorial Hospital (including rules governing the construction of new facilities, funding and management of day-to-day operations). The Act also provided the legal and financial frameworks to support patients who could not afford to pay for healthcare services.

In 1990, the name of the Charlotte Memorial Hospital was changed to Carolinas Medical Center (CMC) to reflect the hospital's increasing focus on education. That year, the facility was designated an "Academic Medical Center Teaching Hospital" by the state of North Carolina (one of only five hospitals in North Carolina to receive the designation). Five years later, the Authority changed the name of the growing hospital network to CHS. In 2007, CHS opened the Levine Children's Hospital, which housed more than 30 medical specialties. In 2010, CHS announced a ten-year, $500 million investment to advance cancer treatment strategies and research through the creation of the Levine Cancer Institute. In 2010, CMC (now a part of CHS) was designated the Charlotte Campus of the University of North Carolina (UNC) School of Medicine and hosted third and fourth-year medical students.

By 2014, CHS had become the biggest healthcare provider in North Carolina with more than 61,000 full-time and part-time employees and an annual budget of over $7.7 billion (see Table 4.1 for selected financial data). Its medical education and research center included over 300 residents and fellows pursuing a variety of medical specialties and had established research relationships with Oxford (stroke), UNC (dementia), Duke, and many other academic centers across the U.S. CHS operated 900 care locations and 7,494 licensed beds in three states, including 39 hospitals (21 of which were managed by CHS, and 18 of which were owned), as well as additional virtual care services. Roughly 75% of patients were located in North Carolina and CHS spent $20 million each year on community outreach in the greater Charlotte, NC area alone. CHS tracked patient satisfaction with mailed surveys or follow-ups within days of an appointment or discharge. Satisfaction was measured by a patient's likelihood to

[1] Patients were considered active if they had engaged with one of the CHS sites (including: primary care facility, hospital, worksite clinic, a virtual visit or a trip to a clinic inside of CVS) at least once in the prior eighteen months. Roughly 13,000 patients fell off of the active rolls each month, many due to relocating out of state, death or attrition.

Table 4.1 Exhibit 1 CHS Summary Financials, 2013

	Dollar Total (million)	*Percentage of Total*
	Revenues	
Tertiary & Acute Care Services	$5,832	68%
Continuing Care Services	$293	4%
Specialty Services	$53	1%
Physician's Services	$1,487	18%
Other Services	$225	3%
Non-Operating Activities	$469	6%
Total Revenues	$8,358	100%
	Expenses	
Wages, Salaries & Benefits	$4,616	55%
Materials, Supplies & Other	$2,615	31%
Depreciation & Amortization	$454	5%
Financing Costs	$125	2%
Funding for Facilities, Equipment & Programs	$547	7%
Total Expenses	$8,358	100%

Source: Company documents.

recommend CHS. As part of its role as a public healthcare system, CHS provided healthcare services to underserved patients and communities. CHS offered financial support to patients without insurance (or who were underinsured), subsidies for Medicare and Medicaid recipients, as well as funding for its education, behavioral health and community health clinics. CHS gave medical supplies and equipment to non-profits valued at over $1.5 million in 2013 (see Table 4.2 for a full list of CHS charitable expenditures for 2013). Roughly 62% of annual revenue came from Medicare and Medicaid patients.

By 2014, the vision of CHS had remained unchanged for two decades: healthcare, education and research. That year, Lovin led an initiative to renew the strategic roadmap to guide CHS's future growth. She worked with her executive team colleagues to craft a strategy that provided for personalized, high quality service across a single, unified enterprise. "Our customers are the consumers and patients first, payers second," said Lovin. The team developed a list of strategic priorities (Table 4.3) and performance measures (Table 4.4) to guide the organization towards its goals.

HEALTH PROVIDER INDUSTRY BACKGROUND

In 2012, healthcare expenditures in the U.S. totaled over $7,600 per capita versus an average of $2,800 per capita among OECD countries.[2] The majority of

[2] "Health Expenditure—OECD Health Statistics 2014," OECD iLibrary, http://www.oecd.org/els/health-systems/health-expenditure.htm, accessed February 2015.

Table 4.2 Exhibit 2 CHS Charitable Expenditures, 2013

Charitable Expenditures	*$, million*
Cost of financial assistance to uninsured patients	$324
Bad debt costs by patients who do not pay for services	$290
Losses incurred by serving Medicare patients[a]	$563
Losses incurred by serving Medicaid patients	$161
Cost of community-building activities and other services	$56
Cost of medical education, research, and cash and in-kind contributions to charities	$146
Total value of uncompensated care and other community benefits	$1,540

Source: Company documents.

[a] Medicare and Medicaid offered fixed compensation per recipient which occasionally fell short of the actual cost of care; hospitals were not permitted to refuse care to these patients.

healthcare expenses were paid for by government-sponsored coverage, such as Medicare and Medicaid,[3] or by health insurance companies that sold plans to employers and individuals (either to those who purchased via healthcare exchanges or those who were eligible for Medicare Advantage[4]). Government reimbursements per Medicare patient to cover healthcare had declined over time (Figure 4.1); however the 2010 Affordable Care Act (ACA) offered providers who were organized as accountable care organizations (ACOs)[5] a share of the cost savings generated in the delivery of care to Medicare patients, so long as minimum quality thresholds were met.

Key changes to the U.S. healthcare landscape over the decade prior had influenced healthcare providers like CHS, and other healthcare stakeholders, to revisit their care delivery models:

- **Fee-for-value instead of fee-for-service** After the ACA's passage, hospital compensation was determined in part by the quality of outcomes, rather than simply on a fee-for-service basis as before. Hospitals faced penalties for high readmission rates and hospital-acquired conditions, but could also receive financial rewards for exceeding clinical quality outcome or patient satisfaction benchmarks. Many healthcare providers sought to quickly build capabilities in analytics and measurement in

[3] Medicare was the federal health insurance program offered to seniors aged 65 and older. Medicaid was offered to low-income individuals who were unable to obtain healthcare via the exchanges or an employer.

[4] Insurers offered Medicare Advantage plans to eligible patients who chose to receive their benefits via the insurer's network.

[5] Qualified ACOs agreed to be accountable for the overall care of their Medicare patients, obtain adequate participation of primary care physicians, create processes around evidence-based medicine, report on quality and costs, and coordinate care.

Table 4.3 Exhibit 3 CHS Strategic Priorities, 2014

Strategic Priority	*Details*
Quality & Patient Experience	Design a customer relationship management tool; increase health literacy; improve critical and diabetes care; improve clinical outcomes via collaboration software.
Integrated System of Care	Deploy the CHS care management platform; manage population health; deploy virtual care; transform service lines, continuing care, community health and point of care.
Strategic Growth	Deliver competitive, consumer-facing retail services; commercialize existing CHS services; develop payer/risk strategies with payers; deliver best-in-class specialty care.
Transformative Operations	Improve processes to reduce patient wait times; share and implement best practices across the organization; put the patient first in operational decisions; leverage engaged workforce.

Source: Company documents.

order to track quality improvements; and to shift the organizational focus towards the continuous improvement of patient care.

- **Physician shortages** In the U.S., there were roughly 2.5 physicians per 1,000 people (versus an average of 3.3 per 1,000 among comparable OECD countries).[6] The ACA was expected to exacerbate the supply-demand shortfall in the future, since it increased the population covered by health insurance. In 2014 alone, nearly 32 million new people entered the healthcare system.[7] The Association of American Medical Colleges estimated that, by 2025, the U.S. would face a shortage of over 130,000 doctors.[8]
- **Digitization of healthcare** In 2011, the U.S. Centers for Medicare and Medicaid Services (CMS) established an incentive system for doctor's offices and hospitals to switch from paper to electronic medical records (EMRs). Hospitals that served Medicare patients could receive up to a $2 million incentive for adopting EMRs.[9] Although patients were free to view and request corrections to the data in their EMRs, the platforms made it difficult for providers to extract and model the data held in the EMRs. In 2014, Google and Apple each announced healthcare dashboards that would aggregate data from wearable devices, including scales, running apps and sleep trackers, into a consumer-friendly dashboard. Apple even partnered with several EMR

[6] "U.S. Health Care Resources Compared to Other Countries Slideshow," Kaiser Family Foundation, http://kff.org/slideshow/u-s-health-care-resources-compared-to-other-countries-slideshow/, accessed February 2015.

[7] "GME Funding: How to Fix the Doctor Shortage," Association of American Medical Colleges, https://www.aamc.org/advocacy/campaigns_and_coalitions/fixdocshortage/, accessed February 2015.

[8] "GME Funding: How to Fix the Doctor Shortage," Association of American Medical Colleges.

[9] "HER Incentives & Certification," HealthIT.gov, January 15, 2013. http://www.healthit.gov/providers-professionals/ehr-incentive-programs, accessed February 2015.

Table 4.4 Exhibit 4 CHS Strategic Performance Measures, 2014

Performance Measures	*Metrics*
Quality & Patient Experience	Inpatient mortality; breast cancer screenings; physician satisfaction; patient likelihood to recommend; patient safety score; diabetes treatment outcomes; appropriate care score (for both ambulatory and acute care).
Integrated System of Care	Readmission rate; CHS/payer collaboration performance; progress against integrated system of care goals; Medicare spend per beneficiary; CHS medical plan performance.
Strategic Growth	Actively managed primary care patients; population share; commercial/managed care population; use rates (versus industry benchmarks); evidence-based screening volumes; commercialized products or services.
Transformative Operations	Average length of stay; emergency department transformation score; operating cash flow margin; productivity improvement; revenue cycle improvement; process enhancement product standardization savings and speed.
Teammate Engagement	Commitment indicator score (percentile ranking)
Community Benefit	Number of individuals screened for pre-diabetes; hours of community service.

Source: Company documents.

companies to make medical records and lab results available to consumers on their iPhone via the single dashboard.

- **Shift to outpatient** In an effort to cut costs and increase access to care, providers encouraged patients to seek care via outpatient facilities, or even via virtual check-ups, rather than at high-cost treatment locations like emergency departments (EDs). Outpatient care comprised 51% of health expenditures in the U.S., whereas the average among OECD countries was 33%.[10] In 2013, CHS chief executive, Michael Tarwater, observed: "More than 90% of our patient encounters now take place in a setting other than the bedside of an inpatient hospital room."[11]
- **New Entrants** The shift to outpatient care led consumers to seek more convenient and inexpensive healthcare services. Retailers (including CVS, Walmart, Target and Krogers) began opening health-care clinics staffed by nurse practitioners in their stores as early as 2000. By 2014, there were 1,600 walk-in clinics in the U.S., and the number

[10] OECD (2013), "Health at a Glance 2013: OECD Indicators," OECD Publishing. http://dx.doi.org/10.1787/health_glance-2013-en, accessed February 2015.

[11] Company documents.

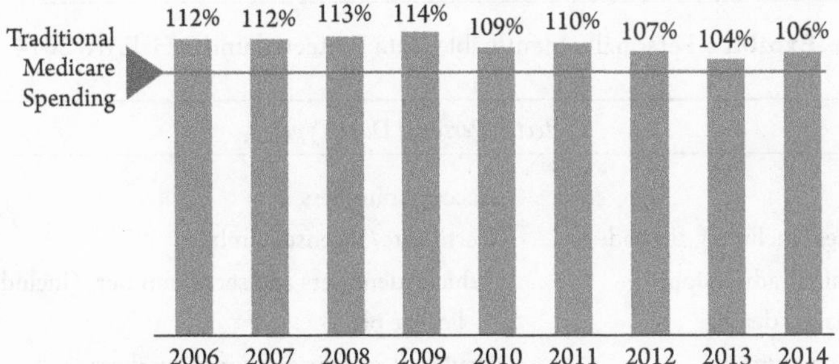

Figure 4.1 Exhibit 5 Medicare Advantage Payments as a Percentage of Traditional Medicare, 2006–2014.

Source: "Medicare at a Glance," *Kaiser Family Foundation*, September 2, 2014, http://www.cdc.gov/obesity/data/adult.html, accessed October 2014.

was expected to reach nearly 3,000 by 2015.[12] Cost of care at the clinics for three common illnesses averaged $110, versus $166 at doctors' offices and $570 in EDs.[13]

HIPAA Regulations

In 1996, the United States House of Representatives passed the Health Insurance Portability and Accountability Act (HIPAA). HIPAA provided for both the portability of employer-provided health insurance (which enabled an individual to keep the same health insurance between jobs), as well as establishing the first set of national security and confidentiality standards for patient health data.[14] The U.S. Department of Health and Human Services (HHS) established a privacy rule to protect individually identifiable patient data, while still enabling stakeholders to access the data needed to provide care. Data protected under HIPAA included: physical or mental health conditions (including those that occurred in the past), health care provided, payments made for healthcare received, and demographic information which could be used to identify the individual (see Box 4.1 for examples).

Health plans (payers), healthcare providers, and healthcare "clearinghouses" (which included billing services, community health management information systems, value-added networks and other business associates) were all subject to

[12] Martha Hamilton, "Why walk-in health care is a fast-growing profit center for retail chains," *Washington Post*, April 4, 2014, http://www.washingtonpost.com/business/why-walk-in-health-care-is-a-fast-growing-profit-center-for-retail-chains/2014/04/04/a05f7cf4-b9c2-11e3-96ae-f2c36d2b1245_story.html, accessed February 2015.

[13] Hamilton, "Why walk-in health care is a fast-growing profit center for retail chains," *Washington Post*, April 4, 2014.

[14] "Summary of the HIPAA Privacy Rule," U.S. Department of Health and Human Services, May 2003, http://www.hhs.gov/ocr/privacy/hipaa/understanding/summary/privacysummary.pdf, accessed February 2015.

Box 4.1 Exhibit 6 Personally Identifiable Data Protected under HIPAA, 2014

Protected Personal Data Types	
Names	Account numbers
Addresses (including zip code)	Certificate/License numbers
Dates (birth, admission, discharge, death)	Vehicle identifiers and serial numbers (including license plate)
Telephone numbers	Device identifiers and serial numbers
Fax numbers	Web Universal Resource Locators (URLs)
E-mail addresses	Internet Protocol (IP) addresses
Social security numbers	Biometric identifiers, including finger and voice prints
Medical record numbers	Full face photographic images and any comparable images
Health plan beneficiary numbers	Any other unique identifying number, characteristic, or code.

Source: Adapted from "HIPAA Background," Office of Corporate Compliance The University of Chicago Medical Center, February 2010, http://hipaa.bsd.uchicago.edu/background.html, accessed February 2015.

the privacy standards outlined in HIPAA. Healthcare organizations had to notify patients of their privacy rights (including acceptable use of personally identifiable information) and obtain signed authorization from patients for any use of individual data beyond treatment, payment and healthcare operations.[15] Restrictions on data use could be waived if data were "de-identified," either by the formal assessment of a statistician to prove individual anonymity was retained, or by the removal of indicators used to identify the individual and his or her relatives, employer, or household members.[16] De-identified data became propriety to the company that held it.

HIPAA supported use of patient data to perform analysis necessary to make improvements to healthcare systems, including: quality reviews, utilization reviews and population reviews (often for a given condition, such as diabetes). Such information could be shared with other entities also subject to HIPAA, such as payers. Employers like CHS, who both provided healthcare and self-funded insurance to their employees, were not permitted to view their employees' disaggregated healthcare data; in addition, employee information collected through the human resources department was kept separately from employee health data. Those who contravened

[15] "HIPAA Background," Office of Corporate Compliance The University of Chicago Medical Center, February 2010, http://hipaa.bsd.uchicago.edu/background.html, accessed February 2015.

[16] "Summary of the HIPAA Privacy Rule," U.S. Department of Health and Human Services, May 2003.

the HIPAA privacy rule could be subject to civil and/or criminal charges and fines of over $1 million.[17]

DICKSON ADVANCED ANALYTICS (DA²)

Following Carolinas Medical Center's designation as a teaching hospital in 1990, CHS established partnerships with eleven academic research centers. There was no medical school located in Charlotte at the time, so one of the independent centers was designated a branch of the University of North Carolina (UNC). The "Dickson Institute for Health Studies," as the center was known, provided education and training facilities to 300 residents, nurses and graduate students. It partnered with UNC—Charlotte and UNC—Chapel Hill to provide health data-focused projects to PhD candidates. The Dickson Institute initially focused on improving acute care quality, but the mission was later broadened to cover an array of healthcare projects under the leadership of Dr. Roger Ray, executive vice president and chief physician executive at CHS. Although The Dickson Institute conducted research, data analysis and public reporting of key metrics for CHS, Ray noted that its activities did not influence the majority of day-to-day operations that occurred within the CHS network.

Beginning in the 2000s, CHS embarked on a visioning and process-development project to determine what data analytics capabilities would be integral to CHS's operations in the future. They determined they would need to develop a distributed data system and create a corporate data warehouse; and decided to coalesce analytics personnel who were currently working in small silos throughout the organization to achieve the vision. CHS Information Services leadership anticipated that cost of data storage would plummet, based upon their experience implementing the EMR-system at CHS in 2006, so the team decided to build generous data storage to support the new analytics team. Prior to CHS's adoption of EMR, most of the data it collected was financial data generated through transactions. The EMR roll-out served as a proof-of-concept that patient data and financial data could be combined to provide decision support. With increasing computing power, CHS and other providers could collect, store and model a variety of clinical data (including unstructured data) that it could not have assembled previously.

CHS hired consultants to advise the organization on the creation of a unified analytics group through the development of a high-level road map. Lovin was interviewed by the consultant group and asked to provide executive leadership for the initiative, and she recruited Dulin to help execute on CHS's vision of creating a unified, data-driven system. Dulin was trained in electrical and biomedical engineering and worked as a quality control specialist for a microchip manufacturer prior to attending medical school. At the time, there were many groups within CHS that handled analytics, but most were tied to a particular business, function, or geography with no integration. CHS decided to differentiate on the basis of its analytics capability and made investments to raise the analytics "IQ" of the organization. CHS leadership and others believed the system

[17] "HIPAA Background," Office of Corporate Compliance The University of Chicago Medical Center, 2010.

could move beyond its current analytics-related KPIs to include data in key decisions that would change patient care and save money over the long term. The new analytics group could have adopted a hybrid model structure wherein descriptive analysis linked to performance metrics was performed internally and more rigorous analytics were outsourced; but CHS instead chose to develop both its foundational descriptive analytics and more advanced predictive and prescriptive models in-house.

Creation of DA^2

Dickson Advanced Analytics (DA^2) was launched in 2011 with an annual budget of $14 million. It was initially composed of 70 people sourced from the disparate internal analytics groups that preceded DA^2. Much of DA^2's capacity was devoted to providing tools to support CHS-affiliated hospitals in delivering best-in-class healthcare to patients; although, over time, DA^2 also developed analytical tools for evidence-based population health management, personalized patient care and predictive modeling.

The success criterion for DA^2 was to improve outcomes, rather than increase the size of CHS. As Ray explained, "healthcare is a massive cottage industry." He estimated that one-third of clinical work was "non-standard," meaning that it diverged from a care plan and/or choices were made in the absence of evidence. Deploying analytics could help improve outcomes for work that was previously considered "non-standard." DA^2 also played an important role in the communication strategy, since improving quality of outcomes often required engaging the patient to change his or her behavior. Many at CHS believed the key to DA^2's success was a continuing commitment to build strong relationships with the physicians and nurses. The data DA^2 used was collected at many points of care through the CHS networks; in addition, any recommendations and tools derived from the data had to be implemented by the physicians (often by the clinical lead).

DA^2 sat outside of the organization's businesses, but still operated as a cost center. DA^2 reported into Lovin and the strategy function, rather than information services. As a result, Dulin and his team created a business plan for DA^2 to show its ROI over the long term, and prioritized projects of strategic importance to the organization. DA^2 was composed of five groups: "Applied Outcomes Research," "Data Services," "Client Services," "Project Management," and "Advanced Analytics." Compulsory reporting was one of DA^2's core responsibilities: most of the staff of 120, including 12 PhD level analysts, worked on reports submitted to the government. Within DA^2, over time, a 15-person team dedicated to serving the medical group performed predictive work. A smaller research team worked to help measure the strength of the models and the interventions they delivered. Another DA^2 team studied cost analytics to measure the ROI of quality-increasing investments. The businesses focused on identifying revenue opportunities and DA^2 helped to assess what each opportunity would be worth. Patient data could be used to support investment decisions, such as which surgical devices to purchase, since patient data contained information on the quality of outcomes (which DA^2 then combined with cost and device lifespan to assess ROI). One of Dulin's responsibilities was managing DA^2's internal customers, whose demand for analytics quickly outstripped the team's capacity. Many saw the potential for DA^2 to become an additional revenue stream by outsourcing its analytics services to third parties in the future.

Shortly after DA^2 launched, the team received more than twice as many requests as they had capacity to accept. DA^2 created an Advisory Board for issues related to effectiveness, priority setting, and other key focus areas. Then, CHS created a priority-setting process for developing predictive analytics: first, DA^2 conducted interviews with the clinical teams and an internal focus group (which was incorporated into the proposals for each project); then DA^2 determined each proposal's alignment with existing systems and CHS strategy, then balanced the resources the proposal required against those needed for DA^2 to conduct on-going reporting and data warehouse management responsibilities, before finally assessing the projects against a matrix of criteria, including: size, patient impact, mortality vs. quality-of-life improvements, speed of implementation, cost, and commercial viability. Included in the process, DA^2 would provide updates to the Clinical Integration Council (CIC), the highest physician leadership team.

DA^2 sought outside partners to improve the breadth and quality of its data. In 2013, CHS partnered with four healthcare systems and IBM to form the Data Alliance Collaborative (DAC), which focused on improving population health by creating scalable data models. The healthcare partners contributed data to a communal warehouse, which contained data from over 100 hospitals and 1,600 non-acute care sites serving 28 million patients.[18] IBM provided the data infrastructure, which could incorporate clinical, claims and financial data, to support the analytics.[19]

CHS used strategic partnerships to incorporate provider and payer data with consumer data into its predictive algorithms. Dulin believed that such data would give DA^2 additional insight into communities and patient populations, and provide indications for early interventions for potential problems beyond EMR data. The spending data, along with other inputs, were used to create a risk score for admitted patients, which were then distributed to doctors and other healthcare providers to reprioritize care delivery. This approach allowed the hospital system to focus limited resources on high-risk patients to improve their outcomes and their health status.

DA^2 and the Data Governance Committee

In 2012, CHS established a data governance committee, headed by Alicia Bowers, vice president of corporate privacy, and Michael Trumbore, assistant vice president of advanced analytics (and sponsored by Ray). The group included representatives from DA^2, clinical and translational research, information services, human resources, financial services, audit services, systems business and the office of the general counsel. Members of the CHS institutional review board (IRB)[20] also had seats on the

[18] Ken Terry, "Healthcare Collaborative, IBM Partner On Big Data Platform," *Information Week*, June 18, 2013, http://www.informationweek.com/healthcare/clinical-information-systems/healthcare-collaborative-ibm-partner-on-big-data-platform/d/d-id/1110419?, accessed February 2014.

[19] Terry, "Healthcare Collaborative, IBM Partner On Big Data Platform," *Information Week*, June 18, 2013.

[20] The IRB was a committee formed to protect the welfare of human subjects involved in research, including maintaining the subjects' privacy. All IRBs were registered with the Office for Human Research Protections, a division of the U.S. Department of Health and Human Services.

committee. Since CHS was a research organization, it followed the IRB standards to guide its handling of data. For example, one of the IRB privacy standards dealt with creating a geographically informed dataset and prevented disclosure of information if fewer than 50 people lived within a single census tract.

The data governance group was formed to protect, manage and determine accountability for the data generated in the day-to-day operations of CHS. CHS recognized that the organization had a data strategy, whether or not it was made explicit. With the formation of the data governance group, it hoped to signal executive support for DA² and facilitate engagement with the information services, clinical and business groups. The group met monthly to:

- Create data governance policies.
- Prioritize data governance initiatives (including pilot-programs).
- Define data governance policies, standards, processes, metrics and principles.
- Communicate the vision and activities of the group to the broad CHS organization.
- Address the governance structure, data access and data quality.

A key initiative of the advisory group was the appointment of "domain owners," who were responsible for upholding governance standards for the data and business processes in a given domain. Domains referred to clusters of data that were organized around CHS businesses. For example, the research domain might contain documentation of patient consent, IRB compliance and grant information; whereas the patient domain could contain EMR information and treatment plans. The domain owners led multifunctional teams composed of process owners, data stewards and project managers, as well as representatives from information services and data governance who were responsible for tracking performance against KPIs, data quality, and compliance with internal data governance policies. The domain owners reported to the Strategic Governance Council, chaired by Dulin, who ultimately reported to the Executive Governance Council, led by Lovin (see Figure 4.2 for an organization chart).

DA² in 2014

By November 2014, DA² had achieved three key results: it collected and handled vast amounts of data efficiently; it created a data governance structure; and it helped shift the organization away from an anecdotal culture to an evidence-based one. The year prior, DA² had spent $5 million[21] to create its enterprise data warehouse (EDW). The EDW initially contained 10 Terabytes of data derived from the system's 1.5 Petabytes of data, which doubled in size by 2015. The data warehouse incorporated clinical, billing and claims data, which enabled DA² to create models including hundreds of different patient variables. In 2014, DA² had a pipeline of nearly a dozen predictive risk models in development and consistently more requests from the organization than it had capacity to accept. Lovin said: "We went from having

[21] Joe Carlson, "Carolinas centralizes data analytics to reduce readmissions and redesign care," *Modern Healthcare*, December 9, 2013, accessed via Factiva, October 2014.

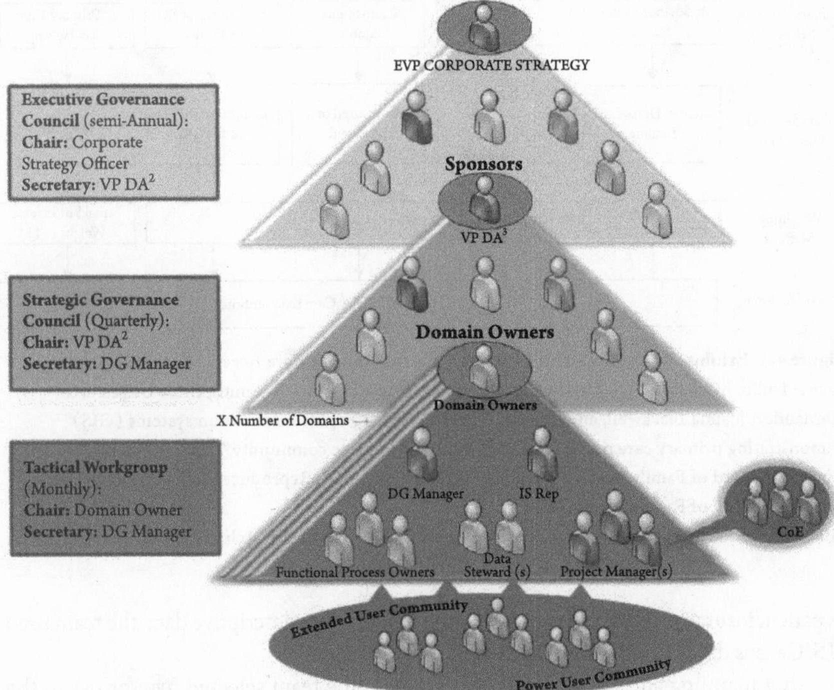

Figure 4.2 Exhibit 7 Data Governance Committee Organizational Chart, 2014.
Source: Company documents.

no DA² to wanting to check their opinion on everything." DA² had made progress towards changing the culture of CHS to be evidence-based and data-driven; however, its success meant DA²'s capacity was strained by demand for its analytics services. DA² began to provide the business lines with tools and education so that some analytics could be performed independently and DA² could reserve capacity for more complex questions.

Key DA² Pilots

In 2014, the three on-going strategic priorities for DA² were: predict health needs; continually enhance patient outcomes; and drive transformative solutions to address community health issues. By that time, DA² had launched a number of successful pilots covering a variety of medical conditions, geographies and functional capabilities.

Mapping Underserved Communities In 2009, the Dickson Institute launched a project to reduce unnecessary emergency department (ED) utilization in Charlotte by identifying areas underserved by primary care facilities. The project leveraged descriptive data and clinical data from local primary care and ED facilities in Charlotte to find the best variables to indicate poor access to primary care. Over 367,000 clinical records were sourced from all 2007 patient visits to CHS primary care and ED facilities. Data that did not contain the patient's address, or from patients who lived outside of the county, was excluded, which left a dataset of 187,000 ED visits and 50,000 primary care visits, as well

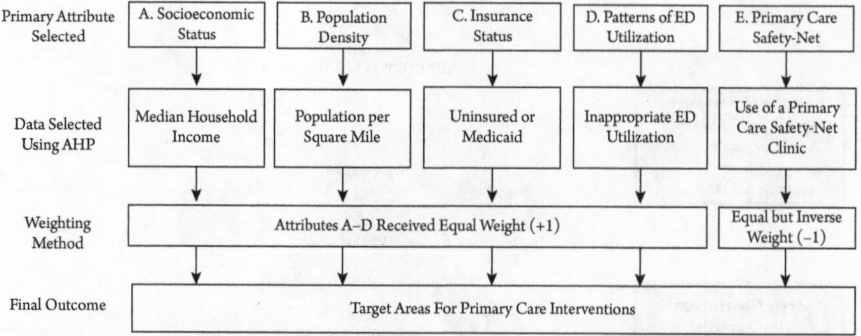

Figure 4.3 Exhibit 8 Variable Definition Process for the Primary Care Access Model,[a] 2013.
Source: Dulin, Michael F., Thomas M. Ludden, Hazel Tapp, Heather A. Smith, Brisa Urquieta de Hernandez, Joshua Blackwell, and Owen J. Furuseth. "Geographic information systems (GIS) demonstrating primary care needs for a transitioning Hispanic community." The Journal of the American Board of Family Medicine 23, no. 1 (2010): 109–120. Reproduced by permission of the American Board of Family Medicine.
[a] ED referred to emergency departments; AHP referred to analytic hierarchical process.

as patient insurance status,[22] to be used in the model.[23] For descriptive data, the team used U.S. Census data at a census tract level.[24]

After mapping and testing multiple variables, the team selected five for use in the primary care access model: population density, median household income, the uninsured/Medicaid population, the incidence of ED utilization for primary care-treatable or preventable conditions, and the proportion of the population who currently used primary care facilities.[25] Equal weight was given to each variable in the model, although the use of primary care facilities was given an inverse, but still equal, weight (see Figure 4.3 for variables). The numeric value of each variable was calculated for each census tract before being combined to create the single measure of need for primary care facilities in that area. Census tracts with values greater than one standard deviation above the mean were highlighted as high-need areas (see Figure 4.4 for map).

The geo-tagging technique was relatively inexpensive and could quickly identify community candidates for additional primary care clinics. The U.S. Census data was free to the public; and, once all data was geocoded, the process of building a new model with weighted attributes took only a few hours. The team believed a similar approach could be used to anticipate localized future demand for healthcare professionals, to

[22] Patient insurance status contained five categories: Medicare, Medicaid, commercial, uninsured and other.

[23] Dulin, Michael F., Thomas M. Ludden, Hazel Tapp, Heather A. Smith, Brisa Urquieta de Hernandez, Joshua Blackwell, and Owen J. Furuseth. "Geographic information systems (GIS) demonstrating primary care needs for a transitioning Hispanic community." *The Journal of the American Board of Family Medicine* 23, no. 1 (2010): 109–120.

[24] Census tracts were geographic regions defined by U.S. Census Bureau that contained between 1,200 and 8,000 people. Census tracts were typically slightly smaller than zip codes.

[25] Dulin, et. al. "Geographic information systems (GIS)," *Journal of the American Board of Family Medicine*, 2010.

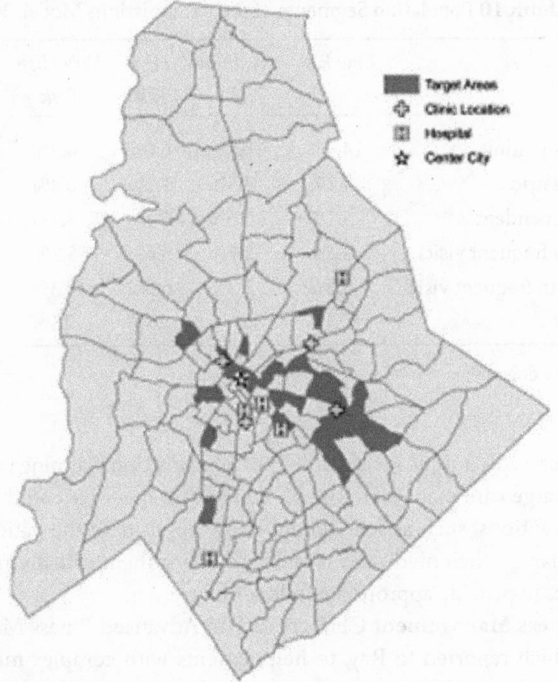

Figure 4.4 Exhibit 9 Map of High-Need Areas in Charlotte Produced by the Primary Care Access Model, 2013.
Source: Dulin, Michael F., Thomas M. Ludden, Hazel Tapp, Heather A. Smith, Brisa Urquieta de Hernandez, Joshua Blackwell, and Owen J. Furuseth. "Geographic information systems (GIS) demonstrating primary care needs for a transitioning Hispanic community." The Journal of the American Board of Family Medicine 23, no. 1 (2010): 109–120. Reproduced by permission of the American Board of Family Medicine.

develop interventions to improve access to primary care facilities, to provide data to support policy decisions regarding healthcare initiatives, and to measure the impact of interventions designed to improve healthcare access.

Reducing Readmissions The Readmission Predictive Risk Model was launched by DA² in 2013 to help the clinical teams in CHS hospitals identify high-risk patients. DA² developed an algorithm that calculated a "readmission risk score" for each admitted patient. The score was modeled from data on the thousands of patients that had been discharged from one of the CHS facilities in the prior two years. Out of 600 variables in the data, DA² found 40 to be highly predictive of readmission, including: history of ED visits, sodium levels, language and late-stage renal disease.[26] Patients who were identified as high risk for readmission within thirty days of discharge received extra focus from clinicians while still in the hospital. The model had an accuracy rate of 79% in predicting a patient's risk of readmission within thirty days of discharge. In addition, the model clustered patients into one of five segments (see Table 4.5),

[26] Carlson, "Carolinas centralizes data analytics," *Modern Healthcare*, 2013.

Table 4.5 Exhibit 10 Population Segments of the Readmissions Model, 2013

Segments	*Low Risk*	*Medium Risk*	*High Risk*	*Very High Risk*	*Total*
Insured Healthy Adult	14.4%	10.9%	6.0%	4.2%	35.5%
Medicaid Pediatric	4.1%	2.5%	1.2%	0.4%	8.2%
Medicare Independent	5.1%	6.6%	6.1%	5.1%	22.9%
Medicare with frequent visits	0.8%	2.7%	5.6%	5.2%	14.2%
Middle age with frequent visits	0.6%	2.3%	6.0%	10.3%	19.1%
Total	25%	25%	25%	25%	100%

Source: Company documents.

each of which possessed a unique set of guidelines for transition planning (which were given to the discharge care manager). The discharge care manager could then select appropriate interventions, such as scheduling follow-up visits to the patient's home, helping patients manage their medications and connecting them with dietitians, trainers and/or coaches to provide appropriate follow-up care.

Advanced Illness Management CHS created an Advanced Illness Management Group (AIM), which reported to Ray, to help patients with complex medical conditions avoid hospital stays. Those patients carried a higher risk of hospital readmission, so the program offered access to a team of experts who helped the patients better understand their health conditions, symptoms, medications and lifestyle choices in order to empower them to manage their own health and reduce unnecessary ED visits and hospitalizations. Eligible patients had at least two chronic conditions, had visited the ED or hospital more than twice over the last six months, took multiple medications to treat the same condition, and were not actively involved in another care management or intensive health program.

The first AIM cohort included 25 patients who collectively visited the hospital 96 times (the ED 41 times and were hospitalized 55 times) in the six months prior to the start of the program in 2014. The multidisciplinary AIM team included licensed clinical social workers, nurse practitioners, licensed practical nurses and registered nurses. For each patient, the team assessed the unmet educational, psycho-social and resource needs, and created a care plan in conjunction with the physician's medical plan. The team was in frequent contact with patients to monitor changes in health status, social circumstances and/or psychosocial needs; to answer questions regarding medications or medical jargon; to discuss care options before going to the ED; and to remind patients of upcoming doctor's appointments. In select cases, licensed practical nurses attended the appointments with the patients. Patients in the first cohort experienced less pain, improved quality of care and increased satisfaction, while also incurring lower costs to the healthcare system. The patients collectively visited the hospital only 33 times in the six months following the start of AIM. Due to the initial success of the AIM program, CHS enrolled additional patients in cohorts 2 and 3.

Patient Segmentation Model In 2014, CHS reviewed the data of 2.2 million active patients who received care within the system and collected 2,000 data points per patient, including clinical data, medication compliance, education attainment, socioeconomic factors, and consumer spending profiles (DA^2 hoped to one day add genetic data and data generated by wearables). DA^2 created a segmentation model which grouped patients into one of seven distinct segments (e.g. "high risk of cancer") so that patients in each group could receive care and communications tailored to their specific needs. Within each segment, DA^2 selected a sub-group from which to gather qualitative data on segment-specific lifestyle and healthcare needs. The qualitative data in turn influenced the recommendations for the communication plans for the sufferers of various disease groups within each segment (a process managed by the Advanced Illness Management group, which partnered with care managers, social workers, pharmacists, rehabilitative and palliate care centers).

The benefits to CHS were two-fold: segmentation helped clinicians to identify high risk patients quickly and help them change harmful behaviors; segmentation also helped CHS to estimate the expected cost of providing care to each segment and influenced how CHS bid on new business contracts with healthcare payers. Providers like CHS were often at a disadvantage when negotiating with payers, since the payers frequently had more information on the patients than the providers who often lacked well-developed analytics capabilities. Since CHS acted as a payer for its own employees, it was aware of the types and quality of data the payers possessed. Trumbore believed that the CHS possessed better data than the average payer, as payers could only see what happened (e.g. claims data), rather than the clinical treatment process. Over time, CHS would use the insights gleaned from the segment analysis to optimize its care delivery model.

KEY CHALLENGES AHEAD FOR DA^2

As Dulin and his team prepared their strategic plan for the next three years, he pondered which of the existing pilots might be extended to different yet related issues without requiring the design and implementation of an entirely new model. The internal demand for DA^2's services could fill its current capacity several times over. CHS identified many opportunities for DA^2 to reduce waste while also improving outcomes, but recognized the need to satisfy as many internal constituents as possible. CHS leadership was interested in exploring external business opportunities that could potentially turn DA^2 into a source of profit for CHS, particularly given the mounting investments DA^2 had received for its technological infrastructure. However, high internal demands for DA^2's services constrained Dulin's ability to test DA^2's capabilities in the external marketplace. Another key focus for DA^2 was ensuring insights translated into action through the creation of user-friendly reports (such as a huddle, summary and decision support reports), and ultimately, consistent care plans and sets of orders to follow for patients with a given condition. Engaging with clinicians to ensure that data from the predictive models improved their workflow would be a core focus of DA^2 for years to come.

5

PHILIPS HEALTHCARE

MARKETING THE HEALTHSUITE DIGITAL PLATFORM

John A. Quelch and Margaret L. Rodriguez

The healthcare landscape is rapidly changing, and it is essential to seamlessly and securely connect devices, systems and people across the entire health continuum, from healthy living, prevention and diagnosis, to treatment, recovery and home care
Jeroen Tas, *CEO, Philips Healthcare Informatics Solutions and Services.*

Philips was very much a device company, not a software company. Even though devices contained software for many years, we now realize we must build devices around the software instead of the reverse.
Jorgen Behrens, *head of technology & strategy, Philips Personal Health Solutions.*

In June 2014, leading healthcare and consumer technology company, Royal Philips ("Philips"), announced its HealthSuite Digital Platform to house healthcare data and enable applications used by physicians and patients. Philips had strong equity in the healthcare technology space, due to its extensive portfolio of medical devices and related software sold primarily to hospitals. Philips designed the first two apps for the platform (eCareCoordinator and eCareCompanion) in-house, but it planned to open it up to third-party developers who would create an array of health-focused apps. Healthcare had long lagged behind other industries in adoption of technology as well as patient-relationship management. However, many health players had recently increased investment in new infrastructure and data analytics. Would the new Philips HealthSuite Digital Platform find success in the rapidly evolving industry?

THE CHANGING HEALTHCARE LANDSCAPE

In 2014, healthcare spending in the U.S. exceeded $3 trillion and was expected to reach $4.5 trillion by 2020.[1] Costs were expected to increase as the U.S. population

[1] Dan Munro, "Annual U.S. Healthcare Spending Hits $3.8 Trillion," *Forbes,* February 2, 2014 http://www.forbes.com/sites/danmunro/2014/02/02/annual-u-s-healthcare-spending-hits-3-8-trillion/,accessed April 2015.

aged and incidence of chronic conditions rose. In 2009, those 60 years and older were 11% of the U.S. population and were expected to be 22% by 2050.[2] In 2013, roughly 133 million people suffered from chronic diseases in the U.S.[3] By 2020, it was estimated that nearly half of the U.S. population would be living with a chronic condition (over 150 million people) and around 81 million would suffer from multiple conditions.[4] As Jeroen Tas, chief executive of Philips' Informatics Solutions and Services business group stated: "I have hypertension, my daughter has juvenile diabetes, and my dad has cancer. We are a normal family."

The combined pressures on the healthcare system in the U.S., as well as the passage of the Affordable Care Act (ACA) in 2010, led to a shift among healthcare providers towards fee-for-value models rather than fee-for-service (FFS). The ACA stipulated that hospital compensation be determined in part by the quality of outcomes, rather than on a simple FFS basis as before. Hospitals could receive financial rewards for high quality outcomes or patient satisfaction scores, but also faced penalties for high rates of readmission or hospital-acquired conditions. The shift to fee-for-value presented new opportunities for providers to focus on holistic wellness and population health management initiatives that would not have been as easy under the old FFS model. Many healthcare providers needed better analytics and measurement capabilities in order to track quality improvements and shift the organizational focus onto integrated delivery of care and continuous improvement of patient outcomes.

Healthcare providers invested in a host of IT-based solutions, including electronic medical records (EMRs), acute care information systems, telehealth services, health information exchanges and analytics. The growing investment was reflected in venture capital funding for healthcare IT companies, which increased from $1.9 billion in 2013 to $2.4 in the first six months of 2014 alone.[5] In 2011, the U.S. Centers for Medicare and Medicaid Services (CMS) established incentives for doctor's offices and hospitals to switch from paper to EMRs. Hospitals that served Medicare patients received up to $2 million for adopting EMRs.[6] Patients could view and request corrections to their medical records, but EMR vendors made it difficult for providers to extract EMR data for use in other healthcare applications or services. Comprehensive efforts to upgrade healthcare IT in hospitals were often limited by poor interconnectivity between data systems, difficulty extracting data from its home network, and lack of training for physicians on how to incorporate data and analytics into their workflows. In addition to these challenges, healthcare providers in developing countries also dealt with poor infrastructure and staff shortages.

[2] World Population Ageing—Department of Economic and Social Affairs, United Nations, http://www.un.org/esa/population/publications/worldageing19502050/, accessed April 2015.

[3] "About Chronic Diseases," National Health Council, July 29, 2014, http://www.nationalhealthcouncil.org/sites/default/files/NHC_Files/Pdf_Files/AboutChronicDisease.pdf, accessed April 2015.

[4] "About Chronic Diseases," National Health Council, 2014, accessed April 2015.

[5] Dan Mangan, "Health-care IT investment boom: Who's the next winner?," *CNBC*, July 14, 2014, http://www.cnbc.com/id/101829949, accessed April 2015.

[6] "HER Incentives & Certification," HealthIT.gov, January 15, 2013. http://www.healthit.gov/providers-professionals/ehr-incentive-programs, accessed February 2015.

As hospitals ramped up their IT investments, consumers began using technology to become more engaged and better educated about their health than ever before. Although healthcare lagged other industries in terms of digitization, consumers had shown a willingness to engage. The success of sites like J&J's Babycenter,[7] which reached 40 million parents each month, demonstrated the consumer interest in digital health resources.[8] Consumers had access to more health data than ever before; not only could they access their medical records, they could also track their health status and wellness with devices from new entrants like FitBit, Apple, Google and others. In 2014, Google and Apple each launched consumer-friendly healthcare dashboards that aggregated data from wearable devices (including scales, running apps and sleep trackers). Apple even partnered with several EMR vendors to incorporate medical records and lab results into its Healthkit iOS dashboard.[9]

PHILIPS COMPANY BACKGROUND

Philips was established in 1891 as a light bulb factory in the Netherlands. In 2014, Philips had sales of EUR 21.4 billion[10] (see Table 5.1) and over 105,000 employees worldwide. Philips was organized into three sectors: healthcare (which included imaging devices, hospital to home monitoring equipment, other devices sold to hospitals and clinics), lighting, and consumer lifestyle (such as toothbrushes, electric razors, and fryers sold directly to consumers). Roughly 35% of Philips' headcount worked in the healthcare sector, with 36% in lighting and 16% in consumer lifestyle. Innovation, Group & Services (IG&S) accounted for the remainder of the workforce (~13%). Philips primary competitors varied by business sector, but in healthcare Philips competed primarily against General Electric (GE) and Siemens AG to sell medical devices to hospitals. Philips was organized in a matrix; it included centralized "innovation to market" (I2M) teams, and market organizations which were responsible for sales. In the healthcare sector, the I2M and market organizations had joint responsibility for in-market product performance and customer support.

Creation of the HealthTech Organization

In 2013, Philips chief executive, Frans van Houten, led a transformation of Philips' organizational structure in order to better support the consumer journey. Philips started by analyzing the journeys experienced by consumers who suffered from specific health conditions, such as pregnancy or diabetes, along a "health continuum" This included six stages: healthy living, prevention, diagnosis, treatment, recovery and

[7] J&J's Babycenter was a website and mobile app designed for expectant mothers and families with infants to receive health education and build a community.

[8] "Company overview," Babycenter Website, http://www.babycenter.com/help-about-company, accessed April 2015.

[9] David F. Carr, "Apple Partners With Epic, Mayo Clinic For HealthKit," *Information Week*, June 3, 2014, http://www.informationweek.com/healthcare/mobile-and-wireless/apple-partners-with-epic-mayo-clinic-for-healthkit/d/d-id/1269371, accessed April 2015.

[10] Estimated at an exchange rate of $1.22 per Euro.

Table 5.1 Exhibit 1 Philips Selected Financial Data (billions), 2014

	Group		*Healthcare*		*Consumer Lifestyle*		*Lighting*	
	2014	Annual Growth	2014	Annual Growth	2014	Annual Growth	2014	Annual Growth
Sales	EUR 21,391	–3%	EUR 9,186	–4%	EUR 4,731	3%	EUR 6,869	–4%
EBITA[a]	EUR 821	–64%	EUR 616	–59%	EUR 573	19%	EUR 293	–49%

Source: Company documents.

[a] EBITA = Earnings before interest, taxes and amortization.

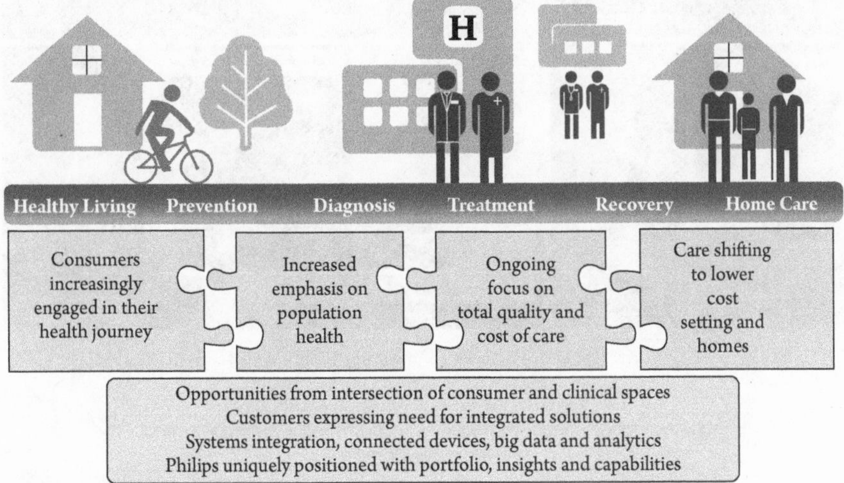

Figure 5.1 Exhibit 2 Philips Health Continuum, 2014.
Source: Company documents.

home care (see Figure 5.1). For example, a common consumer journey was "mother and child", which might begin with fertility and diet in the healthy living stage and extend all the way to infant care in the home care stage. Philips had 18 different teams / product lines across multiple businesses with products which were part of the mother/ child journey, but the product teams did not interact heavily. The team that designed the light therapy blanket (used by hospitals for newborns with Vitamin D deficiency) did not collaborate much with the team that made baby monitors, even though the same consumer might use both products. It was clear to Philips' leaders that these businesses should be connected and aligned to the same strategy to better serve its hospital customers, enable care transitions and increase brand visibility to consumers.

As part of the next phase of the company's transformation program, Philips announced a plan in September 2014 to separate the company into two market-leading independent companies focused on the vast opportunities in health technology (HealthTech) and lighting solutions. HealthTech combined the Philips healthcare and consumer lifestyle[11] sectors. The separation process would take approximately 12–18 months. The new structure would enable Philips to identify gaps in its HealthTech portfolio along the health continuum and spur collaboration across its various divisions. See Figure 5.2 for Philips businesses mapped against the health continuum. The new HealthTech organization comprised eight groups: Personal care; domestic appliances (including kitchen, garment care); health & wellness; imaging systems; patient care and monitoring; healthcare informatics, solutions and services (HISS); customer services; and home healthcare solutions. Prior to the reorganization, each Philips business group developed separate channel strategies; however, in the new HealthTech organization, the sales teams focused their efforts to shift towards enterprise account-based selling. This enabled Philips to better leverage established

[11] All consumer lifestyle products would be folded into HealthTech

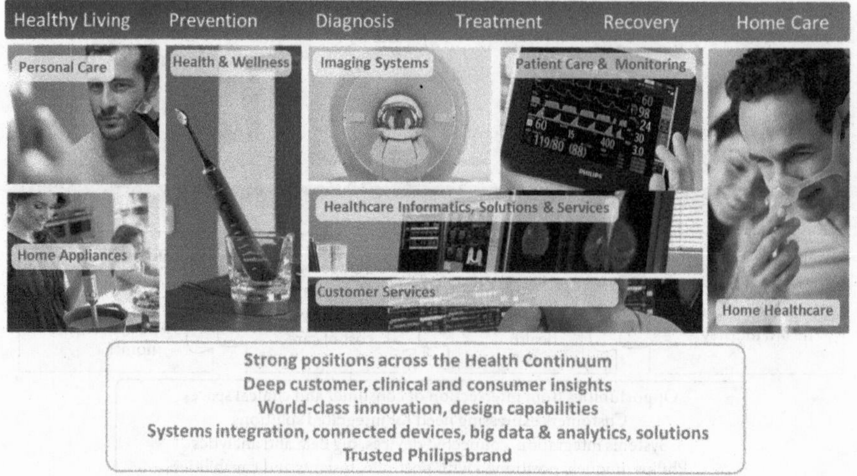

Figure 5.2 Exhibit 3 Share of Philips HealthTech Annual Sales by Business, 2013–2014.
Source: Company documents.

relationships with its hospital customers; some at Philips believed the organization would one day appoint account managers who would manage solutions based on all relevant Philips products and services at each hospital.

In 2013, Philips' HealthTech business generated revenues of EUR 15 billion. Philips Healthcare sales (excluding consumer lifestyle) declined roughly 4% between 2013 and 2014. Healthcare revenues included those from the sales of imaging systems (~35% of Healthcare sales), patient care & monitoring solutions (~32% of Healthcare sales), healthcare informatics solutions and services (HISS), which was led by Tas (~6% of Healthcare sales) and Customer Services (~27% of Healthcare sales). Roughly 40% of healthcare sales were from North America.

HISS Group

In January 2014, Philips created a new business group, Healthcare Informatics, Solutions and Services, which was designed to identify emerging opportunities in healthcare created by new technologies such as social media, mobile, cloud, big data and the Internet of Things. Philips believed it was uniquely positioned to offer its customers, (primarily hospital and clinics) and patients healthcare informatics; Philips planned to leverage its clinical expertise as a maker of medical devices and related informatics services, the library of data its devices generated, its portfolio of products and solutions which spanned the health continuum, and its sales operations that covered customers in many markets. The primary customers for HISS products and services were providers (with the exception of home monitoring products, under the brand "Lifeline," which were also sold directly to consumers).

Initially, HISS had three key roles which were intended to support Philips' transition to the new HealthTech organization: create a "cross-domain" digital platform, develop new healthcare solutions, which combine products and services to address specific customer needs, and establish new businesses. Most healthcare providers did not possess a pool of data that integrated all of a patient's information (e.g., medical records, monitoring data, diagnostic images, physicians' notes and patient generated data), so Philips set out to create one. HISS also oversaw the Healthcare Transformation Services (HTS) business. HTS developed consulting, analytics and managed services capabilities that leveraged data collected from Philips devices and other sources. HTS worked with Philips clients to assist with large, multi-year, transitions to value-based healthcare delivery, which could include projects like optimizing care flows, including the upgrade of diagnostic equipment and backend processing for an entire hospital group. HISS also had new businesses focused on care coordination and population health, including: hospital to home (H2H) and primary and secondary care solutions (PSCS). Philips expected to create even more solutions businesses (centered around oncology, neurology and other specialty departments) with data from the cross-domain digital platform, including newly established capabilities for genomics and digital pathology. In 2014, HISS contributed ~6% to the revenues of Philips Healthcare.

PHILIPS HEALTHSUITE DIGITAL PLATFORM

In June 2014, Philips announced the creation of a cloud-based data platform for healthcare providers: the HealthSuite Digital Platform (HDSP). Philips HSDP was an open cloud-based, data infrastructure that supported the secure collection of data related to health and lifestyle, allowing for hospitals and care provider to integrate and analyze data. By providing a secure and private home for all data collected from Philips and health and lifestyle products, the HSDP allowed care professionals and consumers to use the information to improve decision making. The development of the HSDP was headed by Philips' HISS group, which led a large team spread among offices in Best, The Netherlands; Bangalore, India; Foster City, CA and Tel Aviv/Haifa, Israel. The platform development included an alliance with Salesforce.com to leverage the company's leadership in enterprise cloud computing, innovation and customer engagement. HSDP would incorporate state of the art privacy and data security elements for sensitive healthcare data and allow additional applications to be layered on top. Philips planned to open the platform to third-party app developers who could use the data it held to create apps covering the health continuum (see Figure 5.3). Philips executives believed that a unified hardware and software offering from Philips would drive incremental sales.

HSDP, and its app ecosystem, were intended for use in both continuous healthcare delivery as well as personal health management to collect and exchange data between multiple stakeholders, such as: patients, GP's, diagnostic centers, clinics, hospitals, home care organizations and pharmacies (see Figure 5.4). Philips mapped numerous consumer journeys to identify gaps in their experiences, and concluded that HSDP's first apps should support care delivery in triage and screening, cardiac non-acute diagnosis and chronic disease management, and maternity and obstetric care. HSDP primary users would be Philips' customers: the hospitals. HSDP would store and carry images and information essential to patient care across different hospital departments, while also offering only the most relevant information to each doctor. Unlike EMRs, which were typically built upon legacy platforms that were decades old, HSDP was supported by new cloud and data technologies, which meant

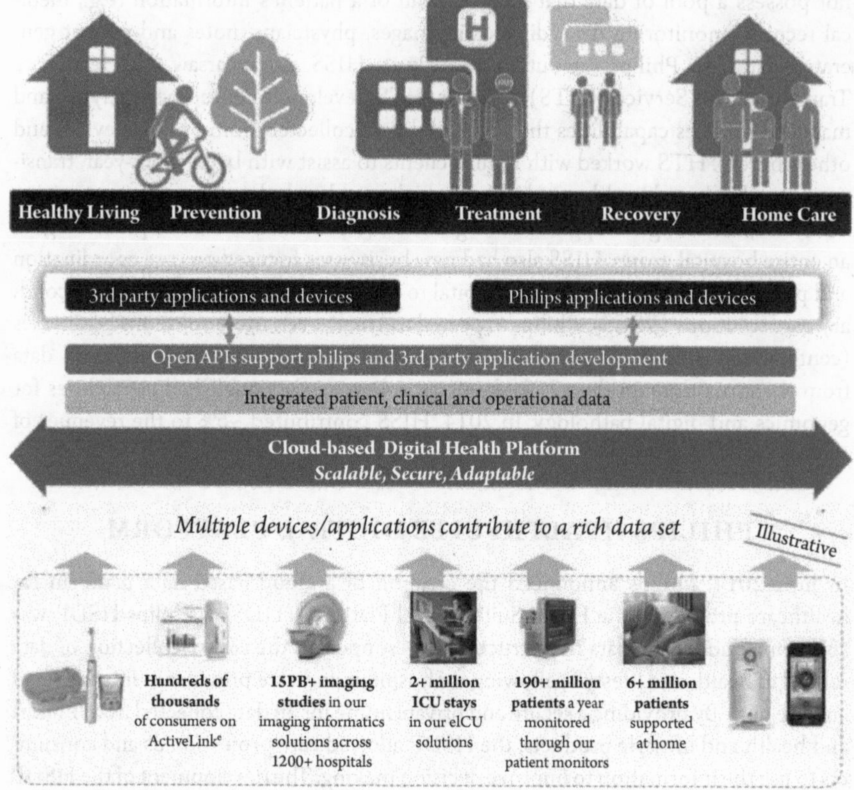

Figure 5.3 Exhibit 4 Digital Health Suite Platform Development, 2014.[a]
Source: Company documents.
[a] APIs referred to application program interface (a defined set of protocols and tools for applications); ICU referred to intensive care unit.

it was fast to retrieve information, fast to write apps, and would be usable by clients for many years. HSDP would help Philips become an even more trusted clinical partner by supporting customized hospital workflows that produced better outcomes at a lower cost. Patients could also use the platform's apps to access and update their health records.

In addition to helping patients and customers, HSDP would enable Philips' business units to avoid steep investment in individual information technology capabilities, help to integrate products and applications across business units (to better serve consumers and cross-sell), rapidly develop and test new applications, easily scale applications through the cloud, decrease operating expenses, and support in-market innovation by opening up access to a common platform.

Partner Alliances

Philips and Salesforce, the world's largest CRM and enterprise cloud computing service provider, had worked together since 2011. Salesforce generated revenues through

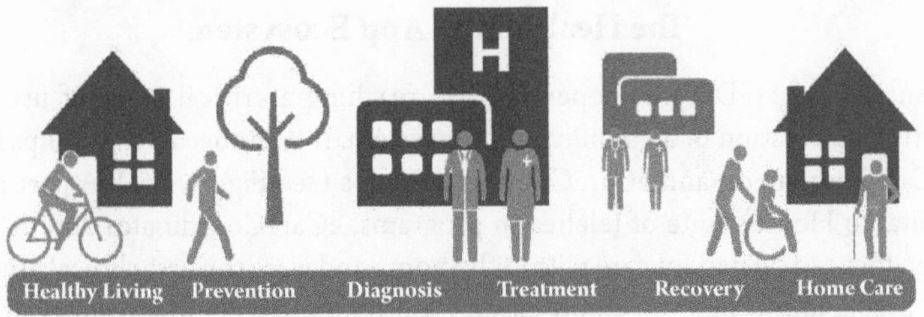

- **Extend beyond the healthcare enterprise** to embrace virtualized patient care
- **Integrate workflows and pathways**
- **Reduce complexity of managing continuous data streams**
- **Optimize the EMR** to support both structured and unstructured health data
- **Minimize disruption to current exiting IT infrastructure**
- **Improve operational performance**

Figure 5.4 Exhibit 5 Supporting Continuous Healthcare Delivery, 2014.
Source: Company documents.

sale of software subscriptions. By 2013, Philips had become one of Salesforce's most important customers in the healthcare sector. That year, Salesforce announced the creation of customized solutions for industry verticals. Philips and Salesforce observed a "perfect storm" occurring in healthcare: healthcare providers worldwide were straining to keep pace with increasing demand and constrained resources, while the declining cost of data storage made building an extensive library of clinical data easier than ever. Salesforce chief executive, Marc Benioff commented: "We have entered a new transformative era for healthcare, and technology is enabling the industry to connect to, care for and engage with patients and each other in a profound new way."[12]

In addition to Salesforce, Philips tapped several other firms to support HSDP so that it could focus on leveraging its core strengths, such as knowledge of the healthcare data regulatory landscape, clinical workflows and integration of medical devices. Philips engaged Amazon Web Services ("AWS") to provide cloud infrastructure as a service, including raw data storage, computing power, and analytical tools. Given that Philips imaging software was expected to generate 1 Petabyte of data per month, Philips needed the ability to scale quickly and economically. On top of the infrastructure layer, Philips used Pivotal, a cloud platform as a service provider, to enable other types of infrastructure as needed for hospital customers who had specific needs or legacy infrastructure that would be utilized beyond AWS. Philips was also building or collaborating with other companies to create tracking and metering tools, so as to enable multiple types of business models. HSDP wanted to retain flexibility to create models that would attract to app developers, hospitals, and other potential partners.

[12] "Philips and Salesforce.com announce a strategic alliance to deliver cloud-based healthcare information technology," Company Press Release, June 26, 2014, http://www.newscenter.philips.com/us_en/standard/news/press/2014/20140626-Philips-and-Salesforce-announce-a-strategic-alliance-to-deliver-cloud-based-healthcare-information-technology.wpd#.VRq3__nF92C, accessed April 2015.

The HealthSuite App Ecosystem

The success of HSDP was dependent on reaching a critical mass of users, which required the creation of an application ecosystem. In October 2014, Philips launched its eCareCompanion and eCareCoordinator apps (see Figure 5.5.). A part of Philips Hospital to Home's suite of telehealth programs, eCareCoordinator and eCareCompanion focused on patient care within the home and were the first clinical applications to be available through the cloud-based HealthSuite Digital platform. eCareCoordinator was a population health management tool designed to give clinicians real-time access to vital signs data (as well as output from patient questionnaires and notes from the care team) and combine this with the patient's medical profile. The app would assist clinicians' daily review of their patients to prioritize interventions and adjust treatments. eCareCompanion was a personalized app designed to help patients engage with and self-manage their care. Patients could receive medication reminders and answer questions about their health, and send data on their health status to their clinicians. The app also connected to devices such as scales, blood pressure meters, oximeters and medication dispensers. In October 2014, the eCareCoordinator and eCareCompanion apps received pre-market approval from the U.S. Food and Drug Administration (FDA).

Third party developers were expected to create many types of apps for HSDP, including consumer-facing apps that incorporated data from devices like FitBit, once the APIs were launched. HSDP offered developers an open system and access to the clinical data collected from Philips devices. HSDP was architected as an open platform from the beginning in order to allow large numbers of consumers and third party developers to leverage the HSDP data to develop useful applications and algorithms for customers. HSDP's philosophy of openness differed significantly from its competitors in the healthcare space, many of whom operated closed systems which prevented data sharing between apps and limited the functionality of any given app.

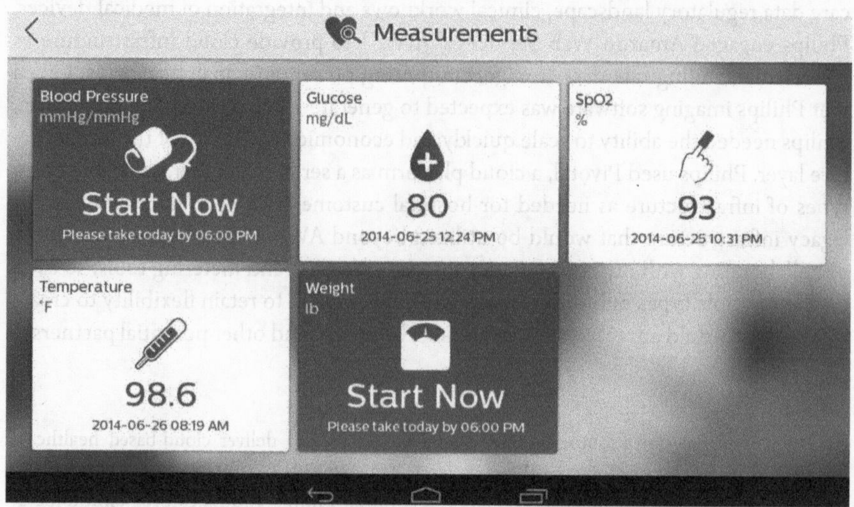

Figure 5.5 Exhibit 6 Philips eCareCompanion App Interface, 2014.
Source: Company documents.

Philips hoped developers would create specialized apps for various conditions, e.g., pregnancy, heart failure, etc.

Go-to-Market Strategy

When HSDP was announced, Philips was in the process of rationalizing its sales force following the company reorganization. Before the ACA was passed, Philips sales teams sold devices to departments within the hospital, such as radiology. The shift to fee-for-value care delivery led many hospitals to centralize purchasing decisions and focus more on cost-control (rather than buying the top-of-the-line machine for a given department). Initially, the leaders of HSDP visited Philips' top customers personally to explain the value proposition of the platform. Philips also saw the potential of HSDP's data for use by pharmacies and pharmaceutical companies, which were not visited by the Philips sales force at that time. Some at Philips believed that it could easily leverage its existing sales team and contacts to expand HSDP's reach to include pharmacies and other outlets. Philips performed very little direct-to-consumer marketing in the initial stage of the HSDP launch, as consumers typically engaged with Philips clinical devices through providers or payers (with the exception of pregnancy-related products and services). Products and services that supported consumer journeys, like pregnancy, where more purchases were made directly by consumers were promoted and priced differently than those that supported consumer journeys, like heart disease, where the clinicians (and payers) bore the majority of the costs.

Competitors

Philips' believed its knowledge of the clinical landscape, its credibility with doctors, its portfolio of devices and proven track record in obtaining FDA approval would be difficult for competitors to replicate. Many at Philips believed the new HealthTech organization's singular focus and investment in healthcare gave it an advantage over more diversified competitors. HSDP itself was designed to stand out from competition; its open system (which supported third-party developers), library of Philips clinical data (including over 18 petabytes of imaging studies, more than 275 million patients monitored through the Philips patient monitoring solutions, etc.[13]), and support for secure and private storage for health and lifestyle data were unique to the industry. Philips faced decisions on whether to collaborate or compete with incumbents in the broader healthcare IT space (including traditional competitors like GE, Electronic Medical Records providers, and other niche healthcare IT providers) as well as generalist IT companies (such as IBM and Oracle).

In 2014, GE was a leading medical device manufacturer, with roughly 30% market share across its healthcare businesses. In 2012, GE launched its "Industrial Internet," a massive data platform intended to collect data from GE hardware (from jet engines to

[13] Data produced enabled the home monitoring group to anticipate heart attacks six hours in advance. The data would be made available to third-party developers (in accordance with FDA and EU regulations).

ultrasound machines) to support the creation of data analytics software and drive predictive maintenance.[14] Despite its impressive data platform, Philips perceived GE's lack of a strong portfolio of consumer facing products to be to its advantage. Large EMRs like Epic and Cerner (which had acquired Siemens health software and EMR business in August 2014)[15] stored data that were essential to hospital operations and many hospitals had been using EMR platforms for over a decade. However, many clinicians complained that the EMR platforms were difficult to access and use. Epic, one of the largest EMRs, was built on old systems dating from the 1960s, which made it difficult to connect EMR databases with other information systems inside hospitals. Many EMRs were also difficult to adapt to care sites that were not hospitals or acute care locations.

Philips did not perceive Apple or Google to be competitors, despite their ownership of the world's largest app stores, since HSDP had the capability to integrate data from the technology companies' health dashboard (like Apple's Healthkit). Philips believed its deep understanding of clinicians' needs and hospital workflows set it apart from competitors like Google Health and Microsoft HealthVault, whose healthcare databases had failed to engage either clinicians or patients. Google Health was shuttered in 2011.[16]

DIGITAL HEALTH PLATFORM AND THE RADBOUD UNIVERSITY MEDICAL CENTER

In October 2014, Philips and Radboud university medical center (Radboudumc), an innovative teaching hospital and medical center based in Nijmegen, Netherlands, partnered to launch a new care approach for patients with chronic obstructive pulmonary disease (COPD). In the U.S., COPD was the third leading cause of death[17] and it was estimated that nearly 13 million adults suffered from the disease.[18] COPD was a progressive disease that required complex treatments and frequently resulted in higher rates of hospital admissions. In the past, the typical assessment used to determine the diagnosis of COPD required a two-hour test that had a margin for error of +/– 30%. Readmissions were very costly for hospitals, so a platform that could help clinicians identify and prioritize care for patients most at-risk for readmission could yield significant savings.

[14] Jon Gertner, "BEHIND GE'S VISION FOR THE INDUSTRIAL INTERNET OF THINGS," *Fast Company*, June 18, 2014, http://www.fastcompany.com/3031272/can-jeff-immelt-really-make-the-world-1-better, accessed April 2015.

[15] "Cerner to Acquire Siemens Health Services for $1.3 Billion," company press release, august 5, 2014, http://www.cerner.com/newsroom.aspx?id=17179877489&blogid=2147483710&langType=1033, accessed April 2015.

[16] Brian Dolan, "10 Reasons why Google Health failed," *Mobihealth news*, June 27, 2011, http://mobihealthnews.com/11480/10-reasons-why-google-health-failed/, accessed April 2015.

[17] Centers for Disease Control and Prevention. National Center for Health Statistics. National Vital Statistics Report. Deaths: Final Data for 2010. May 2013; 61(04).

[18] Centers for Disease Control and Prevention. National Center for Health Statistics. National Health Interview Survey Raw Data, 2011. Analysis performed by the American Lung Association Research and Health Education Division using SPSS and SUDAAN software.

Philips and Radboudumc piloted a program that would produce a more accurate diagnosis by leveraging inexpensive sensor technology and HSDP. During the first visit to the Radboudumc clinic, patients thought to have COPD were given a small sensor (to be worn on the chest), a spirometer,[19] and a tablet with an EKG[20] sensor wrapped around it. The sensors tracked the patient's physical activity (or inactivity), heart rate variability, heart rhythm, sleeping patterns and respiration. All of the sensor data was fed into the two Philips-created HSDP apps: the eCareCompanion and the eCareCoordinator. In addition, the eCareCompanion application on the tablet prompted patients to answer questions, like how they felt that day. Both the sensor data and qualitative data were tracked and shared with doctors through the eCareCoordinator app. The Radboudumc clinic allowed patients to call at any time to receive triage care from its medical staff. Tas commented: "Unlike other wearable solutions recently introduced to the market, this prototype collects more than just wellness data from otherwise healthy people. We are demonstrating the power of harnessing both clinical and personal health information to better manage chronic disease patients across the health continuum, from healthy living, prevention, diagnosis, treatment, recovery and home care."

Radboudumc was the first European academic hospital to use HSDP in a clinical practice; it even created its own app, Hereismydata, to offer its patients a single location to access all of their medical data (from lab results to fitness wearables), make additions and changes, or share data with clinicians, family members or others in the Radboucumc patient network with the same condition.[21] In a different pilot, Philips partnered with an academic hospital to demonstrate that monitoring cardiac chronic patients at home resulted in a 67% reduction in emergency room visits and estimated per patient cost reduction of $27,000 per year. Similar results could be expected for the COPD pilot with Radboud.

SUCCESS AHEAD FOR HSDP?

Although Tas was satisfied with HSDP's initial results, he wondered whether the platform would be successful in attracting both app developers and providers. Each of Philips' competitors knew that digital platforms were the next big opportunity in healthcare, so speed-to-market was essential. Given the structure of ecosystems, there was a significant advantage to being first to market with a widely adopted platform. Furthermore, hospitals sought technology partners who could grow with them over a 10–15 year period since the cost to the hospital of starting over with a new platform and new supplier was high. Philips had to insure that the data HSDP housed (e.g., EMR data, images, and vital signs) could be combined effectively into a total view of the patient that could drive clinical decision-making.

[19] Spirometers were medical devices used to measure the volume of air the lungs took-in and expelled.

[20] EKG, or electrocardiogram, referred to a device which tested the electrical activity of the heart.

[21] "Hereismydata," Hereismydata.com (Radboudumc), http://www.hereismydata.com/, accessed April 2015.

In the long run, Philips hoped that HSDP's success would be measured by the number of patients who lived longer and better lives as a result of the platform. In the short term, Tas and his team needed to insure that HSDP was leveraged by the other Philips HealthTech businesses, deployed to a significant portion of Philips' customers, and had adequate quantities of information (from EMRs, medical devices and consumer products) and apps so that the platform could deliver on its promise to support cutting-edge analytics.

PART III

Prevention and Adherence

6

CANCER SCREENING IN JAPAN

MARKET RESEARCH AND SEGMENTATION

John A. Quelch and Margaret L. Rodriguez

In November 2013, Jun Fukuyoshi (HBS '08) and Yoshiki Ishikawa (HSPH '08) met in their Tokyo office for a periodic strategic review meeting that coincided with the company's fifth anniversary. Since founding CancerScan in 2008, they had helped to improve cancer screening rates in Japan. The founders had focused in particular on breast cancer. They had noted that, between 2005 and 2007, awareness of breast cancer in Japan rose from 55% to 70%, but the incidence of breast cancer screenings remained constant.[1] Jun and Yoshiki applied marketing research techniques to increase the screening rate for breast cancer, a disease which killed over 10,000 Japanese women in 2011. Cancer screening initiatives accounted for 60% of the company's 2013 sales of $2.5 million. Breast cancer screening projects accounted for about one third of the cancer-related revenues.

HEALTH CARE IN JAPAN

In 2012, Japanese citizens enjoyed the highest life expectancy of any country in the Organisation for Economic Co-operation and Development (OECD), at 86.4 years for women, and 79.6 years for men.[2] Japan's developed economy offered its citizens a public health infrastructure which provided every advantage to achieve a long and happy life: government subsidized diagnostic tests, a comprehensive health care system, and ready access to specialists. The Japanese government's comprehensive health care system was established in 1961, and supplied individual insurance coverage through employers, or directly from the national government.[3] Participation in the national health insurance

[1] Jun Fukuyoshi, Akio Yonekura, "A social marketing approach by increasing breast cancer screening in Japan," PowerPoint presentation, November 11, 2010, Harvard School of Public Health, Boston, MA.

[2] OECD iLibrary, "OECD Factbook 2013," *Organisation for Economic Co-operation and Development*, January 9, 2013. http://www.oecd-ilibrary.org/economics/oecd-factbook-2013/life-expectancy_factbook-2013-95-en. Accessed October 2013.

[3] Kenji Shibuya, Hideki Hashimoto, Naoki Ikegami, Akihiro Nishi, Tetsuya Tanimoto, Hiroaki Miyata, Keizo Takemi, Michael R. Reich, "Future of Japan's system of good health at low cost with equity: beyond universal coverage," *The Lancet*, Volume 378, Issue 9798, 1–7 October 2011, Pages

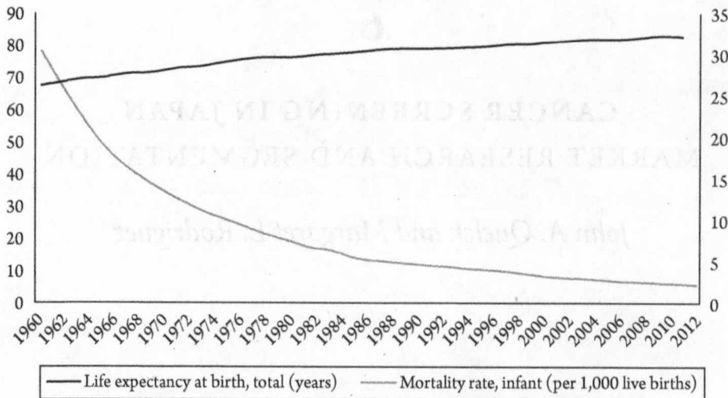

Figure 6.1 Exhibit 1 Life Expectancy and Infant Mortality in Japan, 1961–2012.
Source: Casewriter, adapted from the World DataBank, The World Bank Group. Accessed October 2013.

program was mandatory; this helped to redistribute costs from high-risk to low-risk individuals. By 2011, virtually every person in Japan was covered by one of the 3,500 insurance plans available.[4] In the fifty years following its launch, Japan's health care system had contributed huge increases to life expectancy and decreases in infant mortality (see Figure 6.1 for life expectancy and infant mortality progress in Japan).

Cost Structure of Japan's Health Care System

The health care system in Japan prohibited profits for medical insurance companies, limited doctors' fees and retained tight control of drug prices.[5] In 2009, total health care expenditure in Japan was relatively low, about 8% of Japan's GDP, or about half of the proportion of the United States' spending on health care costs.[6] Japan's low health care costs were helped by the government's uniform fee schedule (which reduced administrative costs for doctors and insurers).[7] Japan's health care system used a fee-per-service system, but the out-of-pocket costs were typically low. Co-payments were 30% (except for those who were low-income and 70 years or older; and children

1265–1273, ISSN 0140-6736, http://dx.doi.org/10.1016/S0140-6736(11)61098-2. Accessed via Google Scholar, October 2013.

[4] Ibid.

[5] Blaine Harden, "Health Care in Japan: Low-Cost, for Now," *The Washington Post*, September 7, 2009. http://articles.washingtonpost.com/2009-09-07/world/36813795_1_medical-care-health-care-health-care. Accessed September 2013.

[6] Ibid.

[7] Hideki Hashimoto, Naoki Ikegami, Kenji Shibuya, Nobuyuki Izumida, Haruko Noguchi, Hideo Yasunaga, Hiroaki Miyata, Jose M. Acuin, Michael R. Reich, "Cost containment and quality of care in Japan: is there a trade-off?", *The Lancet*, Volume 378, Issue 9797, 24–30 September 2011, pp. 1174–1182, ISSN 0140-6736, http://dx.doi.org/10.1016/S0140-6736(11)60987-2. Accessed via Google Scholar, October 2013.

younger than six years old).[8] The government subsidized monthly co-pays that exceeded $863 per individual per month.[9] The low cost of health care services in Japan contributed to high utilization: on average, individuals in Japan visited the doctor fourteen times per year (about four times more often than individuals in the United States).[10] The Japanese government paid for roughly one quarter of health care costs, and the rest were paid by individuals or employers.[11] The health care system in Japan was funded by taxes, fees collected from employers and co-payments. Employees in Japan paid about 4% of their salaries to their employers for insurance; on average, workers paid $1,931 in 2009.[12]

Unsustainable Financial Future

Some feared that the low-cost, high quality Japanese health care system would be unsustainable as the population aged. In 2012, Japan had the oldest population in the world with a median age of 44.4 years for men, and 47.2 years for women (versus the global median age of 28.7 for men and 30.2 years for women).[13] The proportion aged 65 and older was projected to grow from 24%[14] in 2012 to 40% of Japan's population by 2050.[15] Of those in Japan who were 65 and older in 2010, 16.9% lived alone, an increase of 3.1% since 2001.[16] In 2010, 26% of all Japanese households were single person,[17] as compared to 27% in the United States.[18] Over 30% of single person

[8] Naoki Ikegami, Byung-Kwang Yoo, Hideki Hashimoto, Masatoshi Matsumoto, Hiroya Ogata, Akira Babazono, Ryo Watanabe, Kenji Shibuya, Bong-Min Yang, Michael R. Reich, Yasuki Kobayashi, "Japanese universal health coverage: evolution, achievements, and challenges," *The Lancet*, Volume 378, Issue 9796, 17–23 September 2011, Pages 1106–1115, ISSN 0140-6736, http://dx.doi.org/10.1016/S0140-6736(11)60828-3. Accessed via Google Scholar, October 2013.

[9] Blaine Harden, "Health Care in Japan: Low-Cost, for Now," *The Washington Post*, September 7, 2009. http://articles.washingtonpost.com/2009-09-07/world/36813795_1_medical-care-health-care-health-care. Accessed September 2013.

[10] Ibid.

[11] Ibid.

[12] Ibid.

[13] The World Factbook, "Median Age," *Central Intelligence Agency*, https://www.cia.gov/library/publications/the-world-factbook/fields/2177.html. Accessed October 2013.

[14] The World Bank, "Population ages 65 and above (% of total)," http://data.worldbank.org/indicator/ SP.POP.65UP.TO.ZS. Accessed October 2013.

[15] Blaine Harden, "Health Care in Japan: Low-Cost, for Now," *The Washington Post*, September 7, 2009. http://articles.washingtonpost.com/2009-09-07/world/36813795_1_medical-care-health-care-health-care. Accessed September 2013.

[16] Comprehensive Survey of Living Conditions, "Graphical Review of Japanese Households," 2010. Accessed October 2013.

[17] Comprehensive Survey of Living Conditions, "Graphical Review of Japanese Households," 2010. Accessed October 2013.

[18] U.S. Census, 2010, "Households by Presence of People 65 Years and Over, Household Size, and Household Type," *2010 Census Summary File 1*. http://factfinder2.census.gov/faces/tableservices/jsf/pages/ productview.xhtml?pid=ACS_12_1YR_B23001&prodType=table. Accessed October 2013.

households in Japan were located in Tokyo, as opposed to just over 4% of U.S. single person households located in the New York City metropolitan area.[19]

The total population of Japan was expected to decrease from 128 million in 2012[20] to 95 million in 2050.[21] In 2009, the OECD estimated that Japan's health care costs would double as a percentage of GDP, to reach a level similar to that of the United States, by 2020, unless changes were made to the system's cost structure.[22] In 2008, the government of Japan mandated annual health check-ups for citizens between 40-74 years, in an attempt to identify problems early and mitigate rising costs.[23] In 2010, 32% of Japanese adults aged twenty years and older had not had an annual health check-up (25% of those who were employed did not get a check-up, as opposed to 44% of those who were not employed).[24] (See Figure 6.2 for key barriers to getting screened in Japan). The Japanese government faced strict budget constraints for all of its programs, following the burst of Japan's economic bubble in 1991. Japan's national debt had swelled to a size twice that of the country's GDP by 2011.[25] Japan's aging population was also expected to erode the tax base for payroll taxes, as older Japanese citizens exited the workforce.[26]

[19] U.S. Census, 2010, "Households by Presence of People 65 Years and Over, Household Size, and Household Type," *2010 Census Summary File 1*. http://factfinder2.census.gov/faces/tableservices/jsf/pages/ productview.xhtml?pid=ACS_12_1YR_B23001&prodType=table. Accessed October 2013.

[20] The World Bank, "Japan," http://www.worldbank.org/en/country/japan. Accessed October 2013.

[21] Statistics Bureau, Ministry of Internal Affairs and Communications, "Population of Japan: final report of the 2005 population census," *Tokyo: Japan Statistical Association*, 2010. Quoted in Nayu Ikeda, Eiko Saito, Naoki Kondo, Manami Inoue, Shunya Ikeda, Toshihiko Satoh, Koji Wada, Andrew Stickley, Kota Katanoda, Tetsuya Mizoue, Mitsuhiko Noda, Hiroyasu Iso, Yoshihisa Fujino, Tomotaka Sobue, Shoichiro Tsugane, Mohsen Naghavi, Majid Ezzati, Kenji Shibuya, "What has made the population of Japan healthy?", *The Lancet*, Volume 378, Issue 9796, 17–23 September 2011, pp. 1094–1105, ISSN 0140-6736, http://dx.doi.org/10.1016/S0140-6736(11)61055-6. Accessed October 2013.

[22] OECD, "OECD health data 2011: statistics and indicators," *Paris: Organization for Economic Co-operation and Development*, 2011. http://www.oecd.org/els/health-systems/49105858.pdf. Accessed October 2013.

[23] Ministry of Health, Labour and Welfare. Standard health examination and guidance program. *Tokyo: Ministry of Health, Labour and Welfare*, 2007. Quoted in Nayu Ikeda, Eiko Saito, Naoki Kondo, Manami Inoue, Shunya Ikeda, Toshihiko Satoh, Koji Wada, Andrew Stickley, Kota Katanoda, Tetsuya Mizoue, Mitsuhiko Noda, Hiroyasu Iso, Yoshihisa Fujino, Tomotaka Sobue, Shoichiro Tsugane, Mohsen Naghavi, Majid Ezzati, Kenji Shibuya, What has made the population of Japan healthy?, *The Lancet*, Volume 378, Issue 9796, 17–23 September 2011, pp. 1094-1105, ISSN 0140-6736, http://dx.doi.org/10.1016/S0140-6736(11)61055-6. Accessed October 2013.

[24] Comprehensive Survey of Living Conditions, "Graphical Review of Japanese Households," 2010. Accessed October 2013.

[25] OECD, "Economic Outlook 2010," *Organisation for Economic Co-operation and Development*, Paris (2011).

[26] Associated Press, "Decline in U.S. birth rates slows," *CBS News*, October 3, 2012. http://www.cbsnews.com/8301-204_162-57524977/decline-in-u.s-birth-rates-slows/. Accessed October 2013.

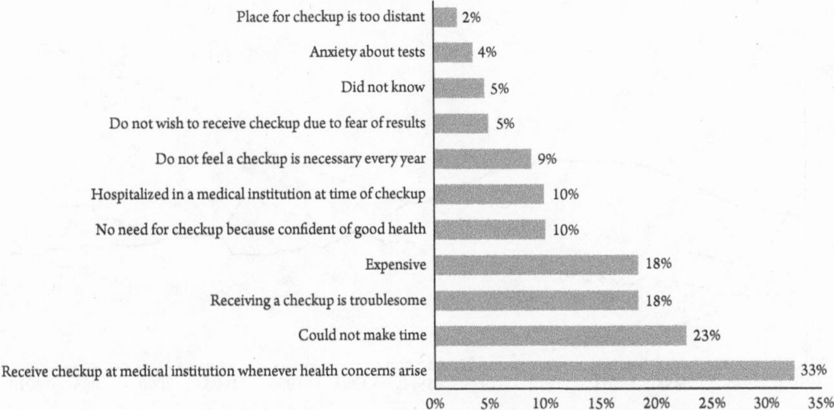

Figure 6.2 Exhibit 2 Key Barriers to Japanese Citizens Seeking Health Screenings, 2010.
Source: Casewriter, adapted from the Comprehensive Survey of Living Conditions, "Graphical Review of Japanese Households," 2010. Accessed October 2013.

THREAT OF CANCER IN JAPAN

Due to the health and longevity of Japan's citizens, degenerative diseases like cancer and cardiovascular afflictions were among the leading causes of death. A Japanese baby born in 2012 was more than 50% likely to die of cancer, heart disease or cerebrovascular disease (the three leading causes of death in Japan) over his lifetime.[27] In 2011, more than 357,000 Japanese citizens died of cancer (144,000 of whom were women).[28] In 2011, cancer-related deaths accounted for 28.5% of all deaths in Japan.[29] (See Figure 6.3 for the leading causes of death in Japan). Five types of cancer[30] accounted for over 60% of all cancer cases.[31] One in two Japanese citizens was expected to be diagnosed with cancer during his/her lifetime.[32] In 2011, it was estimated that one in four Japanese men and one in six Japanese women would die of cancer.[33] In 2007, the

[27] Ministry of Health, Labour and Welfare, "Fact sheet of abridged life tables for Japan 2010," 2011. http://www.mhlw.go.jp/toukei/saikin/hw/life/life10/index.html. Accessed October 2013.

[28] Center for Cancer Control and Information Services, "Cancer Statistics in Japan '12," *National Cancer Center*, January 15, 2013. http://ganjoho.jp/pro/statistics/en/backnumber/2012_en.html. Accessed October 2013.

[29] Ibid.

[30] Among men, the five most common cancer types were: stomach, large intestine, lung, liver and prostate gland. Among women, the five most common cancers were: large intestine, breast, stomach, uterus and lung.

[31] Ministry of Health, Labour and Welfare, "Detailed Data: Statistics Related to Cancer," 2011. http://www.mhlw.go.jp/english/wp/wp-hw4/dl/health_and_medical_services/P76.pdf. Accessed October 2013.

[32] Center for Cancer Control and Information Services, "Cancer Statistics in Japan '12," *National Cancer Center*, January 15, 2013. http://ganjoho.jp/pro/statistics/en/backnumber/2012_en.html. Accessed October 2013.

[33] Ibid.

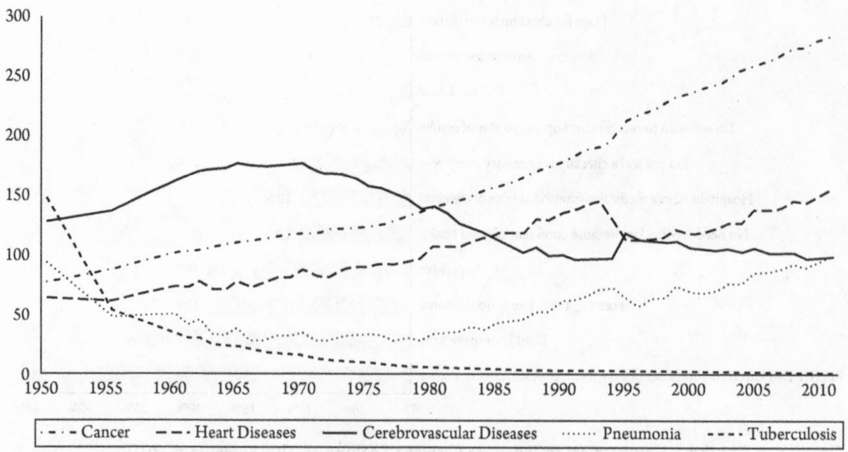

Figure 6.3 Exhibit 3 Leading Causes of Death in Japan (rate per 100,000), 1950–2011.
Source: Casewriter, adapted from the Center for Cancer Control and Information Services, "Cancer Statistics in Japan '12," National Cancer Center, January 15, 2013. http://ganjoho.jp/pro/statistics/en/backnumber/2012_en.html Accessed October 2013.

expenditure on cancer care in Japan was 2.696 trillion yen[34], or 10.5% of the total general practice medical expenditures.[35] In 2008, that Japanese government legislated to provide cancer screenings in every community to combat the disease.[36]

Cancer Legislation

Cancer became the leading cause of death in Japan in 1981. Three years later, in 1984, the Japanese government crafted its first comprehensive piece of legislation to address the threat of cancer, the "Comprehensive 10-year Strategy for Cancer Control."[37] A second ten year plan was created in 1994, followed by a third in 2004, "The 3rd term Comprehensive 10-year Strategy for Cancer Control."[38] Beginning in 2004, the Japanese government officially recommended that all women in Japan over age forty receive mammography

[34] In 2007, $1.00 USD was equal to roughly 116 yen.

[35] Ministry of Health, Labour and Welfare, "Detailed Data: Statistics Related to Cancer," 2011. http://www.mhlw.go.jp/english/wp/wp-hw4/dl/health_and_medical_services/P76.pdf. Accessed October 2013.

[36] Japan Ministry of Health, Labour and Welfare 2007. Quoted in Kazuhiro Harada, Kei Hirai, Hirokazu Arai, Yoshiki Ishikawa, Jun Fukuyoshi, Chisato Hamashima, Hiroshi Saito, and Daisuke Shibuya. "Worry and Intention among Japanese Women: Implications for an Audience Segmentation Strategy to Promote Mammography Adoption." *Health Communication* 0, no. 0 (0): 1–9. doi:10.1080/10410236.2012.711511.

[37] Center for Cancer Control and Information Services, "Cancer Statistics in Japan '12," *National Cancer Center*, January 15, 2013. http://ganjoho.jp/pro/statistics/en/backnumber/2012_en.html. Accessed October 2013.

[38] Ibid.

screenings once every two years.[39] In 2007, the Japanese government enacted a new "Cancer Control Act" which was designed to reduce the prevalence and death rate of cancer in Japan.[40] The Cancer Control Act included a "Basic Plan to Promote Cancer Control Programs," which aimed to decrease cancer deaths by 20%, in age-adjusted mortality, for persons under 75 years old.[41] Early discovery of cancer was a core strategy of the plan, which stipulated the percentage of the population screened for cancers increase to 50% within five years.[42] In 2009, the Japanese Ministry of Health, Labour and Welfare created the headquarters of the initiative for "50% Cancer Screening Rate," in order to promote cancer screening (in support of the Cancer Control Act's goals).[43] The Basic Plan to Promote Cancer Control Program was revised in June 2012, and extended to cover five additional fiscal years, through 2016.[44] In 2012, the Ministry of Health, Labour and Welfare in Japan budgeted 35.7 billion yen for cancer control efforts. (See Figure 6.4 for the cancer budget allocation over time). The National Cancer Center was tasked with identifying methods to increase cancer screening rates.[45] A research group in the Center received research grants from the Ministry of Health, Labour and Welfare, which in turn it helped distribute to organizations dedicated to increasing cancer screening rates.[46]

Japanese Women and Breast Cancer

Beginning in 1986, women in Japan had the highest life expectancy of any female population in the world.[47] In 2009, life expectancy at birth for Japanese women was 86 years.[48]

[39] Ken Uchia, Hitoshi Ohashi, Satoki Kinoshita, Hiroko Nogi, Kumiko Kato, Yasuo Toriumi, Akinori Yamashita, Makiko Kamio, Rei Mimoto, Hiroshi Takeyama, "Breast cancer screening and the changing population pyramid of Japan," *The Japanese Breast Cancer Society*, April 9, 2013. Accessed October 2013, via Google Scholar.

[40] Ministry of Health, Labour and Welfare, "Health and Medical Services: Cancer Control," 2011. Pp. 74–78. http://www.mhlw.go.jp/english/wp/wp-hw2/part2/p3_0026.pdf. Accessed October 2013.

[41] Ken Uchia, Hitoshi Ohashi, Satoki Kinoshita, Hiroko Nogi, Kumiko Kato, Yasuo Toriumi, Akinori Yamashita, Makiko Kamio, Rei Mimoto, Hiroshi Takeyama, "Breast cancer screening and the changing population pyramid of Japan," *The Japanese Breast Cancer Society*, April 9, 2013. Accessed October 2013, via Google Scholar.

[42] Ibid.

[43] Center for Cancer Control and Information Services, "Cancer Statistics in Japan '12," *National Cancer Center*, January 15, 2013. http://ganjoho.jp/pro/statistics/en/backnumber/2012_en.html. Accessed October 2013.

[44] Ibid.

[45] Jun Fukuyoshi, "RE: Cancerscan Case Study,"email message to John Quelch, November 8, 2013.

[46] Jun Fukuyoshi, "RE: Cancerscan Case Study,"email message to John Quelch, November 8, 2013.

[47] Nayu Ikeda, Eiko Saito, Naoki Kondo, Manami Inoue, Shunya Ikeda, Toshihiko Satoh, Koji Wada, Andrew Stickley, Kota Katanoda, Tetsuya Mizoue, Mitsuhiko Noda, Hiroyasu Iso, Yoshihisa Fujino, Tomotaka Sobue, Shoichiro Tsugane, Mohsen Naghavi, Majid Ezzati, Kenji Shibuya, "What has made the population of Japan healthy?," *The Lancet*, Volume 378, Issue 9796, 17–23 September 2011, pp. 1094–1105, ISSN 0140-6736, http://dx.doi.org/10.1016/S0140-6736(11)61055-6. Accessed October 2013.

[48] WHO, "World health statistics 2011," Geneva: *World Health Organization*, 2011. http://www.who.int/%20whosis/whostat/2011/en/Accessed October 2013.

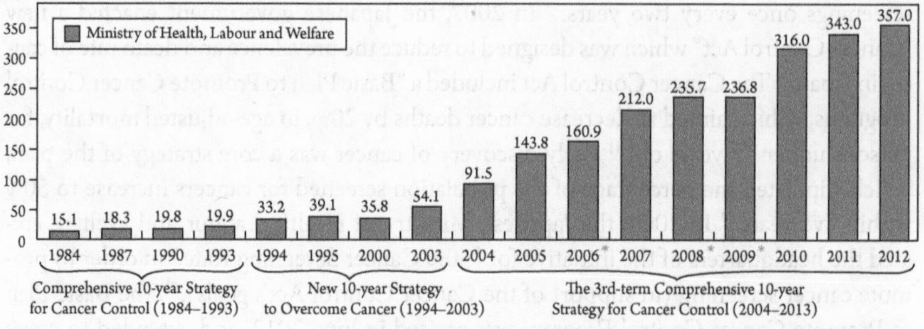

Figure 6.4 Exhibit 4 Ministry of Health, Labour and Welfare's cancer budget (100 million yen), 1984–2012.

Source: Center for Cancer Control and Information Services, "Cancer Statistics in Japan '12," National Cancer Center, January 15, 2013. p. 7. http://ganjoho.jp/pro/statistics/en/backnumber/2012_en.html Accessed October 2013.

A relatively lower proportion of women in Japan was employed. In 2012, roughly 59% of Japanese women between the ages of twenty and sixty-five were employed,[49] in contrast to 66% of women aged between sixteen and sixty-five in the United States.[50] Breast cancer was one of the most common types of cancer among Japanese women. (See Figure 6.5). In 2011, over 10,000 Japanese women died of breast cancer,[51] or 8.8% of all female deaths due to cancer in Japan. [52] Breast cancer had the fifth highest mortality rate of all cancers among Japanese females. The proportion of Japanese women who elected to receive mammography screening from local municipalities was low, only 17.6% in 2005,[53] (compared to 70% of women who received screenings in the United States).[54] (See Figure 6.6 for the cancer screening rate among Japanese women). The majority of breast cancer cases in Japan were identified after the cancer had reached stage II[55], likely as a result of failure to screen early for symptoms.[56]

[49] Portal Site of Official Statistics of Japan, "Japan Current Population Estimates," 2012. http://www.e-stat.go.jp/SG1/estat/ListE.do?lid=000001109855. Accessed October 2013.

[50] U.S. Census Bureau, "American Community Survey 1-Year Estimates," 2012. Accessed October 2013.

[51] Center for Cancer Control and Information Services, "Cancer Statistics in Japan '12," *National Cancer Center*, January 15, 2013. http://ganjoho.jp/pro/statistics/en/backnumber/2012_en.html. Accessed October 2013.

[52] Ibid.

[53] Kumiko Saika, Tomotaka Sobue, "Epidemiology of Breast Cancer in Japan and the US," JMAJ 52(1)39–44, 2009. Accessed October 2013, via Google Scholar.

[54] Harvard School of Public Health, "Antares: Alumni," http://www.hsph.harvard.edu/antares/alumni/. Accessed October 2013.

[55] Stage referred to the cancer's progression within the body, taking into account the size of the tumor, spread of the cancer beyond the initial organ to lymph nodes, tissues or other organs. Stages range from zero to four.

[56] Center for Cancer Control and Information Services, "Cancer Statistics in Japan '12," *National Cancer Center*, January 15, 2013. http://ganjoho.jp/pro/statistics/en/backnumber/2012_en.html. Accessed October 2013. p. 20

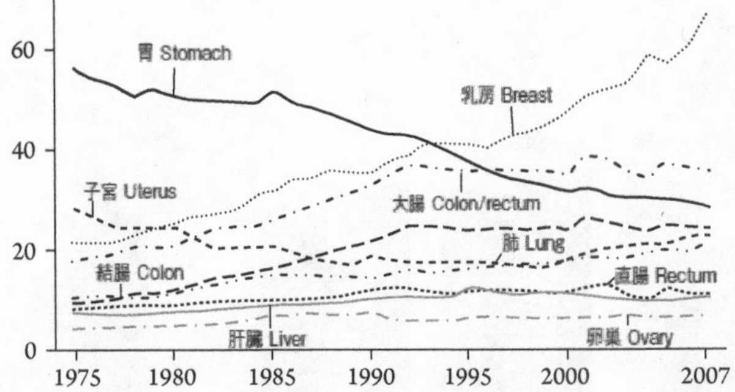

Figure 6.5 Exhibit 5 Incidence of Cancers in Japanese Women (rate per 100,000, log scale), 1975–2007.

Source: Center for Cancer Control and Information Services, "Cancer Statistics in Japan '12," National Cancer Center, January 15, 2013. p. 36. http://ganjoho.jp/pro/statistics/en/backnumber/2012_en.html Accessed October 2013.

Research published by the Japanese Cancer Society in 2013 identified the primary barriers for Japanese women below sixty years to seek mammography screenings as expense and scheduling, whereas the primary barrier for women aged sixty years and older was low awareness of the risk of breast cancer.[57] A 2012 study published by the Sookmyung Women's University in South Korea studied the response of Japanese women and American women to different types of advertisements promoting cancer prevention. The study found that Japanese women responded more favorably to ads which featured collectivistic appeals (e.g. those which mentioned the impact cancer could have on families) and American women preferred ads which featured individualistic appeals.[58] (See Table 6.1 for the results of the study).

CANCERSCAN RESEARCH

CancerScan set out to use market segmentation strategies to increase breast cancer screenings among Japanese women. Segmentation called for dividing a heterogeneous population into smaller, more homogeneous groups on the basis of shared demographic, behavioral or psychological traits.[59] A segmentation pilot was conducted between 2009 and 2010 in Tokyo with a sample of over 8,000 women, aged

[57] Ken Uchia, Hitoshi Ohashi, Satoki Kinoshita, Hiroko Nogi, Kumiko Kato, Yasuo Toriumi, Akinori Yamashita, Makiko Kamio, Rei Mimoto, Hiroshi Takeyama, "Breast cancer screening and the changing population pyramid of Japan," *The Japanese Breast Cancer Society*, April 9, 2013. Accessed October 2013, via Google Scholar.

[58] Kyoo-hoon Han, Samsup Jo, "Does Culture Matter?: A Cross-National Investigation of Women's Responses to Cancer Prevention Campaigns," *Health Care for Women International*, 33:75–94, 2012. Accessed via Google Scholar, October 2013.

[59] Kazuhiro Harada, Kei Hirai, Hirokazu Arai, Yoshiki Ishikawa, Jun Fukuyoshi, Chisato Hamashima, Hiroshi Saito, and Daisuke Shibuya. "Worry and Intention Among Japanese Women: Implications for an Audience Segmentation Strategy to Promote Mammography Adoption." *Health Communication* 0, no. 0 (0): 1–9. doi:10.1080/10410236.2012.711511.

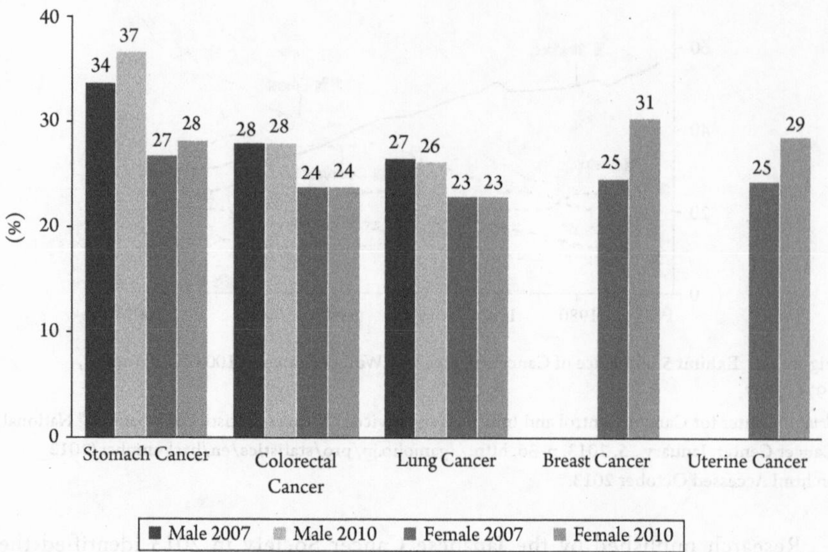

Figure 6.6 Exhibit 6 Cancer Screening Rates for Japanese Men and Women (aged 40–69 years old[a]), 2007–2011.

Source: Center for Cancer Control and Information Services, "Cancer Statistics in Japan '12," National Cancer Center, January 15, 2013. http://ganjoho.jp/pro/statistics/en/backnumber/2012_en.html Accessed October 2013. P. 49.

[a]The age range for Uterine Cancer screening rates was 20–69 years old.

between 51 and 59 years, to test the effectiveness of targeted messages in influencing behavior change. In October 2009, 8,100 women were identified as potential survey candidates from the local health department's database.[60] A mail survey was sent to them to obtain attitudes and opinions regarding cancer and cancer screening. The local government's web site contained details of the study and the women signaled their consent for enrollment by returning the questionnaire, (of the 8,100 women who were sent the survey, 3,236 replied).[61] However, 1,362 women were excluded based on not meeting the eligibility criteria, and 15 were excluded due to missing data.[62] Following the baseline survey, a total of 1,859 eligible women were randomly assigned to one of two conditions: approximately 75% of the sample (n = 1394) to the tailored interventions and 25% (n = 465) to the control group who received the non-tailored intervention.[63] Only 12.2% of eligible women (forty years and older) in the area had received screening through the local government's clinics prior to the pilot.[64] The cost of a mammogram to the consumer in the area was 1,000 yen (about $12).[65]

[60] Jun Fukuyoshi, "RE: Cancerscan Case Study,"email message to John Quelch, November 8, 2013.

[61] Jun Fukuyoshi, "RE: Cancerscan Case Study,"email message to John Quelch, November 8, 2013.

[62] Jun Fukuyoshi, "RE: Cancerscan Case Study,"email message to John Quelch, November 8, 2013.

[63] Jun Fukuyoshi, "RE: Cancerscan Case Study,"email message to John Quelch, November 8, 2013.

[64] Yoshiki Ishikawa, Kei Hirai, Hiroshi Saito, Jun Fukuyoshi, Akio Yonekura, Kazuhiro Harada, Aiko Seki, Daisuke Shibuya, Yosikazu Nakamura, "Cost-effectiveness of a tailored intervention designed to increase breast cancer screening among a non-adherent population: a randomized controlled trial,"BMC. *Public Health* 2012, 12:760. http://www.biomedcentral.com/1471-2458/12/760. Accessed October 2013, via Google Scholar.

[65] Ibid.

Table 6.1 Exhibit 7 Attitudes Towards Cancer Communication Types by Nationality, 2012

Country	*Appeal Type*	*N*	*M*[a]	*SD*	*t*	*p-value*
Japan	Individualistic	160	3.639	.565	−2.016	.045
	Collectivistic	161	3.771	.580		
United States	Individualistic	165	3.911	.657	1.665	.097
	Collectivistic	165	3.792	.637		

Source: Adapted from Kyoo-hoon Han, Samsup Jo, "Does Culture Matter?: A Cross-National Investigation of Women's Responses to Cancer Prevention Campaigns," *Health Care for Women International*, 33:75–94, 2012. Accessed via Google Scholar, October 2013.

[a]M refers to the score an advertisement's appeal on a five-point Likert scale.

To be read as, Japanese women were statistically significantly more likely to prefer collectivistic cancer ads (p-value <0.05); whereas American women were statistically significantly more like to prefer individualistic cancer ads (p-value <0.1).

CancerScan segmented the 1,394 women into four groups, according to their awareness of breast cancer, the perceived urgency of the issue and their strength of motivation to obtain a breast cancer screen.[66] (See Figure 6.7 for the segmentation model). Survey questions were limited to attitudes and opinions regarding cancer, as CancerScan was not permitted to ask demographic questions on the survey due to privacy restrictions.[67] Each participant was placed into one of four segments based upon answers to the survey (so the number of women in each segment varied). The four segments included a group labeled "regular screening takers,"[68] group A, group B and group C. The control group used in the study comprised a weighted sample drawn from groups A, B and C. The participants also answered questions in the survey regarding potential barriers to undergoing breast cancer screening. (See Figure 6.8 for survey responses for each main barrier, aggregated by segment).

Profiling Segments

Prior to the participants being sorted into the four groups according to their survey responses, around twenty one-on-one qualitative interviews were conducted to better understand what drove the low rates of screening. Survey respondents who demonstrated high awareness of breast cancer, more urgency regarding the risk of breast cancer and high motivation to receive breast cancer screening were labeled as "regular screening takers." Additional interviews were not conducted among this group, as they offered no resistance to screening. Women sorted into group A had high awareness of breast cancer and its urgency, but lacked the motivation to receive screenings. Using

[66] Jun Fukuyoshi, Akio Yonekura, "A social marketing approach by increasing breast cancer screening in Japan," PowerPoint presentation, November 11, 2010, Harvard School of Public Health, Boston, MA.

[67] Jun Fukuyoshi, "RE: Cancerscan Case Study," email message to John Quelch, November 8, 2013.

[68] Based upon their response to the survey, women in this group were assumed to already receive regular breast cancer screenings, given their high awareness, urgency and motivation.

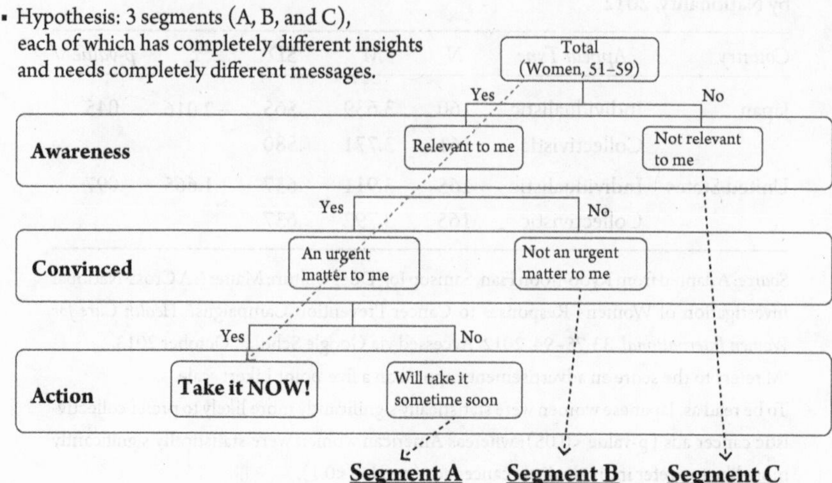

Figure 6.7 Exhibit 8 Segmentation Model for Women Eligible for Breast Cancer Screenings, 2009–2010.

Source: Jun Fukuyoshi, Akio Yonekura, "A social marketing approach by increasing breast cancer screening in Japan," PowerPoint presentation, November 11, 2010, Harvard School of Public Health, Boston, MA.

the survey responses regarding barriers and qualitative interviews, Jun and Yoshiki identified the principal barrier faced by women in group A as a lack of understanding on how to begin the process to get screened for breast cancer. Women sorted into group B exhibited high awareness of breast cancer, but low urgency and motivation to obtain screenings. The responses group B gave regarding barriers in the survey and in the interviews indicated that they were afraid to undergo screenings because of the risk that they could find out that they had cancer. Those participants who were sorted into group C had low awareness, urgency and motivation to receive screenings. Participants in group C believed that cancer was not an issue about which they needed to worry, given their current state of health.

From Barriers to Messages

Next, CancerScan created messages designed to address the barriers to screening for each group. The participants in group A needed further information on where to get breast cancer screenings in their community, so CancerScan crafted a mailer for group A (see Figure 6.9) which included instructions on how to schedule an appointment for a breast cancer screening at the local, government-contracted clinic. The communication also addressed financial barriers by offering a 90% discount off the price of the scan. Participants in group A also received information on the disease, including their level of risk, the disease severity, and the benefits of early screenings.

Women in group B avoided being screened for fear that they would find out that they had cancer. For them, Jun and Yoshiki developed a non-threatening mailer which included a cartoon illustration of the screening process, instructions for self-examinations

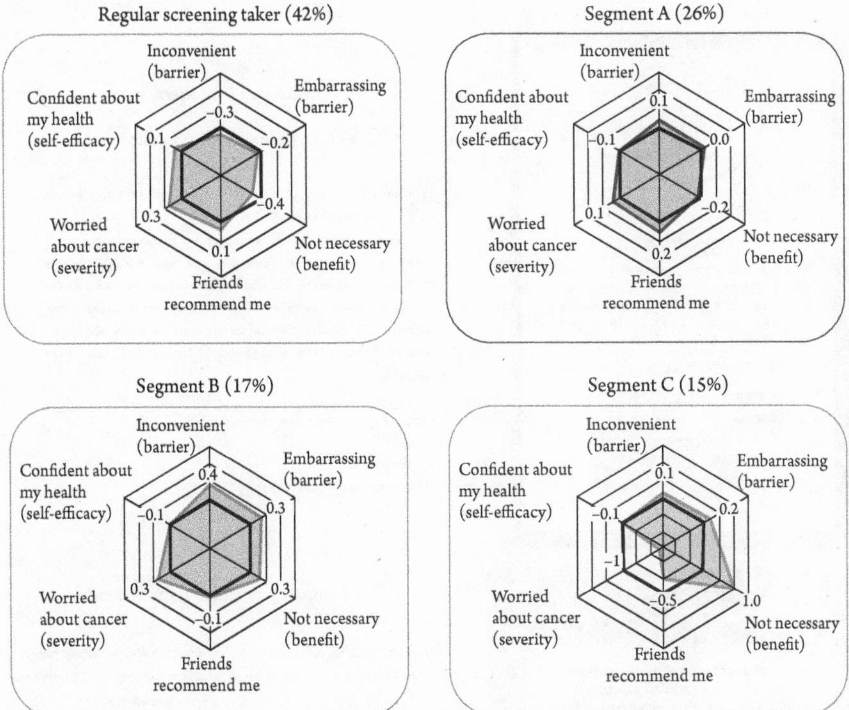

Figure 6.8 Exhibit 9 Key Barriers to Obtaining Breast Cancer Screenings, by Segment 2009–2010. *Source:* Jun Fukuyoshi, Akio Yonekura, "A social marketing approach by increasing breast cancer screening in Japan," PowerPoint presentation, November 11, 2010, Harvard School of Public Health, Boston, MA.

for breast cancer and a list of the benefits obtained from the early detection of breast cancer, (see Figure 6.10). Study participants in group C were unaware or unwilling to acknowledge the threat posed by breast cancer. CancerScan developed a mailer that emphasized the severity of the disease and the importance of screening (see Figure 6.11). The mailer received by group C contained an x-ray photo of a malignant cancer tumor in the breast, as well as statistics regarding cancer's status as a major cause of death among middle-aged women in Japan. Women in the control group were sent the standard reminder message that had been used within the community prior to the study.

Results

The incidence of breast cancer screenings was three times greater across the intervention groups A, B and C, which received targeted mailers, versus the control group, which received the current standardized mailer.[69] (The "regular screening takers" group

[69] Jun Fukuyoshi, Akio Yonekura, "A social marketing approach by increasing breast cancer screening in Japan," PowerPoint presentation, November 11, 2010, Harvard School of Public Health, Boston, MA.

(a)

Tachikawa City offers

¥9,000 mammography subsidy

Tachikawa City provides a subsidy of around ¥9,000 to female residents that are 40 years old and older.

Discretionary breast cancer screening by mammography is an expensive diagnostic test and can cost over ¥10,000. Female residents of Tachikawa City who are 40 years old or above on the day of the exam, and who did not take a mammography exam offered by Tachikawa City in the previous year, are eligible to receive a ¥9,000 subsidy from the city*. (The patient's share of the cost is ¥1,000).

Exam fee	Approximately	¥10,000
Subsidy		¥9,000
Patient cost		¥1,000

*The subsidy is not paid in cash.

受診予約メモ

2009年度乳がん検診受診の最終申し込み締め切り日は平成22年1月29日(金)必着。検診受診期間は平成22年3月31日までです。今年度の検診の予約はお済みですか？ご希望の場所と時間で受けられるようにできるだけ早く予約をしましょう。

検診場所の電話番号

医療機関

日時

メモ

立川市

Exam appointment reminder card

Enrollment for the Tachikawa City breast cancer screening program in FY2009 must be made by no later than January 29, 2010 (Friday). Examinations are scheduled to be performed through March 31, 2010. **Have you made your appointment for a mammography exam this year? Call early to schedule, to ensure you are able to take the exam at the time and location of your choice.**

Hospital/clinic telephone number:

Name of hospital/clinic:

Date and time:

Notes:

Health Promotion Section, Welfare and Health Department, Tachikawa City
Health Care Hall (Kenko Kaikan)
3-22-9 Takamatsu-cho, Tachikawa City Tokyo 190-0011
Tel: (042) 527-3272 Fax: (042) 521-0422

Figure 6.9 Exhibit 10 CancerScan Six Page Direct Mail Message, Customized for Group A, 2009–2010.
Source: Company documents.

was excluded from the analysis of the results). Group A recorded the highest screening rate at 25.5%..[70] Groups B and C recorded screening rates of 17.3% and 13.3%, respectively.

[70] Yoshiki Ishikawa, Kei Hirai, Hiroshi Saito, Jun Fukuyoshi, Akio Yonekura, Kazuhiro Harada, Aiko Seki, Daisuke Shibuya, Yosikazu Nakamura, "Cost-effectiveness of a tailored intervention designed to increase breast cancer screening among a non-adherent population: a randomized controlled trial,"BMC. *Public Health* 2012, 12:760. http://www.biomedcentral.com/1471-2458/12/760. Accessed October 2013, via Google Scholar.

(b)

This Year's Breast Cancer Screening Program

Medical exam planning card

Breast cancer screening program FY2009
Get a mammography exam every two years once you turn 40

Tachikawa City

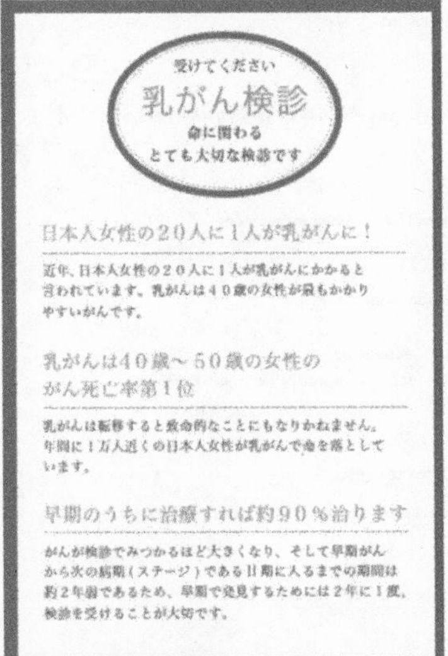

Get tested today

Breast cancer screening

An important test that could save your life

One-in-twenty Japanese women are diagnosed with breast cancer!
In recent years, some studies show that one in every twenty Japanese women develop breast cancer. It is most frequent in women in their 40s.

Breast cancer is the leading cause of cancer death among women in the 40-50 year old age range
Breast cancer can be fatal if it spreads to other parts of the body. In Japan, nearly 10,000 women a year lose their lives to breast cancer.

Nearly 90% of women who receive treatment for early-stage breast cancer are cured
A tumor large enough to be detected during a breast cancer exam can progress from early-stage cancer to Stage II cancer in less than two years. This is why it is important that women have a routine mammography exam once every two years, to enable cancer detection in the early stages.

Figure 6.9 Continued

The overall screening rate across the three test conditions was 19.9%.[71] The screening rate of the control group was 5.8%; women randomly assigned to the control condition from Group A screened at 7.3%, Group B at 4.7% and Group C at 4.6%. The tailored interventions were more expensive to implement ($6 per person versus $3 per person for

[71] Yoshiki Ishikawa, Kei Hirai, Hiroshi Saito, Jun Fukuyoshi, Akio Yonekura, Kazuhiro Harada, Aiko Seki, Daisuke Shibuya, Yosikazu Nakamura, "Cost-effectiveness of a tailored intervention designed to increase breast cancer screening among a non-adherent population: a randomized controlled trial,"BMC. *Public Health* 2012, 12:760. http://www.biomedcentral.com/1471-2458/12/760. Accessed October 2013, via Google Scholar.

(c)

Step 1. Schedule your exam

Enroll for your mammography screening

Enroll by sending in a postcard or letter containing your personal information. A medical card will be mailed to you.

Enrollments must be received by no later than January 29, 2010 (Friday).

Please include the following information on a postcard or in a letter. Indicate that you are enrolling to take a mammogram. Print your name (also provide your name in katakana), date of birth, address and telephone number.

Send to: Health Promotion Section, Tachikawa City
Health Center (Kenko Kaikan)
3-22-9 Takamatsu-cho, Tachikawa City
Tokyo 190-0011

You do not need to enroll for screening if you already have your medical card and coupon for FY2009. People who had a mammogram in FY2008 are not eligible for screening this year.

Make an appointment by phone at one of the selected hospitals/clinics

Once you receive your medical card, call and schedule an appointment at your preferred hospital/clinic from among those listed (see the list of selected hospitals and clinics included with your medical card). In FY2009, breast cancer screening is scheduled to be conducted through March 21, 2010 (final date).

Tel: 042 – selected hospital/clinic

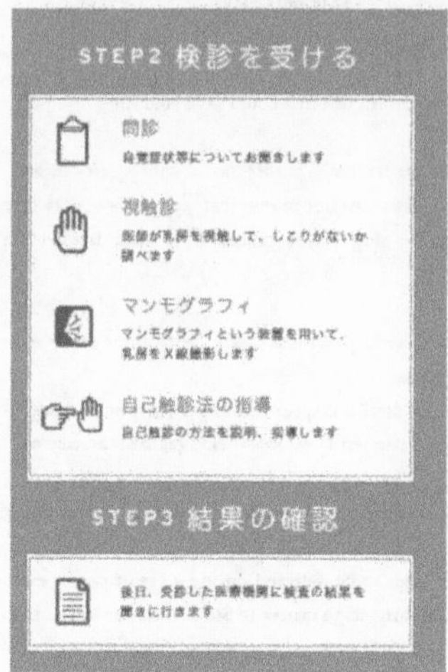

Step 2. Take the exam

Medical interview

The doctor will ask you questions, such as the symptoms you may be experiencing.

Physical examination

The doctor will look and feel for lumps in the breasts.

Mammography

X-rays will be taken using a mammograph.

Guidance on breast self-examination

The doctor will explain and provide instruction on self-examination

Step 3. Get your exam results

Go back to the hospital/clinic where you had your mammogram to get your results

Figure 6.9 Continued

the standardized mailer); yet the cost was lower, at $30 on average per incremental screening across the three test conditions versus $52 per screening for the control group which received the current standard message.[72]

[72] Yoshiki Ishikawa, Kei Hirai, Hiroshi Saito, Jun Fukuyoshi, Akio Yonekura, Kazuhiro Harada, Aiko Seki, Daisuke Shibuya, Yosikazu Nakamura, "Cost-effectiveness of a tailored intervention designed to increase breast cancer screening among a non-adherent population: a randomized controlled trial,"BMC. *Public Health* 2012, 12:760. http://www.biomedcentral.com/1471-2458/12/760. Accessed October 2013, via Google Scholar.

(a)

いま実に日本人女性の２０人にひとりが
乳がんにかかると言われています
がん死亡率
ナンバーワン
自己触診では
みつからないケースが
たくさんある
マンモグラフィはこんな検査
マンモグラフィは
いわゆるおっぱいの
レントゲン

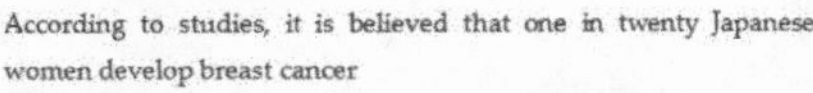

According to studies, it is believed that one in twenty Japanese women develop breast cancer

Breast cancer is no longer someone else's problem! Women in their 40s are at the highest risk

Breast cancer is the leading cause of cancer death in women in their 40s

In recent years, about 10,000 women die annually from breast cancer in Japan. The incidence of breast cancer is most frequent in women in their 40s and 50s.

This means that one or two mothers in your child's class could have breast cancer

In many cases, cancer is undetectable with breast self-examination

It is difficult to detect breast cancer solely by self-examination. Routine mammography screening and physical examinations are important tools for early detection.

I might not catch it in time with self-examination...

Mammography screening

What type of exam is mammography? Some people feel worried or anxious about taking the test. However, by understanding what happens during a mammogram, you will have nothing to worry about when you go in for your exam!

Mammography is basically an X-ray of the breasts

Mammography is sometimes referred to as breast x-raying. A mammogram is an x-ray of your breast. The x-ray image is taken by placing the breast between a plastic plate and an X-ray plate.

here is a slight queeze

ou have to remain till for 5 seconds... here, it's over!

This is a state-of-the-art imaging method that can detect lumps that are 1 centimeter or less

Mammography is an advanced imaging method that can detect lumps measuring 1 centimeter or less. Breast cancer screening consists of mammography together with a medical interview, physical examination, and when necessary, instructions on how to do breast self-examination. If you have any concerns about your breasts, feel free to consult with the doctor.

1cm以下のしこりまで
見つけられる
優れた画像検査法

* Please note that the attending doctor is not always female

Figure 6.10 Exhibit 11 CancerScan Six Page Direct Mail Message, Customized for Group B, 2009–2010.

Source: Company documents.

CANCERSCAN'S GROWTH OPPORTUNITIES

As Jun and Yoshiki reached the end of CancerScan's fifth year, they faced strategic choices in planning the company's future. CancerScan had achieved over $2.5 million dollars in project revenues by 2013 and the business had been profitable since year one. The National Cancer Center was CancerScan's primary client, since the Center was tasked with increasing cancer screening but lacked the internal capability to research and develop behavioral interventions.[73] CancerScan developed relationships

[73] Jun Fukuyoshi, "RE: Cancerscan Case Study," email message to John Quelch, November 8, 2013.

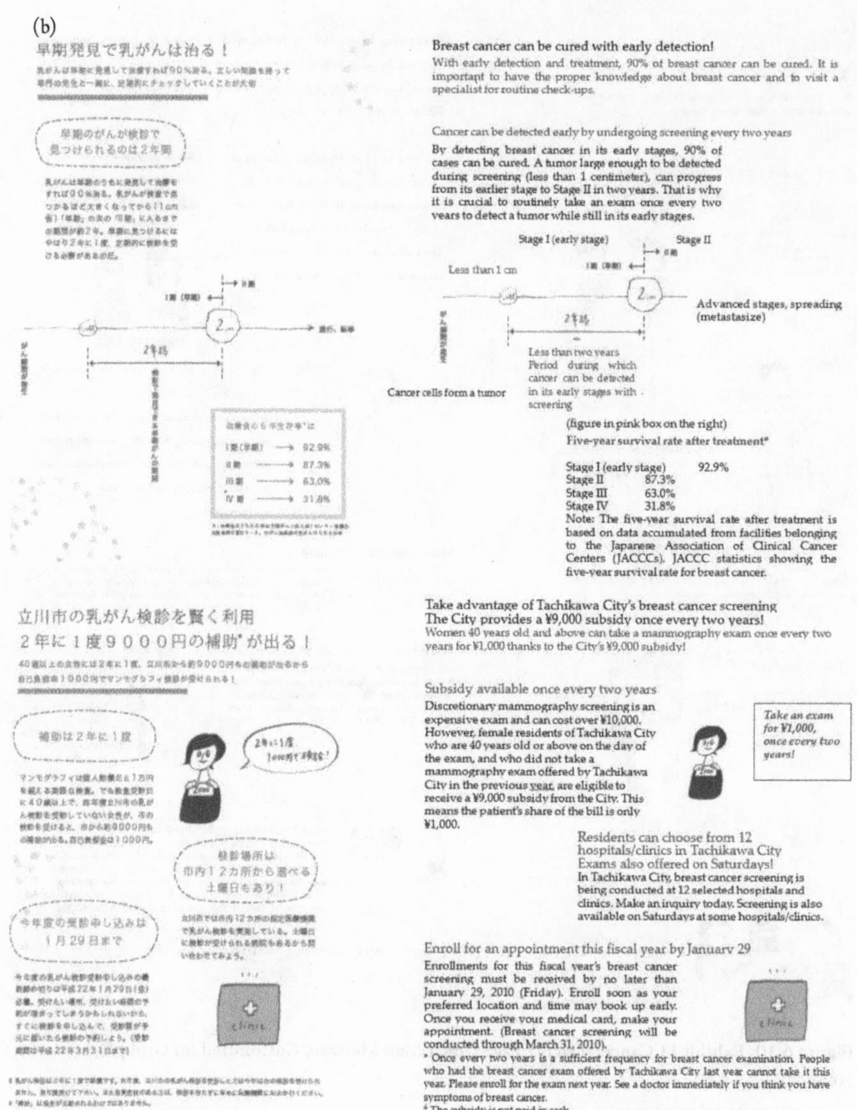

Figure 6.10 Continued

with local municipalities which fielded research studies that were then funded primarily through the National Cancer Center.[74] CancerScan partnered with eight municipalities in 2009, and expanded to thirteen by 2013.[75]

CancerScan was well-known for its cancer screening campaigns and faced no competition within its field in Japan. The only potential threat to CancerScan's business came from advertising agencies, but they were often unable to work within the

[74] Jun Fukuyoshi, "RE: Cancerscan Case Study,"email message to John Quelch, November 8, 2013.

[75] Jun Fukuyoshi, "RE: Cancerscan Case Study,"email message to John Quelch, November 8, 2013.

(c)

Breast cancer screening procedures

1. Apply for your exam

Apply by sending in a postcard or letter containing your personal information. A medical card will be mailed to you.
Applications must be received by no later than January 29, 2010 (Friday)
Please include the following information on a postcard or in a letter. Indicate that you are enrolling to take a mammogram. Print your name (also provide your name in katakana), date of birth, address and telephone number.

Send to: Health Promotion Section, Health Care Hall (Kenko Kaikan)
3-22-9 Takamatsu-cho, Tachikawa City Tokyo 190-0011

You do not need to enroll for screening if you already have your medical card and coupon for FY2009. People who had a mammogram in the previous year are not eligible for screening this year.

2. Select a hospital or clinic and make an appointment by phone

Once you receive your medical card, call and schedule an appointment at your preferred hospital/clinic from among those listed (see the list of selected hospitals and clinics included with your medical card).

3. Take the exam

Medical interview	The doctor will ask you questions, such as the symptoms you may be experiencing
Physical exam	The doctor will look and feel for lumps
Mammography	X-rays will be taken of your breasts
Guidance on breast self-examination	The doctor will explain and provide instruction on self-examination

4. Get your exam results

Go back to the hospital/clinic where you had your mammogram to get your results

Health Promotion Section, Welfare and Health Department, Tachikawa City
Health Care Hall (Kenko Kaikan) 3-22-9 Takamatsu-cho, Tachikawa City Tokyo 190-0011
Tel:042-527-3727 Fax: 042-521-0422

Let's go for a mammography exam!

Get a mammogram once you turn 40

State-of-the-art imaging method that can detect tumors that cannot be discovered with self-examination

Health Promotion Section, Welfare and Health Department, Tachikawa City

Figure 6.10 Continued

budgets of local governments, and they tended to offer strong advertising copy concepts but few consumer insights derived from research.[76] Cancer-related projects accounted for 60% of CancerScan's revenue in 2013. The remainder was composed of nursing-related projects, health check-ups, suicide prevention and non-health care related consulting.[77] The company's revenue growth had been steady at 10% per year for the prior three years. But increasing CancerScan's growth rate was a key focus of Jun and Yoshiki's strategy meeting.

[76] Jun Fukuyoshi, "RE: Cancerscan Case Study,"email message to John Quelch, November 8, 2013.
[77] Jun Fukuyoshi, "RE: Cancerscan Case Study,"email message to John Quelch, November 8, 2013.

がんの知識

乳がん

平成21年度

近年の日本では、2人に1人はがんになり3人に1人はがんで亡くなっています

乳がんは40代女性のがん死亡率第1位

立川市 福祉保健部 健康推進課

Cancer knowledge

Breast cancer

2009

In recent years, in Japan, one-in-two people will get cancer

One-in-three people die of cancer

Breast cancer is the leading cause of cancer death among women in their 40s

Health Promotion Section, Welfare and Health Department, Tachikawa City

"40代女性のがん" 乳がんの実態

40代の日本人女性に急速に広がる乳がん

40代の日本人女性における乳がんの致死性

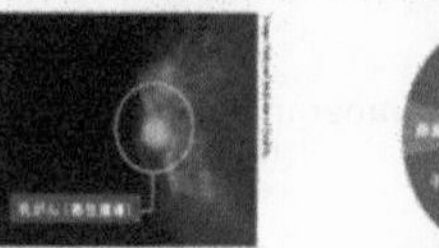

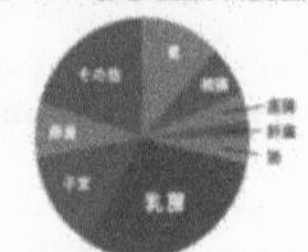

Cancer in women in their 40s" Breast cancer trends

Sharp increase in the incidence of breast cancer among Japanese women in their 40s

The frequency of breast cancer in Japanese women has risen sharply in the past decade or so. Today, the incidence of breast cancer has escalated to the point where it is believed one out of two Japanese women' will get the disease. Moreover, breast cancer is most frequent in women in their 40s. It is the most common type of cancer in women in their 40s.

Figure 1. Mammogram (breast x-ray)

Breast cancer (malignant tumor)

(b) **Breast cancer mortality among Japanese women in their 40s**

Breast cancer is alarming not only due to its onset at a young age. The most concerning aspect is that the mortality rate is the same as in other cancer patients. Since 2000, breast cancer has been the leading cause of cancer death in women in their 40s. Nearly 10,000 women a year lose their lives to breast cancer.

Figure 2. Cancer deaths by type in women 40-44 years old

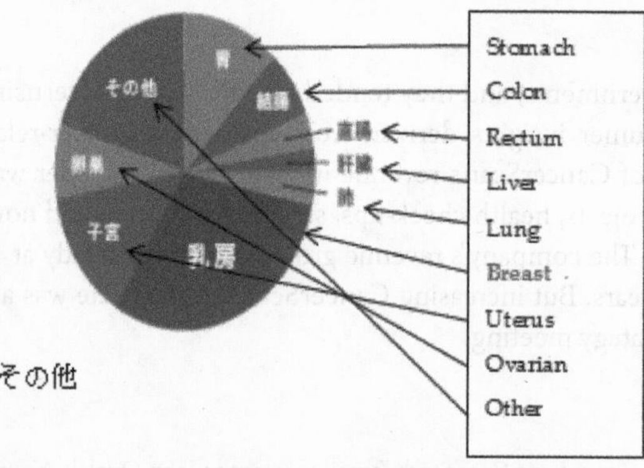

その他

Figure 6.11 Exhibit 12 CancerScan Six Page Direct Mail Message, Customized for Group C, 2009-2010.
Source: Company documents.

(c)

「自覚症状が出てから」では手遅れ

立川市から約9000円の助成

検査費用	約10000円
助成金	ー約9000円
自己負担額	1000円

Too late after you "begin feeling symptoms"

The earlier breast cancer is detected, the better chance you have of beating it. However, it is difficult to detect breast cancer in its early stages with self examination, unless you are a medical practitioner with special training. Mammography screening is essential for women, so that they do not miss the opportunity to detect cancer early, before it has spread to other parts of the body.

Five-year survival rate after treatment*

Stage I (early stage)	Stage II	Stage III	Stage IV
92.9%	87.3%	63.0%	31.8%

Note: The five-year survival rate after treatment is based on data accumulated from facilities belonging to the Japanese Association of Clinical Cancer Centers (JACCCs). JACCCs statistics showing the five-year survival rate for breast cancer.

(page 2, left page, bottom right half of the page)

Tachikawa City offers a subsidy of about ¥9,000

Discretionary mammography screening is an expensive exam and can cost over ¥10,000. However, female residents of Tachikawa City who are 40 years old or above on the day of the exam, and who did not take a mammography exam offered by Tachikawa City in the previous year, are eligible to receive a ¥9,000 subsidy from the City. This means the patient's share of the bill is only ¥1,000.

Exam fee	Approx.	¥10,000
Subsidy	Approx.	¥9,000
Patient cost		¥1,000

*The subsidy is not paid in cash.

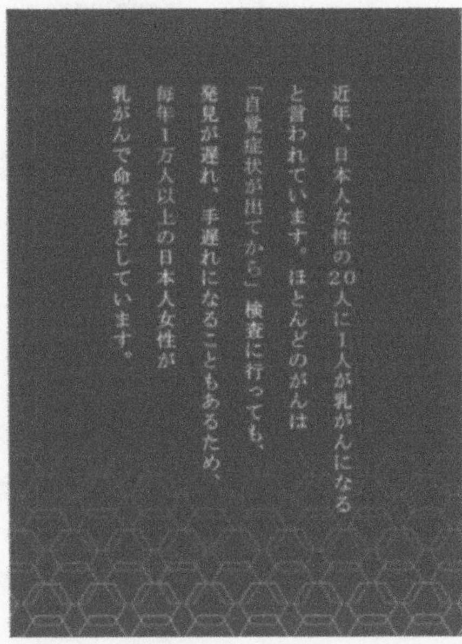

近年、日本人女性の20人に1人が乳がんになる
と言われています。ほとんどのがんは
「自覚症状が出てから」検査に行っても、
発見が遅れ、手遅れになることもあるため、
毎年1万人以上の日本人女性が
乳がんで命を落としています。

In recent years, it is said that one out of every twenty Japanese women develop breast cancer. For most cancers, late detection as a result of waiting to get tested after experiencing symptoms, can result in death. Consequently, more than 10,000 women a year lose their lives to breast cancer in Japan.

Figure 6.11 Continued

Growth Potential in Breast Cancer

The Cancer Control Act's screening goal of 50% had not been met by 2012 (the observed screening rate was closer to 30% across all cancers). The incidence of breast cancer screening was better than those of other cancers, but there was still opportunity to improve. Breast cancer benefited from high awareness in Japan, due in part to the efforts of NGOs, volunteers and merchants under the "Pink Ribbon" awareness campaign. (See Figure 6.12 for the breast cancer awareness campaign which lit the Tokyo Tower in pink for breast cancer awareness month in October). Although Japan had about 1,700 municipalities which could conduct independent campaigns, CancerScan's marketing director, Akio Yonekura (HBS '13) suggested that the

(d)

乳がん検診について

乳がん検診受診の流れ

1. 検診を申し込む

2. 予約の電話

3. 検査当日

4. 結果について

立川市

Breast cancer screening

Tachikawa City recommends that all female residents over 40 get examined

Breast cancer screening procedures

1. Apply for your mammography screening

Apply by sending in a postcard or letter containing your personal information. A medical card will be mailed to your home.

Applications must be received by no later than January 29, 2010 (Friday)

Please include the following information on a postcard or in a letter. Indicate that you are enrolling to take a mammogram. Print your name (also provide your name in katakana), date of birth, address and telephone number.

Send to: Health Promotion Section
Health Care Hall (Kenko Kaikan)
3-22-9 Takamatsu-cho, Tachikawa City, Tokyo 190-0011

*You do not need to apply for screening if you already have your medical card and coupon for this year.

*A breast cancer exam should be taken once every two years. People who took the breast cancer exam offered by Tachikawa City in the previous year cannot take it this year.

2. Make an appointment by phone

Once you receive your medical card, call and schedule an appointment at the selected hospital/clinic of your choice (**see the list of selected hospitals and clinics included with your medical card**).

3. Exam day

Details of the exam

Medical interview The doctor will ask you questions, such as the symptoms you may be experiencing

Physical exam The doctor will look and feel for lumps

Mammography X-rays will be taken of your breasts

Guidance on breast self-examination The doctor will explain and provide instruction on self-examination

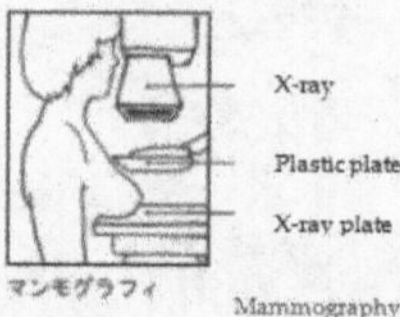

Mammography

4. Get your exam results

Go back to the hospital/clinic where you had your mammogram to get your results

Tachikawa City

Health Promotion Section, Welfare and Health Department, Tachikawa City
Health Care Hall (Kenko Kaikan)
3-22-9 Takamatsu-cho, Tachikawa City
Tokyo 190-0011
Tel: (042) 527-3272 Fax: (042) 521-0422

Figure 6.11 Continued

company shift its focus to consumers rather than municipalities, in order to change the behavior of more people more rapidly.

Opportunities in Other Cancers

CancerScan could extend its marketing research skills to other cancers. Stomach cancer, lung cancer and colon cancer killed more Japanese women than breast cancer, and these cancers also posed a significant health risk to Japanese men. (See Table 6.2 for

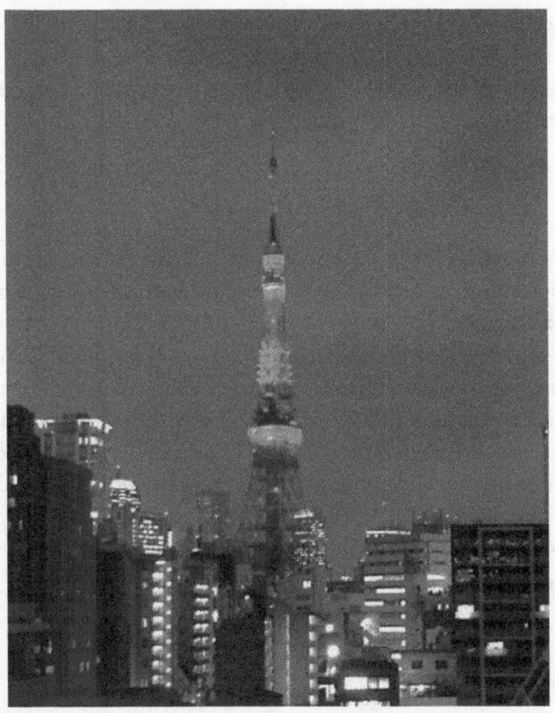

Figure 6.12 Exhibit 13 Pink Ribbon Breast Cancer Awareness Campaign: Tokyo Tower, 2007.
Source: jonny-mt, "Tokyo Tower lit up for Breast Cancer Awareness Month. Taken on October 1, 2007," Wikimedia Commons, http://commons.wikimedia.org/wiki/File:Tokyotowerpink.jpg, Accessed February 2014.

Table 6.2 Exhibit 14 Cancer Incidence and Death Rate in Japan by Gender, 2007–2011[a]

Rank by incidence	*Highest incidence among men*	*Incidence among men, per 100,000*	*Deaths among men, per 100,000*	*Highest incidence among women*	*Incidence among women, per 100,000*	*Deaths among women, per 100,000*
1	Stomach	128.7	53.3	Breast	93.2	19.7
2	Lung	104.7	82.6	Stomach	56.7	26.3
3	Prostate	75.9	17.6	Colon	49.8	24.1
4	Colon	61.9	25.2	Lung	43.0	30.1
5	Liver	48.5	34.1	Uterus	42.5	9.4

[a]Incidence data was gathered in 2007 by the Center for Cancer Control and Information Services, National Cancer Center. Mortality rate data was gathered by the same organization in 2011. Numbers for incidence rates in 2011was not available.

Source: Compiled from Center for Cancer Control and Information Services, "Cancer Statistics in Japan '12," National Cancer Center, January 15, 2013. http://ganjoho.jp/pro/statistics/en/backnumber/2012_en.html Accessed October 2013. pp. 62–65, pp. 70–73.

cancer incidence and mortality among Japanese men and women). The other cancers did not enjoy the same level of awareness in Japan as breast cancer. It was unclear whether CancerScan's segmentation approach to breast cancer screening would be applicable to other cancers.

Other Public Health Campaigns

CancerScan could also address other public health issues. The company had previously developed campaigns to help prevent suicide and to encourage blood donation in Japan. CancerScan's behavioral research methods could be applied to issues like suicide, to deter a one-time act, but also to issues like smoking cessation with the aim of achieving sustainable changes in habits. The Japanese government planned to devote increasing budget resources to efforts to combat obesity, smoking and other lifestyle threats to public health. CancerScan's method of communicating with consumers and tracking results would likely need to be adjusted to reflect the desired sustainability of behavior change interventions. Jun questioned whether expanding CancerScan's scope to address broader public health issues might unrealistically move the company away from its core competency in cancer screening.

7A

"DUMB WAYS TO DIE" ADVERTISING TRAIN SAFETY (A)

John A. Quelch

Metro Trains Melbourne (MT) was increasingly concerned about the number of passenger-related accidents on and around its train platforms. Foolhardy behaviors included daredevil teenagers sprinting over tracks as trains approached and impatient drivers circumventing level crossing gates after they were already down. In 2011, 6 pedestrians and 11 vehicles were reportedly hit at level crossings, resulting in two and three deaths, respectively.[1] Serious incidents involving train operations in the state of Victoria (of which Melbourne was the capital) totaled 21 in 2008, 24 in both 2009 and 2010, and 27 in 2011.[2]

MT was the for-profit, licensed operator of the passenger rail system in the Melbourne metropolitan area. MT employed around 4,000 staff and moved more than 400,000 customers daily through 218 stations. MT trains traveled 5.4 million kilometers every three months over approximately 800 kilometers of track with 177 level crossings.[3]

Traditional public service ads focusing on deaths and maiming caused by such behaviors, together with instructions delivered over station loudspeakers to stand back from the platform edge, did not seem to have an impact on the statistics. MT therefore turned to the McCann advertising agency to help develop a new style of public service campaign focused on train safety that could reach a young, skeptical audience.[4] The media budget for the campaign was limited to around $200,000.[5]

[1] Adam Carey, "Black Humour Latest Weapon in Railway Safety," *The Age*, November 17, 2012, http://newsstore.theage.com.au/apps/viewDocument.ac?page=1&sy=age&kw=adam+carey&pb=age&dt=selectRange&dr=1year&so=relevance&sf=text&sf=author&rc=100&rm=200&sp=nrm&clsPage=1&docID=AGE121117BSF207D2KS9, accessed August 2013.

[2] 2012 Annual incident statistics, Victoria Train Operators, published by Transport Safety Victoria. Includes Melbourne Trains and other operators.

[3] Metro Trains, "Who We Are," http://www.metrotrains.com.au/who-we-are/, accessed August 2013.

[4] Rowan Dean, "Ad Awards and Adoration to Die For," *Australian Financial Review*, June 24, 2013, http://afr.com/p/business/marketing_ad-awards-and-adoration-to-die-for, accessed August 2013.

[5] In 2012, the advertising cost per thousand impressions for online media sites in Australia was around $20.

John Mescall, Executive Creative Director, McCann Australia, described the brief given to the agency:

> The brief was to make something invisible visible. . . . Metro had a problem that there were accidents and deaths on the system due to unthinking carelessness. . . . No one was thinking that being careless around trains could actually get you hurt. Our brief was to talk to a broad cross-section but mostly young people to put the idea of rail safety on the agenda for them, to make it part of their discussion. . . . The brief was to try and do something that would actually work for once because nothing that had ever been done [before] worked.[6]

[6] Presentation at Cannes 2013, http://mumbrella.com.au/pre-roll-video-cpms-experience-surge-in-price-146798.

7B

"DUMB WAYS TO DIE"
ADVERTISING TRAIN SAFETY (B)

John A. Quelch

After consulting with platform staff and train drivers, John Mescall, executive creative director at McCann Melbourne, wrote the copy for the ad, with animation by Julian Frost. The catchy jingle was written by The Cat Empire keyboardist, Ollie McGill, and performed by Tinpan Orange singer, Emily Lubitz.[1] The ad itemized 18 dumb ways to die (including, for example, "Keep a rattlesnake as pet, Sell both kidneys on the internet"), followed by three train-safety-related messages about not standing on the platform edge, not driving around level crossing boom gates, and not running across train tracks between platforms. The text of the three-minute ad is reproduced in Box 7B.1 and a storyboard of the ad is shown in Figure 7B.1a and 7B.1b.

The accompanying animated video showed egg-shaped, pastel-colored characters being blown up, poisoned, electrocuted, or otherwise killing themselves, all to a cheery and memorable nursery rhyme tune.

Mescall, who described the ad as "dark humor delivered with joy," summarized the purpose of the campaign: "We want to create a lasting understanding that you shouldn't take risks around trains, that the prospect of death or serious injury is ever-present and that we as a community need to be aware of what constitutes both safe and dumb behavior."[2]

The media budget for the campaign was limited to around $200,000. MT could extend the campaign to signage on its trains and at its stations where the tune was played without lyrics on station platforms. Some advertising time was purchased in cinemas showing youth-oriented movies. But a major objective was to attract free public relations coverage in traditional and social media. The agency tried to increase shareability by creating clips from the video and sharing them via Tumblr. Apart from uploading the "Dumb Ways to Die" public service announcement on YouTube on November 14, 2013 writing the first comment, and providing links to buy the song

[1] Barbara Lippert, "'Dumb Ways To Die' Is Charmingly Gruesome," MediaPost.com, June 2013, http://www.mediapost.com, accessed September 2013.

[2] Lucinda Beaman, "Stupidity Goes Viral as it Finds an Audience to Die For," *The Times* (London), December 1, 2012, http://www.thetimes.co.uk/tto/news/world/australia-newzealand/article3616388.ece, accessed August 2013.

Box 7B.1 Exhibit 1"Dumb Ways to Die" Lyrics

Set fire to your hair
Poke a stick at a grizzly bear
Eat medicine that's out of date
Use your private parts as piranha bait

Dumb ways to die
So many dumb ways to die
Dumb ways to die
So many dumb ways to die

Get your toast out with a fork
Do your own electrical work
Teach yourself how to fly
Eat a two week old unrefrigerated pie

Dumb ways to die
So many dumb ways to die
Dumb ways to die
So many dumb ways to die

Invite a psycho-killer inside
Scratch a drug dealer's brand new ride
Take your helmet off in outer space
Use your clothes dryer as a hiding place

Dumb ways to die
So many dumb ways to die
Dumb ways to die
Keep a rattlesnake as pet
Sell both the kidneys on the internet
Eat a tube of super-glue
"I wonder what's this red button do?"

Dumb ways to die
So many dumb ways to die
Dumb ways to die
So many dumb ways to die

Dress up like a moose during hunting season
Disturb a nest of wasps for no good reason
Stand on the edge of a train station platform

Drive around the boom gates at a level crossing
Run across the tracks between the platforms
They may not rhyme but they're quite possibly

Dumbest ways to die
Dumbest ways to die
Dumbest ways to die
So many dumb
So many dumb ways to die

SPOKEN: [Be safe around trains. A message from Metro]
So many dumb ways to die

vocalist: Emily Lubitz, from the band Tinpan Orange.
music: Ollie McGill, from the band the Cat Empire.

Source: http://www.anysonglyrics.com/lyrics/t/Tangerine-Kitty/Dumb-Ways-To-Die.htm, September 16, 2013.

on iTunes, agency personnel did not give media interviews or try to promote the campaign in any way.[3]

The video was soon posted on the Internet humor site 9gag, where it obtained over 37,000 Facebook shares and 27,000 up votes within 10 days. The song quickly reached the top 10 on iTunes and sold 10,000 copies within three weeks on Nielsen SoundScan. By early December, the video spawned at least 80 cover versions (including classic rock), 90 parodies, and 30 million YouTube hits.[4] Samples of the parodies are presented in Figure 7B.2. MT launched a karaoke version of the song.

Leah Waymark, MT's general manager for corporate relations, commented: "To have young people singing about safety around trains is just a terrific outcome for us.

[3] McCann Australia, "All Work," http://www.mccann.com.au/project/dumb-ways-to-die, accessed August 2013.

[4] Nancy Szokan and M. Fard, "Video on 'Dumb Ways to Die' Attracts Millions of Online Viewers," *Washington Post*, December 4, 2012, http://www.washingtonpost.com/national/health-science/video-on-dumb-ways-to-die-attracts-millions-of-online-viewers/2012/12/03/a1fbb290-6964-11e1-acc6-32fefc7ccd67_story.html, accessed August 2013.

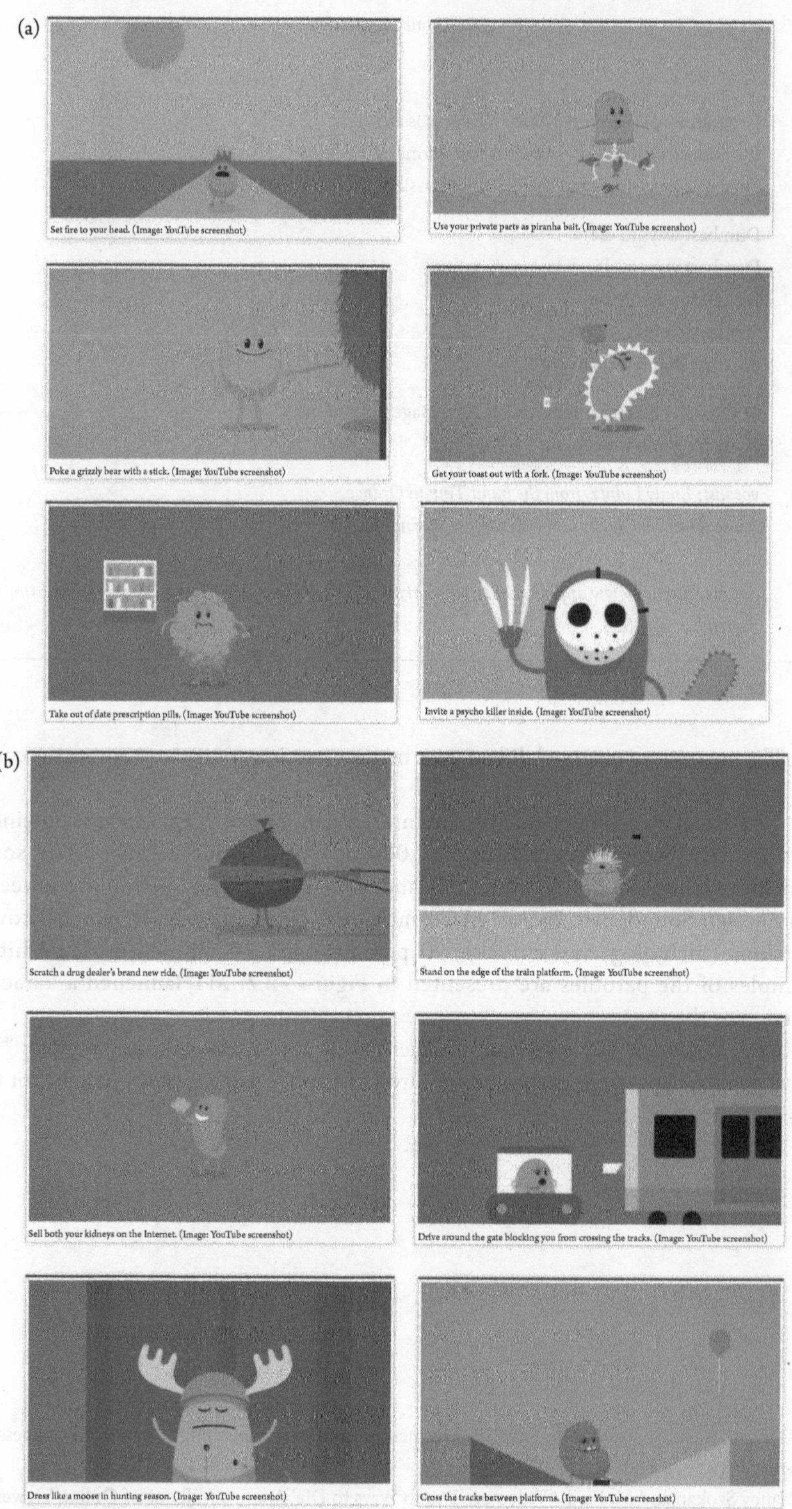

(a)
Set fire to your head. (Image: YouTube screenshot)
Use your private parts as piranha bait. (Image: YouTube screenshot)
Poke a grizzly bear with a stick. (Image: YouTube screenshot)
Get your toast out with a fork. (Image: YouTube screenshot)
Take out of date prescription pills. (Image: YouTube screenshot)
Invite a psycho killer inside. (Image: YouTube screenshot)
(b)
Scratch a drug dealer's brand new ride. (Image: YouTube screenshot)
Stand on the edge of the train platform. (Image: YouTube screenshot)
Sell both your kidneys on the Internet. (Image: YouTube screenshot)
Drive around the gate blocking you from crossing the tracks. (Image: YouTube screenshot)
Dress like a moose in hunting season. (Image: YouTube screenshot)
Cross the tracks between platforms. (Image: YouTube screenshot)

Figure 7B.1 a and 1b Exhibit 2 Storyboard for "Dumb Ways to Die".
Source: Illustrations excerpted from Liz Klimas, *The Blaze*, http://www.theblaze.com/stories/2012/11/21/this-is-the-viral-australian-dumb-ways-to-die-psa-that-glenn-beck-loves-and-will-be-stuck-in-your-head-all-day/, accessed August 2013.

The Walking Dead + Dumb Ways
Dumb Ways to Die
Uploaded by WarPig

Dumb Ways To Die Parody: Dumb...
Dumb Ways to Die
Uploaded by Alex Mercer

[♪] Portal - Dumb Ways To Die
Dumb Ways to Die
Uploaded by BongDong DingDong

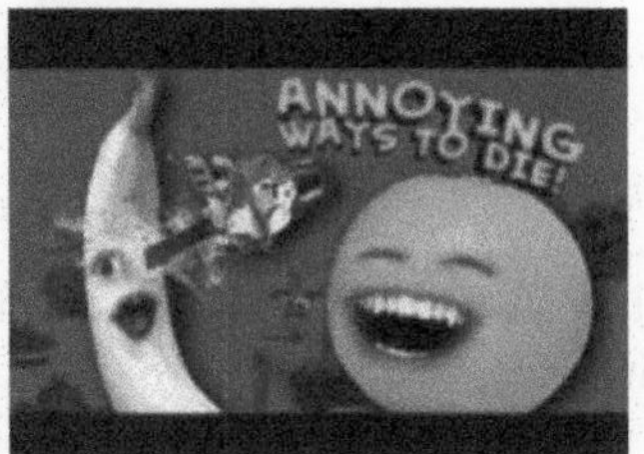

Annoying Orange - Annoying Wa..
Dumb Ways to Die
Uploaded by ♔Leonidas Da King♚

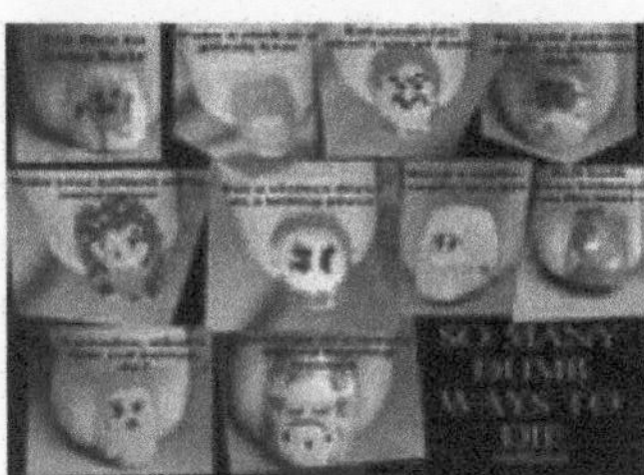

Dumb Ways to Die
Uploaded by Don

Figure 7B.2 Exhibit 3 "Dumb Ways to Die" Parody Samples.
Source: Illustrations excerpted from http://knowyourmeme.com/memes/dumb-ways-to-die, accessed August 2013.

Some people might have an issue of us making light of a serious topic, but if we can save one life or avoid serious injury, that's how we'll measure success."[5]

By December, Mescall concluded: "It's entered popular culture."[6]

[5] "Safety ads a global hit," *TheAge*, June20, 2013, http://newsstore.theage.com.au/apps/viewDocument.ac?page=1&sy=age&kw=dumb+w+to+die&pb=age&dt=selectRange&dr=6months&so=relevance&sf=text&sf=author&rc=100&rm=200&sp=nrm&clsPage=1&docID=AGE1306206-F7ML7VO74F, accessed August 2013.

[6] Asher Moses, "Safety Video Goes Viral, Not Bad for a Dumb Idea," *Sydney Morning Herald*, November 30, 2012.

7C

"DUMB WAYS TO DIE"

ADVERTISING TRAIN SAFETY (C)

John A. Quelch

The "Dumb Ways to Die" (DWTD) campaign stole the show at the June 2013 Cannes Lions festival, international advertising's annual awards event. DWTD captured a record five Cannes Grand Prix.[1]

David Gallagher, chair of the Cannes Public Relations Lions awards jury, stated: "The content was based on real human insight—it was fun, engaging and immensely shareable. And it led to a 21% reduction in serious train accidents, so it was very effective."[2]

John Mescall, executive creative director at McCann and the copywriter on DWTD, commented: "We could have shown documentary film in which people get hit by trains, but we were going for entertainment rather than shock value. . . . We didn't preach, we didn't threaten, we didn't lecture. . . . We wanted to engage a young audience who are wired to resist lectures and warnings from authorities, but would share recommendations peer-to-peer. It allows you to call out your friends without losing your cred."[3]

Speaking at Cannes, Mescall said: "When you're trying to achieve behavioral change in a world of blunt instruments, it's far more effective to bring people along than hit them with your message. . . . Rather than repel young people who didn't want to hear a message about train safety, DWTD made it socially acceptable to discuss something as boring as being safe around trains."[4]

DWTD was extended across the full range of media. There was even a DWTD mobile phone app in which players had to prevent characters from dying a gruesome

[1] Official campaign site, http://dumbwaystodie.com/, accessed August 2013.

[2] Bruce Kennedy, "Why 'Dumb Ways to Die' Became A Viral Hit," What's Trending on Money (blog), MSN.com, June 18, 2013, http://money.msn.com/now/blog--why-dumb-ways-to-die became-a viral-hit, accessed August 2013.

[3] Barbara Lippert, "'Dumb Ways To Die' Is Charmingly Gruesome," MediaPost.com, June 2013, http://www.mediapost.com, accessed September 2013.

[4] Darren Davidson, "A Not So Dumb Way to Sell Rail Safety Acclaimed," *The Australian*, June 20, 2013, http://www.theaustralian.com.au/media/a-not-so-dumb-way-to-sell-rail-safety-acclaimed/story-e6frg996-1226666544520#, accessed August 2013.

death. Supermodel Kate Moss revealed in an interview that this was her favorite phone app. "It is totally addictive," she said.[5] The game climbed to number one in 17 countries. The app also invited players to pledge "not to do dumb stuff around trains."[6]

Between November 2012 and July 2013, the DWTD public service announcement was viewed 57 million times and garnered 3.8 Facebook shares, making it the most-shared PSA in history.[7] Eight months after launch, DWTD was still the fourth most-shared ad of the month. One million online pledges were received.[8] Commentators estimated the value of free media coverage—including stories about the ad—at $60 million.[9] The song charted in 28 countries.[10]

Commenting on the low budget campaign's effectiveness, Mescall stated: "You don't need a lot of money to do something outstanding. . . . It gives heart to marketers everywhere."[11]

Metro Trains reported a 30% reduction in near-miss accidents, from 13.29 near-misses per million kilometers traveled from November 2011 to January 2012, to 9.17 near-misses per million kilometers traveled from November 2012 to January 2013.[12]

[5] Annette Sharp et al., "Sydney Confidential," *Daily Telegraph* (Australia), July 22, 2013, http://www.dailytelegraph.com.au/entertainment/sydney-confidential/kate-moss-reveals-favourite-phone-app-is-aussie-train-safety-campaign-dumb-ways-to-die/story-fni0cvc9-1226682740289, accessed August 2013.

[6] McCann Australia, "Transformation," http://www.mccann.com.au/project/dumb-ways-to-die, accessed August 2013.

[7] Lippert, " 'Dumb Ways To Die' Is Charmingly Gruesome."

[8] Shawn Amos, "WATCH: Content Shines at Cannes," *Huffington Post*, http://www.huffingtonpost.com/shawn-amos/watch-content-shines-at c_b_3484442, accessed August 2013.

[9] Darren Davidson, "Safety Ad Puts McCann on Track," *The Australian*, June 24, 2013, http://www.theaustralian.com.au/media/train-ad-puts-mccann-on-track/story-e6frg996-1226668433366#, accessed August 2013.

[10] Asher Moses, "Safety Video Goes Viral, Not Bad for a Dumb Idea," *Sydney Morning Herald*, November 30, 2012.

[11] Davidson, "A Not So Dumb Way to Sell Rail Safety Acclaimed."

[12] Stephen Cauchi, "No dumb luck: Metro claims safety success," *The Age*, February 14, 2013, http://www.theage.com.au/victoria/no-dumb-luck-metro-claims-safety-success-20130214-2eelt.html

8

CVS HEALTH
PROMOTING DRUG ADHERENCE

Leslie K. John, John A. Quelch, and Robert Huckman

"Drugs don't work in people who don't take them."
C. Everett Koop, *Former U.S. Surgeon General.*

In July 2013, Helena Foulkes, Executive Vice President, Health Care Strategy and Marketing for CVS Health (CVS), relaxed in her office on the secluded, wooded campus of the company's Woonsocket, Rhode Island headquarters as she reviewed her copy of an internal report on helping patients better adhere to their medication regimens. The report, whose lead author was CVS Health's Chief Medical Officer, Dr. Troyen Brennan, highlighted the state of the art in the science of pharmacy care and noted its potential to help patients with chronic health conditions. As she flipped through the report, her eyes were drawn to a page highlighting the cost savings of increased medication adherence. She was excited by the potential for CVS Health to improve its own performance while simultaneously increasing benefits for the company's customers. Foulkes understood that given the unique structure of CVS Health—operating both a retail pharmacy and a pharmacy benefit manager (PBM)—the company's leaders constantly had to balance helping PBM clients save on their pharmacy spend while providing plan members with access to cost-effective medications and improved health outcomes.

Foulkes was preparing for a meeting with CVS Health CEO Larry J. Merlo, during which she was to make the case for a significant marketing spend for each of the next three years to further develop CVS Health's Pharmacy Advisor Program—an initiative aimed at using the latest in pharmacy science to boost medication adherence. The results of the pilot for the Pharmacy Advisor Program had just come in; Foulkes would use these results to request funding for further development of the program. She sought to expand its focus to a chronic condition such as diabetes, high cholesterol, or depression. The significance of the program's development was not lost on Foulkes—she knew that achieving promising results would be essential for its widespread roll out. The new iteration of the program would be launched through CVS' PBM channel due to its strategic importance to the company.

In making her pitch to Merlo, Foulkes would, first and foremost, have to justify the value of investing in adherence. Although she was excited by the results of the first

Figure 8.1 Exhibit 1 The First CVS Retail Store.
Source: Company documents.

Pharmacy Advisor Program pilot, she realized that, in a company where a significant majority of the annual marketing budget was allocated to traditional promotions such as weekly circulars[1], making the case for continued and increased investment in this new program could be challenging. How would she show that investing in adherence would have a noticeable and positive impact on CVS Health's profitability?

CVS HEALTH BACKGROUND

The company had its roots in retail pharmacy and was originally known as Consumer Value Stores. The first CVS retail store was founded in 1963 in Lowell, Massachusetts (Figure 8.1). Within one year, the chain had grown to 17 stores. In 1967 pharmacies were added to the retail stores and by 2014 there were more than 7,800 CVS/pharmacy retail stores across the United States.

In 2007 CVS Corporation, the parent company of CVS/pharmacy, merged with Caremark Rx, Inc., a PBM. The resulting company had two primary channels: retail pharmacy and PBM (described below). The merged company's mission was to help "people on their path to better health."[2] The company's core values were innovation, collaboration, caring, integrity, and accountability (Figure 8.2).

[1] Weekly circulars were flyers that were disseminated widely and highlighted a store's promotions for the given week.

[2] CVS Health, "Company History," http://www.cvshealth.com/about-us/our-story/company-history.

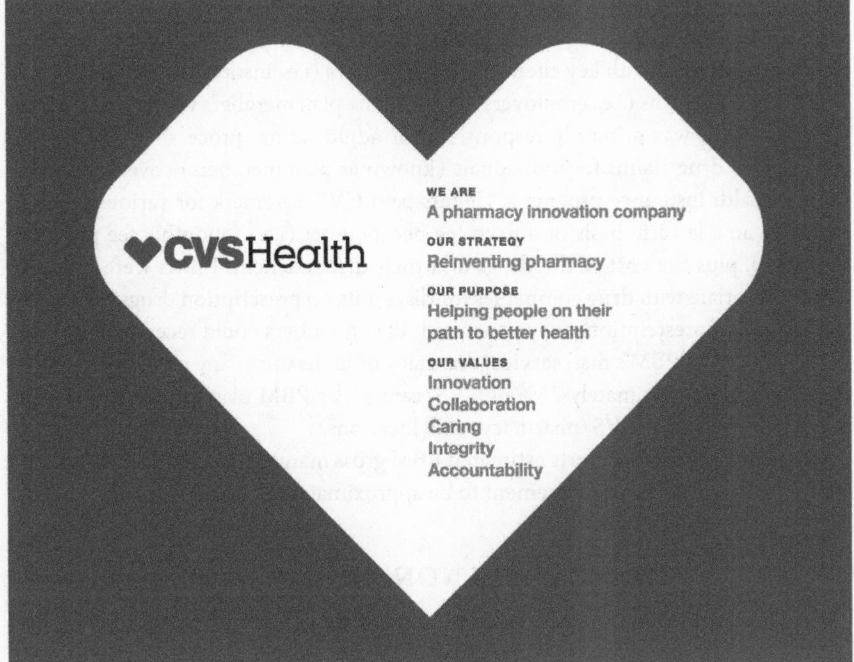

CVSHealth
WE ARE
A pharmacy innovation company
OUR STRATEGY
Reinventing pharmacy
OUR PURPOSE
Helping people on their path to better health
OUR VALUES
Innovation
Collaboration
Caring
Integrity
Accountability

Figure 8.2 Exhibit 2 CVS Health's Mission and Core Values.
Source: http://info.cvshealth.com/about-us/our-purpose-building-bridge-better-health.

Retail Business

Within retail, sales were divided into "front-store sales" and "pharmacy sales." The former included sales of products that did not require a prescription, ranging from over-the-counter (OTC) allergy medication to potato chips. Approximately 60% of CVS/pharmacy retail channel customers were almost exclusively front-store sales customers. Around five percent of retail channel customers came to CVS/pharmacy primarily to get their prescriptions filled. The remaining 35% of retail channel customers made purchases from both the front store and the pharmacy.

Each pharmacy filled an average of 1,900 prescriptions per week, about half of which were new prescriptions. In recent years, the pharmacies had seen an increase in the use of electronic prescriptions, or e-prescriptions, whereby a prescription was sent directly and electronically from a physician's office to the pharmacy. By 2014 about half of all CVS/pharmacy prescriptions were e-prescriptions, which was believed to be similar to that of its major competitors.

Drug revenues and margins varied widely depending on whether generic alternatives for a given product were available. Generic drug revenues were lower than those of brand-name drugs, but this was typically offset by their dramatically higher gross margins.

Pharmacy Benefit Management (PBM) Business

Through its PBM business known as CVS/caremark, CVS Health served as the administrator of the prescription drug benefit within larger health insurance plans.

Integration of the retail pharmacy and PBM businesses was seen as a promising way to improve prescription drug access, quality, user satisfaction and efficiency. The PBM business contracted with key clients including payers (i.e., insurers who hired CVS as a PBM) and the firms (i.e., employers) at which the plan members worked. As a PBM, CVS/caremark was primarily responsible for adjudicating, processing, and paying prescription drug claims for individuals (known as plan members) covered by their clients' health insurance programs. Clients paid CVS/caremark for various services either on an a la carte basis or a fixed fee per member (i.e., a monthly fee per "covered life"), plus the cost of the drugs and their disbursement. PBMs were typically able to negotiate with drug companies for discounts on prescription drugs because of the volume of prescriptions they generated. Plan members could receive their drugs directly from the PBM's mail service pharmacy or in person at any retail pharmacy in the network. Approximately 25% of CVS/caremark's PBM plan members had their prescriptions filled at CVS/pharmacy retail locations.

In general, industry experts estimated PBM gross margins on clients' payments for generic drugs and their disbursement to be approximately 30%.[3]

MEDICATION NON-ADHERENCE

Despite widespread evidence of the clinical effectiveness of medications for the treatment of chronic conditions, an alarming number of patients failed to adhere to their medication regimens. Some failed to take their medications altogether. Others strayed from the regimens prescribed by their physicians in more subtle ways. Up to 30% of patients prescribed medications for newly diagnosed illnesses failed to fill their initial prescription (known as "primary non-adherence"), although this figure was notably lower—around 10%—for e-prescriptions.[4] Among those who had picked up their first prescription of a drug, half stopped taking their prescribed medications within a year of starting therapy (known as "secondary non-adherence"). The vast majority of secondary non-adherent patients stopped taking their medicines between their first and second prescription fills. Secondary non-adherence also increased when patients with chronic conditions failed to call or visit their doctor to obtain additional refills when their initially prescribed number of refills had been exhausted.

Medication non-adherence was often measured by the medication possession ratio (MPR). The MPR was the ratio of the *total* days that a patient had a drug available to the number of *possible* days the patient could have had the drug on hand based on his or her prescription dosage. Foulkes explained, "The MPR measures the proportion of time that a patient has access to his medication. For example, take the case of a patient whose dosage is one pill per day. If he has five pills on hand but isn't planning on going in to get a refill for another 10 days, then his MPR is 0.50. As another example, a patient who has a medication supply for 255 days in a given year would have an MPR of 0.70—that is, 255 days of possession divided by a total possible 365 days. Patients with an MPR of .80 or higher are considered optimally adherent." See Table 8.1 for examples.

[3] Fein, A.J., Drug Channels, http://www.drugchannels.net/

[4] E-prescriptions were sent directly, electronically, from the physician's office to the pharmacy.

Table 8.1 Industry experts' estimates of the percent of those currently medicated for the given ailment who are optimally adherent (i.e., have an MPR of .80 or higher)*

Ailment	*Cholesterol*	*Diabetes*	*Depression*
Percent optimally adherent	46%	65%	42%

* Alexander, A. "CVS Caremark study notes lack of adherence to cholesterol-lowering medications," Drug Store News, August 26, 2009, http://www.drugstorenews.com/article/cvs-caremark-study-notes-lack-adherence-cholesterol-lowering-medications; Kleinman, N.L., Schaneman, J.L., Lynch, W.D. (2008). "The association of insuling medication possession ratio, use of insulin glargine, and health benefit costs in employees and spouses with type 2 diabetes," Journal of Occupational and Environmental Medicine, 50(12), PubMed, http://www.ncbi.nlm.nih.gov/pubmed/19092494; Lee, W.C., Balu, S., Cobden, D., Joshi, A.V., Pashos, C.L. (2006). "Medication adherence and the associated health-economic impact among patients with type 2 diabetes mellitus converting to insulin pen therapy: an analysis of third-party managed care claims data," Clinical Therapeutics, 28(10), PubMed, http://www.ncbi.nlm.nih.gov/pubmed/17157128; Prukkanone, B., Vos, T., Burgess, P., Chaiyakunapruk, N., Bertram, M. (2010). "Adherence to antidepressant therapy for major depressive patients in a psychiatric hospital in Thailand," BMC Psychiatry, 10(64), BioMed Central, http://www.biomedcentral.com/1471-244X/10/64; North, F., DeJesus, R., Katzelnick, D. (2014). "EPA-0910—Medication possession ratio among depressed patients enrolled in collaborative care," European Psychiatry, 29(1), Science Direct, http://www.sciencedirect.com/science/article/pii/S0924933814782355

Source: Company Records.

There were many reasons for non-adherence. While some patients simply forgot to take their medications regularly, others—particularly those paying out-of-pocket—found adherence cost-prohibitive and sometimes rationed their medications by splitting pills or skipping doses. Other patients found their drugs' side effects unacceptable, an issue that could sometimes be resolved by altering the dosage or switching to an alternative drug. Psychological reasons for non-adherence were typically more difficult to address and often required intervention by specially trained medical professionals. These psychological factors varied by the type of medication. For example, anger, denial, and even stigma were common for ailments such as diabetes and human immunodeficiency virus (HIV).

Strategies to boost medication adherence generally fell into one of three categories.[5] *Informational* interventions focused on patient education, including the benefits of compliance and risks of non-compliance. *Behavioral* interventions attempted to modify situational factors to make medication compliance "frictionless." A variety of new technologies had been introduced recently, including pill bottles that chimed when a medication was due to be taken (and that did not stop until the bottle was opened). Finally, *complex* interventions typically addressed the systemic barriers to compliance. For example, patients with chronic conditions often took multiple drugs and coordinating refills of those drugs posed a significant barrier to adherence. CVS Health had begun to test a program designed to sync a patient's refills across drugs to allow all of them to be obtained in a single store visit.

[5] Ito, K., Shrank, W.H., Avorn, J., Patrick, A.R., Brennan, T.A., Antman, E.M., Choudry, N. (2007). "Comparative-Cost Effectiveness of Interventions to Improve Medication Adherence after Myocardial Infarction," Health Services Research.

Table 8.2 Exhibit 3 CVS Health Income Statement

In millions, except per share amounts	*2013*	*2012*[4]	*2011*	*2010*	*2009*
	Statement of operations data:				
Net revenues	**$ 126,761**	$ 123,120	$ 107,080	$ 95,766	$ 98,144
Gross profit	**23,783**	22,488	20,562	20,215	20,348
Operating expenses	**15,746**	15,278	14,231	14,082	13,933
Operating profit	**8,037**	7,210	6,331	6,133	6,415
Interest expense, net	**509**	557	584	536	525
Loss on early extinguishment of debt	—	348	—	—	—
Income tax provision[1]	**2,928**	2,436	2,258	2,178	2,196
Income from continuing operations	**4,600**	3,869	3,489	3,419	3,694
Income (loss) from discontinued operations, net of tax[2]	**(8)**	(7)	(31)	2	(4)
Net income	**4,592**	3,862	3,458	3,421	3,690
Net loss attributable to noncontrolling interest[3]	—	2	4	3	—
Net income attributable to CVS Health	**$ 4,592**	$ 3,864	$ 3,462	$ 3,424	$ 3,690
	Per common share data:				
	Basic earnings per common share:				
Income from continuing operations attributable to CVS Health	**$ 3.78**	$ 3.05	$ 2.61	$ 2.50	$ 2.58
Loss from discontinued operations attributable to CVS Heath	**$ (0.01)**	$ (0.01)	$ (0.02)	—	—
Net income attributable to CVS Health	**$ 3.77**	$ 3.04	$ 2.59	$ 2.50	$ 2.57

Table 8.2 Continued

In millions, except per share amounts	*2013*	*2012* [(4)]	*2011*	*2010*	*2009*
		Diluted earnings per common share:			
Income from continuing operations attributable to CVS Health	**$ 3.75**	$ 3.02	$2.59	$ 2.49	$ 2.55
Loss from discontinued operations attributable to CVS Health	**$ (0.01)**	$ (0.01)	$ (0.02)	—	—
Net income attributable to CVS Health	**$ 3.74**	$ 3.02	$ 2.57	$ 2.49	$ 2.55
Cash dividends per common share	**$ 0.900**	$ 0.650	$ 0.500	$ 0.350	$ 0.305
		Balance sheet and other data:			
Total assets	**$ 71,526**	$ 66,221	$ 64,852	$ 62,457	$ 61,919
Long-term debt	**$ 12,841**	$ 9,133	$ 9,208	$ 8,652	$ 8,755
Total shareholders' equity	**$ 37,938**	$ 37,653	$ 38,014	$ 37,662	$ 35,732
Number of stores (at end of year)	**7,702**	7,508	7,388	7,248	7,095

Source: http://investors.cvshealth.com/financial-information/five-year-financial-summary.aspx.

CVS HEALTH RESEARCH ON ADHERENCE

The cost of unnecessary medical treatment to the American health care system resulting from non-adherence was estimated at $290 billion annually[6], largely because of the failure to adhere to medication regimens for chronic diseases including high cholesterol and diabetes. Foulkes noted, "If we find ways to improve patient adherence, we can improve health care quality and lower overall medical costs." She was quick to add that "helping people is smart business for us, too." CVS Health had therefore invested more than $5 million in conducting research resulting in over 40 scientific studies published in prominent, peer-reviewed medical, pharmacy care, and economics journals. The studies' primary goals were to assess the benefit of increasing adherence and test the effectiveness of programs aimed at reducing non-adherence. The Pharmacy Advisor Program was CVS Health's cornerstone in this effort.

[6] New England Health Institute, Thinking Outside the Pillbox: A System-wide Approach to Improving Patient Medication Adherence for Chronic Disease, August 2009.

In a study published in 2011, CVS Health compared the health care utilization of non-adherent and adherent patients.[7] Specifically, CVS Health aimed to determine whether adherent patients' "health care costs are lower because they are adherent, or [whether] they have lower costs and use fewer health care resources because they are simply healthier individuals who make good lifestyle choices (e.g., healthy diet, regular exercise)."[8]

The study focused on quantifying the value of adherence for common chronic conditions including diabetes and high cholesterol—each of which could commonly be controlled with generic medications. High cholesterol occurred when cholesterol, a waxy, fat-like substance, built up on the arterial walls. Like hypertension, it was typically symptomless.[9,10] Diabetes was a disease in which blood glucose levels were chronically above normal. If not controlled by medication such as insulin, it could cause a variety of complications, including heart disease and kidney failure.[11,12] Diabetics typically began to notice adverse symptoms such as headaches and blurred vision rapidly after missing a dose of insulin. Depression was characterized by consistent and pervasive low mood and self-esteem.[13] Depression medications were highly effective for some patients, although the medication typically took several weeks to both take effect and to wear off.

Results of the study are shown in Figure 8.3. For all three ailments, the report concluded that "medication adherence reduces total annual health care spending."[14] Using this and other research, Brennan spent 2012 and 2013 developing the proprietary Pharmacy Care Economic Model (PCEM). The model compared the system-wide costs and benefits of increasing medication adherence. Brennan explained that the model "calculates the potential cost-savings that could be achieved by improving medication adherence and reducing unnecessary health care interventions, enabling us to provide an estimate of medical cost avoidance that could result from improving medication adherence."

[7] Some data have been adjusted and masked for case analysis purposes.

[8] Roebuck, C., Liberman, L.N., Gemmil-Toyama, M., and Brennan, T.B. (2011). "Medication Adherence Leads To Lower Health Care Use And Costs Despite Increased Drug Spending," Health Affairs, 30(1).

[9] Centers for Disease Control and Prevention, "High Cholesterol," http://www.cdc.gov/cholesterol/

[10] Briesacher, B.A., Andrade, S.E., Fouayzi, H., Chan, K.A. (2008). "Comparison of Drug Adherence Rates Among Patients with Seven Different Medical Conditions," Pharmacotherapy, 28(40), PubMed Central, http://www.ncbi.nlm.nih.gov/pmc/articles/PMC2737273/

[11] Centers for Disease Control and Prevention, "Diabetes 101," http://www.cdc.gov/diabetes/basics/index.html

[12] Briesacher, B.A., Andrade, S.E., Fouayzi, H., Chan, K.A. (2008). "Comparison of Drug Adherence Rates Among Patients with Seven Different Medical Conditions," Pharmacotherapy, 28(40), PubMed Central, http://www.ncbi.nlm.nih.gov/pmc/articles/PMC2737273/

[13] National Institute for Mental Health, "What is Depression" http://www.nimh.nih.gov/health/topics/depression/index.shtml

[14] Roebuck, C., Liberman, L.N., Gemmil-Toyama, M., and Brennan, T.B. (2011). "Medication Adherence Leads To Lower Health Care Use And Costs Despite Increased Drug Spending," Health Affairs, 30(1), p. 97.

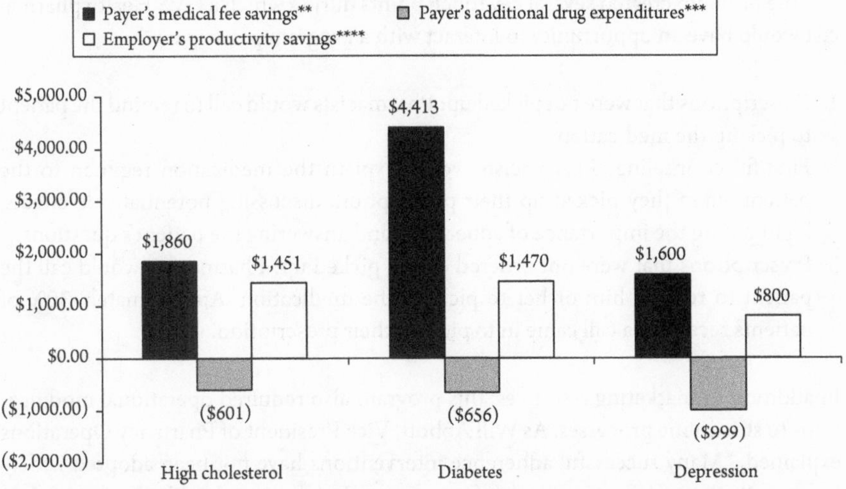

Figure 8.3 Exhibit 4 Financial Implications of Adherence, Per Adherent Patient, Per Year, from the perspective of CVS' Pharmacy Benefit Manager clients (largely HMOs) and the Employers they serve.*

*An adherent patient is a patient with a Medical Possesion Ratio of at least .80.

**An adherent patient incurs fewer medical fees to the payer, including emergency department visits and outpatient physical visits.

***An adherent patient uses more drugs, for which the payer must pay.

****An adherent patient incurs fewer expenses to his employer; for example by taking fewer sick days.

Source: Company documents.

Brennan further explained, "Regardless of where I am or who I am speaking to, people listen up when I tell them that there is a $290 billion expense that could be avoided *if only* patients took their medications properly." He continued, "but when it comes to communicating that value to our PBM clients and even internally, it is sometimes hard because they don't see the savings . . . Although our PCEM model is designed to help, it is harder to sell the indirect cost savings attributable to medication adherence than the immediate, direct, and highly quantifiable cost savings of, say, switching from brand-name to generic medication."

PHARMACY ADVISOR PROGRAM

The Pharmacy Advisor Program employed elements of all three strategies—informational, behavioral, and complex—to improve adherence rates. The program consisted of counseling from pharmacists who had specific information about the patient's treatment and had been trained to advise patients on managing their ailments. For PBM plan members who used CVS/pharmacy locations, counseling was conducted primarily face-to-face, as patients typically came into the pharmacy to drop off prescriptions and pick up medications. For PBM plan members who chose to use a pharmacy other than CVS/pharmacy, counseling was usually provided over the phone by CVS/caremark pharmacists.

The program created several key touch points during which a CVS Health pharmacist would have an opportunity to interact with a program participant:

1. Prescriptions that were not picked up: Pharmacists would call to remind the patient to pick up the medication.
2. First-fill counseling: Pharmacists would explain the medication regimen to the patient when they picked up their prescription, discussing potential side effects, highlighting the importance of adherence, and answering the patient's questions.
3. Prescriptions that were not ordered or not picked up: Pharmacists would call the patient to remind him or her to pick up the medication. Approximately 30% of patients receiving a call came in to pick up their prescription.

In addition to marketing resources, this program also required operational modifications to streamline processes. As Will Abbott, Vice President of Pharmacy Operations explained, "Many successful adherence interventions have not been adopted widely because they require specialized infrastructure. In creating the Pharmacy Advisor Program, we overhauled, and continue to overhaul, existing care processes and communication channels." He anticipated that with these continued increases in operating efficiencies, plus the influx of funding that Foulkes was attempting to obtain, the Pharmacy Advisor Program's variable cost could be lowered to $15 per plan member.

A sophisticated computer program deployed at CVS/pharmacy retail stores managed the pharmacist's workflow and streamlined the prescription-management process. For example, a "drop-off dialog" appeared on the pharmacist's screen when a patient dropped off a prescription to be filled. The dialog prompted the pharmacist if the patient was past due filling other prescriptions and, if so, encouraged the pharmacist to talk to the patient about the importance of medication adherence. The system also automatically provided relevant information about the drug (e.g., side effects or dosage) for the pharmacist to communicate easily to the patient upon medication pick-up. During slower times, the system prompted the pharmacist to contact patients who had not yet picked up their medications. Finally, the program included an extensive reporting mechanism: store-level adherence to system prompts and effectiveness in influencing patient behavior were automatically recorded in a centralized database. The store then received customized action guides on the highest-priority opportunities for performance improvement. Figure 8.4 illustrates the computer-aided workflow.

Brennan led a team of researchers in evaluating the effectiveness of the initial version of the Pharmacy Advisor Program.[15] Working with a PBM client, the team implemented the Pharmacy Advisor Program in a large Midwestern manufacturing firm among its employees (and their qualifying dependents) who had diabetes. The program was administered for six months, at which point the researchers compared adherence rates of the 5,123 study participants to those of a matched control group. The latter consisted of 24,124 patients who also had diabetes and demographic attributes similar to those of the study participants.

[15] Brennan, T.A., Dollear, T.J., Hu, M., Matlin, O.S., Shrank, W.H., Choudry, N.K., Grambley, W. (2012). "An Integrated Pharmacy-Based Program Improved Medication Prescription And Adherence Rates in Diabetes Patients," Health Affairs, 31(1).

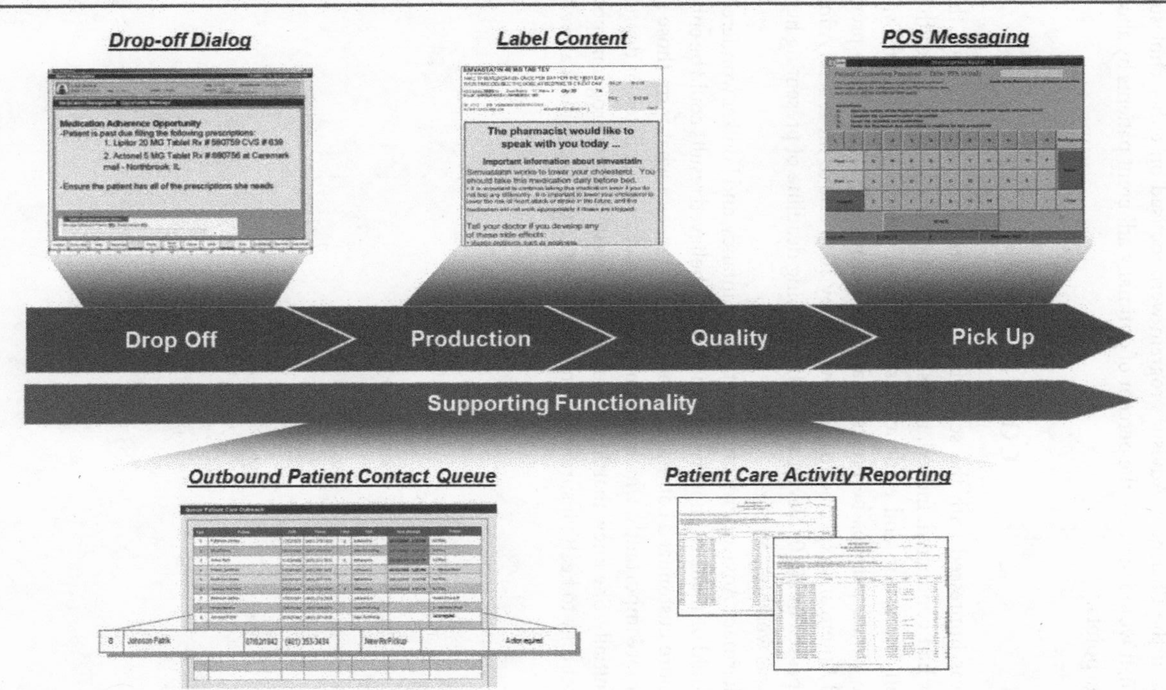

Pharmacy Advisor Program's Point-of-Sale Automated System for Pharmacists

Figure 8.4 Pharmacy Advisor Program's Point-of-Sale Automated System for Pharmacists.
Source: Company documents.

Medication adherence rates for study participants increased by 2.1% during the six months that the Pharmacy Advisor pilot program was administered. Given that on average 65% of medicated diabetics is optimally adherent, the study can be assumed to have increased this percent to 66.4% (i.e., a 1.4 percentage point increase). Among control group participants, medication adherence remained unchanged. It was estimated that if the Pharmacy Advisor program were focused on either cholesterol or depression, it would increase the percent of optimally adherent patients by about one percentage points.

CONCLUSION

Foulkes was impressed with the scientific rigor of the empirical research that her colleagues had conducted. Indeed, it was very much in line with CVS Health's deep interests in innovation and evidence-based pharmacy. Further, the future value of adherence would perhaps be greater than ever before, with 32 million previously uninsured Americans expected to gain coverage by 2019 due to the federal Affordable Care Act passed in 2010. Nevertheless, the looming deadline of presenting her pitch to Merlo was weighing on her.

The Pharmacy Advisor Program was still in its infancy, and Foulkes wondered what changes could be made to improve it. Although she believed results could be enhanced through more customized communications, she was unsure what form those should take, and more importantly, which ailment (high cholesterol, diabetes, or depression) to target initially. She knew that Merlo would be interested in the program's potential benefits not only to health insurers and employers but to CVS/caremark as well.

PART IV

Consumer Access and Affordability

9

THE SLINGSHOT
IMPROVING WATER ACCESS

John A. Quelch, Margaret L. Rodriguez, and Carin-Isabel Knoop

In your lifetime, my lifetime, we will see water be a really scarce, valuable commodity. We believe the world needs a slingshot to take care of its Goliath of a problem in water. So we decided to build a small machine and give it to the little Davids.[1]
Dean Kamen, *DEKA Founder and CEO, 2009.*

Wherever you go in the world, there is one product you can buy—a Coke. They have figured out how to build the most effective distribution system for a product that has to sell for pennies in the most remote places in the world.[2]
Dean Kamen, *2012.*

In September 2012, inventor and entrepreneur Dean Kamen was on the verge of seeing one of his dreams come true: providing safe drinking water to the more than 1 billion of the world's people living where there was a scarcity of potable or drinkable water,[3,4] 300 million of them living in Africa alone.[5] Kamen's water purification system, known as Slingshot, now had the muscle and resources of the Coca-Cola Company behind the invention. Kamen had been convinced for years that Slingshot was one answer to the global water problem, but he did not have the resources to mass-produce

[1] Ryan Bergeron, "Segway inventor takes aim at thirst with Slingshot," *CNN*, September 11, 2009, http://www.cnn.com/2009/TECH/09/11/kamen.water.slingshot/index.html#cnnSTCText, accessed May 2013.

[2] "Coca-Cola Teams with DEKA R&D," Professional Services Close-up, September 29, 2012, via ABI Inform Complete, accessed May 1, 2013.

[3] WHO Fact File, "Water Scarcity," http://www.who.int/features/factfiles/water/water_facts/en/index2.html, accessed May 8, 2013.

[4] Only about 2% of water on earth was drinkable. For much of the earth's population, getting fresh water was a daily struggle. Some 300,000 people died annually from illness, malnutrition, or other factors due to lack of clean water. Source: "Coca-Cola Teams with DEKA R&D," "Professional Services Close-up, September 29, 2012, via ABI Inform Complete, accessed May 1, 2013.

[5] Dave Solomon, "Dean Kamen's Slingshot heard 'round the world," *New Hampshire Union Leader*, October 6, 2012, http://www.unionleader.com/article/20121007/NEWS02/710079913&source=RSS, accessed May 1, 2013.

the machine and deploy it in thousands of locations. What Kamen called a 10-year science project had reached a multimillion-dollar partnership with Coca-Cola.[6]

DEKA BACKGROUND

Kamen grew up on Long Island, New York, the son of an artist who contributed to *Mad* maga-zine.[7] When he was 20 years old, Kamen invented a pump to deliver drugs to children suffering from cancer. The device, the AutoSyringe, was later reconfigured to serve a larger population: diabetics. Kamen figured out a way to deliver a precise dose of insulin exactly when patients needed it.

In 1976, he founded his first medical device company, AutoSyringe, Inc., to manufacture and market the pumps. At age 30, he sold the company to Baxter Healthcare Corporation. By then, he had added a number of other infusion devices, including the first wearable insulin pump for diabetics.

Following the sale of AutoSyringe in 1982, Kamen founded DEKA Research & Development Corporation to develop internally generated inventions as well as to provide research and development for major corporate clients. Located in New Hampshire, DEKA innovated around its core technologies, with most of its projects falling into one of four categories: (1) fluid management, (2) mobility, (3) power, and (4) water.[8] The company employed 400 people in 2012. According to one observer, "There was a steampunk quality to the combination of nineteenth and twenty-first-century technology in this lab, which can be seen as the descendent of the Edison invention factory in the 1890s or Bell Labs in the 1940s and 1950s."[9]

Over 30 years, DEKA developed a variety of innovations. Notable ones included an in-home dialysis system, components of a device to treat T-cell lymphoma, a cardiovascular stent, and an advanced prosthetic arm in development for the Defense Advanced Research Projects Agency, part of the U.S. Department of Defense, to improve the quality of life for returning injured soldiers.[10] Kamen held more than 440 U.S. and foreign patents, many of them for innovative medical devices that expanded the frontiers of health care worldwide.[11]

Of all of Kamen's and DEKA's inventions, the most well-known was the Segway Human Transporter (see Figure 9.1), a self-balancing scooter, introduced in 2001 to great fanfare. Kamen positioned the "revolutionary" electric scooter as an alternative to cars that would transform the way people moved around cities and towns. Investors, including Kleiner Perkins, Credit Suisse, and Kamen himself, spent more than $100 million to commercialize the machine. But it proved to be too expensive—and

[6] Solomon, "Dean Kamen's Slingshot heard 'round the world."

[7] Phil Patton, "Slingshot: Inventor Dean Kamen's Revolutionary Clean Water Machine," Coca-Cola website, November 2, 2012, http://www.coca-colacompany.com/stories/slingshot-inventor-dean-kamens-evolutionary-clean-water-machine, accessed May 8, 2013.

[8] DEKA Research & Development Corporation, "Our Founder," DEKA website, http://www.deka-research.com/founder.shtml, accessed February 2014.

[9] "Coca-Cola Teams with DEKA R&D," "Professional Services Close-up."

[10] DEKA Research & Development Corporation, "Our Founder."

[11] DEKA Research & Development Corporation, "Our Founder."

Figure 9.1 Exhibit 1 Dean Kamen unveils the Segway Personal Transporter, a two-wheeled, self-balancing scooter, on *Good Morning America*.
Source: Dylan Tweney, "Dec. 3, 2001: Segway Starts Rolling," *Wired*, December 3, 2009, http://www.wired.com/thisdayintech/2009/12/1203segway-unveiled/, accessed May 8, 2013.

too impractical—for the U.S. mass market.[12] James "Jimi" Heselden, a prominent British entrepreneur, acquired Segway in 2009. In 2013, Segway was acquired by Summit Strategic Investments. The product did eventually find some success in niche markets such as law enforcement and tourism.

SLINGSHOT

Kamen began working on Slingshot around 1999. In 2003 he showed off his prototype on the mainstream American news television show *60 Minutes*. In 2008, he appeared on *The Colbert Report*, a late-night U.S. television comedy show, operating a Slingshot on the air and drinking its product.

Slingshot was a portable, low-power water purification system. It boiled and evaporated water from any source—rivers, oceans, even raw sewage—then allowed the pure water to condense and be collected (see Box 9.1 for details). Earlier versions were much

[12] Michael V. Copeland, "Dean Kamen (still) wants to save the world," *Fortune*, May 10, 2010, http://money.cnn.com/2010/04/22/technology/dean_kamen.fortune/index.htm, accessed May 8, 2013.

Box 9.1 Exhibit 2 Slingshot Water Cleaning Process

1. A heat exchanger heats the input water to approximately 100 degrees Celsius and cools the clean water and the return water to ambient temperature.
2. Dirty water is heated in the boiling chamber and evaporates as steam.
3. The compressor slightly raises the pressure and temperature of the steam.
4. Clean water condenses on the relatively cooler surfaces of the condensing chamber. Heat released by the condensing water is recycled into the boiling chamber.
5. Separated contaminants are collected and discharged.
6. Clean water is collected and ready to drink.

Source: Adapted from Phil Patton, "Slingshot: Inventor Dean Kamen's Revolutionary Clean Water Machine," November 2, 2012, http://www.cocacolacompany. com/stories/slingshot-inventor-dean-kamens-revolutionary-clean-water-machine, accessed May 1, 2013.

larger and required more electricity. The smaller pre-production model could produce 10 gallons of clean water an hour while consuming less than 1 kilowatt of electricity, less than the power needed for a handheld blow-dryer. It could be plugged into any wall socket or powered by solar cells, batteries, or DEKA's own Stirling electric generator, which ran on biogases such as methane from local waste sources.

The machine's name came from the biblical battle between David and Goliath, in which the shepherd boy defeated the giant with a slingshot. "The Goliath of the 21st century for millions of people is bad water," Kamen said, "and all those little villages need a slingshot to deal with that Goliath. The 21st-century slingshot is right here."[13]

In summer 2006, Kamen delivered two Slingshots to a small community in Honduras. "The machine worked very well down there, taking virtually any water that the people from that village brought to us," he said. "All the water that we got from the machine was absolutely pure water."[14] But there was a problem: each Slingshot cost several thousand dollars to build. Kamen looked to partner with companies and organizations to distribute Slingshots around the world, but he said that more engineering work was needed to lower the production costs.[15] One Slingshot machine could supply about 250 gallons of water a day, which was enough for 100 people.[16]

For several years, Kamen had been talking about the Slingshot to people at the United Nations and various nongovernmental organizations (NGOs). "But we realized the NGOs aren't the ones who can help us get the machine into production, scale it up, bring down the cost curve," said Kamen.[17] Creating a device that delivered clean water from almost any source was one thing. Getting them built and deployed in sufficient numbers

[13] Solomon, "Dean Kamen's Slingshot heard 'round the world."

[14] Bergeron, "Segway inventor takes aim at thirst with Slingshot."

[15] Bergeron, "Segway inventor takes aim at thirst with Slingshot."

[16] Bergeron, "Segway inventor takes aim at thirst with Slingshot."

[17] Jessie Scanlon, "Dean Kamen Reinvents Coke's Soda Fountain," *Bloomberg Businessweek*, October 7, 2009, http://www.businessweek.com/innovate/content/oct2009/id2009107_810817.htm, accessed May 8, 2013.

to have global impact was another. "We went from big companies to foundations; we went from foundations to the World Health Organization, and they all said, 'This is a big idea; it's fantastic, but we can't do the part you're not doing.' "[18]

ALLIANCE WITH COCA-COLA

As part of his day job as an inventor-for-hire, Kamen developed a next-generation soda fountain for Coca-Cola called the Freestyle (see Figure 9.2) and, in the process, started talking up the Slingshot.

Kamen's relationship with Coca-Cola had been forged earlier when the beverage company became a sponsor of Kamen's nonprofit FIRST,[19] which aimed to encourage children's interest in science and technology, with the hope that this could motivate them to careers in those fields. Through Coca-Cola's FIRST sponsorship, Kamen met Nilang Patel, the head of Coca-Cola's research lab.[20]

In early 2005, Patel's team started thinking about how to reinvent the company's fountain business, which controlled 75% of the market but had not changed in decades. Patel approached Kamen to help. Kamen was happy to develop closer ties with a FIRST sponsor, and he saw Coca-Cola as a potential future partner in his plan to deploy the Slingshot.[21]

Using technology adapted from systems that DEKA previously had developed to deliver small but steady doses of chemotherapy drugs, the Freestyle could combine tiny amounts of concentrated ingredients, stored in cartridges, with carbonated water and sweetener to mix a beverage on the spot. Each new machine gave customers a choice of up to 100 different soft drinks, from favorites such as Coke Classic to customized offerings like grape Fanta. That was a 12½-fold increase from the selections at most machines found in fast-food restaurants and movie theaters.[22] By 2012, more than 10,000 Freestyle machines, offering 127 flavor combinations, were in the field at restaurants such as Five Guys Burgers and Fries.

"For years, we looked for a partner who could help us get the Slingshot machine into production, scale it up, bring down the cost curve, and deliver and operate the units in the places where the need is the greatest. Now we have that partner with Coca-Cola," Kamen said.[23] "We figured if we exceeded their expectations on [the Freestyle] commercial partnership, we would get their attention."[24] It worked. Coca-Cola committed

[18] Solomon, "Dean Kamen's Slingshot heard 'round the world."

[19] For Inspiration and Recognition of Science and Technology (FIRST) was an organization dedicated to motivating the next generation to understand, use, and enjoy science and technology. Founded in 1989, FIRST served more than 300,000 young people, ages 6 to 18, in more than 50 countries in 2012. High-school-aged participants were eligible to apply for more than $15 million in scholarships from leading colleges, universities, and corporations. Source: DEKA, "Our Founder," DEKA website, http://www.dekaresearch.com/founder.shtml, accessed May 1, 2013.

[20] Scanlon, "Dean Kamen Reinvents Coke's Soda Fountain."

[21] Scanlon, "Dean Kamen Reinvents Coke's Soda Fountain."

[22] Scanlon, "Dean Kamen Reinvents Coke's Soda Fountain."

[23] Solomon, "Dean Kamen's Slingshot heard 'round the world."

[24] Solomon, "Dean Kamen's Slingshot heard 'round the world."

Figure 9.2 Exhibit 3 Coca-Cola's Freestyle Vending Machine.
Source: Casewriter, compiled from Mbrstooge, "Coca Cola Freestyle," Wikipedia Commons, December 17, 2010, accessed February, 2014; Phillip, "Red Coca-Cola Freestyle soda machine at a Burger King," Wikipedia Commons, October 23, 2012, accessed February, 2014.

millions to the development, production, and deployment of the Slingshot machines in what it called a long-term global clean water partnership.[25]

Before entering into the partnership, Coca-Cola and DEKA conducted a successful field trial of the Slingshot technology at five schools outside Accra, Ghana, in 2011, providing 140,000 liters of clean drinking water to 1,500 schoolchildren over a six-month period. The Slingshot systems experienced very few issues and were able to operate based on the available electricity supply, working despite frequent power outages in the villages where they were located.[26]

An updated version of the Slingshot was displayed at the Coca-Cola pavilion during the 2012 Summer Olympics in London so that Coca-Cola personnel could demonstrate its potential to a worldwide audience and measure the feedback. Continuing to promote the partnership, Coca-Cola's chairman and CEO, Muhtar Kent, was on the stage with former U.S. president Bill Clinton at the Clinton Global Initiative plenary session in New York in October 2012, where Clinton expressed his own enthusiasm for the emerging partnership.

The next step was to have 50 Slingshots built by a contract manufacturer in Massachusetts. These began to roll off the assembly line within a few weeks of

[25] Solomon, "Dean Kamen's Slingshot heard 'round the world."

[26] "Coca-Cola Teams with DEKA R&D," "Professional Services Close-up."

the partnership announcement. Completed by November 2012, 20 were brought to DEKA for rigorous testing, while 30 were field-tested by Coca-Cola in South Africa, Mexico, and Paraguay. (The latest version of the Slingshot could purify up to 365,000 liters of water each year—enough daily drinking water for roughly 300 people.)[27] The companies partnered with Africare, an NGO in Africa, to field-test Slingshot units in health clinics in the Eastern Cape of South Africa in 2013. The units would provide clean drinking water to the health clinics, which operated an HIV/AIDS intervention program that Africare was leading with support from the Coca-Cola Foundation.[28]

If all of the tests proved out, the machine would move into mass production by the middle of 2013. Kamen said Coca-Cola stood ready to invest "tens of millions of dollars"[29] to build the manufacturing equipment needed for mass production that could ultimately put 1 to 2 million Slingshots in the field.

"Water is the lifeblood of our business, and our commitment is to ensure we're doing our part to replenish the water we use and give it back to communities around the world," Kent said. Coca-Cola had set a goal of "no net loss of water" in the production of its beverages by 2020, and Kent explained that Slingshot dovetailed with this goal.[30]

The idea was to eventually use the company's delivery infrastructure to place Slingshot machines in remote villages; perhaps carried by hand over dirt roads, traversing the proverbial "last mile" that was often the key hurdle to distributing technology and medicine. Kamen hoped to place machines in India, the Middle East, and Africa. Eventually, the partnership was expected by Coca-Cola to add more than half a billion liters of clean drinking water per year to the global water supply.[31]

Kamen said:

> For years, we looked for a partner who could help us get the Slingshot machine into production, scale it up, bring down the cost curve, and deliver and operate the units in the places where the need is greatest. Now we have that partner with Coca-Cola, which brings unparalleled knowledge of working, operating and partnering in the most remote places of the world.[32]

On another occasion, Kamen said:

> The Coca-Cola system has more than 700,000 employees, 300,000 people in Africa. That is an incredible resource for getting the word out about Slingshot. . . . Invention is part of innovation. The rest is the infrastructure to support and deliver the solutions.[33] . . . We are now at the point where even the skeptics would have to say, "Wow, this could actually have a major impact on global health."[34]

27 "Coca-Cola Teams with DEKA R&D," "Professional Services Close-up."

28 "Coca-Cola Teams with DEKA R&D," "Professional Services Close-up."

29 Solomon, "Dean Kamen's Slingshot heard 'round the world."

30 "Coca-Cola Teams with DEKA R&D, "Professional Services Close-up."

31 "Coca-Cola Teams with DEKA R&D, "Professional Services Close-up."

32 Patton, "Slingshot: Inventor Dean Kamen's Revolutionary Clean Water Machine."

33 "Coca-Cola Teams with DEKA R&D," "Professional Services Close-up."

34 "Coca-Cola Teams with DEKA R&D," "Professional Services Close-up."

COCA-COLA'S WATER POLICY

The Coca-Cola Company had taken steps to proactively address the coming water crisis. Coca-Cola was a founding member of the 2030 Water Resources Group (WRG), a public-private partnership under the International Finance Corporation.[35] The WRG helped countries diagnose gaps in their water systems and implement sustainable, long-term solutions. Coca-Cola invested $2 million in WRG between 2012 and 2013. Between 2005 and 2013, Coke had also helped fund over 380 projects that were designed to improve water systems. The company estimated that 1.6 million people had benefited from the initiatives, which increased water access and sanitation.[36]

Coca-Cola had made strides to improve the water usage of its production facilities. The company focused on decreasing its "water ratio," the amount of water needed to produce a liter of product. Between 2008 and 2012, Coca-Cola reduced the ratio by 20%.[37] The company also sought to replenish the water used in its final products. Between 2005 and 2011, Coca-Cola balanced about 35% of the water used in its finished products (based on 2011 production volume).[38] By 2020, the company intended for its production operations to be "water neutral."[39]

THE WATER PROBLEM

At the end of 2011, nearly 90% of the world's population had access to a potable-water supply, and 55% had a piped source on the premises.[40] About 770 million people across the globe were left without access to an improved drinking water source (one that was adequately protected from contamination, particularly from human waste). Diarrhea resulting from contaminated water was a major threat to public health, killing as many children as HIV/AIDS in 2006.[41] Of those who lacked access to potable water, 185 million relied on surface water for their daily needs.[42] Lack of potable water was greater among populations that lived in rural areas: 83% of people who lacked access to a potable water source lived in rural communities, and 71% of people who lived without sanitation also lived in rural areas.[43] Research by the United Nations found that the poorest populations paid nearly 10 times more for water than wealthier households.[44] Many

[35] Water Resources Group, http://www.coca-colacompany.com/promoting-policy-reform-through-he-2030-water-resources-group, accessed September 2013.

[36] Coca-Cola Company, "Water Stewardship," http://www.coca-colacompany.com/sustainability-report/world/water-stewardship.html, accessed September 2013.

[37] Coca-Cola Company, "Water Stewardship."

[38] Coca-Cola Company, "Water Stewardship."

[39] Coca-Cola Company, "Water Stewardship."

[40] World Health Organization, "2.4 billion people will lack improved sanitation in 2015," WHO website, May 13, 2013, http: //www.who.int/mediacentre/news/notes/2013/sanitation_mdg_20130513/en/index.html, accessed September 2013.

[41] United Nations Development Programme, "Human Development Report, 2006: Beyond Scarcity," 2006.

[42] World Health Organization, "2.4 billion people will lack improved sanitation in 2015."

[43] World Health Organization, "2.4 billion people will lack improved sanitation in 2015."

[44] United Nations Development Programme, "Human Development Report, 2006."

of the people who lived without access to potable water were located in sub-Saharan Africa and Oceania; less than one third of their populations had access to piped water on premises.[45] Their communities disproportionately relied on surface water as a source of drinking water.

Access to water was a growing problem that would impact more people in the coming years. The 2013 Bonn Declaration on Global Water Security estimated that, within one or two generations, the global population of 9 billion would face severe pressure on its water resources.[46] Projections of population growth and economic development suggested that, by 2030, demand for water would be 30% greater than the available supply.[47] One-third of the world's population, mostly located in developing countries, would live in areas where demand was 50% greater than supply.[48] The current approaches to water management and security were detrimental to the health of water ecosystems, and were unsustainable in the long term. It was expected that the current system would be increasingly strained, leading to potentially irreversible changes in the globe's water ecosystems.[49]

COMPETING SOLUTIONS

Kamen's Slingshot was not the only product that could take contaminated water and produce potable output in the areas where it was needed most. (See Table 9.1 for a summary of different products and costs for water purification.) Tata's Swach, the University of Kassel's Portable Aqua Unit for Lifesaving (PAUL), and Lifesaver's C2 effectively removed contaminates, producing safe drinking water from rivers and other sources.

In 2009, Tata, the Indian conglomerate, launched the Swach water purifier. Swach used silver-coated filters to remove impurities from water. The purifier required no electricity in order to produce clean water and could filter 30–40 liters per day.[50] Swach was inexpensive, with a retail price of about $16, and the annual cost of replacement filters was around $21. While Swach was designed primarily for single household use, other systems, like the PAUL and the LifeSaver C2 unit, were designed to serve multifamily communities.

PAUL was developed in 2010 by faculty at the University of Kassel in Germany under the direction of Franz-Bernd Frechen. PAUL purified water using a membrane

[45] "Progress on Sanitation and Drinking-Water, 2013 Update," World Health Organization, Unicef, 2013, http://apps.who.int/iris/bitstream/10665/81245/1/9789241505390_eng.pdf, accessed September, 2013.

[46] Global Water System Project, "The Bonn Declaration on Global Water Security," 2012, http://www.gwsp.org/fileadmin/documents_news/Bonn_Water_Declaration_final.pdf, accessed September 2013.

[47] 2030 Water Resources Group, "Charting Our Water Future," 2009, http://www.2030waterresourcesgroup.com/water_full/Charting_Our_Water_Future_Final.pdf, accessed September 2013.

[48] 2030 Water Resources Group, "Charting Our Water Future."

[49] Global Water System Project, "The Bonn Declaration on Global Water Security."

[50] Tata Swach Company, "Know Tata Swach," Tata Swach website, http://www.tataswach.com/shopping/product_index.aspx, accessed September 2013.

Table 9.1 Exhibit 4 Summary of Costs for Water Purification Products, 2013

	Liters per Day	*People Served per Day*	*Initial Cost per Product*	*Fuel Required, per Day*	*Cost of Fuel, per Day*	*Mainten-ance Costs*	*Operating Life (years)*
Slingshot	1,000	250	$5,200[a]	<10 KWh	$0[b]	None	5
PAUL	1,200	300	$1,350[c]	None	N/A	None	10
LifeSaver C2	3,600	900	$8,000	None	N/A	None	0.38
Tata Swach	30–40	10	$16	None	N/A	None	0.3

Source: Compiled from LifeSaver, "C2 Data," LifeSaver website, http://www.lifesaversystems.com/documents/LS_C2_Data _PRINT.pdf; Tata Swach website, http://www.tataswach.com/shopping /product_index.aspx; Nigel Powell, "Dean Kamen's Slingshot water purifier and Stirling generator tech—low cost water and power for the developing world," *Red Ferret*, March 29, 2008; PAUL website, http://www.water-backpack.org/; Hilfswerk der Deutschen Lions e.V., "Water filter PAUL—Portable Aqua Unit for Lifesaving," http://www.lions-hilfswerk.de/nationale-undinternationale-hilfsprojekte/wasserfilter-paul.html, accessed September 2013.

[a] Includes the cost of the DEKA-produced generator needed to run Slingshot.

[b] The generator was capable of burning dung, which could be acquired for little to no cost.

[c] Each PAUL unit cost 1,000 euros in 2013, which was equivalent to roughly $1,350.

filter that removed 99% of bacteria.[51] Six PAUL units were dispatched to Haiti to aid victims of the 2010 earthquake.[52] In 2011, 135 more devices were distributed to villages in Pakistan impacted by floods.[53] By 2012, over 700 PAUL units had been distributed to 20 countries in Asia, South America, and Africa.[54] Each PAUL was capable of supplying water to 300 people per day.[55]

Michael Pritchard founded Lifesaver in the United Kingdom in 2007 after 2004's Indian Ocean tsunami and 2005's Hurricane Katrina illustrated the need for water purification systems in the wake of natural disasters.[56] His first product was the personal use Lifesaver bottle, which used a carbon filter and hand pump, and could hold 750 milliliters. Between 2007 and 2013, Pritchard developed Lifesaver purification systems in a variety of sizes and sold them to the military, camping enthusiasts, and humanitarian organizations. The Lifesaver C2 was the largest product sold by the company and could serve the needs of 900 people per day, but, unlike the designs of Slingshot and PAUL, the filter of the C2 would last less than one year when used at maximum capacity.[57]

FROM SLINGSHOT TO EKOCENTER

In September 2013, Muhtar Kent, the chairman and chief executive of Coca-Cola, unveiled a new product to address public health issues in developing markets, the EKOCENTER, at the Clinton Global Initiative meeting.[58] Dubbed by Coke a "downtown in a box,"[59] each EKOCENTER was built in a shipping container shell fitted with a Slingshot to provide clean water.[60] Powered by solar panels, the EKOCENTER could

[51] Hilfswerk der Deutschen Lions e.V. (Lions Foundation Germany), "Hundred Help for clean water in Haiti—Hundreds PAULs in use," October 1, 2012, http://www.lions-hilfswerk.de/nationale-und-internationale-hilfsprojekte/katastrophenhilfe/haiti/100-pauls-im-einsatz.html, accessed September 2013.

[52] Kinderhilfswerk Global-Care, "PAUL water backpack on the way to Haiti," November 17, 2010, http://www.global-care.de/index.php?option=com_content&view=article&id=351%3Acholera-epedemie-haiti&catid=61%3Akatastrophenhilfe-allgemein&Itemid=537&lang=de, accessed September2013.

[53] Nighat Aziz, "PAUL—Systems," Humanity Care Foundation, 2011, http://www.humanity-care-stiftung.de/erlebnisberichte-aus-pakistan/paul-systeme.html, accessed September 2013.

[54] Waterbackpack Blog, "PAUL is more and more a citizen of the world," University of Kassel, August 6, 2012, http://wasser rucksack.de/Blog, accessed September 2013.

[55] Waterbackpack Website, University of Kassel, August 6, 2012, http://www.waterbackpack.org/, accessed September 2013.

[56] LifeSaver Company, "About Us," LifeSaver website, http://www.lifesaversystems.com/about-us, accessed September 2013.

[57] LifeSaver Company, "LifeSaver C2 Data," LifeSaver website, http://www.lifesaversystems.com/documents/LS_C2_Data_ PRINT.pdf, accessed September 2013.

[58] Donald G. McNeil Jr., "Coca-Cola Plans Kiosks with Water and Internet," *New York Times*, October 1, 2013, via Factiva, accessed October 2013.

[59] McNeil, "Coca-Cola Plans Kiosks with Water and Internet."

[60] Dominic Basulto, "Why entrepreneurs have an edge over governments in shaping global development," *Washington Post (online)*, October 22, 2013, via Factiva, accessed October 2013.

Box 9.2 Exhibit 5 EKOCENTER Partner Roles by Company, 2013

In addition to providing financial support and expertise, each partner company had specific responsibilities:

The Coca-Cola Company and its bottling partners will lead the project, managing the site selection, installation and maintenance of each EKOCENTER. They also will utilize their local operations to support on-the-ground needs and serve as a distribution channel for EKOCENTER placements. The Company led the EKOCENTER vision and design as well as the creation and installation of the prototype unit in South Africa.

The Coca-Cola Company & DEKA R&D will supply the Slingshot™ water purification system as well as design and infrastructure expertise to build and install EKOCENTER. DEKA R&D supported the design and creation of the first EKOCENTER test site in South Africa and also has an additional partnership with Coca-Cola to deliver safe drinking water using the Slingshot technology at schools, health clinics and community centers in Africa and Latin America.

IBM will contribute technology and business consulting services to provide high-level business plan development and technology plan development for EKOCENTER. IBM also will explore and advise on potential technology applications for treating return water.

IDB will provide funding and implementation support for EKOCENTER placements in Latin America. It also will help establish relationships with local non-governmental organizations (NGOs) to support health and sanitation education for communities receiving EKOCENTERs. IDB is a funding and implementation partner for Coca-Cola's existing safe drinking water partnership with DEKA R&D in Latin America.

McCann Health, a part of McCann Worldgroup, will work with Coca-Cola and other partners to create a micro-business model for EKOCENTER. Additionally, it also will develop consumer-focused health and sanitation programs and messaging for communities receiving an EKOCENTER.

NRG is the official energy partner for EKOCENTER, providing solar panels and battery storage to power EKOCENTER, enabling each one to be a self-sustaining, off-the-grid operation. NRG also is assisting DEKA R&D with development of the Stirling™ engine technology which could provide another energy option for EKOCENTER in the long-term. NRG provided solar panels and battery storage for the first EKOCENTER test site earlier this year.

Qualcomm Technologies, Inc., a wholly-owned subsidiary of Qualcomm Incorporated, will provide guidance to Coca-Cola on the inclusion of wireless communications technologies, such as mobile devices and wireless Internet connectivity, for EKOCENTER.

UPS will serve as a logistics partner, providing technical expertise on global operations and deployment of EKOCENTER.

Source: "Coca-Cola Launches Global EKOCENTER Partnership to Deliver Safe Drinking Water and Basic Necessities to Rural Communities," Business Wire, September 24, 2013, via ABI ProQuest, accessed October 2013.

accommodate a small retail store that could sell Coca-Cola products. It would also offer locally tailored services, which might include WiFi, electricity, temperature-controlled storage for vaccines, and health education services.[61] Women in the local communities would be recruited and given business skills training to operate the EKOCENTERs.[62] Coke and Kamen partnered with IBM, McCann Health, NRG Energy, Inter-American Development Bank, UPS, and Qualcomm to craft the EKOCENTER.[63] (See Box 9.2 for the role of each partner.)

In October 2013, one EKOCENTER was piloted in Heidelberg, South Africa.[64] Coke and its partner companies planned to place between 1,500 and 2,000 EKOCENTERs in 20 countries across Asia, Africa, North America, and South America by the end of 2015.[65] "Through EKOCENTER we have the ability to change lives by offering access to safe drinking water and other needed resources, all while empowering local entrepreneurs. What started as an aspiration is now becoming a reality as we welcome our partners across the golden triangle of business, government and civil society to scale and improve this innovation," said Kent.[66] Kamen's pre-existing agreement with Coke to distribute Slingshots to communities in Africa and South America continued, even as the EKOCENTERs were piloted.[67]

[61] "Coca-Cola Launches Global EKOCENTER Partnership to Deliver Safe Drinking Water and Basic Necessities to Rural Communities," Business Wire, September 24, 2013, via ABI ProQuest, accessed October 2013.

[62] "Coca-Cola Launches Global EKOCENTER Partnership," Business Wire.

[63] "Coca-Cola Launches Global EKOCENTER Partnership to Deliver Safe Drinking Water and Basic Necessities to Rural Communities," *ENP Newswire*, September 24, 2013, via Factiva, accessed October 2013.

[64] McNeil, "Coca-Cola Plans Kiosks with Water and Internet."

[65] "Coca-Cola Launches Global EKOCENTER Partnership," Business Wire.

[66] "Coca-Cola Launches Global EKOCENTER Partnership," Business Wire.

[67] "Coca-Cola Launches Global EKOCENTER Partnership," Business Wire.

10

VAXESS TECHNOLOGIES, INC.

John A. Quelch and Margaret L. Rodriguez

In February 2014, Michael Schrader, chief executive of Vaxess Technologies, Inc., was assessing the start-up healthcare company's 2014 marketing plan. On December 31, 2013, Vaxess had obtained an exclusive license to a series of patents for a silk protein technology that, when added to vaccines, reduced or removed the need for refrigeration between manufacturing and delivery to the end patient. Schrader and his colleagues had to decide which vaccines to focus on and whether and how to target the drug companies that manufactured the vaccines or the quasi-government organizations (such as UNICEF and PAHO) and nongovernment organizations (such as GAVI) that purchased large quantities of vaccines for the developing world.

VACCINES

Vaccines exposed the immune system to safe amounts of a stimulus that triggered an immune response in order to develop protection against specific diseases. The exposure created antibodies that prevented the immunized individual from contracting the disease in the future. Vaccinated individuals typically required 2 to 10 days following injection or ingestion to develop antibodies, and the protection afforded by vaccines could last for years.[1] Vaccines offered the opportunity to prevent many from falling sick to begin with, and thus reduced the need for costly health services.

Vaccines began to degrade the moment they left the factory. As much as 80% of the price paid for vaccines was allocated to the process to keep vaccines cold until they reached the point of use.[2] By some estimates, failure to regulate temperature resulted in waste of nearly half of all vaccine doses worldwide.[3] All vaccines were temperature sensitive and had to be stored either frozen (3%) or at temperatures between 2 degrees

[1] Alison Sahoo, "Vaccines 2012," *Kalorama Information Market Intelligence Report*, September 2012, p. 2; and Marketresearch.com, accessed January 2014.

[2] National Institutes of Health, "Global Health Matters," 11, no. 4 (July-August 2012), ISSN: 1938-5935, http://www.fic.nih.gov/News/GlobalHealthMatters/july-august-2012/Documents/ghmjul-aug2012.pdf, accessed February 2014.

[3] National Institutes of Health, "Global Health Matters."

<table>
<tr><th rowspan="2"></th><th rowspan="2">Primary vaccine store
Up to 6 Months</th><th colspan="2">Intermediate vaccine store</th><th rowspan="2">Health centre
Up to one month</th><th rowspan="2">Health post
Up to one month</th></tr>
<tr><th>Region-up to 3 months</th><th>District-up to one month</th></tr>
<tr><td>OPV</td><td colspan="2">−15°C to −25°C</td><td colspan="3" rowspan="12">+2°C to +8°C</td></tr>
<tr><td>BCG</td><td colspan="2" rowspan="6">2°C to +8°C
(−15°C to −25°C also possible)</td></tr>
<tr><td>Measles, MR, MMR</td></tr>
<tr><td>YF</td></tr>
<tr><td>Hib freeze-dried</td></tr>
<tr><td>Meningococcal A&C</td></tr>
<tr><td>HepB</td></tr>
<tr><td>IPV</td><td colspan="2" rowspan="5">+2°C to +8°C
Never Freeze!</td></tr>
<tr><td>DT, DTP, DTP Hep B</td></tr>
<tr><td>Hib liquid</td></tr>
<tr><td>Td</td></tr>
<tr><td>TT</td></tr>
</table>

Figure 10.1 Exhibit 1 Vaccine Storage Temperatures, 2014.
Source: Simona Zipursky, "Beyond the cold chain," TechNet Meeting, February 5, 2013, http://www.technet-21.org/resources/documents/immunization-delivery-strategies/1591-beyond-the-cold-chain-taking-advantage-of-the-true-heat-stability-of-vaccines, accessed February 2014.

Celsius and 8 degrees Celsius (97%). Viral vaccines (those for measles, mumps, rubella, yellow fever, and influenza, for example) tended to be more subject to temperature stability problems than most other types of vaccines. As a result, most live viral vaccines were freeze dried. (See Figure 10.1 for storage temperatures by vaccine type.)

If the storage conditions were not shielded from temperature swings, the vaccine could degrade, reducing or entirely eliminating the effectiveness of the vaccine. Oftentimes identifying which vaccine doses had been exposed to temperature deviations and were no longer effective was problematic.

Around 2.4 million people died each year of diseases that could have been prevented by vaccinations.[4] One in five children worldwide did not receive basic vaccines, often for a host of reasons, including political or financial limitations but also because of the cost and complexity of cold storage distribution.

VACCINE MANUFACTURERS

In 2010, 23 billion vaccine doses were manufactured worldwide. This number was expected to reach over 35 billion doses by 2015.[5] The global market for vaccines was far smaller than that for pharmaceuticals (one-fortieth the size in dollars), yet totaled

[4] Bill & Melinda Gates Foundation, "Global Health Program Fact Sheet," https://docs.gatesfoundation.org/Documents/GlobalHealthProgramFactSheet.pdf, accessed May 2014.

[5] Jon Evans, "Vaccine Production," *Kalorama Information Market Intelligence Report*, February 2012, p. 9, Marketresearch.com, accessed January 2014.

$19.8 billion (at manufacturer prices) in 2011 and was estimated to reach $30.4 billion by 2016.[6] The estimated compound annual growth rate between 2011 and 2016 was 8.9% for all adult vaccines (which accounted for 44% of worldwide vaccine market value, pediatric vaccines accounting for the remainder).[7] In 2013, there were more than 120 new vaccine candidates in the development pipeline worldwide.[8]

Five pharmaceutical companies accounted for 85% of vaccines sold worldwide in 2013. Sanofi Pasteur led with 23.1% of the market, followed by Merck with 22.0%, GlaxoSmithKline (GSK) with 21.9% (each had over $5 billion in vaccine sales), Pfizer with 17.1%, and Novartis with 5.8%.[9] GSK and Sanofi took a global approach to their vaccine businesses, with discriminatory pricing driving higher margins in developed regions and large volumes allowing them to derive a small profit in more cost-sensitive regions. GSK's polio vaccine for children, for example, was sold at 10 times the price in developed versus developing markets. (See Table 10.1 for vaccine prices in developing and developed markets.) Merck was moving its vaccines business from a developed country focus to a more global strategy. Pfizer focused on vaccines for the developed world; sales of Prevnar (and Prevnar 13) for pneumococcal infection were $1.85 billion in the first half of 2012 alone.[10]

Other pharmaceutical companies, including Johnson & Johnson and Takeda, aspired to become larger global players in vaccines and were acquiring companies with promising late-stage vaccines under development. Takeda, for instance, had a strong vaccine business in Japan but almost no international sales. A third group of companies included regional players such as the Serum Institute of India, which focused primarily on creating low-cost versions of vaccines developed by major manufacturers. Vaccines were subject to the same 20-year patent protections as drugs, but because they were created through a biological process rather than a chemical process, they were much harder to create in generic format (which limited the opportunities for competitors to enter the market). The biological nature of vaccines meant that generic products could be subject to almost the same regulatory approval process as new products (see Figure 10.2 for the FDA approval process), even if they were based upon existing vaccines.

VACCINE PROCUREMENT[11]

The largest customers for vaccines were governments and international organizations. Governments and international organizations pledged $25 billion to fund

[6] Sahoo, "Vaccines 2012," p. 10.

[7] Sahoo, "Vaccines 2012," p. 12.

[8] Miloud Kaddar, "Global Vaccine Market Features and Trends," World Health Organization Presentation, 2012, http://who.int/influenza_vaccines_plan/resources/session_10_kaddar.pdf, accessed January 2014.

[9] Compiled from Fierce Vaccines, "Top 5 Vaccine Companies by Revenue—2012," http://www.fiercevaccines.com/special-reports/top-5-vaccine-companies-revenue-2012, accessed January 2014.

[10] Kaddar, "Global Vaccine Market Features and Trends."

[11] John A. Quelch and Margaret L. Rodriguez, "Vision 2020: Takeda and the Vaccine Industry," HBS No. 514-084 (Boston: Harvard Business School Publishing, 2014), p. 9.

Table 10.1 Exhibit 2 Vaccine Prices in Developing and Developed Markets, 2011

Vaccines	*United States*[a]	*South Africa*	*PAHO*	*GAVI/UNICEF*
Pentavalent[b]	$51.15[c]	$9.35	$2.95	$1.75
Rotavirus	$89.25	$7.75	$7.50	$2.50
PCV	$97.21	$26.00	$14.85	$7.00

Source: Compiled from Medecins Sans Frontieres, "The Right Shot," MSFAccess.org, April 2012, http://www.msfaccess.org/sites/default/files/MSF_assets/Vaccines/Docs/VACC_report_RightShot_ENG_2012Update.pdf, accessed February 2014; and Centers for Disease Control and Prevention, "Archived CDC Vaccine Price List as of December 15, 2011," http://www.cdc.gov/vaccines/programs/vfc/awardees/vaccinemanagement/price-list/2011/2011-12-15.html, accessed February 2014.

[a] Prices for the United States and South Africa reflect those paid by government agencies to obtain vaccines.

[b] The pentavalent vaccine purchased by South Africa, PAHO, and GAVI/UNICEF addressed five diseases: diphtheria-tetanus-pertussis (DTP), hepatitis B (HepB), and Haemophilius influenzae type b (Hib).

[c] U.S. pricing information for the pentavalent vaccine sold to South Africa, PAHO, and GAVI/UNICEF was unavailable; the price above is for the DTP, HepB, and Polio pentavalent manufactured by GSK under the brand name "Pediarix" and sold in the U.S.

immunizations between 2011 and 2015.[12] They pressed for much lower prices on vaccines than those sold in the private sector. The U.S. government received discounts of 30%–80% off of private-sector prices.[13] In 2013, a dose of influenza vaccine might be sold to a government health agency for $3.30,[14] while a pharmacy chain would pay $15 and then sell the vaccine directly to consumers at an in-store clinic for $30 per dose.[15]

The Bill & Melinda Gates Foundation, the world's largest private foundation, distributed grants through three subdivisions: the Global Health Program, the Global Development Program, and the United States Program.[16] The Global Health Program provided funding to numerous immunization programs, including the children's vaccine program; Global Alliance for Vaccines and Immunization (GAVI), the Aeras global TB vaccine foundation, and the neglected tropical diseases initiative.

[12] WHO, UNICEF, and World Bank, "State of the world's vaccines and immunization," 3rd ed., World Health Organization, 2009, http://whqlibdoc.who.int/publications/2009/9789241563864_eng.pdf?ua=1, accessed February 2014.

[13] Sahoo, "Vaccines 2012,"p. 70.

[14] Pan American Health Organization, "Expanded Program of Immunization Vaccine Prices for Year 2014," http://www.paho.org/hq/index.php?option=com_content&view=article&id=1864&Itemid=4135, accessed January 2014.

[15] Marty Lariviere, "What explains the price of a flu vaccine?," post on blog "The Operations Room," Kellogg School of Management, January 22, 2013, http://operationsroom.wordpress.com/2013/01/22/what-explains-the-price-of-a-flu-vaccine/, accessed January 2014.

[16] The Bill & Melinda Gates Foundation, "Home Page," http://www.gatesfoundation.org/, accessed January 2014.

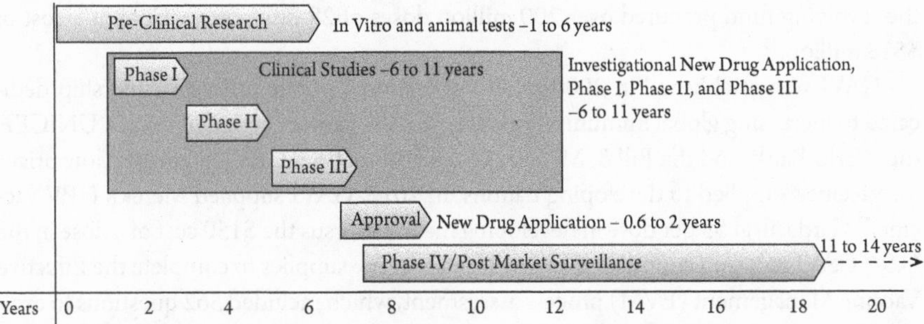

Figure 10.2 Exhibit 3 FDA Approval Process.
Source: Casewriter, adapted from company documents.

In 2007, the Bill & Melinda Gates Foundation funded "Project Optimize" a five-year, $34 million program involving the World Health Organization (WHO) and the Program of Appropriate Technology in Health (PATH).[17,18] Project Optimize aimed to improve the vaccine supply chain, as well as define the ideal characteristics of health products. As part of its cold chain mission, Project Optimize developed global policies and profiles of new technologies such as heat-stable containers for vaccines that would operate in environments lacking power.[19] Project Optimize also developed a vaccine cold-chain costing tool that transformed operational variables into economic measures (e.g., cost per dose administered, cost by location or activity).[20] The Bill & Melinda Gates Foundation also participated in the Last Mile Partnership (LMP), along with the Coca-Cola Company and Accenture Development Partnerships. LMP improved the cold chain through partnerships with the private sector: in Ghana, for example, Coke shared its refrigerator maintenance work process and best practices to improve the performance of cold chains.[21]

The Pan American Health Organization (PAHO) was the regional office of WHO for the Americas. Founded in 1902, PAHO was the oldest international public health agency. Through its revolving fund, PAHO and WHO offered a cooperative purchasing mechanism for vaccines, which were then distributed throughout the Americas. In 2012,

[17] PATH brought together representatives from industry and developing countries to implement new vaccine supply chain technologies, such as "smart" refrigerators, which kept temperatures at ideal levels for vaccines; new technologies for more efficient cooling; and lower-cost solar refrigerators.

[18] UNICEF, "Cold Chain and Logistics Taskforce Workshop," November 2009, http://www.unicef.org/immunization/files/CCL_Workshop_Report_Nov_2009.pdf, accessed February 2014.

[19] PATH and WHO, "Cool innovations for vaccine transportation and storage," July 2012, http://www.path.org/publications/files/TS_opt_cool_innov.pdf, accessed February 2014.

[20] PATH and WHO, "Building next-generation vaccine supply systems," May 2012, http://www.path.org/publications/files/TS_opt_evm_hermes_fs.pdf, accessed February 2014.

[21] David Sarley, Adrian Ristow, and Edward Llewellyn, "Coca-Cola's Refrigeration Equipment Maintenance Model," Last Mile Partnership, July 2013, http://www.technet-21.org/resources/documents/cold-chain-equipment/1710-ghana-health-services-vaccines-intervention-implementation-of-cold-chain-uptime-coca-colas-refrigeration-equipment-maintenance-model, accessed February 2014.

the revolving fund procured over 200 million doses of 28 different vaccines at a cost of $518 million.[22]

GAVI was established in 2000 as an international public-private partnership dedicated to increasing global immunization rates. GAVI's donors included WHO, UNICEF, the World Bank, and the Bill & Melinda Gates Foundation. GAVI negotiated low prices for vaccines supplied to developing nations. In 2012, GAVI supplied Merck's HPV vaccine,[23] Gardasil, at $5 per dose in developing markets versus the $150 cost of a dose in the U.S.[24] GAVI required countries applying for its vaccine supplies to complete the Effective Vaccine Management (EVM) process assessment, which included 562 questions to evaluate the vaccine supply chain within the country. By May 2012, over 50 countries had completed assessments of their vaccine supply chains.[25,26] By 2014, GAVI had secured over $8.4 billion in funding through 2016 to help supply the world's poorest countries with vaccines.[27]

UNICEF was the world's largest supplier of vaccines, procuring vaccines for over 80 countries.[28] UNICEF obtained vaccines at affordable prices via partnerships with manufacturers. UNICEF vaccines ultimately reached about 36% of the world's children.[29] In 2012, 50% of global vaccine doses were purchased by UNICEF, but they accounted for only about 5% of worldwide vaccine sales in dollars.[30] In 2009, all of GAVI's vaccine supply was purchased with the help of UNICEF, at a cost of $390 million.[31] In 2011, UNICEF and PAHO together procured $1.43 billion of vaccines, or roughly 7.5% of total vaccines sold by value (a fivefold increase since 2000).[32] The growth of vaccine purchases was driven by the scaling of campaigns, new vaccines, price increases, a strong emphasis on eradicating polio, and the creation of GAVI.[33]

[22] "PAHO/WHO Revolving Fund helps countries provide free vaccines during Vaccination Week in the Americas," Pan American Health Organization, April 26, 2013, http://www.paho.org/HQ/index.php?option=com_content&view=article&id=8598%3Apahowho-revolving-fund-helps-countries-provide-free-vaccines-during-vaccination-week-in-the-americas&catid=740%3Anews-press-releases&Itemid=1926&lang=en, accessed January 2014.

[23] Human papillomavirus (HPV) was a sexually transmitted infection that could result in health problems such as recurrent respiratory papillomatosis (throat warts), genital warts, and cervical cancer.

[24] Sahoo, "Vaccines 2012,"p. 22.

[25] B. Y. Lee, T. M. Assi, and J. Rajgopal et al., "Impact of introducing the pneumococcal and rotavirus vaccines into the routine immunization program in Niger," *American Journal of Public Health* 102, no. 2 (2012): 269–276.

[26] B. Y. Lee, T. M. Assi, and K. Rookkapan et al., "Replacing the measles ten-dose vaccine presentation with the single-dose presentation in Thailand," *Vaccine* 29, no. 21 (2011): 3811–3817.

[27] GAVI Alliance, "Advocacy Statistics," http://www.gavialliance.org/advocacy-statistics/, accessed January 2014.

[28] UNICEF, "Cold Chain and Logistics Taskforce Workshop," http://www.unicef.org/.

[29] UNICEF, "Immunization," http://www.unicef.org/immunization/, accessed January 2014.

[30] Kaddar, "Global Vaccine Market Features and Trends."

[31] GAVI Alliance, "UNICEF," http://www.gavialliance.org/about/governance/gavi-board/composition/unicef/, accessed January 2014.

[32] Kaddar, "Global Vaccine Market Features and Trends."

[33] Kaddar, "Global Vaccine Market Features and Trends."

In addition to procuring vaccines, UNICEF also helped to procure cold chain equipment, offered technical guidance on cold chain systems, and assisted with national and subnational installation. In 2007, UNICEF conducted the first "Cold Chain Logistics" task force meeting to address six "rights": "right amount of right commodity to the right place at the right time at the right quality for the right cost."[34] In 2008, a grant from the government of Japan for pandemic prevention provided $8 million to improve cold chain systems in 17 countries; UNICEF oversaw the implementation of the grant.[35]

COLD CHAIN DISTRIBUTION

The cold chain referred to the system for temperature-controlled storage and transport of vaccines from production to point of use. (See Figure 10.3 for an illustration of the cold chain.) Cold chain systems were complex and included management information systems to collect and report data; inventory management systems, temperature-controlled storage capacity; distribution and maintenance systems for transport; and trained personnel at every stage.[36] Vaccines were typically stored in refrigerators, while transportation required cold boxes and ice packs.[37] Cold boxes were insulated transportation containers that had internal divisions to separate the ice packs from the vaccines (to prevent freezing). (See Figure 10.4 for an image of a cold box.)

Cold chain systems had been in place for over 30 years in some areas and helped to achieve vaccine coverage of 85% of the world's population by 2011.[38] Despite the success of cold chains in select geographies, cold chains were difficult to maintain in places with unreliable electricity, poor maintenance of equipment, and far-flung communities. In 2013, the total global cost of cold chain logistical services for biologic products (including vaccines, medicines, and other temperature-controlled medical products) was $7.5 billion (and estimated to reach $9.3 billion in 2017).[39] The cost to maintain and expand cold chain systems to accommodate additional vaccines and medicines was typically paid by government agencies, while GAVI provided one-off introductory grants for new vaccines,[40] and the Gates Foundation, international aid

[34] UNICEF, "Cold Chain and Logistics Taskforce Workshop."

[35] UNICEF, "Cold Chain and Logistics Taskforce Workshop."

[36] UNICEF, "Cold Chain and Logistics Taskforce Workshop."

[37] State of New Jersey Department of Health, "Guidelines for maintaining vaccine cold chain," http://www.state.nj.us/health/er/documents/coldchain.pdf, accessed February 2014.

[38] "Global vaccine coverage is estimated by tracking the percentage of children receiving the third dose of diphtheria-pertussis-tetanus vaccine," World Health Organization (WHO) and United Nations Children's Fund (UNICEF) coverage estimates 1980–2010, July 2010, 2011 revision, accessed February 2014.

[39] "Pharmaceutical Commerce's Biopharma Cold Chain Sourcebook, 4th ed. Is published," *Pharmaceutical Commerce*, April 17, 2013, http://pharmaceuticalcommerce.com/latest_news?articleid=26834, accessed February 2014.

[40] Medecins Sans Frontieres, "The Right Shot," MSFAccess.org, April 2012, http://www.msfaccess.org/sites/default/files/MSF_assets/Vaccines/Docs/VACC_report_RightShot_ENG_2012Update.pdf, accessed February 2014.

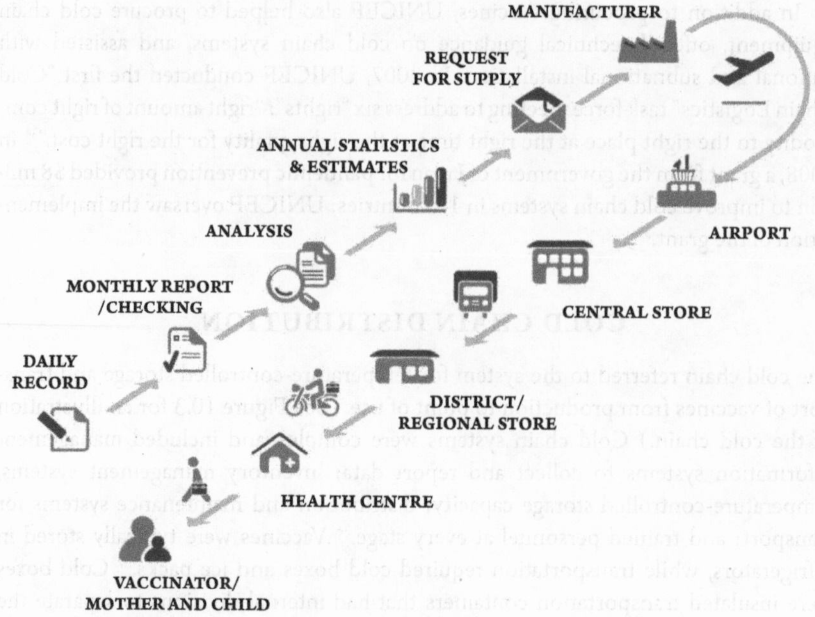

Figure 10.3 Exhibit 4 Cold Chain Illustration, 2014.
Source: Simona Zipursky, "Beyond the cold chain," TechNet Meeting, February 5, 2013, http://www.technet21.org/resources/documents/immunization-delivery-strategies/1591-beyond-the-cold-chain-taking-advantage-of-the-true-heat-stability-of-vaccines, accessed February 2014.

organizations like Doctors Without Borders, and pharmaceutical companies also contributed.[41]

Cold Chain Capacity and Costs

WHO created the Expanded Programme on Immunization (EPI) in 1974 to immunize children younger than one year old against six diseases.[42,43] The 2000s saw the addition of Hepatitis B (HepB), Haemophilus influenza type B (Hib), pneumococcal conjugate (PCV), rotavirus (RV), and human papilloma virus (HPV) vaccines. In 2011, the cost per child to administer these vaccines was nearly $39 (not including wastage).[44] (See Figure 10.5 for immunization cost over time.) Around 14%–20% of the cost of an average immunization was related to the need for cold storage.[45]

[41] Pharmaceutical companies were reluctant to contribute refrigeration equipment because the logistics and servicing were unfamiliar and they could not restrict storage to just their own products.

[42] Medecins Sans Frontieres, "The Right Shot."

[43] The six vaccines in EPI were diphtheria, pertussis, tetanus, polio, measles, and tuberculosis.

[44] Medecins Sans Frontieres, "The Right Shot."

[45] "Comparison of Costs Incurred in Dedicated and Diffused Vaccine Logistics Systems," October 2009, *VillageReach*, http://villagereach.org/vrsite/wp-content/uploads/2010/10/091009-VillageReach-Cost-Study-Report.pdf, accessed February 2014.

Figure 10.4 Exhibit 5 Insulated Cold Box with Ice Packs, 2011.
Source: Givewell, "Vaccine Cold Chain," Wikimedia Commons, April 8, 2011, http://commons.wikimedia.org/wiki/File: VillageReach_vaccine_cold_chain.jpg, accessed February 2014.

The existing cold chain systems worldwide had sufficient capacity to store and deliver the six vaccines that comprised the early EPI[46] (roughly 40 cubic centimeters per child).[47] By 2009, the immunization schedule used by UNICEF required about 60 cubic centimeters of refrigerated vaccine storage per fully immunized child.[48] The roll-out of rotavirus and pneumococcal vaccines in the 2010s threatened to further strain the existing cold chain capacity. WHO estimated at least 150 cubic centimeters would be needed per child to accommodate existing plus new vaccines.[49] UNICEF estimated the additional cost to expand the cold chain by 100 cubic centimeters per child would be between $1 and $20, depending upon the type of cold storage equipment needed.[50] Other medicines that required cold storage (such as rapid diagnostic tests and oxytocin) further increased the amount of cold storage needed per person.[51] Combination vaccines, such as the pentavalent vaccine,[52] effectively reduced the cold chain capacity requirements but not enough to offset the extra space needed for new vaccines.

[46] PATH and WHO, "Building next-generation vaccine supply systems," May 2012, http://www.path.org/publications/files/TS_opt_evm_hermes_fs.pdf, accessed February 2014.

[47] UNICEF, "Cold Chain and Logistics Taskforce Workshop."

[48] UNICEF, "Cold Chain and Logistics Taskforce Workshop."

[49] UNICEF, "Cold Chain and Logistics Taskforce Workshop."

[50] UNICEF, "Cold Chain and Logistics Taskforce Workshop."

[51] UNICEF, "Cold Chain and Logistics Taskforce Workshop."

[52] The pentavalent vaccine administered by GAVI addressed five diseases: diphtheria-tetanus-pertussis (DTP), hepatitis B (HepB), and Haemophilius influenzae type b (Hib).

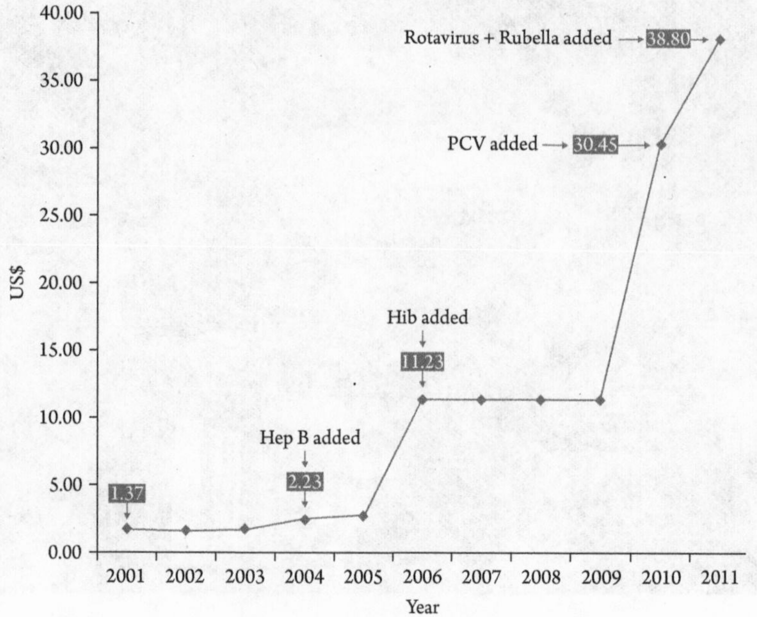

Figure 10.5 Exhibit 6 Immunization Cost per Child, 2001–2011.
Price of an individual vaccine is defined as the average price per dose offered by contracted suppliers to UNICEF in a given year, multiplied by the WHO-recommended number of doses.
Calculations do not include wastage rates factored into vaccine forecasting and purchasing.
Source: Medecins Sans Frontieres, "The Right Shot," MSFAccess.org, April 2012, http://www.msfaccess.org/sites/default/ files/MSF_assets/Vaccines/Docs/VACC_report_RightShot_ENG_2012Update.pdf, accessed February 2014.

Even if the cold chain had the capacity to easily accept new vaccines, the quality of refrigeration was often poor. Storing vaccines in low-cost and easily serviced refrigerators designed for domestic use was common (even in the U.S.).[53] However, domestic refrigerators were not designed for vaccine storage, and poor temperature regulation resulted in higher wastage. In 2012, the U.S. Inspector General released a report that found that 76% of selected clinics in the U.S. had exposed vaccines to inappropriate temperatures for at least five hours over a two-week period (the study did not include data on the impact of the exposure on the efficacy of the vaccines).[54] Costs per refrigeration unit ranged between \$500 and \$5,000, rising to between \$1,000 and \$7,000 when the cost of installation and spare parts were included, which made upgrades to the cold chain costly. (See Figure 10.6 for the cost by refrigeration type.)

[53] PATH and WHO, "Cool innovations."

[54] Daniel R. Levinson, "Vaccines for Children Program: Vulnerabilities in Vaccine Management," U.S. Department of Health and Human Services, June 2012, http://oig.hhs.gov/oei/reports/oei-04-10-00430.pdf, accessed February 2014.

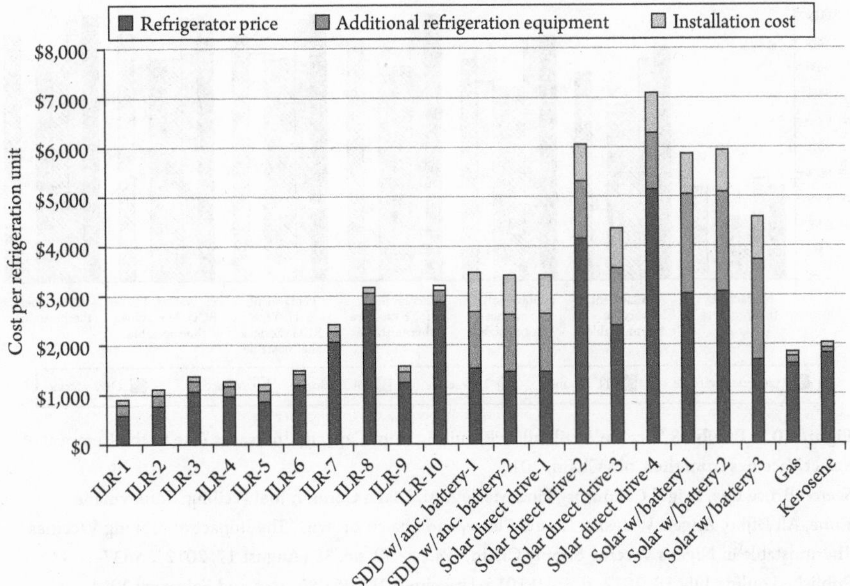

Figure 10.6 Exhibit 7 Comparative Cost of Refrigeration Type, 2014.
SDD = solar direct drive; SDD w/ anc. Battery = solar direct drive with ancillary battery; ILR = ice-lined electric refrigerator.
Source: Solo Kone, Sophie Newland, Tina Lorenson, and Dereje Haile, "Refrigerator Cost Comparison Tool," TechNet21, February 2013, http://www.technet-21.org/resources/documents/cold-chain-equipment/1621-refrigerator-cost-comparison-tool-a-tool-to-inform-cold-chain-equipment-selection, accessed February 2014.

In existing cold chain systems, 50% of vaccine doses were wasted due to expiry, temperature spikes (hot or cold), or other supply chain disruptions.[55] Waste was especially significant for new vaccines, the cost of which could be 50 times higher than mature vaccines.[56] As a result, cold chain wastage represented a significant and growing concern to international organizations and governments that bought vaccines in bulk. Cold chain cost analysis showed that significant savings could come from fewer ice packs (which needed to be collected and returned to storage; and ice stores maintained); less cold-storage space required (as more temperature-stable vaccines or combination vaccines were introduced); and fewer delivery trips to the point of use (previous capacity limited by the size of the iceboxes used to transport vaccines).[57]

55 "WHO. Monitoring Vaccine Wastage at Country Level: Guidelines for Programme Managers," WHO Department of Vaccines and Biologicals, 2005, http://www.who.int/vaccinesdocuments/DocsPDF05/www.811.pdf, accessed February 2014.

56 UNICEF Supply Division, "Vaccine price data page," UNICEF website, http://www.unicef.org/supply/index_57476.html, accessed February 2014.

57 SimonaZipursky,"Beyondthecoldchain,"TechNetMeeting,February5,2013,http://www.technet-21.org/resources/documents/immunization-delivery-strategies/1591-beyond-the-cold-chain-taking-advantage-of-the-true-heat-stability-of-vaccines, accessed February 2014.

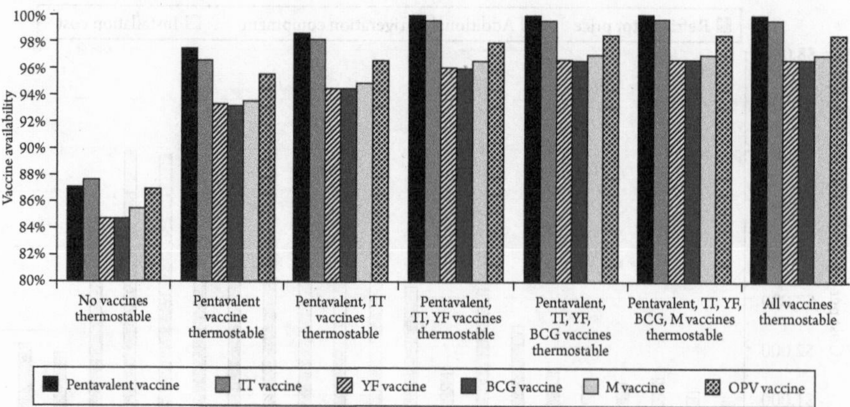

Figure 10.7 Exhibit 8 Vaccine Availability Resulting from Capacity Increases Due to the Removal of Select Vaccines from the Cold Chain, 2012.
Source: Bruce Lee, Brigid Cakouros, Tina-Marie Assi, Diana Connor, Joel Welling, Souleymane Kone, Ali Dijbo, Angela Wateska, Lionel Pierre, and Shawn Brown, "The Impact of Making Vaccines Thermostable in Niger's Vaccine Supply Chain," *Vaccine* 30, no. 38 (August 17, 2012): 5637–5643. Published online July 10, 2012, doi: 10.1016/j.vaccine.2012.06.087, accessed February 2014.

Thermostable Vaccine Technologies

Since a vaccine's efficacy began to degrade immediately upon leaving the factory, any process that could make vaccines hardier could significantly reduce waste and costs. In addition, removing a vaccine from the cold chain would free up additional capacity so that those vaccines that still required temperature-controlled storage could become more widely available (see Figure 10.7). Nongovernment organizations, research labs, and companies worldwide were working to improve the thermo-stability of vaccines.

In 2012, PATH and Bend Research partnered to produce a thermo-stable influenza vaccine using a "spray dry" technique.[58] The process produced a vaccine that maintained effectiveness, even when stored at 50 degrees Celsius for over two months.[59] The researchers believed the technology could be applied to other vaccines. In 2013, the Biomedical Advanced Research and Development Authority (BARDA) gave PATH a $2.5 million grant to develop a scalable production process and share the results with vaccine manufacturers.[60] Separately, a research team at Tufts School of Medicine developed a technique to protect vaccines from extreme temperatures by encapsulating them in harmless bacterial spores that were naturally heat resistant and could be taken orally or intranasally.[61] The team piloted the technology with

[58] Spray drying was the process commonly used in pharmaceutical and food production to create powders with uniform particle sizes (such as powdered milk). Liquids were sprayed through an atomizer and dried quickly with a hot gas.

[59] "New technology for producing thermostable vaccines," PATH, http://www.path.org/news/press-room/149/, accessed February 2014.

[60] "PATH receives follow-up funding to scale up production of thermostable influenza vaccines," PATH, February 12, 2013, http://www.path.org/news/press-room/123/, accessed February 2014.

[61] "Bacterial Spores as Vaccine Delivery Systems," *Grand Challenges in Global Health*, http://www.grandchallenges.org/ImproveVaccines/Challenges/HeatStable/Pages/BacterialSpores.aspx#Collaborators, accessed February 2014.

strains of diphtheria, tetanus, pertussis, and rotavirus. Third, researchers at Oxford and Nova Bio-Pharma Technologies found that sealing vaccines in glass made from sugar enabled the vaccine to be transported and stored at 37 degrees Celsius for up to one year without significant degradation.[62] The sugar suspended the vaccine until the point of use, at which time the sugar was dissolved with water.

Other approaches used additives to modify a vaccine's properties. Techniques including the addition of salts, polyols,[63] and sugars were commonly used in pharmaceutical production but had only recently begun to be tried in vaccine production. Researchers at Endo Pharmaceuticals tested over 200 formulations of a polymer, Pluronic F127, to stabilize measles and HepB vaccines between negative 10 and 45 degrees Celsius.[64] PATH developed a freeze-protection technology for vaccines that contained aluminum adjuvant and released it into the public domain for use by manufacturers.[65]

Professors Fiorenzo Omenetto and David Kaplan of Tufts University discovered new uses for silk as a medium for photonics, medical, optoelectronics, and high-technology applications. They found that the addition of a solution of purified fibroin protein derived from silk stabilized mumps vaccine at 45 degrees Celsius for over six months.[66] Harvard Kennedy School graduate, Livio Valenti, introduced Omenetto and Kaplan to Vaxess.

VAXESS GOES TO MARKET

Company Background

Vaxess was founded in 2012 by four young entrepreneurs: Michael Schrader, the chief executive, (a graduate of Harvard Business School); scientist Kathryn Kosuda, vice president of research and development; lawyer Patrick Ho, vice president of operations and legal affairs; and Livio Valenti, vice president of policy and strategy. Vaxess aimed to improve access to vaccines worldwide by removing the need for cold storage of the product between manufacture and use. Vaxess licensed the discovery of the properties of fibroin as a vaccine stabilizer from Tufts University and sought to commercialize the technology. First, Tufts granted Vaxess an exclusive option to license the technology. Then, on December 31, 2013, Vaxess and Tufts converted

[62] "Sugar preserves vaccines without refrigeration," *CBC News*, February 17, 2010, http://www.cbc.ca/news/technology/sugar-preserves-vaccines-without-refrigeration-1.933492, accessed February 2014.

[63] Polyol was a type of alcohol, which included sugar alcohols used to artificially sweeten food products.

[64] "Thermostable Vaccines with Improved Stability at Non Refrigerated Temperatures," *Grand Challenges in Global Health*, http://www.grandchallenges.org/ImproveVaccines/Challenges/HeatStable/Pages/Thermo stable.aspx#top, accessed February 2014.

[65] "Vaccine freeze-protection technology: frequently asked questions," PATH, http://www.path.org/projects/vaccine-stabilization-freeze-faqs.php, accessed February 2014.

[66] Jeney Zhang, Eleanor Pritchard, Xiao Hu, Thomas Valentin, Bruce Panilaitis, Fiorenzo G. Omenetto, and David L. Kaplan, "Stabilization of vaccines and antibiotics in silk and eliminating the cold chain," *PNAS* 109, no. 30 (2012): 11981–11986; published ahead of print, July 9, 2012, doi:10.1073/pnas.1206210109, accessed February 2014.

the exclusive option into an exclusive license. Vaxess would retain the exclusive right to Tufts' patents related to the vaccine stabilization technology (through the licensing of seven patent families, which included a number of U.S. and foreign patents and patent applications) until the patents expired (the last was expected to expire in 2033). The team at Vaxess had high expectations for the technology and hoped to use it to stabilize multiple vaccines.

Vaxess raised an initial $160,000 as the winner of three business plan competitions in 2012 and 2013. In May 2013, Vaxess secured $3.75 million in financing, principally from Norwich Ventures, enough to fund the company for at least two years. Vaxess's operating budget for 2014 was roughly $1.2 million.

Research Agenda

In November 2013, Vaxess launched a laboratory space in Cambridge, Massachusetts, and hired two senior scientists and one research associate led by Kosuda. The first task was to replicate the experiments performed by the professors at Tufts with the measles, mumps, and rubella (MMR) vaccine in the Vaxess lab. This work was to be followed by efforts to stabilize a wide range of vaccine candidates, further validating the platform nature of the technology. The team needed to demonstrate the efficacy of the silk in vitro (which would illustrate its stabilization properties) and in vivo (which would show that the addition of silk fibroin did not have an impact on the efficacy of the vaccine antigens). The in vitro tests required the silk solution to be added to a vaccine and placed into stability chambers to assess the formulation's stability at high temperatures. The total time needed to complete the in vitro test, from formulation through stability testing, was six months per vaccine target. Evaluation of in vivo performance required testing on animal and human subjects, the cost of which could range from approximately $300,000 (for small animals) to millions of dollars (for human trials) per vaccine. Due to the resources required Vaxess chose, in some cases, to work with external organizations in performing the in vivo tests.

In parallel with the replication of the MMR experiments, the Vaxess team also planned to optimize the silk stabilizer formula to ready it for mass production. The U.S. Food and Drug Administration (FDA) stipulated that nonclinical research studies for vaccines had to be conducted in facilities that upheld "good laboratory practices" (GLP).[67] FDA requirements for facilities to uphold "good manufacturing practices" (GMP) carried even higher standards for product testing and quality assurance than GLP.[68] The silk used to create the stabilizer was an organic product sourced from different providers. In order to prepare to meet the GMP standards, Vaxess had already begun working to improve sourcing and extracting processes to ensure the quality and consistency of the stabilizer.

[67] "Good Laboratory Practice for Nonclinical Laboratory Studies," Title 21, U.S. Code of Federal Regulations, Chapter 21, Part 58, 2013, http://www.accessdata.fda.gov/scripts/cdrh/cfdocs/cfcfr/CFRSearch.cfm?CFRPart=58&showFR=1&subpartNode=21:1.0.1.1.23.1, accessed February 2014.

[68] U.S. Federal Food and Drug Administration, "Pharmaceutical cGMPS for the 21st Century," 2009, http://www.fda.gov/drugs/developmentapprovalprocess/manufacturing/questionsandanswersoncurrentgoodmanufacturingpracticescgmpfordrugs/ucm071836.htm, accessed February 2014.

Vaxess faced the challenge of transforming a technology developed in an academic setting into a product marketable to global organizations. Regulatory requirements for clinical trials of thermo-stable vaccines meant, according to Schrader, up to six years of further research and development before a commercial product could be brought to market.

Selecting Vaccine Targets

The Vaxess team set out to delineate criteria for vaccines that would be good candidates for its technology. In the short term, the team decided to focus on live attenuated[69] and lyophilized[70] vaccine types where the value-added potential of adding the fibroin solution could be greatest. (See Table 10.2 for the drug prices of top-selling vaccines.)

Over the long term, Vaxess intended to partner with government agencies and vaccine makers to defray the costs of research. Organizations such as the U.S. Centers for Disease Control and Prevention (CDC), the U.S. National Institutes of Health (NIH), PATH, the Task Force for Global Health, and the Gates Foundation had all expressed interest and willingness to support efforts to improve vaccine stability. Vaxess aimed to have at least two vaccine targets complete in vitro testing by the end of 2014. Vaxess also partnered with multiple universities and contract research organizations to outsource a portion of the laboratory testing.

Kosuda explained the vaccine targets would be selected by Vaxess according to a "balance of science, business and public health concerns." Preliminary scientific research indicated that the technology could potentially be used to stabilize a range of biological compounds. Ho believed that business and public health objectives could be largely aligned within the vaccine industry. This was because large international organizations like GAVI worked to pool demand and create markets for these vaccines with the greatest public health impact. He stated: "GAVI is trying to guide the market and businesses, including ours, to focus on areas of importance to public health." The Vaxess team recognized the need to balance the profit incentives of Big Pharma (which could limit the distribution of the silk formulation via exclusive contracts) with time to market (such firms would likely get the formulation into the market more quickly than organizations operating without a profit incentive).

SELLING THE CONCEPT

After a year of engaging with prospective pharmaceutical partners and the global health community, Vaxess decided to focus its initial sales efforts on the leading manufacturers of vaccines rather than on GAVI, UNICEF, and government healthcare agencies in emerging economies. According to Schrader:

> Government organizations haven't been able to move at the pace we want to. Big pharmaceutical companies get the idea we are selling, the problem that it helps to resolve and the benefits of moving quickly to get it to market.

69 Live attenuated vaccines stimulated immune response by using weakened forms of the living virus or bacteria.

70 Lyophilized vaccines were freeze dried to increase shelf life. Many of the vaccines included in the EPI programme, and roughly half of those distributed to the developing world, were lyophilized.

Table 10.2 Exhibit 9 Drug Prices for Top-Selling Vaccines, 2012

Vaccine[a]	*Type*	*Manufacturer*	*Price per Dose, Developed*[b]	*Price per Dose, Developing*
Prevnar 13	Pneumococcal	Pfizer	$128.16	$7.00
Gardasil	HPV	Merck	$141.38	$4.50
Pediarix	DTP, Polio, HIB	GSK	$70.72	N/A
Hepatitis Franchise	Hep A, Hep B	GSK	$92.50	N/A
Varivax	Varicella	Merck	$94.14	N/A
Cervarix	HPV	GSK	$128.75	$4.60
Rotateq	Rotavirus	Merck	$75.20	$5.00
Synflorix	Pneumococcal	GSK	N/A	$7.00

Source: Compiled from Alison Bryant, "20 Top-selling Vaccines—H1 2012," *Fierce Vaccines*, September 25, 2012, http://www.fiercevaccines.com/special-report/20-top-selling-vaccines/2012-09-25, accessed March 2014; UNICEF, "Vaccine Price Data," http://www.unicef.org/supply/index_57476.html, accessed March 2014; and Centers for Disease Control and Prevention, "CDC Vaccine Price List as of March 12, 2014," http://www.cdc.gov/vaccines/programs/vfc/awardees/vaccine-management/price-list/, accessed February 2014.

[a] Top-selling vaccines based upon sales data for the first six months of 2012.

[b] U.S. private-sector prices in 2014, unless otherwise noted.

Much depended on one or more drug companies championing the Vaxess solution. Adding fibroin solution might enable a drug manufacturer to achieve the same level of vaccine efficacy over time with less antigen. In the U.S., manufacturer vaccine prices typically incorporated a strong gross margin of up to 95%, and the largest cost component in most vaccines was the antigen or active ingredient. (Other variable costs included manufacturing, packaging, storage and shipping, tracking and monitoring, and replacement of defective product.) In the U.S., the larger drug companies stored their vaccines in their own refrigerated warehouses and then shipped them to drugstore chains, large hospitals, and secondary distributors, as needed. Vaxess estimated that its technology could cut vaccine costs for manufacturers anywhere from 2%–25%, depending on the product, geography, and market dynamics. (This included savings across a variety of areas such as eliminating the need for storing products in refrigerated environments, reduced monitoring of storage conditions, and reduction in spoiled product.)

In addition to reducing the warehousing and transportation costs for vaccine manufacturers, Vaxess' technology could also increase demand through differentiation. Jim Connolly, a non-executive director of Vaxess and former head of Wyeth's global vaccine business, explained:

> If Vaxess partners with a vaccine manufacturer in a given category (e.g., measles or rabies), that partner will probably want exclusivity. If you were UNICEF and you were considering two comparable vaccines, but one is much more stable, that's the one you'd choose, prices being equal.

After performing additional tests, Vaxess concluded that its solution should be added to a vaccine during the formulation stage of the manufacturing process. The optimal percentage of Vaxess solution in the final formulation varied by vaccine (between 0.1% and 10%). Vaxess was aware of the competition it faced from other emerging thermo-stable technologies, such as the sugar glass approach, but management believed these technologies were not as effective as the Vaxess solution. Schrader summarized the challenge:

> Our technology is superior but, from Big Pharma's viewpoint, potentially riskier. Silk protein material is on the market today in numerous medical devices but has never before been FDA-approved in an injectable format.

Kosuda believed that so-called "competitive" technologies could present opportunities for collaboration. The silk fibroin formula could conceivably be used in conjunction with other additives with the same thermo-stability objective.

PARTNERSHIP APPROACHES

Thanks to its presentations at scientific conferences and referrals, Vaxess was known to the major vaccine manufacturers by the end of 2013. To help get the company up and running and attract Series A funding, Vaxess chose to pursue a partnership agreement whereby a pharmaceutical company would pay Vaxess to license the technology for select vaccines and would cover portions of the R&D costs. In return, Vaxess would agree to meet specific milestones, including a demonstration that the technology would successfully increase the stability of the selected vaccines. Despite entering into conversations with several pharmaceutical companies early on, negotiations of the contract terms stretched over an entire year.

With the security provided by the Series A funding and its initial agreement, Vaxess was then in a position to select partnerships that would closely match its capabilities and mission. Vaxess could maximize its impact by partnering with many pharmaceutical companies to increase the thermo-stability of as many vaccines as possible as fast as possible. However, big pharmaceutical companies considered the silk technology a means to achieve differentiation, and in most cases, preferred exclusive contracts. In addition, Big Pharma was focused not only on reducing distribution costs for existing vaccines but also on the development of new vaccines. In the U.S., the cold chain was already in place, although it still required annual investment for replacement equipment and monitoring.

Big Pharma's engagement style with Vaxess' technology varied widely across firms. In general, there seemed to be four main approaches: science-driven, business development-driven, business need-driven, and wait-and-see.

Several companies exhibited a desire to lead with science. Prior to any discussion of specific vaccine targets or long-term partnership strategies, these companies wanted to run a battery of tests to validate the silk technology. They wished to confirm that the silk-enhanced vaccine formulation: (a) successfully stabilized the vaccine, and (b) still met all of the other vaccine performance targets. These studies varied from simple, quick laboratory tests to more extensive animal studies. This approach provided pharmaceutical companies with technical validation before investing, but it exposed them to the risk of losing the rights to other companies that were willing to pay up front. The second approach focused on business development, wherein pharmaceutical partners sought long-term, worldwide rights to the silk technology for one or more vaccines. Before initiating any expensive scientific studies, these partners wanted to ensure that long-term agreements were in place. While this approach protected the partners, it often imposed higher costs on them and also lengthened the negotiation time.

The third approach was driven by market need. In these pharmaceutical companies, certain departments had specific stability issues, and they wanted to understand if Vaxess' technology could help. These issues ranged from early-stage research with highly unstable targets to manufacturing challenges regarding distribution logistics. At one pharmaceutical company, Vaxess engaged with four internal groups, including research, manufacturing, and business development. The company had cut spending on internal research and development in favor of partnering with third parties. The downside to the approach was that the involvement of multiple departments slowed down the company's decision-making process.

The fourth approach, wait and see, was the most cautious. Certain prospective partners, especially those dedicated to launching new vaccines versus upgrading existing vaccines, decided to wait for more data before engaging. This approach often saved the pharmaceutical companies time and money in the short term, but carried a higher price if the company wished to gain access to the technology at a later date.

Schrader felt it was critical to evaluate the different approaches in terms of what offered the most value to the pharmaceutical partner, as well as to Vaxess, so that a mutually beneficial partnership and path to market could be established. Some at Vaxess debated whether it was better to partner with the larger vaccine manufacturers (which possessed established global marketing and distribution capabilities) or with the smaller, emerging vaccine companies (which were eager to grow their market share). Although the team felt a natural urgency to bring the silk formulation to the market as quickly as possible, the company lacked the financial resources to sustain a lengthy research program.

11

ACCESS HEALTH CT

MARKETING AFFORDABLE CARE

John A. Quelch and Michael Norris

Kevin Counihan stood up from his desk and glanced at his watch: 12:20 a.m. It was April 1, 2014. Open enrollment in health insurance plans had just ended at Access Health CT (AHCT),[1] where Counihan was the CEO. In the last week, more than 25,000 people had enrolled in Connecticut's Medicaid program or in qualified health plans (QHPs) offered by private insurers on accesshealthct.com, the state's online insurance exchange. This final surge brought the total number of enrollments to over 200,000 since the beginning of open enrollment on October 1, 2013, which was double the goal that the federal government had set for the state. Local and national media outlets were pointing to AHCT as an important success story in the nationwide push to increase insurance coverage through the Patient Protection and Affordable Care Act (ACA). Relatively affluent, Connecticut had only about 345,000 uninsured individuals before open enrollment began, or 9.4% of its population of 3.6 million, well below the national average of 15% uninsured. Counihan thought that achieving twice the goal in a state with already high insurance penetration and the fourth-highest insurance premiums in the country was particularly gratifying.

Although he was proud of AHCT's success, Counihan still had concerns for 2015. For example, the federal funding that had been AHCT's sole source of revenue since its inception would cease at the end of 2014. AHCT had a funding model to make it financially viable on its own—the ability to assess a tax on any individual or small group medical or dental carrier capable of offering a health plan on the exchange, whether they did or did not offer a plan—but Counihan believed that these funds would cover only about 80% of the projected 2015 budget (see Table 11.1a **and** Table 11.1b for 2012–2014 budget information). He would need to find new sources of funds to sustain AHCT's success.

Counihan and his senior staff also worried about 2015 enrollments. AHCT had invested in an extensive marketing push with the help of marketing firm Pappas MacDonnell in 2013 and 2014. The campaign had raised awareness about the ACA

[1] The organization was named "Access Health CT," but referred to itself as "Access Health Connecticut."

Table 11.1a Exhibit 1a AHCT's Revenues, Expenses, and Change in Net Position, 2012–2013 (FY July 1–June 30)

	2012	*2013*
Operating revenues:		
Government grants and contracts	$3,448,792	$45,463,090
Other income	–	513
Total revenues	3,448,792	45,463,603
Operating expenses:		
Wages	309,049	2,734,791
Fringe benefits	79,796	626,199
Consultants	1,357,315	16,838,212
Equipment	7,280	217,628
Supplies	4,076	21,882
Travel	17,220	99,891
Administration	67,657	249,885
Maintenance	8,424	875,491
Depreciation and amortization	1,064	1,509,001
Total operating expenses	1,851,881	23,172,980
Change in net position	1,596,911	22,290,623
Net position, beginning of year	–	1,596,911
Net position, end of year	$1,596,911	$23,887,534

Source: Company documents.

and AHCT, improved education and engagement about the law and health insurance in general, and spurred enrollment. It had not come cheap, however, and the federal grants that had funded the marketing in 2013–2014 would run out in the midst of the open enrollment period in 2014–2015. If AHCT's highly visible 2013–2014 marketing campaign could not convince, or perhaps even reach, tens of thousands of uninsured individuals throughout the state, what chance did AHCT have of connecting with the uninsured in 2014–2015?

Finally, Counihan had some concerns about the health-care law itself. The law allowed insurance carriers to change premiums the following year, subject to state insurance commissioner approval, if they determined that the risk pool warranted it. Would Connecticut's risk pool be too heavily weighted towards older or sicker individuals, leading insurers to raise rates on everyone in the individual market? Would bad experiences with insurance companies, including potential rate increases, lead to a negative perception of AHCT? Individuals who bought insurance plans on AHCT and received subsidies for their purchases would have to be re-qualified every year, but there was no system in place yet to automate or standardize the annual re-enrollment process. Would next year's open enrollment be as relatively smooth as this year's had been?

Table 11.1b Exhibit 1b AHCT's Marketing Budget, November 2012–March 2014 (part of "Consultants" in **Exhibit 1a**)

Category	*Pre-Enrollment (Nov. 2012–Sep. 2013)*	*Enrollment Period (Oct. 2013–Mar. 2014)*	*Total*
Public relations	$351,397	$140,000	$491,397
Paid media, creative, production	2,057,591	5,625,034	7,682,625
Direct response acquisition	34,253	240,355	274,608
Outreach including staff, storefronts, events, fairs	2,349,359	1,902,086	4,251,445
Collateral & promotions	146,542	323,538	470,080
Learn website, interactive tools, content development	524,971	390,866	915,837
Social media, email & text messaging	115,791	137,931	253,722
Small business, broker marketing	257,051	125,639	382,690
Customer database set-up	84,810	15,334	100,144
Marketing strategy, planning, branding	949,439	348,465	1,297,904
Research, testing, analytics	164,249	323,386	487,635
Total	$7,035,454	$9,572,634	$16,608,088

Source: Company documents.

Counihan knew the stakes were high. He, and AHCT, had received immense support from Connecticut's political establishment so far, but he knew that could change if significant operational issues surfaced.

HEALTH INSURANCE IN THE UNITED STATES AND THE AFFORDABLE CARE ACT

The ACA was signed into law by President Barack Obama on March 23, 2010, and the majority of the law was upheld by the Supreme Court in June 2012. While certain ACA provisions took effect immediately, other provisions, including the creation of insurance "marketplaces" (referred to as exchanges in the ACA) and the imposition of the individual mandate to have health insurance, were implemented over time. By 2014, most provisions of the law were in place, although due to delays in writing certain rules and implementing some technology, combined with political and industry lobbying, other provisions, such as the requirement for businesses with 50 or more employees to provide health insurance for their workers or face a penalty, were delayed (see Table 11.2 for a timeline of major provisions). The ACA promised to change the U.S. health insurance market, which comprised three segments: those covered by government insurance programs, those covered by private insurance (either employer-sponsored or individually purchased), and the uninsured.

Government insurance programs President Lyndon Johnson signed the government-run health insurance programs, Medicare and Medicaid, into law in 1965. Medicare, administered and funded at the federal level, covered the elderly (65 and older), and Medicaid, administered and jointly funded by the states, covered the poor and permanently disabled. About 50 million people relied on Medicare for some or all of their health-care needs in 2014, including about 42 million elderly people, more than 98% of the U.S. elderly population. About 8 million permanently disabled people (half of that population) relied on Medicare, and many were also eligible for Medicaid.[2] Medicaid or other public insurance programs were the primary health insurance for about 55 million people, many of whom were children; virtually any poor child was eligible for Medicaid.[3] Each state's Medicaid program had different eligibility requirements and benefits. About 43% of the funding for Medicaid came out of state budgets, and these funds often accounted for 10% or more of the total state budget.

Employer-sponsored private insurance Most non-elderly people in the U.S., about 150 million people,[4] obtained health insurance through their employer from a for-profit insurance company, a mutual insurance company, a Blue Cross Blue Shield plan,[5] or their employer's self-funded insurance offerings (see Figures 11.1a and 11.1b). This system had developed during World War II when a 1942 wage control law allowed employers to offer health insurance rather than higher wages to attract highly qualified employees, often as a result of collective bargaining by trade unions. After World War II, a tax break on these employer-sponsored plans was made permanent, encouraging more employers to offer plans for their employees. By 2014, about 57% of firms offered insurance plans, including 99% of firms with more than 200 employees.[6] Annual premiums[7] for individuals under employer-sponsored plans ranged from about $860 annually for those working in small firms to about $1,000 annually for employees of larger firms; the corresponding premiums for families ranged from

[2] Kaiser Family Foundation, "The Uninsured: A Primer—Key Facts about Health Insurance on the Eve of Coverage Expansions," October 23, 2013, http://kff.org/uninsured/report/the-uninsured-a-primer-key-facts-about-health-insurance-on-the-eve-of-coverage-expansions/, accessed April 2014.

[3] Kaiser Family Foundation, "The Uninsured: A Primer."

[4] Kaiser Family Foundation, "The Uninsured: A Primer."

[5] These plans were regulated differently in different states, but were historically nonprofit corporations. By 2014, many had become for-profit companies.

[6] Kaiser Family Foundation and Health Research & Educational Trust, "2013 Kaiser/HRET Employer Health Benefits Survey," http://www.kff.org/private-insurance/report/2013-employer-health-benefits/, accessed April 2014.

[7] A premium was the amount an insured individual paid to their insurer every month, a deductible was the amount the insured had to pay out-of-pocket each year for health services before the insurance started paying, and copayments and coinsurance were the small payments that patients made each time they visited a doctor's office.

Table 11.2 Exhibit 2 Major Provisions of the Affordable Care Act

Provision	*In Effect As of*
Consumer protections; guaranteed issue[a] children	March 2010
Free preventive care must be included in all plans	2010, 2012, 2014
Begin to close the Medicare Part D "donut hole"	March 2010
Children can stay on parents' insurance until age 26	March 2010
Begin Medicaid expansion	March 2010
Cost-cutting innovations	January 2011
Medical loss ratio	January 2011
Open enrollment begins	October 2013
State health exchanges open	October 2013
Individual mandate	January 2014
Guaranteed issue[a] adults	January 2014
Essential health benefits	January 2014
Full Medicaid expansion	January 2014
"Cadillac tax" on high-cost insurance plans	January 2018
Employer mandate penalty	Delayed until January 2015 for businesses with 100+ employees, January 2016 for businesses with 50–99 employees

Source: Casewriter, from Kaiser Family Foundation, "Health Reform Implementation Timeline," http://kff.org/interactive/implementation-timeline/, accessed April 2014.

[a] "Guaranteed issue" meant that insurers could not deny coverage due to preexisting conditions. The ACA mandated guaranteed issue for children beginning in 2010 and for adults beginning in 2014.

$4,000 annually.[8] The cost for the employer was typically four times the employee's contribution.[9]

The individual market for private insurance Those individuals who did not qualify for Medicare or Medicaid and were unemployed, self-employed, worked part-time for an employer that did not offer insurance to part-time workers, or worked for an employer that did not offer insurance at all, had to buy health insurance on their own or go without it. Buying health insurance of the coverage level that would be offered in an employer-sponsored health plan was often prohibitively expensive for an individual, so many people who bought their own health insurance (often subject to long waiting periods, and sometimes, limited to only emergency coverage) were considered "underinsured." Average yearly premiums for those who bought their own insurance topped $2,400 in 2010.[10] In addition, many of these plans had very high

[8] Kaiser Family Foundation, "The Uninsured: A Primer."

[9] Kaiser Family Foundation, "Average Single Premium per Enrolled Employee For Employer-Based Health Insurance," http://kff.org/other/state-indicator/single-coverage/, accessed April 2014.

[10] Kaiser Family Foundation, "The Uninsured: A Primer."

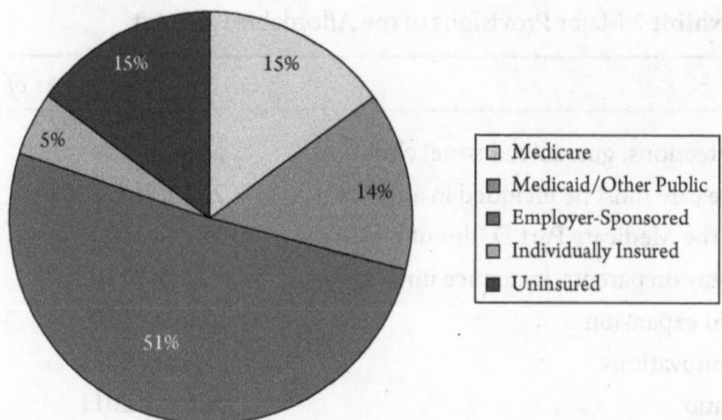

Figure 11.1a Exhibit 3a U.S. Population's Health Insurance Coverage, 2012.
Source: Casewriter, adapted from Kaiser Family Foundation, "The Uninsured: A Primer—Key Facts about Health Insurance on the Eve of Coverage Expansions," October 23, 2013, http://kff.org/uninsured/report/the-uninsured-a-primer-key-facts-about-health-insurance-on-the-eve-of-coverage-expansions/, accessed April 2014.

deductibles. About 15 million people annually bought their own health insurance before the individual mandate of the ACA went into effect.

The uninsured A main goal of the ACA was to reduce the number of uninsured people in the U.S., estimated at 47 million people in 2012.[11] About 12 million people in this group were undocumented immigrants. A further 9 million were documented non-citizens. Around 5 million of the 47 million were children.[12] Before the ACA became law, insurance companies were able to deny coverage to people with preexisting conditions, preventing them from buying insurance; this population was estimated at 25 million.[13] About 40% of the uninsured lived below the federal poverty line (FPL) (annual income less than 11,670 for an individual or $23,850 for a family of four in 2014), while about 10% of the uninsured earned more than 400% of the FPL (more than $46,680 annually for an individual or $95,200 for a family of four in 2014).[14]

Objectives and Methods of the Affordable Care Act

The ACA aimed to increase the number of people with health insurance and its affordability in the U.S., primarily through two methods. The law created health insurance exchanges in all 50 states where under- or uninsured individuals could buy coverage, or currently insured people could switch to cheaper and/or more comprehensive plans. If a state chose not to create its own exchange, the federal government would create and oversee the exchange for that state. By grouping individual purchasers into these state exchanges and mandating coverage so that young, healthy people would

[11] Kaiser Family Foundation, "The Uninsured: A Primer."

[12] Ezekiel J. Emanuel, *Reinventing American Health Care* (New York: Public Affairs Press, 2014), p. 49.

[13] U.S. Department of Health and Human Services, "At Risk: Pre-Existing Conditions Could Affect 1 in 2 Americans," http://aspe.hhs.gov/health/reports/2012/pre-existing/, accessed April 2014.

[14] Emanuel, *Reinventing American Health Care*, p. 51.

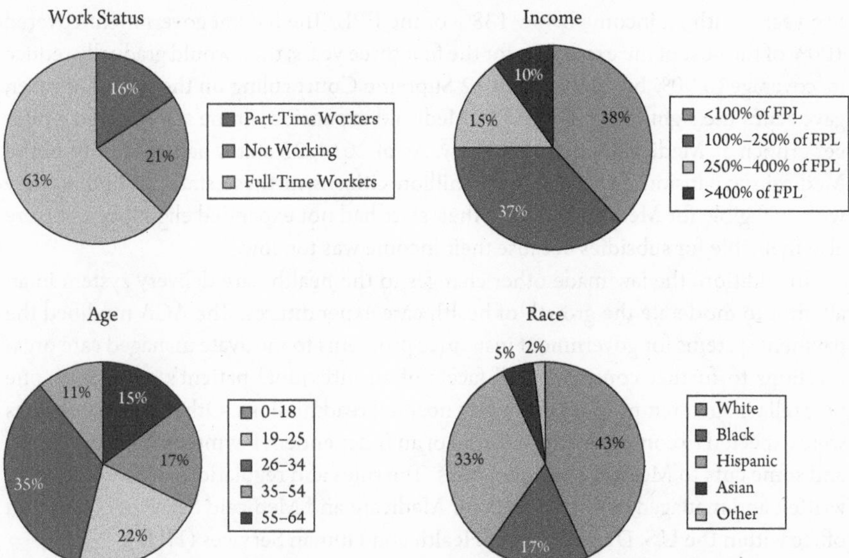

Figure 11.1b Exhibit 3b Demographic Characteristics of the Uninsured in the U.S., 2012.
Source: Casewriter, adapted from Kaiser Family Foundation, "The Uninsured: A Primer—Key Facts about Health Insurance on the Eve of Coverage Expansions," October 23, 2013, http://kff.org/uninsured/report/the-uninsured-a-primer-key-facts-about-health-insurance-on-the-eve-of-coverage-expansions/, accessed April 2014.

buy insurance or face a penalty,[15] the law pooled the risk for the insurance companies, implemented adjustment mechanisms to balance the risk across carriers, and made it cheaper for any one individual to buy coverage. At the same time, the law banned certain insurance practices, such as charging more or denying coverage to someone with a preexisting condition, and offered subsidies for low-income individuals to make health insurance even more affordable. These subsidies were available to individuals with incomes between 138% and 400% of the FPL to cover premiums for insurance bought on state exchanges, and, for individuals who were ineligible for Medicaid with incomes up to 250% of the FPL, the law offered subsidies to help pay for deductibles and copayments.[16]

The law also changed the eligibility requirements for Medicaid to give coverage to those who, even after subsidies, could not afford to buy their own health insurance. Rather than a means-tested program to provide insurance for certain low-income groups, such as pregnant women, children, and the disabled poor, with different rules for qualification in each state, the ACA aimed to transform Medicaid into a program that offered insurance to any legal U.S. resident (who had been in the country at least

[15] In 2014, the penalty was whichever was greater of: 1% of household income with a maximum of the price of the average premium for a bronze plan, or $95 per individual up to a maximum of $285 per household. The penalty was scheduled to rise in 2015 to 2% of income or $325 per person, in 2016 to 2.5% of income or $695 per person, and thereafter was pegged to inflation.

[16] Emanuel, *Reinventing American Health Care*, p. 216.

five years) with an income below 138% of the FPL. The federal government covered 100% of the cost of the expansion for the first three years, then would gradually reduce its coverage to 90% by 2020. The 2012 Supreme Court ruling on the ACA, however, gave states the right to opt out of this Medicaid expansion. Some states feared a budget crunch as Medicaid enrollment grew. As of 2014, 25 states had opted out of the Medicaid expansion, leaving some 5 million citizens in these states in limbo. They were ineligible for Medicaid because their state had not expanded eligibility, but were also ineligible for subsidies because their income was too low.[17]

In addition, the law made other changes to the health-care delivery system in an attempt to moderate the growth of health care expenditures. The ACA modified the payment systems for government insurance programs to motivate managed care organizations to further consolidate all facets of an individual patient's care under one umbrella in an attempt to reduce costly hospital readmissions. Other medical savings were expected to come from the creation of an Independent Payments Advisory Board and some cuts to Medicare payment rates. The rules and regulations of the ACA were written and managed by the Centers for Medicare and Medicaid Services (CMS), an office within the U.S. Department of Health and Human Services (HHS).

CONNECTICUT'S HEALTH EXCHANGE: ACCESS HEALTH CT

A 2011 law created Connecticut's state health exchange, a quasi-governmental organization called Access Health CT (AHCT). As the law defined it, "a body politic and corporate, constituting a public instrumentality and political subdivision of the state . . . which shall not be construed to be a department, institution or agency of the state."[18] Funding for the health insurance marketplace came entirely from federal grants. By August 2011, AHCT had been awarded almost $8 million in federal grants to begin operations and start information technology (IT) planning for its website. In August 2012, it received a $107 million grant to fund its operations through the end of 2014.

AHCT was governed by a 14-member board of which 8 members were political appointees and 6 were *ex officio* state officers. Eleven of the members had voting rights, including three of the *ex officio* members. Appointment powers were split between the governor and the majority and minority party leadership of the state's House and Senate. The statute defined appointees' expertise requirements; for example, of the governor's two appointees, one needed expertise in individual insurance coverage and the other in small business insurance coverage, while the Speaker of the House's appointee needed to be "knowledgeable in health-care benefits plan administration."[19]

[17] Kaiser Family Foundation, "The Coverage Gap: Uninsured Poor Adults in States that Do Not Expand Medicaid," October 23, 2013, http://kff.org/health-reform/issue-brief/the-coverage-gap-uninsured-poor-adults-in-states-that-do-not-expand-medicaid/, accessed March 2014.

[18] AHCT, "Our Charter," http://www.ct.gov/hix/cwp/view.asp?a=4295&q=532142, accessed April 2014.

[19] AHCT, "Our Charter."

The board was fully constituted by September 2011. It selected Counihan to be CEO of the exchange in April 2012, and he started work in July. Prior to becoming CEO of AHCT, Counihan had served as president of Choice Administrators, a California-based private health insurance exchange, and before that as chief marketing officer of the Massachusetts Health Connector.[20] He had begun his career in the health insurance industry at CIGNA and Tufts Health Plan in Massachusetts, working in the private sector for more than two decades.

GETTING TO WORK: JULY 2012–JANUARY 2013

Days after moving into the CEO's office, Counihan took stock of AHCT:

> About two weeks after starting, I went to visit CMS in Washington, D.C. I spent most of the day detailing my plans for designing and building AHCT as Connecticut's exchange. That evening, I joined a senior CMS official for dinner and she said to me: "Kevin, your plans sound great and all, but right now Connecticut is on our watch list. We assume you are going to fail at building your own exchange and default to the federal exchange because you are starting so late." That opened my eyes to how fast we needed to move.

Within a few weeks, Counihan filled the senior-level positions at the exchange, mainly with former health insurance executives: Chief Operating Officer (COO) Peter Van Loon was an executive specializing in underwriting and finance for several health insurance companies, including CIGNA and Aetna, after serving for many years in the U.S. Navy. Chief Information Officer (CIO) Jim Wadleigh had spent more than a decade in various positions at CIGNA. Chief Financial Officer (CFO) Stephen Sigal had worked for 10 years at Travelers Insurance before moving to Aetna for 17 years. And Chief Marketing Officer (CMO) Jason Madrak began his career in marketing at the *Wall Street Journal*, then worked at Aetna before joining AHCT (see Box 11.1 for backgrounds of the board and executive team members).

Counihan worked with the board of directors to make AHCT's executive salaries competitive enough to attract these insurance industry executives. He explained:

> I needed a staff that was used to working under high pressure with limited resources and a crazy schedule. I also wanted to bring private-sector business practices to the public sector because I thought that would be the only way that AHCT could succeed in such a short amount of time. But at the end of the day, even with the compensation structure I worked with the board to create, my pitch when hiring these executives was, "Do you want a regular job, or do you want to make history?" I was lucky to put together such an accomplished team. Everyone was on board by August 2012.

In mid-July, the newly formed team began addressing the line items of the CMS blueprint for approval to create a state health insurance exchange. The blueprint

[20] This state health insurance exchange was the nation's first, signed into law in April 2006 by then Governor Mitt Romney. The law sought to ensure that all of the state's residents would have health-care coverage. In many ways, the Massachusetts law set the example for the national plan.

Box 11.1 Exhibit 4 Backgrounds of AHCT Board and Executive Team

Board

Board Member	*Title*	*Appointed by*
Nancy Wyman, Chair	CT Lieutenant Governor	Governor
Mary Fox	Former Senior Vice President, Aetna	Governor
Paul Philpott	Principal Consultant, Quo Vadis Advisors LLC	Legislature
Grant A. Ritter	Senior Scientist, Schneider Institutes for Health Policy	Legislature
Robert E. Scalettar	Former Chief Medical Officer, Anthem Blue Cross Blue Shield	Legislature
Robert F. Tessier	Executive Director, CT Coalition of Taft-Hartley Health Funds	Legislature
Cecilia J. Woods	Former Vice-Chair, Permanent Commission on the Status of Women	Legislature
Maura Carley	President and CEO, Healthcare Navigation, LLC	Legislature
Roderick L. Bremby	Commissioner, Department of Social Services	Ex-Officio
Victoria Veltri, Co-Chair	State Healthcare Advocate, Office of the Healthcare Advocate	Ex-Officio
Benjamin Barnes	Secretary, Office of Policy & Management	Ex-Officio
Anne Melissa Dowling	Deputy Commissioner, Connecticut Insurance Department	Non-Voting
Jewel Mullen	Commissioner, Department of Public Health	Non-Voting
Patricia Rehmer, MSN	Commissioner, Department of Mental Health and Addiction Services	Non-Voting

Management

Executive	*Position*	*Background*
Kevin Counihan	CEO	Former CMO, Massachusetts Health Connector; Tufts Health Plan; Kellogg MBA
Peter Van Loon	COO	Insurance industry, including CIGNA and Aetna; U.S. Navy; Wharton MBA
Steven Sigal	CFO	Insurance industry, including Aetna and Travelers; CPA
Jim Wadleigh	CIO	Insurance industry, mainly at CIGNA; MS in finance

Jason Madrak	CMO	Print media industry; Insurance industry Aetna and Wellpoint; NYU MBA
Julie Lyons	Director	Insurance industry, including Health Net and Hartford
Virginia Lamb	General Counsel	Former senior vice president Eastern Connecticut Health Network; American University JD

Source: Company documents.

had more than 150 items to fulfill, ranging from the simple: "1.2b: The Exchange has a formal, publicly-adopted charter or bylaws,"[21] to the complex: "3.12 The Exchange and SHOP have the capacity to process QHP selections and terminations in accordance with 45 CFR 155.400 and 155.430, compute actual APTC, and report and reconcile QHP selections, terminations, and APTC/advance CSR information in coordination with issuers and CMS. This includes exchanging relevant information with issuers and CMS using electronic enrollment transaction standards."[22] Explained Madrak, "By late August we had worked through 85% of the blueprint. We updated CMS on our progress and they were amazed, comparing Connecticut to Maryland which, at the time, was deemed the most promising state exchange."

By October 2012, AHCT had contracted with consulting firm Deloitte to help design, create, and implement the state's health exchange website, accesshealthct.com. Deloitte had worked with several states before 2012 on Medicaid system overhauls, and had contracted with several other states to help develop their health exchanges. Nonetheless, as Counihan explained, "This would be a major project for any firm to handle. In addition to building our exchange, it is important to note that we also integrated our Medicaid systems onto this single platform.[23] It was a $42.5 million contract with Deloitte, the largest single expense we had."

The website was one of the biggest challenges AHCT faced. Noted Counihan, "Deloitte developed an extensive plan for the website, but by January 2013 it was clear that not everything would be developed in time to launch. We knew it was absolutely necessary to have a functional website on October 1 [the start of open enrollment], so we worked with Deloitte in January to scale back the technological requirements for the site by 30%."

Another important early task AHCT faced was to determine the requirements for the insurance plans that would be sold on the exchange. Counihan had

[21] Centers for Medicare and Medicaid Services, "Blueprint for Approval of Affordable State-Based and State Partnership Insurance Exchanges," http://www.cms.gov/CCIIO/Resources/Files/Downloads/hie-blueprint-11162012.pdf, accessed April 2014.

[22] Centers for Medicare and Medicaid Services, "Blueprint for Approval of Affordable State-Based and State Partnership Insurance Exchanges."

[23] Connecticut's Medicaid system was relatively simple with only four eligibility categories.

to balance the quality requirements that would ensure that consumers would be offered good plans with worries that insurers might balk at such requirements and choose not to offer any plans. To achieve the best balance, Counihan decided to develop a standard plan for each coverage tier,[24] and require every insurer on the exchange to offer a standard plan for each tier. These standard plans could only differ in price, provider network, and brand name (see Table 11.3 for a sample standard plan). Once an insurer offered a standard plan in each tier, it could then offer several nonstandard plans in each tier. These requirements ensured quality for consumers, decreased confusion in the marketplace, and facilitated comparison shopping. Three of the four largest insurers in Connecticut's individual market—Anthem Blue Cross Blue Shield; ConnectiCare, an HMO that had operated in the state since the early-1980s; and HealthyCT, an insurance co-op, a new type of nonprofit insurance company made possible by the ACA—decided to offer plans on the exchange in 2013–2014. UnitedHealthcare, the only one of the top four that did not participate in the individual exchange in 2014, was involved in the exchange for the Small Business Health Options Program (SHOP)[25] in 2014, and was planning to enter the individual exchange in 2015. AHCT was also in talks with Harvard Pilgrim Health Care to join the individual exchange in 2015 (see Box 11.2 for more on these insurers).

A final important decision was the hiring, in November 2012, of Pappas MacDonnell, a Southport, Connecticut–based firm that specialized in marketing for the financial services, insurance, business services, and health-care industries. The marketing professionals began working with Deloitte to integrate as much educational, customer-focused content as possible into the exchange website, but, by late January 2013, when they saw a mock-up of the site, Kyle MacDonnell, principal at the agency, realized that the plan needed refining. She noted, "We realized we would not be able to get all of our desired educational content on the exchange site. Deloitte's focus, rightly, was on the technical systems that the site had to have by October 1—the plumbing that would handle eligibility and enrollment—but we were pushing to include educational content in plain language. We had to make some tradeoffs in the interest of simplicity."

MARKETING THE EXCHANGE: JANUARY–OCTOBER 2013

Even before they knew what would happen with the exchange website, Pappas MacDonnell's marketers had begun developing plans and content to understand the market for the exchange, how best to educate consumers, and how to reach the uninsured during open enrollment.

[24] The ACA specified that insurers had to develop plans in three tiers. Bronze plans had to cover at least 60% of medical costs, Silver plans at least 70%, and Gold plans at least 80%. Insurers could also develop Platinum plans that covered at least 90%, and "catastrophic coverage" plans that were below the Bronze level, but only available to people under age 30.

[25] The SHOP program was another part of the ACA that created an exchange for small businesses, only available to businesses with 50 or fewer employees in 2014. The AHCT marketing program did not place a heavy emphasis on the SHOP exchange.

Table 11.3 Exhibit 5 Example of Standard Silver Plan

Plan Overview	*In-Network Member Pays*	*Out-of-Network Member Pays*
	Medical Deductible:	
Individual:	$3,000	$6,000
Family:	$6,000	$12,000
(copays are not applied to deductible)		
	Prescription Drug Deductible:	
Individual:	$400	Medical and Prescription Deductibles are combined
Family:	$800	
	Out-of-Pocket Maximum:	
Individual:	$6,250	$12,500
Family:	$12,500	$25,000
	Physician Office Visits:	
Preventive Care/Screenings/ Immunizations	$0	40% coinsurance
Primary Care (injury or illness)	$30 copay	40% coinsurance[b]
Specialist	$45 copay	40% coinsurance[b]
	Emergency/Urgent Care:	
Urgent Care Center or Facility	$75 copay	40% coinsurance[b]
Emergency Room	$150 copay	$150 copay
Ambulance	$0	
	Hospital Services:	
Inpatient	$500 copay per day to a maximum of $2,000 per admission	40% coinsurance[b]
Outpatient (performed at hospital or ambulatory facility)	$500 copay	40% coinsurance[b]
Skilled Nursing Facility 90 day calendar year maximum	$500 copay per day to a maximum of $2,000 per admission[a]	40% coinsurance[b]
	Mental Health, Substance Abuse & Behavioral Health Care:	
Mental Health, Substance Abuse & Behavioral Health Services	Covered same as any other illness	Covered same as any other illness

(*continued*)

Table 11.3 Continued

Plan Overview	*In-Network Member Pays*	*Out-of-Network Member Pays*
	Hospice Care:	
Hospice Services	$0	40% coinsurance[b]
	Outpatient Services:	
Home Health Care 100 visit calendar year maximum	$0	25% coinsurance subject to a $50 deductible
Advanced Radiology (CT/ PET Scan, MRI)	$75 copay per service up to a combined calendar year maximum of $375 for MRI and CT scans; $400 for PET scans	40% coinsurance[b]
Non-Advanced Radiology (X-ray, Diagnostic)	$45 copay	40% coinsurance[b]
Laboratory Services	$30 copay	40% coinsurance[b]
Rehabilitative & Habilitative Therapy (Physical, Speech, Occupational) combined 40 visit calendar year maximum	$30 copay	40% coinsurance[b]
Chiropractic Care 20 visit calendar maximum	$45 copay	40% coinsurance[b]
	Other Services:	
Durable Medical Equipment	40% coinsurance	40% coinsurance[b]
Prosthetics	40% coinsurance	40% coinsurance[b]
Diabetic Supplies & Equipment	40% coinsurance	40% coinsurance[b]
	Prescription Drugs:	
Generic Drugs	$10 copay	40% coinsurance[b]
Preferred Brand Drugs	$25 copay[c]	40% coinsurance[b]
Non–Preferred Brand Drugs	$40 copay[c]	40% coinsurance[b]
Specialty Drugs	40% coinsurance	40% coinsurance[b]
	Pediatric-Only Services (for children under age 19):	
	Pediatric Dental Care:	
Diagnostic & Preventive (Oral Exam, Cleaning, X-ray)	$0	50% coinsurance[b]
Basic Restorative (Filling, Simple Extraction)	40% coinsurance	50% coinsurance[b]

Table 11.3 Continued

Plan Overview	*In-Network Member Pays*	*Out-of-Network Member Pays*
Major Restorative (Endodontic, Crown)	50% coinsurance	50% coinsurance[b]
Orthodontia Services *medically necessary only*	50% coinsurance	50% coinsurance[b]
	Pediatric Vision Care:	
Routine Eye Exam	$30 copay	40% coinsurance
Prescription Eye Glasses *one pair of frames & lenses per calendar year*	lenses: collection frames: non-collection frames: Members choosing to upgrade from a collection frame to a non-collection frame will be given a credit equal to the cost of the collection frame and will be entitled to a negotiated discount	100% coinsurance

Source: Company documents.

Note: Only services marked by an "a," "b," or "c" were subject to a deductible. A copay or coinsurance was a small payment that was made by the patient at the time the care was received. A copay was a specified dollar amount that depended on the type of care being received, while a coinsurance payment was a certain percentage of the cost of the care.

[a] After in-network deductible is met.

[b] After out-of-network deductible is met.

[c] After in-network prescription drug deductible is met.

Market Research and Segmentation

Market research Through public data, telephone and in-person surveys, and interviews throughout Connecticut, Pappas MacDonnell developed an understanding of the health insurance market in the state. Of the 3.6 million people in Connecticut, 345,000 were uninsured; 120,000 of the uninsured lived at or below 138% of the poverty line and so were eligible for Medicaid; and 176,000 had incomes between 138% and 400% of the poverty line, making them eligible for federal subsidies.

About 14% of the state population was over the age of 65, and 42% of people were between the ages of 35 and 64. African Americans made up about 10% of the population, Latinos about 15%, Asian Americans about 5%, and non-Hispanic whites about 70%. About 10% of the population lived below the poverty line, and median family income in the state was around $70,000 in 2012, about a third higher than the national average. The state had about 8% unemployment in 2014 (see Table 11.4 for Connecticut's demographics).

Box 11.2 Exhibit 6 Connecticut's Insurance Companies

Anthem Blue Cross Blue Shield

Connecticut's Blue Cross Blue Shield affiliate had about 300,000 customers in 2013, making it the largest insurer in the state. It was the most popular insurer across all types of purchasers—individuals, small groups, and large groups. Anthem Blue Cross Blue Shield was a member of WellPoint, the largest for-profit Blue Cross Blue Shield company in the U.S.

ConnectiCare

An HMO that had operated in Connecticut since 1981, ConnectiCare was, by 2014, part of the EmblemHealth network of insurers serving the greater New York City area. ConnectiCare had about 240,000 members in 2013. The insurer covered all of Connecticut, parts of Western Massachusetts, and the New York metro area, with 22,000 providers and 126 hospitals in-network.

HealthyCT

A newly founded nonprofit co-op, HealthyCT was owned and governed by its members through their participation in selecting a board of directors. HealthyCT was one of 24 co-ops throughout the U.S. to receive federal start-up and operational funding. It was sponsored by the Connecticut State Medical Society, an independent association of providers in the state. The insurer was focused on delivering care around patient-centered medical homes, a health-care system that increased provider cooperation and tied provider payments to quality outcomes in an attempt to improve systemwide health and decrease costs.

United Healthcare

United Healthcare was the largest insurance company in the U.S. in 2014, with operations in all 50 states. The insurer's Connecticut operations had more than 100,000 customers, most of whom were in the small group market. While United Healthcare did not participate on the individual exchange in 2014, it did offer its products on Connecticut's small business exchange, known as SHOP, and was planning on joining the individual exchange in 2015.

Harvard Pilgrim

Harvard Pilgrim was a large insurer in the Northeast that did not offer insurance in Connecticut in 2014. However, it was among the largest insurers in neighboring Massachusetts, with about 700,000 customers. As of May 2014, Harvard Pilgrim was considering offering its products through AHCT during the next open enrollment period.

Source: Anthem Blue Cross Blue Shield information from: Kaiser Family Foundation, "Insurance Market Competitiveness," http://kff.org/state-category/health-insurance-managed-care/insurance-market-competitiveness/, accessed April 2014. ConnectiCare information from: "ConnectiCare's Corporate Fact Sheet," http://connecticare.com/CorporateFacts.aspx, accessed April 2014. HealthyCT information from: "about us," http://www.healthyct.org/about-us/, accessed April 2014. United Healthcare information from: Kaiser Family Foundation, "Insurance Market Competitiveness," http://kff.org/state-category/health-insurance-managed-care/insurance-market-competitiveness/, accessed April 2014. Harvard Pilgrim Information from: Kaiser Family Foundation, "Insurance Market Competitiveness," http://kff.org/state-category/health-insurance-managed-care/insurance-market-competitiveness/, accessed April 2014.

Table 11.4 Exhibit 7 Connecticut Demographic Information

Connecticut's population	3.6 million
Uninsured population	345,000
Medicaid eligible uninsured	120,000
Subsidy eligible uninsured	176,000
Female uninsured	148,000
Male uninsured	197,000
Uninsured by race:	
• White	55%
• Hispanic	25%
• African American	12%
• Other	8%

Source: Company documents.

Low-income residents were clustered in three of the four largest cities in the state: Bridgeport (1), New Haven (2), and Hartford (4). Each of these cities was home to many uninsured individuals. Stamford, the third-largest city, had somewhat higher average incomes, and a lower proportion of the population lived in poverty. Nonetheless, a higher than average percentage of Stamford's population was uninsured. Men made up about 57% of the uninsured population. Overall, the uninsured population was about 55% white, 25% Latino, and 12% African American.

Market segmentation The marketing firm initially tried to use as much demographic information as possible to break down the health insurance market into various segments, but quickly found that no single set of characteristics defined the insured, uninsured, or underinsured population of the state. Instead, Pappas MacDonnell profiled four different portraits, revealed in quantified segmentation research, that characterized Connecticut consumers' attitudes toward health insurance. *Confident rejectors,* who made up about 15% of consumers, were mostly uninsured men who viewed themselves as healthy and not needing insurance. *Cautious optimists,* about 40% of consumers, many of whom were Latinos and were typically family-oriented, were excited about the prospect of being able to buy insurance. About 20% were *stoic skeptics,* older, often single people who doubted the success of health insurance reform. The final 25% of *stressed and strained* individuals supported the idea of the government ensuring that people could get insurance, but were too overwhelmed by life to spend much time thinking about it. These portraits informed Pappas MacDonnell's messaging. For example, the marketers anticipated that the *confident rejectors* might most respond to messaging about the individual mandate, while *stressed and strained* individuals would respond more to affordability messaging. As it turned out, affordability was the dominant concern across all segments, to a greater or lesser extent.

Awareness

Pappas MacDonnell then worked to raise awareness of both the new health insurance law and the AHCT brand. Early research showed that in April 2013, fewer than 30% of Connecticut residents had heard of AHCT, even though it had been promoted, and anything having to do with the ACA was often met with skepticism and even negativity.

The marketing team's first ad spend was on search engine marketing in the first months of 2013. "We began with paid search ads because those were individuals who had, in essence, raised their hand to say that they were interested in health insurance," explained Philip Stevens, executive vice president of Pappas MacDonnell. At the same time, the marketing firm was building an educational, consumer-facing website that included the content that it had wanted in the official insurance enrollment site. The educational site went live in late February 2013, several months before the enrollment site was ready.

Soon after the educational site debuted, Pappas MacDonnell began buying branded search terms rather than generic health-care-related terms. This change had two positives for AHCT: the branded terms (such as "Access Health Connecticut") were less expensive than the generic terms (such as "insurance exchange") (see Figure 11.2

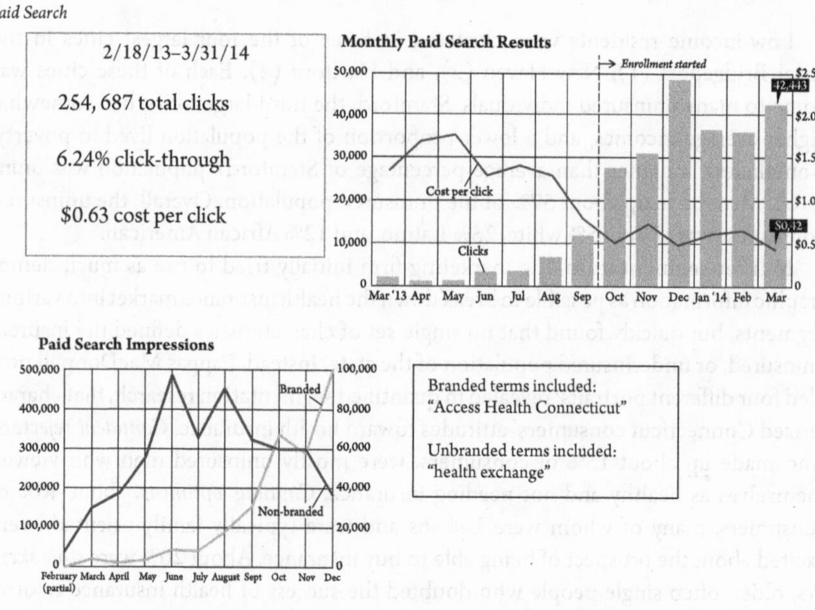

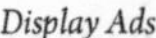

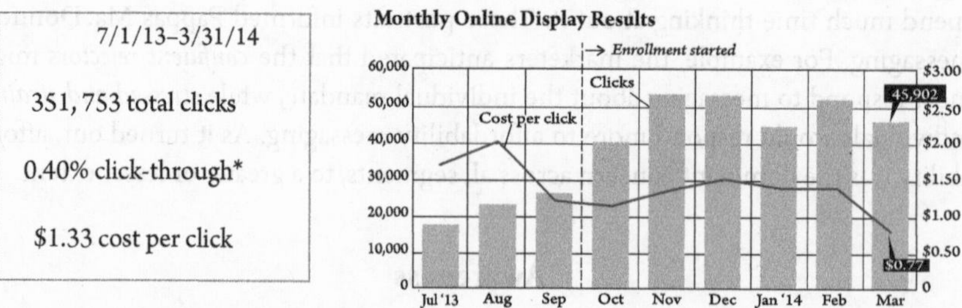

Figure 11.2 Exhibit 8 Digital Advertising Results.
Source: Company documents.

for data); and the branded terms gave the team a sense of how brand awareness was improving in general. Clicks on the paid-search ads led people to the AHCT educational site. Online display ads followed the paid search ads, also pointing users to the educational site.

As Pappas MacDonnell was rolling out the digital marketing campaign in early 2013, the firm was also working with AHCT to host a series of "Healthy Chats" throughout Connecticut, especially in cities and towns with higher rates of uninsured individuals. These community meetings included a presentation on the exchange and a question-and-answer session, giving citizens a chance to interact with AHCT board members, local politicians, and other health-care experts. These sessions also gave AHCT a chance to gather leads on interested individuals and hone its marketing messaging based on how different people responded.

By June 2013, Pappas MacDonnell and AHCT decided it was time for a major advertising push across every format: TV, radio, print media, billboards, direct mailing, bus signage, text messaging, and even aerial billboard flyovers at beaches and summer events (see Table 11.5 for ad spending and reach data and Figure 11.3 for sample ads). Explained Stevens, "TV ended up being the most important channel. Most people that we surveyed heard about AHCT on TV. Radio underperformed our expectations in part because it was harder to measure and therefore seemingly less efficient, while direct mailings overperformed. We were still getting inquiries from our direct mail campaigns months after we mailed them out."

AHCT collaborated with Hartford's NBC TV station to deploy several promotional initiatives and assisted with many news stories about the exchange and health insurance in general. The station's marketing manager, Terese Guerrero, explained, "NBC Connecticut decided very early that we wanted to be the station that would explain the health insurance exchange to Connecticut residents. We ran hundreds of stories over the summer and participated in a series of promotions." By the end of September, AHCT and Pappas MacDonnell considered the ad push to be a success. Awareness of the exchange rose to more than 50% of the population (see Figure 11.4 for people's awareness of AHCT).

Table 11.5 Exhibit 9 Ad Spending and Reach Data

Medium	*Impressions*	*% of Ad Budget*
Billboards	28 million	4%
Bus cards	8.5 million	4%
Posters	4.5 million	10%
Out of home total:	41 million	18%
Print	6.5 million	7%
TV	15 million	46%
Radio	14 million	11%
Traditional media total:	35.5 million	64%
Digital:	100 million	18%

Source: Company documents.

English Language Online Display Ad *Spanish Language Newspaper Ad*

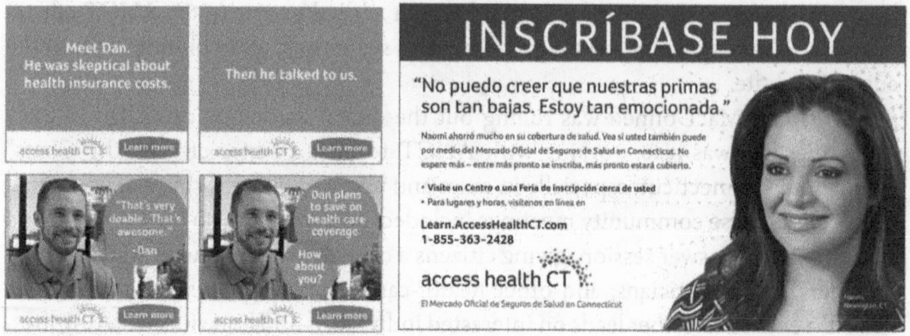

Figure 11.3 Exhibit 10 Sample Ads.
Source: Company documents.

Education and Engagement

The teams from Pappas MacDonnell and AHCT believed wholeheartedly in integrated marketing, so while they raised awareness of AHCT, they also worked to educate and engage with their target populations. The firm employed several channels to make as many connections as possible. Pappas MacDonnell principal, Susan Pappas, explained, "We believed that about 80% of enrollments would require at least some in-person contact somewhere along the process. That could happen at the beginning with information about the exchange, in the middle to answer questions that might come up, or at the end to close the sale of insurance. We wanted to make sure we had enough staff, resources, and information for every channel that a consumer might use."

Navigators and in-person assisters The ACA required state exchanges to develop a system of navigators and in-person assisters who could reach out to the uninsured population within a state, educate them on the exchange, and help them enroll. AHCT developed a system in which six regional navigators managed the outreach efforts of about 200 in-person assisters. The navigators were large regional organizations such

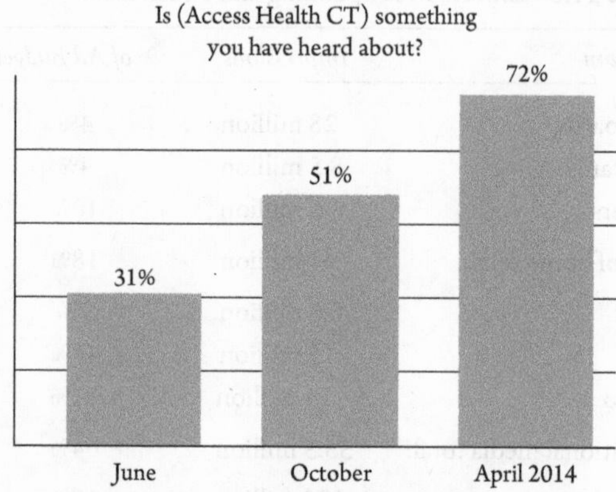

Figure 11.4 Exhibit 11 Raising Awareness of AHCT (percent of people answering yes).
Source: Company documents.

as the city of New Haven Department of Health and the Hartford County Hispanic Health Council, which interfaced regularly with uninsured populations in their region (see Figure 11.5 for a map of the navigators' regions). Navigators were funded in 2013–2014 from outside grants because the ACA stipulated that they could not be funded with the federal grant money that funded the rest of the exchange. The assister organizations were divided among the six navigator regions, with each navigator managing a certain number of grassroots community organization assisters, depending on the number of uninsured people in their region. The 160 assister organizations, which included community health centers, small business, and faith-based partnerships, were each given a $6,000 stipend (from federal grants), a secure laptop, and a goal of engaging with 300 people and enrolling 100 people during open enrollment. After passing a criminal background check, personnel at the assister organizations were given 35 hours of training on the ACA and AHCT during August and September. About 33% of assisters spoke Spanish. Although assistor organizations did not start getting paid until October, some assisters began fieldwork over the summer.

Outreach workers While the assisters were being trained, the exchange hired a team of about 50 outreach workers. Explained Stevens, "Our outreach workers were focused on getting people enrolled in private individual insurance, or QHP. Most of the outreach workers had worked on political campaigns, were passionate about making the law a success, and had free time in the fall of a non-election year to work for us." These outreach workers were salaried employees who reported directly to AHCT. They began work in June 2013 and stayed on through the end of open enrollment, March 31, 2014.

The toolkit Before the beginning of open enrollment, the main task for AHCT was education. AHCT and Pappas MacDonnell developed a suite of tools to help workers

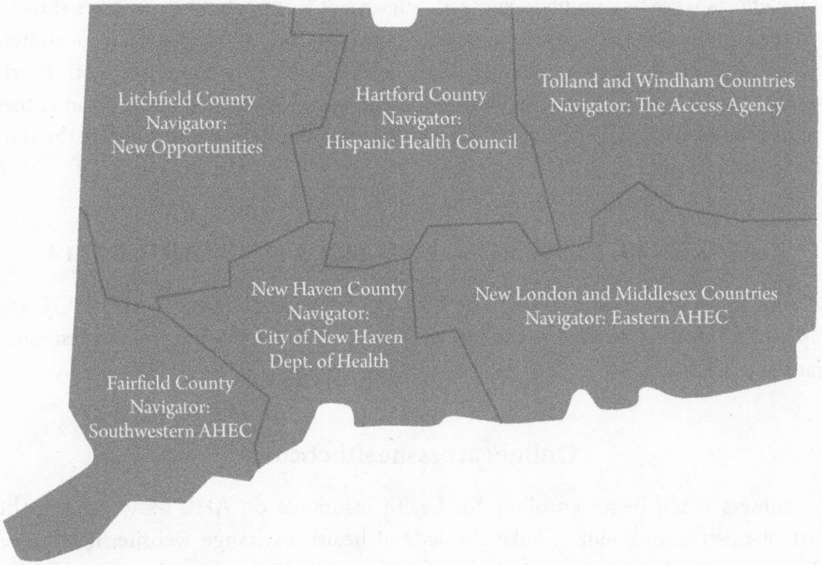

Figure 11.5 Exhibit 12 Regional Navigators.
Source: Company documents.

educate the people they talked to. These tools were also available to the general population on the educational AHCT site described above. Pappas explained, "The most important tool we had was the savings calculator. It was available on our website, and outreach workers in the field had it on iPads to show to consumers. All the consumer had to do was input their age, income, and family composition, and they were given an estimated price for insurance that included all the subsidies they were eligible for." Other tools included a myth-vs.-fact quiz that tested the users' knowledge of the ACA, AHCT, and health insurance in general, and a "Making the Right Choice" interactive tool where users could follow a decision tree to see the consequences of their health insurance choices based on their profiles (e.g., single parent).

Healthy Chats The series of "Healthy Chats" held throughout Connecticut from August to November 2013 provided another opportunity for assisters and outreach workers to connect with interested consumers at locations all around the state. At the start of open enrollment (October 1), these meetings migrated from informational and educational content toward a focus on enrollment.

Nurturing leads At every opportunity to talk to interested consumers, whether at the Healthy Chats, on the beach, at concerts, or in shopping centers, the assisters and outreach workers took care to get as much information as possible from the consumers. To manage these leads, AHCT used the customer relationship management (CRM) system that the 2012 Obama campaign had developed to track potential voters, called the Voter Activation Network (VAN). Explained Madrak, "As far as I know, Connecticut was the only state using the VAN tool in conjunction with the insurance exchange. It allowed us to know who was interested in insurance and how they could be contacted in the future." Regular e-mail blasts maintained a connection to qualified leads. AHCT eventually aggregated a core e-mail list of more than 23,000 such people and a text-messaging list of more than 13,000.

By late September 2013, AHCT and Pappas MacDonnell believed their educational efforts were beginning to succeed. Surveys of Connecticut consumers showed that they understood health insurance exchanges and the ACA better than consumers nationally. From June to September 2013, AHCT's workers connected with nearly 14,000 people over the phone, in shopping centers, and at summer concerts and other events. The educational website received over 100,000 unique visitors before the start of open enrollment.

OPEN ENROLLMENT: OCTOBER 2013–MARCH 2014

As with the multichannel strategy to raise education and engagement, AHCT and Pappas MacDonnell used as many methods as possible to enroll people in insurance plans and Medicaid.

Online: accesshealthct.com

Consumers could begin enrolling for health insurance on AHCT's website at the start of open enrollment. Unlike the federal health exchange website, healthcare.gov, Connecticut's exchange was largely free from glitches and service interruptions. Nonetheless, the healthcare.gov issues did cause some confusion for Connecticut consumers. Counihan explained, "Despite the fact that healthcare.gov automatically transferred Connecticut consumers to accesshealthct.com, many people thought that our exchange was experiencing problems. We did a November marketing push to try to dispel that confusion, and by late December we started seeing higher enrollment numbers." Even though the site operated well, it could have been improved. Madrak explained:

> We ran into some problems with eligibility verification, especially with immigration and incarceration issues. People were being told they were ineligible because they were incarcerated when they were very clearly not in jail. There was also the issue of educational material on the actual exchange site. The educational site was integrated with a button on the homepage of accesshealthct.com, but, when you were in the process of enrolling in health insurance, it was difficult to get information to answer any questions you might have had.

Enrolling on accesshealthct.com without any AHCT accredited outside help accounted for just under half of enrollments, even though AHCT predicted that only 20% would come through the website without the help of assisters, outreach workers, or brokers (see Table 11.6 for projected and actual enrollment by channel). A higher percentage of website shoppers and applicants proved to be more self-sufficient than originally expected.

Call Centers

AHCT had employed a business process outsourcing (BPO) strategy since its inception. The organization's management believed that delegation of key operational services to private-sector firms enabled them to focus on the customer-facing activities most valued by its target markets. Examples of this delegation included the call center, SHOP exchange, premium billing, and broker commission payment.

AHCT call-center representatives served several functions for callers. First, they could answer basic questions about the ACA, AHCT, and the enrollment process.

Table 11.6 Exhibit 13 Projected and Actual Enrollment by Channel (excluding Medicaid enrollments).

Channel	*Projected*		*Actual*	
Online unassisted	16,000	20%	41,549	48%
Call center	28,000	35%	5,548 [a]	6%
Broker	8,000	10%	26,184	30%
Navigator/In-person assister/ Certified Application Counselors (CAC)	*28,000*	*35%*	*13,002*	*15%*
Total	80,000	100%	86,283	100%

Source: Company documents.

[a] Some call-center enrollments were counted under "Online unassisted" if the call-center representative talked the enrollee through the process.

Second, the call-center representatives had special administrative privileges on the website, so if a consumer got stuck in the middle of an application because of a technical glitch or other problem, they could call up and the representative could fix the problem for them. Finally, the representatives could directly enroll consumers in two ways. The representatives themselves could open an application on the website, fill out the caller's information, explain their plan choices and prices, and enroll the caller, or they could transfer callers to a telephone-based broker who could close the enrollment. The call center also proved to be a valuable "help desk" when assisters had questions about enrollment.

For the first several months of AHCT's operations, the success of the advertising and outreach meant that the call center turned out to be understaffed, with fewer than 100 representatives trying to handle thousands of calls a day. Noted Counihan, "This led to longer than acceptable wait times and too many dropped calls." A few weeks into open enrollment, the contractor brought on about 300 more representatives. Wait times and dropped calls decreased substantially, and call-center enrollment figures improved.

In Person: Brokers, Outreach Workers, Assisters, and Enrollment Centers and Fairs

A significant number of consumers enrolled in person, either through an insurance broker or on the website with the assistance of outreach workers or assisters. By October 1, all 50 outreach workers and 200 assisters were in the field every day helping people enroll. AHCT's management felt that the two types of workers served two complementary functions. Stevens explained, "While assisters were focused to some extent on QHP enrollments, they were also interested in signing up newly eligible individuals for Medicaid as well as promoting better health outcomes in their communities. Our outreach workers, on the other hand, were more like a sales force. They were more focused on qualifying the right people for QHPs and moving them along to enrollment."

AHCT and Pappas MacDonnell thought insurance brokers could play a major role in enrolling Connecticut consumers because, in terms of insurance, these were the "pros who close." But broker commissions for individual insurance had been dwindling,[26] and it was unclear how enthused brokers would be in spending their time selling individual policies (as opposed to higher-volume employer-sponsored group insurance). The marketing firm came up with a strategy to leverage AHCT's capabilities to empower brokers to support the law and help enroll thousands of people.

There were about 13,000 registered health insurance brokers in Connecticut, but a much smaller number actively sold health insurance plans. These small businesspeople

[26] A provision of the ACA, implemented in 2011, required health insurance carriers to maintain a minimum loss ratio (MLR) of 80% for all individual policies sold (85% for group plans). This meant that no less than 80% of all premium dollars received needed to be paid out to claimants in the form of health benefits. This in turn meant that all other expenses, including administration, marketing, and commissions, needed to be funded from the remaining 20%. As a result, broker commissions had been shrinking.

Table 11.7 Exhibit 14 Broker Compensation Information

Type	*Rate*
Medicaid	$0
QHPs on the exchange	$16/enrollee/month
QHPs directly with insurance companies, not on exchange	Up to $39/enrollee/ month

Source: Company documents.

typically had to engage in a lot of work for each customer, from prospecting and educating to spending the time to fill out forms and help the customer choose a plan. Brokers' customers were typically individuals, families, or small businesses that wanted to provide health insurance to their employees. Customers did not pay the brokers directly; rather, the insurance companies gave the brokers a set fee per enrollee or enrollment group per month (see Table 11.7 for broker compensation information).

Stevens knew it would be a challenge to win support from brokers due to the lower compensation structure for individual health plans on the exchange:

> Brokers receive zero commission for enrolling a consumer in Medicaid, so we knew we had to direct people eligible for Medicaid away from the broker. And because insurance companies paid brokers $16 per individual enrollee per month in each exchange plan versus as much as $39 per enrollee per month in non-exchange plans, we had to find a way to make our proposition appealing. So we did the prospecting for them. We qualified the customers and paired them with brokers at our Enrollment Centers and Enrollment Fairs. You might say that rather than sending qualified leads to brokers, we brought the brokers to the leads.

By grouping customers at these Enrollment Centers and Enrollment Fairs, AHCT was able to reduce brokers' customer acquisition costs by creating economies of scale. AHCT opened two Enrollment Centers—in New Haven and New Britain—that were open seven days a week. These storefront locations were modeled on the Apple Store. Customers could walk in to browse the educational material they had in stock and learn more about the exchanges and health plans, or they could make an appointment with an enrollment specialist. Whether or not customers were Medicaid eligible, these specialists walked them through the application process. Then, when it came time to choose a plan, the non-Medicaid eligible customer would be handed off to a broker who would help them make a choice and sign up. On a typical day, five brokers worked at each enrollment center and saw about 100 customers (see Table 11.8 for data on the centers and fairs).

AHCT's Enrollment Fairs worked similarly to the Enrollment Centers. The fairs were one-day events held around Connecticut. Customers responded to invitations before attending, so brokers got a good sense of how many enrollments they could expect on a given day. Most brokers attending the fairs agreed to assist Medicaid customers enroll, even though they received no commissions for doing so. AHCT held 81 fairs between October and March, accommodating more than 4,000 customers (refer to Table 11.8). One broker noted that she could enroll a customer, from start

Table 11.8 Exhibit 15 Enrollment Center and Enrollment Fair Data

Visits	*Online Browse Only*	*Create Account Only*	*Start Application Only*	*Complete Application*	*Enrollments*	*Enrollments per App.*	*QHPs*	*Medicaid*
				Enrollment Centers				
15,191	518	500	1,370	5,636	7,639	1.36	4,439	3,164
				Enrollment Fairs				
4,302	300	182	761	1,742	2,278	1.31	1,230	1,056

Source: Company documents.

to finish, in about 10 minutes with the help of the staff at the fairs. At the fairs and Enrollment Centers, brokers closed about 75% of applications started, which was about 45% higher than the close rate overall. About 500 brokers participated in enrollment, enrolling more than 30% of all enrollees, much more than the 10% AHCT had initially predicted. Participation was widely dispersed: 80% of brokers' enrollments were written by the top 50% of brokers, as opposed to the typical 80/20 rule (i.e., 80% of the business from the top 20% of brokers) that was expected.

ASSESSING AHCT: APRIL 2014

A week into April, after Counihan and his staff at AHCT had a chance to recover from the exhaustion of open enrollment, they assessed the results. Over 200,000 people had signed up for health coverage—129,000 through Medicaid and about 80,000 in QHPs on the exchange. A majority of enrollees had enrolled after January 1, 2014 (see Figure 11.6 for the enrollment timeline). The team estimated that about 65% of QHP enrollees already had insurance (a detailed census of enrollees was in the works) and were just switching to a cheaper or more comprehensive health plan. Enrollees tended to be older than the population as a whole—as data from the savings calculator had predicted (see Figure 11.7)—and poorer, although younger and better off than what had originally been estimated. About 32% of enrollees were under age 35, and 25% of enrollees were between ages 18 and 34, younger than the average enrollment nationwide. About 77% received subsidies for their QHPs. While ethnicity data was still limited, about 10% of enrollees indicated that they preferred to communicate in Spanish. About 53% of enrollees enrolled in plans with Anthem Blue Cross Blue Shield of Connecticut, 44% enrolled in ConnectiCare, and 3% enrolled in HealthyCT, the new state co-op health plan. About 70% of enrollments were in the standard plans offered by the three carriers at each tier. The most popular single plan, with about 32% of all enrollees, was the ConnectiCare Standard Silver plan (see Table 11.9 for plan enrollment data).

These results were widely viewed as a success for Connecticut and for the ACA in general. One report commented, "The Connecticut exchange has performed better than the federal insurance marketplace and its troubled website, HealthCare.gov, and better than many state-run exchanges."[27] While Counihan noted that the most important success that AHCT had so far was getting so many people to sign up, "Getting so many people into the exchange, whether they were previously insured or not, will help create a balanced risk pool for the participating health insurance companies, which should mitigate against premium increases in the future, and it will help take away any stigma that people might have about getting insurance through AHCT. Both of these factors will ensure that AHCT is politically and financially sustainable."

Despite the praise, Counihan knew that some things could be improved. Potential improvements included upgrading the call-center functionality and adding even more educational content to the exchange website. Counihan also knew

[27] Robert Pear, "Connecticut Plans to Market Health Exchange Expertise," *New York Times*, February 24, 2014, http://www.nytimes.com/2014/02/25/us/connecticut-plans-to-market-health-exchange-expertise.html, accessed April 2014.

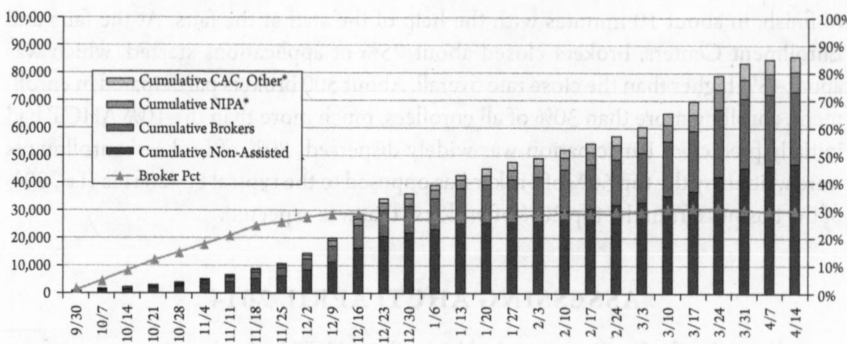

Figure 11.6 Exhibit 16 Enrollment Time Line (QHPs Only).
Source: Company documents.

that AHCT had to work on a method to smooth out re-enrollment, especially for people who received subsidies, to make the process as pain-free as possible for consumers, insurance companies, and AHCT. Would current enrollees re-enroll on their own next year or would another major marketing push be called for? As many as 20% of enrollees might be expected to experience a qualifying life event during the year (i.e., marriage, birth of a child, death of a spouse, etc.) that would change their eligibility for insurance, and any enrollees who received subsidies would have to be re-qualified annually to ensure that they still met the income requirements. Should AHCT budget for maintenance marketing for the next several months to keep enrollees engaged? And if so, where was the demarcation between the role of the insurance carriers and that of AHCT?

Planning for the Future at AHCT

Knowing that AHCT had to be financially viable as of January 1, 2015, Counihan turned his thoughts to the future. AHCT was divided into three business units: the

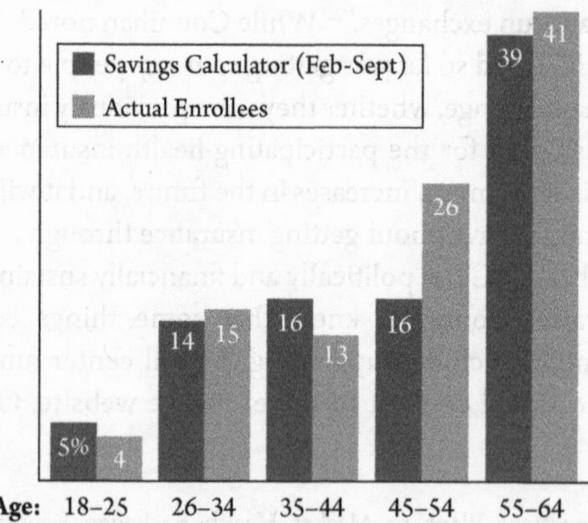

Figure 11.7 Exhibit 17 Savings Calculator Users Mirror Actual Enrollees.
Source: Company documents.

Table 11.9 Exhibit 18 Enrollment Data

Carrier	*Standard Plans*	*Nonstandard Plans*	*Enrollment*
Anthem Blue Cross Blue Shield:			
	Bronze		1,893
	Silver		15,262
	Gold		7,208
		Bronze	8,827
		Silver	9,256
		Gold	3,141
		Other	959
		Total	46,546
ConnectiCare:			
	Bronze		1,054
	Silver		27,840
	Gold		4,475
		Bronze	1,593
		Silver	0
		Gold	0
		Other	1,491
		Total	36,453
HealthyCT:			
	Bronze		1,110
	Silver		864
	Gold		731
		Bronze	0
		Silver	0
		Gold	0
		Other	85
		Total	2,790
Medicaid		Total	129,588

Source: Company documents.

exchange, which Counihan predicted to account for about 80% of AHCT's future revenue, mainly from the 1.35% tax assessment; Access Health Analytics, an insurance data analysis and management business that would sell its services to other states and would account for about 5% of AHCT's revenue; and Access Health Exchange Solutions, AHCT's business to sell complete or partial health exchange services to other states, which would account for about 15% of AHCT's revenue.

Counihan saw Exchange Solutions as AHCT's biggest source of future growth. He noted:

> The success and publicity that Connecticut's exchange has received so far has been great advertising for the services we plan to offer to other states. In the next few years, more states will take over the management of their exchanges, or at least portions of their exchanges, from the federal government. We can provide them with a low-cost way to set up an exchange that they can manage, or can manage the exchange for them after we set it up. We've already received calls from other states asking us to offer these services. This will provide financial security for AHCT and a smoothly running exchange for the other state, and it will allow federal government-averse states to comply with the ACA without having the federal government providing a "one size fits all" approach.

Counihan also considered branching AHCT out into other health insurance products, such as vision care. Could AHCT develop into a recognizable enough brand name to make this possible? Or should it remain focused on distributing health insurance plans from outside carriers? Whether or not AHCT worked to further develop its brand, when consumers ran into service issues with their insurers, or insurers raised premiums, where would exchange enrollees call? Was AHCT the new face for insurance complaints in Connecticut? Would enrollees call the insurance company or the broker they worked with to enroll? Counihan was still unsure.

With the first open enrollment complete and AHCT in a good position entering year two, Counihan wondered about the steps he should take to ensure AHCT's lasting success.

PART V

Consumerism and Paternalism

12A

23ANDME

GENETIC TESTING FOR CONSUMERS (A)

John A. Quelch and Margaret L. Rodriguez

The great loophole in all of health care is that you own your own data and ultimately you can direct your care. We're direct to consumer not because it's easy, but because that's how you create a revolution.
Anne Wojcicki, *co-founder of 23andMe.*[1]

On November 22, 2013, the direct-to-consumer genetic testing provider, 23andMe, received a letter from the U.S. Food and Drug Administration (FDA) ordering the company to halt the sale and promotion of its personal genome service (PGS) which provided inherited condition, health risk and drug response information based on DNA analysis of a saliva sample submitted by a consumer. The FDA stated that the product was marketed as a diagnostic and preventative tool and that it was subject to the agency's regulations for medical devices. Company co-founder Anne Wojcicki and president Andy Page carefully considered the potential impact of the FDA's letter on 23andMe's position in the industry and the sustainability of its operations.

THE DNA TESTING INDUSTRY

In 2003, an international team of scientists successfully completed the thirteen year project to sequence the entire human genome. The Human Genome Project required the work of hundreds of scientists and $2.7 billion to complete.[2] Following the conclusion of the project, genome sequencing services became available to the medical world.

Initially, gene testing services typically sequenced one or more specific genes (there were around 20,000 genes) and were only requested by doctors. Tests were

[1] Evie Nagy, "Fixing Healthcare.gov is the least of it when it comes to reinventing healthcare," *Fast Company*, November 7, 2013, http://www.fastcompany.com/3021310/most-creative-people/fixing-healthcaregov-is-the-least-of-it-when-it-comes-to-fixing-health-, Accessed December 2013.

[2] Elizabeth Murphy, "Inside 23andMe Founder Anne Wojcicki's $99 DNA Revolution," *Fast Company*, October 14, 2013. http://www.fastcompany.com/3018598/for-99-this-ceo-can-tell-you-what-might-kill-you-inside-23andme-founder-anne-wojcickis-dna-r. Accessed December 2013.

developed over time for as many as 2,000 diseases. Genetic tests for BRCA1 and BRCA2 and Huntington's disease, for example, were especially predictive. Gradually the price of sequencing a full genome fell from $350,000 in 2007 to $10,000 in 2013, as new technologies and competitors entered the direct-to-consumer genetic testing industry.

Concurrently alternative lower-cost technologies (called "SNP chips") were developed that did not determine linear DNA sequences, but sampled the genome at hundreds of thousands of points enabling scientists to correlate common genetic variations with hundreds of diseases and human characteristics. These correlations, based on genetic variants that were common in the population, were mostly far less predictive of future disease than the rare variants detected by sequencing genes such as BRCA1 and BRCA2.

At the 2007 meeting of the American Society of Human Genetics, 23andMe, along with two other companies, Navigenics and deCODE Genetics, announced that it would be selling SNP chip genetic testing kits directly to consumers.[3] The announcement was met with concern, as genetic tests had previously been offered to patients only through doctors or insurance companies. Many doctors questioned the accuracy of the tests, suggesting that false positives and false negatives might be frequent. Others argued that consumers would not know how to interpret properly the DNA results, especially when it came to assessing their risk of specific diseases. Some consumers might elect to take drastic action based on the test results without proper communication with genetic specialists. Few doctors, especially general practitioners, had been trained in genetics or in interpreting DNA data. Professor David Hunter of the Harvard School of Public Health commented in a *Los Angeles Times* interview on 23andMe's disease risk interpretative analysis:

> Any reasonable interpretation would assume this is news you can use, until you get the disclaimer. The problem is that we are notoriously poor at estimating risk and communicating relative and absolute risk. We simply don't know a lot about the effect of specific genes or mutations on risk.

Gene Testing Companies

By 2013, Navigenics and deCODE Genetics had both been acquired. Navigenics, which was founded in 2006, chose to cease sales to consumers in 2010 and sold its genetic tests exclusively through doctors until its acquisition by Life Technologies in 2012.[4] (Life Technologies was itself acquired one year later by Thermo Fisher Industries for $13.6 billion).[5] deCODE Genetics, launched in Iceland, went into bankruptcy in 2009 and was later acquired along with its database by Amgen for $415 million

[3] Ricki Lewis, "Why 23andMe is Not for Me—Yet," *DNA Science Blog, PLOS Blog,* November 27, 2013, http://blogs.plos.org/dnascience/2013/11/27/why-23andme-is-not-for-me-yet/. Accessed December 2013.

[4] Christopher R. O'Dea, "Science, Math, Biology," *Korn/Ferry International,* Q1, Winter 2014, Accessed December 2013.

[5] O'Dea, "Science, Math, Biology."

in 2012.[6] Pharmaceutical companies grew interested in acquiring gene testing firms after realizing the potential to use the genome data to contribute to their drug research and discovery efforts.[7]

Meanwhile, new players entered the market. Pathway Genomics originally planned to sell its gene test kit directly to consumers through Walgreens drug stores but, when Walgreens withdrew in 2012, decided to sell its test only through doctors.[8] BGI Shenzen, a Chinese firm which had the production capacity to map 10% to 20% of global genetic data, acquired U.S. firm, Complete Genetics, in 2012.[9] In late 2012, Gene by Gene Ltd. launched a direct-to-consumer service to sequence the entire human genome called "DNA DTC."[10] The company offered raw genome data without analysis or interpretation of the results, which protected it against regulatory challenge.[11]

A sales boost to gene testing companies came in May 2013, when Angelina Jolie elected to have a double-mastectomy after learning she carried the BRCA1 mutation through a gene test. (The mutation increased the likelihood of developing serious breast cancer). Jolie commented in a *New York Times* op-ed: "I choose not to keep my story private because there are many women who do not know that they might be living under the shadow of cancer. It is my hope that they, too, will be able to get gene tested, and that if they have a high risk they, too, will know that they have strong options." Wojcicki commented: "Angelina Jolie talking about a technical subject and saying, 'I did this, you can do this,' is a great thing for us. She did something to prevent the disease and that's exactly what we want people thinking about."[12]

23ANDME

In 2006, Anne Wojcicki (wife of Google co-founder, Sergey Brin), Linda Avey and Paul Cusenza founded 23andMe, a service to provide genetic testing to consumers. The name was derived from the number of chromosome pairs in the human cell. The founders had two goals for the company: empower consumers to manage their own health by giving them access to their genetic information, and aggregating the data from genetic tests into a database to help researchers and medical professionals develop cures.[13] 23andMe began selling kits to consumers in 2007 for $999 each.[14] In 2008, 23andMe's consumer genetic testing kit was named *Time* magazine's invention of the year.[15]

[6] O'Dea, "Science, Math, Biology."
[7] O'Dea, "Science, Math, Biology."
[8] O'Dea, "Science, Math, Biology."
[9] O'Dea, "Science, Math, Biology."
[10] O'Dea, "Science, Math, Biology."
[11] O'Dea, "Science, Math, Biology."
[12] Murphy, "Inside 23andMe."
[13] Murphy, "Inside 23andMe."
[14] Murphy, "Inside 23andMe."
[15] Anita Hamilton, "Invention of the Year," *Time Magazine*, October 29, 2008, http://content.time.com/time/ specials/packages/article/0,28804,1852747_1854493_1854113,00.html. Accessed December 2013.

Figure 12A.1 Exhibit 1 23andMe DNA Test Kit, 2013.
Source: Diane Brady, "23andMe wants to take its DNA test mass-market," *BusinessWeek*, September 30, 2013, http://www.businessweek.com/articles/2013-09-27/23andme-wants-to-take-its-dna-tests-mass-market, Accessed December 2013.

23andMe used SNP (single nucleotide polymorphisms) chip technology that sequenced less than 0.1% of the genome but offered genetic results for 260 factors.[16] Customers visiting the 23andMe website could pay $99 to be sent a DNA test kit (Figure 12A.1) which included a receptacle for a saliva sample. Six to eight weeks after the sample was returned, the customer received an email prompting him or her to log onto the 23andMe website in order to review the PGS results. These summarized the customer's genetically-based predisposition for 53 inherited conditions, 122 health risks, 25 drug responses (for example, to warfarin) and 60 traits (such as the perception of bitter tastes), as well as genetic ancestry information.[17]

The 23andMe website included numerous disclaimers that the test results were "intended for research and educational programs only, and not for diagnostic use." Consumers were encouraged to discuss the results with a doctor and were advised that they should not replace a doctor's professional advice. Certain results for risk of Parkinson's disease and Alzheimer's disease, for example, required the consumer to

[16] Murphy, "Inside 23andMe."
[17] O'Dea, "Science, Math, Biology."

specifically agree to unlock the data before the test results were revealed. There was also an option on the 23andMe website for a customer to forward the results by email to his or her doctor.

23andMe customers were invited to opt-in to the company's research program, which placed their genetic results into an anonymous research database. Those who elected to contribute their results to the database (around 90% chose to do so) were included in surveys, which sought to gather additional data on specific traits from participants. By 2013, 23andMe users had answered over 200 million survey questions.[18] In addition to the surveys, 23andMe stayed connected to those who shared their genetic data by alerting customers to posts about new research studies and other news related to each individual's risk factors.

23andMe sought to give its customers more influence over their health care decisions. "We want to be the last mile of communication and interpretation of genetic data. As more and more people do that, and we establish more partnerships where we become that interface between institutions that are offering the tests [and individuals], we can build communities around certain disease states," said Wojcicki.[19] The company subsidized kits for those with certain conditions: any consumer diagnosed with Parkinson's was eligible to receive a free genetic testing kit. Through its effort, 23andMe soon created the largest database of Parkinson's patients in the world, with more than 10,000 participants.[20]

23andMe also believed its data would be of interest to government health agencies running single-payer systems. "Let's say you genotype everyone in Canada or the United Kingdom or Abu Dhabi, and the government is able to identify those segments of the population that are most at risk for heart disease or breast cancer or Parkinson's. You can target them with preventative messages, make sure they're examined frequently, and in the end live healthier lives, and the government will save massive expenses because they halted someone who's pre-diabetic from getting diabetes. 23andme has been in discussion with a bunch of such societies," said Patrick Chung, a venture capitalist investor in 23andMe.[21]

23andMe's funding came mainly from Google Ventures, Johnson & Johnson and venture capitalists. 23andMe also received over $550,000 in three grants from the National Institute of Health to study allergies and asthma.[22] 23andMe amassed $125 million in funding by 2013. A $59 million round of financing in December 2012 added Yuri Milner as a new investor and enabled the company to reduce the price of the genetic test from $299 to $99. "At $99, we are opening the doors of access. Genetics is part of an entire path for how you're going to live a healthier life," said Wojcicki.[23]

23andMe raised most of its operating revenue from the sale of $99 consumer genetic test kits. The company had not made a profit as of 2013. [24] It broke even on the

[18] Murphy, "Inside 23andMe."

[19] Murphy, "Inside 23andMe."

[20] Murphy, "Inside 23andMe."

[21] Murphy, "Inside 23andMe."

[22] Murphy, "Inside 23andMe."

[23] Murphy, "Inside 23andMe."

[24] Murphy, "Inside 23andMe."

test kits and hope to raise added revenues by monetizing the genetic database created from the test results plus additional user information.[25]

23andMe's customer acquisition was relatively slow following its creation: only 35,000 customers had purchased kits by 2010.[26] Sign-ups rose with increased awareness of genetic testing (helped by the publicity surrounding Angelina Jolie's test).[27] A study by 23andMe released in April 2013 found that 73% of Americans who had not received a genetic test would like to be tested in the future (around 1% of the U.S. population had undergone a genetic test).[28] Of those surveyed, 70% said they would like the test to identify their risks of developing health conditions, and 55% said that they would consider altering their lifestyles (diet, exercise, etc.) based upon such results.[29]

In order to continue acquiring new customers, 23andMe's vice president of marketing, Neil Rothstein (formerly of Netflix), decided to target consumers who were proactive about their health care needs and sought to take control of their health. In August 2013, 23andMe launched a $5 million television, radio and direct mail advertising campaign to reach those consumers. The "Portraits of Health" campaign featured 23andMe customers discovering their results and what they learned about their health from exploring their DNA. The message centered on the preventative health measures that informed consumers could take if they knew their disease risks.

By November 2013, the company had tested the genetics of almost 450,000 consumers, nearly half of whom had signed up during 2013.[30] Wojcicki's original goal had been one million customers by the end of 2013.[31]

Regulation and the FDA Letter

In 2008, Congress passed the Genetic Information Nondiscrimination Act (GINA). GINA prohibited the use of genetic test results by employers or health insurers to assess candidates. Insurers and employers were specifically banned from: requiring candidates undergo DNA testing, using genetic information to restrict enrollment in insurance programs/changing premiums, and using genetic information to determine whom to hire or to set salary levels.[32] However, long-term-care, life and disability insurance providers were not prevented from using genetic test results under GINA.

The FDA was responsible for the regulation of gene test companies. In 2010, concerned about consumer safety and the potential for results to lead to unnecessary medical procedures, Alberto Gutierrez, director of diagnostic test regulation at the FDA, sent letters to five gene testing companies (including 23andMe, deCODE,

[25] Murphy, "Inside 23andMe."

[26] Murphy, "Inside 23andMe."

[27] Murphy, "Inside 23andMe."

[28] O'Dea, "Science, Math, Biology."

[29] O'Dea, "Science, Math, Biology."

[30] Elizabeth Murphy, "To know you is to really know you," *Fast Company*, October 14, 2013, http://www.fastcompany.com/3019323/to-know-you-is-to-really-know-you, Accessed December 2013.

[31] Murphy, "Inside 23andMe."

[32] 23andMe Company, "Customer Care," https://customercare.23andme.com/entries/21252073, Accessed December 2013.

Navigenics, and Illumina, a manufacturer of DNA chips used to complete DNA scans) which stated that the tests were considered "medical devices" and required the companies to seek FDA approval for their tests.[33] According to the definition provided by the FDA, a "medical device" was any tool intended for use in diagnosis, mitigation, cure, prevention or treatment of disease.[34] The FDA required manufacturers of such devices: register the device with the FDA, list the parties connected to the device's manufacture, provide pre-market notification (and, for high risk devices, obtain approval), insure supply quality met FDA standards, label the device, and report incidents in which the device may have contributed to injury or death.[35] Some companies claimed their test kits did not require FDA approval because they were developed and offered by a single laboratory; the FDA had focused on regulating tests that were widely distributed to hospitals, labs and doctors. Other companies cooperated and, on November 19, 2013, DNA test component manufacturer, Illumina, became the first company to receive premarket clearance from the FDA for its DNA sequencing analyzer.[36]

On November 22, 2013, 23andMe received a letter from the FDA ordering the company to halt the sale and promotion of its genetic testing kit until it was in compliance with the standards required for medical devices (Box 12A.1). Wojcicki claimed that 23andMe had been in contact with FDA since 2008, and had submitted applications to obtain clearance of the test kit as a medical device in July and September of 2012.[37] She acknowledged that the FDA had provided feedback on the application in May 2013 and that 23andMe had not responded since. In a statement, she said:

> We recognize that we have not met the FDA's expectations regarding timeline and communication regarding our submission. Our relationship with the FDA is extremely important to us, and we are committed to fully engaging with them to address their concerns.[38]

The FDA gave 23andMe 15 days following its letter to respond to its charges and take the necessary actions to avoid an injunction.

[33] Andrew Pollack, "F.D.A. faults companies on unapproved genetic tests," *New York Times*, June 11, 2010, http://www.nytimes.com/2010/06/12/health/12genome.html, Accessed December 2013.

[34] U.S. Food and Drug Administration, "Medical Devices: Is the Product a Medical Device?," http://www.fda.gov/MedicalDevices/DeviceRegulationandGuidance/Overview/ClassifyYourDevice/ucm051512.htm, accessed December 2013.

[35] U.S. Food and Drug Administration, "Medical Devices: Overview of Device Regulation," http://www.fda.gov/MedicalDevices/DeviceRegulationandGuidance/overview/, accessed December 2013.

[36] Thomas M. Burton, "FDA Approves New Gene-Sequencing Devices," *Wall Street Journal (Online)*, November 20, 2013, http://online.wsj.com/news/articles/SB10001424052702303755504579208551375755402, Accessed December 2013.

[37] Caroline Humer, "Genetic test maker 23andMe stops marketing after FDA warning," *Reuters*, December 2, 2013, http://www.reuters.com/article/2013/12/03/us-23andme-fda-idUSBRE9B202G20131203, Accessed December 2013.

[38] 23andMe, "23andMe statement regarding FDA warning letter," *the 23andMe blog*, November 25, 2013, http://blog.23andme.com/news/23andme-statement-regarding-fda-warning-letter/, accessed December 2013.

Box 12A.1 Exhibit 2 Letter from the FDA to 23andMe, 2013

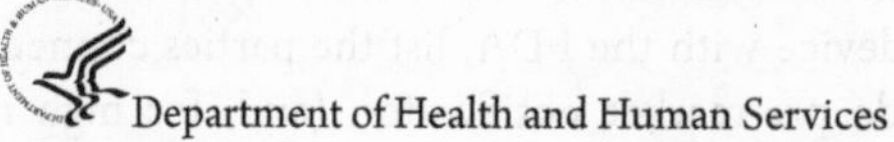
Department of Health and Human Services

Public Health Service
Food and Drug Administration

10903 New Hampshire Avenue
Silver Spring, MD 20993

Nov 22, 2013
Ann Wojcicki
CEO
23andMe, Inc.
1390 Shoreline Way
Mountain View, CA 94043
Document Number: GEN1300666
Re: Personal Genome Service (PGS)
WARNING LETTER
Dear Ms. Wojcicki,

The Food and Drug Administration (FDA) is sending you this letter because you are marketing the 23andMe Saliva Collection Kit and Personal Genome Service (PGS) without marketing clearance or approval in violation of the Federal Food, Drug and Cosmetic Act (the FD&C Act).

This product is a device within the meaning of section 201(h) of the FD&C Act, 21 U.S.C. 321(h), because it is intended for use in the diagnosis of disease or other conditions or in the cure, mitigation, treatment, or prevention of disease, or is intended to affect the structure or function of the body. For example, your company's website at www.23andme.com/health (most recently viewed on November 6, 2013) markets the PGS for providing "health reports on 254 diseases and conditions," including categories such as "carrier status," "health risks," and "drug response," and specifically as a "first step in prevention" that enables users to "take steps toward mitigating serious diseases" such as diabetes, coronary heart disease, and breast cancer. Most of the intended uses for PGS listed on your website, a list that has grown over time, are medical device uses under section 201(h) of the FD&C Act. Most of these uses have not been classified and thus require premarket approval or de novo classification, as FDA has explained to you on numerous occasions.

Some of the uses for which PGS is intended are particularly concerning, such as assessments for BRCA-related genetic risk and drug responses (e.g., warfarin sensitivity, clopidogrel response, and 5-fluorouracil toxicity) because of the potential health consequences that could result from false positive or false negative assessments for high-risk indications such as these. For instance, if the BRCA-related risk assessment for breast or ovarian cancer reports a false positive, it could lead a patient to undergo prophylactic surgery, chemoprevention, intensive screening, or other morbidity-inducing actions, while a false negative could result in a failure to recognize an actual risk that may exist. Assessments for drug responses carry the risks that patients relying on such tests may begin to self-manage their treatments through dose changes or even abandon certain therapies depending on the outcome of the assessment. For example, false genotype results for your warfarin drug response test could have significant unreasonable risk of illness, injury, or death to the patient due to thrombosis or bleeding events that occur from treatment with a drug at a dose that does not provide the appropriately calibrated anticoagulant effect. These risks are typically mitigated by International Normalized Ratio (INR) management under a physician's care. The risk of serious injury or death is known to be high when patients are either non-compliant or not properly dosed; combined with the risk that a direct-to-consumer test result may be used by a patient to self-manage, serious concerns are raised if test results are not adequately understood by patients or if incorrect test results are reported.

Your company submitted 510(k)s for PGS on July 2, 2012 and September 4, 2012, for several of these indications for use. However, to date, your company has failed to address the issues described during previous interactions with the Agency or provide the additional information identified in our September 13, 2012 letter for **(b)(4)** and in our November 20, 2012 letter for **(b)(4)**, as required under 21 CFR 807.87(1). Consequently, the 510(k)s are considered withdrawn, *see* 21 C.F.R. 807.87(1), as we explained in our letters to you on March 12, 2013 and May 21, 2013. To date, 23andMe has failed to provide adequate information to support a determination that the PGS is substantially equivalent to a legally marketed predicate for any of the uses for which you are marketing it; no other submission for the PGS device that you are marketing has been provided under section 510(k) of the Act, 21 U.S.C. § 360(k).

The Office of In Vitro Diagnostics and Radiological Health (OIR) has a long history of working with companies to help them come into compliance with the FD&C Act. Since July of 2009, we have been diligently working to help you comply with regulatory requirements regarding safety and effectiveness and obtain marketing authorization for your PGS device. FDA has spent significant time evaluating the intended uses of the PGS to determine whether certain uses might be appropriately classified into class II, thus requiring only 510(k) clearance or de novo classification and not PMA approval, and we have proposed modifications to the device's labeling that could mitigate risks and render certain intended uses appropriate for de novo classification. Further, we provided ample detailed feedback to 23andMe regarding the types of data it needs to submit for the intended uses of the PGS. As part of our interactions with you, including more than 14 face-to-face and teleconference meetings, hundreds of email exchanges, and dozens of written communications, we provided you with specific feedback on study protocols and clinical and analytical validation requirements, discussed potential classifications and regulatory pathways (including reasonable submission timelines), provided statistical advice, and discussed potential risk mitigation strategies. As discussed above, FDA is concerned about the public health consequences of inaccurate results from the PGS device; the main purpose of compliance with FDA's regulatory requirements is to ensure that the tests work.

However, even after these many interactions with 23andMe, we still do not have any assurance that the firm has analytically or clinically validated the PGS for its intended uses, which have expanded from the uses that the firm identified in its submissions. In your letter dated January 9, 2013, you stated that the firm is "completing the additional analytical and clinical validations for the tests that have been submitted" and is "planning extensive labeling studies that will take several months to complete." Thus, months after you submitted your 510(k)s and more than 5 years after you began marketing, you still had not completed some of the studies and had not even started other studies necessary to support a marketing submission for the PGS. It is now eleven months later, and you have yet to provide FDA with any new information about these tests. You have not worked with us toward de novo classification, did not provide the additional information we requested necessary to complete review of your 510(k)s, and FDA has not received any communication from 23andMe since May. Instead, we have become aware that you have initiated new marketing campaigns, including television commercials that, together with an increasing list of indications, show that you plan to expand the PGS's uses and consumer base without obtaining marketing authorization from FDA.

Therefore, 23andMe must immediately discontinue marketing the PGS until such time as it receives FDA marketing authorization for the device. The PGS is in class III under section 513(f) of the FD&C Act, 21 U.S.C. 360c(f). Because there is no approved application for premarket approval in effect pursuant to section 515(a) of the FD&C Act, 21 U.S.C. 360e(a), or an approved application for an investigational device exemption (IDE) under section 520(g) of the FD&C Act, 21 U.S.C. 360j(g), the PGS is adulterated under section 501(f)(1)(B) of the FD&C Act, 21 U.S.C. 351(f)(1)(B). Additionally, the PGS is misbranded under section 502(o) of the Act, 21 U.S.C. § 352(o), because notice or other information respecting the device was not provided to FDA as required by section 510(k) of the Act, 21 U.S.C. § 360(k).

Please notify this office in writing within fifteen (15) working days from the date you receive this letter of the specific actions you have taken to address all issues noted above. Include documentation of the corrective actions you have taken. If your actions will occur over time, please include a timetable for implementation of those actions. If corrective actions cannot be completed within 15 working days, state the reason for the delay and the time within which the actions will be completed. Failure to take adequate corrective action may result in regulatory action being initiated by the Food and Drug Administration without further notice. These actions include, but are not limited to, seizure, injunction, and civil money penalties.

We have assigned a unique document number that is cited above. The requested information should reference this document number and should be submitted to:

James L. Woods, WO66-5688
Deputy Director
Patient Safety and Product Quality
Office of In vitro Diagnostics and Radiological Health
10903 New Hampshire Avenue
Silver Spring, MD 20993

If you have questions relating to this matter, please feel free to call Courtney Lias, Ph.D. at 301-796-5458, or log onto our web site at www.fda.gov for general information relating to FDA device requirements.

Sincerely yours,

/S/

Alberto Gutierrez
Director
Office of In vitro Diagnostics
and Radiological Health
Center for Devices and Radiological Health

Source: U.S. Food and Drug Administration, "23andMe, Inc. 11/22/13," http://www.fda.gov/iceci/enforcementactions/ warningletters/2013/ucm376296.htm, Accessed December 2013.

12B

23ANDME
GENETIC TESTING FOR CONSUMERS (B)

John A. Quelch and Margaret L. Rodriguez

Following the receipt of the Food and Drug Administration (FDA) letter dated November 22, 2013, 23andMe cofounder and chief executive officer, Anne Wojcicki, posted a blog that stated: "We are behind schedule with our responses."[1] This was followed by an e-mail message to 23andMe customers dated November 27 (see Box 12B.1 for text of e-mail).

The management team at 23andMe had three customer groups to consider: those who had already received complete test results; those who had submitted saliva samples prior to the FDA announcement and had not yet received their results; and those who visited the site and wished to purchase the test kit following the FDA announcement.

23andMe benefited from publicity following the FDA letter, which spurred many new visitors to its website. Figure 12B.1 depicts Google search results for "23andMe" and "DNA Test" over time, relative to total Google searches.

Science writer Razib Khan predicted the FDA's move would matter little, as raw genetic results could be obtained cheaply from international genome sequencing firms, and open source tools to analyze such data using published scientific research were freely available.[2] For example, promethease.com offered to take the raw genetic data supplied by 23andMe and provide the associated disease risk interpretation for only $5.[3]

Ronald Bailey wrote in *Reason* magazine: "The FDA bureaucrats think that they know better than you how to handle your genetic information. This is outrageous."[4] TechFreedom, a nonprofit think tank devoted to technological progress,

[1] AnneW [Wojcicki], "An update regarding the FDA's letter to 23andMe," 23andMe blog, November 26, 2013, http://blog.23andme.com/news/an-update-regarding-the-fdas-letter-to-23andme/, accessed December 2013.

[2] Razib Khan, "The FDA's Battle with 23andMe Won't Mean Anything in the Long Run," *Slate*, November 25, 2013, http://www.slate.com/blogs/future_tense/2013/11/25/fda_letter_to_23andme_won_t_mean_anything_in_the_long_run.html, accessed January 2014.

[3] Promethease, "Promethease," https://promethease.com/ondemand, accessed January 2014.

[4] Ronald Bailey, "FDA Shuts Down 23andMe," Hit & Run (Blog), *Reason*, November 25, 2013, http://archive.today/uUyXG, accessed January 2014.

Box 12B.1 Exhibit 1 November 27, 2013, E-mail to Customers of 23andMe

"Dear 23andMe Customers,

I wanted to reach out to you about the FDA letter that was sent to 23andMe last Friday. It is absolutely critical that our consumers get high quality genetic data that they can trust. We have worked extensively with our lab partner to make sure that the results we return are accurate. We stand behind the data that we return to customers—but we recognize that the FDA needs to be convinced of the quality of our data as well.

23andMe has been working with the FDA to navigate the correct regulatory path for direct-to-consumer genetic tests. This is new territory, not just for 23andMe, but for the FDA as well. The FDA is an important partner for 23andMe and we will be working hard to move forward with them.

I apologize for the limited response to the questions many of you have raised regarding the letter and its implications for the service. We don't have the answers to all of those questions yet, but as we learn more we will update you.

I am committed to providing each of you with a trusted consumer product rooted in high quality data that adheres to the best scientific standards. All of us at 23andMe believe that genetic information can lead to healthier lives.

Thank you for your loyalty to 23andMe. Please refer to our 23andMe blog for updates on this process.

Anne Wojcicki

Co-founder and CEO, 23andMe"

Source: 23andMe, "A letter from the CEO," e-mail message to casewriter, November 27, 2013.

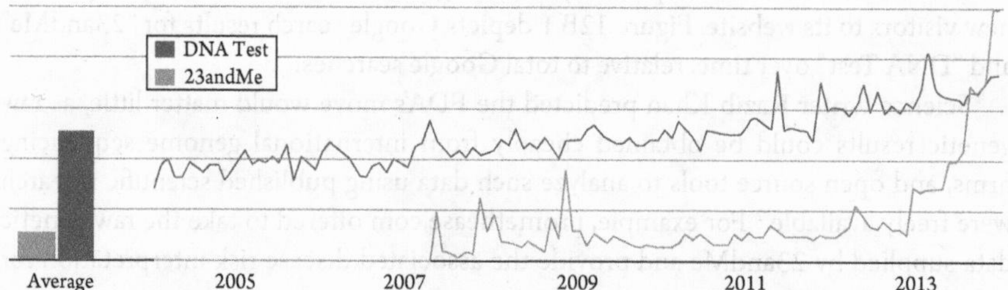

Figure 12B.1 Exhibit 2 Google Search Incidences over Time for "23andMe" and "DNA Test," 2005–2013.
Source: Google, "Google Trends," http://www.google.com/trends/explore#q=23andMe%2C%20DNA%20Test&cmpt=q, accessed December 2013.

created a petition asking the FDA to refrain from banning 23andMe's consumer gene-testing kits.[5] Matthew Herper, staff science writer for *Forbes*, was more critical of 23andMe: "The FDA probably felt it had little choice. This is not the story of a big

[5] Timothy B. Lee, "The FDA should leave 23andMe alone," *Washington Post*, November 25, 2013, http://www.washingtonpost.com/blogs/the-switch/wp/2013/11/25/the-fda-should-leave-23andme-alone/, accessed January 2014.

Welcome to 23andMe.

At this time, we have suspended our health-related genetic tests to comply with the U.S. Food and Drug Administration's directive to discontinue new consumer access during our regulatory review process.

We are continuing to provide you with both ancestry-related genetic tests and raw genetic data, without 23andMe's interpretation.

If you are an existing customer please click the button below and then go to the health page for additional information, including information about refunds.

We remain firmly committed to fulfilling our long-term mission to help people everywhere have access to their own genetic data and have the ability to use that information to improve their lives.

Upon entering the site, please confirm you understand the new changes in our services.

I understand that 23andMe only sells ancestry reports and raw genetic data at this time. I understand 23andMe will not provide health-related reports. However, 23andMe may provide health-related results in the future, dependent upon FDA marketing authorization.

I UNDERSTAND

Figure 12B.2 Exhibit 3 23andMe Website Message about the Removal of Disease Analysis, 2013.
Source: 23andMe Company, "Home Page," https://www.23andme.com/, accessed December 6, 2013.

Box 12B.2 Exhibit 4 December 6, 2013, E-mail Message to 23andMe Customers

"Dear 23andMe Customers,

I'm writing to update you on our conversation with the U.S. Food and Drug Administration and how it impacts you.

If you are a customer whose kit was purchased before November 22, 2013, your 23andMe experience will not change. You will be able to access both ancestry and health-related information as you always have.

23andMe has complied with the FDA's directive and stopped offering new consumers access to health-related genetic results while the company moves forward with the agency's regulatory review processes. Be sure to refer to our 23andMe blog for updates.

We stand behind the data we have generated for customers. Our lab partner adheres to strict quality standards that are part of the Clinical Laboratory Improvement Amendments of 1988—known as CLIA. These are the same standards used in the majority of other health and disease-related tests.

You are among the first people in the world to ever get access to their genomes. You are genetic pioneers. Thank you for your ongoing support and we look forward to continuing to serve you.

Anne Wojcicki

Co-founder and CEO, 23andMe"

Source: 23andMe, "Important update from 23andMe," e-mail message to casewriter, December 6, 2013.

regulator choosing to squash a small company, but of a company that decided that it didn't have to follow the rules."[6]

On December 2, 23andMe ceased advertising its test kit but continued to sell the product via its website. As of December 5, 23andMe announced that it would henceforth be selling only raw genetic data and ancestry-related results.[7] Visitors to the 23andMe website received a welcome message, reproduced here as Figure 12B.2. Refunds were available to consumers who purchased their test kits after November 22, because 23andMe would not be able to provide them with health information. A December 6 e-mail message from Wojcicki to existing customers (those who purchased kits prior to November 22) is reproduced as Box 12B.2.

By mid-December, class action lawsuits citing 23andMe for misleading advertising had been filed in California and Massachusetts.

[6] Matthew Herper, "23andStupid: Is 23andMe Self-Destructing?" *Forbes*, November 25, 2013, http://www.forbes.com/sites/matthewherper/2013/11/25/23andstupid-is-23andme-self-destructing/, accessed Jan. 2014.

[7] 23andMe Company, "Home Page," https://www.23andme.com/, accessed December 6, 2013.

13

DEMARKETING SODA IN NEW YORK CITY

John A. Quelch, Margaret L. Rodriguez, Carin-Isabel Knoop, and Christine Snively

I've got to defend my children, and yours, and do what's right to save lives ... Obesity kills. There's no question it kills ... People are dying every day. This is not a joke. This is about real lives.
—Mayor Michael Bloomberg[1]

This is what makes liberals look like elitist bullies who think they know everything and can tell people what to do. You shouldn't have to clear what you eat with the municipal government.
—Bill Maher, comedian and television host[2]

In the spring of 2013, New York City (NYC) mayor, philanthropist, and billionaire Michael R. Bloomberg (HBS '66) was foiled in his attempt to make it illegal for NYC food-service establishments regulated by the city's health department (including street vendors, bowling alleys, and restaurants) to sell sodas and other sugary drinks in containers larger than 16 ounces (475ml). The city defined a sugary drink as a non-alcoholic beverage that was less than 50% milk and was presweetened by the manufacturer or the vendor with sugar or another caloric sweetener, like high-fructose corn syrup, honey, or agave nectar. Large drink containers would still be available at convenience stores and grocery stores. The ubiquitous convenience store 7-Eleven was exempted, saving its 32-ounce Big Gulp (with its "drink like you mean it" slogan), which contained as much liquid as could be comfortably held by the average human stomach, along with its 50-ounce Double Gulp.[3] When a judge struck down the ruling as "arbitrary" and "capricious," he mentioned such incongruities.

[1] Michael Grynbaum, "Judge Blocks New York City's Limits on Big Sugary Drinks," *New York Times*, March 11, 2013, http://www.nytimes.com/2013/03/12/nyregion/judge-invalidates-bloombergs-soda-ban.html?pagewanted=all&_r=0, accessed May 2013.

[2] Tom Watkins, "Bloomberg: Nanny-in-chief or health crusader?" *CNN U.S.*, March 24, 2013, http:// www.cnn.com/2013/03/24/us/michael-bloomberg-profile, accessed May 2013.

[3] 7-Eleven, "Big Gulp," https://www.7-eleven.com/Thirsty/Cold/Big-Gulp/, accessed May 2013.

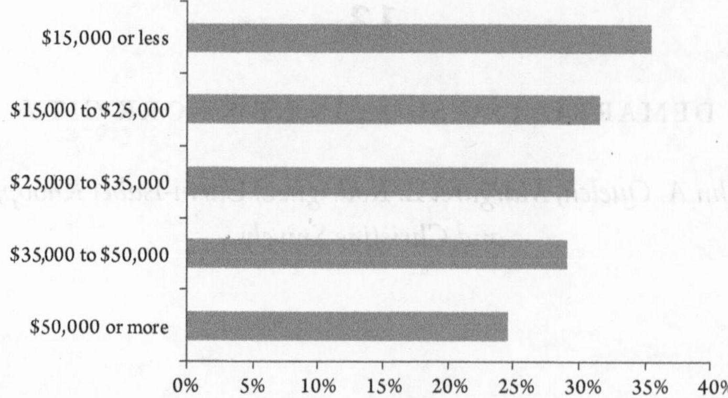

Figure 13.1 Exhibit 1 Obesity Rates by Income Level, 2010.
Source: Adapted from "F as in Fat: How Obesity Threatens America's Future," Trust for America's Health, 2010, http:// healthyamericans.org/reports/obesity2010/Obesity2010Report.pdf, accessed May 2013.

THE OBESITY EPIDEMIC

The term *overweight* was generally used in the U.S. to indicate excess weight, while *obese* referred to excess fat. The U.S. Dietary Guidelines defined those with a Body Mass Index (BMI) of 25.0 to 29.9 as overweight, and those with BMI scores of 30.0 or greater as obese.[4] The BMI-derived definitions of overweight and obese were based on data that showed modest mortality increases among participants whose BMI scores were above 25.0, and more dramatic mortality increases for persons with BMI scores of 30 or above.[5] BMI was calculated using only weight and height, and so failed to account for individual differences in muscle mass or "fatness" in all individuals.[6] While an overweight person always carried excess weight, she might or might not have an excess accumulation of fat. By some estimates, about 78.4 million people in the U.S. were obese and 154.7 million were overweight in 2013.[7] Lower-income Americans, especially those living in "food deserts,"[8] had a greater chance of becoming obese. (See Figure 13.1 for obesity rates by income level.)

[4] Ogden, CL, Yanovski, SZ, Carroll, MD, and Flegal, KM, 2007, "The Epidemiology of Obesity," *Gastroenterology* 132: 2087–2102.

[5] National Institutes of Health, 1998, "Clinical Guidelines on the Identification, Evaluation and Treatment of Overweight and Obesity in Adults: The Evidence Report," http://www.nhlbi.nih.gov/guidelines/obesity/ob_gdlns.htm.

[6] World Health Organization, "Obesity Fact Sheet," http://www.who.int/mediacentre/factsheets/fs311/en/index.html, accessed April 2014.

[7] "Statistical Fact Sheet 2013 Update: Overweight & Obesity," American Heart Association, Inc, 2013, http: //www.heart.org/idc/groups/heart-public/@wcm/@sop/@smd/documents/downloadable/ucm_319588.pdf, accessed August 2013.

[8] A *food desert* was defined as a neighborhood with limited access to supermarkets or other sources of healthy and affordable food.

According to the Centers for Disease Control and Prevention (CDC), the U.S. spent about $190 billion a year (about 13% of the country's medical expenses) treating obesity-related health conditions in 2012.[9] Obese individuals cost the system an additional $1,443 per year per person in health-care expenditures compared to non-obese individuals[10] (overweight individuals cost an additional $266).[11] In 2012, approximately one in three U.S. adults, and one in six U.S. children, were obese. The CDC considered obesity an epidemic that contributed to heart disease, gout, osteoarthritis, sleep apnea, diabetes, cancer, and death.[12] Obesity had led to an increase in type 2 diabetes, which could result in blindness, kidney failure, and amputations.[13] Individuals diagnosed with diabetes incurred on average an additional $6,649 per year in medical costs.[14] Obesity-related expenditures were expected to account for over 21% of the nation's health-care spending by 2018.[15]

Obesity resulted from people consuming more calories than their bodies could burn. Societal, economic, and cultural conditions all contributed to its greater prevalence. Diets had changed over the prior 50 years, as people consumed more processed foods, more food on the run, more fast food, and larger portions. Americans had also become more sedentary and spent more time in front of screens while at home and at work.[16] See Table 13.1.

Obesity-related health-care expenditures in NYC were estimated at $4.7 billion in 2012. (See Table 13.2 for costs of worker absenteeism due to weight). Obesity contributed to over 5,000 deaths annually. In 2012, 23% of 6.5 million New Yorkers over 18 were obese, and an additional 34% were overweight.[17] Of the 1.8 million New Yorkers 18 years

[9] Cawley J, and Meyerhoefer C, "The medical care costs of obesity: an instrumental variables approach," *J Health Econ.* 2012; 31:219–230, as presented on the Harvard School of Public Health website, http://www.hsph. harvard.edu/nutritionsource/sugary-drinks-fact-sheet/, accessed May 2013.

[10] Danielle Tcholaklan, "Judge Forbids Implementing soda ban, Bloomberg vows to appeal," *Metro*, March 11, 2013, http://www.metro.us/newyork/news/local/2013/03/11/judge-forbids-implementing-soda-ban/, accessed May 2013

[11] A.G. Tsai, D.F. Williamson, and H.A. Glick, "Direct medical costs of overweight and obesity in the USA: a quantitative systematic review," *Obesity Reviews*, January 2011, Google Scholar, accessed August 2013.

[12] "The Obesity Epidemic," video, Centers for Disease Control and Prevention, July 22, 2011, http://www.cdc.gov/cdctv/ObesityEpidemic/, accessed May 2013.

[13] "MAYORBLOOMBERG,DEPUTYMAYORGIBBS,HEALTHCOMMISSIONERFARLEYAND SUPPORTERS VISIT RESTAURANT . . .," press release, March 12, 2013, http://www.nyc.gov/portal/site/ nycgov/menuitem.c0935b9a57bb4ef3daf2f1c701c789a0/index.jsp?pageID=mayor_press_release&catID=1194&doc_name=http%3A%2F%2Fwww.nyc.gov%2Fhtml%2Fom%2Fhtml%2F2013a%2Fpr091-13.html&cc=unused 1978&rc=1194&ndi=1, accessed May 2013.

[14] Danielle Tcholaklan, "Judge Forbids Implementing soda ban, Bloomberg vows to appeal."

[15] "MAYOR BLOOMBERG, DEPUTY MAYOR GIBBS, HEALTH COMMISSIONER FARLEY AND SUPPORTERS VISIT RESTAURANT. . . ."

[16] "The Obesity Epidemic," video, Centers for Disease Control and Prevention, July 22, 2011, http://www.cdc.gov/cdctv/ObesityEpidemic/, accessed May 2013.

[17] NYC Community Health Survey (CHS) 2002–2010; Youth Risk Behavior Survey (YRBS), 2001–2011; NYC Fitnessgram 2006–2010, http://www.nyc.gov/html/om/pdf/2012/otf_report.pdf.

Table 13.1 Table A Prevalence of Overweight and Obesity in U.S. Adults between 1965 and 2010

	1965	*1990*	*2010*
% of overweight adults	32%	33%	33%
% of obese adults	13%	23%	36%
Gallons of soda consumed per capita	17.8	48.0	44.7
Average serving size of soda	12 oz.	20 oz.	20 oz.

Source: Compiled from "Overweight and Obesity Statistics," Weight-Control Information Network, National Institute of Health, http://win.niddk.nih.gov/statistics/index.htm#ref2; "An Update on the Dangers of Soda Pop," http://www.ineedce.com/courses/1417/HTML/soda_pop_print.html; "NYC Soda Ban Debate: Half Empty or Half Full?" National Heart, Lung, and Blood Institute, http://www.nhlbi.nih.gov/health/public/heart/obesity/wecan/eat-right/distortion.htm, accessed September 2013.

old and younger, 40% were overweight or obese in 2012. The daily NYC work force was 4 million. Nine of the top ten NYC neighborhoods with the highest obesity rates also consumed the highest amounts of sugary drinks. Almost 70% of residents in NYC's Bronx borough were obese.[18] Hispanic and black New Yorkers were two and three times more likely, respectively, to die from diabetes. (See Figure 13.2 for obesity trends in NYC.)

The Connection between Sugary Drinks and Obesity

A 2004 study showed that Americans increased the proportion of total energy obtained from soft drinks and fruit drinks, while decreasing the proportion of total energy obtained from milk. Total calories from soft drinks increased from 2.8% to 7.0% between 1977 and 2001, and for younger Americans (19 to 39 years old), soft drink intake increased from 4.1% to 9.8% of total calories.[19] Average daily sweetened-beverage caloric intake increased from 70 to 141.[20]

In the U.S., sweetened beverages and milk were consumed primarily at home, with restaurants and fast-food locations increasing in importance.[21] In the 1970s, most soft drinks were made with sucrose, but, beginning in the 1990s, they were made with high-fructose corn syrup. It was unclear how much of a role this change played in the obesity epidemic, but many researchers believed it was a cause for concern.[22] The World Health Organization (WHO) had suggested that added sugars should provide no more than 10% of caloric intake. In 2006, the mean intake of added sugar by

[18] "MAYOR BLOOMBERG, DEPUTY MAYOR GIBBS, HEALTH COMMISSIONER FARLEY AND SUPPORTERS VISIT RESTAURANT . . . "

[19] Samara Joy Nielsen, BS, and Barry M. Popkin, PhD, "Changes in Beverage Intake Between 1977 and 2001," *American Journal of Preventive Medicine*, 27 (3), 2004, accessed May 2013.

[20] Nielsen and Popkin, "Changes in Beverage Intake Between 1977 and 2001."

[21] Nielsen and Popkin, "Changes in Beverage Intake Between 1977 and 2001."

[22] Nielsen and Popkin, "Changes in Beverage Intake Between 1977 and 2001."

Table 13.2 Exhibit 2 Cost of NYC Labor Force Absenteeism Due to Weight Issues, 2011

Group	*Mean unhealthy days per month*[a]	*Proportion of U.S. labor force*	*NYC labor force ('000)*[b]	*Incremental costs to labor force ($ mil)*	*NYC municipal labor force ('000)*[c]	*Incremental costs to municipality($ mil)*
Normal weight, no chronic conditions[d]	0.34	13.9%	556	—	41.7	—
Overweight or obese, no chronic conditions	0.36	17.9%	716	54	53.7	4.05
Overweight or obese, 1-2 chronic conditions	1.08	30.2%	1,208	3,368	90.6	253
Overweight or obese, 2 or more chronic conditions	3.51	17.8%	712	8,504	53.4	638

Source: Compiled from New York State Department of Labor; and Dan Witters, Sangeeta Agrawal, "Unhealthy U.S. Workers' Absenteeism Costs $153 Billion," *Gallup Wellbeing*, October 17, 2011, http://www.gallup.com/poll/150026/ Unhealthy-Workers-Absenteeism-Costs-153-Billion.aspx#1, accessed August 2013.

[a] The study did not include presenteeism. Presenteeism occurred when employees were present at work, but less productive, due to poor health.

[b] The total NYC labor force was 4.00 million in 2013.

[c] The total Municipal labor force was 300,000 in 2013.

[d] Chronic conditions included high blood pressure, high cholesterol, diabetes, cancer, asthma, and/or depression.

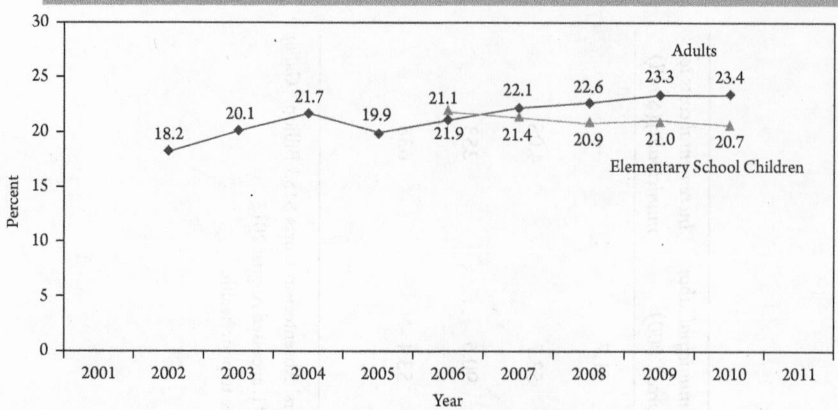

Figure 13.2 Exhibit 3 Trends in Youth and Adult Obesity in NYC, 2001–2011.
Source: NYC Community Health Survey (CHS) 2002-2010, Youth Risk Behavior Survey (YRBS), 2001–2011, NYC Fitnessgram 2006–2010, http://www.nyc.gov/html/om/pdf/2012/otf_report.pdf.

Americans accounted for an estimated 15.8% of daily calories.[23] Soft drinks were the leading source of sugar in the average diet, with average daily sugar consumption at 36.2g for adolescent girls and 57.7g for boys. These figures approached or exceeded the daily limits for total added sugar recommended by the U.S. Department of Agriculture (USDA).[24]

In the U.S., a 12-ounce serving of soda provided an average of 150 calories. If these calories were added to a typical U.S. diet without reducing intake from other sources, one soda per day could lead to a weight gain of 15 pounds in one year.[25] People who regularly consumed one to two sugary drinks or more per day had a 26% greater risk of developing type 2 diabetes than people who rarely had such drinks.[26] (See Figure 13.3 for NYC sugary drink consumption.)

Drink serving sizes had also increased. Before the 1950s, standard soft-drink bottles were 6.5 ounces. In the 1950s, soft-drink makers introduced larger sizes, including the 12-ounce can, which became widely available in 1960.[27] By the early 1990s,

[23] Vasanti S. Malik, Matthias B. Schulze, and Frank B. Hu, "Intake of sugar-sweetened beverages and weight gain: a systematic review," *American Journal of Clinical Nutrition*, vol. 84, pp. 274–288 (2006), accessed May 2013.

[24] David S. Ludwig, Karen E. Peterson, and Steven L. Gortmaker, "Relation between consumption of sugar-sweetened drinks and childhood obesity: a prospective, observational analysis," *The Lancet*, Vol. 357, February 17, 2001, accessed May 2013.

[25] Malik, Schulze, and Hu, "Intake of sugar-sweetened beverages and weight gain: a systematic review."

[26] Malik VS, Popkin BM, Bray GA, Despres JP, Willett WC, and Hu FB, "Sugar-sweetened beverages and risk of metabolic syndrome and type 2 diabetes: a meta-analysis," *Diabetes Care*, 2010; 33:2477–83, as presented on the Harvard School of Public Health website, http://www.hsph.harvard.edu/nutritionsource/sugary-drinks-fact-sheet/, accessed May 2013.

[27] The Coca-Cola Company, "History of Bottling," http://www.thecocacolacompany.com/ourcompany/historybottling.html, accessed May 2013.

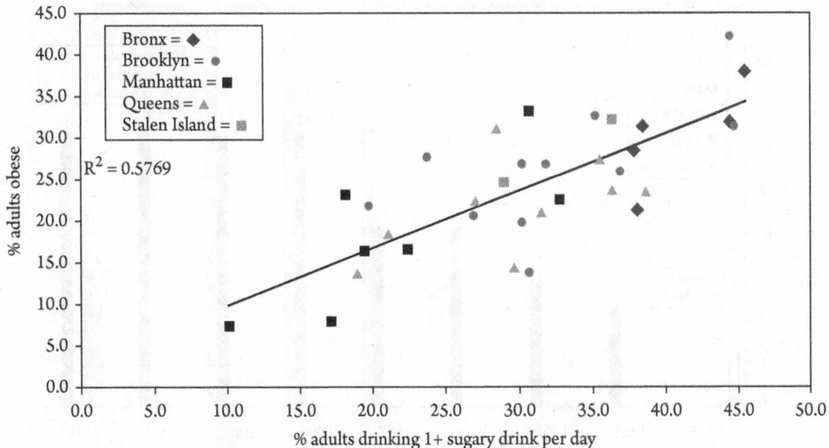

Figure 13.3 Exhibit 4 Sugary-Drink Consumption and Obesity Prevalence in NYC Neighborhoods, 2010.
Source: NYC Community Health Survey (CHS) 2002–2010, http://www.nyc.gov/html/om/pdf/2012/otf_report.pdf.

20-ounce plastic bottles were the norm.[28] (See Figure 13.4 for the size increase of soda sold at McDonalds over the years.) A typical 20-ounce soda contained 15 to 18 teaspoons of sugar and over 240 calories. A 64-ounce fountain cola drink could provide up to 700 calories.[29] Healthy daily caloric intake for adults ranged from 1,800 to 2,400.[30] On any given day, half of the people in the U.S. consumed sugary drinks; one in four consumed at least 200 calories from such drinks; and 5% consumed at least 567 calories from such drinks—equivalent to four cans of soda.[31]

Findings from large cross-sectional studies demonstrated a positive association between greater intakes of sugar-sweetened beverages with weight gain and obesity in both children and adults. Other studies had made apparent that consumers of "liquid candy" did not feel as full as they would have had they eaten an equivalent number of calories, and hence did not compensate for the soda by ingesting fewer solid

[28] Jacobson M., *Liquid Candy: How Soft Drinks are Harming Americans' Health* (Washington, DC: Center for Science in the Public Interest, 2005), as presented on the Harvard School of Public Health website, http://www.hsph.harvard.edu/nutritionsource/sugary-drinks-fact-sheet/, accessed May 2013.

[29] US Department of Agriculture. Nutrient data for 14400, "Carbonated beverage, cola, contains caffeine," National Nutrient Database for Standard Reference, Release 24, 2012, accessed June 21, 2012, http://ndb.nal.usda.gov/ndb/foods/show/4337, as presented on the Harvard School of Public Health website, http://www.hsph.harvard.edu/nutritionsource/sugary-drinks-fact-sheet/, accessed May 2013.

[30] "Estimated Calorie Needs per Day by Age, Gender, and Physical Activity Level," USDA, http://www.cnpp.usda.gov/Publications/USDAFoodPatterns/EstimatedCalorieNeedsPerDayTable.pdf, accessed May 2013.

[31] CL Ogden, BK Kit, MD Carroll, and S. Park, "Consumption of sugar drinks in the United States, 2005–2008," NCHS Data Brief, 2011:1–8.

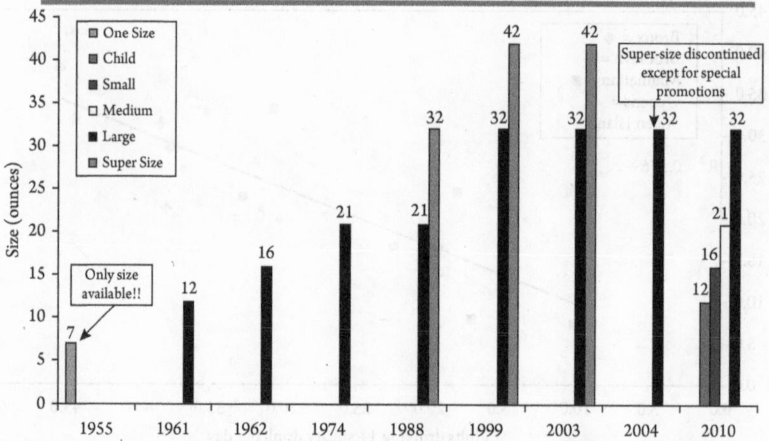

Figure 13.4 Exhibit 5 Size of the Largest Fountain Drinks Sold at McDonalds, 1999–2010.
Source: "Reversing the Epidemic: The New York City Obesity Task Force Plan to Prevent and Control Obesity," May 31, 2012, http://www.nyc.gov/html/om/pdf/2012/otf_report.pdf, accessed May 2013.

calories.[32] Little research had focused on the beneficial impacts of reduced soft-drink and fruit-drink intake, but many researchers believed this would be one of the simpler ways to reduce obesity in the U.S.[33]

Impact on Children

Consensus had emerged that the impact of sugary drinks on childhood obesity was particularly stark. Children and youth in the U.S. averaged 224 calories per day from sugary beverages from 1999 to 2004—nearly 11% of their daily calorie intake.[34] From 1989 to 2008, calories from sugary beverages increased by 60% in children aged 6 to 11, from 130 to 209 calories per day, and the percentage of children consuming them rose from 79% to 91%.[35] Sugary drinks were the top calorie source in teens' diets (226 calories per day), followed by pizza (213 calories per day).[36]

[32] Pan A, and Hu FB, "Effects of carbohydrates on satiety: differences between liquid and solid food," *Curr Opin Clin Nutr Metab Care* 2011; 14:385–390, as presented on the Harvard School of Public Health website, http://www.hsph.harvard.edu/nutritionsource/sugary-drinks-fact-sheet/, accessed May 2013.

[33] Nielsen and Popkin, "Changes in Beverage Intake Between 1977 and 2001."

[34] Wang YC, Bleich SN, and Gortmaker SL, "Increasing caloric contribution from sugar-sweetened beverages and 100% fruit juices among US children and adolescents, 1988–2004," *Pediatrics*, 2008; 121:e1604–e1614

[35] Lasater G, Piernas C, and Popkin BM, "Beverage patterns and trends among school-aged children in the US," 1989–2008, *Nutrition* Journal, 2011; 10:103.

[36] "Mean Intake of Energy and Mean Contribution (kcal) of Various Foods Among US Population, by Age," *National Cancer Institute* NHANES 2005–06. Accessed June 21, 2012, http://riskfactor.cancer.gov/diet/foodsources/, accessed May 2013.

Beverage companies in the U.S. spent roughly $3.2 billion marketing carbonated beverages in 2006, with nearly a half billion dollars of that marketing aimed directly at youth aged 2 to 17.[37] In 2010, preschoolers viewed an average of 213 ads for sugary drinks and energy drinks over the course of a year; children and teens watched an average of 277 and 406 ads, respectively.[38]

A 2001 study aimed to determine the association between the change in sugar-sweetened drink consumption and changes in BMI and obesity among school-age children over a two-year period. The study's findings suggested that sugar-sweetened drink consumption could be an important contributory factor to obesity. Among children, the odds of becoming obese increased 1.6 times for each additional can or glass of sugary beverage they consumed every day.[39]

MAYOR BLOOMBERG

Michael R. Bloomberg was born in Medford, Massachusetts, in 1942. He attended Johns Hopkins University for his undergraduate degree. After earning his MBA at Harvard Business School, he was hired by the Wall Street firm Salomon Brothers, where he worked his way up the ranks until 1981, when the firm was acquired. In 1981 he launched a startup called Bloomberg LP, which grew into a global media company. By 2012 it provided its 310,000 subscribers with financial news and employed over 15,000 people worldwide. As Bloomberg LP grew, Bloomberg turned his attention to philanthropic works. He joined the board of several charitable and cultural institutions.

In 2001 he ran for mayor of New York City and won. He was reelected in 2005, and after persuading the city council to approve a change in term limits, was reelected again in 2009.[40] During his tenure as mayor, his administration achieved a 30% reduction in city crime, teen smoking dropped 50%, high-school graduation rates increased 40%, and over 730 new acres of parks were added to the city. He had also advocated several public-health strategies.[41]

[37] US Federal Trade Commission, *Marketing Food to Children and Adolescents: A Review of Industry Expenditures, Activities, and Self-Regulation* (Washington, DC: US Federal Trade Commission, 2008), as presented on the Harvard School of Public Health website, http://www.hsph.harvard.edu/nutritionsource/sugary-drinks-fact-sheet/, accessed May 2013.

[38] Harris J, Schwartz MB, Brownell KD, et al., *Sugary Drink FACTS: Evaluating Sugary Drink Nutrition and Marketing to Youth* (New Haven, CT: Rudd Center for Food Policy and Obesity, 2011), as presented on the Harvard School of Public Health website, http://www.hsph.harvard.edu/nutritionsource/sugary-drinks-fact-sheet/, accessed May 2013.

[39] David S. Ludwig, Karen E. Peterson, and Steven L. Gortmaker, "Relation between consumption of sugar-sweetened drinks and childhood obesity: a prospective, observational analysis."

[40] Michael M. Grynbaum and Marjorie Connelly, "Good Grade for Mayor; Regret Over his 3rd Term," *New York Times*, August 20, 2012, http://www.nytimes.com/2012/08/21/nyregion/majority-regrets-3rd-term-for-bloomberg-poll-finds.html?ref=nyregion, accessed May 2012.

[41] Biography—Mayor Michael Bloomberg, http://www.nyc.gov/portal/site/nycgov/menuitem.e985cf5219821bc3f7393cd401c789a0/, accessed May 2013.

Bloomberg Leads Health-Care Reforms

In 2005, New York became the first American city to require restaurants and food vendors to eliminate trans fat[42] from the food they sold. Trans fats had been linked to obesity and heart disease. Other cities including Philadelphia and San Francisco had since passed trans-fat bans of their own, along with the state of California.[43] Critics argued that trans-fat bans were burdensome and the costs of compliance could jeopardize the livelihoods of smaller, independent restaurants.[44]

Three years later, in 2008, New York became the first U.S. city to pass a law requiring food-service providers to post calorie counts on menus. Seattle and other cities subsequently passed similar laws, and a federal law was passed in 2012 that required chain restaurants with more than 20 locations to publish calorie counts on their menus.[45]

In 2010, Bloomberg proposed banning the use of food stamps to purchase sugary sodas. The U.S. Department of Agriculture, which administered the food stamp program, rejected the proposal due to enforcement difficulties. Also in 2010, Bloomberg urged state legislators to pass a soda tax that would allow the state to collect an additional $0.01 per ounce of soda. The legislation failed to pass.[46]

Finally, in 2011, the mayor banned smoking[47] in the city's 1,700 public parks, plazas, and 14 miles of public beaches.[48] At the time, 105 municipalities in California, Hawaii, Massachusetts, and New Jersey had already enacted bans on smoking at public beaches, and 507 municipalities in California, Texas, Illinois, Minnesota, and New Jersey had banned smoking in city parks.[49] (See Figure 13.5 for a list of cities that enacted health-care policies similar to NYC). The following year Bloomberg's administration set its sights on sugar. In total, by June 2012, NYC claimed to have launched more than 20 initiatives to combat obesity.[50] (See Table 13.3 for the full list of initiatives.)

THE PROPOSAL

The city proposed a ban in May 2012 on the sale of sugary drinks larger than 16 ounces in restaurants, movie theaters, sports venues, and other establishments regulated by

[42] Trans fat, considered worse for a person than saturated fat, was found in vegetable shortenings, some margarines, and some processed foods, and was made through the chemical process of hydrogenation of oils. Hydrogenation solidified liquid oils and increased the shelf life and the flavor stability of oils and foods that contained them.

[43] Alice Park, "The New York City Soda Ban, and a Brief History of Bloomberg's Nudges," *TIME*, May 31, 2012, http://healthland.time.com/2012/05/31/bloombergs-soda-ban-and-other-sweeping-health-measures-in-new-york-city/#ixzz2SFutqGkv.

[44] Public Health Law Center at William Mitchell College of Law, "Transfat Bans Overview," http://phlc.stylefish.com/topics/healthy-eating/transfat-bans.

[45] Alice Park, "The New York City Soda Ban, and a Brief History of Bloomberg's Nudges."

[46] Alice Park, "The New York City Soda Ban, and a Brief History of Bloomberg's Nudges."

[47] In 2002 Bloomberg banned public smoking in the city's bars and restaurants.

[48] Alice Park, "The New York City Soda Ban, and a Brief History of Bloomberg's Nudges."

[49] Jordana Ossad, "New York City outdoor smoking ban begins," *CNN*, May 24, 2011, http://www.cnn.com/2011/US/05/23/new.york.smoking.ban/index.html, accessed May 2013.

[50] Jason Keyser, "Coca-Cola executive says Bloomberg's proposed New York soda ban is unfair," Associated Press, June 7, 2012, via Factiva, accessed May 2013.

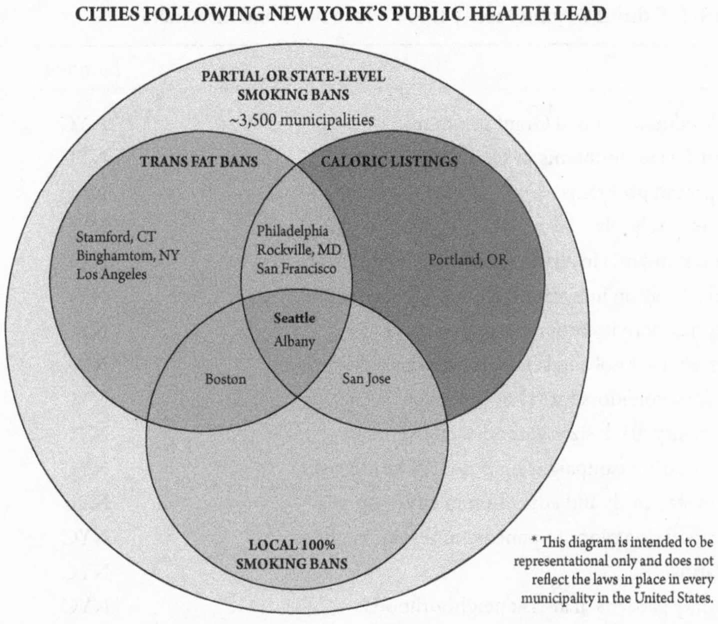

CITIES FOLLOWING NEW YORK'S PUBLIC HEALTH LEAD

PARTIAL OR STATE-LEVEL SMOKING BANS
~3,500 municipalities
TRANS FAT BANS
CALORIC LISTINGS
Stamford, CT
Binghamtom, NY
Los Angeles
Philadelphia
Rockville, MD
San Francisco
Portland, OR
Seattle
Albany
Boston
San Jose
LOCAL 100% SMOKING BANS
* This diagram is intended to be representational only and does not reflect the laws in place in every municipality in the United States.

Figure 13.5 Exhibit 6 Cities That Adopted New York City-Style Health Laws.
Source: Eric Jaffe, "Which City Might Try to Ban Huge Sodas Next?" *The Atlantic Cities*, June 7, 2012, http://www.theatlantic cities.com/arts-and-lifestyle/2012/06/which-city-might-try-ban-huge-sodas-next/2192/, accessed August 20, 2013.

the city's health department. The city argued that the ban would lead New Yorkers to drink less soda and thus help combat the spread of obesity. The city defined a sugary drink as a nonalcoholic beverage of which less than 50% was milk (or milk substitute), and which was presweetened by the manufacturer or vendor with sugar, high-fructose corn syrup, honey, or another sweetener containing calories. The ban was to go into effect on March 12, 2013.[51]

The beverage also had to contain at least 25 calories per eight ounces to be included in the ban. Though known as the "soda ban," it also applied to fruit-juice drinks including lemonade, sports drinks such as Gatorade, energy drinks, iced slushes, smoothies, bubble teas, and coffee- and tea-based sweetened drinks that met that calorific intensity. Fruit smoothies and juices that contained only fruit and fruit juice with no added sweeteners were exempt. Some coffee drinks with high sugar content, such as Starbucks' pumpkin spice *lattes* and *macchiatos,* were also exempt due to their milk content.[52] (See Figure 13.6 for sample beverages and restrictions under the ban.)

Alcoholic beverages were excluded from the proposed ban, but, because nightclubs were subject to the regulation, carafes of mixers (cranberry juice cocktail, tonic) were

[51] Jason Keyser, "Coca-Cola executive says Bloomberg's proposed New York soda ban is unfair."
[52] Vivian Yee, "Your Guide to New York's Soda Ban," *New York Times,* March 11, 2013, http://cityroom. blogs.nytimes.com/2013/03/11/your-guide-to-new-yorks-soda-ban/, accessed May 2013.

Table 13.3 Exhibit 7 Anti-Obesity Initiatives in NYC and Elsewhere

Initiative	*Location*
School Wellness Council Grant program	NYC
Additional water fountains in schools	NYC
School garden programs	NYC
Salad bars in schools	NYC
Nutrition standards in city licensed kid's camps	NYC
Physical education integrated into school curriculum	NYC
Free physical activity programs in city parks	NYC
Daycare, after school and senior center share play space	NYC
Safe walking corridors for school children	NYC
Cap on sugary drink sizes at food establishments	NYC
Public education campaigns on potential health risks	NYC
Nutrition standards and education in city hospitals	NYC
Healthy food donations to pantries and soup kitchens	NYC
Urban farms	NYC
Community gardens in at-risk neighborhoods	NYC
Zone to promote supermarkets in food deserts	NYC
Food stamps accepted at farmers' markets	NYC
Offer healthier food options at retail outlets	NYC
Access to tap water in public spaces	NYC
Easy access to stairs in new and renovated buildings	NYC
Free, city-wide fitness classes	NYC
Bike-sharing programs	NYC
Nutrition and fitness programs for city employees	NYC
Early identification of obese youth via school programs	NYC
Best-practice sidewalk and stairway specifications	NYC
Free, healthy breakfast served at school	DC
Reimbursement for preventative health care	Vermont
Soda removed from school vending machines	Philadelphia
Fryers removed from school kitchens	Philadelphia

Source: Compiled from Bipartisan Policy Center, "Lots to Lose: How America's Health and Obesity Crisis Threatens our Economic Future," http://bipartisanpolicy.org/sites/default/files/5023_BPC_NutritionReport_FNL_Web.pdf; Don Sapatkin, "Obesity among Philadelphia students drops 5% over 4 years" Phila-delphia Inquirer, December 20, 2012, http://mobile.philly.com/health/?wss=/philly/health&id=168862236&viewAll=y; and "Reversing the Epidemic: The New York City Obesity Task Force Plan to Prevent and Control Obesity," May 31, 2012, http://www.nyc.gov/.

restricted to the 16-ounce limit. Plain coffee was exempt, but baristas were restricted to adding three to five teaspoons of sugar to large cups of coffee. However, customers were then free to add as much sugar as they pleased. Refills and the option to purchase additional 16-ounce beverages were allowed under the law. Pizza shops could no

Figure 13.6 Exhibit 8 Examples of 8-Ounce Beverages and How the Proposal Would Apply to Them. *Source:* Natalie Zmunda and Maureen Morrison, "New York's Big-Drink Ban Would Trim Bottom Lines," *Advertising Age*, June 4, 2012, http://adage.com/article/news/sugary-drink-ban-trim-restaurants-bottom-lines/235147/, accessed May 2013.

longer sell two-liter bottles of soda to complement purchases. Convenience stores, not regulated by the city's health department, were exempt.[53] In health-department-regulated establishments, consumers stood to pay higher unit prices for smaller bottles. For example, if a pizzeria charged $3 for a two-liter bottle of Pepsi, the equivalent six 12-ounce cans would cost $7.50.[54]

The plan was praised by many public health officials as a breakthrough in the effort to combat the effects of high-calorie, sugary drinks on public health. Los Angeles, California, and Cambridge, Massachusetts, also considered similar proposals. But in a *New York Times* poll conducted in August 2012, 60% of residents believed that the ban was a bad idea (residents from NYC's Bronx and Queens boroughs showed more resistance than other boroughs).[55]

[53] Vivian Yee, "Your Guide to New York's Soda Ban."

[54] Brad Hamilton, "Bloomberg's ban prohibits 2-liter soda with your pizza and some nightclub mixers," *New York Post*, February 24, 2013, http://www.nypost.com/p/news/local/soda_ban_to_sap_your_4t5pEK0hv o3PoNZEBOdZ2L?utm_medium=rss&utm_content=Local, accessed May 2013.

[55] Michael Grynbaum, "Judge Blocks New York City's Limits on Big Sugary Drinks."

NYC Board of Health Public Hearing

In 2011, the New York City Department of Health employed 5,405 workers (out of 300,000 total municipal employees),[56] including 140 public health inspectors (paid on average $54,000 in 2013).[57] The department was responsible for inspecting 24,000 restaurants for compliance with numerous health codes.[58] If enacted, the ban on large sodas would be enforced by the Department of Health.

The New York City Board of Health held a filled-to-capacity public hearing on July 24, 2012, open to supporters and opponents to voice their opinions on the proposal to ban large sugary drinks. Dr. Thomas Farley, the city's health commissioner, announced before the hearing, "The Health Department will be reviewing all the comments it receives today as well as online in writing, and will be presenting to the board in September the rule [for a vote], along with any modifications that the Health Department feels it should be making." Members of the board were independent health experts appointed by the mayor, and had the final say on the proposal. Though most considered the board's decision a foregone conclusion, attendees on both sides delivered passionate remarks.[59]

Many health experts spoke out in favor of the proposal. Dr. Walter Willett, chairman of the department of nutrition at Harvard School of Public Health and a professor at Harvard Medical School, argued, "Soda in large amounts is metabolically toxic. Soda is indeed the right target." Other health experts accused the soda industry of propagating a campaign about personal freedom, while their real goal was protecting profits.[60]

Because obesity aggravated vulnerability to other diseases, it indirectly contributed to worker absenteeism. One study estimated the cost of absenteeism per day per worker at $341.

Some argued that the mayor had overreached. Daniel Halloran, a member of the city council representing parts of Queens, stated, "When they came for the cigarettes, I didn't say anything. I didn't smoke. When they came for the MSG, I really didn't care because I didn't order it very often. I'm not a big salt eater, so I didn't mind when you guys regulated salt. But what will the government be telling me next?"[61]

Farley compared the proposal to the city's ban on trans fats: "The restaurant industry called it a 'misguided attempt at social engineering by a group of physicians who don't understand the industry.' I have not heard a single complaint about the ban on

[56] Michael R. Bloomberg, Thomas Farley, "Living Healthy 2009–2011," *New York City Department of Health and Mental Hygiene*, http://www.nyc.gov/html/doh/downloads/pdf/report/nycdohmh-triennial09-11.pdf, accessed August 20, 2013.

[57] New York City Careers, www.nyc.gov/careers, accessed August 20, 2013.

[58] New York City Department of Health and Mental Hygiene, "Restaurant Inspection Results (Letter Grades)," http://www.nyc.gov/html/doh/html/services/restaurant-inspection.shtml, accessed August 20, 2013.

[59] Kevin Lori, "New York soda ban proposal: Public hearing gets impassioned," *Christian Science Monitor*, July 24, 2012, available via Factiva, accessed May 2013.

[60] Kevin Lori, "New York soda ban proposal: Public hearing gets impassioned."

[61] Kevin Lori, "New York soda ban proposal: Public hearing gets impassioned."

trans fats in New York City, and I fully expect the same will happen with this rule when it is all put into place."[62]

RULING AND IMPLEMENTATION

The New York City Board of Health voted 8-0 (with one abstention) on September 13, 2012, in favor of the ban on large sugary drinks. "This is the single biggest step any city, I think, has ever taken to curb obesity," Bloomberg said after the vote. "It's certainly not the last step that lots of cities are going to take, and we believe that it will help save lives." The measure was scheduled to take effect on March 12, 2013, unless blocked by a judge. Dr. Joel A. Forman, a member of the Board of Health and a professor at the Mount Sinai School of Medicine, said after the vote, "I can't imagine the board not acting on another problem that is killing 5,000 people per year. The evidence strongly supports a relationship between sweet drinks and obesity." Another member of the board, Dr. Deepthiman K. Gowda, professor of medicine at Columbia University, recognized public concerns: "The same way that we've become acclimatized and normalized to sodas that are 32 ounces, we've started to become acclimatized to the prevalence of obesity in our society. The reality is, we are in a crisis, and I think we have to act on this."[63]

The NYC Department of Health would be responsible for checking compliance with the soda ban at the 24,000 restaurants it surveyed.[64] Health inspectors could issue violations in the form of $200 fines. The city planned to allow a three-month grace period until June to give vendors a chance to adjust.[65] Some restaurants prepared new menus right away, while others opted to wait for the ban to go into effect. Different establishments developed different approaches: some chains, like Dunkin' Donuts and McDonald's, planned to ask customers to add their own sugar and flavored syrups.[66] (See Figure 13.7 for an explanation on display at Dunkin' Donuts.) Many restaurants ordered smaller glasses in preparation for the change. The Barclays Center, the new home of the Brooklyn Nets professional basketball team, planned to implement the new rule at concession stands immediately upon its opening.

Beverage Industry Reactions

In the summer of 2012, the American soft-drink industry undertook a multimillion-dollar campaign to block the legislation, purchasing advertising space in subway stations and flying banners from planes (see Figures 13.8a-c for sample ads in opposition and in favor of the ban).[67] Steve Cahillane, president and

[62] Kevin Lori, "New York soda ban proposal: Public hearing gets impassioned."

[63] Michael M. Grynbaum, "Health Panel Approves Restriction on Sale of Large Sugary Drinks," September 13, 2012, *New York Times*, http://www.nytimes.com/2012/09/14/nyregion/health-board-approves-bloombergs-soda-ban.html?_r=0, accessed May 2013.

[64] New York City Department of Health and Mental Hygiene, "Restaurant Inspections," http://www.nyc.gov/html/doh/html/services/restaurant-inspection.shtml, Accessed August 2013.

[65] Vivian Yee, "Your Guide to New York's Soda Ban."

[66] Vivian Yee, "Your Guide to New York's Soda Ban."

[67] Michael Grynbaum, "Judge Blocks New York City's Limits on Big Sugary Drinks."

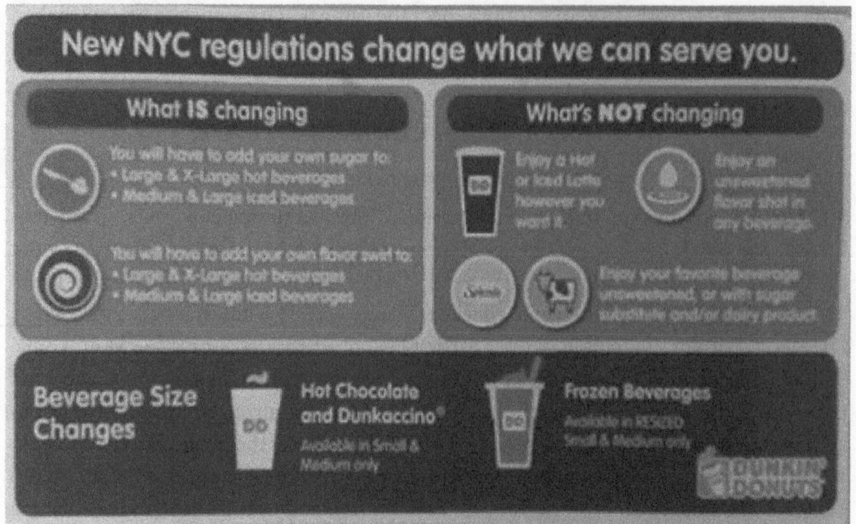

Figure 13.7 Exhibit 9 Dunkin' Donuts Explanation of the New Rules, March 2013.
Source: "Why the New York soda ban was doomed anyway: an illustrated guide," *The Guardian*, March 11, 2012, http:// www.guardian.co.uk/world/us-news-blog/2013/mar/11/new-york-soda-ban-loopholes-exceptions, May 2013.

CEO of Coca-Cola's Refreshments unit, thought the mayor's plan singled out and demonized the industry. "We're not putting our head in the sand and saying there's not an obesity epidemic in this country. There is," Cahillane said in an interview. "But we believe that we can be part of the solution rather than be demonized and discriminated against." He continued, "Obesity is a complex issue. To the extent that anybody says there's a simple solution to it . . . I think fundamentally misleads people."[68]

After the Board of Health voted in favor of the ban, the American soft-drink industry vowed to fight the decision through the courts, if necessary.[69] Eliot Hoff, a spokesman for the soda-industry-funded New Yorkers for Beverage Choices, responded to the vote: "By imposing this ban, the board has shown no regard for public opinion or the consequences to businesses in the city." An ad campaign by the soda industry, which cost more than $1 million, stressed that the policy would restrict consumer freedom.[70]

On October 12, 2012, the American Beverage Association, along with the National Restaurant Association, filed a lawsuit to block the city's ban on large servings of sugary beverages. The suit claimed, "(The rule) unfairly harms small businesses at a time when we can ill afford it." It also argued that the Board of Health, appointed by Bloomberg, did not have the authority to approve the rule. Soda makers and sellers

[68] Jason Keyser, "Coca-Cola executive says Bloomberg's proposed New York soda ban is unfair," *Associated Press*, June 7, 2012, via Factiva, accessed May 2012.

[69] Michael M. Grynbaum, "Health Panel Approves Restriction on Sale of Large Sugary Drinks."

[70] Michael M. Grynbaum, "Health Panel Approves Restriction on Sale of Large Sugary Drinks."

(a)

Figure 13.8a Exhibit 10a Movie Theater Marquee Opposing the Ban, July 2012.
Source: Michelle V. Agins, "At Movies and Beaches, Soda Industry Makes Its Case," July 5, 2012, *New York Times/Redux*, http://cityroom.blogs.nytimes.com/2012/07/05/at-movies-and-beaches-soda-industry-fights-back/, accessed May 2013.

also claimed the city was being a "nanny-like nag" to consumers, while imposing a burden on businesses. (See Table 13.4 for estimated loss of soda revenue for businesses impacted by the ban). The plaintiffs claimed the rules were "ludicrous" and dreamed up by "scientists in the room, working with the mayor, creating a regulation here that is going to cost people a ton of money." A spokesman for the mayor responded that "this predictable, yet baseless, lawsuit fortunately will help put an even greater spotlight on the obesity epidemic."[71]

Regarding the industry approach, the press drew parallels with an earlier ban on lead paint in the U.S. (see details in Box 13.1). An article in *The Atlantic* explained, "In all these cases the industry presents the problem simply as a matter of choice and then blames consumers for not taking simple precautions to protect themselves: smokers who don't quit; parents who don't supervise their children and 'let' them eat lead paint; people who simply have no idea of moderation or the importance of physical activity."[72]

[71] Jennifer Peltz, "NYC Soda Ban Sued by Businesses, Beverage Groups Including National Restaurant Association," *Huffington Post*, October 10, 2012, http://www.huffingtonpost.com/2012/10/13/nyc-soda-ban-sued-by-businesses-national-restaurant-assocation_n_1963615.html, accessed May 2013.

[72] David Rosner and Gerald Markowitz, "Why It Took Decades of Blaming Parents Before We Banned Lead Paint," *The Atlantic*, April 22, 2013, http://www.theatlantic.com/health/archive/2013/04/why-it-took-decades-of-blaming-parents-before-we-banned-lead-paint/275169/, accessed May 2013.

(b)

Figure 13.8b Exhibit 10b City Subway Ad in Support of the Ban, 2012.
Source: April Fulton, "Hold The Ice: Rhetoric Gets Hot Over New York's Big Soda Ban," *NPR*, July 24, 2012, http://www.npr.org/blogs/thesalt/2012/07/24/157290522/hold-the-ice-rhetoric-gets-hot-over-new-yorks-big-soda-ban, May 2013.

LEGAL CHALLENGES

One day before the law was to take effect, Justice Milton A. Tingling of the New York State Supreme Court[73] in Manhattan called the limits "arbitrary and capricious." In his ruling, Justice Tingling agreed with the beverage industry's legal arguments. He echoed the complaints of business owners and consumers who "deemed the rules unworkable and unenforceable, with confusing loopholes and voluminous exemptions."[74] He said the Board of Health overreached in approving the plan and ruled that only the City Council had the power to approve the initiative. He wrote that the administration had interpreted the Board of Health's powers broadly to "create an administrative Leviathan," capable of enacting any rules that were "limited only by the imagination."[75]

The judge also criticized the rules themselves and their application to only certain sugary drinks, and in certain establishments, as well as the exemptions for milk-based beverages sold at restaurants and sugary drinks sold at grocery and convenience stores. The rules would "create uneven enforcement," Tingling noted, "even within a particular city block, much less the city as a whole."[76]

[73] The Supreme Court of New York was not the highest court in the state. It was a trial-level court (with 62 branches, one in each New York state county).
[74] Michael Grynbaum, "Judge Blocks New York City's Limits on Big Sugary Drinks."
[75] Michael Grynbaum, "Judge Blocks New York City's Limits on Big Sugary Drinks."
[76] Michael Grynbaum, "Judge Blocks New York City's Limits on Big Sugary Drinks."

(c)

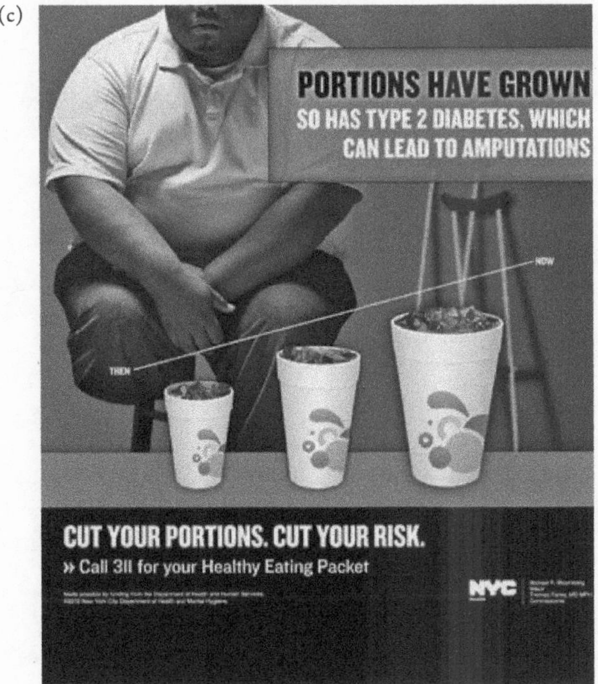

Figure 13.8c Exhibit 10c City Ad Warning about Risks of Sugary Drinks, 2012.
Source: "New York City's big 'soda ban' canned," *Stuff*, March 12, 2012, http://www.stuff.co.nz/world/americas/ 8414362/New-York-Citys-big-soda-ban-canned, accessed May 2013.

A spokesman for the American Beverage Association said the court decision "provides a sigh of relief . . . With this ruling behind us, we look forward to collaborating with city leaders on solutions that will have a meaningful and lasting impact on the people of New York City."[77]

Asked by a reporter whether he thought a drawn-out legal battle would continue into his successor's administration, Bloomberg said, "All of our time is running out. I don't know who is going to be my successor."[78] He expected that the proposal and its defeat had contributed to the conversation about the issue. "When our Administration implemented calorie counts and worked to eliminate trans fats in restaurants, we were taken to court," said Bloomberg. "But today, both reforms are recognized as models. Already our proposal to limit the size of sugary beverages has changed the national conversation around obesity and we are confident that yesterday's court decision will be reversed on appeal."[79]

Following Judge Tingling's ruling, the NYC Department of Health requested an appeal. On July 30, 2013, the Appellate Division of the New York Supreme Court upheld the lower court's ruling. The court found that the Department of Health had

[77] Michael Grynbaum, "Judge Blocks New York City's Limits on Big Sugary Drinks."
[78] Michael Grynbaum, "Judge Blocks New York City's Limits on Big Sugary Drinks."
[79] "MAYOR BLOOMBERG, DEPUTY MAYOR GIBBS, HEALTH COMMISSIONER FARLEY AND SUPPORTERS VISIT RESTAURANT . . ."

Table 13.4 Exhibit 11 Estimated Change in Volume, Revenue, and NYC Sales Tax under the Soda Ban

	Daily kcal decrease for all soda drinkers impacted by ban	*Estimated change in soda volume sold*[a] *(ounces, million)*	*Estimated change in annual soda revenue in NYC ($, million)*[b]	*Estimated change in NYC tax revenue*[c] *($, million)*	*Estimated change in annual profit for establishments covered by the ban ($, million)*[d]
100% substitute	−102.1	(2,341)	(234.1)	(10.5)	(211.0)
80% substitute	−62.6	(1,435)	(143.5)	(6.46)	(129.2)
50% substitute	−3.2	(73)	(7.3)	(0.33)	(6.6)
20% substitute	56.1	1,286	128.6	5.79	115.74
0% substitute	95.7	2,194	219.4	9.87	197.5

Source: Casewriter estimates, based on data from the City of New York; Brent M. Wilson, Stephanie Stolarz-Fantino, and Edmund Fantino, "Regulating the Way to Obesity: Unintended Consequences of Limiting Sugary Drinks Sizes,"*PLoS ONE* 8(4): e61081, Doi:10.1371/journal.pone.0061081, accessed August 2013; Y. Claire Wang and Seanna M. Vine, "Caloric effect of a 16-ounce (473-ml) portion-size cap on sugar-sweetened beverages served in restaurants," *American Society for Nutrition*, 2013, via Google Scholar, accessed August 2013; and Christina Cheddar Berk, "Soft-Drink Providers Seek Ways to Boost Fountain-Product Sales," *Wall Street Journal*, April 13, 2005, via Factiva, accessed September 2013.

[a] Volume refers to sales volume in food-service establishments covered by the soda ban.

[b] Assumes price per ounce of .10; taken from McDonald's price of $1.59 for a 16-ounce soda.

[c] Calculated using the 4.5% sales tax for NYC.

[d] Assumes a profit margin of 90% on sugary beverages sold through food-service establishments covered by the soda ban.

Box 13.1 Appendix The Lead Paint Precedent

Observers likened the beverage industry's approach to that of lead paint manufacturers and tobacco marketers before—with the important distinction that the latter were lethal.

. . . It was hard to remember that once, in the US, the lead pigment lent color and texture to the oil that formed its base made up as much as 70% of a can of paint. As little as a thumbnail-sized chip, though, could send children into convulsions. Since the 1920s, the lead industry had organized to fight bans, restrictions, even warnings on paint-can labels. When public health officials in New York, Baltimore, and Chicago tried to enact regulations in the 1950s that threatened the industry's interests, lobbyists visited legislators and governors to get restrictions lifted. When Baltimore's health department called for the removal of lead from paint, the industry countered by proposing and winning a "voluntary" standard, reducing the lead content in paint. When New York City's health department proposed a warning label saying that the product was poisonous to children, the industry rejected the "poison" label and lobbied successfully for another label that simply advised parents not to use it on "toys, furniture, or interior surfaces that might be chewed by children."

. . . But the industry wouldn't remove all lead from their products. It fought every attempt at regulation. Industry representatives threatened lawsuits against television stations such as CBS that aired popular shows like Highway Patrol in which the product was depicted as dangerous . . . All this despite records that show that the industry knew that their product was poisoning children.

. . . Starting in the 1950s it took local health departments three decades to assert themselves. A couple of bans were passed and then repealed. In 1971, the federal government banned lead-based paints on public housing. Finally, in 1978, the federal government banned the use of lead in virtually any paint intended for sale to consumers.

Source: Excerpted from David Rosner & Gerald Markowitz, "Why It Took Decades of Blaming Parents Before We Banned Lead Paint," The Atlantic, April 22, 2013, http://www.theatlantic.com/health/archive/2013/04/why-it-took-decades-of-blaming-parents-before-we-banned-lead-paint/275169/, accessed May 2013.

violated the "separation of powers" established in *Boreali v. Axelrod*: the power to craft polices resided with the legislature, and administrative agencies were not permitted to create broad policies intended to balance competing priorities (such as economic and public-health outcomes). Administrative agencies were permitted to create policies only to aid the implementation of established legislation. The court noted that the failure of prior legislative proposals to tax or otherwise control the distribution of sugary beverages—as well as the heated debate sparked by the proposed cap on soda—would suggest policies on sugary beverages be created by elected officials in the legislature and not by the Department of Health.

In October 2013, the highest court in New York State announced that it would hear the city's appeal of the decision to strike down the ban on large sugary beverages. The city believed that the Department of Health was an exception to the "separation of powers" standard. Fay Ng, a lawyer for the city of New York, wrote: "[The Court of Appeals] has

Table 13.5 Exhibit 12 Expected Health Outcomes of the Soda Ban, by Substitution Rate, 2013

	Daily kcal decrease for each soda drinker BMI >/ = 25	*Estimated change in weight per year (pounds)*[a]	*NYC obese population (thousand)*	*NYC overweight population (thousand)*
Base	—	—	1,952	2,886
100% substitute[b]	−102.6	−10.3	1,835	2,813
80% substitute	−62.6	−6.3	1,872	2,838
50% substitute	−2.4	−0.24	1,947	2,884
20% substitute	57.7	5.8	2,034	2,926
0% substitute	97.8	9.8	2,095	2,953

Source: Casewriter estimates, based on data from the U.S. Census Bureau; Center for Disease Control; and Y. Claire Wang and Seanna M. Vine, "Caloric effect of a 16-ounce (473-ml) portion-size cap on sugar-sweetened beverages served in restaurants," *American Society for Nutrition*, 2013, via Google Scholar, accessed August 2013.

[a] Calculated using BMI for a person of average male height.

[b] *Substitute* refers to the proportion of the population whose large sugar-sweetened beverage purchases (greater than 16 ounces) would be substituted for a smaller size if the ban were enacted. It is assumed that those who do not substitute purchase two 16-ounce drinks (which is why, beyond 50% substitution, the obese and overweight populations increase).

To be read, for example, as if 80% of all large drinks purchased by overweight New Yorkers were substituted for smaller sizes, the obese population of NYC would be expected to decrease by 80,000 and the overweight (excluding obese) population by 48,000.

long recognized that the board of health is not a typical administrative agency, but rather, is an entity with legislative authority."[80]

RELEVANT RESEARCH

A 2013 study published by the American Society for Nutrition estimated the potential weight loss per overweight person in NYC if the ban were enacted. The researchers used data on the consumption of sugar-sweetened beverage servings over 16 ounces at food-service establishments subject to the ban in order to estimate the caloric savings. For example, if 80% of all large drinks purchased by overweight New Yorkers were substituted for smaller sizes (e.g., 16 ounces or less), the obese population of NYC would be expected to decrease by 80,000, and the overweight (excluding obese) population, by 48,000. Table 13.5 shows the substitution estimates applied to the NYC overweight and obese

[80] Daniel Wiessner, "New York court to hear Bloomberg's appeal to restore soda ban," *Reuters*, October 17, 2013, http://www.reuters.com/article/2013/10/17/us-nycsodaban-appeal-idUSBRE99G0T620131017, accessed February 2014.

Table 13.6 Table B Menu Options in the UC San Diego Soda Research Study

Price	*No Ban Menu*	*16 Ounce Only Menu*	*Bundled Menu*
$1.59	16 ounce bottle	16 ounce bottle	16 ounce bottle
$1.79	24 ounce bottle	—	Two 12 ounce bottles
$1.99	32 ounce bottle	—	Two 16 ounce bottles

Source: Brent M. Wilson, Stephanie Stolarz-Fantino, Edmund Fantino, "Regulating the Way to Obesity: Unintended Consequences of Limiting Sugary Drinks Sizes," *PLoS ONE*, via Google Scholar, accessed August 2013.

Table 13.7 Exhibit 13 UC San Diego Study on Consumer Purchase Behavior under the Soda Ban, 2013

	Participants who bought no soda (%)	*Amount of soda purchased by all*	*Amount spent on soda by all ($)*[d]	*Amount of soda purchased (those who bought only)*	*Amount spent on soda, those who bought only ($)*
No Ban Menu[a]	21%	19 oz	1.50	24 oz	1.90
16 Ounce Only[b]	38%	10 oz	1.00	16 oz	1.60
Bundled Menu[c]	16%	23 oz	1.70	27 oz	2.00

Source: Brent M. Wilson, Stephanie Stolarz-Fantino, and Edmund Fantino, "Regulating the Way to Obesity: Unintended Consequences of Limiting Sugary Drinks Sizes," *PLoS ONE* 8(4): e61081, Doi:10.1371/journal.pone.0061081, accessed August 2013.

[a] The No Ban Menu included 16-ounce soda ($1.59), 24-ounce soda ($1.79), and 32-ounce soda ($1.99) options.

[b] The 16 Ounce Only menu included only a 16-ounce soda ($1.59) option.

[c] The Bundled Menu included 16-ounce soda ($1.59), two 12-ounce sodas ($1.79), and two 16-ounce sodas ($1.99) options.

[d] Average expenditure across all subjects in each treatment group, including those who bought no soda.

populations. The researchers assumed that those who did not substitute would continue to consume large quantities of soda by, for example, purchasing two 16-ounce bottles.

A second study, published in April 2013 and conducted at the University of California at San Diego, examined what drinks people ordered when serving sizes were limited to 16 ounces.[81] One hundred participants were each offered three different menus, as shown in Table 13.6.

Each participant was shown several menus in a randomized order. Prices were equal across all settings, and no limit was placed on the amount of soda participants could order. Participants were asked to specify the quantity of the item, or bundle, they wished to purchase. When exposed to the bundled menu, participants ordered,

[81] Brent M. Wilson, Stephanie Stolarz-Fantino, Edmund Fantino, "Regulating the Way to Obesity: Unintended Consequences of Limiting Sugary Drinks Sizes," *PLoS ONE* 8(4): e61081. Doi:10.1371/journal.pone. 0061081, accessed August 2013.

on average, a larger amount of soda than when exposed to the other two menus. See Table 13.7 for ounces of soda purchased and average dollars spent per person in response to being shown each menu.

The researchers concluded that bundling two small sodas together led to more orders as well as larger orders than those in the scenario where large serving sizes were included.[82] The researchers acknowledged that the study did not measure what the customers drank, only what they purchased. Participants were also not in a real-world setting.[83] A researcher uninvolved with the study believed most people purchasing soda would select the "regular" size (for example, the middle size among a range of three size options), which varied depending on what options the menu included. However, those denied a larger soda would, according to researchers, "display what we call reactance—rebelliousness, a determination to circumvent this policy, an attitude of 'I'll show them.' And the people selling the soda are all too willing to comply."[84]

[82] Sarah Kliff, "Will New York City's large soda ban backfire?," *Washington Post*, April 14, 2013, http:// www.washingtonpost.com/blogs/wonkblog/wp/2013/04/14/will-new-york-citys-large-soda-ban-backfire, accessed May 2013.

[83] Ryan Jaslow, "NYC soda ban would lead customers to consume more sugary drinks, study suggests," *CBS News*, April 11, 2013, http://www.cbsnews.com/8301-204_162-57579172/nyc-soda-ban-would-lead-customers-to-consume-more-sugary-drinks-study-suggests, accessed May 2013.

[84] Ryan Jaslow, "NYC soda ban would lead customers to consume more sugary drinks, study suggests."

PART VI

Emerging Markets, Consumer Behavior, and Public Health

14

FRESNO'S SOCIAL IMPACT BOND FOR ASTHMA

John A. Quelch and Margaret L. Rodriguez

Just as entrepreneurship changed the mind-set in business, [Social Impact Bonds] could change the mind-set in the social sector. It could lead to a paradigm shift in the mind-set of institutional and private investors, corporations, and governments about the way we deal with social issues.
—Sir Ronald Cohen, cofounder, Social Finance, Inc.[1]

In 2014, Social Impact Bonds (SIBs) were quickly gaining popularity as an investment vehicle that joined together private investors and nonprofits to tackle social issues. Although numerous SIB projects and proposals had cropped up across the U.S. following the launch of the first SIB in the U.K. in 2010, none were explicitly focused on healthcare. Fresno, California, announced the first healthcare SIB in 2013 to fund home-based programs to reduce asthma attacks. If successful, the Fresno SIB model would help solve the challenge of delivering preventative care efficiently in at-risk communities.

WHAT WERE SIBS?[2]

SIBs were investment vehicles that united private investors with nonprofits to fund and execute programs to address social issues. SIBs differed from traditional bonds, as investors risked losing their initial investment if the SIB did not result in expected improvements. SIBs aimed to provide high-quality services to at-risk communities more efficiently than government agencies, so that a portion of the savings could be returned to private investors as interest. Investors were only reimbursed if the program administered by the nonprofits met agreed-upon performance targets. SIBs belonged to a larger category of impact investing which included microfinance and other types of investments designed to reach people or communities that were underserved by traditional financial markets.

[1] Shawn Cole, Rawia Abdel Samad, Matt Berner, and Raluca Dragusanu, "Social Finance, Inc.," HBS No. 212-055 (Boston: Harvard Business School Publishing, 2011), p. 8.

[2] Cole, et al., "Social Finance, Inc.," p. 8.

The Peterborough Social Impact Bond exemplifies a new contracting model, focused on outcomes, a new delivery model and a new social investment model

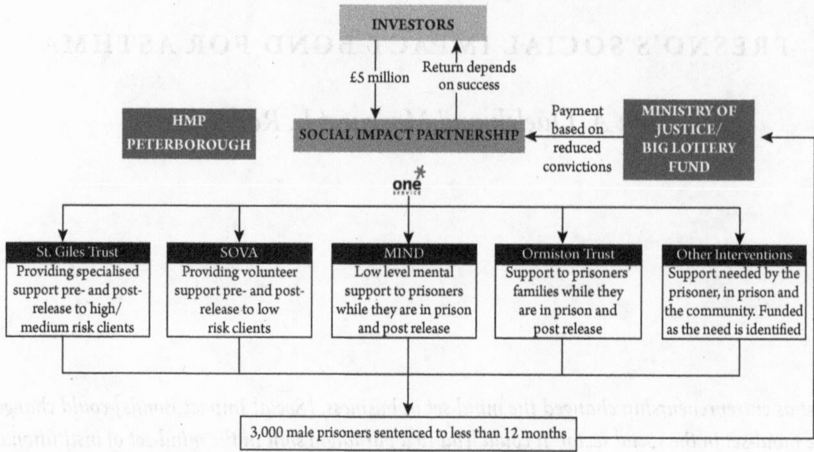

Figure 14.1 Exhibit 1 Peterborough SIB Stakeholder Map, 2011.
Source: Social Finance UK, "Peterborough Social Impact Bond," 2014, http://www.socialfinanceus.org/sites/socialfinanceus.org/files/SF_Peterborough_SIB_0.pdf, accessed August 2014.

History of SIBs

The first SIB was launched in the U.K. in 2010. The SIB funded programs designed to reduce recidivism[3] at the Peterborough prison by supporting the reintegration of newly released prisoners into the community. When the SIB was launched, recidivism at the Peterborough prison was 60%, and the cost of housing a repeat offender could reach $126,000 per year.[4] Social Finance, a nonprofit financial firm, raised roughly $7.4 million[5] for the SIB from 17 investors, mostly philanthropic organizations or high-wealth individuals who sought an investment (rather than a grant-giving) opportunity. Multiple nonprofits, including the St. Giles Trust, YMCA, and Ormiston Trust, would administer the prison programs under the leadership of the "One Service" nonprofit organization (see Figure 14.1 for the Peterborough SIB stakeholders). The U.K. Ministry of Justice and the Big Lottery Fund agreed to pay returns to investors if the project successfully reduced recidivism.

[3] The recidivism measure used by the Peterborough evaluators was the number of reconviction events (e.g., occasions when a former prisoner is convicted in court for a new offense) incurred by Peterborough prisoners within 18 months of release (for crimes committed within one year of release) versus a comparable control group.

[4] Maria Hernandez, S. Len Syme, and Rick Brush, "Impact Investing in Sources of Health," Collective Health, http://collective health.files.wordpress.com/2012/04/impact-investing-in-health_tce-paper_feb-2012.pdf, accessed August 2014.

[5] Converted from pounds using the "Yearly Average Currency Exchange Rate for Translating foreign currency into U.S. dollars" provided by the U.S. Internal Revenue Service. The initial sum of 5 million pounds was converted using the 2010 exchange rate of 0.673 pounds per U.S. dollar.

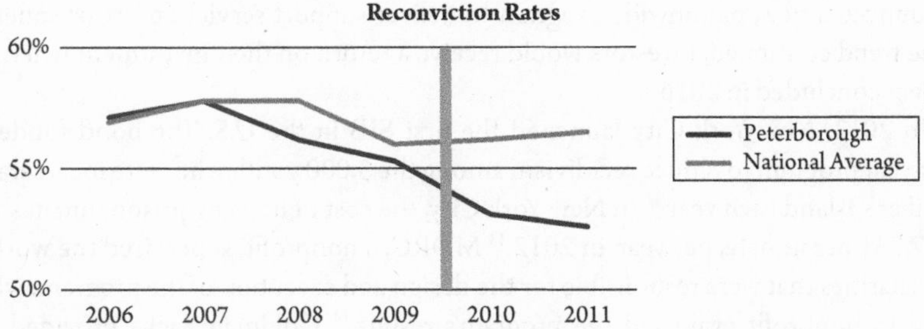

Figure 14.2 Exhibit 2 Partial Peterborough Interim Recidivism Results, 2006–2011.
In October 2013, the U.K. Ministry of Justice released interim results for reconviction rates for the first cohort of the Peterborough SIB program national recidivism rates. The green bar indicates the launch of the Peterborough SIB in early 2010.
Source: Social Finance UK, "Peterborough Interim Figures – 31 October 2013," http://www.socialfinance.org.uk/sites/ default /files/peterborough_interim_figures_october_2013.pdf, accessed August 2014.
Note: The reconviction rates are given for prisoners released during a 16-month window. Data should be read as "For prisoners released during the 16-month period ending in December 2009, the reconviction rate for those incarcerated at Peterborough was 55.3%."

The performance target for the eight-year SIB was for the social programs to reduce recidivism by at least 7.5% among the target cohort (versus a similar group of prisoners released at the same time). (For interim results of the Peterborough SIB, see Figure 14.2.) The payout amount[6] was linked to the level of recidivism reduction achieved:

- If recidivism dropped by less than 7.5%, investors would forfeit their initial investment.
- If recidivism dropped by 7.5% or more, the Ministry of Justice would pay investors an increasing rate of return up to 13.5% per year[7] on their investment, over the eight-year period.[8]

In August 2014, the first official results of the Peterborough prison SIB were released. An independent evaluator found that the SIB-funded program, executed by One Service, reduced recidivism among the first cohort of 1,000 former prisoners by 8.4% (which exceeded the minimum successful reduction of 7.5%).[9] Prisoner engagement with support services increased from 74% to 86% since the start of the SIB, and post-release engagement increased from 37% to 71%.[10]

In addition to reducing recidivism rates, the Peterborough SIB started a national conversation on prisoner rehabilitation, and as a result, the Ministry of Justice

[6] Final payments would be made to investors in 2018.

[7] For example, a 10% reduction in recidivism would result in a 7.5% annual return for investors.

[8] Hernandez, et al., "Impact Investing in Sources of Health."

[9] Social Finance US, "First Official Results Demonstrate Positive Outcomes at Peterborough," Social Finance US (Blog), August 7, 2014, http://socialfinanceusblog.wordpress.com/2014/08/07/first-official-results-demonstrate-positive-outcomes-at-peterborough-3/, accessed August 2014.

[10] Social Finance US, "First Official Results Demonstrate Positive Outcomes at Peterborough."

announced a new, nationwide program to deliver support services to ex-prisoners.[11] If the trend continued, investors would receive a return on their investment when the project concluded in 2016.

In 2012, New York City launched the first SIB in the U.S. The bond funded a four-year program to reduce recidivism among the 3,000 youth who were incarcerated at Riker's Island each year.[12] In New York City, the cost of housing prison inmates was $167,731 per inmate, per year, in 2012.[13] MDRC, a nonprofit, supervised the work of two charities that were responsible for the design and execution of the program, while a fourth nonprofit evaluated the program's results.[14] Goldman Sachs provided the $9.6 million investment (with $7.4 million backed by Bloomberg Philanthropies).[15] The payout amount was made on a sliding scale:[16]

- If recidivism dropped by less than 10%, the city would pay nothing and Goldman Sachs would forfeit its investment.
- If recidivism declined by exactly 10%, Goldman Sachs would receive its initial investment with no additional interest.
- If recidivism declined by more than 10%, Goldman Sachs would receive its initial investment, plus an additional return of up to $2.1 million.[17]

In 2011, U.S. president Barack Obama requested $100 million in the federal budget to fund pay-for-success programs (which included SIBs) for fiscal year 2012. Although his request was denied by Congress, several federal agencies, including the Department of Labor, allocated money to SIBs within their existing budgets. In 2014, the Obama administration successfully obtained $500 million in support for pay-for-success programs in the budget ($300 million of which would be used to incentivize state and municipal governments to develop their own SIBs).[18]

SIB Stakeholders

In order to achieve success, SIBs required the coordination of multiple parties. The new financial vehicles had to balance not only the motivations of private stakeholders and

[11] Social Finance US, "First Official Results Demonstrate Positive Outcomes at Peterborough."

[12] Caroline Preston, "Getting Back More Than a Warm Feeling," NYTimes.com Feed, November 9, 2012, via Factiva, July 2014.

[13] New York City Independent Budget Office, "NYC's Jail Population: Who's There and Why?" New York City by the Numbers, August 22, 2013, http://ibo.nyc.ny.us/cgi-park2/?p=516, accessed August 2014.

[14] Preston, "Getting Back More Than a Warm Feeling."

[15] Preston, "Getting Back More Than a Warm Feeling."

[16] "Illinois to Join Ranks of Social Impact Bond Users," *The Bond Buyer*, April 10, 2013, via Factiva, July 2014.

[17] Preston, "Getting Back More Than a Warm Feeling."

[18] Sonal Shah and Kristina Costa, "Social Impact Bonds: White House Budget Drives Pay for Success and Social Impact Bonds Forward," Center for American Progress, April 23, 2013, http://www.americanprogress.org/issues/economy/news/2013 /04/23/61163/white-house-budget-drives-pay-for-success-and-social-impact-bonds-forward/, accessed August 2014.

governments, but the needs and capabilities of nonprofits as well. Stakeholders had differing motivations, which were reflected in the construction of the SIB contracts.

Nonprofits In the U.S., there were an estimated 1.5 million nonprofit organizations, which collectively addressed virtually every social issue.[19] Many nonprofits found it challenging to balance the dispensation of services with fund-raising activities. Molly Baldwin, executive director of Roca,[20] stated:

> In contrast to the private sector, running a nonprofit is like running two businesses. Doing good work, and raising money. These businesses are often not related: serving more youth does not provide us with more revenue. The level of effort required to get funding is huge.[21]

SIBs offered nonprofits a bridge between the two activities by providing those that were the highest performing in their area of focus with a long-term source of capital to fund their programs. Although many nonprofits were excited about using SIBs to fund social programs, most agreed that SIBs were not appropriate for all causes or organizations. Nonprofit programs seeking funding from investors and governments in the form of SIBs had to meet the following criteria:

- Significant Cost Saving Potential: The expected savings from the preventative, nonprofit programs (versus the comparable government intervention) needed to be large enough to justify the implementation costs of the SIB and fund investor returns.
- Measurable Outcomes: The performance metrics of the nonprofit programs needed to be clear and measurable over the time horizon. Ideally, an independent organization would evaluate the outcomes by comparing the target population to a control group.

Some observers worried that the significant measurement component required by SIBs would interfere with nonprofits' ability to deliver services. Stakeholders recognized the need for nonprofits to have adequate managerial capacity to process all of the data. Third-party private investment or management consulting firms were occasionally tapped to play a role by financing improved data management capabilities at the nonprofit, or by sharing use of their in-house data analytics services.

Government Following the U.S. recession of 2008, government budgets became strained. Collective state budget gaps exceeded $500 billion in 2011.[22] By 2014, stress on state budgets had lessened dramatically; however, 22 states still exceeded their budgets (although the overruns were relatively modest).[23] SIBs offered an alternative to direct government funding, if the stakeholders could successfully navigate

[19] Foundation Center, "Frequently Asked Questions," http://foundationcenter.org/getstarted/faqs/html/howmany.html, accessed August 2014.

[20] Roca was a Massachusetts-based nonprofit organization that worked with at-risk youth.

[21] Cole, et al., "Social Finance, Inc.," p. 5.

[22] National Conference of State Legislature, "State Budget Update: Summer 2011," http://www.ncsl.org/documents/fiscal/ SummerSBU2011FreeVersion.pdf, accessed August 2014.

[23] National Conference of State Legislature, "State Budget Update: Spring 2014."

the bureaucracy and convince government officials of the potential benefits of SIBs. Massachusetts was the first state to formally declare an interest in SIBs; in May 2011, it issued a request for information that was met with 32 responses (mostly nonprofits pitching SIB proposals).

Ironically, cost savings produced by SIBs posed a challenge when selling an idea to government stakeholders, as successful SIBs often produced savings for multiple agencies at different levels of government; this made it difficult to determine which agencies should fund the SIB. For example, projects to reduce recidivism could potentially benefit the Department of Corrections, local police departments, and the Department of Labor.

Some observers worried that the government would eventually use SIBs as a replacement for direct government spending on essential services, rather than as a source of capital to fund experimental, high-impact projects. Given the political nature of government budget discussions, there was some concern that politicians would have an incentive to claim that SIBs were unsuccessful in order to avoid paying for projects approved by their predecessors.

Investors For investors seeking primarily to improve social outcomes, SIBs offered unique upside potential when compared to grants. Grants provided no financial return, regardless of the nonprofit program's success, whereas SIBs allowed investors to receive returns if the program was successful. Investors in the Peterborough SIB were composed entirely of foundations and charitable trusts; however, many SIB partners hoped that future SIB projects would attract both nonprofit philanthropic organizations and for-profit investors.

However, for investors seeking primarily financial returns, SIBs were not appealing due to their high levels of risk (see Figure 14.3). The Peterborough SIB and others stipulated that investors would not recover their investment if recidivism failed to decline; this

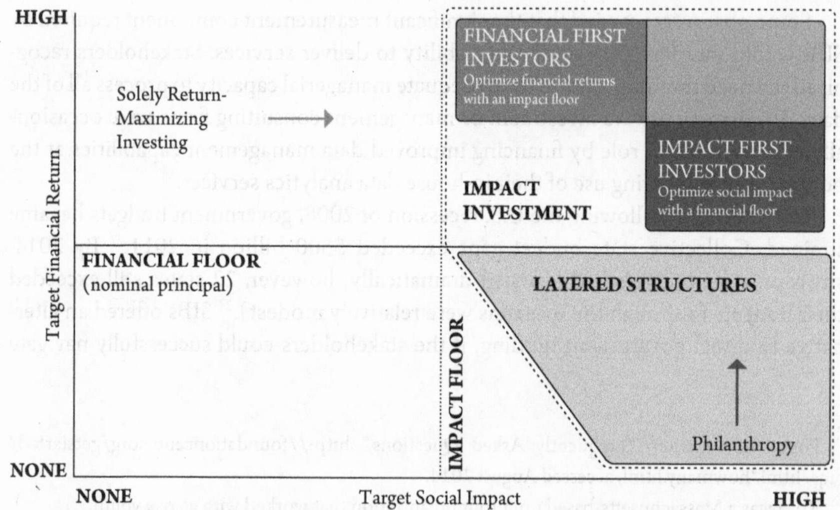

Figure 14.3 Exhibit 3 Segments of Impact Investors by Interest in Financial Return versus Social Impact, 2010.

Source: Bridges Ventures, The Parthenon Group, Global Impact Investing Network, "Investing for Impact," 2010, http://www.parthenon.com/GetFile.aspx?u=%2FLists%2FThoughtLeadership%2FAttachments%2F15%2FInvesting%2520for%2520Impact.pdf, accessed August 2014.

placed a heavy risk on the investors. The upside offered if the intervention was successful (a maximum of 13.5% per year over eight years) was not high enough to balance the risk of losing everything. It was difficult for any SIB to offer returns that matched the risk level, given that the payout made to investors was bound by the amount of savings the intervention could produce. In addition, U.S. government budgeting practices required that the highest potential payout to SIB investors be included in budget projections.

Social Impact Bonds for Healthcare Issues

Many believed that SIBs were ideally suited to tackle public health issues. With federal and state budgets under pressure to cut costs, it was difficult to justify spending on preventative healthcare programs, the savings of which would often not be realized for a year or more. However, it was widely believed that greater preventative investment was essential to curtailing rapidly growing costs of treatment.

FRESNO AND THE FIRST HEALTHCARE SIB

In March 2013, the launch the first health-focused social impact bond in the U.S. was announced. A two-year pilot program would be launched in Fresno, California, to study the impact of home-based interventions on asthma treatment costs. If successful, the asthma prevention program would be scaled up and funded via an SIB.

Why Fresno?

In 2013, Fresno, California, was the 86th-largest U.S. metropolitan area, with a population of over 950,000.[24] Fresno's citizens were younger, less wealthy, and more likely to be an ethnic minority than those of California as a whole[25] (see Table 14.1). In 2012, children under 18 living in Fresno County were more likely to be uninsured (11%) than all children in California (7.7%).[26] Children in Fresno were also more likely than other children in the state to receive insurance via a government program (49.9% versus 40.5%).[27] Among adults in Fresno, rates of chronic diseases such as obesity were higher than for the state as a whole (see Table 14.2).

[24] "Annual Estimates of the Resident Population: April 1, 2010 to July 1, 2013," U.S. Census Bureau, Population Division, March 2014, http://factfinder2.census.gov/faces/tableservices/jsf/pages/productview.xhtml?src=bkmk, accessed August 2014.

[25] U.S. Census Bureau: State and County QuickFacts, "Population Estimates, American Community Survey, Census of Population and Housing, State and County Housing Unit Estimates, County Business Patterns, Nonemployer Statistics, Economic Census, Survey of Business Owners, Building Permits," Last Revised: July 8, 2014, http://quickfacts.census.gov/ qfd/states/06/06019.html, accessed August 2014.

[26] UCLA Center for Health Policy Research, "Child and Teen 2011-2012 Health Profiles: Fresno County," 2012, http://healthpolicy.ucla.edu/health-profiles/Child_Teen/Documents/2011-2012/Counties/Fresno.pdf, accessed August 2014.

[27] UCLA Center for Health Policy Research, "Child and Teen 2011-2012 Health Profiles: Fresno County."

Table 14.1 Exhibit 4 Fresno County Demographics, 2013

	Fresno County	*California*
Population	955,272	38,332,521
Persons under 18 Years	29.1%	23.9%
Black or African American	5.9%	6.6%
Asian	10.5%	14.1%
Hispanic	51.6%	38.4%
White[a]	31.4%	39.0%
Median Household Income, 2008–2012	$42,741	$61,400
Persons below Poverty Level, Percent, 2008–2012	24.8%	15.3%

Source: U.S. Census Bureau: State and County QuickFacts, "Population Estimates, American Community Survey, Census of Population and Housing, State and County Housing Unit Estimates, County Business Patterns, Nonemployer Statistics, Economic Census, Survey of Business Owners, Building Permits," Last Revised, July 8, 2014, http://quickfacts.census.gov/qfd/states/06/06019.html, accessed August 2014.

[a] White alone, not Hispanic.

The California Endowment (TCE) selected Fresno as one of 14 cities in California to participate in a 10-year "Building Healthy Communities" plan to develop communities where children were safe, healthy, and ready to learn.

Why Asthma?

Asthma was a chronic disease that inflamed airways, which caused them to swell and decrease the air supply of afflicted children and adults. Symptoms of asthma included tightness in the chest, coughing, shortness of breath, and wheezing.[28] In some cases, asthma presented as mild symptoms that went away without intervention; in others, symptoms escalated into severe, life-threatening asthma attacks. Asthma could not be cured, but medications were available to ease symptoms. Medications came in two types: quick-relief[29] and long-term control.[30,31] Patients were also encouraged to be proactive in managing their exposure to asthma triggers.[32]

[28] National Heart, Lung and Blood Institute, "What is Asthma?" June 15, 2012, http://www.nhlbi.nih.gov/health/health-topics/topics/asthma/#, accessed August 2014.

[29] Quick-relief medicines relieved the symptoms of an asthma attack, such as shortness of breath.

[30] Long-term control medicines eased the inflammation of the airways. They were often taken daily to prevent asthma symptoms from occurring.

[31] National Heart, Lung and Blood Institute, "How is Asthma Treated and Controlled?" June 15, 2012, http://www.nhlbi.nih. gov/health/health-topics/topics/asthma/treatment.html,accessed August 2014.

[32] National Heart, Lung and Blood Institute, "How is Asthma Treated and Controlled?"

Table 14.2 Exhibit 5 Incidence of Chronic Health Conditions among Adults in Fresno County, 2012

Health Outcomes	*Fresno County (%)*	*California (%)*
Fair or Poor Health (Age-Adjusted)	25.0	19.4
Current Asthma	13.0	7.7
Ever Diagnosed with Diabetes	8.5	8.4
Obese	30.0	24.8
Ever Diagnosed with High Blood Pressure	29.7	27.3

Source: UCLA Center for Health Policy Research, "Child and Teen 2011-2012 Health Profiles: Fresno County," 2012, http://health policy.ucla.edu/health-profiles/Child_Teen/Documents/2011-2012/Counties/Fresno.pdf, accessed August 2014.

Around 1 in 12 adults suffered from asthma in the U.S. versus 1 in 11 children.[33] After children were diagnosed with asthma, they were often prescribed inhaled corticosteroids, a type of long-term control medication.[34] Inhaled corticosteroids carried the risk of slowing growth in the children to whom it was prescribed. However, the slowed growth was typically minor, and many doctors believed the benefits of the medications outweighed the risks.[35]

Asthma mitigation was well suited to funding via SIBs. Asthma was a chronic condition that 25.5 million adults and children[36] suffered from in the U.S. in 2012.[37] Although treatment options existed, little headway had been made to address environmental triggers in patients' homes (such as tobacco smoke, pet dander, dust, or mold) in order to prevent asthma attacks.

Home-based asthma prevention programs had an independently verified track record of success. In 1999, the "Healthy Homes" initiative was piloted in Seattle–King County. Community health workers (CHWs) visited the homes of children who suffered from asthma to assess environmental triggers and offer education to families. The program resulted in significant reductions to healthcare costs, health facility utilization, and days of missed school. (See Box 14.1 for more on the Healthy Homes initiative.)

In 2008, a literature review of 23 research studies found that asthma prevention programs where trained personnel made one or more visits to the patients' homes were very effective in improving health outcomes.[38] Studies of home-based interventions

[33] U.S. Centers for Disease Controls, "Asthma's Impact on the Nation," http://www.cdc.gov/asthma/impacts_nation/asthmafactsheet.pdf, accessed August 2014.

[34] National Heart, Lung and Blood Institute, "How is Asthma Treated and Controlled?"

[35] National Heart, Lung and Blood Institute, "How is Asthma Treated and Controlled?"

[36] In 2012, 18.7 million adults and 6.8 million children suffered from asthma in the U.S.

[37] Centers for Disease Control and Prevention, Guide to Community Preventive Services, "FastStats: Asthma," updated July 14, 2014, http://www.cdc.gov/nchs/fastats/asthma.htm, accessed August 2014.

[38] Centers for Disease Control and Prevention, "Guide to Community Preventive Services, Asthma control: home-based multi-trigger, multicomponent interventions," http://www.thecommunityguide.org/asthma/rrchildren.html, accessed August 2014.

Box 14.1 Appendix: Seattle–King County Healthy Homes Project

The Seattle–King County Healthy Homes Project was designed as an intervention for Medicaid-enrolled children with asthma to receive home visits from community health workers (CHWs) in Seattle–King County in Washington State. The program was later expanded to include in-home support to teach asthma self-management and trigger reduction techniques.

Initially, CHWs performed home assessments to identify environmental triggers, gauge the family's knowledge and skills of asthma self-management, create an action plan, and provide asthma fighting tools (such as vacuums, bedding encasements, etc.). Additional support services, like facilitating pest extermination or advocating on behalf of families for better housing, were provided to some of families.

A randomized controlled trial was conducted using the data from 274 households that participated over the one-year-long intervention. Households were assigned to either a high-intensity group (seven visits from CHWs and a full set of resources) or a low-intensity group (one visit from CHW and limited resources). The "intensity" was not linked to the severity of the asthma.

Table A-1 Results of the Seattle–King County Healthy Homes Project

	Pre-Intervention	*Post-Intervention*
	Urgent Health Care Utilization	
High-Intensity Group	23.4%	8.4%
Low-Intensity Group	20.2%	16.4%
	Days of Limited Activity	
High-Intensity Group	5.6	1.5
Low-Intensity Group	4.3	1.7
	Quality of Life (7 point scale)	
High-Intensity Group	4.0	5.6
Low-Intensity Group	4.4	5.4
	Urgent Health Care Costs	
High-Intensity Group		$201–$334/child
Low-Intensity Group		$185–$315/child
	Missed School in Past 2 Weeks	
High-Intensity Group	31.1.%	12.2%
Low-Intensity Group	28.4%	20.3%

Source: Deborah Bachrach, Helen Pfister, Kier Wallis, and Mindy Lipson, "Addressing Patients' Social Needs," Manatt Health Solutions, May 2014, http://www.manatt.com/uploadedFiles/Content/5_News_and_Events/Newsletters/ Medicaid_Update/

Addressing-Patients-Social-Needs-An-Emerging-Business-Case-for-Provider-Investment.pdf, accessed August 2014.

Note: The study included 214 participants, 110 in the high-intensity group and 104 in the low-intensity group.

High-intensity interventions offered superior cost savings versus the low-intensity intervention. The estimated marginal cost of the high-intensity intervention relative to the low-intensity intervention was an additional $124,000, or $1,124 per child. However, the savings accrued by the high-intensity group in urgent care cost (which included hospital admissions, emergency department visits, and unscheduled clinic visits) during a two-month period ranged from $57 to $80 per child. The observed bimonthly savings were likely to persist for several years.

The study did not collect data on both groups for an extended period, post-test, so it was not known if the lower use of urgent care remained among the high-intensity group. If the low urgent care costs observed at the conclusion of the study among the high-intensity group persisted for several years, the high-intensity intervention would be more cost effective than the low-intensity intervention. The savings per asthma-afflicted child, discounted at 3% per year, would range from $972 to $1,366 for three years and from $1,316 to $1,849 for four years.

Funding for the Seattle–King Healthy Homes Project was sourced entirely from grants, including support from the U.S. Department of Housing and Urban Development, National Institutes of Health, and the Centers for Disease Control and Prevention.

Similar models for asthma management were adopted by public health agencies in Fresno, Boston, Philadelphia, Baltimore, and others.

Source: Bachrach, Pfister, Wallis, and Lipson, "Addressing Patients' Social Needs," pp. 32–33, 35; J. W. Krieger, T. K. Takaro, L. Song et al., "The Seattle-King County Healthy Homes Project: A Randomized, Controlled Trial of a Community Health Worker Intervention to Decrease Exposure to Indoor Asthma Triggers, American Journal of Public Health 95, no. 4 (April 2005):652–659, http://www.ncbi.nlm.nih.gov/pmc/articles/PMC1449237/, accessed August 2014.

for adults with asthma were less common than studies of children; however, three studies found that, while reported quality of life improved, there was no significant improvement in productivity or decreased healthcare use.[39] Home-based interventions proved successful in improving outcomes for children with asthma:

- Five of the studies measured number of school days missed due to asthma and found a median reduction of 12.3 school days per year.[40]
- Eleven studies measured the proportion of children who required at least one asthma-motivated acute care visit, and a median absolute percentage reduction of 5.4% was observed.[41]

The literature review contained 13 studies that discussed the costs of the asthma interventions, expected savings, and return on investment. The study found that

[39] Centers for Disease Control and Prevention, "Guide to Community Preventive Services."

[40] Centers for Disease Control and Prevention, "Guide to Community Preventive Services."

[41] Centers for Disease Control and Prevention, "Guide to Community Preventive Services."

Table 14.3 Exhibit 6 Home-based Asthma Intervention Programs Cost and Return on Investment, 2008[a]

	Minimum Cost	*Maximum Cost*
	Program Cost per Participant	
Major Remediation[b]	$3,796	$14,858
Minor to Moderate Remediation	$231	$1,720
	Return on Investment[c]	
Savings per Dollar Invested	$5.30	$14
Cost per Symptom-Free Day	$12	$57

Source: Centers for Disease Control and Prevention, "Guide to Community Preventive Services, Asthma control: home-based multi-trigger, multicomponent interventions," http://www.thecommunityguide.org/asthma/multicomponent.html, accessed August 2014.

[a] Unless otherwise noted, data in the table represent costs measured across 13 research studies (the majority of which studied interventions for children, and all of which included child participants). Costs and savings are measured in 2007 U.S. dollars.

[b] Major remediation included substantive environmental changes; those patients who received major remediation were not necessarily those whose asthma was most severe.

[c] Return on investment was measured among six studies that provided minor to moderate remediation. Based upon the Seattle–King County Health Home Project (see the **Appendix**), it is reasonable to assume that major remediation would exhibit higher returns on investment than minor to moderate remediation.

home-based, multicomponent (individual education plus household remediation) asthma interventions provided good value-for-money when improvement in "symptom-free days" and productivity, as well as savings arising from averting treatment costs, were all considered.[42] (See Table 14.3 for the minimum and maximum costs, and rates of return for the 13 studies.)

Fresno's Asthma Problem

In 2014, the American Lung Association named Fresno-Madera as suffering the worst exposure to air pollution, including chemicals and soot, of any city in the U.S.[43] Fresno had among the highest rates of asthma in the country, with roughly 20% of children diagnosed with asthma.[44] Tim Tyner, president of the Central California Asthma Collaborative, stated:

[42] Centers for Disease Control and Prevention, "Guide to Community Preventive Services."

[43] Mark Grossi, "Fresno-area air problem ranks as nation's worst," *Fresno Bee*, April 29, 2014, http://www.fresnobee.com/ 2014/04/29/3901583/fresno-area-air-problem-ranks.html, accessed August 2014.

[44] Rebecca Fairfax Clay, "Health Impact Bonds: Will Investors Pay for Intervention?" *Environmental Health Perspectives* 121, no. 2 (February 2013): A45, http://ehp.niehs.nih.gov/pdf-files/2013/Feb/ehp.121-a45_508.pdf, accessed July 2014.

Table 14.4 Exhibit 7 Asthma-Related Emergency Department Visits and Hospitalizations in Fresno, 2010

	Under 18 Years	*18 Years and Older*
Emergency Department Visits	3,669	3,484
Cost per Emergency Department Visit	$1,375	$1,375
Hospitalizations	699	592
Cost per Hospitalization	$16,181	$23,074

Source: Compiled from Rebecca Fairfax Clay, "Health Impact Bonds: Will Investors Pay for Intervention?" *Environmental Health Perspectives* 121, no. 2 (February 2013): A45, http://ehp.niehs.nih.gov/pdf-files/2013/Feb/ehp.121-a45_508.pdf, accessed July 2014; and California Department of Public Health, "Fresno County Asthma Profile," Environment Health Investigations Branch, July 16, 2014, http://goo.gl/qaQoa, accessed August 2014.

Asthma is the leading cause of emergency room and hospital encounters for children in Fresno, and the number one health-related reason kids miss school.[45]

In Fresno, roughly 20 people went to the emergency room for treatment of asthma-related issues each day, and three were hospitalized as a result.[46] The estimated direct cost of such visits was $35 million[47] per year,[48] while indirect costs (such as lost school and work days) contributed an additional $52 million.[49] (For a breakout of direct costs, see Table 14.4.)

SIB Pilot Design

Two nonprofits—Social Finance, Inc., and Collective Health—proposed an SIB to fund in-home interventions for low-income children with asthma in Fresno. A two-year pilot program was designed to demonstrate the efficacy of the intervention, which, if successful, could be scaled up to serve more children who suffered from asthma in the Fresno area.

The pilot provided the families of 200 low-income children suffering from moderate to severe asthma with home-based care, educational materials, and support to

[45] "The California Endowment Awards Grant to Social Finance and Collective Health," Social Finance press release, March 25, 2013, on the Nonprofit Finance Fund website, http://payforsuccess.org/sites/default/files/fresno_asthma_demonstration_ project_press_release.pdf, accessed July 2014.

[46] "The California Endowment Awards Grant to Social Finance and Collective Health," Social Finance press release.

[47] The $35 million included the cost of hospitalizations (nearly 1,300 each year, totaling $24.6 million), emergency room visits (7,000 each year), and other costs related to the treatment of asthma that were paid by the public.

[48] Rob Waters, "Pay Now, Or Pay (More) Later: The Crying Need to Fund Community Prevention," *Forbes*, February 4, 2013, http://www.forbes.com/sites/robwaters/2013/02/04/pay-now-or-pay-more-later-the-crying-need-to-fund-community-prevention/, accessed August 2014.

[49] Clay, "Health Impact Bonds: Will Investors Pay for Intervention?"

reduce environmental triggers (such upgraded vacuum cleaners to better remove dust mites). Similar interventions had been proven to significantly lower healthcare costs in other areas.[50] The pilot focused on children who averaged 1.5 emergency department visits per year and were hospitalized for 50% of visits.[51] "Some of these children go to the emergency department almost every week," says Rick Brush, founder and chief executive officer of Collective Health and former executive of Cigna Healthcare.[52]

Under the program, community health workers visited the participants' homes to assess indoor triggers for asthma and suggest solutions (such as cleaning or replacing carpets, monitoring medication compliance, and removing dust, mold, or pests). The community health workers performed follow-ups in the form of monthly phone calls and quarterly home visits to provide further assistance and to ensure that suggested changes were made.[53]

The program provided for the collection and evaluation of data to show progress against the social and financial goals of the project. Children were only included in the pilot if they had been diagnosed with asthma and had received insurance coverage through Medi-Cal, the California State Medicaid program. Enrollment in Medi-Cal was necessary to ensure that the pilot executors could access historical claims data for asthma-related expenses to accurately measure savings resulting from the pilot. After one year, historical asthma-related claims data (including the number of emergency department visits and hospitalizations) were compared to the cost of treatment, post-pilot intervention.[54] The asthma SIB in Fresno was expected to result in 30% to 40% savings in reduced emergency visits.[55]

The Fresno SIB Pilot Program Stakeholders

The stakeholders for Fresno's two-year SIB pilot program included a host of nonprofit, private entities that were responsible for providing funding, designing and implementing the program, and measuring the program outcomes. If Fresno's small two-year pilot was successful, the stakeholders intended to scale up the project to include more families and a broader selection of investors and government agencies.

Funding The California Endowment, a nonprofit, granted $660,000 to fund the pilot.[56] The California Endowment's grant was sufficient to fund the entire project over the two-year period. Since the money provided was given as a grant, the California Endowment did not expect a return on the investment, even if the project was

[50] "The California Endowment Awards Grant to Social Finance and Collective Health," Social Finance press release.

[51] Clay, "Health Impact Bonds: Will Investors Pay for Intervention?"

[52] Clay, "Health Impact Bonds: Will Investors Pay for Intervention?"

[53] Clay, "Health Impact Bonds: Will Investors Pay for Intervention?"

[54] Clay, "Health Impact Bonds: Will Investors Pay for Intervention?"

[55] Manuela Badawy, "California city seeks to cut asthma rate via bond issue," Reuters, October 19, 2012, http://www.reuters. com/article/2012/10/19/us-investing-impactbonds-health-idUSBRE89I0U120121019, accessed August 2014.

[56] "The California Endowment Awards Grant to Social Finance and Collective Health," Social Finance press release.

successful.[57] As a result, the project stakeholders of the pilot did not need to determine which government agencies would be responsible for funding returns to investors.

Designing and implementing the program The asthma management program was designed and executed by the Central California Asthma Collaborative and Clinica Sierra Vista, with technical support provided by the Regional Asthma Management and Prevention program and strategic guidance given by Social Finance.

The Central California Asthma Collaborative was a nonprofit that ran numerous programs in Fresno and surrounding areas to reduce asthma among children. One such program, "Fresno Kicks Asthma," taught a class on asthma management strategies to middle school children.[58] Regional Asthma Management and Prevention was a nonprofit dedicated to improving asthma-related health outcomes by influencing state-level policy on land-use and transportation issues, as well as providing technical support to other asthma-focused nonprofits.[59] Clinica Sierra Vista, a local medical clinic with more 40 locations, was primarily responsible for the home assessments and patient education. Its involvement with prior studies on home-based asthma intervention, as well as its reputation as a healthcare provider, helped give the SIB pilot credence.[60] Social Finance, the U.S.-based sister-organization to the firm that procured funding for the Peterborough SIB, provided strategic guidance on the program's implementation and helped locate the initial funding needed for the pilot.

Measuring the program Collective Health, a healthcare-focused social enterprise organization, helped to procure funding for the pilot, but also played a key role in the data collection and analysis for the healthcare savings resulting from the project. The children in the pilot were selected based upon their asthma diagnosis as well as related expenses captured in claims data from Medi-Cal. Matching each child's pre- and post-intervention treatment costs was essential to the calculation of savings resulting from preventive care.

INVESTMENT APPEAL

After analyzing the cost savings generated from the pilot, Social Finance and Collective Health decided to launch an SIB to scale the program up by 1,000–3,500 additional children (depending upon the capital raised). Possible investors for the SIB included foundations, government agencies, self-insured private companies, individuals, and investment firms.[61] The California Endowment agreed to contribute a second investment of $1.1 million to fund the expanded program.[62] Collective Health and Social

57 "The California Endowment Awards Grant to Social Finance and Collective Health," Social Finance press release.

58 Central California Asthma Collaborative, "Fresno Kicks Asthma," http://www.centralcalasthma.org/fresno-kicks-asthma-17, accessed August 2014.

59 Public Health Institute, "Regional Asthma Management and Prevention Program," http://www.phi.org/focus-areas/?program=regional-asthma-management-and-prevention-program, accessed August 2014.

60 Hernandez, et al., "Impact Investing in Sources of Health."

61 Clay, "Health Impact Bonds: Will Investors Pay for Intervention?"

62 Clay, "Health Impact Bonds: Will Investors Pay for Intervention?"

Finance then determined that the expanded SIB would cover treatment for 1,100 households.[63] Brush, CEO of Collective Health, stated:

> We know that prevention is a better investment than paying for care in the ER or the hospital. The challenge is that most of the nation's health care dollars are spent after people get sick. This project will demonstrate the financial value of expanding a proven prevention program to a much greater number of children who will benefit. We are aiming for a 30% reduction in emergency room visits and 50% reduction in hospitalizations, which would yield an approximate net savings of $5,000 per child per year. There's significant potential to make a real impact here.[64]

Costs

Initially, Collective Health estimated that the cost of providing home-based assessments and interventions to 1,100 households with asthma in Fresno would cost $1.1 million.[65] The $1,000 per household would cover the salaries of the community health workers and the costs of any support provided (e.g., new vacuum cleaners). However, after speaking with service providers in the Fresno area, Collective Health revised the expected cost per participant upward to $2,500.[66] The increased cost provided for the delivery of health education in the home ($500) and an average of $2,000 for remediation, which could include cleaning services, slipcovers for pillows and mattresses, weatherizing windows, or pest extermination.[67]

Collective Health estimated that the direct healthcare costs of asthma among the cohort of 1,100 participants would be $17.1 million (47% of which was paid for by Medi-Cal).[68] However, Collective Health noted that the cost of care would vary based upon the severity of the asthma. (See Table 14.5 for average cost of care by level of asthma severity.) Collective Health calculated the revised estimate of the average cost of care for the target population, given the moderate to severe asthma conditions of the area, to be $10,212 per person or $11.2 million total.[69]

Expected Savings

The expected savings were calculated by subtracting the cost of preventative care from the total cost of asthma treatment. While the investment of $1.1 million would help reduce utilization of costly healthcare treatments for asthma, it would not eliminate their usage entirely. As a result, the expected savings from the SIB were initially

[63] "The California Endowment Awards Grant to Social Finance and Collective Health," Social Finance press release.

[64] "The California Endowment Awards Grant to Social Finance and Collective Health," Social Finance press release.

[65] Hernandez, et al., "Impact Investing in Sources of Health."

[66] Hernandez, et al., "Impact Investing in Sources of Health."

[67] Hernandez, et al., "Impact Investing in Sources of Health."

[68] Hernandez, et al., "Impact Investing in Sources of Health."

[69] Hernandez, et al., "Impact Investing in Sources of Health."

Table 14.5 Exhibit 8 Average Baseline Cost of Asthma Care by Severity, 2012

	Mild Asthma	*Moderate Asthma*	*Severe Asthma*
Annual Cost of Care per Patient	$2,646	$4,530	$12,813

Source: Maria Hernandez, S. Len Syme, and Rick Brush, "Impact Investing in Sources of Health," Collective Health, http://collective health.files.wordpress.com/2012/04/impact-investing-in-health_tce-paper_feb-2012.pdf, accessed August 2014.

estimated to be approximately $6 million[70]—$3 million of which would be savings accrued by Medi-Cal.[71] If the SIB program successfully generated the $6 million savings target, the bond would pay investors a return of 5% and the remaining savings would be reinvested into care.[72]

However, after increasing the expected cost of care per participant from $1,000 to $2,500 and altering the medical costs due to asthma to reflect the risk profile of the target population (a decrease in the cost per participant from $17.1 million to $11.2 million), the total expected savings dropped from over $6 million to $4.6 million among the 1,100 participants.[73]

Rate of Return

The positive outcomes generated by the SIB could take like multiple forms, such as increased productivity or a decreased number of lost school days. However, Collective Health chose, for simplicity, to calculate the return on investment (ROI) using the direct medical cost savings resulting from the asthma prevention program divided by the costs of the prevention program (see Table 14.6). It was understood that the total savings of the program were likely greater than the ROI figure.[74]

THE FUTURE OF HEALTHCARE SIBS

In August 2014, initial results of the Fresno pilot were still unpublished. Some observers expressed concerns about the ability to scale SIBs to other health issues. Due to its chronic nature, asthma was particularly well suited to the rate-of-return and time horizons expectations of SIBs. John Capitman, executive director of the Central Valley Health Policy Institute at Fresno State, said:

[70] A portion of the remaining savings would go to local companies with self-insured healthcare plans ($2.3 million), as well as to accountable care organizations, local healthcare providers in capitated payments contracts, and similar firms ($1 million).

[71] Hernandez, et al., "Impact Investing in Sources of Health."

[72] Joe Moore, "Social Impact Bond May Fund Asthma Prevention in Fresno," KVPR, October 30, 2012, http://kvpr.org/post/social-impact-bond-may-fund-asthma-prevention-fresno, accessed August 2014.

[73] Hernandez, et al., "Impact Investing in Sources of Health."

[74] Hernandez, et al., "Impact Investing in Sources of Health."

Table 14.6 Exhibit 9 Collective Health's Asthma Mitigation in Fresno Example, 2012

		Notes
Target Population	1,100	Children with asthma emergencies related to home-based environmental triggers
Savings Opportunity	$17.1 million	Medical costs pre-intervention
	($10.8 million)	Medical costs post-intervention
	$6.3 million	37% savings
Financial Stakeholders	$3 million	Projected savings to Medi-Cal
	$2.3 million	Projected savings to employers
	$1 million	Projected savings to healthcare providers
Bond Term Sheet	$1.1 million	Capital required
	18	Months
	5%	Return[a]
Stakeholder ROI	5.68:1	Based upon projected total savings of $6.3 million over 18 months (from which the initial investment of $1.1 million plus 5% return are subtracted).

Source: Adapted from Collective Health, "Example: Asthma Mitigation in Fresno," 2011–2012, http://collectivehealth.net/new/about_files/CH_fresno%20asthma%20value%20model.pdf, accessed August 2014

[a] Obligation to pay the bondholders. Bond investors are high-net-worth/social impact investors, institutional investors, and foundations.

> I think that for many health issues the changes that people need to make in their lives and in their environments are probably more expensive than that, or have longer returns on investment than may be acceptable to social impact bond investors. I think there are a limited number of health issues that this might work with.[75]

However, other observers noted that, if successful, healthcare-focused SIBs would be an ideal investment vehicle for insurers, since the Affordable Care Act placed limits on the amount of profit insurers could disperse to shareholders. Kevin Hamilton, deputy chief of programs at Clinica Sierra Vista Inc., said:

> The money will be used to reduce the expense associated with the care of their patients and in turn make more money. Not only that, they will likely get to write this money off because it is going to a bond with social impact while still making money for their shareholders.[76]

[75] Moore, "Social Impact Bond May Fund Asthma Prevention in Fresno."

[76] Badawy, "California city seeks to cut asthma rate via bond issue."

15

E-CIGARETTES
MARKETING VERSUS PUBLIC HEALTH

John A. Quelch and Margaret L. Rodriguez

We are at the dawn of a revolution in the fight against tobacco.
—Brice Lepoutre, president of the Independent Association of Electronic Cigarette Users[1]

The [e-cigarette] market is producing, at no cost to the tax-payer, an emerging triumph of public health.
—Clive Bates, former director of Action on Smoking and Health, a British advocacy group[2]

In 2013, the public health debate regarding electronic cigarettes, "e-cigarettes," was lighting up. Developed as a safer alternative to tobacco cigarettes, e-cigarettes delivered nicotine to users through the vaporization of chemical cartridges, rather than the combustion of tobacco. By 2012, retail sales of e-cigarettes were $1.7 billion in the U.S. and were expected to reach $3 billion in 2013[3] E-cigarettes contained far fewer toxins than tobacco cigarettes, and did not produce second-hand smoke. Some observers were concerned about potential risks to public health as a result of the product's positioning as a break-through smoking cessation aid. Many were concerned that e-cigarettes would instead serve as a gateway for young people to eventually smoke tobacco cigarettes, due to the addictive properties of the nicotine found in most e-cigarettes.

[1] "E-cigarettes: Kodak Moment," *The Economist*, September 28, 2013. http://www.economist.com/news/ business/21586867-regulators-wrestle-e-smokes-tobacco-industry-changing-fast-kodak-moment. Accessed October 2013.

[2] Ibid.

[3] Andrea Felstad, "WH Smith and Gamucci forge e-cigarette alliance," *Financial Times*, August 5, 2013. Accessed via Factiva, October 2013.

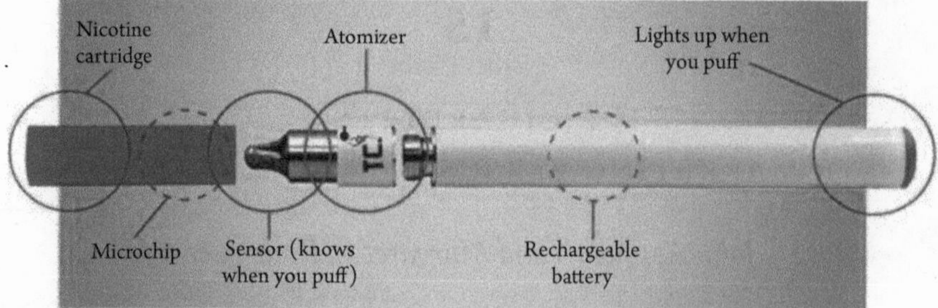

Figure 15.1 Exhibit 1 E-cigarette Product Design, 2013.
Source: Consumer Reports, "Do e-cigarettes help smoker quit?" May 2012. http://www.consumerreports.org/cro/magazine/ 2012/04/do-e-cigarettes-help-smokers-quit/index.htm. Accessed October 2013.

THE EMERGENCE OF E-CIGARETTES

E-cigarettes were hailed as disruptive technology that would revolutionize the consumption of nicotine. Developed in 2003 by Hon Lik,[4] a pharmacist in China, e-cigarettes used small batteries to vaporize a nicotine-laced solution, which consumers then inhaled.[5] The e-cigarette design allowed smokers to closely mimic the sensorial experience of smoking by inhaling vapor from a tube placed in the mouth, a behavior called "vaping" (see Figure 15.1 for e-cigarette design). In 2013, Goldman Sachs called e-cigarettes one of the top eight disruptive technologies to watch.[6] The firm estimated that, by 2020, e-cigarettes could reach sales of $10 billion, delivering 10% of the sales volume and 15% of the profits for the entire tobacco industry.[7] E-cigarettes could be made to deliver zero nicotine, or more nicotine than traditional cigarettes. E-cigarettes contained far fewer toxins than tobacco cigarettes and did not produce second-hand smoke, because they did not require the burning of tobacco.[8] According to the Centers for Disease Control and Prevention (CDC), roughly 6% of all adults in the U.S. had tried an e-cigarette in 2011 (roughly double the percentage in 2010).[9]

[4] Barbara Demick, "A High-tech Approach to Getting a Nicotine Fix." *Los Angeles Times*, April 25, 2009. http: //articles.latimes.com/2009/apr/25/world/fg-china-cigarettes25. Accessed October 2013.

[5] "Sending the Wrong Smoke-signal." *The Economist*. September 28, 2013. http://www.economist.com/ news/leaders/21586855-european-lawmakers-should-reject-proposals-control-electronic-cigarettes-strictly. Accessed October 2013.

[6] Tyler Durden, "Goldman's Top Disruptive Themes," *Zero Hedge*, August 8, 2013. http://www.zerohedge. com/news/2013-08-08/goldmans-top-disruptive-themes. Accessed October 2013.

[7] Ibid.

[8] "Sending the Wrong Smoke-signal." *The Economist*.

[9] Sabrina Tavernise, "Rise is Seen in Students who Use E-cigarettes," *New York Times*, September 6, 2013. Accessed via Factica, October 2013

Market for E-Cigarettes

In the U.S., around 300 million e-cigarettes were sold in 2013.[10] E-cigarettes represented roughly 2-3% of the $100 billion retail tobacco market in the U.S.[11] According to *The Economist*, in 2013, almost all users of e-cigarettes were smokers or those who had smoked previously.[12] A 2013 study published by the CDC found that six in ten U.S. adults were aware of e-cigarettes, up from four in ten in 2010.[13] In 2011, one out of five current smokers in the U.S. had tried an e-cigarette.[14] The CDC found that the proportion of high school students who had tried e-cigarettes had increased from 4.7% in 2011 to 10% in 2012. The percentage in middle school rose from 1.4% in 2011 to 2.7% in 2012. The study found that, in total, 1.8 million middle and high school students in the U.S. had tried e-cigarettes in 2012.[15] Of those who smoked e-cigarettes within 30 days of the survey (about one third of the 1.8 million), about 80% had also smoked a tobacco cigarette within the same period.[16] (See Table 15.1 for estimated conversions between e-cigarette and tobacco cigarette users.)

Pricing and Distribution

Part of the appeal of e-cigarettes to smokers was their cheapness relative to tobacco cigarettes. Cigarettes cost about $7.50 a pack of twenty versus $75-$115 for an e-cigarette starter pack, which included the rechargeable e-cigarette and five cartridges (equivalent to around 10 packs of 20 cigarettes). A set of five refill cartridges for e-cigarettes ranged in retail price between $15 and $25.[17] In 2012, $3.16 per pack of cigarettes sold was collected by U.S. government agencies via excise taxes, fees and settlement payments.[18] E-cigarettes were not subject to excise taxes, and retailer margins on e-cigarettes were 30% to 40% (versus the 5% to 15% margins on tobacco cigarettes).[19] (See Table 15.2 for pricing comparison between e-cigarettes and tobacco cigarettes.) CFO of Philip Morris, Jacek Olczak, attributed the growing popularity of e-cigarettes to the "phenomena of price" and asserted that the flavor of e-cigarette products was

10 "Sending the Wrong Smoke-signal." *The Economist.*

11 Mike Esterl, "E-Cigarette Use Rises Sharply" *Wall Street Journal*, September 6, 2013. *Wall Street Journal.* A5.

12 "Sending the Wrong Smoke-signal." *The Economist.*

13 Michael Felberbaum, "CDC smoking chief says awareness, use of electronic cigarettes underscores need for regulation," *Associated Press*, February 28, 2013. Accessed via Factiva, October 2013.

14 Centers for Disease Control and Prevention, "About one in five U.S. adult cigarette smokers have tried an electronic cigarette," February 28, 2013. http://www.cdc.gov/media/releases/2013/p0228_electronic_cigarettes.html. Accessed October 2013.

15 Sabrina Tavernise, "Rise is Seen in Students who Use E-cigarettes."

16 Centers for Disease Control and Prevention, "Notes from the Field: Electronic Cigarette Use Among Middle and High School Students—United States, 2011-2012," *Morbidity and Mortality Weekly Report* 2013; 62(35):729–730. http://www.cdc.gov/mmwr/preview/mmwrhtml/mm6235a6.htm?s_cid=mm6235a6_w. Accessed October 2013.

17 Steve Warden, "Some Indiana smoker turning to e-cigarettes, seeing vapor devices as better option," *The Journal Gazette*, August 6, 2013. Accessed via Factiva, October 2013.

18 Tyler Durden, "Goldman's Top Disruptive Themes."

19 Ibid.

Table 15.1 Exhibit 2 Estimated Conversion from E-cigarettes to Tobacco Cigarettes in the U.S., 2011

	Tobacco Smokers	*Non-smokers*
Population	43.8 million	270 million
Population who tried e-cigarettes	8.8 million	Adults: 5.6 million[a] Youth: 1.8 million
Estimated proportion of those who tried e-cigarettes habitually smoking e-cigarettes	40%*	Adults: 33% Youth: 50%
Estimated population smoking e-cigarettes	3.5 million	Adults: 1.9 million Youth: 0.9 million
Estimated proportion of e-cigarette smokers who convert to tobacco cigarettes	N/A	Adults: 33% Youth: 80%
Estimated net change to number of smokers	(3.5million)	+ 0.6 million Adults + 0.7 million Youths[b]

Source: Casewriter estimates based on data from U.S. Census Bureau, 2011 Population Clock, http://www.census.gov/ main/www/popclock.html; Centers for Disease Control and Prevention, "Notes from the Field: Electronic Cigarette Use Among Middle and High School Students — United States, 2011-2012," http://www.cdc.gov/mmwr/preview/mmwrhtml/mm6235a6.htm?s_cid=mm6235a6_w. Accessed October 2013; "About one in five U.S. adult cigarette smokers have tried an electronic cigarette," Centers for Disease Control and Prevention, February 28, 2013. http://www.cdc.gov/media/releases/ 2013/p0228_electronic _cigarettes.html. Accessed October 2013.

[a]6% of the U.S. adult population tried e-cigarettes, or roughly 18.7 million. One in five tobacco smokers tried e-cigarettes, or roughly 8.8 million. 9.9 million Adult non-smokers tried e-cigarettes (18.7 million–8.8 million).

[b]To be read: The net decrease in tobacco smokers as a result of e-cigarettes was estimated to be 2.2 million in 2011. The population of non-smokers fell by 2.7 million and the population of e-cigarette smokers increased by 4.9 million.

not comparable to tobacco cigarettes.[20] Research by the U.S. Department of Health and Human Services estimated that an increase of 10% in the price of tobacco cigarettes would reduce overall cigarette consumption by 3–5%.[21]

When first sold in the U.S. in the mid-2000s, e-cigarettes were only available online and at shopping mall kiosks.[22] Kiosks allowed vendors to demonstrate how the product worked, including its ability to be smoked indoors and the variety of flavors available. (See Table 15.3 for e-cigarette flavors.) In 2010, Wal-Mart briefly sold e-cigarettes on its website, but removed them the same year due to lower than anticipated demand.[23]

[20] "Philip Morris Int'l CFO Jacek Olczak talks about the electronic cigarette market," *Associated Press*, July 18, 2013. Accessed via Factiva, October 2013.

[21] Centers for Disease Control and Prevention, "Economic Facts About U.S. Tobacco Production and Use," August 1, 2013. http://www.cdc.gov/tobacco/data_statistics/fact_sheets/economics/econ_facts/. Accessed October 2013.

[22] Michael Felberbaum, "Firms dusts off tobacco marketing playbook amid pending regulation of electronic cigarettes," *Associated Press*, August 3, 2013. Accessed via Factiva, October 2013.

[23] David Kesmdoel, Danny Yadron, "E-cigarettes Spark New Smoking War," *The Wall Street Journal*, august 25, 2010. Accessed via Factiva, October 2013.

Table 15.2 Exhibit 3 Price Comparison of E-Cigarettes and Tobacco Cigarettes in the Drugstore Channel

Brand	*Retail Price*[a]	*Taxes*[b]	*Retailer Margin*[c]	*Manufacturer Selling Price*
Marlboro	$9.37	$3.51+0.59	$1.41	$4.45
Newport	$9.22	$3.51+0.58	$1.38	$4.33
Camel	$9.32	$3.51+0.58	$1.40	$4.41
Blu eCigs	$7.50	.47	$3.00	$4.50
NJOY	$11.00	.69	$4.40	$6.60

Source: E-Cigarette Forum, "No, one carto is NOT equivalent to a pack of cigarettes," January 29, 2012. http://www.e-cigarette-forum.com/forum/ecf-library/263069-no-one-carto-n-o-t-equivalent-pack-cigarettes.html; Jack Lepiarz, "With Higher Cigarette Taxes, Concerns About Smuggling," *90.9WBUR (NPR Affiliate)*, July 31, 2013. http://www.wbur.org/2013/07/31/cigarette-taxes-smuggling; Massachusetts Department of Revenue, "Cigarette Minimum Price List," October 3, 2013. http://www.mass.gov/dor/docs/dor/cigarette/pdfs/minimum-pricelist.pdf.

[a]Retail prices are for 20-count pack of cigarettes equivalent. Assumes 2.5 cartridges equal one 20-pack of tobacco cigarettes.

[b]The Massachusetts tobacco tax ($3.51 per pack) and sales tax rates (6.25%) are used. Taxes are included in the retail price.

[c]Assumes retail margins on tobacco cigarettes of 15%, and margins on e-cigarettes of 40%.

Costco Wholesale Corp. sold e-cigarettes on its website but pulled them in 2010, because of the uncertainty around potential FDA regulation of the products.[24] In 2013, e-cigarettes were widely available at convenience stores, grocery stores, drug stores, mall kiosks and liquor/specialty stores. In most drug stores, e-cigarettes were stocked alongside tobacco cigarettes behind the checkout counters rather than in the aisles. Shelf space allocated to e-cigarette brands was comparable to that of mid-volume cigarette brands (such as Pall Mall, Camel and Newport), but much smaller than the amount of space allocated to the leading brand, Marlboro. Sales of e-cigarettes online in 2013 were estimated to be $500 to $625 million.[25]

E-CIGARETTES ENTRANTS AND ACQUISITIONS

In 2013, the e-cigarette category included over 200 brands.[26] The e-cigarette industry in the U.S. was initially composed of corporate start-ups, following the introduction of the

[24] Ibid.

[25] Rob Wile, "E-Cigarettes Just Passed the $1 billion Sales Mark," *Business Insider*, August 28, 2013. http:// www.businessinsider.com/e-cigarettes-passes-1-billion-sales-2013-8. Accessed October 2013.

[26] Chris Burritt, "Camel Maker Returns to TV With E-Cig Ad 43 Years Later," *Bloomberg*, August 26, 2013. http://www.bloomberg.com/news/2013-08-26/camel-maker-returns-to-tv-with-e-cig-ad-43-years-later-retail.html. Accessed October 2013.

Table 15.3 Exhibit 4 E-cigarette Flavors from Leading Brands, 2013

Brand	*Flavor*
Blu eCigs	Classic Tobacco
Blu eCigs	Magnificent Menthol
Blu eCigs	Java Jolt
Blu eCigs	Cherry Crush
Blu eCigs	Vivid Vanilla
Blu eCigs	Pina Colada
Blu eCigs	Peach Schnapps
NJOY	Traditional (Tobacco)
NJOY	Menthol
Logic eCigs	Original (Tobacco)

Source: Logic eCig, "Products," http://store.logicecig.com/all-new-400-puff-logic-platinum-extra-high-2-4-nicotine-by-volume/, accessed October 2013. blu Cigs, "Cartridges," http://www.blucigs.com/cartridges, accessed October 2013. NJOY, "Buy Online," http://www.njoy.com/njoy-kings.html, accessed October 2013.

product in the mid-2000s. Later, large tobacco companies began to develop and acquire companies with e-cigarette product portfolios to capitalize on the industry's growth.

E-Cigarette Start-ups

In the U.S., Logic eCig, NJOY and blu (owned by Lorillard) led the category in market shares. Logic eCig was founded in 2010 in New Jersey (see Figure 15.2 for packaging).[27] Total U.S. market share numbers were not available for Logic, but it was known to hold 15% of the value share of e-cigarettes sales in convenience stores, in comparison to blu's 40% share, and NJOY's 28% share.[28]

NJOY was founded in 2006 in Scottsdale, Arizona by Craig Weiss (see Figure 15.3 for packaging). NJOY's mission was " to obsolete cigarettes." Using advertising slogans such as "friends don't let friends smoke" and "cigarettes—you've met your match," NJOY offered its King e-cigarette, a disposable model that retailed for $7.99, and was designed to deliver the same nicotine as a 20-pack of tobacco cigarettes.[29] The NJOY King was

[27] Market Wired, "E-cigarette Reviewed Digs into Claims of 'Industry Best' With New Logic Electronic Cigarette Review," August 8, 2013. http://www.marketwired.com/press-release/ecigarettereviewed-digs-into-claims-industry-best-with-new-logic-electronic-cigarette-1819055.htm. Accessed October 2013.

[28] "Cigarettes in the U.S.," August 2012. Euromonitor International, accessed October 2013.

[29] Matt Richtel, "As market grows, e-cigarette maker battles with Big Tobacco," *International New York Times*, October 28, 2013. Accessed via Factiva, October 2013.

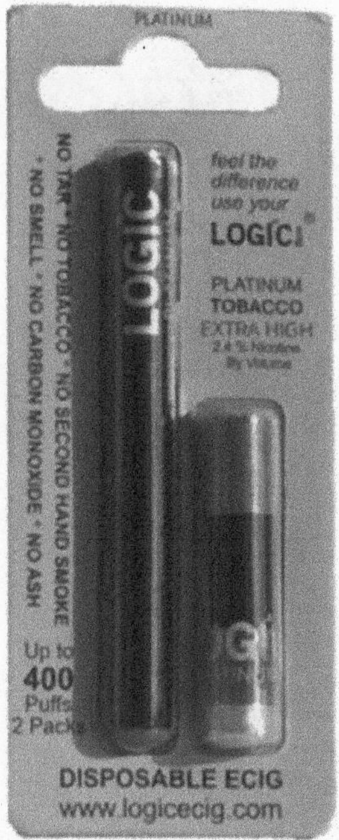

Figure 15.2 Exhibit 5 Logic E-cigarette Packaging, 2013.
Source: Casewriter, February 2014.

intended to mimic as closely as possible the experience of smoking a tobacco cigarette. Roy Anise, NJOY's executive vice president of sales said, "An e-cigarette that doesn't look like a cigarette but looks like a silver tube with a white light at the end, is anything but an exquisite experience."[30] By 2013, the brand was sold in over 60,000 retail outlets in all fifty states and held 32% of the U.S. market.

Blu eCigs, known for its distinctive blue-tipped e-cigarettes, was founded in 2009 by Jason Healy (see Figure 15.4 for packaging).[31] The North Carolina-based brand recorded $30 million in online revenues in 2011.[32] In 2013, blu held roughly 37% of the U.S. market for e-cigarettes[33]. The blu brand ran a television spot with actor Stephen Dorff in 2012, and another with Jenny McCarthy in 2013. Both ads featured the actors "vaping" on the blue-tipped e-cigarettes. The ads presented blu as a "smarter alternative" to tobacco cigarettes

30 Ibid.

31 "blu Cigs Appoints Jim Raporte As New President," *Yahoo! Finance*, May 9, 2013. http://finance.yahoo. com/news/blu-ecigs-appoints-jim-raporte-130000365.html. Accessed October 2013.

32 Austin Carr, "E-Cig Maker Develops Fourquare-Style Check-In for Hookup Hunting Nicotine Addicts," *Fast Company*, April 19, 2011. http://www.fastcompany.com/1748493/e-cig-maker-develops-foursquare-style-check-hookup-hunting-nicotine-addicts. Accessed October 2013.

33 Amy Ho, "Smoker and Mirrors: European Parliament May Clear the Air on E-Cigarettes," *Daily Finance*, October 7, 2013. http://www.dailyfinance.com/2013/10/07/smoke-and-mirrors-european-parliament-may-clear-th/. Accessed October 2013.

Figure 15.3 **Exhibit 6** NJOY E-cigarette Packaging, 2013.
Source: Casewriter, February 2014.

Big Tobacco Makes Its Move

The president and CEO of Lorillard, Murray S. Kessler, estimated that 2 billion tobacco cigarettes would not be smoked in 2013 as a direct result of smokers switching to e-cigarettes.[34] The large tobacco companies weighed the risk of cannibalizing their tobacco cigarette business against the growth potential and comparative profit margin of the emerging e-cigarettes segment. Mr. Kessler acknowledged in 2013 that e-cigarettes were less profitable than tobacco cigarettes, but expressed hope that the margins would grow over time.[35] In 2012, Lorillard acquired blu for $135 million.[36] Mr. Kessler described blu's products as "edgy" and "cool," well-positioned to make blu a "complete replacement" for tobacco cigarettes.[37] Mr. Kessler said, "I don't want to emulate a cigarette. The big idea isn't to try to keep people in cigarettes, but to normalize smoking e-cigarettes and vaping as the next generation."[38] He hoped the blu's unique appearance would help to "solve the social stigma issue" regarding smoking in public places.[39] In a little over a year following its acquisition by Lorillard, blu was

[34] Murray S. Kessler, "E-cigarettes could reduce harm: Opposing view," *USA Today*, September 22, 2013. http://www.usatoday.com/story/opinion/2013/09/22/electronic-cigarettes-blu-ecigs-editorials-debates/2850859/. Accessed October 2013.

[35] Matt Richtel, "As market grows, e-cigarette maker battles."

[36] Mike Esterl, "Lorillard to buy U.K. E-cig maker," *The Wall Street Journal*, October 2, 2013. Accessed via Factiva, October 2013.

[37] Matt Richtel, "As market grows, e-cigarette maker battles."

[38] Ibid.

[39] Ibid.

Figure 15.4 Exhibit 7 blu E-cigarette Packaging, 2013.
Source: Casewriter, February 2014.

distributed in 125,000 stores and its market share in convenience stores increased from 12% to 39%, while NJOY's share dropped from 48% to 30% over the same period.[40] It was estimated that, by the end of 2013, blu would account for 5% of Lorillard's total sales in the U.S.[41] In 2013, Lorillard acquired the British e-cigarette maker, Skycig, for roughly $100 million.[42]

In 2012, British American Tobacco acquired CN Creative, a British start-up devoted to cigarette substitutes, for an undisclosed sum. BAT's chief executive, Nicandro Durante, estimated that tobacco alternatives could account for up to 40% of BAT's revenues by 2020.[43] In 2013, Reynolds American, Inc. (which owned the second largest tobacco company in the U.S.), launched its own e-cigarette product, Vuse, which it claimed delivered a more consistent smoke than existing e-cigarettes.[44] Later that year, the largest cigarette maker in the U.S., Altria, marketed its first e-cigarette brand, MarkTen.[45] Tobacco companies which entered the market for e-cigarettes brought distribution networks honed over decades, large marketing budgets, and

[40] Ibid.

[41] Tyler Durden, "Goldman's Top Disruptive Themes."

[42] Mike Esterl, "Lorillard to buy U.K. E-cig maker."

[43] Christopher Thompson, "BAT acquires ecigarette start-up," *Financial Times*, December 19, 2012. Accessed via Factiva, October 2013.

[44] Michael Felberbaum, "Firms dusts off tobacco marketing playbook."

[45] Ibid.

Table 15.4 Exhibit 8 U.S. Cigarette Company Volume Shares, 2011

Companies	*Volume Share*
Philip Morris USA Inc.	46.2
RJ Reynolds Tobacco Co.	26.8
Lorillard Tobacco Co.	13.1
Liggett Group Inc.	3.7
Commonwealth Brands Inc.	3.7

Source: Adapted from "Cigarettes in the U.S.," August 2012. Euromonitor International, accessed October 2013.

databases filled with customer contact information, all of which placed them at an advantage over the start-ups.[46]

TOBACCO CIGARETTES: A DECLINING MARKET

In 2012, the estimated retail sales of tobacco cigarettes in the U.S. were $80 billion.[47] Sales of tobacco cigarettes had been declining for more than a decade: consumption of smoked tobacco fell 27% between 2000 and 2011 in the U.S.[48] The decline was driven in part by increases in tobacco taxation, which in turn drove up retail prices. Between 2008 and 2011, the unit retail price of cigarettes increased by 31%.[49] In 2009, the U.S. government increased the excise tax per pack of twenty cigarettes from $0.39 to $1.01.[50] Volume sales of cigarettes were expected to decline by 7% over the five year period between 2011 and 2016, due to increasing awareness of the health risks posed by cigarettes and increasing retail prices.[51]

In 2011, the cigarette industry in the U.S. was consolidated, with three firms accounting for 86% of the volume. Philip Morris held 46%, with Reynolds American and Lorillard holding 27% and 13%, respectively. (See Table 15.4 and Table 15.5 for category shares by company and by brand). Lorillard gained 1.6% in volume share in 2011, due to the success of its Newport brand, which increased in volume by 9% that year.[52] Newport, the most successful brand of menthol cigarettes and the second most popular brand overall, benefitted from the increased popularity of menthol among cigarette consumers. Menthol cigarettes accounted for 28% of cigarette category volume in 2011. In 2013, the U.S. Food and Drug Administration (FDA) was considering a

[46] Matt Richtel, "As market grows, e-cigarette maker battles."

[47] Tyler Durden, "Goldman's Top Disruptive Themes."

[48] Alan Rappeport, "E-cigarette makers fear taxes and regulation will vaproise growth," *Financial Times*, January 22, 2013. Accessed via Factiva, October 2013.

[49] "Cigarettes in the U.S.," Euromonitor International.

[50] Ibid.

[51] Ibid.

[52] Ibid.

Table 15.5 Exhibit 9 Cigarette Brand U.S. Volume Shares by Company, 2011

Brand	*Company*	*Volume Share*
Marlboro	Philip Morris USA Inc.	39.5
Newport	Lorillard Tobacco Co.	11.8
Pall Mall	RJ Reynolds Tobacco Co.	7.9
Camel	RJ Reynolds Tobacco Co.	7.9
Doral	RJ Reynolds Tobacco Co.	3.4
Basic	Philip Morris USA Inc.	2.8
Winston	RJ Reynolds Tobacco Co.	2.4
USA Gold	Commonwealth Brands Inc.	2.2
Pyramid	Liggett Group Inc.	2.0
Kool	RJ Reynolds Tobacco Co.	2.0

Source: Adapted from "Cigarettes in the U.S.," August 2012. Euromonitor International, accessed October 2013.

ban on menthol cigarettes,[53] as it had banned all other flavored cigarettes (including fruit and clove flavors) under the Tobacco Control Act in 2009.[54] Flavored cigars or cigarillos, "little cigars," were exempt from the ban. In 2013, 5% of high school students and 1% of middle school students had tried flavored cigarillos (which included fruit and candy flavored products).[55] Of those students who smoked tobacco, 36% smoked flavored cigarillos. Intention to quit smoking was lower among teens who smoked flavored cigarillos (60% said they had no intention of quitting, versus 49% among those who smoked unflavored cigarillos).[56]

The marketing of tobacco cigarettes was limited by the federal prohibitions on certain types of advertising, including television advertising and advertising targeting young people. Cigarette makers had to incorporate age verification into their websites and in their mail offers (occasionally, a cigarette package pin was also required to verify that the recipient was already a smoker). Due to advertising restrictions, tobacco firms relied on point-of-sale promotions, in-store signage and share of shelf space to drive volume. Tobacco cigarettes could be purchased in grocery stores, tobacco specialty stores, convenience stores and forecourt retailers.[57] (See Table 15.6 for volume distribution by channel.) Online sales of cigarettes to U.S. consumers were effectively banned, as delivery services like FedEx and UPS voluntarily prohibited the delivery

[53] Toni Clarke, Tom Miles, "FDA considers tightening rules on menthol cigarettes," *Reuters*, July 23, 2013. http://www.reuters.com/article/2013/07/23/us-tobacco-fda-idUSBRE96M0T320130723. Accessed October 2013.

[54] U.S. Food and Drug Administration, "Youth & Tobacco," http://www.fda.gov/TobaccoProducts/ProtectingKidsfromTobacco/default.htm. Accessed October 2013.

[55] Deborah Kotz, "More teens trying flavored cigars, study finds," *The Boston Globe*, October 23, 2013. Accessed via Factiva, October 2013.

[56] Ibid.

[57] Forecourts were small retail formats attached to gas stations and supermarkets.

Table 15.6 Exhibit 10 Volume Sales of Cigarettes by Distribution Channel, 2011

Distribution Format	*Volume Share*
Grocery Retailers	10.8
Convenience Stores	15.8
Forecourt Retailers	47.5
Tobacco Specialty Stores	21.0
Pharmacies & Drug Stores	3.7
Vending & Internet	0.2
Bars, Restaurants, Hotels	0.8

Source: Adapted from "Cigarettes in the U.S.," August 2012. Euromonitor International, accessed October 2013.

of tobacco products, and the U.S. Postal Service was banned from delivering tobacco products under the Family Smoking Prevention and Tobacco Control Act in 2009.

PUBLIC HEALTH RISKS OF CIGARETTES

A 2010 study published by the Independent Scientific Committee on Drugs found tobacco caused more harm than amphetamines or cannabis. (See Figure 15.5 for most harmful drugs.) Between 2000 and 2004, cigarette smoking in the U.S. cost more than $193 billion ($97 billion in productivity loss and $96 billion in health care expenditures).[58] Tobacco cigarettes contained over 7,000 chemicals,[59] of which hundreds were toxic and roughly 70 caused cancer.[60] Traditional cigarette smoking contributed to the incidence of heart disease, cancer, stroke and lung diseases.[61] (See Figure 15.6 for health benefits of smoking cessation.) In 2013, over 40 million people in the U.S. were tobacco smokers.[62]

[58] Centers for Disease Control and Prevention, "Smoking and Tobacco Use; Fact Sheet; Fast Facts." http://www.cdc.gov/tobacco/data_statistics/fact_sheets/fast_facts/. Accessed October 2013.

[59] National Toxicology Program, "Report on Carcinogens, Twelfth Edition," *Research Triangle Park (NC): U.S. Department of Health and Human Sciences, National Institute of Environmental Health Sciences, National Toxicology Program,* 2011. http://ntp.niehs.nih.gov/?objectid=03C9AF75-E1BF-FF40-DBA9EC0928DF8B15. Accessed October 2013.

[60] U.S. Department of Health and Human Services, "How Tobacco Smoke Causes Disease: The Biology and Behavioral Basis for Smoking-Attributable Disease," *Atlanta: U.S. Department of Health and Human Services, Centers for Disease Control and Prevention, National Center for Chronic Disease Prevention and Health Promotion, Office on Smoking and Health,* 2010. http://www.cdc.gov/tobacco/data_statistics/sgr/2010/index.htm. Accessed October 2013.

[61] Centers for Disease Control and Prevention, "Smoking and Tobacco Use; Fact Sheet; Fast Facts." http://www.cdc.gov/tobacco/data_statistics/fact_sheets/fast_facts/. Accessed October 2013.

[62] Centers for Disease Control and Prevention, "Current Cigarette Smoking Among Adults—United States, 2011-2012," *Morbidity and Mortality Weekly Report* 2012; 61(44):889–8940. http://www.cdc.gov/mmwr /preview/mmwrhtml/mm6144a2.htm?s_cid=mm6144a2_e. Accessed October 2013.

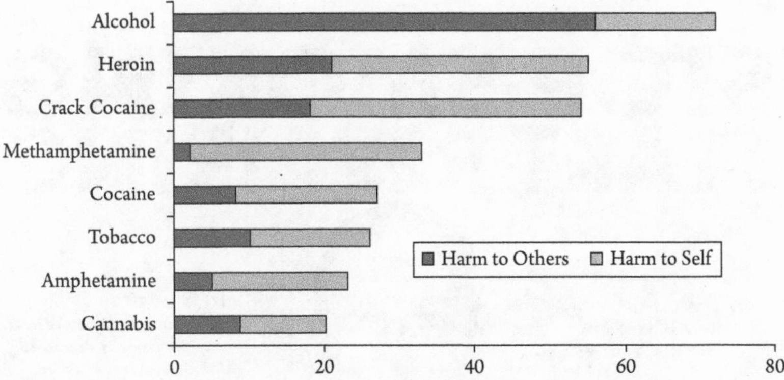

Figure 15.5 Exhibit 11 Harm to Self and to Others Caused by Drugs (maximum = 100), 2010. *Source:* Adapted from "Scoring drugs," The Economist (online), November 2, 2010. http://www.economist.com/blogs/ dailychart/2010/11/drugs_cause_most_harm, accessed October 2013.

More than 400,000 died in the U.S. each year from tobacco use (nearly 50,000 of whom died from exposure to secondhand smoke).[63] For every person who died, it was estimated that 20 more suffered from at least one serious illness.[64] (See Table 15.7 for estimated public health impact of e-cigarettes and tobacco cigarettes.)

Youth smoking rates declined from highs in the mid-1990s to a rate of roughly 10% of teens smoking regularly in 2010 (see Figure 15.7).[65] In a 2011 study, the CDC found that 18.1% of high school students, and 4.3% of middle school students, had tried a cigarette in the prior month.[66] Young people were particularly at-risk as they had greater sensitivity to nicotine and could develop dependencies more easily than adults.[67] Nearly nine out of ten adult smokers had begun smoking by age 18.[68] The CDC identified advertising, peer group pressure and easy access as important in promoting youth tobacco use.[69]

[63] U.S. Department of Health and Human Services, "How Tobacco Smoke Causes Disease."

[64] Centers for Disease Control and Prevention, "Cigarette Smoking-Attributable Morbidity—United States, 2000," *Morbidity and Mortality Weekly Report 2003*;52(35):842–4. http://www.cdc.gov/mmwr/preview/ mmwrhtml/mm5235a4.htm. Accessed October 2013.

[65] U.S. Department of Health and Human Services, "Trends in Adolescent Tobacco Use." http://www.hhs. gov/ash/oah/adolescent-health-topics/substance-abuse/tobacco/trends.html. Accessed October 2013.

[66] Centers for Disease Control and Prevention. "Youth and Tobacco Use." http://www.cdc.gov/tobacco/ data_statistics/fact_sheets/youth_data/tobacco_use/index.htm. Accessed October 2013.

[67] Ibid.

[68] American Cancer Society, "Child and Teen Tobacco Use," http://www.cancer.org/cancer/ cancercauses/tobaccocancer/childandteentobaccouse/child-and-teen-tobacco-use-child-and-teen-tobacco-use. Accessed October 2013.

[69] Centers for Disease Control and Prevention. "Youth and Tobacco Use." http://www.cdc.gov/tobacco/ data_statistics/fact_sheets/youth_data/tobacco_use/index.htm. Accessed October 2013.

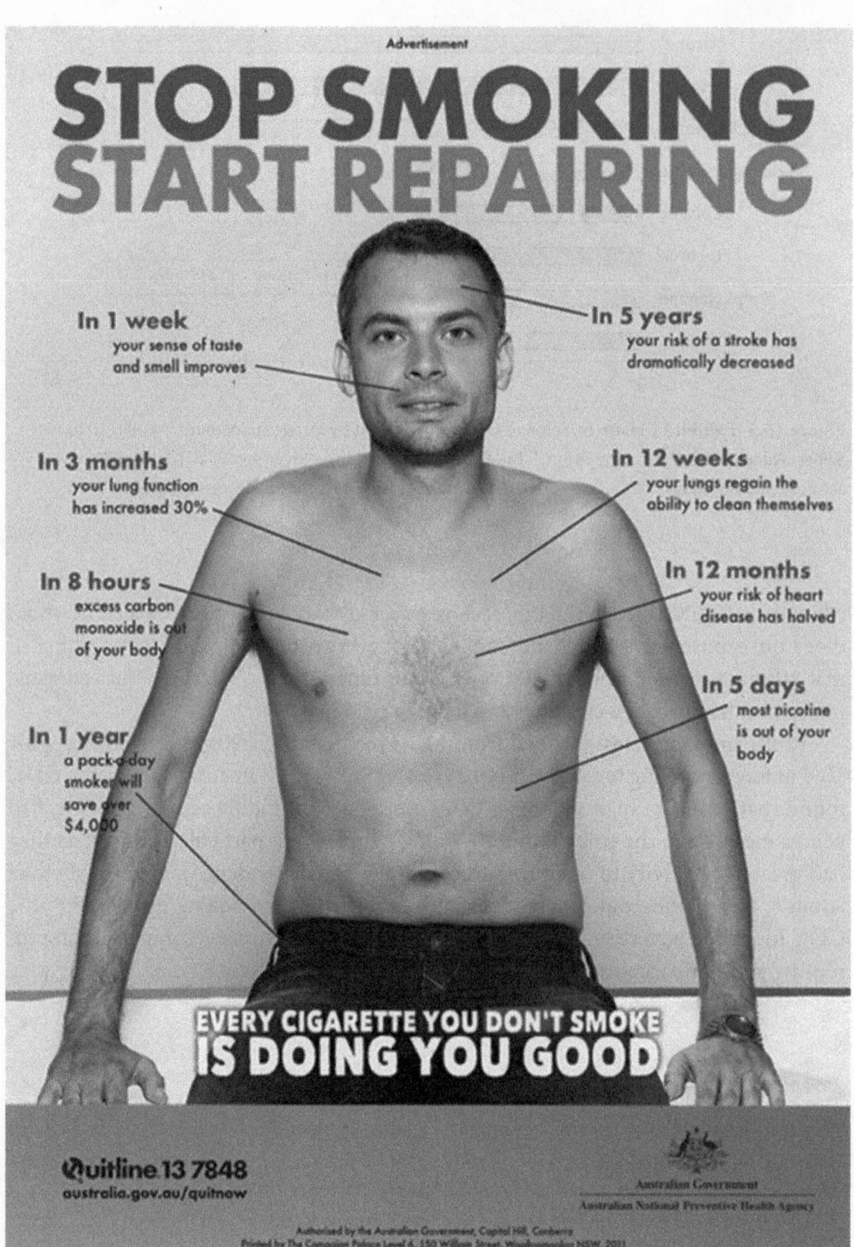

Figure 15.6 Exhibit 12 Health Benefits of Smoking Cessation, 2013.

Source: Australian Government "Benefits of Quitting," http://www.quitnow.gov.au/internet/quitnow/publishing.nsf/ Content/0F70F614594EC954CA257A0D001F11F9/$File/printm3.pdf. Accessed October 2013.

Table 15.7 Exhibit 13 Expected Public Health Impact of E-cigarettes in the U.S., 2013

	Tobacco Smokers	*E-cigarette Smokers*	*Non-smokers*
Population	43.8 million	16.2 million	196 million
Health Care Costs due to Smoking, per year[a]	$48.3 billion	Unknown	0
Cost per Capita	$1,102	Unknown	0
Annual Deaths due to Smoking in the U.S.	390,600	Unknown	49,400
Deaths per Capita	1 per 112 smokers	Unknown	1 per 886 smokers
Estimated Net Population Change	(2.2 million)	+4.9 million	(2.7 million)[b]
Estimated Annual Health Care Savings	$2.4 billion	N/A	N/A
Estimated Lives Saved Annually	19,600	N/A	2,500

Source: Casewriter estimates based on information in the case, U.S. Census Bureau, 2011 Population Clock (link), Centers for Disease Control and Prevention, "Notes from the Field: Electronic Cigarette Use Among Middle and High School Students -- United States, 2011-2012," Morbidity and Mortality Weekly Report 2013; 62(35):729–730. http://www.cdc.gov/mmwr/ preview/mmwrhtml/ mm6235a6.htm?s_cid=mm6235a6_w. Accessed October 2013. "About one in five U.S. adult cigarette smokers have tried an electronic cigarette," Centers for Disease Control and Prevention, February 28, 2013. http://www.cdc.gov/media/releases/2013/p0228_electronic_cigarettes.html. Accessed October 2013.

[a]Total health care costs attributable to smoking amounted to over $193 billion between 2000 and 2004. Cost per year was estimated by dividing the total sum by four to reach $48.3 billion.

[b]Casewriter estimates likely too low as current figure does not account for those who switch from tobacco cigarettes to e-cigarette to no smoking at all.

To be read as, e-cigarettes were estimated to result in over two billion dollars in annual health care savings, due to a reduced population of smokers. E-cigarettes were estimated to save over 22,000 lives per year (including smokers and non-smokers). (All savings are calculated from tobacco smokers switching to e-cigarettes. Currently, unique health risks or benefits attributable to e-cigarettes are unknown).

REGULATION OF TOBACCO CIGARETTES

In 2012, Australia enacted regulation that stripped cigarette packaging of logos and color and replaced them with images of diseased body parts and ill children, all caused by smoking cigarettes.[70] Different brands were distinguished by name only, printed in identical font on all packages. The goal of the regulation was to prevent young people from smoking; studies showing that people who had not begun smoking by age 26

[70] "Cigarette plain packaging laws come into force in Australia," *theguardian.com*, December 1, 2012, www. theguardian.com/world/2012/dec/01/plain-packaging-australian-cigarette-tobacco/print. Accessed September 2013.

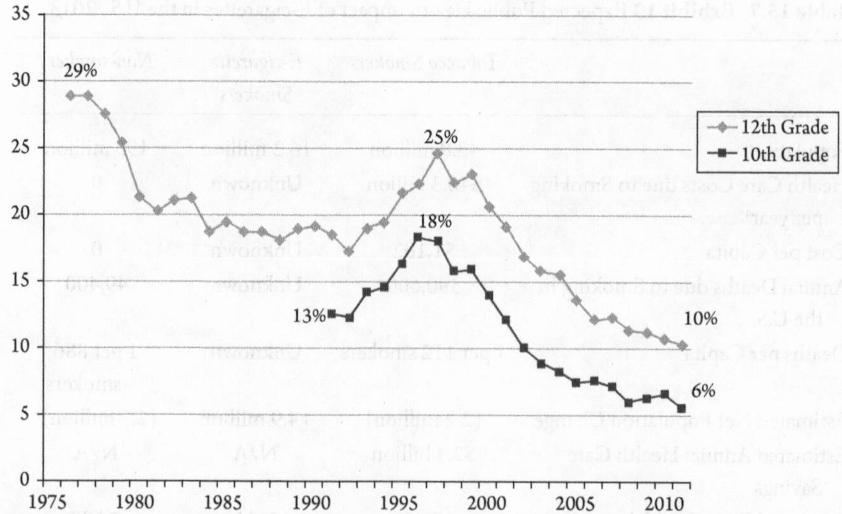

Figure 15.7 Exhibit 14 Prevalence of Daily Cigarette Use Among Youths in 10th Grade and 12th Grade, 1975-2011.

Source: U.S. Department of Health and Human Services, "Trends in Adolescent Tobacco Use." http://www.hhs.gov/ ash/oah/adolescent-health-topics/substance-abuse/tobacco/trends.html. Accessed October 2013.

were likely to never begin were used to support the regulation.[71] In 2001, Canada had become the first country to place photographic warnings on cigarette packaging.[72] By 2012, more than forty countries had adopted similar rules for cigarette packaging.[73]

U.S. Regulation

In 1965, the U.S. government crafted the Federal Cigarette Labeling and Advertising Act, which required cigarette packages to include health warnings, and called for annual reports on the tobacco industry's advertising and labeling practices.[74] In 1970, the Public Health Cigarette Smoking Act prohibited the advertising of cigarettes on television and radio, and in 1986, smokeless tobacco products (including chewing tobacco and snus[75]) were also banned from advertising on television and radio. The 1992 Synar amendment to the Alcohol, Drug Abuse and Mental Health Administration Reorganization Act banned the sale of tobacco products to minors

[71] Ibid.

[72] Ibid.

[73] Ibid..

[74] BeTobaccoFree.Gov, "Laws/Policies," http://betobaccofree.hhs.gov/laws/index.html. Accessed October 2013.

[75] Snus was a moist variant of snuff. In a similar manner as American dipping tobacco or chewing tobacco, snus was consumed by placing the product into the mouth (but unlike dipping tobacco, snus did not require spitting).

in an effort to reduce the availability of tobacco products to young people under age eighteen.[76]

In 1998, the attorneys general of 46 U.S. states and the District of Columbia crafted the Master Settlement Agreement (MSA) with the four largest U.S. tobacco companies (and by 2013, forty additional tobacco companies had signed the agreement).[77] The MSA included provisions which barred tobacco companies from advertising to minors (particularly, the use of cartoons in cigarette advertising). The MSA also limited the amount of outdoor and public transit advertising available to tobacco companies.

The 2009 Family Smoking Prevention and Tobacco Control Act included restrictions on advertising, including: limiting the design of cigarette packaging and advertisements, prohibiting event sponsorships and banning use of cigarette brands on non-tobacco items.[78] The Act also required tobacco companies to submit reports to the FDA on the behavioral, psychological and toxicological effects of tobacco products, banned the sale of flavored cigarettes (excluding menthol), and required tobacco companies to obtain an order or exemption from the FDA before introducing new products. In 2010, the Prevent All Cigarette Trafficking Act prohibited the mailings of tobacco products through the U.S. Postal Service and required online cigarette retailers to include age verification requirements.[79]

In 2011, the U.S. FDA attempted to require cigarette makers to include new warning labels on cigarette packaging and advertisements under new rules included in the Family Smoking Prevention and Tobacco Control Act.[80] The new labels would include color graphics illustrating the negative health outcomes associated with smoking. In 2012, the rule was challenged by several cigarette companies based on First Amendment claims of free speech and overturned by the U.S. Court of Appeals for the District of Columbia.[81] The government's petition for a rehearing of the rule was denied.

SMOKING CESSATION AIDS

Nicotine was a psychoactive drug found in tobacco products. Dependence on nicotine was the most common form of chemical dependence in the U.S. in 2010.[82] Research suggested that nicotine was as addictive as heroin, cocaine or alcohol.[83] The CDC

[76] Ibid.

[77] Ibid.

[78] Ibid.

[79] Ibid.

[80] U.S. Food and Drug Administration, "Cigarette Health Warnings," http://www.fda.gov/TobaccoProducts/Labeling/Labeling/CigaretteWarningLabels/default.htm. Accessed October 2013.

[81] Ibid.

[82] American Society of Addiction Medicine, "Public Policy Statement on Nicotine Dependence and Tobacco,"*Chevy Chase (MD): American Society of Addiction Medicine*, 2010. http://www.asam.org/advocacy/find-a-policy-statement/view-policy-statement/public-policy-statements/2011/12/15/nicotine-addiction-and-tobacco. Accessed October 2013.

[83] National Institute on Drug Abuse, "Research Report Series: Tobacco Addiction," *Bethesda (MD): National Institutes of Health, National Institute on Drug Abuse*, 2009. http://www.drugabuse.gov/publications/research-reports/tobacco-addiction Accessed October 2013.

conducted a study in 2010 which found that 52.4% of U.S. smokers had attempted to quit at least once in the prior year, but only 6.2% of smokers had done so.[84] Of those who attempted to quit, 30% used medication and 6% used counseling.[85]

Smokers who wanted to quit had a variety of counseling and medicinal options available. Those who sought counseling could choose to obtain a clinical intervention from a doctor, group counseling, online or telephone hotline resources or behavioral cessation therapies. A variety of smoking cessation medicinal aids was available, including over-the-counter products (e.g. nicotine gum, patches or lozenges) and prescriptions (e.g. nicotine nasal sprays or inhalers).[86] The size of the market for over-the-counter smoking cessation products in the U.S. was $528 million in 2012.[87] Smokers who used both counseling and medications had higher rates of cessation than those who used only one approach.[88] Pharmaceutical companies typically made and marketed the chemical smoking cessation aids such as nicotine patches.[89] The pharmaceutical companies viewed e-cigarettes as competition to their smoking cessation products. Unlike the smoking cessation products manufactured by pharmaceutical companies, e-cigarettes did not need to meet pharmaceutical safety standards or secure prior approval from the FDA.[90]

The Efficacy of E-cigarettes as Smoking Cessation Aids

Research conducted by the University of Catania in Italy found that e-cigarettes were helpful cessation aids for some smokers. Between 2010 and 2012, researchers tracked 300 smokers who were given e-cigarettes to help them quit.[91] On average, 8.7% of study participants were no longer smoking traditional cigarettes after one year (the quit rates varied depending on the differing levels of nicotine in the e-cigarettes given to participants). Of those who gave up tobacco cigarettes, 73.1% had also ceased use of e-cigarettes after one year.[92] The participants in the study who were given e-cigarettes that contained no nicotine had a quit rate of 4%.[93] Another study conducted by researchers at the University of Auckland found e-cigarettes to be more effective than patches in helping smokers to quit. The study found that 7.3% of smokers who switched to e-cigarettes had quit smoking

[84] Mike Esterl, "E-Cigarettes Found to Provide Some Benefit," *The Wall Street Journal*. June 25, 2013.

[85] Ibid.

[86] Centers for Disease Control and Prevention, "Quitting Smoking Among Adults—United States, 2001–2010," *Morbidity and Mortality Weekly Report* 2011;60(44):1513–19 http://www.cdc.gov/tobacco/data_statistics/ mmwrs/byyear/2011/mm6044a2/intro.htm Accessed October 2013.

[87] "Nicotine Replacement Product Manufacturing OTC,"U.S., December 2012.IBIS World, accessed October 2013.

[88] Fiore MC, Jaén CR, Baker TB, Bailey WC, Benowitz NL, Curry SJ, Dorfman SF, Froelicher ES, Goldstein MG, Froelicher ES, Healton CG, et al.,"Treating Tobacco Use and Dependence: 2008 Update—Clinical Practice Guidelines," *Rockville (MD): U.S. Department of Health and Human Services, Public Health Service, Agency for Healthcare Research and Quality*, 2008. http://www.ncbi.nlm.nih.gov/books/NBK63952/. Accessed October 2013.

[89] "Sending the Wrong Smoke-signal." *The Economist*.

[90] "E-cigarettes: Kodak Moment," *The Economist*.

[91] Mike Esterl, "E-Cigarettes Found to Provide Some Benefit," *The Wall Street Journal*. June 25, 2013.

[92] Ibid.

[93] Ibid.

traditional cigarettes after six months.[94] By comparison, only 5.8% of those smokers who were given nicotine patches were able to quit smoking.

REGULATION OF E-CIGARETTES

In 2010, the FDA sent warning letters to five e-cigarette makers to stop claiming unproven health benefits and improve their poor manufacturing practices.[95] Product claims regarding the treatment of diseases, such as nicotine addiction, were prohibited under the Food, Drug and Cosmetics Act, unless the safety and effectiveness of the product had been proven.[96] In a concurrent letter to the Electronic Cigarette Association, the FDA stipulated that the letters did not reflect an effort to ban all e-cigarettes and encouraged the trade group to promote clinical trials for e-cigarette products in order to verify the products' effectiveness as smoking cessation aids.[97] E-cigarette manufacturers contended that e-cigarettes fell under tobacco laws (as a nicotine product), rather than drug laws, and that the FDA lacked the authority to regulate e-cigarettes.[98] In 2010, the Federal Court in Washington, D.C., ruled that e-cigarettes would be regulated as tobacco products.[99] In January 2011, the FDA appealed the ruling, but its appeal was rejected.[100] The previous year, the FDA had banned imports of e-cigarettes to the U.S., claiming that the products were drug delivery devices.[101]

State and Local Legislation

Although U.S. federal laws prohibited the sale of traditional tobacco products to children under eighteen, no such provision existed for e-cigarettes.[102] In 2011, the City of Boston passed legislation prohibiting the sale of e-cigarettes to minors and banning their use in the workplace.[103] However, as of 2013, the state of Massachusetts did not regulate the sale of e-cigarettes.[104] More than two dozen U.S. states had

[94] Christopher Bullen, Colin Howe, Murray Laugesen, Hayden McRobbie, Varsha Parag, Jonathon Williman, Natalie Walker, "Electronic cigarettes for smoking cessation: a randomized controlled trial," *The Lancet (Early Online Publication)*, September 9, 2013. http://www.thelancet.com/journals/lancet/article/PIIS0140-6736(13)61842-5/abstract. Accessed October 2013.

[95] Michael Felberbaum, "FDA warns 5 electronic cigarette companies about making health claims," *Associated Press*, September 9, 2010. Accessed via Factiva, October 2013.

[96] Claudia W. Esbenshade, "Electronic cigarettes ignite debate," *Associated Press*, March 26, 2011, Accessed via Factiva, October 2013.

[97] Michael Felberbaum, "FDA warns 5 electronic cigarette companies."

[98] Claudia W. Esbenshade, "Electronic cigarettes ignite debate."

[99] Ibid.

[100] Claudia W. Esbenshade, "Electronic cigarettes ignite debate."

[101] Michael Felberbaum, "FDA warns 5 electronic cigarette companies."

[102] Mike Esterl. "E-Cigarette Use Rises Sharply" *Wall Street Journal*, September 6, 2013. *Wall Street Journal*. A5.

[103] "E-cigarettes May Have a Place — Just Not with Minors," *The Boston Globe*, July 11, 2013. http://www.bostonglobe.com/opinion/editorials/2013/07/11/cigarettes-may-have-place-just-not-with-minors /aIJcHjP5LJZL6k7cLjQ8OK/story.html. Accessed October 2013.

[104] Ibid.

enacted legislation to ban the sale of e-cigarettes to minors.[105] As of 2013, Minnesota was the only state to enact a tax on e-cigarettes similar to the existing tax on tobacco cigarettes.[106]

International Legislation Governing E-Cigarettes

On October 8, 2013, the European parliament voted on a new tobacco-control initiative to prevent children from starting to smoke and reduce the consumption of those who already smoked.[107] The regulation required cigarette and e-cigarette packages to include larger warning labels on the packaging, banned flavored products and prohibited e-cigarettes from advertising on television. The marketing of e-cigarettes under the brand names of tobacco cigarette products was also outlawed.[108] The outcome of the vote was viewed as a victory by the e-cigarette industry because a prior version of the proposal would have treated e-cigarettes as medicinal products. If e-cigarettes were considered medicinal, the products would have been subject to higher standards of consumer safety prior to product launch.[109] Such legislation would likely have resulted in increased prices and a narrower selection of e-cigarette products in Europe. As of 2013, sales of e-cigarettes were banned entirely in Germany, Australia,[110] New Zealand, Brazil and Canada.[111]

Regulating the Advertising of E-Cigarettes

In 2013, the FDA did not consider e-cigarettes to be tobacco products, so e-cigarettes were not subject to the federal ban on TV advertising. Total advertising for e-cigarettes in the U.S. exceeded $20 million in 2012, up from $7.2 million in 2011 and $2.7 million in 2010.[112] Lorillard, the parent company of blu, planned to spend $40 million marketing the brand in 2013, which was equivalent to 35% of blu's sales in the first half of the year.[113] Skeptics were concerned that the unlimited advertising of e-cigarettes could undo decades of work to discourage smoking behaviors.[114]

In September 2013, attorneys general from forty U.S. states petitioned the FDA to regulate the ingredients, sale and advertising of e-cigarettes to minors.[115] In their letter,

105 Mike Esterl. "E-Cigarette Use Rises Sharply."

106 Alan Rappeport, "E-cigarette makers fear taxes and regulation."

107 Gabriele Steinhauser, "EU Votes for Tougher Cigarette Regulations," *The Wall Street Journal*, October 9, 2013. Accessed via Factiva, October 2013.

108 Ibid.

109 "Sending the Wrong Smoke-signal." *The Economist*.

110 Andrew Jack, "Advert for electronic cigarette breaks the mould," *Financial Times*, January 19, 2013. Accessed via Factiva, October 2013.

111 Mark Wembridge, Christopher Thompson, "Big Tobacco works on its e-cigarette habit," *Financial Times*, August 13, 2012. Accessed via Factiva, October 2013.

112 Ibid.

113 Matt Richtel, "As market grows, e-cigarette maker battles."

114 Ibid.

115 Mike Esterl, "States urge e-cigarette rules," *The Wall Street Journal*, September 25, 2013. Accessed via Factiva, October 2013.

the attorneys general referenced the targeting of children by e-cigarette companies through the use of cartoon characters in advertising and candy-flavored products.[116] In October 2013, 41 attorneys general sent the FDA another letter which reiterated the petition to halt the advertising of e-cigarettes to minors.[117] The FDA intended to propose regulations for the e-cigarette industry by the end of October.[118]

[116] "North Carolina AG Cooper signed letter with colleagues asking for e-cigarette regulations," *Associated Press*, September 25, 2013. Accessed via Factiva, October 2013.

[117] Matt Richtel, "As market grows, e-cigarette maker battles."

[118] Mike Esterl, "States urge e-cigarette rules."

PART VII

Consumer Power in Shaping Public Health

16A

RANA PLAZA
WORKPLACE SAFETY IN BANGLADESH (A)

John A. Quelch and Margaret L. Rodriguez

On April 24, 2013, the Rana Plaza factory building collapsed in the Savar industrial district outside of Dhaka, the capital of Bangladesh. Over 1,100 people were killed in the worst industrial accident[1] since 1984 when over 2,000 people were killed (and 150,000 injured) in the Union Carbide plant gas leak in Bhopal, India.[2] Most of the victims worked for the five garment factories housed in Rana Plaza, whose primary clients were European, U.S., and Canadian firms. Export contracts to such firms had helped Bangladesh become the world's second-largest clothing exporter.[3] Rana Plaza was not the first tragedy to occur in Bangladesh's garment industry, and without intervention, more might follow. After the Rana Plaza disaster, international brand owners, domestic and foreign governments, labor unions, and non-governmental organizations (NGOs) began to discuss responsibilities for improving conditions for Bangladeshi garment workers.

THE BANGLADESH GARMENT INDUSTRY

Following independence from Pakistan in 1971, the Bangladesh government began privatizing industries to spur economic growth. The garment industry became a major force in Bangladesh after the Multi-Fiber Arrangement (MFA) was enacted in 1974. The MFA regulated the sale of garments and textiles from developing countries to First World countries. The MFA, which was in effect until 2004, imposed quotas on garment exports from Korea, China, Hong Kong, and India.[4] No quotas were

[1] "Disaster at Rana Plaza," *The Economist*, May 4, 2013, http://www.economist.com/news/leaders/21577067-gruesome-accident-should-make-all-bosses-think-harder-about-what-behaving-responsibly, accessed August 21, 2013.

[2] "Few Lasting Health Effects Found among India Gas-Leak Survivors," *New York Times*, December 20, 1984, via Factiva, accessed August 2013.

[3] Victor Mallet, "Bangladesh garment makers chase growth despite factory disasters," *Financial Times*, July 29, 2013, http://www.ft.com/intl/cms/s/0/24a9552c-f7ed-11e2-87ec-00144feabdc0.html#axzz2cdA6Ou30, accessed August 20, 2013.

[4] Bjorn Claeson, *Deadly Secrets* (Washington, DC: International Labor Rights Forum, 2012), p. 12.

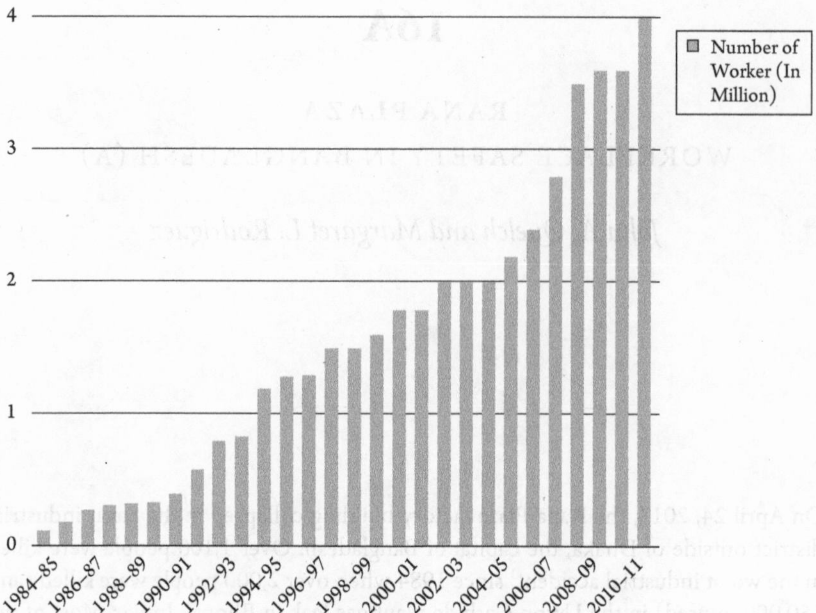

Figure 16A.1 Exhibit 1 Bangladesh Garment Industry Employment.
Source: BGMEA Statistics.

imposed on Bangladesh's garment exports, and its industry grew from $12,000 worth of exports in 1978 to over $21 billion in 2012. Even after the MFA expired, Bangladesh maintained export volume, thanks to its low labor costs. In 2012, Bangladesh was the second-largest garment exporter in the world, after China.[5]

The garment industry was a major force in the Bangladesh economy. The industry employed 3.6 million people (and an additional 6 million, through indirect employment) or roughly 2% of the population.[6] The garment industry accounted for 13% of GDP.[7] It was the single-largest source of exports, 78% in 2011.[8] (See Figure 16A.1 for growth in garment industry employment over time.) Workers in garment factories were paid approximately 13% more than workers in other industries.[9] The vast majority of garment workers were women. In 2011, around 12% of Bangladeshi women between 15 and 30 years of age were employed in the garment industry.[10]

[5] Ibrahim Hossain Ovi, "RMG export defiant against all odds," *Dhaka Tribune*, July 12, 2013, http://www. dhakatribune.com/commerce/2013/jul/12/rmg-export-defiant-against-all-odds, accessed August 20, 2013.

[6] Claeson, *Deadly Secrets*, pp. 12–13.

[7] Ibid., p. 13.

[8] Ibid., p. 13.

[9] Mehul Srivastava and Arun Devnath, "Bangladesh's Paradox for Poor Women Workers," *Bloomberg Businessweek*, May 9, 2013, http://www.businessweek.com/articles/2013-05-09/bangladeshs-paradox-for-poor-women-workers, accessed August 20, 2013.

[10] Ibid.

Table 16A.1 Exhibit 2 Destinations of Bangladesh Garment Exports, 2012

Destination	*Percent of Exports*
Europe	47%
United States	35%
Canada	5%
Other	13%

Source: BGMEA, via EPB, compiled by RDTI Cell, BGMEA.

Global Customers

The vast majority of garments produced in Bangladesh were exported. In 2013, 2,000 of 5,000 garment factories had export contracts, with many of the remaining 3,000 factories working as subcontractors that provided additional capacity for the factories with international orders.[11] Some multinational brands imposed strict limitations on the use of subcontractors in their contracts with primary suppliers (in certain cases, processes existed for MNCs to grant permission for use of subcontractors). It was also common for brands to employ agents to locate production capacity on their behalf. Nearly 90% of garments produced in Bangladesh were exported to the United States, Europe, and Canada (see Table 16A.1 for proportionate export volume). In 2012, the U.S. alone received $4.9 billion worth of garment exports from Bangladesh.

Many U.S. and European fashion brands sourced items from Bangladesh. Brands with operations in Bangladesh included well-known global fast-fashion labels such as H&M, Inditex (Zara), and Loblaw's (Joe Fresh), as well as other low- to mid-priced labels like Walmart, Gap, and PVH (Calvin Klein, Tommy Hilfiger, Timberland). Many brands required garment production to align with the seasonal release of new clothing collections (in spring, summer, fall, and winter). These production schedules caused large spikes in demand for capacity, with little room for errors, around the seasonal release dates and lower demand at other times.

Low-cost production and large capacity were key incentives for multinational corporations (MNCs) to produce garments in Bangladesh. The minimum wage in 2012 was $37 per month and had only increased by $29 over the past 30 years.[12] In comparison, China, the largest clothing exporter, had a minimum wage four times that of Bangladesh and saw its labor costs increase by 30% in 2011 alone.[13] As shown in Figure 16A.2, Bangladesh's minimum and average wages were far lower than those of other developing countries that produced garments for export.

[11] Tripti Lahiri and Christina Passariello, "Why Retailer Don't Know Who Sews Their Clothing," *Wall Street Journal*, July 24, 2013, http://online.wsj.com/article/SB10001424127887324436104578579552855683948.html, accessed August 20, 2013.

[12] Claeson, *Deadly Secrets*, p. 29.

[13] Ibid., p. 13.

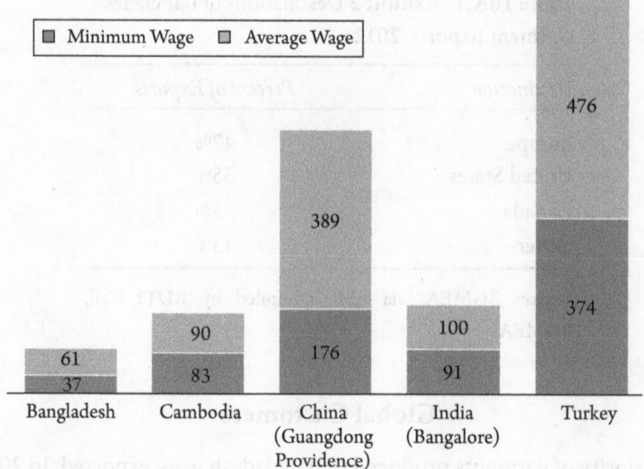

Figure 16A.2 Exhibit 3 Garment Industry Monthly and Minimum Wages by Country.
Source: Adapted from H&M, "Conscious Action Sustainability Report 2012," p. 49, http://about.hm.com/ content/dam/hm/about/documents/en/CSR/reports/Conscious%20Actions%20 Sustainability%20Report%202012_en.pdf, accessed August 2013.

Combined labor cost differentials were expected to help Bangladesh's garment industry to reach $30 billion by 2015.[14]

Factory Conditions

More than 1,000 garment workers were thought to have died and 3,000 to have been injured working in Bangladesh's garment industry since 1990.[15] (See Table 16A.2 for a list of industrial buildings that had collapsed in Bangladesh.) The quick growth of the garment industry had resulted in fast construction of factories, often at the expense of adhering to building codes. The government feared foreign investment and export contracts would flow to other low-cost garment-producing countries if MNCs perceived Bangladesh's factory safety record and labor disputes as risks to their brands. In 2012, the U.S. ambassador to Bangladesh shared with the Bangladesh Garment Manufacturers and Exporters Association (BGMEA) details of a call he received from the U.S. CEO of one of Bangladesh's largest garment export customers. The CEO stated his concern that "the tarnishing of the Bangladesh brand may be putting our company's reputation at risk."[16]

The BGMEA claimed to regularly monitor member factories for safety compliance. However, it was unclear the extent to which compliance was enforced. Following the Tazreen garment factory fire caused by unsafe storage of flammable materials in November 2012, which killed over 100 workers, BGMEA inspectors were sent to member factories

[14] Ibid., p. 13.

[15] Ibid., p. 19.

[16] "Mozena fears 'perfect storm' in garment sector," *Daily Star*, June 7, 2012, http://archive.thedailystar.net/newDesign/news-details.php?nid=237309, accessed August 21, 2013.

Table 16A.2 Exhibit 4 Timeline of Bangladesh Building Collapses

Year	*Building That Collapsed*	*People Killed*
2004	Shankhari Bazar in Old Dhaka	11
2005	Spectrum Sweater Factory	64
2006	Phoenix Garments	21
2010	Begun Bari	23

Source: "Looking beyond Rana Plaza," *Dhaka Tribune*, July 29, 2013, http://www.dhakatribune.com/safety/2013/jul/29/looking-beyond-rana-plaza, accessed August 2013.

to check labor and safety compliance. Four of the buildings inspected, which belonged to BGMEA president Atiqul Islam, were found to have multiple violations.[17]

Numerous NGOs sought to improve labor and safety conditions for Bangladesh's garment workers. Care Bangladesh partnered with MNCs to create programs to help female garment workers develop leadership skills. The Global Women's Economic Empowerment Initiative, a partnership between Care Bangladesh and Walmart, helped nearly 24,000 female garment workers learn their legal rights and develop communication skills.[18] Gap worked with Care Bangladesh to form the Personal Advancement and Career Enhancement Initiative for around 500 female garment workers employed in Gap's supplier factories.[19] Other NGOs, like the Awaj Foundation, empowered garment workers to understand and act upon their legal rights. The Awaj Foundation's network included 255,719 garment workers and offered programs for workers on Bangladesh labor laws, fire safety, and health-care services, among others.[20] The Worker Rights Consortium inspected Bangladesh garment factories for labor violations but, over three years, it had only checked the factories associated with three factory owners.[21] In 2007, the Bangladesh Center for Worker Solidarity (an affiliate of the American Federation of Labor and Congress of Industrial Organizations) petitioned the U.S. government to suspend trade privileges for Bangladesh, in light of workers' rights violations in the garment industry.[22]

[17] "BGMEA probe accuses building, factory owners," *Dhaka Tribune*, June 26, 2013, http://www.dhakatribune.com/labour/2013/jun/26/rana-plaza-bgmea-probe-accuses-building-factory-owners, accessed August 21, 2013.

[18] Care Bangladesh, "Care Bangladesh Current Project Information—2013," http://www.carebangladesh.org/cw_oproject.php, accessed August 2013.

[19] Ibid.

[20] Awaj Foundation, "About," Facebook, https://www.facebook.com/pages/Awaj-Foundation/263243713738253?id=263243713738253&sk=info, accessed August 2013.

[21] Worker Rights Consortium, "Factory Investigations," http://www.workersrights.org/Freports/index.asp#freports, accessed August 2013.

[22] Solidarity Center, "Bangladesh," http://www.solidaritycenter.org/content.asp?contentid=448, accessed August 2013.

The Bangladesh government tried to suppress activities by labor unions and other groups that attempted to highlight poor safety conditions in the country's garment factories. Bangladesh police and security forces were suspected in the 2012 murder of labor activist Aminul Islam, the president of the Bangladesh Garment and Industrial Workers Federation in Savar and organizer of the Bangladesh Center for Worker Solidarity, a labor rights group. He was detained and beaten by Bangladesh security forces, and his body showed signs of torture after being recovered in 2012.[23]

RANA PLAZA

On April 23, the day before it collapsed, workers observed cracks in the walls of the Rana Plaza building. The building housed five garment factories, as well as a bank and shopping mall.[24] That morning, an engineer who had previously consulted for Sohel Rana, the building owner,[25] deemed the building unsafe and recommended that the workers be evacuated.[26] Later that day, a local government official met with Rana. After the meeting, the official declared the building was safe, pending another inspection.[27] The workers of the Brac Bank branch heeded the advice of the engineer and vacated the building.[28] Garment workers, however, were informed that they were expected to return to work in the building the next morning to fulfill overdue orders, or risk losing their jobs.[29]

On April 24, 2013, the nine-story Rana Plaza building collapsed, killing 1,100 workers and injuring 2,500 more.[30] Sohel Rana was in his office in Rana Plaza when the disaster occurred; he fled but was arrested later at the Indian border. The disaster was caused by numerous structural problems (see Box 16A.1 for a list of additional causes for the collapse):[31]

[23] Ibid., p. 16.

[24] Mohammad Zakaria, "Over 6,000 workers killed in the last 12 years: BILS," *Dhaka Tribune*, April 28, 2013, http://www.dhakatribune.com/labour/2013/apr/28/over-6000-workers-killed-last-12-years-bils, accessed August 2013.

[25] Farid Hossain, "Bangladesh Official: Disaster Not 'Really Serious,'" Associated Press, May 3, 2013, http://bigstory.ap.org/article/430-dead-so-far-bangladesh-building-collapse-0, accessed August 21, 2013.

[26] "BGMEA probe accuses building, factory owners."

[27] Syed Zain Al-Mahmood, "Nexus of politics, corruption doomed Rana Plaza," *Dhaka Tribune*, April 26, 2013, http://www.dhakatribune.com/politics/2013/apr/26/nexus-politics-corruption-doomed-rana-plaza, accessed August 21, 2013.

[28] Charles Kenny, "Why You Shouldn't Stop Buying From Bangladesh," *Business Week*, May 5, 2013, http://www.businessweek.com/articles/2013-05-05/why-you-shouldnt-stop-buying-from-bangladesh, accessed August 21, 2013.

[29] Syed Zain Al-Mahmood, "Dhaka: many dead as garment factory building that supplied west collapses," *The Guardian*, April 24, 2013, http://www.theguardian.com/world/2013/apr/24/bangladesh-building-collapse-shops-west, accessed August 21, 2013.

[30] Emran Hossain, "Rana Plaza Collapse Victims Still Waitng for Compensation," *Huffington Post*, August 6, 2013, http://www.huffingtonpost.com/2013/08/06/rana-plaza-collapse-victims-compensation_n_3713408.html, accessed August 21, 2013.

[31] Daniel M. Sabet and Afsana Tazreen, "Looking Beyond Rana Plaza," *Dhaka Tribune*, July 29, 2013, http://www.dhakatribune.com/safety/2013/jul/29/looking-beyond-rana-plaza, accessed August 2013.

Box 16A.1 Exhibit 5 Causes of the Rana Plaza Collapse

- In 2006, a four-story building with supporting walls was built without permission.
- Floors from 5th to 8th were built between 2008 and 2012 without any supporting walls.
- 9th floor was under construction at time of collapse.
- The building was constructed upon a filled-in pond.
- Debris revealed poor construction materials, with thin metal rods used as main pillars.
- Six garment factories were housed on 3rd through 8th floors.
- The day before the collapse, cracks were noticed across the building and it was evacuated.
- More than 2,500 people were inside the building when all of its floors collapsed.
- The collapse caused a neighboring three-story building, also occupied, to cave in.

Source: Adapted from Shaheen Mollah and Wasim Bin Habib, "It crumbles like a pack of cards," Daily Star, April 25, 2013, http://www.thedailystar.net/beta2/news/like-a-pack-of-cards-it-crumbles/, accessed August 2013.

- Four additional floors were constructed illegally upon the existing four stories, with a ninth floor under construction.
- The building lacked the supporting walls needed to hold heavy industrial machines and generators used by the factories.
- The lot where Rana Plaza stood was formerly a pond, which was filled only with sand.
- Inferior building materials were used to construct Rana Plaza.

INITIAL REACTIONS TO THE TRAGEDY

Garment Workers

After the collapse of Rana Plaza, rescue workers began excavating to locate the employees killed or trapped in the rubble.[32] "I would never return to that death trap," said a survivor, who had worked in the button division of one of the factories in Rana Plaza.[33] In the two days following the tragedy, thousands of garment workers rioted in the industrial districts in and around Dhaka, causing the closure of many local garment factories.[34]

[32] Farid Hossain and Tim Sullivan, "Owner is at the Nexus of Bangladesh Politics, Business," Associated Press, April 28, 2013, http://bigstory.ap.org/article/bangladesh-owner-nexus-politics-business, accessed August 2013.

[33] "Rana Plaza survivors want to go back home," *Dhaka Tribune*, April 28, 2013, http://www.dhakatribune.com/bangladesh/2013/apr/28/rana-plaza-survivors-want-go-back-home, accessed August 2013.

[34] "RMG factories close for two days," *Dhaka Tribune*, April 26, 2013, http://www.dhakatribune.com/bangladesh/2013/apr/26/rmg-factories-closed-two-days, accessed August 2013.

None of the workers in the Rana Plaza garment factories belonged to a union. Under Bangladesh's labor laws, 30% of the workforce had to petition in order for a union to be formed.[35] This was hard to achieve since, by law, the names on the petition were open to inspection by the factory owners. Workers had few opportunities to change the garment industry from within.

Alternative employment options were limited, even for workers who were not maimed by the building collapse. It was difficult to find other jobs that offered the salary needed to live in Dhaka. Many of those who chose to leave work in the garment industry after the collapse returned to their home villages in rural Bangladesh to work in agriculture. The Clean Clothes Campaign, a not-for-profit worker advocacy group based in Europe, estimated that $71 million would be needed to compensate the victims who died or were injured in Rana Plaza.[36]

Consumers

As news of the Rana Plaza collapse broke internationally, consumers who purchased products from MNC retailers with operations in Bangladesh expressed their concerns on the retailers' websites and in social media. Many consumers condemned the retailers for taking advantage of Bangladeshi workers and subpar working conditions, and a few inquired about the retailers' supply chain safety programs.[37] In response, many retailers claimed ignorance of their own supply chains and blamed their suppliers for placing the retailers' orders with unapproved and unsafe subcontractor factories.[38]

A survey by *Retail Week*, an industry publication, found that 44% of consumers were no more likely to ask retailers where their clothes were produced than before the Rana Plaza disaster (in contrast to the 35% who said they were "a lot" or "a little" more likely to ask).[39] (See Table 16A.3 for the survey question and results.) Some observers were concerned that certain consumers' preference for low prices would be greater than their desire for safe production.

[35] Krishnadev Calamur, "New Bangladeshi Law Lets Workers Unionize More Freely," National Public Radio, July 15, 2013, http://www.npr.org/blogs/parallels/2013/07/15/202348027/new-bangladesh-law- lets-workers-unionize-more-freely, accessed August 2013.

[36] Gordon Fairclough, "World News: Plight of Bangladesh Amputees—After Garment Factory Collapses, Workers Who Lost Limbs Have Poor Job Prospects," *Wall Street Journal Europe*, May 24, 2013, via Factiva, accessed August 2013.

[37] Emily Jane Fox, "Shoppers lash out at stores over Bangladesh," CNN Money, May 2, 2013, http://money.cnn.com/2013/05/01/news/companies/bangladesh-factory-shoppers/index.html, accessed August 2013.

[38] Matthew Mosk, "Wal-Mart Fires Supplier After Bangladesh Revelation," ABC News, May 15, 2013, http:// abcnews.go.com/Blotter/wal-mart-fires-supplier-bangladesh-revelation/story?id=19188673, accessed August 2013.

[39] Michael Skapinker, "Bangladesh and the clothes on our backs," *Financial Times*, May 22, 2013, http://www.ft.com/intl/cms/s/0/cb3c1fb2-c202-11e2-ab66-00144feab7de.html#axzz2dm3WdZLk, accessed August 2013.

Table 16A.3 Exhibit 6 Retail Week Consumer Survey, May 2013
Question: To what extent has the Bangladesh factory building collapse made you more likely, if at all, to ask retailers about where the clothes you buy are produced?

Percentage[a]	*Response*
13%	a lot more likely
22%	a little more likely
44%	it has made no difference
7%	I have not heard of the Bangladesh Factory building collapse
14%	don't know

Source: ICM Research, on behalf of *Retail Week*, "Retail Week—May 2013, Bangladesh Building Collapse," May 2013, http://www.retail-week.com/Journals/2013/05/14/w/e/m/ICM-Poll—Bangladesh.pdf, accessed August 2013.
[a] The survey was conducted online with 2,025 respondents.

Bangladesh Government

After the incident, the government moved to arrest the owner of the building, Sohel Rana, as well as the owners of the garment factories housed there.[40] The charges brought against Rana and the factory owners by the Labor Court were intended to punish negligence, rather than to compensate victims for loss of life or earning potential.[41] The mayor of Savar and the engineer who inspected the building the day prior were suspended.[42]

Rana Plaza revealed the extent to which the government organizations tasked with inspecting factories and enforcing the building codes were understaffed. Responsibility to inspect factories was split incoherently among different entities. Local government and the Ministry of Textiles both conducted random inspections, while some MNCs did their own audits, and other factories were inspected by the BGMEA. There was no comprehensive or coordinated approach to factory inspections, and no organization had the resources to take on all of the inspections alone. The local Dhaka development organization, Rajuk, had only 40 inspectors for all of Dhaka's factories, estimated at 1 million (of which the garment industry represented only a small percentage).[43]

[40] "11 cases filed with labour court against 5 apparel factory owners," *Dhaka Tribune*, April 29, 2013, http:// www.dhakatribune.com/bangladesh/2013/apr/29/11-cases-filed-labour-court-against-5-apparel-factory-owners, accessed August 2013.

[41] Muktasree Chakma Sathi, "Cases filed won't benefit victims," *Dhaka Tribune*, April 29, 2013, http:// www. dhakatribune.com/law-amp-rights/2013/apr/29/cases-filed-won%E2%80%99t-benefit-victims, accessed August 2013.

[42] Hossain, "Bangladesh Official: Disaster Not 'Really Serious.'"

[43] Jim Yardley, "After Disaster, Bangladesh Lags in Policing Its Maze of Factories," *New York Times*, July 2, 2013, http://www.nytimes.com/2013/07/03/world/asia/bangladeshi-inspectors-struggle-to-avert-a-new-factory-disaster.html?pagewanted=1&_r=2&hp, accessed August 2013.

The government entities were not sufficiently staffed to inspect factories, let alone enforce building codes in non-compliant factories. Lack of resources was not the only barrier to enforcing building codes. More than 25 members of Bangladesh's parliament had a direct stake in the garment industry.[44] Officials from the inspection department said that factory owners were often given advance warning of inspections, since maintaining good relations with the owners was a priority for the department.[45] The government sought to avoid widely publicizing the scope of the non-compliance problem, for risk of scaring away foreign investment. The prime minister, Sheikh Hasina, stated in an interview with CNN following the disaster, "Anywhere in the world, any accident can take place," she said. "You cannot predict anything."[46]

BGMEA

The day after the tragedy, BGMEA president Islam announced the creation of three committees intended to help the victims and families with treatment and compensation.[47] He pledged that the organization would pay for medical treatment for the workers injured at Rana Plaza and would also compensate the families of the victims.[48] The proposed compensation per deceased worker was equivalent to roughly seven months of salary. After the disaster, the BGMEA quickly assembled a team of engineers to inspect factories; 19 were closed as a result of the inspections.[49]

Global Labor Activists

Activists called for reform of Bangladesh's strict thresholds for the formation of unions and for greater stringency of building inspections. None of the garment factories operating in Rana Plaza was unionized.[50] According to Brad Adams, the Asia director for Human Rights Watch, unions could have saved workers' lives: "Had one or more of the Rana Plaza factories been unionized, workers could have refused to enter the building the day it collapsed."[51]

[44] T. J., "The new collapsing building," *The Economist*, April 25, 2013, http://www.economist.com/blogs/banyan/2013/04/disaster-bangladesh, accessed August 2013.

[45] "Tragedy shows urgency of worker protections: HRW," Star Online Report, *Daily Star*, April 26, 2013, http://www.thedailystar.net/beta2/news/tragedy-shows-urgency-of-worker-protections-hrw/, accessed August 2013.

[46] Tom Watkins, "Bangladesh's prime minister: 'Accidents happen,'" Amanpour (blog), CNN, May 2, 2013, http://amanpour.blogs.cnn.com/2013/05/02/prime-minister-says-bangladesh-is-reforming-its-garment-industry/, accessed August 2013.

[47] "Biggest tragedy to strike RMG sector: BGMEA," *Dhaka Tribune*, April 25, 2013, http://www.dhakatribune.com/law-amp-rights/2013/apr/25/biggest-tragedy-strike-rmg-sector-bgmea, accessed August 2013.

[48] Ibid.

[49] Yardley, "After Disaster, Bangladesh Lags in Policing Its Maze of Factories."

[50] Human Rights Watch, "Bangladesh: Tragedy Shows Urgency of Worker Protections," April 25, 2013, http: //www.hrw.org/news/2013/04/25/bangladesh-tragedy-shows-urgency-worker-protections, accessed August 2013.

[51] Ibid.

Activists uncovered further holes in the rigor of the inspections process. Scott Nova of the Worker Rights Consortium revealed that, while many MNC audits evaluated important labor issues such as working hours and use of child labor, prior to Rana Plaza, most audits did not include any inspections of factory structure and safety.[52]

U.S. Government

Prior to the disaster, the U.S. government was set to review Bangladesh's inclusion in the Generalized System of Preferences (GSP) in June 2013. Participation in GSP granted Bangladesh tariff exemption on certain imports to the U.S. Worker rights and labor standards were considered as criteria for a country's inclusion in GSP, and the administration had been "concerned about the worker rights situation in Bangladesh for some time."[53]

THE WAY FORWARD

MNCs with operations in Bangladesh had several options on how to respond to the Rana Plaza tragedy.

Business as Usual

MNCs were not directly responsible for the disaster, and many MNCs that had already been conducting factory inspections (like Walmart) would continue to do so and retain private records of infractions with no obligations to alert workers of safety hazards. There was low risk of consumers of the MNCs' products substituting for apparel not made in Bangladesh. Consumers, especially those with lower incomes, were unlikely to alter their purchase decisions based upon a garment's origins (and even if they wished to, the size of the Bangladesh garment industry made it difficult to avoid Bangladesh-made apparel).

Relocate Production

The Disney Corporation decided to shift all of its production away from Bangladesh to other, lower-risk countries.[54] Due to the significant gap in labor costs between

[52] "Avoiding the fire next time," *The Economist*, May 4, 2013, http://www.economist.com/news/business/21577078-after-dhaka-factory-collapse-foreign-clothing-firms-are-under-pressure-improve-working, accessed August 2013.

[53] Brian Wingfield, "Bangladesh Trade Was Under U.S. Review Prior to Factory Collapse," Bloomberg, May 3, 2013, http://www.bloomberg.com/news/2013-05-03/bangladesh-trade-was-under-u-s-review-prior-to- factory-collapse.html, accessed August 2013.

[54] Liana Foxvog and Judy Gearhart, "Disney's Disgrace," *New York Times*, May 2, 2013, http://www.nytimes.com/roomfordebate/2013/05/02/when-does-corporate-responsibility-mean-abandoning-ship/disneys-decision-to-pull-out-of-bangladesh-is-a-mistake, accessed August 2013.

Factory owner Tipu Munshi says safety in Bangladesh's garment industry could be ensured if retailers stopped haggling and paid the 90¢ per pair it costs to sew jeans, like the Walmart-ordered pair below, in a safe facility. Buyers often bargain down to what Munshi calls a danger zone, where rivals make cuts that threaten safety. "Let us earn those few cents, and nobody has to die while making basic jeans."

Made in Bangladesh
The shell fabric is 63 percent cotton, 36 percent polyester, and 1 percent elastane at a cost of $3.69 per pair
A 20-millimeter fancy shank button costs 6¢
The 4.5-inch metal zipper costs 15¢
Sepal charges 90¢ per pair for cutting and making the jeans, which includes labor and factory expenses such as rent, energy, and safety measures
Monthly wages for garment workers
$48 $100 $235
$1,440
Bangladesh
Vietnam
China
Oklahoma
The country's garment industry has spawned 5,000 factories and produced $18 billion in exports in 2012
A company called Round House has produced jeans in Shawnee for 110 years
Munshi's Sepal Garments, one of Bangladesh's biggest apparel producers, makes these jeans for Asda, a Wal-Mart Stores subsidiary in Britain
After materials, assembly, and 26¢ profit, Sepal sells the jeans to Hong Kong middleman Li & Fung for ...
Shipping cost, plus profit for Li & Fung and Walmart:
Asda store costs, profit, tax, and other expenses:
Price for Asda customers in Britain:
$7.29 + $4.33 + $10.50 = $22.12
JEANS: PHOTOGRAPH BY AARON DYER FOR BLOOMBERG BUSINESSWEEK; DATA: SEPAL GARMENTS, BLOOMBERG INDUSTRIES ESTIMATES

Figure 16A.3 Exhibit 7 Cost of Garment Production in Bangladesh, 2013.
Source: Mehul Srivastava, "Correlations: Perilous Arithmetic for Bangladesh's Factories," *Bloomberg Businessweek*, June 6, 2013, http://www.businessweek.com/articles/2013-06-06/correlations-perilous-arithmetic-for-bangladeshs-factories.

Table 16A.4 Exhibit 8 ROI for Compliant and Non-Compliant Garment Factories in Bangladesh, 2012[a]

Factory name	*(A) Initial investment*	*(B) Initial investment for compliance (B)*	*(C) Annual running cost (C)*	*(D) Annual running cost for compliance (D)*	*(E) Annual Turnover (E)*	*(F) Annual Profit (=E-C-D)*	*(G) Profit-to-initial investment ratio (= F/A+B)*
				Compliant Factories			
Shine fashion	305.31	43.75	173.52	3.36	1000	836.58	2.40
Mascot Knit Ltd.	284.76	9.52	162.34	1.08	1000	716.4	2.44
Zaara Composite	280.88	3.57	199.88	0.72	917	676.76	2.38
Knit Plus Ltd.	274.82	0.71	196.56	1.68	875	789.75	2.87
Knit Asia Ltd.	273.83	0.29	159.41	0.84	950	768.52	2.80
Average	283.92	11.57	178.34	1.54	948.4	757.60	2.58
				Noncompliant Factories			
Harun garments Ltd.	92.14		44.3		267	222.70	1.97
Alim Knit Wear Ltd.	113.10		64.43		250	185.57	1.23
Green Knit Wear	151.40		64.28		350	285.72	2.33
Step Two Garments	122.86		63.09		300	236.91	1.66
Texcon Textile Ltd.	142.75		64.68		375	310.32	2.49
Average	124.45		60.16		308.40	248.00	1.94

Source: L. M. Baral, "Comparative Study of Compliant and Non-Compliant RMG Factories in Bangladesh," *International Journal of Engineering & Technology* (2010), as compiled by World Bank, "Consolidating and Accelerating Exports in Bangladesh," Bangladesh Development Series, Paper No. 29, June 2012, http://www-wds.worldbank.org/external/default/WDSContentServer/WDSP/IB/2012/07/04/000333037_20120704022441/Rendered/PDF/708450NWP0BDS20tsinBanglades h0BDS29.pdf, accessed August 2013.

[a] All figures in US $ million. Compliant investment implies the absence of child labor, health and safety or environmental issues, and harassment of employees.

Bangladesh and the next cheapest supplier, Cambodia, shifting operations would incur higher production costs, but could lessen the risk of negative press or irresponsible labor practices tainting the Disney brand. (See Figure 16A.3 for example of production costs.) The larger the proportion of a retailer's supply chain produced in Bangladesh, the more costly to move production to another country (Disney's operations in Bangladesh were a relatively low percentage of its total garment production).

Collaborate to Invest in Safety Standards

MNCs could decide to remain in Bangladesh and partner with factories to improve safety conditions in the garment industry. The Worker Rights Consortium, a labor advocacy group based in Washington, D.C., estimated the cost to improve conditions in all 5,000 garment factories at $3 billion or $600,000 per factory, paid over five years.[55] A sample of 300 factories in Dhaka revealed that about 90% of facilities were in need of serious repairs or demolition.[56] In order to sustain improvements in factory conditions, retailers (and/or the Bangladesh government) would need to provide for on-going inspections and enforcement. Not all factories had contracts with international retailers, although many subcontracted from factories that did, so determining which factories belonged to each MNC's supply chain was itself a challenge.

Factory owners were hesitant to invest large sums to improve safety unless they could be assured that their MNC customers would not shift contracts from their factories to lower-cost, lower-safety options. A 2012 study by the World Bank of 10 of the largest Bangladeshi garment factories suggested some productivity benefits to factories that were in compliance with international labor standards. The return on investment (ROI) for compliant factories was 2.58, whereas non-compliant factories had an ROI of 1.94 (see Table 16A.4).[57]

[55] Suzanne Kapner and Shelly Banjo, "Plan B for Bangladesh," *Wall Street Journal*, June 27, 2013, via Factiva, accessed August 2013.

[56] Mehul Srivastava and Sarah Shannon, "A Scary Tour of Bangladesh's Factories," *Bloomberg Businessweek*, June 3, 2013.

[57] World Bank, "Consolidating and Accelerating Exports in Bangladesh," Bangladesh Development Series, Paper No. 29, June 2012, http://www-wds.worldbank.org/external/default/WDSContentServer/WDSP/IB/ 2012/07/04/000333037_20120704022441/Rendered/PDF/708450NWP0BDS20tsinBangladesh0BDS29.pdf, accessed August 2013.

16B

RANA PLAZA

WORKPLACE SAFETY IN BANGLADESH (B)

John A. Quelch and Margaret L. Rodriguez

In the wake of the 2013 Rana Plaza building collapse, which killed more than 1,100 Bangladeshi garment workers, a group of retailers formed a pact to prevent future disasters. Some firms hesitated to sign the legally binding contract, fearing litigation. The labor unions and European firms that created the pact were concerned about the lack of cooperation and the implications for reform in Bangladesh.

BANGLADESH FIRE AND SAFETY ACCORD

On July 8, 2013, over 80 global retailers, mainly European, and two labor unions proposed a five-year plan to improve working conditions in Bangladesh garment factories called the Bangladesh Fire and Safety Accord (BFSA).[1] Features of the pact included:

- Independent inspections of factories, with safety violations made public on the Internet.
- Retailers to underwrite mandatory repairs and building improvements at factories.
- Fire and building safety training to be given by trade unions.
- Trade unions to have a seat on the accord's governing board.
- Legally binding arbitration for noncompliance, led by the accord's steering committee.

The pact required inspection of factories working for the signatories over two years.[2] During that period, signatories of the accord agreed to maintain production in Bangladesh. Participating retailers would share information about the factories they

[1] Sarah Labowitz, "The $250 Million commitment to Bangladesh's factories misses the point," *Quartz*, July19,2013,http://qz.com/105852/the-250-million-commitment-to-bangladeshs-factories-misses-the-point/, accessed August 2013.

[2] Shelly Banjo and Christina Pasariello, "Promises in Bangladesh," *Wall Street Journal*, May, 13 2013, http:// online.wsj.com /article/SB10001424127887323716304578480883414503230.html, accessed August 2013.

used, and each of those factories would be inspected within nine months.[3] Factories found to be unsafe would close for repairs, and workers would be paid up to six months' salary during that time.[4] The cost of implementation would be split according to the proportion of production each brand had in Bangladesh—with a maximum outlay per retailer of $2.5 million over five years.[5] If a retailer failed to provide funding or continued production in unsafe factories, the signatories could file complaints. A committee composed of three labor group representatives, three brand representatives, and one member from the International Labour Organization (ILO) would enforce the accord's terms.[6] Disputes would be referred to arbitration, as needed, and the outcome would be legally binding in the brand's home country. No penalty provisions were included in the pact.[7]

By October 2013, the accord had grown to include over 90 international retailers.[8] Since the formation of the accord, its signatories had been compiling a list of factories in Bangladesh that they used for production. On October 2, 2013, the list of nearly 1,600 factories used by members of the accord was published on the organization's website.[9] The factories on the list employed more than 2 million workers.[10] Inspections of all factories that produced garments for the accord's signatories would commence in April 2014 and would be led by the accord's soon-to-be-appointed safety inspector.[11]

ALLIANCE FOR BANGLADESH WORKER SAFETY

Although more than 90 retailers signed the BFSA pact, the absence of U.S. firms was conspicuous. Only a few U.S. companies, including Abercrombie and PVH (Calvin Klein, Tommy Hilfiger) had signed. Walmart and Gap argued that the legally binding arbitration clause carried too high a risk of litigation.[12] European firms did not face the same financial risk, since the European legal environment did not facilitate

[3] Emma Thompson, "Retailers plan Bangladesh factory inspections under safety pact," Reuters, July 7, 2013, http://www.reuters.com/article/2013/07/07/bangladesh-retailers-accord-idUSL5N0FB2IK20130707, accessed August 2013.

[4] Barney Jopson, "Bangladesh factories face inspection after safety deal," *Financial Times*, July 8, 2013, http://www.ft.com/intl/cms/s/0/1edd8ce2-e76e-11e2-aa48-00144feabdc0.html#axzz2dm3WdZLk, accessed August 2013.

[5] Banjo and Pasariello, "Promises in Bangladesh."

[6] Robert Kuttner, "Sweat & Tears," *The American Prospect*, July/August 2013, pp. 61–66.

[7] Jopson, "Bangladesh factories face inspection after safety deal."

[8] "Bangladesh Safety Accord Publishes Unprecedented Wealth of Factory Data," Industriall, October 3, 2013, http://www.industriall-union.org/bangladesh-safety-accord-publishes-unprecedented-wealth-of-factory-data, accessed October 2013.

[9] Ibid.

[10] Ibid.

[11] Christina Passariello, "Retailers' Group Publishes List of Bangladeshi Factories," *Wall Street Journal* (Online), October 3, 2013, via Factiva, accessed October 2013.

[12] Suzanne Kapner and Shelly Banjo, "Plan B for Bangladesh," *Wall Street Journal*, June 27, 2013, via Factiva, accessed August 2013.

class action lawsuits with unlimited damages.[13] On July 10, 2013, U.S. retailers and brand-name manufacturers, including Walmart, VF, and Gap, announced the creation of the Alliance for Bangladesh Worker Safety (ABWS). The features of this five-year pact were largely similar to the BFSA (including inspections for members' factories, with factories to be notified of safety violations),[14] but it was not legally binding and there were some other differences:

- Retailers' direct funding of repairs would be smaller (maximum per retailer of $1 million vs. $2.5 million), but $100 million of loans would be available to factories to fund repairs.[15]
- Retailers would be able to leave the alliance at any time, provided the initial funds they had promised were paid (up to $1 million).[16]

Responsibility to comply with safety standards fell to factory owners. The alliance would identify violations and offer loans and financial support, but would assume no legal obligation for improvements to be made. The threat of loss of business would, it was argued, be sufficient to enforce factories' safety compliance.[17]

The alliance numbered 20 retailers by October 2013. Since its inception, the alliance had drafted a set of uniform fire and building codes with the Bangladeshi government and the ILO.[18] The unified codes would be used in the inspections of members' supplier factories, to be completed by July 2014. The alliance also developed fire and safety training courses and, in the fall of 2013, was seeking Bangladeshi partners to help with implementation of training. By October, signatories of the alliance had completed the list of the 620 factories[19] they used and submitted it to the Fair Factories Clearinghouse, a nonprofit funded by the industry, which helped the companies share data on factory conditions with one another.[20]

[13] European courts generally prohibited class action lawsuits, did not allow the successful litigant to collect contingency fees, and required the loser to pay legal fees for both parties. As a result, fewer lawsuits were filed.

[14] Alliance for Bangladesh Worker Safety, "Alliance of Leading Retailers in North America join Forces in Comprehensive, Five-Year Commitment to Improve Factory Safety Conditions for Workers in Bangladesh," press release, http://az204679.vo.msecnd.net/media/documents/bangladesh-alliance-press-release_ 130179348 070616796.pdf, accessed August 2013.

[15] Labowitz, "The $250 Million commitment to Bangladesh's factories misses the point."

[16] Steven Greenhouse and Stephanie Clifford, "U.S. Retailers Offer Plan for Safety at Factories," *New York Times*, July 10, 2013, http://www.nytimes.com/2013/07/11/business/global/us-retailers-offer-safety-plan-for- bangla deshi-factories.html?pagewanted=all&_r=0, accessed August 2013.

[17] Ibid.

[18] "Statement on the Achievement of September 10 Milestones As Outlined in the Bangladesh Worker Safety Initiative," The Alliance for Bangladesh Worker Safety, September 10, 2013, http://www.bangladeshworker safety.org/news/statement-on-september-10-milestones, accessed October 2013.

[19] Shelly Banjo, "Wal-Mart, Gap Press Safety in Bangladesh," *Wall Street Journal*, October 23, 2013, http://stream.wsj.com/story/latest-headlines/SS-2-63399/SS-2-361600/, accessed October 2013.

[20] Ibid.

THE ILO AND THE U.S. GOVERNMENT

In October 2013, the ILO announced a $24.2 million program, a portion of which would help support the implementation of the National Tripartite Plan of Action on Fire Safety and Structural Integrity,[21] developed through a collaboration between the ILO and the Bangladesh government.[22] These factories were thought to include many of the least-safe operations. Around $15 million of the funding was contributed by the Dutch and British governments.[23] ILO representatives in Bangladesh noted that factory owners were slowly but surely making changes to improve workplace safety.[24]

Some believed that the garment industry in Bangladesh could be improved by learning from measures adopted in Cambodia. In 2002, with the assistance of the ILO, Cambodia implemented a workplace rights program that included provisions for collective bargaining and arbitration.[25] The ILO initiated the Cambodian Arbitration Council, a three-person panel (one labor representative, one employer representative, and a neutral arbitrator) to resolve disputes under collective bargaining agreements. All awards were decided within 15 days of the submission of the dispute to the council. Eighty percent of the cases heard by the council came from the garment industry.[26] The council was considered successful because it was less susceptible to bribes than the courts, and the disputes were resolved quickly.

Others argued that the success of the Cambodian Arbitration Council was predicated upon the U.S.–Cambodia Trade Agreement on Textiles and Apparel, enacted in 1999.[27] The agreement increased the import quota for Cambodia's garment and textile exports to the U.S., as long as working conditions in Cambodia's garment factories were in compliance with ILO workplace standards. Such a system would, it was argued, be difficult to replicate in Bangladesh in 2013. The World Trade Organization (WTO) prohibited its members, including the U.S., from raising tariffs against each other on a discriminatory basis.[28]

In June 2013, President Obama removed Bangladesh from the Generalized System of Preferences (GSP) due to labor and safety issues. The GSP waived tariffs on imports into the U.S., but garments and textiles were excluded.[29] Of the $4.9 billion worth of goods imported into the U.S. from Bangladesh in 2012, the GSP applied to only

[21] The National Tripartite Plan was signed by representatives from the Bangladesh government, the BGMEA, and Bangladesh workers unions in July 2013. The plan was designed to integrate and standardize building and fire safety initiatives in Bangladesh.

[22] Ibid.

[23] Ibid.

[24] Srinivas Reddy, "Online Conference on Minimal Global Standards for Worker Safety," speech given at Boston Global Forum, Online, November 18, 2013.

[25] Arnold M. Zack, "How Labor Arbitration Has Changed the Workplace Landscape in Cambodia," *Dispute Resolution Journal*, May–July 2009, pp. 77–81.

[26] Ibid.

[27] Ibid.

[28] Kent Jones, "RE: Boston Global Forum Interview," e-mail message to Khanh Ngo, September 24, 2103.

[29] Jopson, "Bangladesh factories face inspection after safety deal."

$34.7 million.[30] The GSP termination sent a warning to the Bangladesh government, but did nothing to change the position of U.S. retailers or improve factory conditions.

Separately, the U.S. Food and Drug Administration proposed new legislation in July 2013 to make food importers legally responsible for ensuring that their food imports met domestic safety standards.[31] Some believed that similar legislation could be applied to garment importers to prevent safety and labor failures, such as those that caused the Rana Plaza disaster. Some states had already passed laws requiring that products purchased by state agencies (including, for example, uniforms) be sourced either from American factories or from importers that certified the products were made overseas in factories complying with U.S. standards.

Another approach to certifying production standards in supply chains was the "Fair Trade" label. The label could be placed on products manufactured in compliance with the International Labor Conventions[32] recommended by the ILO.[33] Independent non-profit organizations typically performed the audits. Fair Trade products often carried higher prices, reflecting the higher cost structure associated with fair labor practices.

A WORKPLACE IN PROGRESS

During the three months following the formation of the BFSA and ABWS pacts, Bangladesh garment workers went on strike to obtain better working conditions. Workers demanded an increase in the Bangladesh minimum wage from 3,000 taka to 8,000 taka per month ($38 to roughly $100).[34] "It is all connected," said Kalpona Akter, the executive director of the Bangladesh Center for Worker Solidarity. "The low wages, the cycle of poverty, and the unsafe factories."[35] Garment factory owners balked; the Bangladesh Garment Manufacturers and Exporters Association offered to increase the wage by 20% (to about $46 per month).[36]

In September 2013, garments workers in Bangladesh held a strike to protest the low wages and poor working conditions offered by the factories. The three-day worker strike culminated on September 23, 2013, with over 100 garment factories

[30] Richard McGregor, "US curbs Bangladesh trade privileges," *Financial Times*, June 28, 2013.

[31] U.S. Food and Drug Administration, "FDA takes step to help ensure the safety of imported food," FDA News Release, July 26, 2013, http://www.fda.gov/NewsEvents/Newsroom/PressAnnouncements/, accessed August 2013.

[32] The ILO conventions protected the freedom to associate and to receive fair remuneration, and also prevented the use of child labor. In order for the conventions to prevent another disaster like Rana Plaza, additional protections for worker safety and structural compliance would be needed.

[33] Fair Trade USA, "Principles: Fair Trade Standards," February 2013, http://www.fairtradeusa.org/sites/ all/files/wysiwyg/filemanager/standards/FTUSA_Standards_Principles.pdf, accessed August 2013.

[34] Syed Zain Al-Mahmood, "Corporate News: Strife Over Wages Roils Bangaldesh," *Wall Street Journal*, September 23, 2013, via Factiva, accessed October 2013.

[35] Kalpona Akter, "Keynote Address," speech given at Mary Robinson Speaker Series, "The Rana Plaza Disaster in Bangladesh: Taking Stock Half a Year On—And marking one year since the Tazreen factory fire," New York, NY, November 20, 2013.

[36] Ibid.

forced to close. A BBC documentary aired on the same day showed factories with ties to H&M, Gap, and Lidl forcing workers to take shifts longer than 15 hours.[37] The legal limit on daily working hours in Bangladesh was 10 hours, which included 2 hours of overtime.[38] Nevertheless, during the period between July and September 2013, the value of Bangladesh's garment exports rose 24% over the same period in 2012.[39]

Fire in the Aswad Textile Mill

On October 9, 2013, three months after the formation of the accord and the alliance, a fire broke out in the Aswad Composite Mills Ltd. textile factory outside of Dhaka. The factory made fabric rather than finished garments, but the fabric was used in factories that made finished garments for signatories to both the accord and the alliance. The fire at the Aswad factory killed 7 people and injured 50 more.[40] The Aswad Mill housed 200 workers at the time of the fire, and the neighboring Aswad garment factory employed 3,000 more during peak hours.[41] The disaster took place outside of normal working hours and was contained in the mill, which helped to reduce the casualties.

The event sparked renewed conversations on the urgency of workplace safety issues in Bangladesh and how to ensure the safety of workers at subcontractors used by suppliers to the signatories of the accord and the alliance. "The safety accord in and of itself doesn't change anything, which is why this fire underscores the urgency of getting factory inspections and renovations under way," said Scott Nova, director of the Washington, D.C.–based nonprofit, Worker Rights Consortium.[42]

Meanwhile, survivors and families of those who died at Rana Plaza struggled to obtain compensation. "Corporations are coming up with the best public relations solution that money can buy, rather than paying the victims of Tazreen and Rana Plaza," said Akter.[43] IndustriALL, a global union federation with operations in Bangladesh, demanded $74 million compensation on their behalf, $35 million to be paid by the retailers that sourced from Rana Plaza, the remainder to be paid by factory owners and the government.[44] In September 2013, the ILO and IndustriALL invited

[37] Sarah Butler, "Workers for Lidl, H&M and Gap in Bangladesh work 15-hour shifts," *The Guardian*, September 23, 2013, http://www.theguardian.com/fashion/2013/sep/23/workers-in-bangladesh-long-hours, accessed October 2013.

[38] National Bangladesh Workers Federation, http://www.nadir.org/nadir/initiativ/agp/s26/banglad/, accessed October 2013.

[39] Shelly Banjo, "Bangladesh Racks Up Exports," *Wall Street Journal*, October 11, 2013, via Factiva, accessed October 2013.

[40] Syed Zain Al-Mahmood, "Deadly Fire Hits Bangladesh Factory," *Wall Street Journal*, October 8, 2013, via Factiva, accessed October 2013.

[41] Al-Mahmood, "Deadly Fire Hits Bangladesh Factory."

[42] Al-Mahmood, "Deadly Fire Hits Bangladesh Factory."

[43] Akter, "Keynote Address."

[44] Syed Zain Al-Mahmood and Christina Passariello, "Bangladesh Victims Demand Payback," *Wall Street Journal*, October 24, 2013, http://on.wsj.com/1gFDB5M, accessed October 2013.

28 companies that sourced garments from Rana Plaza to a Geneva meeting but only 10 sent representatives.[45] However, 4 of these (Benetton of Italy, El Corte Ingles of Spain, Primark of the U.K., and Loblaw of Canada) formed a committee to create an accident fund.[46] On October 24, 2013, Primark unilaterally decided to pay six months of wages to surviving Rana Plaza workers and the families of the deceased,[47] pending the resolution of long-term compensation.

45 Ibid.

46 Ibid.

47 "Bursting at the seams," *The Economist*, October 26, 2013, http://www.economist.com/news/business /21588393-workers-continue-die-unsafe-factories-industry-keeps-booming-bursting-seams, accessed October 2013.

17

NOTE ON MOBILE HEALTHCARE

John A. Quelch and Margaret L. Rodriguez

Delivering healthcare to the global population was a challenge. Healthcare costs accounted for 10% of world GDP by 2013. In the U.S., healthcare costs were expected to top $3.1 trillion in 2014.[1] New technologies, shortages of trained personnel, and lengthening life expectancies were accelerating the growth of healthcare costs. Physicians often failed to engage patients in preventative care, which many believed would help combat the rising costs of treating chronic conditions. Diabetes and hypertension, in particular, afflicted many developed nations and were a growing threat in the developing world. Mobile health (mHealth) used networked devices to distribute or collect medical information from patients and/or medical personnel. Given its low cost and broad reach, many wondered if and how mHealth could help solve the global healthcare crisis.

WHAT IS MHEALTH?

mHealth referred to the delivery of healthcare services wherever and whenever they were needed through mobile phones and other networked devices. mHealth included many services, such as the use of cellphone cameras to gather data to perform medical diagnostics, automated sensing to collect data on location or other context-based factors, applications for fall detection using smartphones' integrated tri-axial accelerometer,[2] and short message service (SMS) texts to provide medical advice. (See Table 17.1 for a typology of mHealth applications developed by the World Health Organization, Johns Hopkins, and UNICEF.)[3] By 2013, mHealth services were available for many

[1] Centers for Medicare and Medicaid Services, "National Health Expenditure Projections 2011-2021," http:// www.cms.gov/Research-Statistics-data-and-Systems/Statistics-Trends-and-Reports/NationalHealthExpend Data/Downloads/Proj2011PDF.pdf, accessed March 2014.

[2] Peter Baum and Fabienne Abadie, "Market Developments—Remote Patient Monitoring and Treatment, Telecare, Fitness/Wellness and mHealth," *European Commission—JRC Scientific and Policy Reports*, 2013, p. 43, ftp://ftp.jrc.es/pub/EURdoc/JRC71141.pdf, via Google Scholar, accessed September 2013.

[3] The framework was developed to describe mHealth services related to reproductive, maternal, newborn, and child health, but the classifications below can be understood to describe mHealth services related other types of care.

Table 17.1 Exhibit 1 Common Mobile Health Types, 2013

Common mHealth and ICT Applications	*Examples of Mobile Phone Functions*	
Client education and behavior change communication	Short Message Service (SMS) Multimedia Messaging Service (MMS) Images	Interactive Voice Response Voice communication Video clips
Sensors and point-of-care diagnostics	Mobile phone camera Tethered accessory sensors, devices	Built-in accelerometer
Registries and event tracking	Short Message Service (SMS) Voice communication	Digital forms
Data collection and reporting	Short Message Service (SMS) Voice communication	Digital forms
Electronic Health Records (EHRs)	Digital forms	Mobile web
Electronic decision support (protocols, consultation)	Stored information "apps" Interactive Voice Response	Mobile web
Provider-to-provider communication	Short Message Service (SMS) Multimedia Messaging Service (MMS)	Mobile phone camera
Provider work planning and scheduling	Interactive electronic client list Short Message Service (SMS) alerts	Mobile phone calendar
Provider training and education	Short Message Service (SMS) Multimedia Messaging Service (MMS) Interactive Voice Response (IVR)	Voice communication Audio or video clips, images
Human resource management	Web-based performance dashboards Global Positioning Service (GPS)	Digital forms Short Message Service (SMS)
Supply chain management	Web-based supply dashboards Global Positioning Service (GPS)	Digital forms Short Message Service (SMS)
Financial transaction and incentives	Mobile money transfers and banking services	Transfer of airtime minutes

Source: Adapted from Alain B. Labrique, Lavanya Vasudevan, Erica Kochi, Robert Fabricant, and Garrett Mehl, "mHealth innovations as health system strengthening tools: 12 common applications and a visual framework," *Global Health: Science and Practice*, 2013, http://www.ghspjournal.org/content/1/2/160.full.pdf+html, via Google Scholar, accessed November 2013.

medical specialties, including allergy/immunology, anesthesiology, cardiology, dentistry, dermatology, emergency medicine, endocrinology, family practice, gastroenterology, genetics, geriatric care, infectious diseases, obstetrics, gynecology, pediatric care, psychiatry, and more.[4]

In 2012, PwC estimated that the global mHealth market would reach $23 billion by 2017.[5] Europe and Asia were expected to have 30% of the mHealth market; the U.S. and Canada, 28%; Latin America, 7%; and Africa, 5%.[6] Monitoring services were expected to account for about 65% of the global market (driven by growth of chronic diseases in developed countries); diagnostic services, 15% of the market (driven primarily by developing markets); and support services for healthcare administration, 6%; with the remainder comprising wellness, prevention, and other services.[7]

TECHNICAL INFRASTRUCTURE AND COSTS

mHealth Value Chain

The mHealth category included many types of non-application mHealth services, but the value chain for smartphone mHealth apps described the relationships underlying many mHealth products. In these cases, the phone or device manufacturer and the telecom company always played a key role. (See Figure 17.1 for an mHealth value chain diagram.) The value chain included a variety of stakeholders, including device manufacturers, telecom networks, operating system developers, peripherals manufacturers, and healthcare professionals.

Device manufacturers Hardware specifications and device features (such as high-resolution cameras) determined the applications the device could host. Device manufacturers had an interest in offering standardized operating systems and cutting-edge hardware on their phones or devices in order to host a large array of applications that would attract customers.

Telecom companies The telecom companies provided the networks required for mHealth services to function and often distributed the phone handsets. Telecoms typically derived revenue from a subscription model and/or by charging for data usage. mHealth apps, which provided diagnostics (and thus required the transmission of high-bandwidth images or video) or offered automatic data collection, were valuable to telecoms because they raised data usage and, therefore, revenues. Select mHealth devices or services could increase consumer demand for a given telecom carrier (and thus offered a differentiation opportunity to the telecoms). In addition, the advanced sensor technologies used for mHealth applications generated large sets of data, which presented telecoms with both challenges and market opportunities.[8]

[4] Baum and Abadie, "Market Developments," p. 43.

[5] Siddharth Vishwanath, Kaushal Vaidya, Ravi Nawal, Amit Kumar, Srikanth Parthasarathy, and Snigdha Verma, "Touching lives through mobile health," PwC India, February 2012, pp. 4–5, http://www.pwc.in/ assets/pdfs/telecom/gsma-pwc_mhealth_report.pdf, accessed November 2013.

[6] Vishwanath et al., "Touching lives through mobile health," pp. 4–5.

[7] Vishwanath et al., "Touching lives through mobile health," pp. 4–5.

[8] Baum and Abadie, "Market Developments," p. 50.

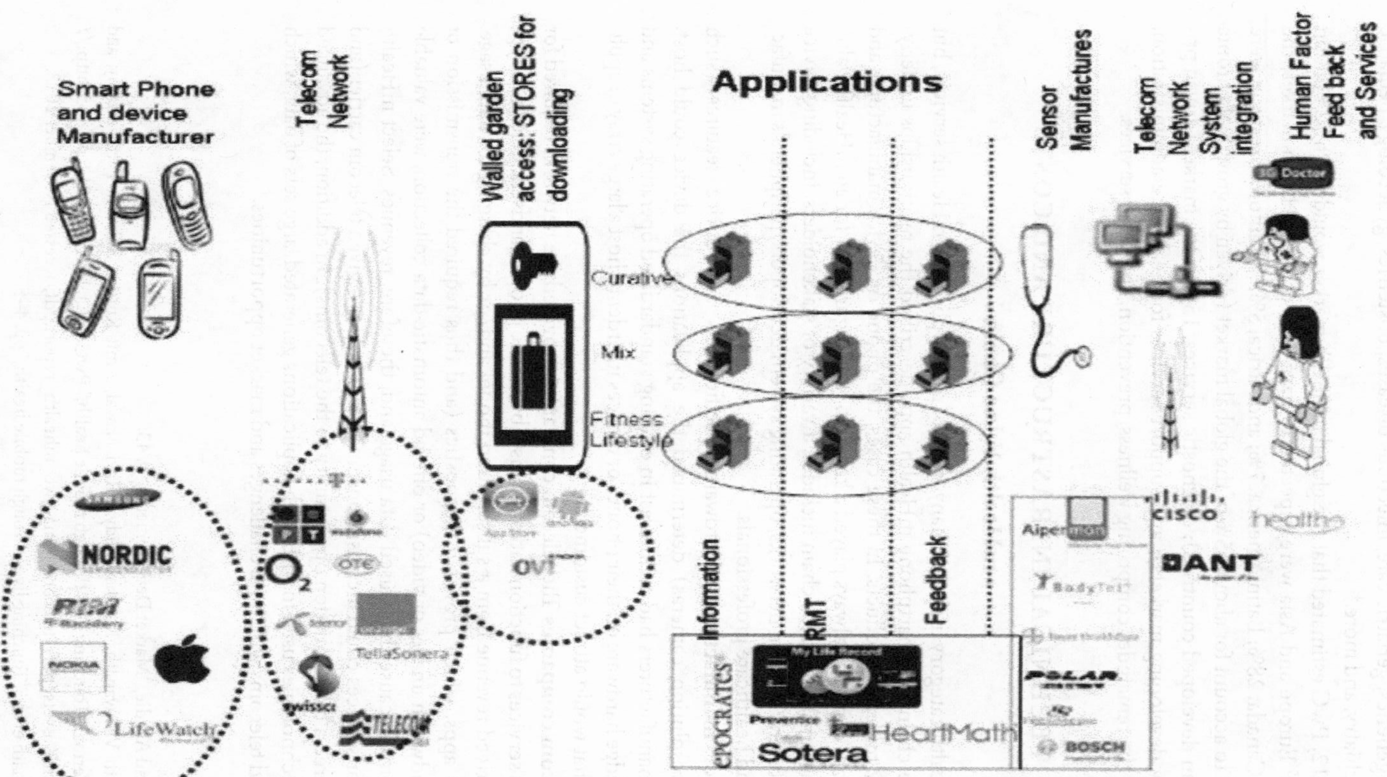

Figure 17.1 **Exhibit 2** Mobile Health Smartphone Applications Value Chain with Company Examples.

Source: Peter Baum and Fabienne Abadie, "Market Developments—Remote Patient Monitoring and Treatment, Telecare, Fitness/Wellness and mHealth," *European Commission—JRC Scientific and Policy Reports*, 2013, Figure 15, p. 43, ftp://ftp.jrc.es/pub/EURdoc/JRC71141.pdf, via Google Scholar, accessed September 2013.

Operating system (OS) developers Companies like Apple and Google, which produced the leading operating systems for smartphones in the U.S., provided the platforms on which mHealth applications were distributed and run; hence, the OS developers acted as gatekeepers for mHealth apps to reach consumers' phones. In 2014, OS developers began to experiment with creating their own mHealth platforms and apps, rather than simply allowing third-party developers to sell mHealth apps on the devices. (Occasionally, the telecom carrier, rather than an outside company, would provide the operating system and app store.) Revenue from app sales was important to the business operations of OS developers.[9]

Peripheral manufacturers Certain mHealth services required additional hardware beyond the smartphone itself, such as electric sensors to capture electrocardiogram (ECG) readings. The peripheral hardware was produced mainly by medical device manufacturers and sports equipment makers.[10] Medical device and sports equipment manufacturers could enter the mHealth category with relative ease by releasing products that had (1) network connectivity, and (2) tapped partnerships with healthcare institutions (to perform data analysis and/or lend credibility). Manufacturers of peripherals gained revenues from the sales or rental of their products, or through the sale of usage-based additions (e.g., disposable test strips used by diabetics for blood sugar testing).

Healthcare professionals For mHealth apps or services that provided expert medical advice to consumers, healthcare professionals represented the last link in the value chain. These professionals provided individual counseling on healthcare issues to users, whether through Q&A forums, data analysis, or individual consultation via telemedicine or SMS.[11] Hospitals and clinics also had an interest in developing applications to assist with patient care or acquisition within their organization. Pharmaceutical companies could also play a role in the mHealth value chain, particularly for mHealth services that dealt with supply chain logistics (such as pharmacy inventory management).

BENEFITS OF MHEALTH

Consumers

Consumers found using many healthcare services to be inconvenient and, when expenses were paid out-of-pocket, costly. Patients in developed markets did not believe healthcare was on par with other service industries in terms of user experience.[12] The top drivers for consumers to consider using mHealth services were increased convenience, followed by reduced costs and greater control over their personal health. (See Table 17.2 for list of consumer concerns addressed by mHealth.)

[9] Baum and Abadie, "Market Developments," p. 43.

[10] Baum and Abadie, "Market Developments," p. 43.

[11] Baum and Abadie, "Market Developments," p. 43.

[12] David Levy, "Emerging mHealth: Paths for growth," PwC, 2012, p. 10, http://www.pwc.com/en_GX/gx/healthcare/mhealth/assets/pwc-emerging-mhealth-full.pdf, accessed November 2013.

Table 17.2 Exhibit 3 Consumers' Healthcare Benefits Delivered by mHealth, 2012

Top drivers for patients to consider beginning to use or increasing use of mHealth applications/ services

Drivers	*Response Rate*
Ability to access my healthcare providers more conveniently, effectively	46%
Ability to reduce my own healthcare costs	43%
Ability to take greater control over my own health	32%
Ability to obtain information that is difficult or impossible for me to obtain from other sources	28%
Ability to access better-quality healthcare	25%

Source: Adapted from David Levy, "Emerging mHealth: Paths for growth," PwC, 2012, p. 10, http://www.pwc.com/en_GX/gx/ healthcare/mhealth/assets/pwc-emerging-mhealth-full.pdf, accessed November 2013.

The Economist Intelligence Unit identified patients most likely to seek out mHealth services as those who suffered from chronic conditions and/or those who spent more than 30% of their household income on medical services.[13] Chronic conditions required frequent contact with medical staff to monitor changes to health status and treatment efficacy. mHealth monitoring solutions helped those who suffered from chronic conditions reduce the time spent in hospitals, hospital readmissions, and doctor visits. As populations aged, the incidence of chronic conditions tended to rise.

Doctors

The key drivers of mHealth adoption among doctors were improved quality of care and access to care for existing patients, followed by the reduction of administrative tasks required of doctors. Doctors believed that a decrease in administrative work would result in increased time for patients.[14] (See Table 17.3 for list of physician concerns addressed by mHealth.)

Payers

Regardless of the healthcare market type (e.g., private insurance, national healthcare systems), insurers in every market aimed to reduce the cost of claims (both expenditures on healthcare services and administration costs) and establish a competitive advantage versus other insurers. The key drivers of payer interest in mHealth were the reduction of the administrative burden on medical personnel, improved health

[13] Economist Intelligence Unit Survey, 2012, commissioned for inclusion in David Levy, "Emerging mHealth," p. 12.

[14] Levy, "Emerging mHealth," p. 10.

Table 17.3 Exhibit 4 Physicians' Healthcare Benefits Delivered by mHealth, 2012

What would spur doctor adoption of mHealth?

Drivers	*Response Rate*
Improved quality of care; better health outcomes	36%
Easier access to care for existing patients	32%
Reduction in administrative time for medical personnel, allowing greater time for patients	32%
More efficient internal processes, communication	29%
Ability to reach previously unreachable patients	28%
Patient expectations, demand	26%
Lower overall cost of care for patients	25%
Opportunity to provide new services, tap into new markets	17%
Ubiquity of smartphones and applications in all areas of life	16%
Encouragement by regulators	14%
Expectation, demand of medical personnel or employees	13%

Source: Adapted from David Levy, "Emerging mHealth: Paths for growth," PwC, 2012, p. 12, http://www.pwc.com/en_GX/gx/ healthcare/mhealth/assets/pwc-emerging-mhealth-full.pdf, accessed November 2013.

outcomes, and lowered costs (see Table 17.4 for full list). Insuring medication adherence and tracking patient conditions via mHealth were inexpensive ways to avoid utilization of costly hospital resources downstream. In 2014, consumers (rather than insurance companies) mostly paid for mHealth services out-of-pocket, whether the services were for wellness (medical or fitness advice) or recommended by medical professionals as part of a treatment plan.[15]

MHEALTH EXAMPLES

Mobile healthcare offerings addressed the needs of different communities within the healthcare system: physicians and medical professionals, patients, and payers. This note focuses primarily on mobile health products designed for use by consumers and medical professionals (although payers still benefited indirectly from such products via reduced healthcare system costs). Although the examples selected below represented leaders in mobile health innovation, gaps still existed in the market's understanding of which business opportunities represented sustainable and scalable solutions to challenges in the healthcare system.

15 Levy, "Emerging mHealth," p. 10.

Table 17.4 Exhibit 5 Payers' Healthcare Benefits Delivered by mHealth, 2012
What would spur payer adoption of mHealth?

Drivers	*Response Rate*
Reduction in administrative time for medical personnel, allowing greater time for patients	30%
Improved quality of care; better health outcomes	29%
Lower overall cost of care for patients	28%
Ability to reach previously unreachable patients	26%
Easier access to care for existing patients	24%
Patient expectations, demand	23%
Opportunity to provide new services, tap into new markets	22%
More efficient internal processes, communication	21%
Expectation, demand of medical personnel or employees	19%
Ubiquity of smartphones and applications in all areas of life	16%
Encouragement by regulators	16%

Source: Adapted from David Levy, "Emerging mHealth: Paths for growth," PwC, 2012, p. 12, http://www.pwc.com/en_GX/gx/healthcare/mhealth/assets/pwc-emerging-mhealth-full.pdf, accessed November 2013.

Numerous devices and services, particularly in the developing world, aimed to substitute for or improve upon existing healthcare systems. Remote diagnostics enabled people without access to medical practitioners or resources to receive healthcare advice via SMS, phone calls, or video chats. In developed countries, diagnostic devices could help consumers determine whether to seek medical attention for changes in their conditions. Although a wave of new mHealth devices brought increased diagnostic capabilities, the broader mHealth market encompassed many products dedicated to preventative care, whether by incenting physical fitness, avoiding hospitalization due to medication non-adherence, or enabling doctors to improve their prognoses by supplying synthesized, easily accessed patient data. (See Table 17.5 for mHealth market segmentation.)

CONSUMER-FACING PREVENTATIVE SERVICES

Medication Adherence

Failure to comply with a prescribed medication regimen occurred due to patient forgetfulness or concerns about costs. Around 20% to 30% of prescriptions in the U.S. were never filled, and in many other cases, patients did not take all of the pills or did not take them at the prescribed intervals.[16] It was estimated that

[16] U.S. Centers for Disease Control and Prevention, "Medication Adherence," March 27, 2013, http://www. cdc.gov/primarycare/materials/medication/docs/medication-adherence-01ccd.pdf, accessed March 2014.

Table 17.5 Table 1 Health Product Market Segmentation Framework

Service Type	*Consumer-Facing*	*Medical-Personnel-Facing*
Preventative[a]	Medication Adherence	Data Integration
	Vitality GlowCap	Practice Fusion
		Medic Mobile
	Fitness/Wellness	2Net
	Fitbit	HealthPal
	Location/Context-Based	Monitoring
	Propeller Health	Guard2me
	Data Integration	
	Google Fit	
	Apple HealthKit	
	Philips and Salesforce.com	
Therapeutic	Remote Diagnostics	Portable Hardware
	MERA Doctor	PEEK
		Mobisante
	Diagnostic Hardware	
	Scanadu Scout	Connecting Medical Professionals
	ECG Check	Doximity
	Behavioral Interventions for Chronic Conditions	
	Text2Quit Smoking Cessation	

Source: Casewriter.
[a] Includes mHealth monitoring services.

the cost of suboptimum medication adherence in the U.S. could be up to $289 billion.[17]

Vitality GlowCap GlowCap was a smart prescription bottle produced by Vitality that incorporated a microchip to record when the bottle was opened. The product helped increase medication adherence by sending medication reminders to the patient and/or caregiver via AT&T's broadband network. The GlowCap prescription bottle included a push button that sent refill requests directly to the pharmacist (see Figure 17.2 for a photo). The GlowCap collected data on medication adherence and produced reports for the patient and physician to review. Vitality was piloting additional products in the GlowCap line that would feature tiered reminders (e.g., the product would glow at

[17] Meera Viswanathan, Carol E. Golin, Christine D. Jones, Mahima Ashok, Susan J. Blalock, Roberta C.M. Wines, Emmanuel J. L. Coker-Schwimmer, David L. Rosen, Priyanka Sista, and Kathleen N. Lohr, "Interventions to Improve Adherence to Self-administered Medications for Chronic Diseases in the United States: A Systematic Review," *Annals of Internal Medicine* 157, no. 11 (December 2012): 785–795, http://annals.org/article.aspx?articleid=1357338, accessed March 2014.

Figure 17.2 Exhibit 6 Vitality GlowCap, 2009.
Source: Juhan Sonin, "GlowCap," Flickr Commons, https://www.flickr.com/photos/juhansonin/3475944227/, accessed March 2014.

medication time; glow and play a song at one hour past; and send a call reminder to the patient at two hours past).

A June 2011 study found that GlowCaps helped hypertensive patients to reach 98% medication adherence,[18] a 27% improvement versus those who did not use GlowCaps.[19] Vitality next planned to test the impact of GlowCaps coupled with various financial incentives on medication adherence among high-cholesterol patients.[20]

When GlowCaps launched in 2009, the devices (then only Wi-Fi-enabled) were sold directly to consumers for $99 via Amazon.com.[21] In 2011, the AT&T networked device was released on Amazon, also for $99. The company was acquired by Nant Health shortly thereafter, and Amazon stopped selling GlowCaps.[22] GlowCaps were

[18] Jonah Comstock, "GlowCaps now sold through CVS, new randomized control trial launches," *MobiHealth News*, March 11, 2013, http://mobihealthnews.com/20750/glowcaps-now-sold-through-cvs-new-randomized-control-trial-launches/, accessed April 2014.

[19] "AT&T Connected Vitality GlowCaps Wins 2011 Global Mobile Award," AT&T, February 16, 2011, http://www.att.com/ gen/press-room?pid=19064&cdvn=news&newsarticleid=31610&mapcode=, accessed April 2014.

[20] Each group, including the control group, would use Vitality GlowCaps as a medication reminder, but each experimental group would also enroll in a different sweepstake: for group one, patients would be entered to win money each time they remembered to take their medication; the second group would be entered only if they took medication prior to being reminded; and a third group would accumulate money for each on-time dose taken, but they would only be eligible for a prize if they reached a certain overall adherence level. Results of the study would be delivered in August 2016.

[21] Comstock, "GlowCaps now sold through CVS, new randomized control trial launches."

[22] Comstock, "GlowCaps now sold through CVS, new randomized control trial launches."

sold to pharmaceutical companies and self-insured employers for two years before again selling directly to consumers via CVS in February 2013.[23] GlowCaps were sold on CVS.com for $79.99, with an additional monthly fee for use of the AT&T network.

Fitness/Wellness

In 2014, mHealth applications and devices on sale allowed consumers to variously track their daily physical activity, food consumption, sleeping patterns, heart rate, blood sugar, and mood with increasing levels of precision. Dramatic increases in phone hardware features, such as the inclusion of superior cameras, accelerometers, computing power, and other improvements, resulted in devices that could capture accurately vast amounts of consumer health information. Certain mHealth companies elected to produce devices (such as wristbands, watches, or visors) that would capture data without requiring the use of a phone. Many mHealth fitness and wellness devices offered data analysis (via an application or website) to help users track and share their results with their friends or doctors. The majority of these fitness and wellness products were paid for out-of-pocket by consumers (rather than on the advice or prescription of a physician).

Fitbit Fitbit was the leading manufacturer of body trackers with 67% of the U.S. market in 2013[24] (see Figures 17.3a-c for examples of Fitbit products and output). Fitness devices dominated the wearables category (9 out of 10 devices sold),[25] and 2014 sales for the wearables category were estimated to reach 10 million devices and $3 billion in sales.[26] Fitbit offered a range of wearable trackers that captured steps taken, calories burned, sleep quality and quantity, active time, and distance traveled.[27]

Fitbit's CEO James Park said: "People tend to increase their activity level by 30-40% after using a Fitbit tracker for 12 weeks and Fitbit users take 43% more steps than non-Fitbit users."[28] Fitbit users lost 13 pounds on average while using the device.[29] In 2012, early results from an obesity study performed by HealthCore found 41% of

[23] Sumathi Reddy, "Ring, Buzz, Flash: It Must Be Time to Take Your Medicine," *Wall Street Journal*, January 8, 2013, http://online.wsj.com /news/articles/SB10001424127887323706704578227861587228102?KEYWORDS=national+health+policy+institute&mg=reno64wsj&url=http%3A%2F%2Fonline.wsj.com%2Farticle%2FSB10001424127887323706704578227861587228102.html%3FKEYWORDS%3Dnational%2Bhealth%2Bpolicy%2Binstitute, accessed April 2014.

[24] Jason Feifer, "Most Innovative Companies 2014: 23, Fitbit," *Fast Company*, February 10, 2014, http://www.fastcompany.com/most-innovative-companies/2014/fitbit, accessed March 2014.

[25] Connie Guglielmo and Parmy Olson, "The Case Against Wearables," *Forbes*, March 3, 2014, http://www. forbes.com/sites/connieguglielmo/2014/02/12/the-case-against-wearables/, accessed March 2014.

[26] Guglielmo and Olson, "The Case Against Wearables."

[27] Fitbit, Inc., "Products," http://www.fitbit.com/flex#syncs-wirelessly-container, accessed March 2014.

[28] Megan Humphreys, "7 FitBit Hacks to Burn More Calories in 2014," *Daily Beast*, January 6, 2014, http://www.thedaily beast.com/articles/2014/01/06/7-fitbit-hacks-to-burn-more-calories-in-2014.html, accessed April 2014.

[29] Jennifer Wang, "How Fitbit Is Cashing in on a High-Tech Fitness Trend," *Entrepreneur*, July 27, 2012, http://www.entrepreneur.com/article/223780, accessed April 2014.

(a)

Figure 17.3a Exhibit 7a Fitbit Ultra, 2012.
Source: Zack Copley, "FitBit Ultra," Flickr Commons, https://www.flickr.com/photos/zcopley/6651251857/, accessed March 2014.

Fitbit users lost at least five pounds in six months; and Fitbit users who were also given professional weight-loss coaching lost an average of 7.5 pounds.[30]

Fitbit products contained a social feature, as its mobile app offered users the chance to compete with friends.[31] Fitbit also partnered with employers to enhance corporate wellness programs (the inclusion of Fitbit in such programs helped spur sign-ups above the average rate of 20%).[32] Fitbit planned next to create devices that interfaced with phones (e.g., caller ID displayed on the scrolling Fitbit screen).[33] Prices ranged from $59.95 for the Fitbit Zip (a more basic step and calorie counter) to $99.95 for the Fitbit Flex (a premium model that captured physical activity and sleep).[34]

[30] Wang, "How Fitbit Is Cashing in on a High-Tech Fitness Trend."

[31] Guglielmo and Olson, "The Case Against Wearables."

[32] Guglielmo and Olson, "The Case Against Wearables."

[33] Jason Feifer, "Most Innovative Companies 2014: 23, Fitbit," *Fast Company*, February 10, 2014, http://www.fastcompany.com/most-innovative-companies/2014/fitbit, accessed March 2014.

[34] Fitbit, Inc., "Compare Devices," https://www.fitbit.com/comparison/trackers, accessed March 2014.

(b)

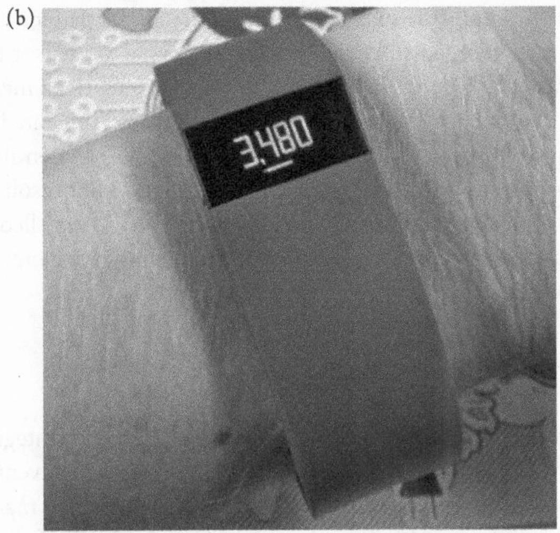

Figure 17.3b Exhibit 7b Fitbit Force, 2013.
Source: Becky Stern, "FitBit Force," Flickr Commons, https://www.flickr.com/photos/bekathwia/11502871793/, accessed March 2014.

(c)

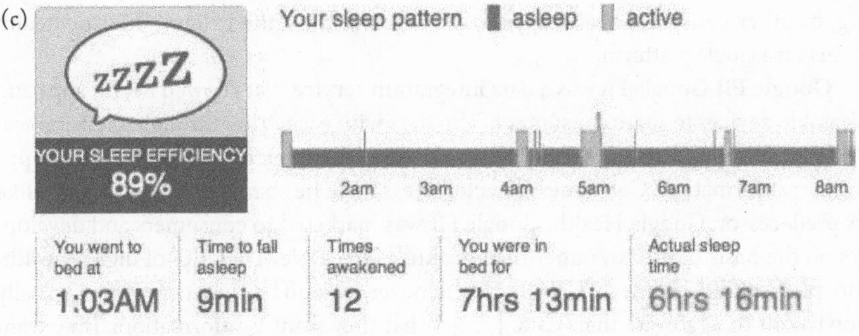

Figure 17.3c Exhibit 7c Fitbit Sleep Metrics Output, 2013.
Source: Todd Huffman, "FitBit," Flickr Commons, https://www.flickr.com/photos/oddwick/4209197542/, accessed March 2014.

Location/Context Based

The portable nature of mHealth applications and devices allowed for the capture of accurate data on the impact of time, location, temperature, and other ambient factors on an individual's health status. Such data could be used to identify patterns that might lead to more severe illness and to craft improvements in treatment plans.

Propeller Health asthma tracker In the U.S., approximately 25 million people suffered from asthma (and 2 million visited the emergency room for asthma each year).[35] Physicians recommended that asthma patients track their symptoms, triggers,

[35] Propeller Health, "Respiratory health matters," http://propellerhealth.com/solutions/payers/, accessed March 2014.

and medications, but capturing such records was onerous for patients (and, as a result, records were often incomplete). Propeller Health designed a sensor to be placed on the asthma inhaler (see Figure 17.4 for a photo) that would track medication adherence (including the time and location of each dose taken). The data from the sensor synced with an app to produce medical reports to help patients identify their environmental triggers and share the results with their doctors.[36] Pilot results indicated that patients using the product were more likely to have "well-controlled" asthma (over two-thirds, versus one-third for non-users), and the technology increased medication adherence by up to 80%.[37]

Data Integration

In 2014, a new generation of consumer-targeted healthcare data integration products emerged. Previous data integration platforms emphasized the convenience of storing health information, like medical records, in one location. However, many past incarnations of personal health records (PHRs), such as Google Health, failed due to lack of participation from medical institutions, consumer concerns over privacy, or low consumer interest in aggregated medical records.[38] The new generation of data integration platforms not only combined lab results and other clinical data into one interface, but also broke down the "silos" around the data stored in different fitness, calorie counting, or other consumer health apps to present and track the patient's holistic health status on a single platform.

Google Fit Google Fit was a data integration service that allowed health apps and wearable devices to share consumer health data with each other through open application programming interfaces (APIs), which were sets of instruction that allowed apps to share information. Consumers selected the data to be shared between apps. Unlike its predecessor, Google Health, Google Fit was marketed to consumers and developers on the basis of fitness, rather than health.[39] Derek Newell, CEO of digital healthcare platform Jiff, claimed: "Google Health never took off because consumers actually don't want to aggregate their data. [. . .] What they want is information. They want meaning, rewards and a feedback loop."[40]

[36] Propeller Health, "Home," http://propellerhealth.com/, accessed March 2014.

[37] Erica St. Angel, "Asthmaoplis Relaunches as Propeller Health to Advance Broader Respiratory Mission," Propeller Health, September 10, 2013, http://propellerhealth.com/2013/09/asthmapolis-relaunches-as-propeller-health-to-advance-broader-respiratory-mission/, accessed April 2014.

[38] Leo Sun, "Can Google Really Save 100,000 Lives?" *The Motley Fool*, July 6, 2014, http://www.fool.com/investing/general/2014/07/06/can-google-really-save-100000-lives.aspx, accessed July 2014.

[39] Neil Versel, "Google Fit Intro at I/O Conference Wisely Shies Away from 'Health'," *Forbes*, June 27, 2014, http://www.forbes.com/sites/neilversel/2014/06/27/google-fit-intro-at-io-conference-wisely-shies-away-from-health/, accessed July 2014.

[40] Parmy Olson, "Exclusive: Google Wants to Collect Your Health Data with 'Google Fit'," *Forbes*, June 12, 2014, http://www.forbes.com/sites/parmyolson/2014/06/12/exclusive-google-to-launch-health-service-google-fit-at-developers-conference/?ss=future-tech, accessed July 2014.

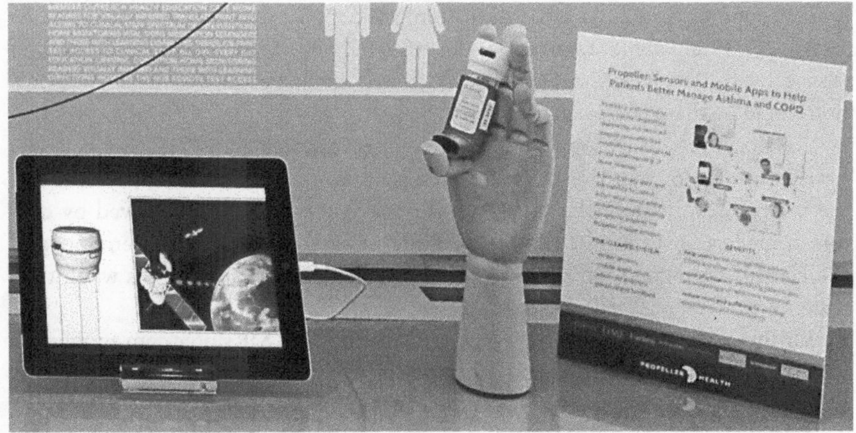

Figure 17.4 Exhibit 8 Propeller Health Asthma Sensor, 2013.
Source: Ted Eytan, "Excited for new @propellerhealth display," Flickr Commons, https://www.flickr.com/photos/ taedc/10407443535/, accessed March 2014.

When announced in June 2014, Google Fit had not formally contracted with any electronic health record (EHR) or clinical partners. Some observers believed that, without such partners, Google Fit would not be able to funnel data collected from consumer health apps into the patient's EHR, and thus would not be able to influence point-of-care decisions.[41] If true, Google would also be unable to benefit from data mining holistic patient healthcare profiles.[42] However, a leading EHR provider, Practice Fusion, publicly commented on the potential of Google Fit to improve its clinician-facing platform. Chris Hogg, a data scientist at Practice Fusion, said: "We could easily integrate these kinds of devices and data streams and give more information back to physicians at point-of-care."[43] Numerous consumer-facing apps had agreed to participate in Google Fit, including Nike+, Withings (a smart scale), Runkeeper Basic, Adidas, and Mio (a wristband heart rate monitor).[44]

Apple HealthKit Apple's HealthKit was similar to Google Fit in that it was a framework that enabled wearable devices and healthcare apps to share data. A native iOS8 enabled-iPhone app, called Health, aggregated the data from the apps, devices, and clinical sources into "Dashboards" that allowed users to track their health status over time. Health also supplied data for an "emergency card" lock screen for the iPhone, which could display the user's medical contact, blood type, and allergy information. Third-party developers would be able to request access to Health (much like other

[41] Sun, "Can Google Really Save 100,000 Lives?"

[42] Sun, "Can Google Really Save 100,000 Lives?"

[43] Parmy Olson, "For Google Fit, Your Health Data Could Be Lucrative," *Forbes*, June 26, 2014, http://www.forbes.com /sites/parmyolson/2014/06/26/google-fit-health-data-lucrative/, accessed July 2014.

[44] Parmy Olson, "Google Unveils Its Hub for Health Tracking, Google Fit," *Forbes*, June 25, 2014, http://www.forbes.com /sites/parmyolson/2014/06/25/google-unveils-its-hub-for-health-tracking-google-fit/, accessed July 2014.

types of apps requested access to a user's contacts or photos).[45] Both Healthkit and the Health app would come standard with the iOS 8 mobile operating system, slated for launch in fall 2014. As with Google Fit, consumers would decide what health information would be shared between apps.

To launch HealthKit, Apple partnered with Epic Systems, an EHR company that covered roughly 50% of U.S. patients.[46] The Epic partnership would help ensure that the information held on the phone would match the information viewed by doctors at medical institutions. The Mayo Clinic, another HealthKit partner, hoped to use HealthKit's data in the Mayo Clinic app, which would alert doctors when their patients' vital statistics fell outside of normal ranges.[47]

Philips and Salesforce.com In June 2014, Philips and Salesforce.com announced a partnership to create a healthcare platform to aggregate and share consumer health data. The two companies would adapt the existing Salesforce platform to accept data from medical devices such as MRI scanners or heart monitors, and then aggregate the data in a manner compliant with privacy laws.[48] At the time of the announcement, Philips had designed two apps for use on the platform: eCareCompanion and eCareCoordinator. The platform launch was planned for the end of summer 2014, and access to the platform would be available to third-party developers.

eCareCoordinator was a consumer-facing app that aggregated healthcare data into a single interface. Unlike the Google Fit, which was positioned as a fitness tracker, the eCareCoordinator was explicitly positioned for healthcare applications, such as taking data from[49] Banner Health's hospitals and specialized healthcare facilities.[50]

CONSUMER-FACING THERAPEUTIC SERVICES

Remote Diagnostics

In many developing countries, the majority of the population was served by rudimentary healthcare delivery systems. The ratio of doctors to the total population in developing nations was lower than in developed markets (see Figure 17.5). Africa suffered one-quarter of the cases of disease worldwide, but possessed only 3% of the world's medical professionals.[51] It was common for people living in poor or rural areas to lack healthcare facilities and medical staff; those in need of care had to travel for days (incurring cost of travel and lost workdays) to facilities in larger metropolitan areas.

[45] Olson, "Exclusive: Google Wants to Collect Your Health Data with 'Google Fit.'"

[46] Sun, "Can Google Really Save 100,000 Lives?"

[47] Neil Versel, "Apple's HealthKit Connects With Mayo and Epic, but Don't Call it Revolutionary," *Forbes*, June 3, 2014, http://www.forbes.com/sites/neilversel/2014/06/03/apples-healthkit-connects-with-mayo-and-epic-but-dont-call-it-revolutionary/, accessed July 2014.

[48] Klint Finley, "Salesforce and Philips Connect Doctors to Your Fitness Tracker," *Wired*, June 26, 2014, http://www.wired.com /2014/06/salesforce_phillips/, accessed July 2014.

[49] Finley, "Salesforce and Philips Connect Doctors to Your Fitness Tracker."

[50] Finley, "Salesforce and Philips Connect Doctors to Your Fitness Tracker."

[51] "Private Health Care in Africa: A Middle Way?" *The Economist*, November 16, 2013, http://www.economist.com/news/middle-east-and-africa/21589925-insurers-have-spotted-opening-no-frills-life-saving-health-care, accessed March 2014.

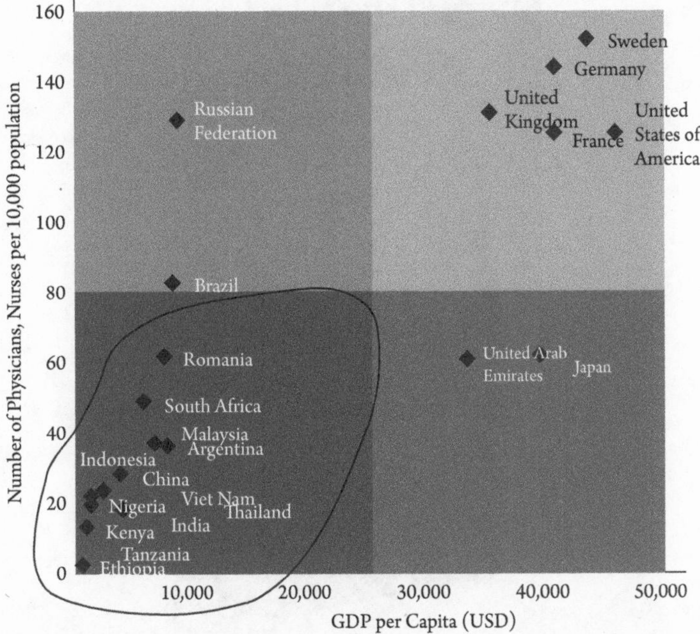

Figure 17.5 Exhibit 9 GDP per Capita (US$) and Number of Physicians and Nurses per 10,000 People, 2010.

Source: Siddharth Vishwanath, Kaushal Vaidya, Ravi Nawal, Amit Kumar, Srikanth Parthasarathy, and Snigdha Verma, "Touching lives through mobile health," PwC India, February 2012, p. 7, http://www.pwc.in/assets/pdfs/telecom/gsma-pwc_mhealth_report.pdf, accessed November 2013.

If a rural community had a clinic, it might be staffed by community health workers (CHWs) who had less medical training than nurses or physicians. mHealth technology offered people in remote areas the opportunity to connect with medical professionals for advice on treatment and care.

MERA Doctor MERA Doctor was a subscription telemedicine service, based in Mumbai, that connected patients to doctors who could analyze data sent via phone to generate a diagnosis. Up to six patients per family could call the helpline as many times as they needed, for about $5 per three-month subscription.[52] The doctors provided advice on which over-the-counter medicine (or home remedy) the patient should take for his or her sickness via a follow-up SMS after the call. When needed, the doctors could refer patients to hospitals to obtain specific tests to determine treatment for more complex cases.

Diagnostic Hardware

Patients in developed countries generally had access to healthcare services, but often found the services to be inconvenient and expensive to use. Physicians also struggled

[52] Uttarika Kumaran, "Feeling under the weather? Ring a doctor now," *DNA India*, June 20, 2011, http:// www.dnaindia.com/mumbai/report-feeling-under-the-weather-ring-a-doctor-now-1556945, accessed March 2014.

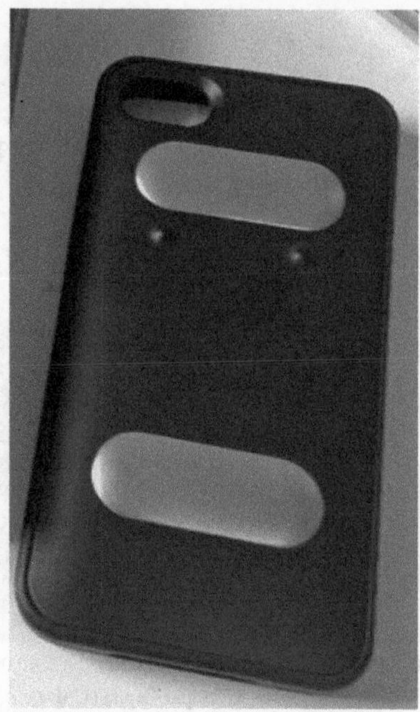

Figure 17.6 Exhibit 10 Smartphone ECG Example, 2013.
Source: Maarten den Braber, "Just received this new case for my iPhone," Flickr Commons, https://www.flickr.com/photos/mdbraber/8683589632/, accessed March 2014.

to engage patients in preventative practices to safeguard against poor health outcomes. A market niche emerged for products that enabled consumers to measure their health status to help them determine whether or not to go to a clinic or hospital for medical care.

Cardiac Designs ECG Check The ECG Check was a mobile heart monitor attachment designed for the iPhone to capture the user's heart rate and check for arrhythmias (see Figure 17.6 for an example of a smartphone ECG device). The ECG Check was the first over-the-counter heart monitor to be cleared by the U.S. Federal Food and Drug Administration (FDA).[53] ECG readings were taken when the user pressed his fingers against the sensors in the iPhone attachment; the readings were then displayed and stored on the phone application. The ECG Check Web Center received and analyzed the ECG readings and immediately returned test results to the users.[54] The ECG Check retailed for $99 and was sold directly to consumers.

Scanadu Scout The Scout was a medical monitoring device designed for use by consumers to measure key vital signs each day, including blood pressure, temperature,

[53] ECG Check, "ECG Check Heart Monitor," http://www.ecgcheck.com/media/1009/prescription.pdf, accessed March 2014.

[54] "Cardiac Designs to exhibit ECG Check at 5th Annual mHealth Summit in Washington, DC," December 6, 2013, http://www.prnewswire.com/news-releases/cardiac-designs-to-exhibit-ecg-check-at-5th-annual-mhealth -summit-in-washington-dc-234826501.html, accessed March 2014.

heart rate, ECG, oximetry (saturation of hemoglobin), and heart rate variability. The device provided consumers with information on their health status and alerted them to changes that indicated a doctor visit was needed (and shared the data with doctors). The Scout was initially funded via crowdsourcing on Indiegogo ($1.7 million) and received an additional $10.5 million in Series A funding in November 2013.[55] The Scout, which was expected to launch in late 2014, was the first device in Scanadu's planned ecosystem of consumer medical devices (the next device, Scanaflo, would be a consumer urine-testing device).

Behavioral Interventions for Chronic Conditions

Mobile technology offered the potential to deliver health-related interventions to individuals who would not otherwise be present for in-person treatment. Text messaging (short message service, SMS), being the most ubiquitous form of mobile communication, was a promising method for reaching millions of individuals.

Text2Quit Smoking Cessation[56] SMS mHealth educational programs were found to be effective for various applications, including delivering neonatal and pregnancy advice. Text-based mHealth services were especially useful in addressing healthcare issues that required continuous intervention, such as smoking cessation. Text2Quit was a smoking cessation program developed by Voxiva, which used text messages, e-mails, and web to help users quit. While users would interact directly with the service, Voxiva marketed the platform to employers, public health departments, and health plan providers.[57]

MEDICAL PERSONNEL–FACING PREVENTATIVE SERVICES

Data Integration

With the array of new devices and applications to gather data on patient health, physicians and medical professionals were confronted with massive amounts of data and little time to analyze and incorporate such data into treatment plans. Physicians saw time spent on administrative tasks as taking away from time spent with patients. The technological infrastructures within hospitals and other medical facilities were not standardized, so staff found it difficult to synthesize data from different departments on individual patients, let alone incorporate new data from mHealth devices outside of their healthcare

[55] Eliza Brooke, "Scanadu Closes $10.5M Series A Round, Gearing Up to Send Its Medical Tricorder Through Clinical Testing," Techcrunch, November 12, 2013, http://techcrunch.com/2013/11/12/scanadu-closes-10-5m-series-a-round-gearing-up-to-send-its-medical-tricorder-through-clinical-testing/, accessed March 2014.

[56] B. Bock, K. Heron, E. Jennings, K. Morrow, V. Cobb, J. Magee, J. Fava, C. Deutsch, and R. Foster, "A Text Message Delivered Smoking Cessation Intervention: The Initial Trial of TXT-2-Quit: Randomized Controlled Trial," *JMIR Mhealth Uhealth* 1, no. 2 (2013): e17, http://mhealth.jmir.org/2013/2/e17/,doi: 10.2196/mhealth.2522, via Google Scholar, accessed September 2013.

[57] Brian Dolan, "Text2Quit launch follows Text4Baby's lead," *MobiHealth News*, June 9, 2011, http://mobihealthnews.com/ 11167/text2quit-launch-follows-text4babys-lead/, accessed April 2014.

organizations. EHRs aimed to address the former, whereas start-ups began to emerge to fulfill the second need.

Practice Fusion In 2013, the research firm Black Book ranked Practice Fusion as the number-one EHR for primary care practices for the third year in a row, based upon consumer polls covering over 600 medical software providers.[58] Practice Fusion offered free, ad-supported EHR records, including charting, prescriptions, lab work, and scheduling. The online system was available wherever there was an Internet connection, carried no additional expense to upgrade, and could be set up in minutes.[59] Practice Fusion was the largest cloud-based EHR system in the U.S. (with 6.4% of the market)[60] used by over 100,000 medical professionals each month,[61] who had access to the health records of 33 million patients.[62] In 2013, Practice Fusion was selected as a "Technology Pioneer" by the World Economic Forum (previous award recipients included Mozilla, Mint, and Dropbox).[63]

Medic Mobile (formerly FrontlineSMS) Medic Mobile was an application developed to streamline patient health records captured by community health workers (CHWs) in Malawi, India, and other areas (see Figure 17.7 for a photo). The suite of Medic Mobile software included disease surveillance, immunization records, postnatal care coordination, and remote treatment support. In rural or poor areas, CHWs served as the primary care provider, although technology helped connect specialists to CHWs to provide advice on treatment and care for complex cases. CHWs often had less medical training and expertise than nurses or doctors, but possessed valuable Mobile's superior record-keeping system had saved hospital staff 1,200 hours of follow-up care and over $3,000 in motorbike fuel.[64] More than 100 patients started tuberculosis treatment after CHWs spotted the symptoms in the field and reported them to the hospital via text message.[65] A pilot conducted in India showed that Medic Mobile could increase immunization coverage by over 20% by sending mothers an SMS reminder when their children were due for vaccinations.[66]

Qualcomm 2Net 2Net was a cloud-based service designed to synthesize mHealth data collected from an entire ecosystem of devices (see Figure 17.8 for Qualcomm's

[58] Practice Fusion, Inc., "Practice Fusion Voted #1 EHR," http://www.practicefusion.com/brown-wilson-black-book-rankings/, accessed March 2014.

[59] Christina DesMarais, "17 Game-Changing Health Start-ups," *Inc. Magazine*, http://www.inc.com/ss/christina-desmarais/17-game-changing-health-tech-start-ups.html#5, accessed March 2014.

[60] Practice Fusion, Inc., "Report: Practice Fusion Nabs Top Spot as the Largest Cloud-Based EHR in the U.S.," http://www.practicefusion.com/pages/pr/skanda-ranks-pf-largest-cloud-ehr.html, accessed March 2014.

[61] Practice Fusion, Inc., "Report: Practice Fusion Nabs Top Spot as the Largest Cloud-Based EHR in the U.S."

[62] DesMarais, "17 Game-Changing Health Start-ups."

[63] Practice Fusion, Inc., "World Economic Forum Names Practice Fusion a 2013 Technology Pioneer," http://www.practicefusion.com/pages/pr/world-economic-forum-2013.html, accessed March 2014.

[64] Isaac Holeman, "New Name, Same Mission," *Medic Mobile*, http://medicmobile.org/2010/12/21/new-name-same-mission/, accessed March 2014.

[65] Holeman, "New Name, Same Mission."

[66] Holeman, "New Name, Same Mission."

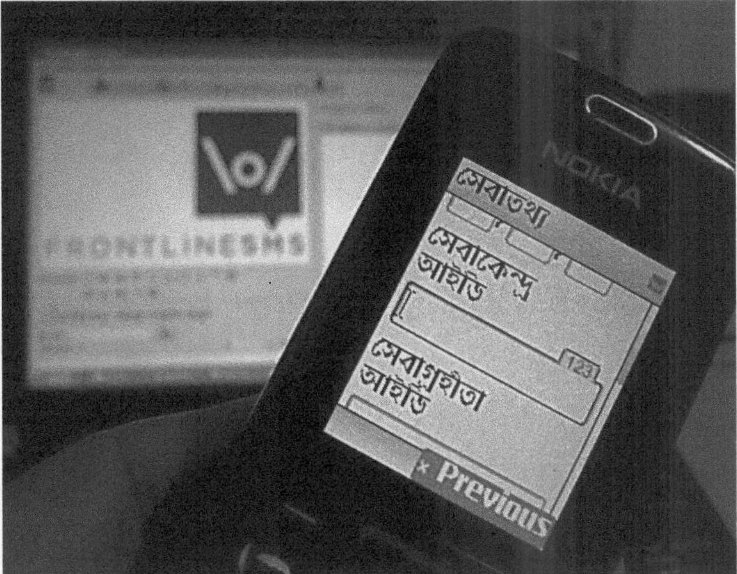

Figure 17.7 Exhibit 11 Medic Mobile Phone and Web Interface, 2011.
Source: Medic Mobile, "SSFP 003," Flickr Commons, https://www.flickr.com/photos/medicmobile/5888338025/, accessed March 2014.

2Net Pavilion at CES). 2Net received data sent from a variety of mHealth devices and apps (including third-party devices, mobile phones, and embedded devices that produced clinical data collected at the point-of-care) over a short-range wireless system, and then encrypted and uploaded all data to the cloud. Healthcare professionals could then access the data, which had been tagged and sorted using unique patient identity codes, and produce charts.[67] The 2Net hardware and platform were approved by the FDA and helped to uphold the privacy standards stipulated by the U.S. Health Insurance Portability and Accountability Act of 1996 (HIPAA).[68] The 2Net mobile portal won "Best of Innovations: Health & Fitness" at the 2014 CES.[69]

Alere HealthPal The HealthPal produced by Alere was a portable wireless device that transmitted health metrics from glucose meters, pulse oximeters, scales, or blood pressure monitors directly to a patient's EHR (which could then be accessed by the patient or a physician).[70] Due to the direct transmission of the metrics from the HealthPal to the patient's EHR, the need for a smartphone intermediary was

[67] Stephen Lawson, "Qualcomm's health-device platform wins over home care provider," PC World, March 6, 2014, http://www.pcworld.com/article/2105700/qualcomms-healthdevice-platform-wins-over-home-care-provider.html, accessed March 2014.

[68] Qualcomm Life, "The Future of Mobile Health," http://www.qualcommlife.com/images/pdf/2net_Platform_White_Paper.pdf, accessed March 2014.

[69] CES, "CES Innovations Design and Engineering Awards," http://www.cesweb.org/Awards/CES-Innovations-Awards/2013.aspx#inline_content7989, accessed March 2014.

[70] CES, "CES Innovations Design and Engineering Awards."

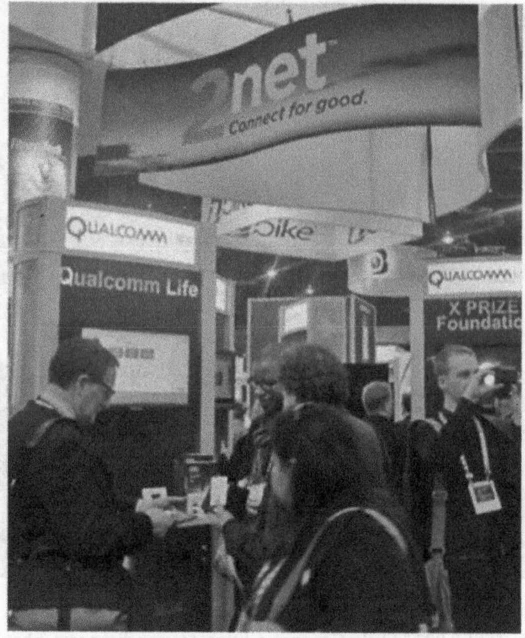

Figure 17.8 Exhibit 12 Qualcomm 2Net Pavilion at CES, 2013.
Source: Jill Gilbert, "Qualcomm Life Pavilion @ Digital Health Summit CES," Flickr Commons, https://www.flickr.com/photos/jilbert/6723224463/, accessed March 2014.

eliminated, as were any charges associated with data usage that similar products used to send data to physicians via the patient's phone.[71]

Monitoring

In 2005, 133 million people in the U.S. had at least one chronic condition that required ongoing medical care and/or interfered with the activities of daily living.[72] By 2020, the figure was expected to reach 157 million.[73] The aging U.S. population was driving the increase, along with the growing prevalence of youth obesity, diabetes, and asthma.[74] In 2009, it was estimated that chronic conditions accounted for roughly 75% of the $2 trillion spent on healthcare in the U.S.[75]

[71] Brian Dolan, "Alere to pay as much as $22M for MedApps," *MobiHealth News*, January 2, 2013, http://www.alere.com/us/en/product-details/alere-healthpal.html, accessed March 2014.

[72] S. Y. Wu and A. Green, "Projection of chronic illness prevalence and cost inflation" (Santa Monica, CA: RAND Health; 2000), quoted in U.S. Centers for Disease Control and Prevention, "Chronic Diseases and Health Promotion," http://www.cdc.gov/chronicdisease/overview/index.htm?s_cid=ostltsdyk_govd_203, accessed March 2014.

[73] Nicholas Freudenberg and Kenneth Olden, "Getting Serious About the Prevention of Chronic Diseases," U.S. Centers for Disease Control and Prevention, July 4, 2011, http://www.cdc.gov/pcd/issues/2011/jul/10_0243.htm, accessed March 2014.

[74] Freudenberg and Olden, "Getting Serious About the Prevention of Chronic Diseases."

[75] U.S. Centers for Disease Control and Prevention, "Chronic diseases: the power to prevent, the call to control, at-a-glance 2009," Atlanta, GA: U.S. Department of Health and Human Services,

LOSTnFOUND guard2me Guard2me was a wearable mobile-tracking device (designed to also function as a watch) used to locate individuals with Alzheimer's or dementia. Location information was relayed to a smartphone app held by a caretaker or family member, which placed the lost individual's position into Google Maps for easy location.[76] The wearable device also included a panic button for use by the lost individual. The device retailed for $800. The guard2me device and application was an honoree for the "Best of Innovations: Health & Fitness" at the 2014 CES.[77]

MEDICAL PERSONNEL-FACING THERAPEUTIC SERVICES

Portable Hardware

Poor or remote communities often lacked the diagnostic equipment found in hospitals or large clinics, as well as staff trained in their use. A significant opportunity existed for innovative diagnostic tools that could travel to remote communities and were less expensive and easier to operate than traditional devices. Since individuals living in those hard-to-reach areas were often underserved by the existing medical infrastructure, any increase in access to healthcare equipment was incremental.

Portable Eye Exam Kit (PEEK) PEEK was a mobile diagnostic tool that used a clip-on eyepiece designed for use with smartphones to instantly perform vision tests and diagnose common ocular problems (such as cataracts). The test could be performed without specialized medical training, and the results could be shared with vision experts worldwide. The device used high-resolution mobile device hardware and software to identify common eye disorders and geo-tagged each patient's test to enable follow-up care, as needed.[78] In 2013, 285 million people were vision-impaired and 39 million were blind worldwide, and 90% of those with impaired vision lived in developing countries.[79] Blind patients who were identified as candidates for corrective surgeries by the PEEK device were later located by hospital workers who used the geo-tagged patient logs to provide appropriate follow-up care.

MobisanteMobisante was a portable ultrasound machine that worked with smartphones and tablets (see Figure 17.9). The battery-powered device could be taken to patients who lived off-grid, and the ultrasound images could be stored or shared (via Wi-Fi or mobile network).[80] The Mobisante ultrasound tool could be used by obstetricians, as well as for medical professionals whose patients suffered from trauma or

2009, http://www.cdc.gov/chronicdisease/resources/publications/aag/chronic.htm, accessed March 2014.

[76] LOSTnFOUND, "How it works," http://www.guard2me.com/guard2me/how-it-works-preview/how-it-works/, accessed March 2014.

[77] CES, "CES Innovations Design and Engineering Awards," http://www.cesweb.org/Awards/CES-Innovations-Awards/2013.aspx#inline_content7989, accessed March 2014.

[78] Peekvision, "Features," http://www.peekvision.org/index.html#features, accessed March 2014.

[79] World Health Organization, "Visual impairment and blindness," October 2013, http://www.who.int/ mediacentre/factsheets/fs282/en/, accessed March 2014.

[80] Mobisante, "Products," http://www.mobisante.com/products/tc2/, accessed March 2014.

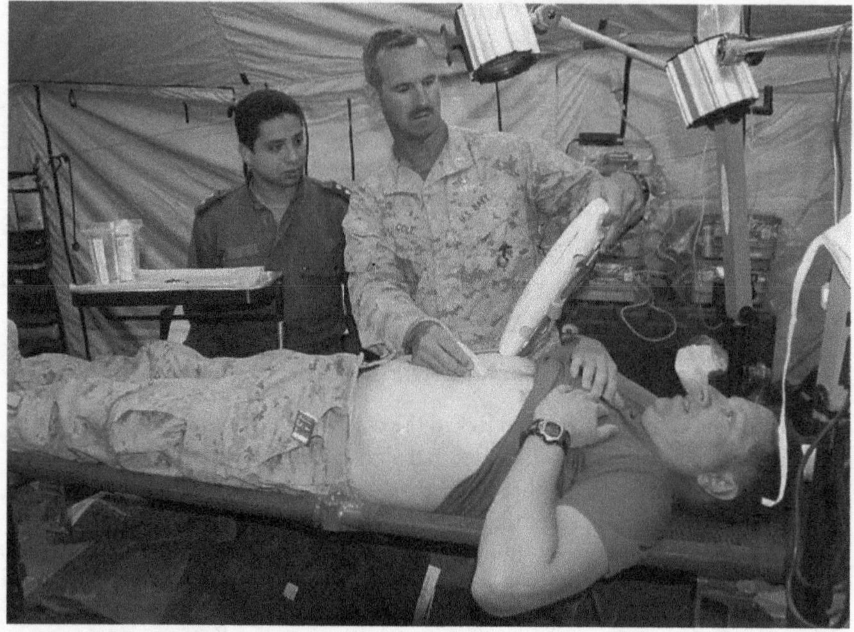

Figure 17.9 Exhibit 13 Portable Ultrasound Example, 2013.
Source: Major Paul Greenberg, "USMC-100608-M-0493G-043," Wikimedia Commons, http://commons.wikimedia.org/wiki/ File:USMC-100608-M-0493G-043.jpg, accessed March 2014.

abdominal pain, or required routine internal screening. In addition to assisting internal examination, Mobisante could be used to guide the accuracy and efficiency of biopsies, removal of foreign bodies, IV placement, and anesthesia.[81]

Connecting Medical Professionals

Just as Stack Overflow successfully created a professional question-and-answer forum for programmers, websites promising to connect physicians and other medical professionals to each other began to appear. Such networks benefited participants by offering access to specialists in a variety of fields for assistance on difficult patient cases, giving physicians a means to build their reputation by helping their peers and forging new connections to others in their field.

Doximity Doximity was a platform to allow physicians to consult and collaborate with their peers to treat difficult cases. Each physician created a profile that included their training, the insurance they accepted, languages they spoke, papers they wrote,

[81] Mobisante, "Products."

and clinical trials they conducted—all of which was searchable by other members of the site.[82] About 1,000 doctors a week joined the network,[83] and, by 2013, the site hosted nearly 30% of U.S. doctors or roughly 200,000 physicians.[84] Doximity also connected users to market research firms that sought expert input on new medical devices (members were paid $250–$500 an hour for such input).[85]

82 DesMarais, "17 Game-Changing Health Start-ups."
83 DesMarais, "17 Game-Changing Health Start-ups."
84 Doximity, Inc., "About," https://www.doximity.com/about, accessed March 2014.
85 DesMarais, "17 Game-Changing Health Start-ups."